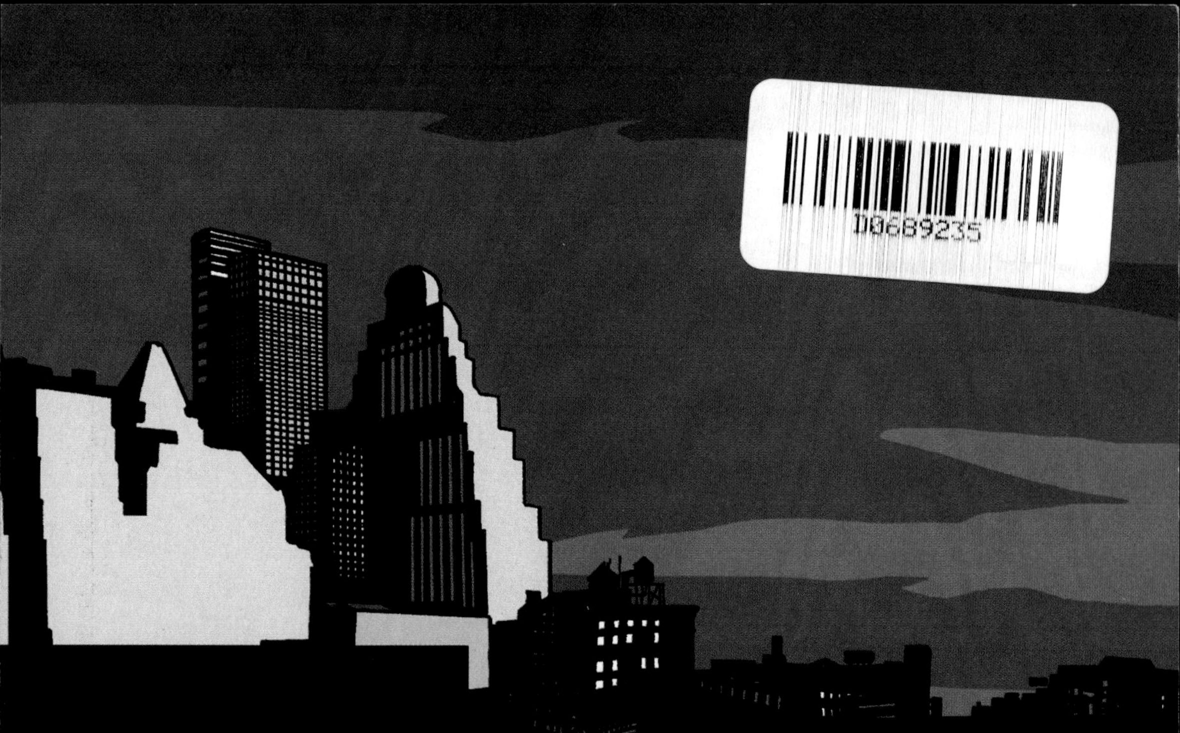

POW

CREATED AN

BRIAN MICHAEL BENDI

COLOR ART BY
PAT GARRAHY
SEPARATION ASSISTS BY OJO CALIENTE STUDIOS

LETTERING BY
GARRAHY AND BEND

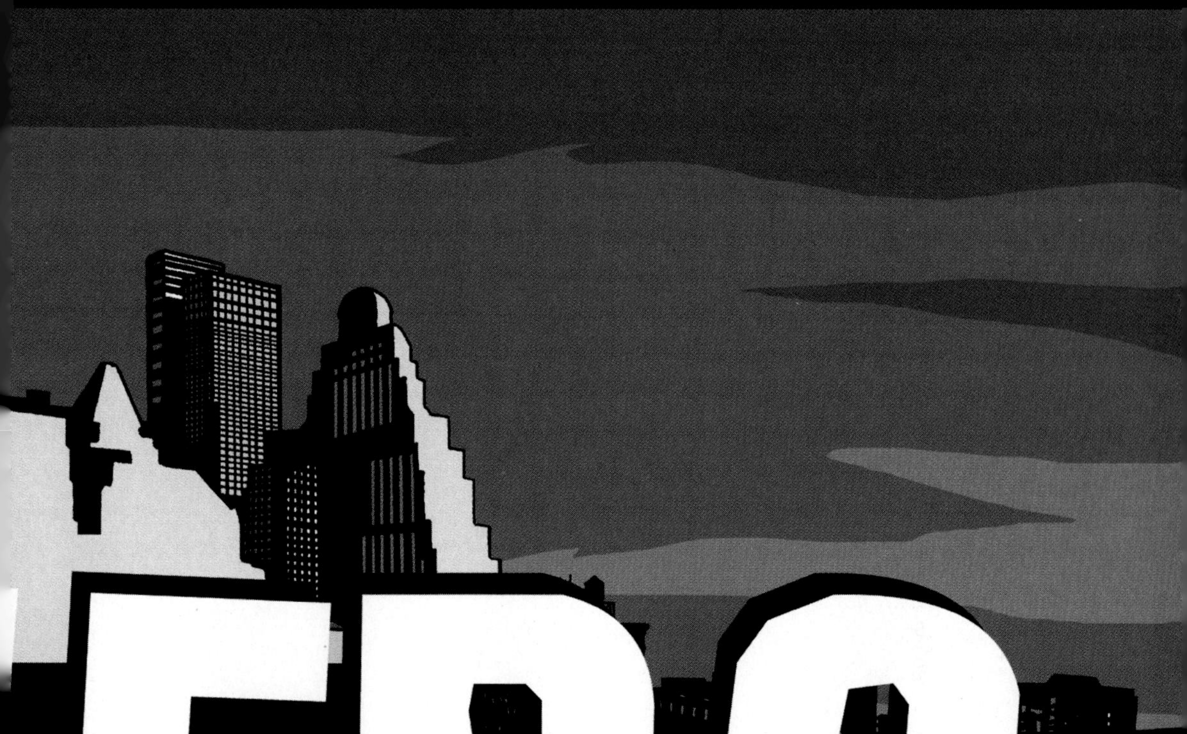

ERS

RODUCED BY

AND MIKE AVON OEMING

EDITOR
KC MCCRORY

BUSINESS AFFAIRS
ALISA BENDIS

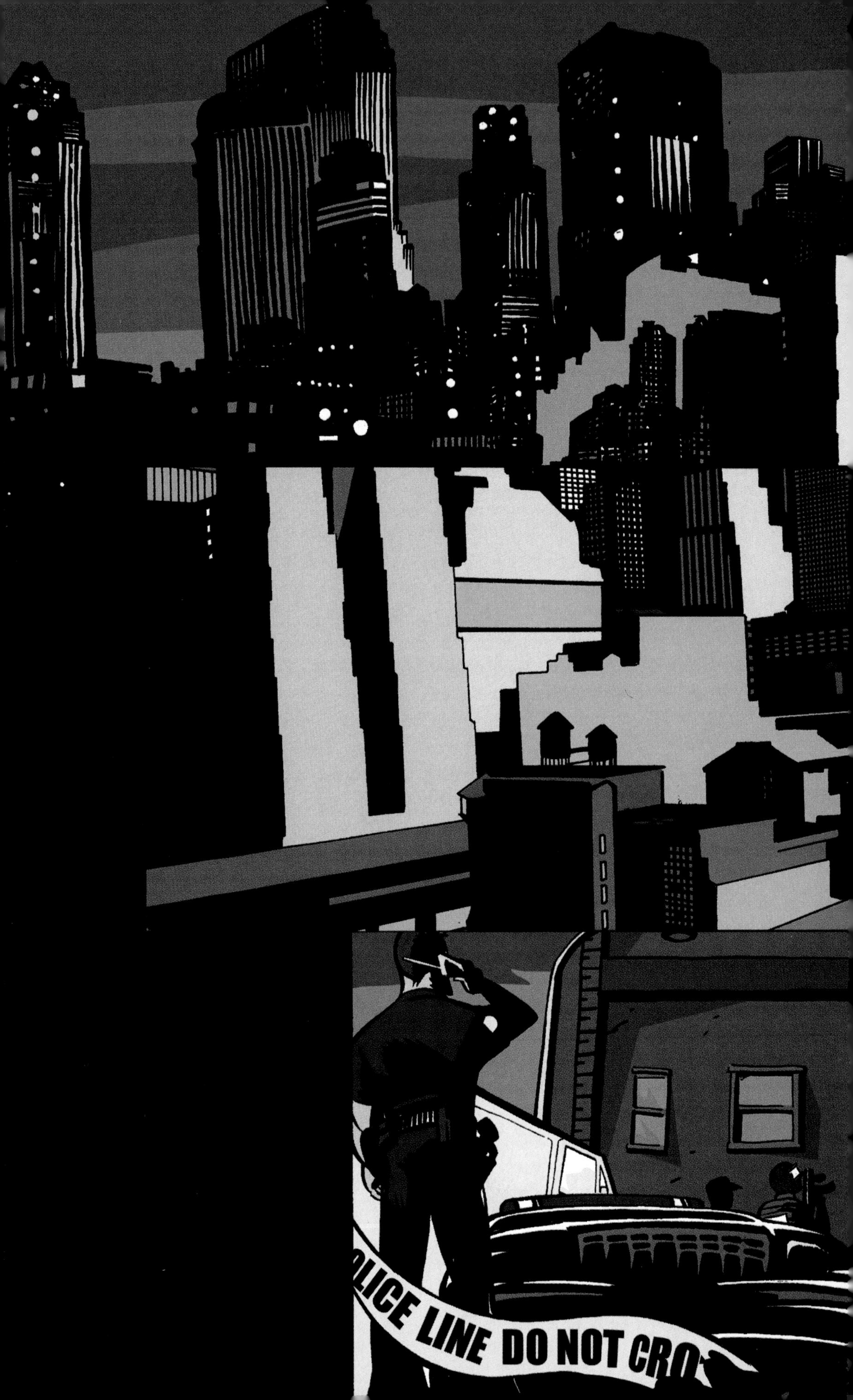
OLICE LINE DO NOT CRO

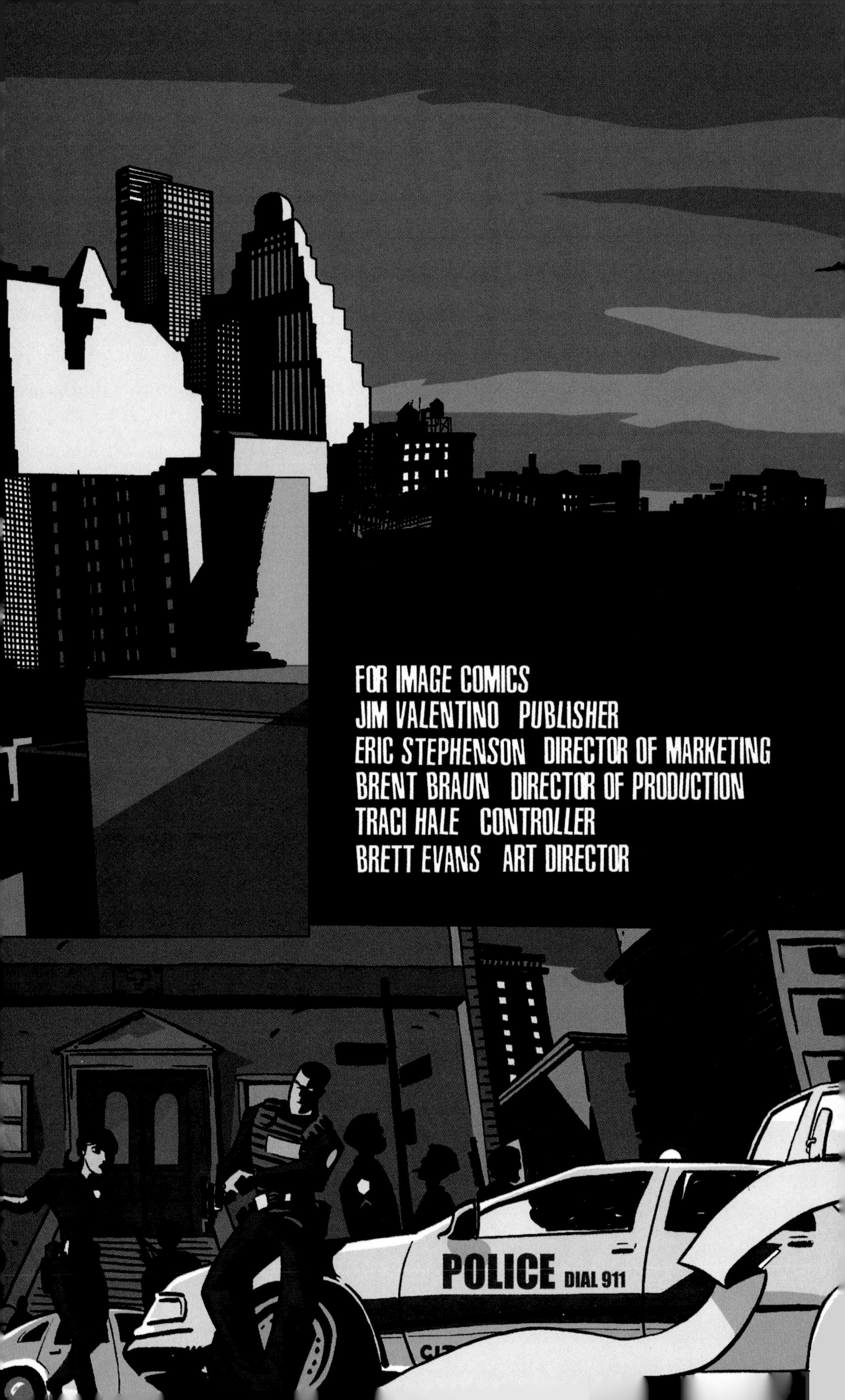
POLICE DIAL 911

FOR IMAGE COMICS
JIM VALENTINO PUBLISHER
ERIC STEPHENSON DIRECTOR OF MARKETING
BRENT BRAUN DIRECTOR OF PRODUCTION
TRACI HALE CONTROLLER
BRETT EVANS ART DIRECTOR

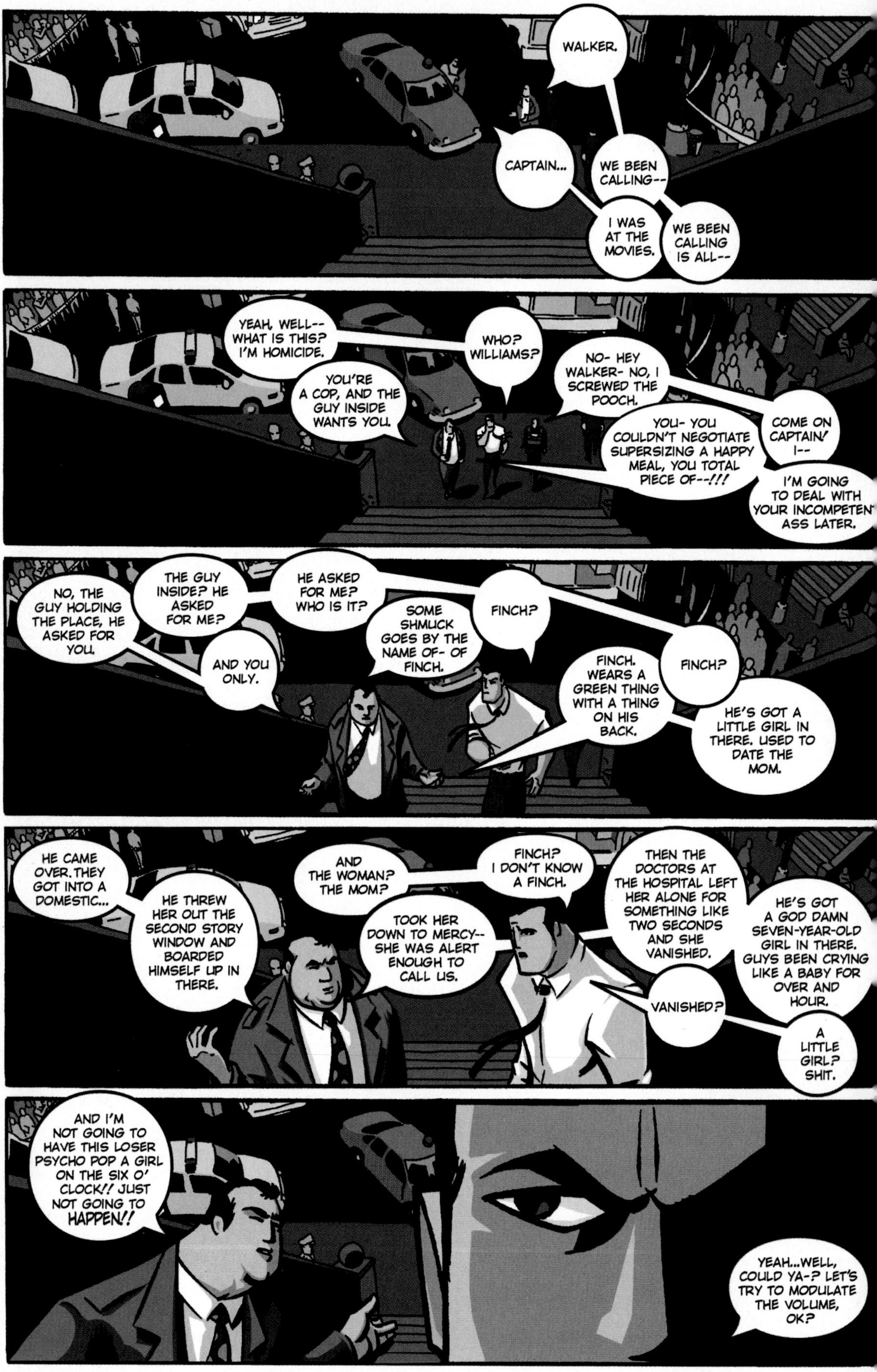
WALKER.
CAPTAIN...
WE BEEN CALLING--
I WAS AT THE MOVIES.
WE BEEN CALLING IS ALL--
YEAH, WELL-- WHAT IS THIS? I'M HOMICIDE.
WHO? WILLIAMS?
YOU'RE A COP, AND THE GUY INSIDE WANTS YOU.
NO- HEY WALKER- NO, I SCREWED THE POOCH.
COME ON CAPTAIN! I--
YOU- YOU COULDN'T NEGOTIATE SUPERSIZING A HAPPY MEAL, YOU TOTAL PIECE OF--!!!
I'M GOING TO DEAL WITH YOUR INCOMPETEN ASS LATER.
NO, THE GUY HOLDING THE PLACE, HE ASKED FOR YOU.
THE GUY INSIDE? HE ASKED FOR ME?
AND YOU ONLY.
HE ASKED FOR ME? WHO IS IT?
SOME SHMUCK GOES BY THE NAME OF- OF FINCH.
FINCH?
FINCH?
FINCH. WEARS A GREEN THING WITH A THING ON HIS BACK.
HE'S GOT A LITTLE GIRL IN THERE. USED TO DATE THE MOM.
HE CAME OVER. THEY GOT INTO A DOMESTIC...
HE THREW HER OUT THE SECOND STORY WINDOW AND BOARDED HIMSELF UP IN THERE.
AND THE WOMAN? THE MOM?
TOOK HER DOWN TO MERCY-- SHE WAS ALERT ENOUGH TO CALL US.
FINCH? I DON'T KNOW A FINCH.
THEN THE DOCTORS AT THE HOSPITAL LEFT HER ALONE FOR SOMETHING LIKE TWO SECONDS AND SHE VANISHED.
VANISHED?
HE'S GOT A GOD DAMN SEVEN-YEAR-OLD GIRL IN THERE. GUYS BEEN CRYING LIKE A BABY FOR OVER AND HOUR.
A LITTLE GIRL? SHIT.
AND I'M NOT GOING TO HAVE THIS LOSER PSYCHO POP A GIRL ON THE SIX O' CLOCK!! JUST NOT GOING TO HAPPEN!!
YEAH...WELL, COULD YA-? LET'S TRY TO MODULATE THE VOLUME, OK?

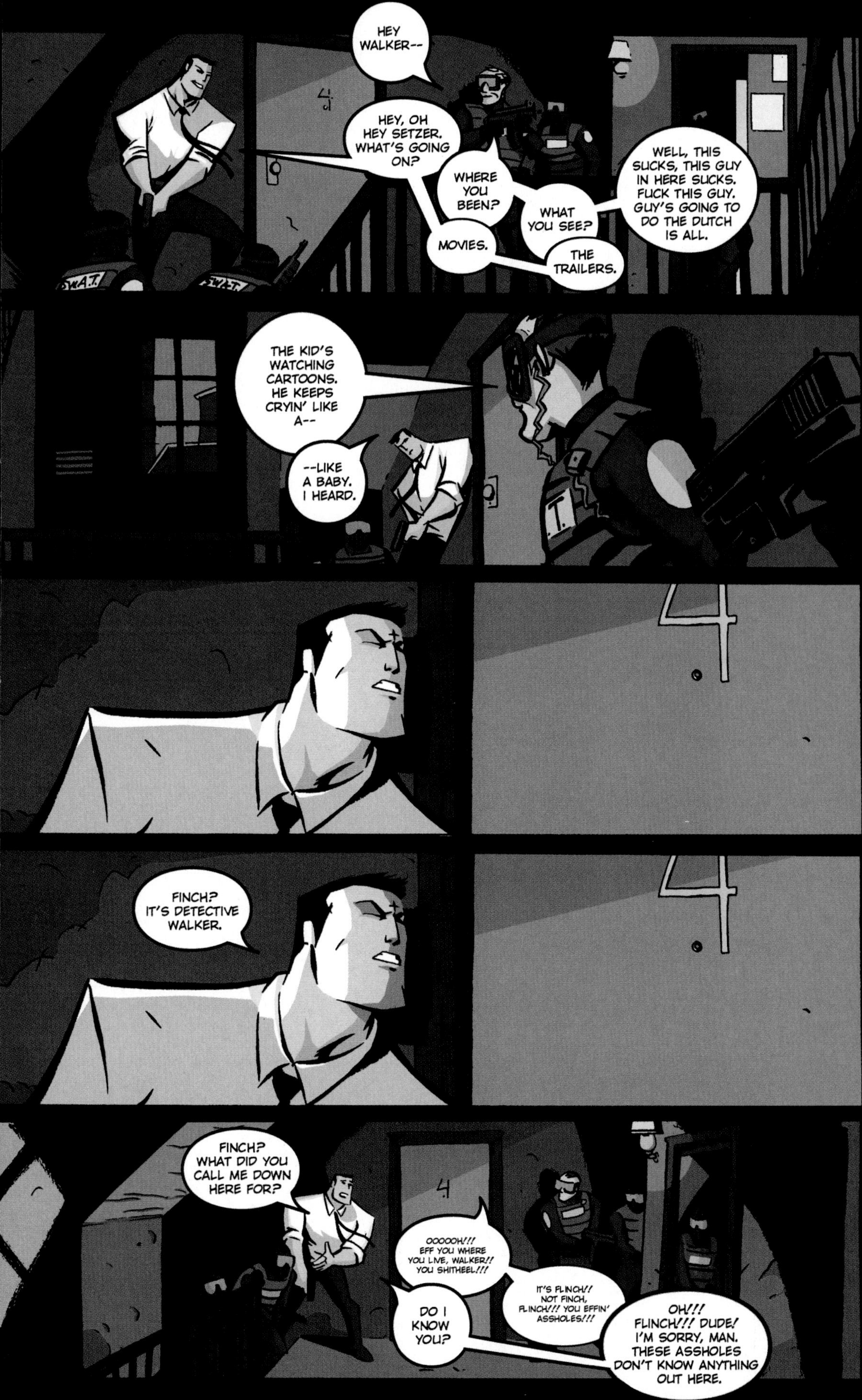
HEY WALKER--
HEY, OH HEY SETZER. WHAT'S GOING ON?
WHERE YOU BEEN?
MOVIES.
WHAT YOU SEE?
THE TRAILERS.
WELL, THIS SUCKS, THIS GUY IN HERE SUCKS. FUCK THIS GUY. GUY'S GOING TO DO THE DUTCH IS ALL.
THE KID'S WATCHING CARTOONS. HE KEEPS CRYIN' LIKE A--
--LIKE A BABY. I HEARD.
FINCH? IT'S DETECTIVE WALKER.
FINCH? WHAT DID YOU CALL ME DOWN HERE FOR?
OOOOOH!!! EFF YOU WHERE YOU LIVE, WALKER!! YOU SHITHEEL!!!
DO I KNOW YOU?
IT'S FLINCH!! NOT FINCH, FLINCH!!! YOU EFFIN' ASSHOLES!!!
OH!!! FLINCH!!! DUDE! I'M SORRY, MAN. THESE ASSHOLES DON'T KNOW ANYTHING OUT HERE.

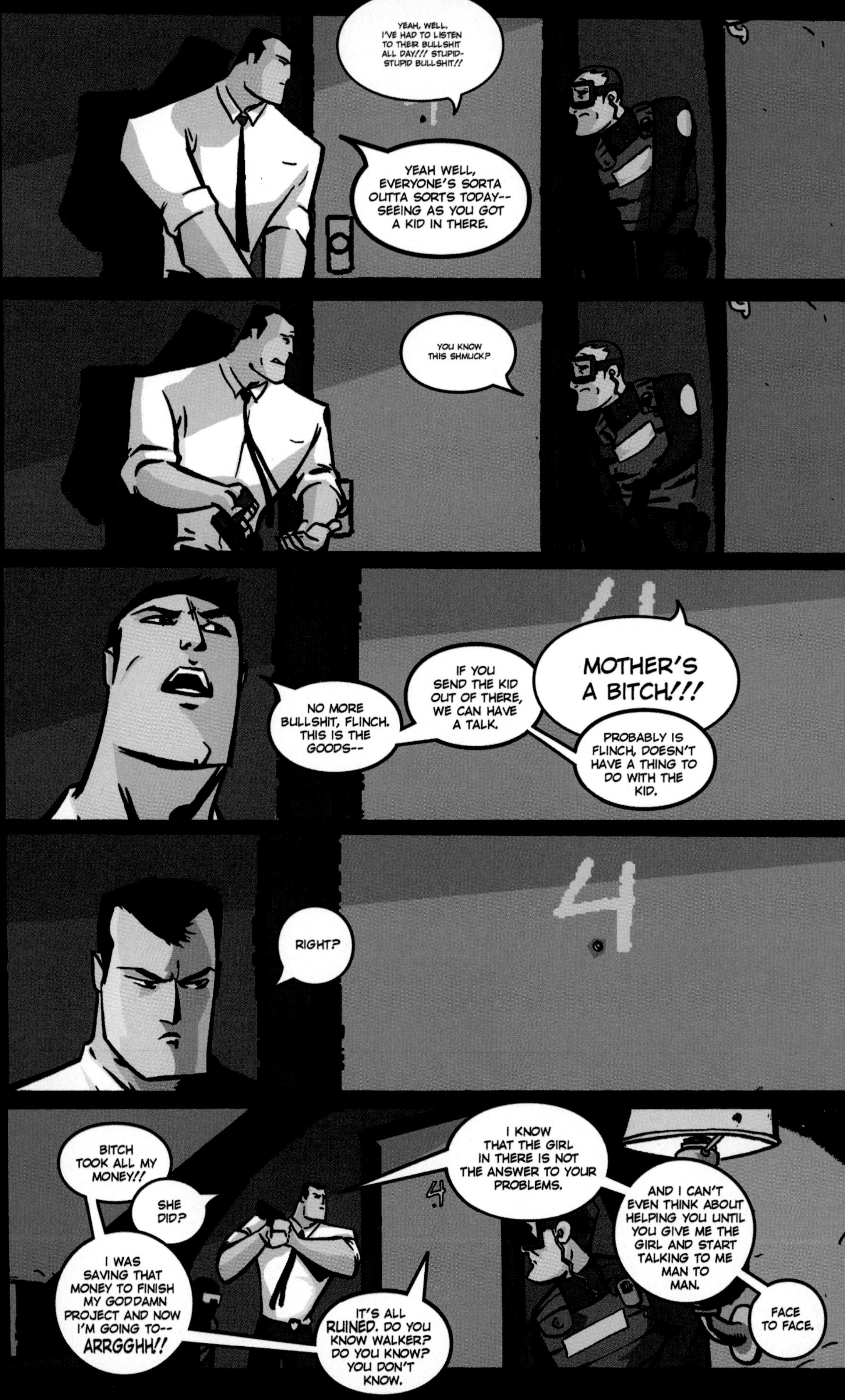
YEAH, WELL. I'VE HAD TO LISTEN TO THEIR BULLSHIT ALL DAY!!! STUPID-STUPID BULLSHIT!!
YEAH WELL, EVERYONE'S SORTA OUTTA SORTS TODAY-- SEEING AS YOU GOT A KID IN THERE.
YOU KNOW THIS SHMUCK?
NO MORE BULLSHIT, FLINCH. THIS IS THE GOODS--
IF YOU SEND THE KID OUT OF THERE, WE CAN HAVE A TALK.
MOTHER'S A BITCH!!!
PROBABLY IS FLINCH, DOESN'T HAVE A THING TO DO WITH THE KID.
RIGHT?
BITCH TOOK ALL MY MONEY!!
SHE DID?
I WAS SAVING THAT MONEY TO FINISH MY GODDAMN PROJECT AND NOW I'M GOING TO-- ARRGGHH!!
IT'S ALL RUINED. DO YOU KNOW WALKER? DO YOU KNOW? YOU DON'T KNOW.
I KNOW THAT THE GIRL IN THERE IS NOT THE ANSWER TO YOUR PROBLEMS.
AND I CAN'T EVEN THINK ABOUT HELPING YOU UNTIL YOU GIVE ME THE GIRL AND START TALKING TO ME MAN TO MAN.
FACE TO FACE.

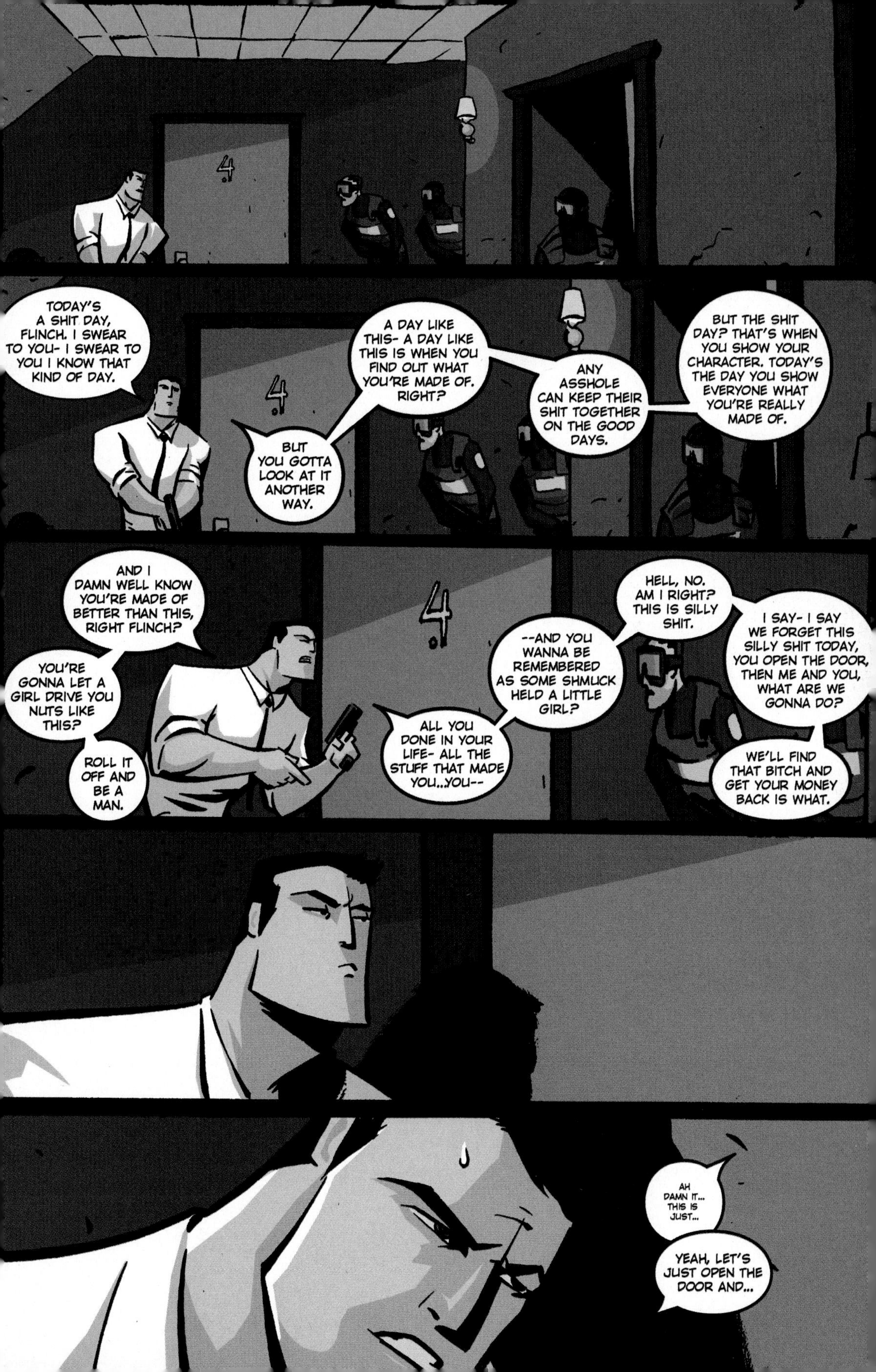

TODAY'S A SHIT DAY, FLINCH. I SWEAR TO YOU- I SWEAR TO YOU I KNOW THAT KIND OF DAY.
BUT YOU GOTTA LOOK AT IT ANOTHER WAY.
A DAY LIKE THIS- A DAY LIKE THIS IS WHEN YOU FIND OUT WHAT YOU'RE MADE OF. RIGHT?
ANY ASSHOLE CAN KEEP THEIR SHIT TOGETHER ON THE GOOD DAYS.
BUT THE SHIT DAY? THAT'S WHEN YOU SHOW YOUR CHARACTER. TODAY'S THE DAY YOU SHOW EVERYONE WHAT YOU'RE REALLY MADE OF.
AND I DAMN WELL KNOW YOU'RE MADE OF BETTER THAN THIS, RIGHT FLINCH?
YOU'RE GONNA LET A GIRL DRIVE YOU NUTS LIKE THIS?
ROLL IT OFF AND BE A MAN.
ALL YOU DONE IN YOUR LIFE- ALL THE STUFF THAT MADE YOU...YOU--
--AND YOU WANNA BE REMEMBERED AS SOME SHMUCK HELD A LITTLE GIRL?
HELL, NO. AM I RIGHT? THIS IS SILLY SHIT.
I SAY- I SAY WE FORGET THIS SILLY SHIT TODAY, YOU OPEN THE DOOR, THEN ME AND YOU, WHAT ARE WE GONNA DO?
WE'LL FIND THAT BITCH AND GET YOUR MONEY BACK IS WHAT.
AH DAMN IT... THIS IS JUST...
YEAH, LET'S JUST OPEN THE DOOR AND...

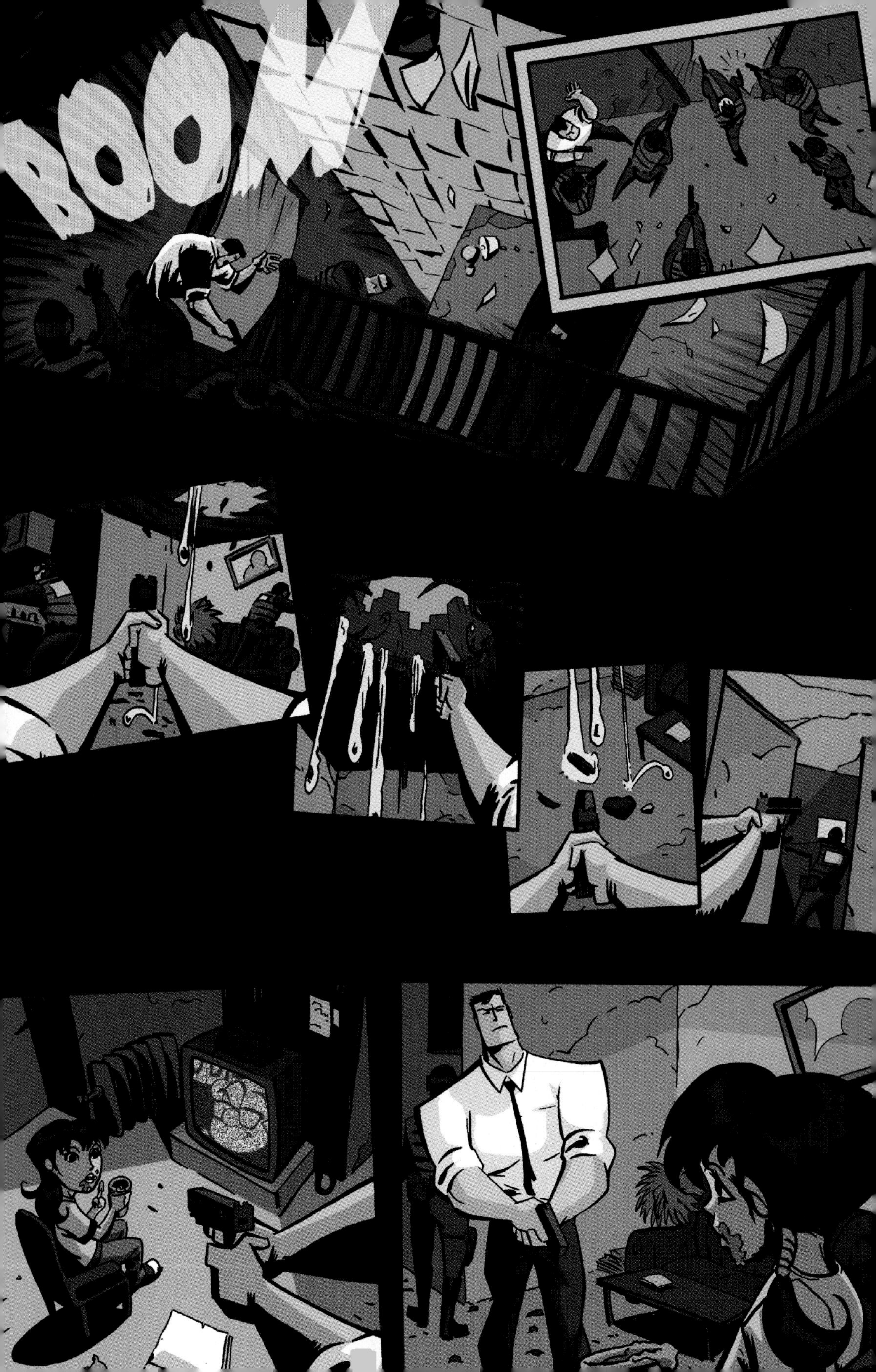
BOOM

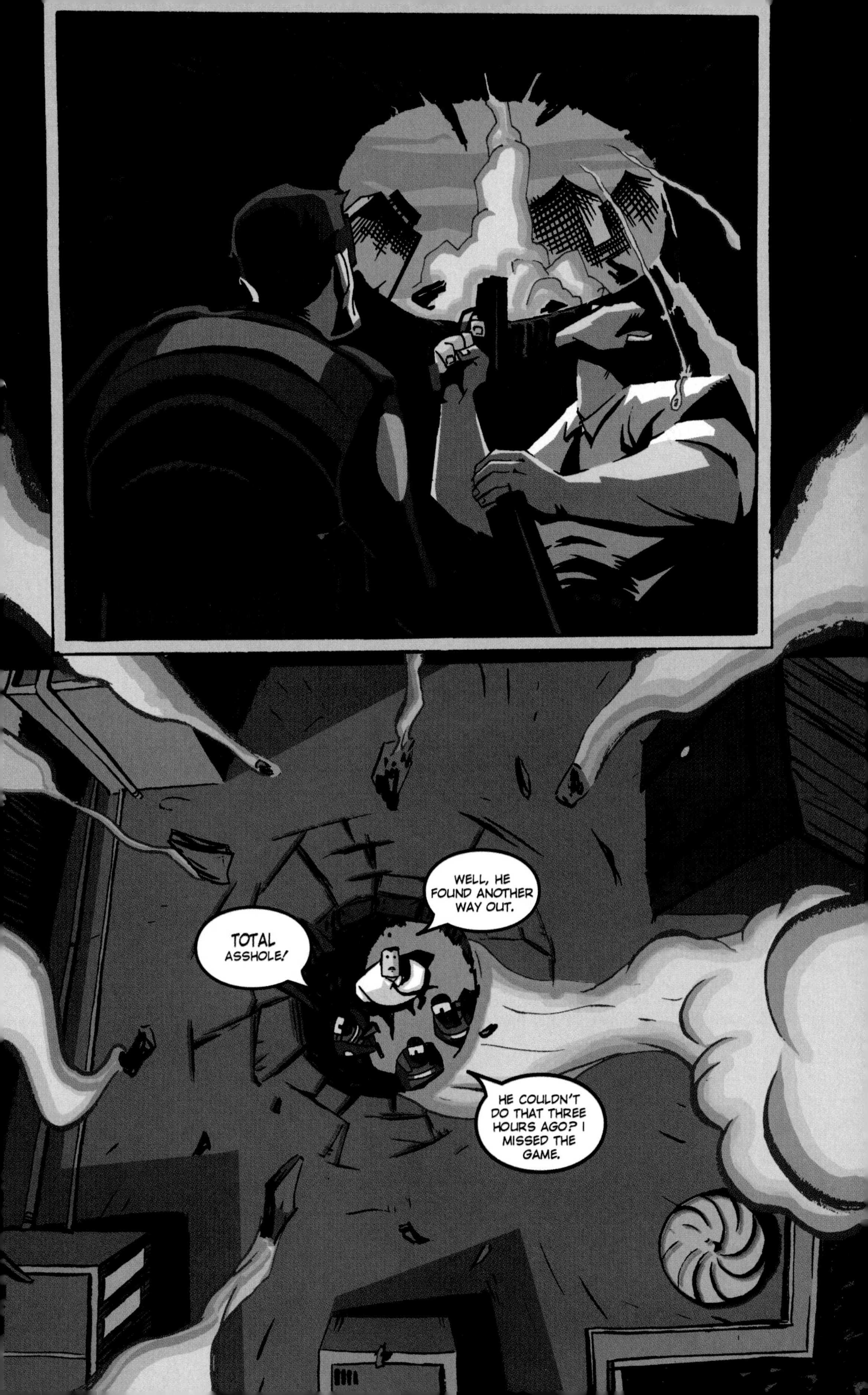
TOTAL ASSHOLE!
WELL, HE FOUND ANOTHER WAY OUT.
HE COULDN'T DO THAT THREE HOURS AGO? I MISSED THE GAME.

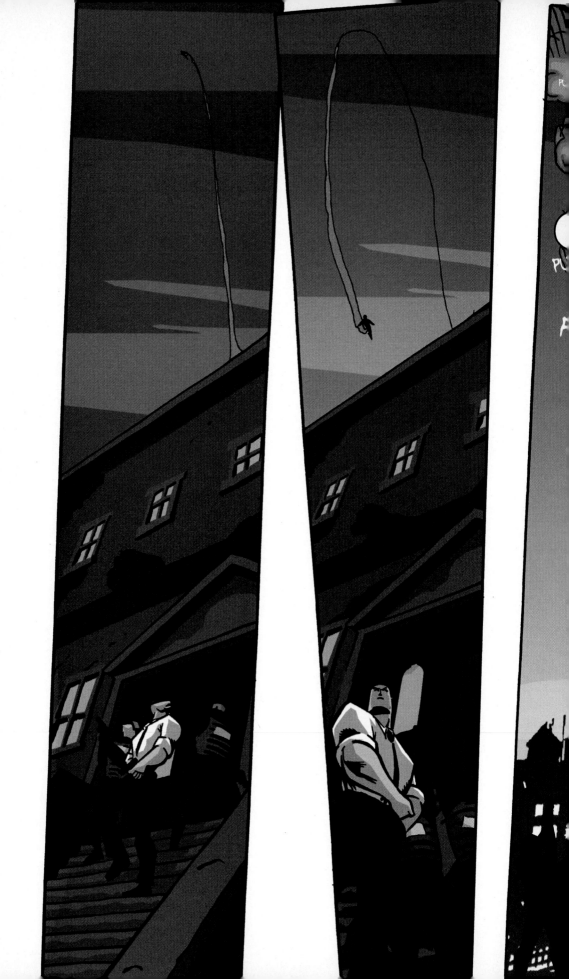

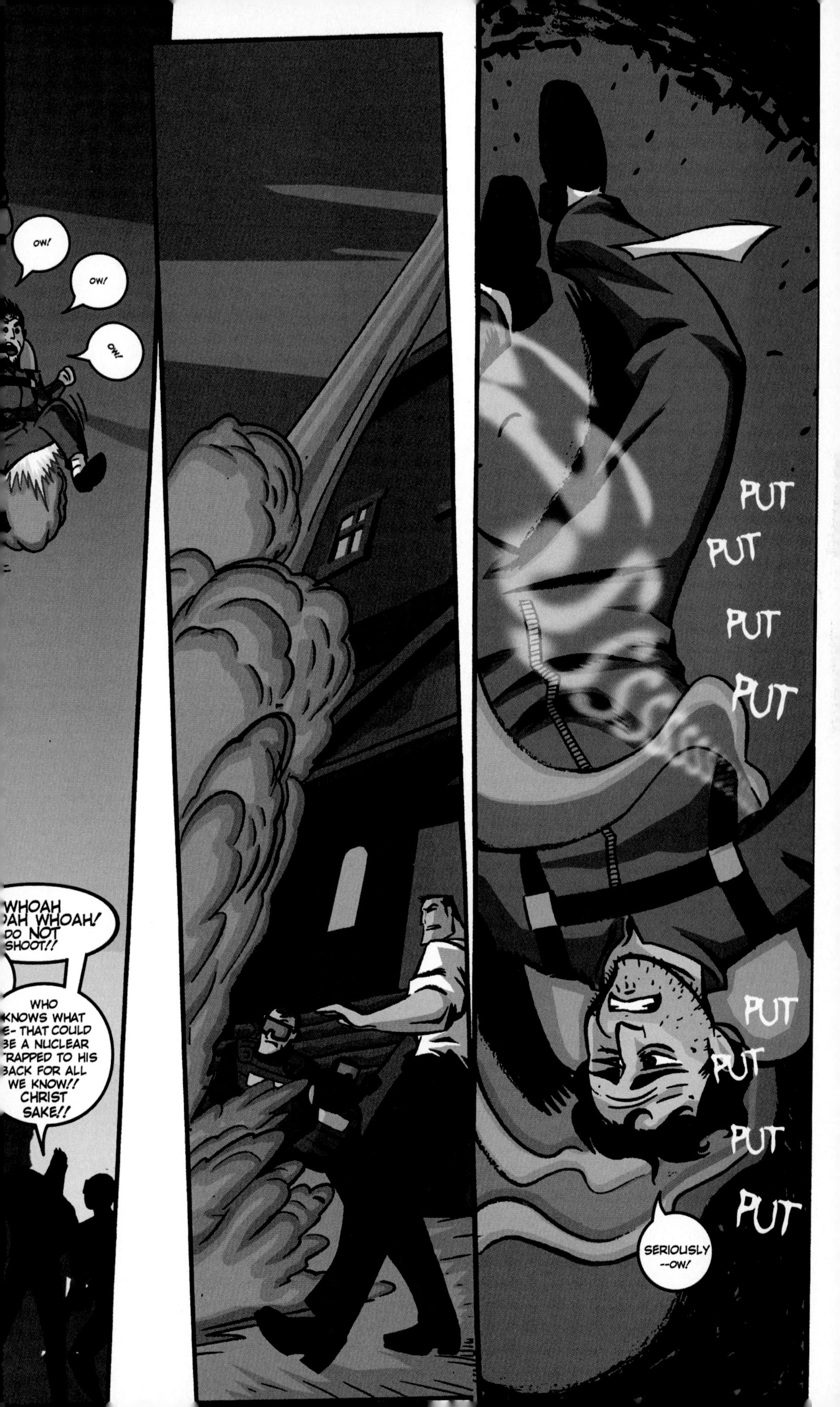

OW!
OW!
OW!
WHOAH
OAH WHOAH!
DO NOT
SHOOT!!
WHO
KNOWS WHAT
E- THAT COULD
BE A NUCLEAR
TRAPPED TO HIS
BACK FOR ALL
WE KNOW!!
CHRIST
SAKE!!
PUT
PUT
PUT
PUT
PUT
PUT
PUT
PUT
SERIOUSLY
--OW!

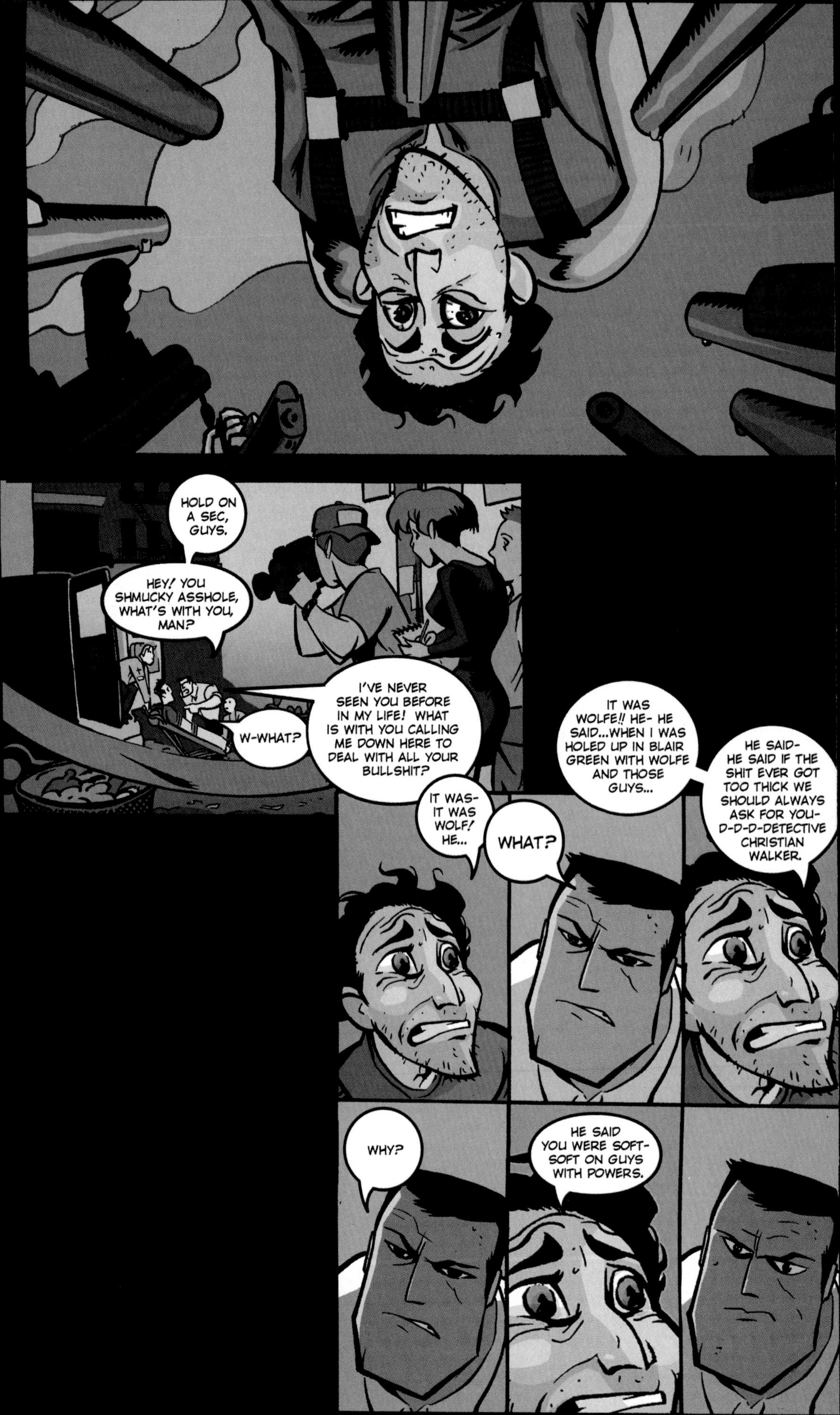
HOLD ON A SEC, GUYS.
HEY! YOU SHMUCKY ASSHOLE, WHAT'S WITH YOU, MAN?
I'VE NEVER SEEN YOU BEFORE IN MY LIFE! WHAT IS WITH YOU CALLING ME DOWN HERE TO DEAL WITH ALL YOUR BULLSHIT?
W-WHAT?
IT WAS- IT WAS WOLF! HE...
WHAT?
IT WAS WOLFE!! HE- HE SAID...WHEN I WAS HOLED UP IN BLAIR GREEN WITH WOLFE AND THOSE GUYS...
HE SAID- HE SAID IF THE SHIT EVER GOT TOO THICK WE SHOULD ALWAYS ASK FOR YOU- D-D-D-DETECTIVE CHRISTIAN WALKER.
WHY?
HE SAID YOU WERE SOFT- SOFT ON GUYS WITH POWERS.

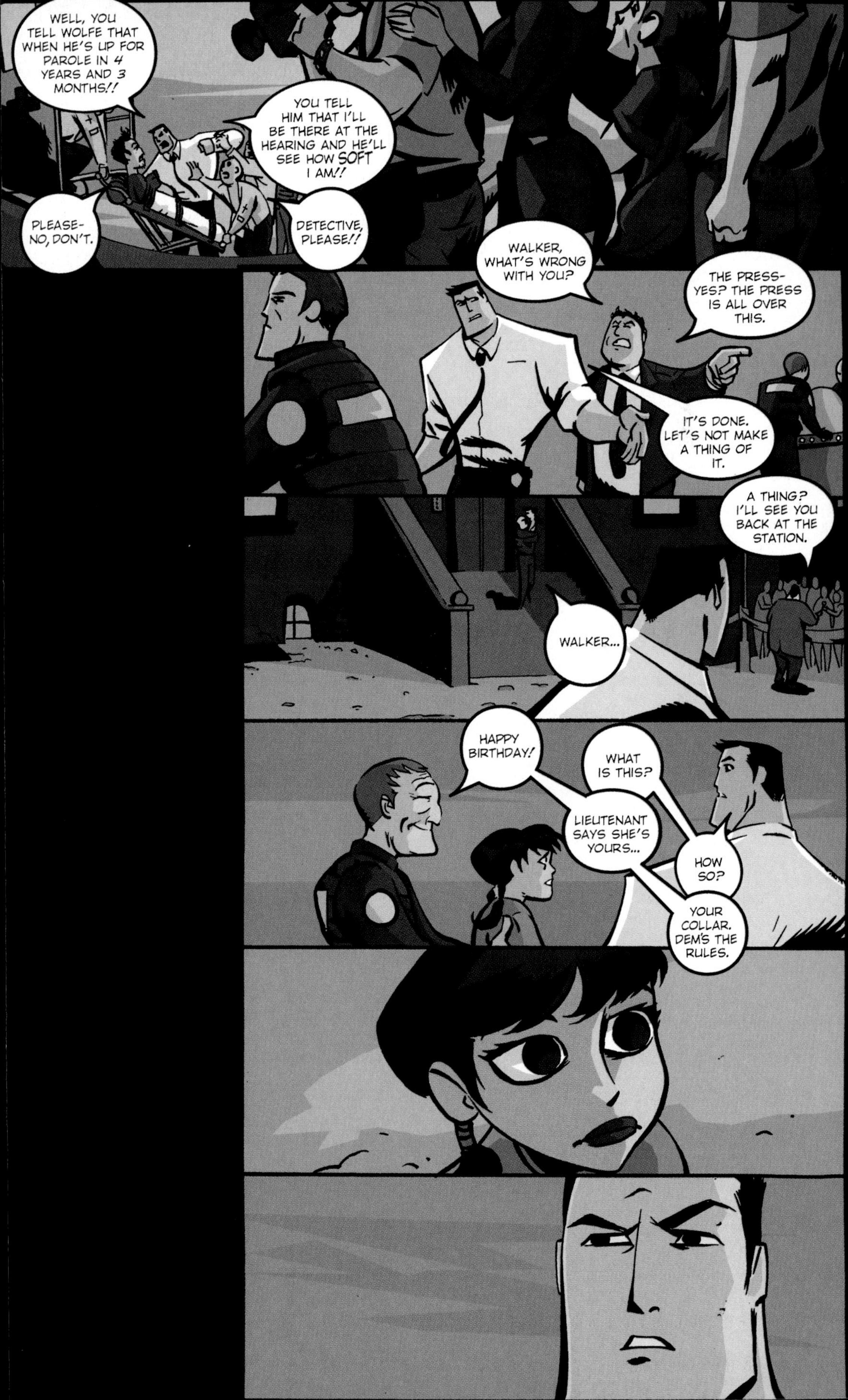
WELL, YOU TELL WOLFE THAT WHEN HE'S UP FOR PAROLE IN 4 YEARS AND 3 MONTHS!!
YOU TELL HIM THAT I'LL BE THERE AT THE HEARING AND HE'LL SEE HOW SOFT I AM!!
PLEASE- NO, DON'T.
DETECTIVE, PLEASE!!
WALKER, WHAT'S WRONG WITH YOU?
THE PRESS- YES? THE PRESS IS ALL OVER THIS.
IT'S DONE. LET'S NOT MAKE A THING OF IT.
A THING? I'LL SEE YOU BACK AT THE STATION.
WALKER...
HAPPY BIRTHDAY!
WHAT IS THIS?
LIEUTENANT SAYS SHE'S YOURS...
HOW SO?
YOUR COLLAR. DEM'S THE RULES.

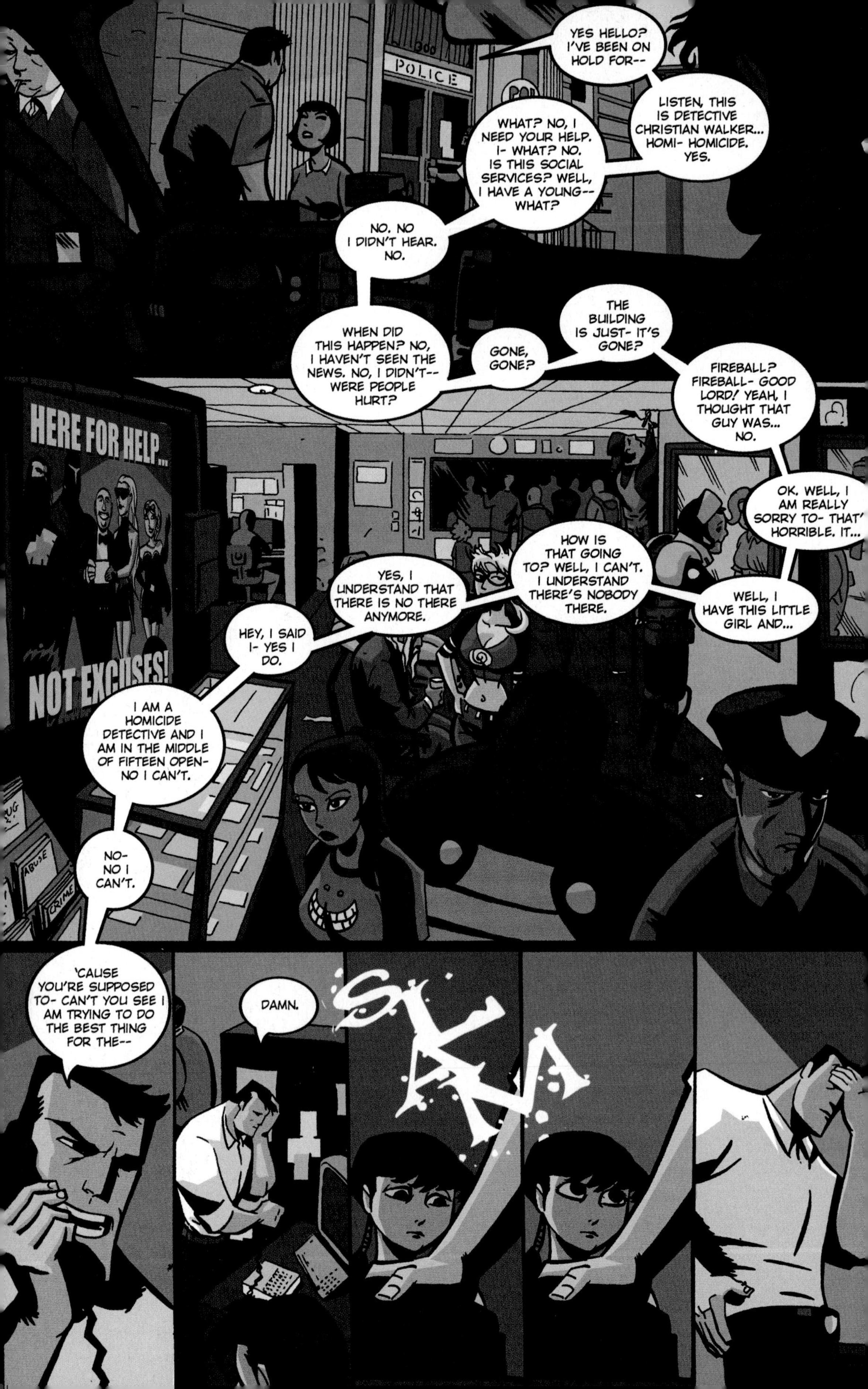
POLICE
YES HELLO? I'VE BEEN ON HOLD FOR--
LISTEN, THIS IS DETECTIVE CHRISTIAN WALKER... HOMI- HOMICIDE. YES.
WHAT? NO, I NEED YOUR HELP. I- WHAT? NO. IS THIS SOCIAL SERVICES? WELL, I HAVE A YOUNG-- WHAT?
NO. NO I DIDN'T HEAR. NO.
WHEN DID THIS HAPPEN? NO, I HAVEN'T SEEN THE NEWS. NO, I DIDN'T-- WERE PEOPLE HURT?
GONE, GONE?
THE BUILDING IS JUST- IT'S GONE?
FIREBALL? FIREBALL- GOOD LORD! YEAH, I THOUGHT THAT GUY WAS... NO.
OK. WELL, I AM REALLY SORRY TO- THAT' HORRIBLE. IT...
WELL, I HAVE THIS LITTLE GIRL AND...
HOW IS THAT GOING TO? WELL, I CAN'T. I UNDERSTAND THERE'S NOBODY THERE.
YES, I UNDERSTAND THAT THERE IS NO THERE ANYMORE.
HEY, I SAID I- YES I DO.
I AM A HOMICIDE DETECTIVE AND I AM IN THE MIDDLE OF FIFTEEN OPEN- NO I CAN'T.
NO- NO I CAN'T.
HERE FOR HELP...
NOT EXCUSES!
ABUSE
CRIME
'CAUSE YOU'RE SUPPOSED TO- CAN'T YOU SEE I AM TRYING TO DO THE BEST THING FOR THE--
DAMN.
SLAM

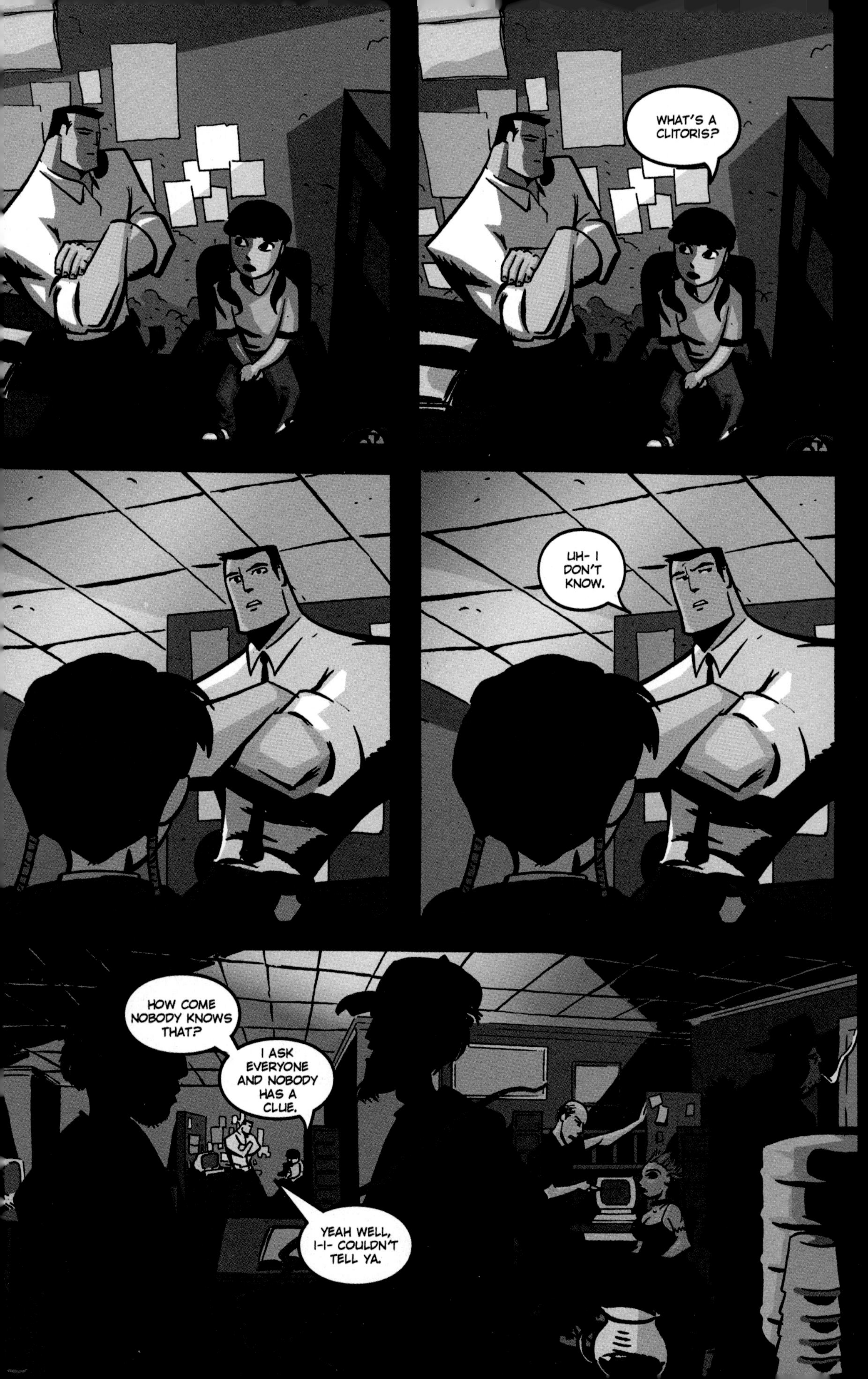
WHAT'S A CLITORIS?
UH- I DON'T KNOW.
HOW COME NOBODY KNOWS THAT?
I ASK EVERYONE AND NOBODY HAS A CLUE.
YEAH WELL, I-I- COULDN'T TELL YA.

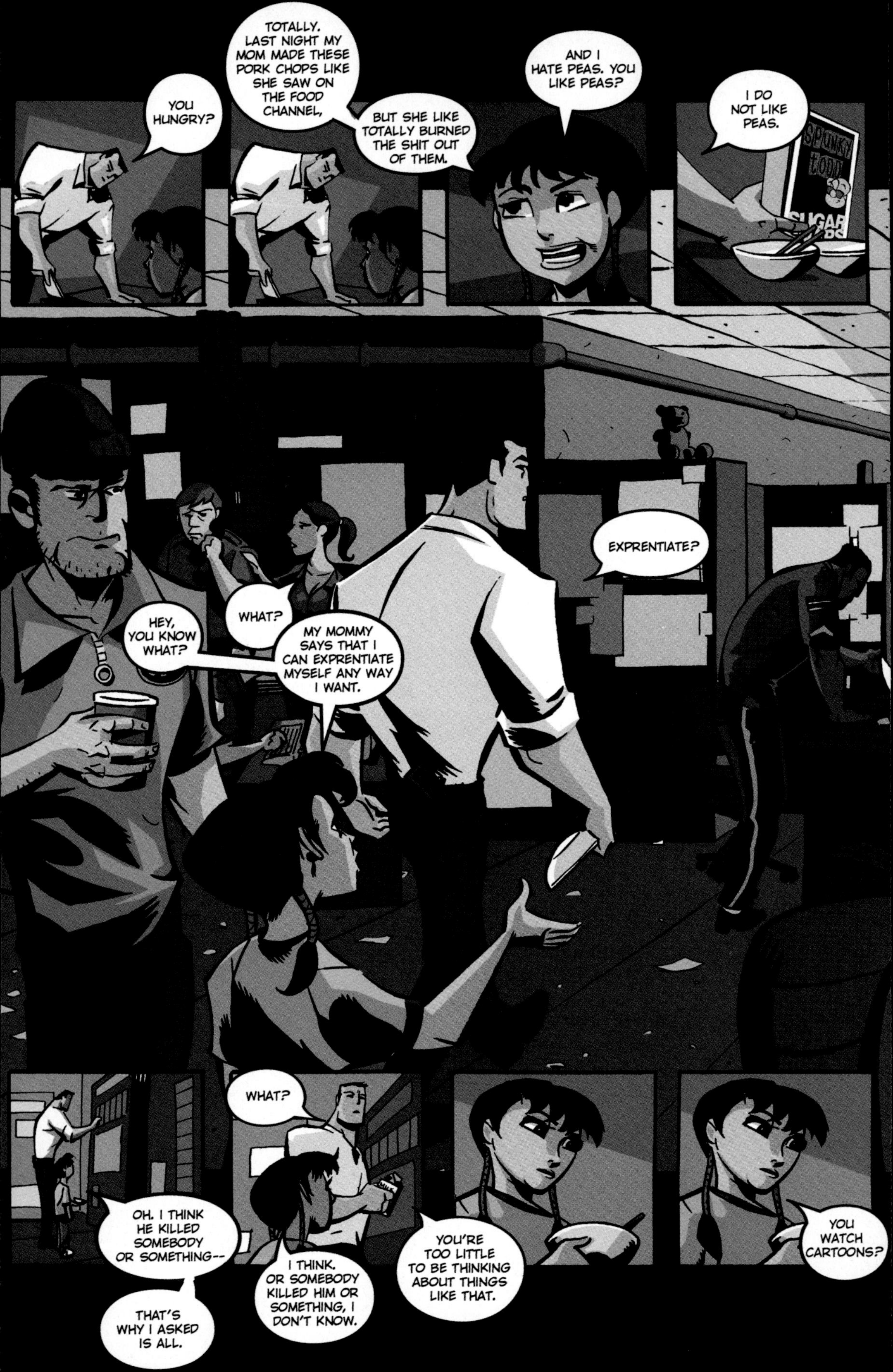
YOU HUNGRY?
TOTALLY. LAST NIGHT MY MOM MADE THESE PORK CHOPS LIKE SHE SAW ON THE FOOD CHANNEL,
BUT SHE LIKE TOTALLY BURNED THE SHIT OUT OF THEM.
AND I HATE PEAS. YOU LIKE PEAS?
I DO NOT LIKE PEAS.
SPUNKY TODD
SUGAR
EXPRENTIATE?
HEY, YOU KNOW WHAT?
WHAT?
MY MOMMY SAYS THAT I CAN EXPRENTIATE MYSELF ANY WAY I WANT.
WHAT?
OH. I THINK HE KILLED SOMEBODY OR SOMETHING--
THAT'S WHY I ASKED IS ALL.
I THINK. OR SOMEBODY KILLED HIM OR SOMETHING, I DON'T KNOW.
YOU'RE TOO LITTLE TO BE THINKING ABOUT THINGS LIKE THAT.
YOU WATCH CARTOONS?

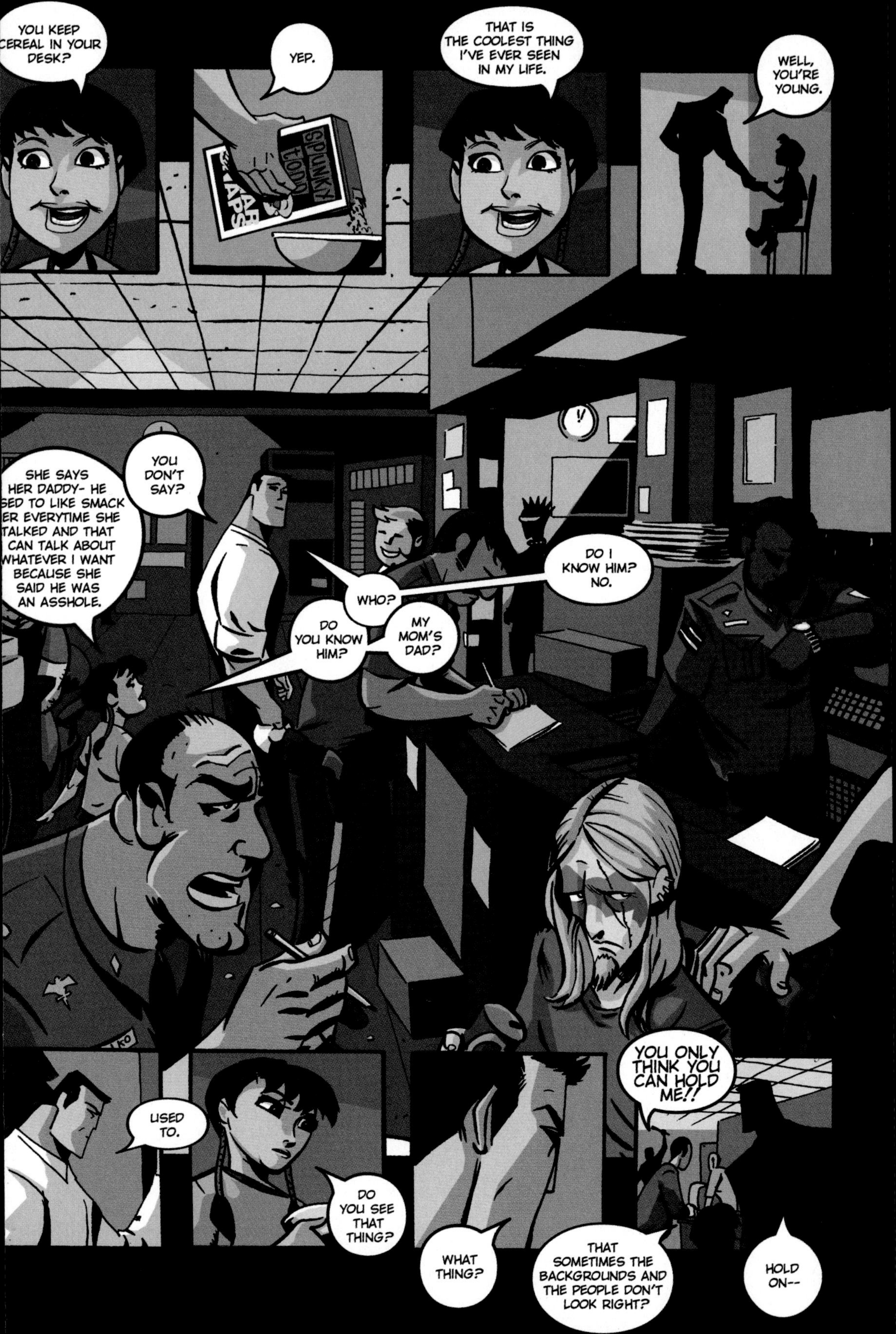

YOU KEEP CEREAL IN YOUR DESK?
YEP.
SPUNKY TODD
THAT IS THE COOLEST THING I'VE EVER SEEN IN MY LIFE.
WELL, YOU'RE YOUNG.
SHE SAYS HER DADDY- HE SED TO LIKE SMACK ER EVERYTIME SHE TALKED AND THAT CAN TALK ABOUT WHATEVER I WANT BECAUSE SHE SAID HE WAS AN ASSHOLE.
YOU DON'T SAY?
WHO?
MY MOM'S DAD?
DO YOU KNOW HIM?
DO I KNOW HIM? NO.
USED TO.
YOU ONLY THINK YOU CAN HOLD ME!!
DO YOU SEE THAT THING?
WHAT THING?
THAT SOMETIMES THE BACKGROUNDS AND THE PEOPLE DON'T LOOK RIGHT?
HOLD ON--

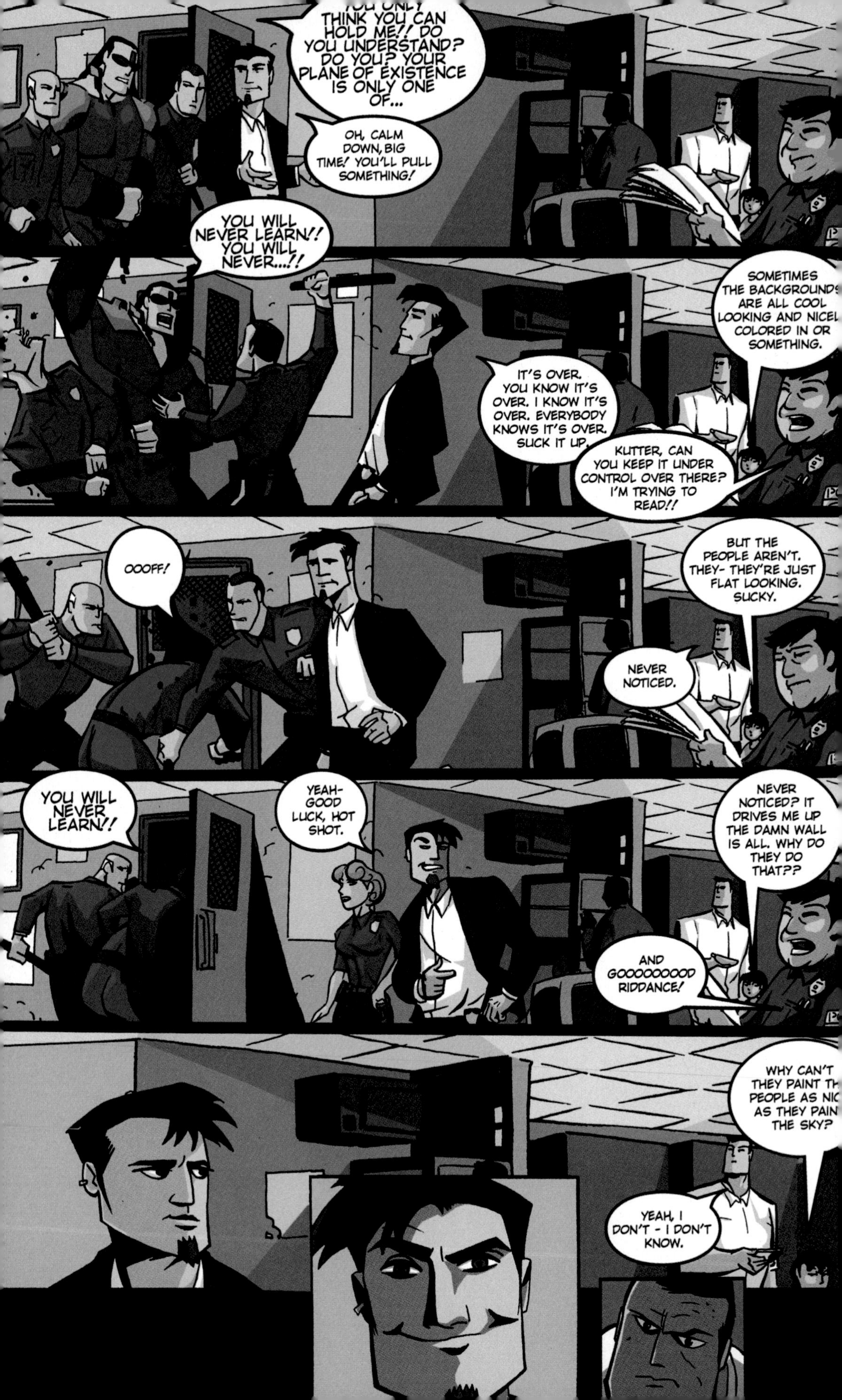

THINK YOU CAN HOLD ME!! DO YOU UNDERSTAND? DO YOU? YOUR PLANE OF EXISTENCE IS ONLY ONE OF...
OH, CALM DOWN, BIG TIME! YOU'LL PULL SOMETHING!
YOU WILL NEVER LEARN!! YOU WILL NEVER...!!
IT'S OVER. YOU KNOW IT'S OVER. I KNOW IT'S OVER. EVERYBODY KNOWS IT'S OVER. SUCK IT UP.
SOMETIMES THE BACKGROUNDS ARE ALL COOL LOOKING AND NICEL COLORED IN OR SOMETHING.
KUTTER, CAN YOU KEEP IT UNDER CONTROL OVER THERE? I'M TRYING TO READ!!
OOOFF!
BUT THE PEOPLE AREN'T. THEY- THEY'RE JUST FLAT LOOKING. SUCKY.
NEVER NOTICED.
YOU WILL NEVER LEARN!!
YEAH- GOOD LUCK, HOT SHOT.
NEVER NOTICED? IT DRIVES ME UP THE DAMN WALL IS ALL. WHY DO THEY DO THAT??
AND GOOOOOOOOD RIDDANCE!
WHY CAN'T THEY PAINT TH PEOPLE AS NIC AS THEY PAIN THE SKY?
YEAH, I DON'T - I DON'T KNOW.

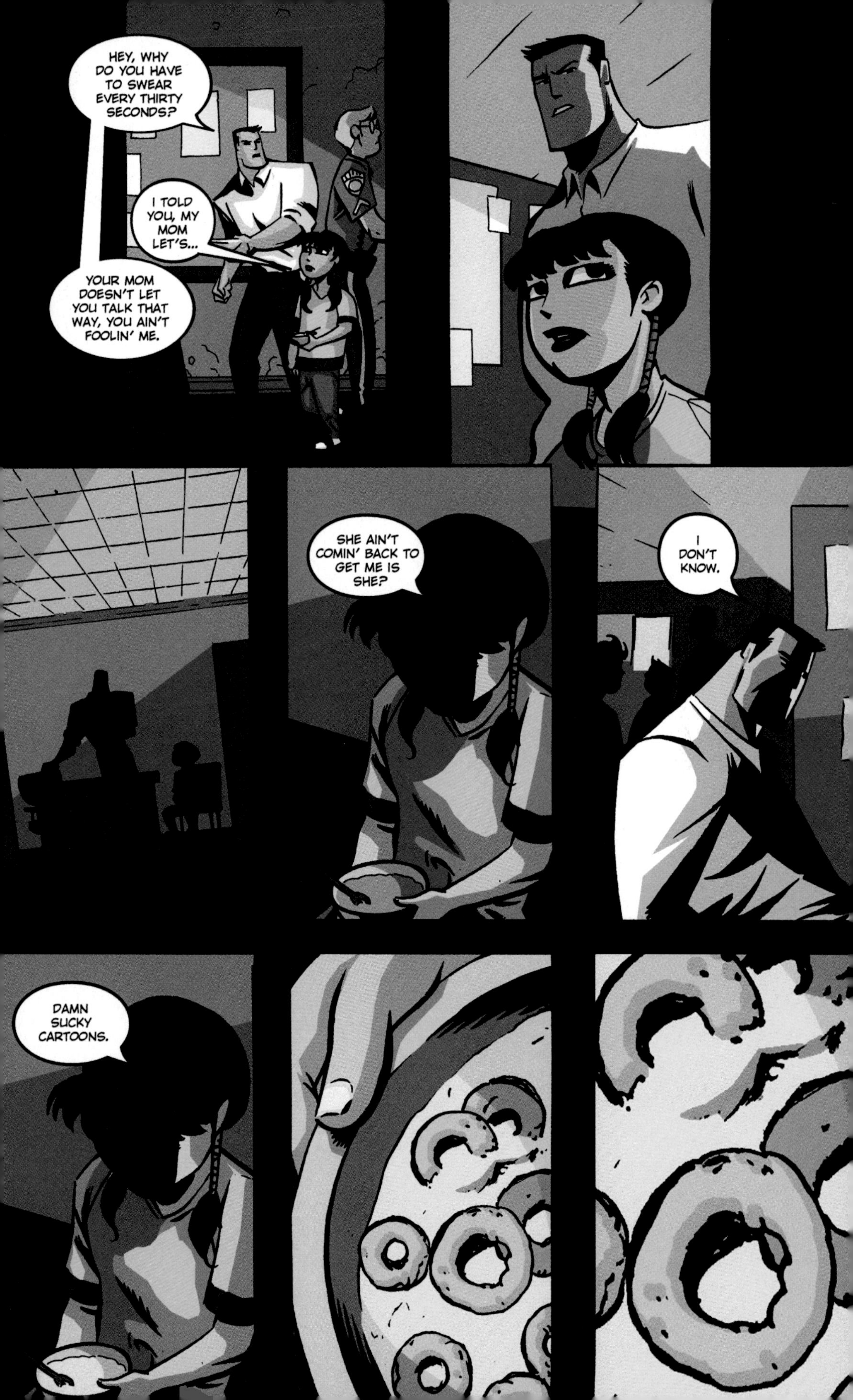
HEY, WHY DO YOU HAVE TO SWEAR EVERY THIRTY SECONDS?
I TOLD YOU, MY MOM LET'S...
YOUR MOM DOESN'T LET YOU TALK THAT WAY, YOU AIN'T FOOLIN' ME.
SHE AIN'T COMIN' BACK TO GET ME IS SHE?
I DON'T KNOW.
DAMN SUCKY CARTOONS.

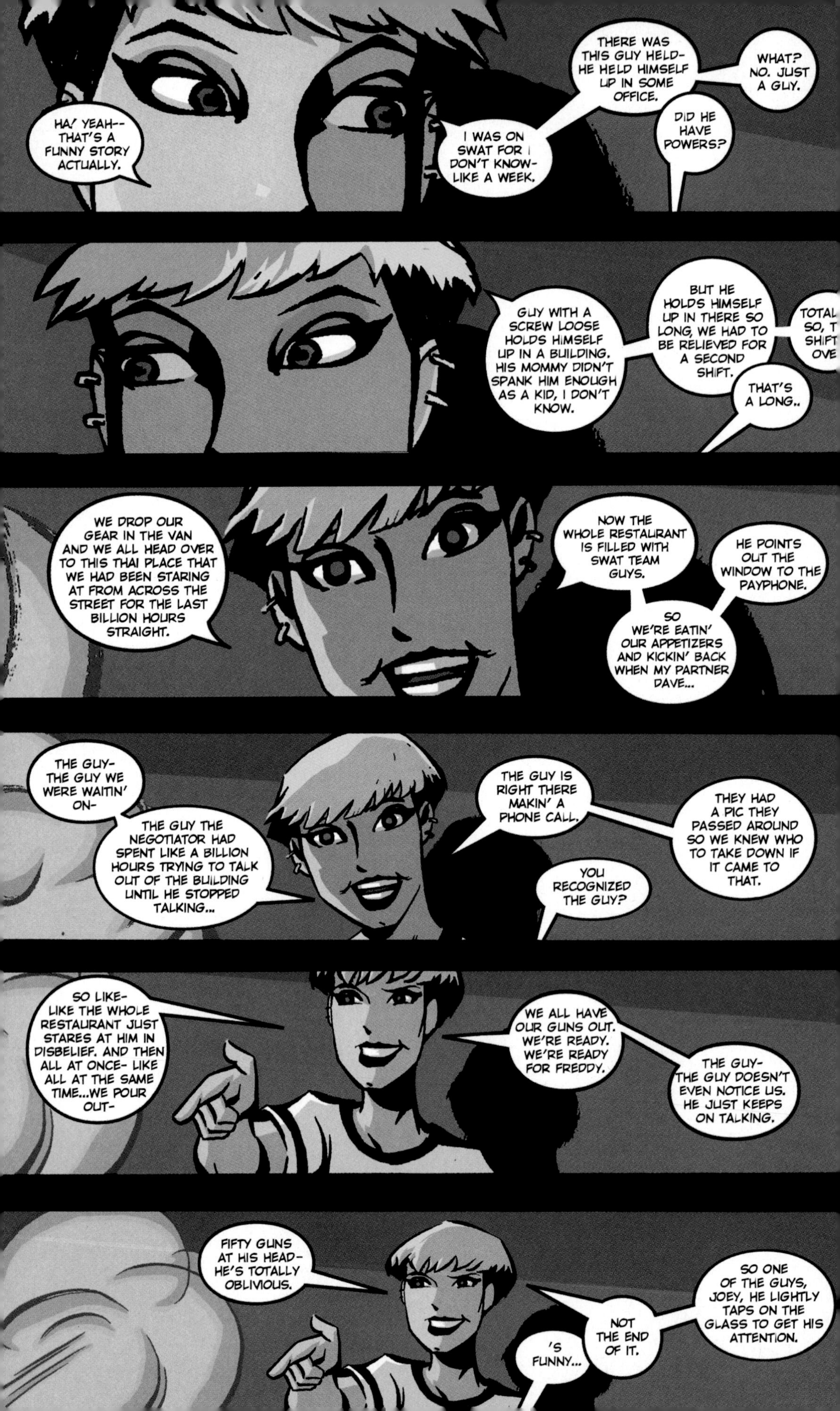

HA! YEAH-- THAT'S A FUNNY STORY ACTUALLY.
I WAS ON SWAT FOR I DON'T KNOW- LIKE A WEEK.
THERE WAS THIS GUY HELD- HE HELD HIMSELF UP IN SOME OFFICE.
DID HE HAVE POWERS?
WHAT? NO. JUST A GUY.
GUY WITH A SCREW LOOSE HOLDS HIMSELF UP IN A BUILDING. HIS MOMMY DIDN'T SPANK HIM ENOUGH AS A KID, I DON'T KNOW.
BUT HE HOLDS HIMSELF UP IN THERE SO LONG, WE HAD TO BE RELIEVED FOR A SECOND SHIFT.
THAT'S A LONG..
WE DROP OUR GEAR IN THE VAN AND WE ALL HEAD OVER TO THIS THAI PLACE THAT WE HAD BEEN STARING AT FROM ACROSS THE STREET FOR THE LAST BILLION HOURS STRAIGHT.
NOW THE WHOLE RESTAURANT IS FILLED WITH SWAT TEAM GUYS.
SO WE'RE EATIN' OUR APPETIZERS AND KICKIN' BACK WHEN MY PARTNER DAVE...
HE POINTS OUT THE WINDOW TO THE PAYPHONE.
THE GUY- THE GUY WE WERE WAITIN' ON-
THE GUY THE NEGOTIATOR HAD SPENT LIKE A BILLION HOURS TRYING TO TALK OUT OF THE BUILDING UNTIL HE STOPPED TALKING...
THE GUY IS RIGHT THERE MAKIN' A PHONE CALL.
YOU RECOGNIZED THE GUY?
THEY HAD A PIC THEY PASSED AROUND SO WE KNEW WHO TO TAKE DOWN IF IT CAME TO THAT.
SO LIKE- LIKE THE WHOLE RESTAURANT JUST STARES AT HIM IN DISBELIEF. AND THEN ALL AT ONCE- LIKE ALL AT THE SAME TIME...WE POUR OUT-
WE ALL HAVE OUR GUNS OUT. WE'RE READY. WE'RE READY FOR FREDDY.
THE GUY- THE GUY DOESN'T EVEN NOTICE US. HE JUST KEEPS ON TALKING.
FIFTY GUNS AT HIS HEAD- HE'S TOTALLY OBLIVIOUS.
'S FUNNY...
NOT THE END OF IT.
SO ONE OF THE GUYS, JOEY, HE LIGHTLY TAPS ON THE GLASS TO GET HIS ATTENTION.

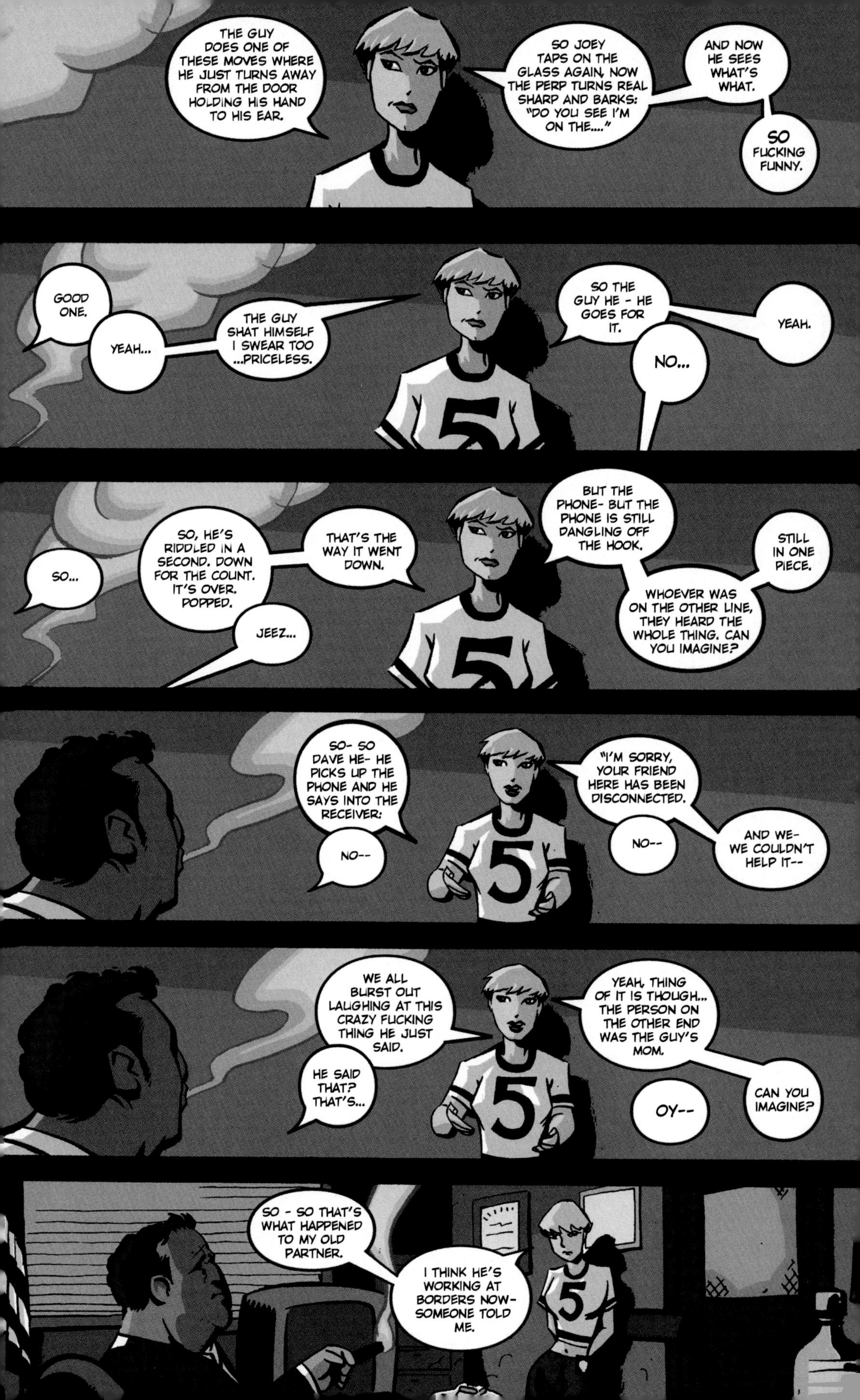
THE GUY DOES ONE OF THESE MOVES WHERE HE JUST TURNS AWAY FROM THE DOOR HOLDING HIS HAND TO HIS EAR.
SO JOEY TAPS ON THE GLASS AGAIN, NOW THE PERP TURNS REAL SHARP AND BARKS: "DO YOU SEE I'M ON THE...."
AND NOW HE SEES WHAT'S WHAT.
SO FUCKING FUNNY.
GOOD ONE.
YEAH...
THE GUY SHAT HIMSELF I SWEAR TOO ...PRICELESS.
SO THE GUY HE - HE GOES FOR IT.
YEAH.
NO...
SO...
SO, HE'S RIDDLED IN A SECOND. DOWN FOR THE COUNT. IT'S OVER. POPPED.
JEEZ...
THAT'S THE WAY IT WENT DOWN.
BUT THE PHONE- BUT THE PHONE IS STILL DANGLING OFF THE HOOK.
STILL IN ONE PIECE.
WHOEVER WAS ON THE OTHER LINE, THEY HEARD THE WHOLE THING. CAN YOU IMAGINE?
SO- SO DAVE HE- HE PICKS UP THE PHONE AND HE SAYS INTO THE RECEIVER:
NO--
"I'M SORRY, YOUR FRIEND HERE HAS BEEN DISCONNECTED.
NO--
AND WE- WE COULDN'T HELP IT--
WE ALL BURST OUT LAUGHING AT THIS CRAZY FUCKING THING HE JUST SAID.
HE SAID THAT? THAT'S...
YEAH, THING OF IT IS THOUGH... THE PERSON ON THE OTHER END WAS THE GUY'S MOM.
OY--
CAN YOU IMAGINE?
SO - SO THAT'S WHAT HAPPENED TO MY OLD PARTNER.
I THINK HE'S WORKING AT BORDERS NOW- SOMEONE TOLD ME.

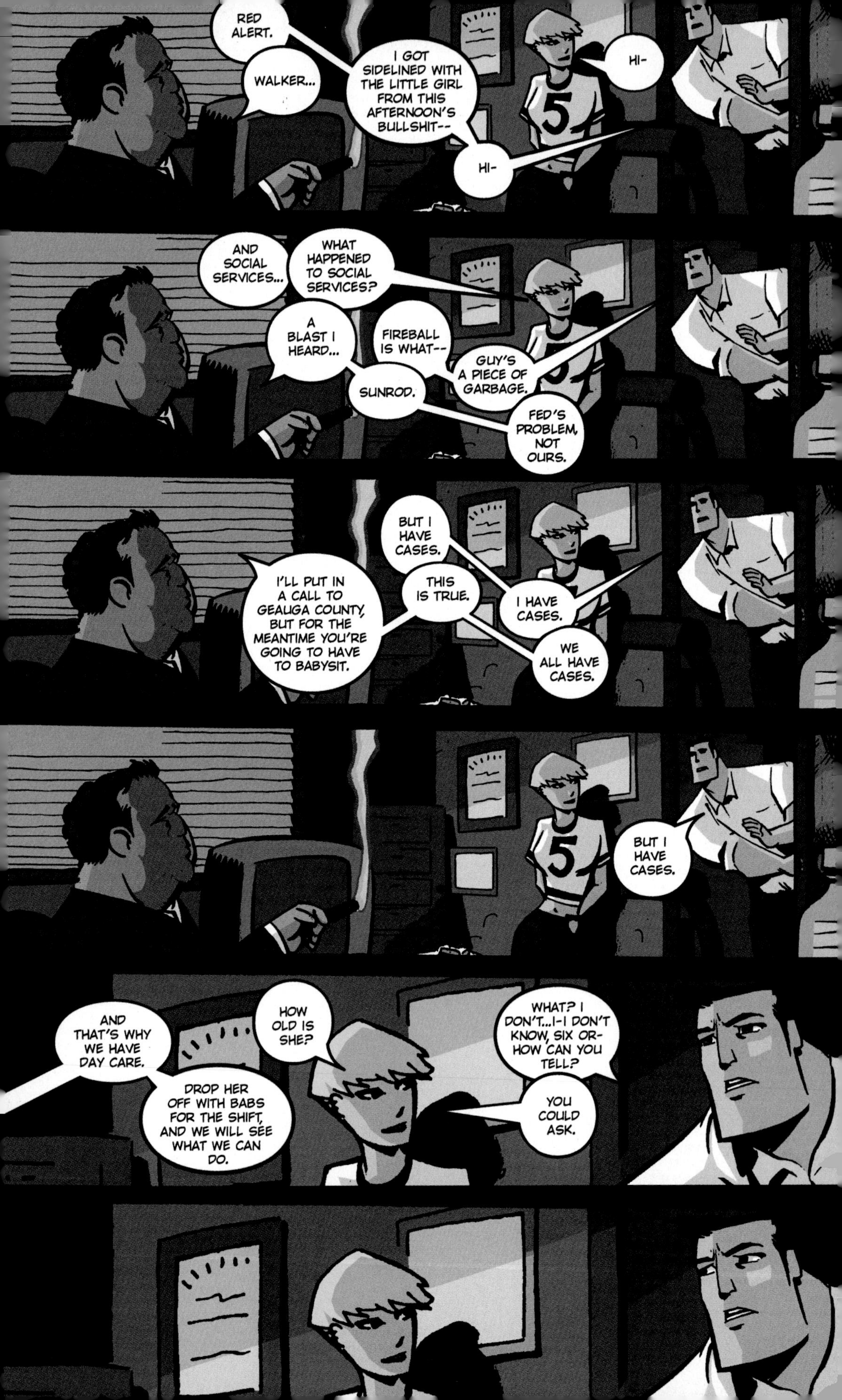
RED ALERT.
WALKER...
I GOT SIDELINED WITH THE LITTLE GIRL FROM THIS AFTERNOON'S BULLSHIT--
HI-
HI-
AND SOCIAL SERVICES...
WHAT HAPPENED TO SOCIAL SERVICES?
A BLAST I HEARD...
FIREBALL IS WHAT--
SUNROD.
GUY'S A PIECE OF GARBAGE.
FED'S PROBLEM, NOT OURS.
I'LL PUT IN A CALL TO GEAUGA COUNTY, BUT FOR THE MEANTIME YOU'RE GOING TO HAVE TO BABYSIT.
BUT I HAVE CASES.
THIS IS TRUE.
I HAVE CASES.
WE ALL HAVE CASES.
BUT I HAVE CASES.
AND THAT'S WHY WE HAVE DAY CARE.
DROP HER OFF WITH BABS FOR THE SHIFT, AND WE WILL SEE WHAT WE CAN DO.
HOW OLD IS SHE?
WHAT? I DON'T...I-I DON'T KNOW, SIX OR- HOW CAN YOU TELL?
YOU COULD ASK.

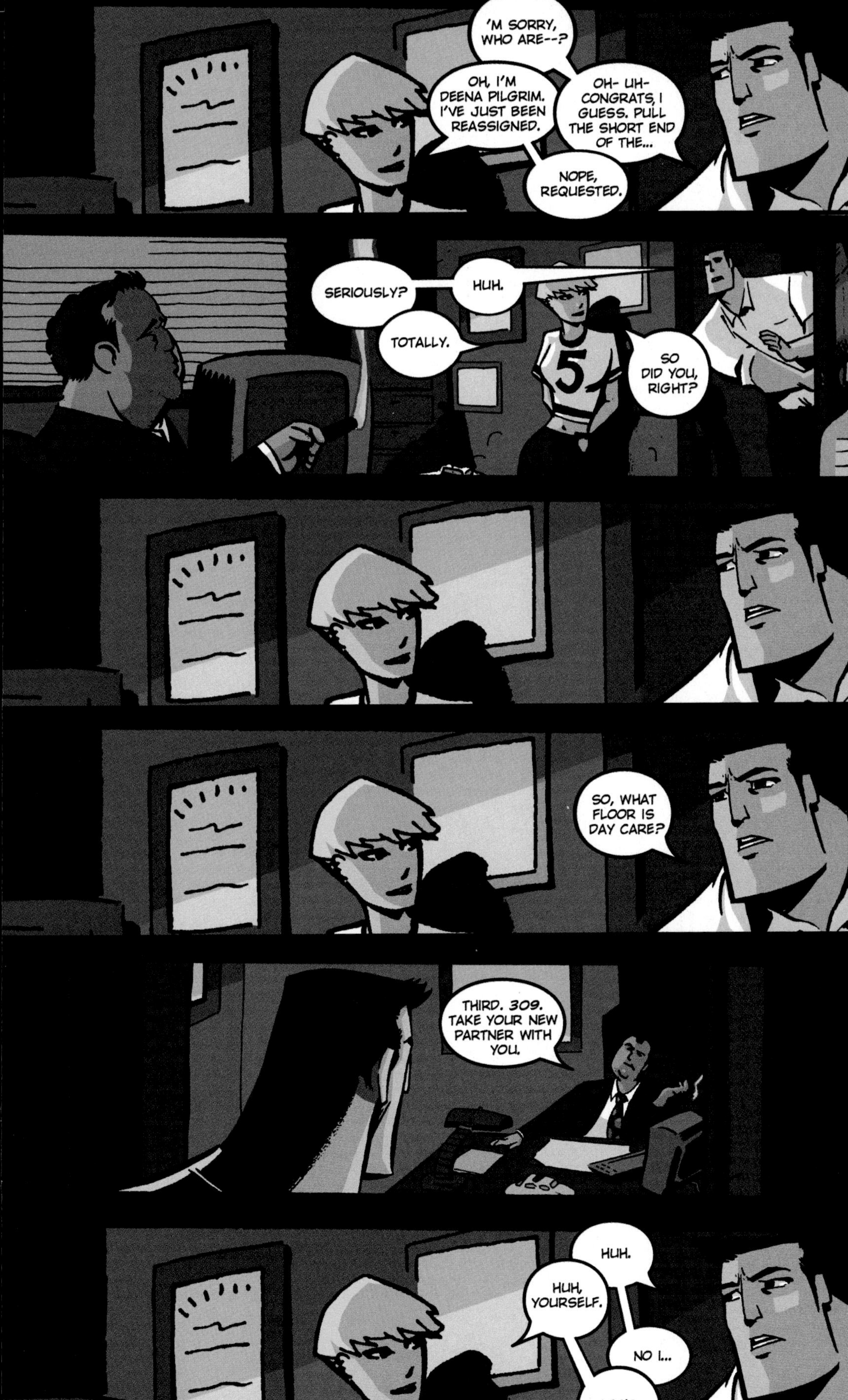
'M SORRY, WHO ARE--?
OH, I'M DEENA PILGRIM. I'VE JUST BEEN REASSIGNED.
OH- UH- CONGRATS, I GUESS. PULL THE SHORT END OF THE...
NOPE, REQUESTED.
SERIOUSLY?
HUH.
TOTALLY.
SO DID YOU, RIGHT?
SO, WHAT FLOOR IS DAY CARE?
THIRD. 309. TAKE YOUR NEW PARTNER WITH YOU.
HUH.
HUH, YOURSELF.
NO I...

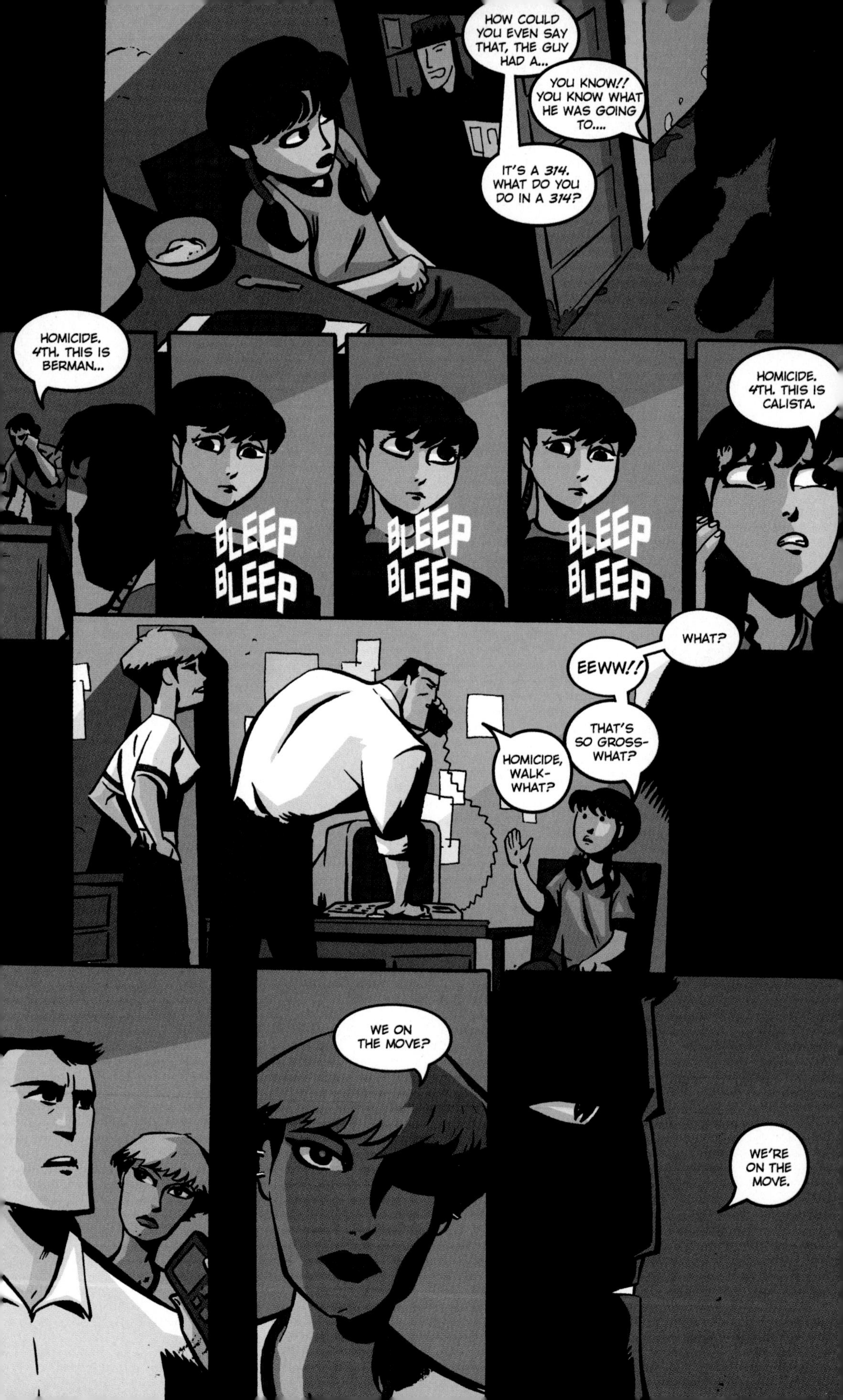
HOW COULD YOU EVEN SAY THAT, THE GUY HAD A...
YOU KNOW!! YOU KNOW WHAT HE WAS GOING TO....
IT'S A 314. WHAT DO YOU DO IN A 314?
HOMICIDE. 4TH. THIS IS BERMAN...
BLEEP BLEEP
BLEEP BLEEP
BLEEP BLEEP
HOMICIDE. 4TH. THIS IS CALISTA.
WHAT?
EEWW!!
THAT'S SO GROSS-WHAT?
HOMICIDE, WALK-WHAT?
WE ON THE MOVE?
WE'RE ON THE MOVE.

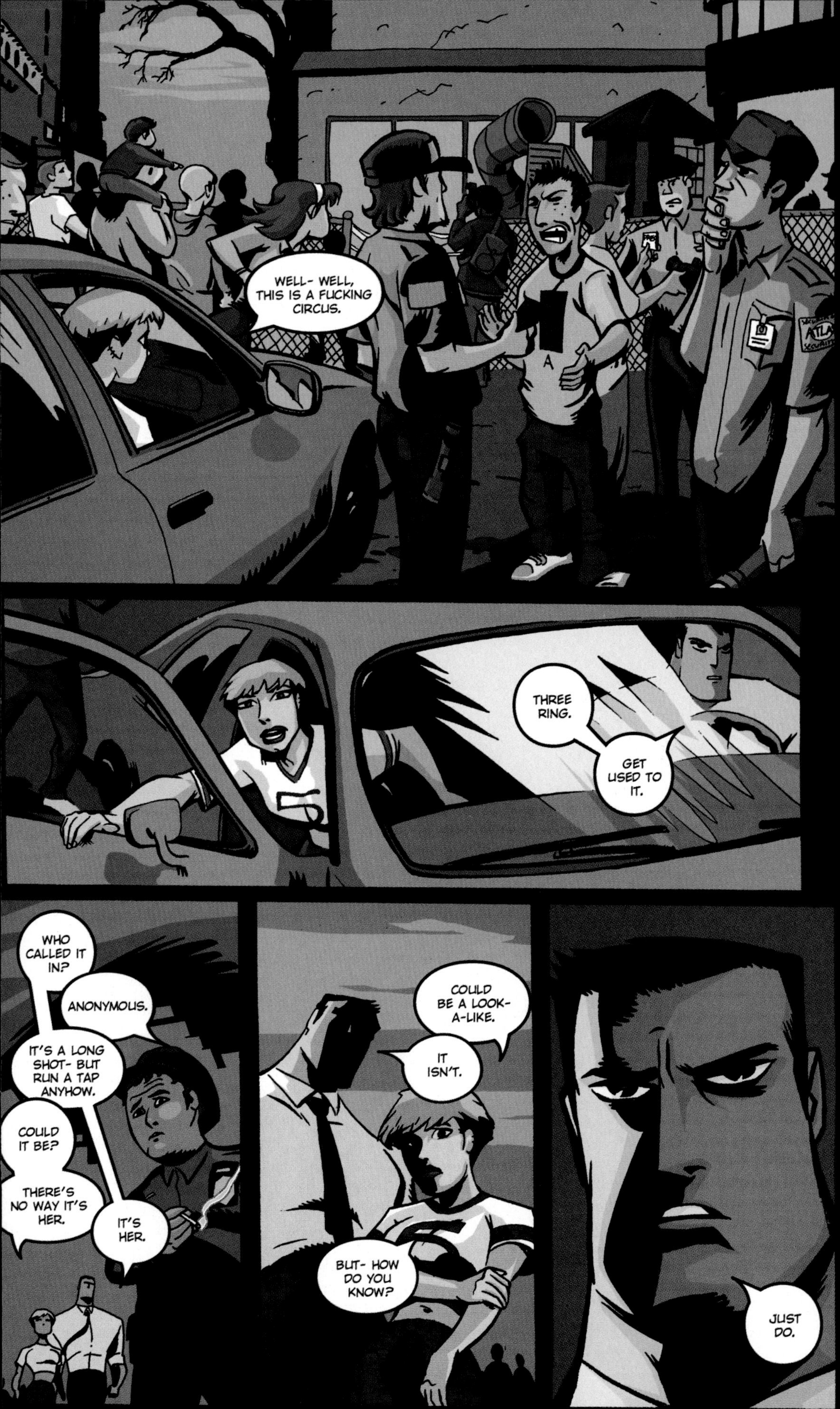
WELL- WELL, THIS IS A FUCKING CIRCUS.
THREE RING.
GET USED TO IT.
WHO CALLED IT IN?
ANONYMOUS.
IT'S A LONG SHOT- BUT RUN A TAP ANYHOW.
COULD IT BE?
THERE'S NO WAY IT'S HER.
IT'S HER.
COULD BE A LOOK-A-LIKE.
IT ISN'T.
BUT- HOW DO YOU KNOW?
JUST DO.

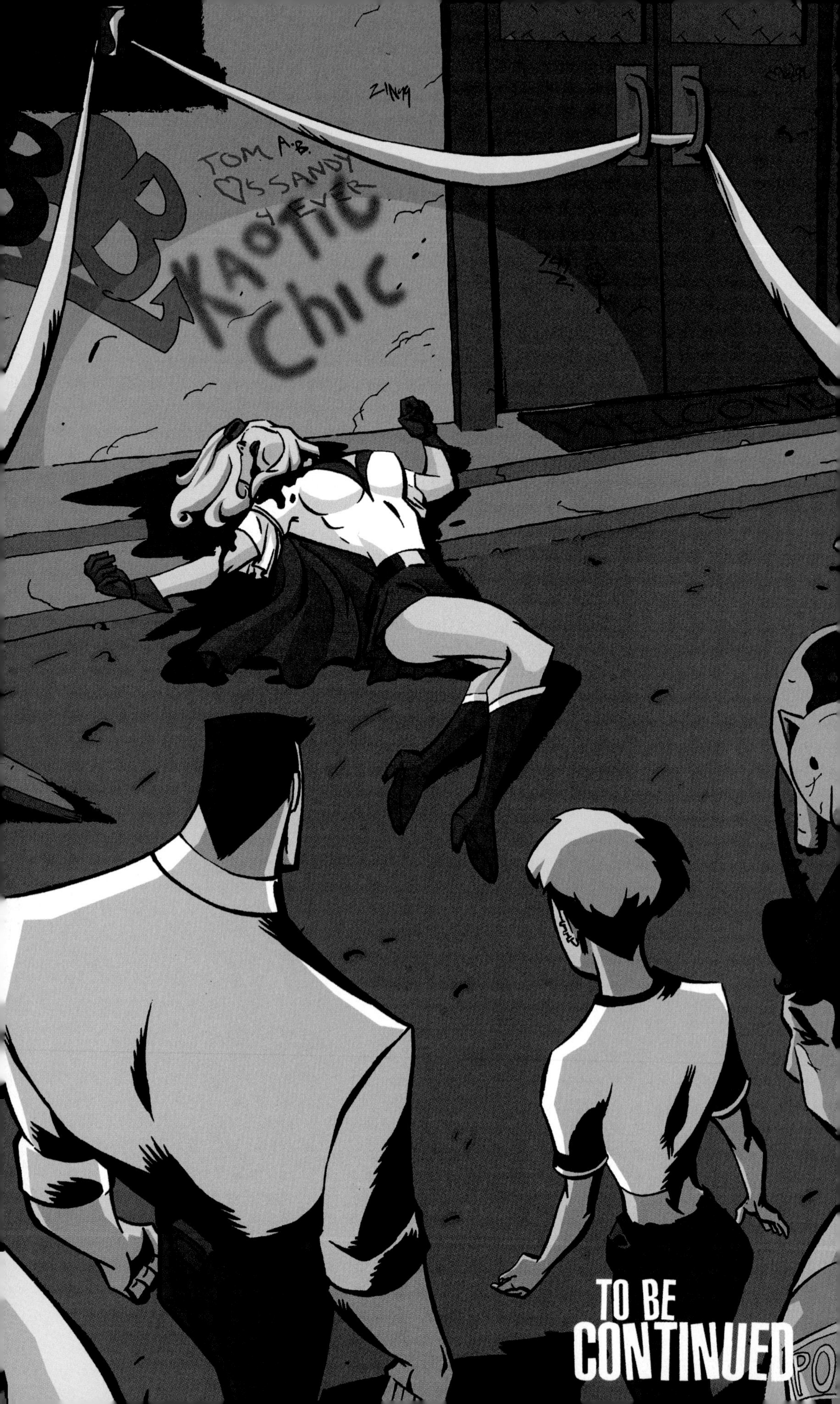
TOM A.B.
♡SSANDY
4 EVER
KAOTIC
Chic
TO BE
CONTINUED

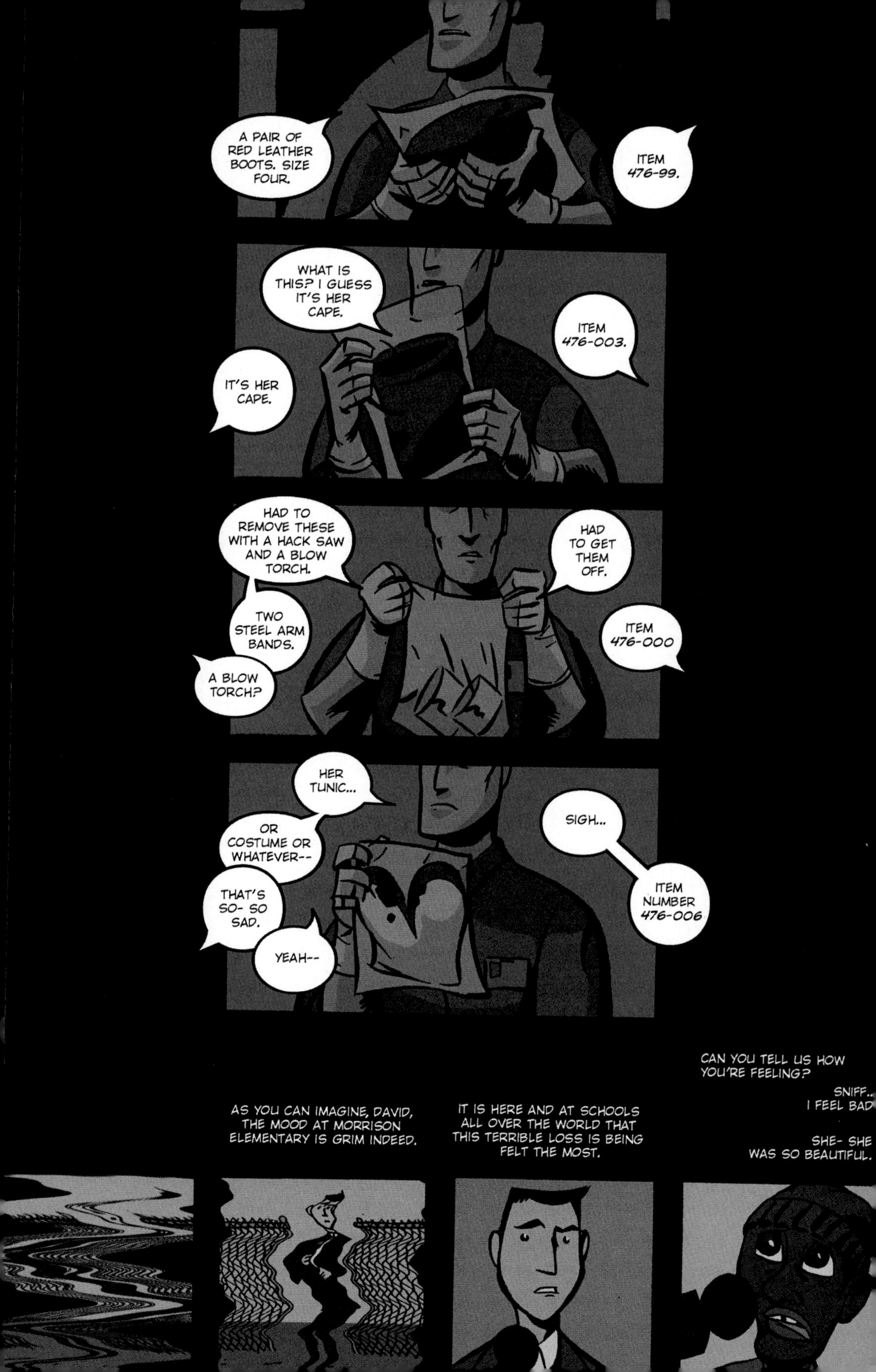
A PAIR OF RED LEATHER BOOTS. SIZE FOUR.
ITEM 476-99.
WHAT IS THIS? I GUESS IT'S HER CAPE.
ITEM 476-003.
IT'S HER CAPE.
HAD TO REMOVE THESE WITH A HACK SAW AND A BLOW TORCH.
HAD TO GET THEM OFF.
TWO STEEL ARM BANDS.
ITEM 476-000
A BLOW TORCH?
HER TUNIC...
OR COSTUME OR WHATEVER--
SIGH...
THAT'S SO- SO SAD.
ITEM NUMBER 476-006
YEAH--
AS YOU CAN IMAGINE, DAVID, THE MOOD AT MORRISON ELEMENTARY IS GRIM INDEED.
IT IS HERE AND AT SCHOOLS ALL OVER THE WORLD THAT THIS TERRIBLE LOSS IS BEING FELT THE MOST.
CAN YOU TELL US HOW YOU'RE FEELING?
SNIFF.. I FEEL BAD
SHE- SHE WAS SO BEAUTIFUL.

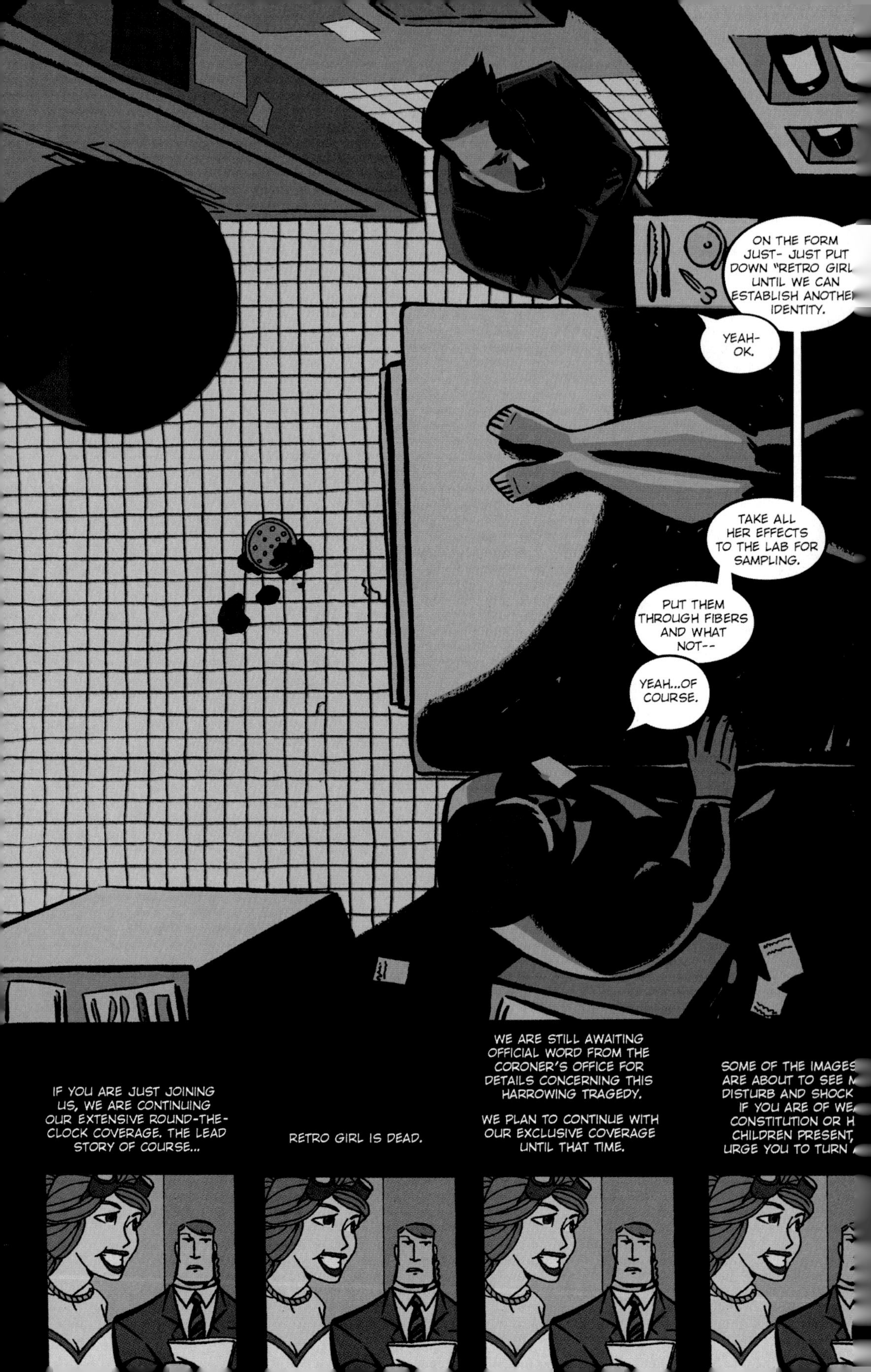
ON THE FORM JUST- JUST PUT DOWN "RETRO GIRL UNTIL WE CAN ESTABLISH ANOTHE IDENTITY.
YEAH- OK.
TAKE ALL HER EFFECTS TO THE LAB FOR SAMPLING.
PUT THEM THROUGH FIBERS AND WHAT NOT--
YEAH...OF COURSE.
IF YOU ARE JUST JOINING US, WE ARE CONTINUING OUR EXTENSIVE ROUND-THE-CLOCK COVERAGE. THE LEAD STORY OF COURSE...
RETRO GIRL IS DEAD.
WE ARE STILL AWAITING OFFICIAL WORD FROM THE CORONER'S OFFICE FOR DETAILS CONCERNING THIS HARROWING TRAGEDY.
WE PLAN TO CONTINUE WITH OUR EXCLUSIVE COVERAGE UNTIL THAT TIME.
SOME OF THE IMAGES ARE ABOUT TO SEE DISTURB AND SHOCK IF YOU ARE OF WE CONSTITUTION OR H CHILDREN PRESENT, URGE YOU TO TURN

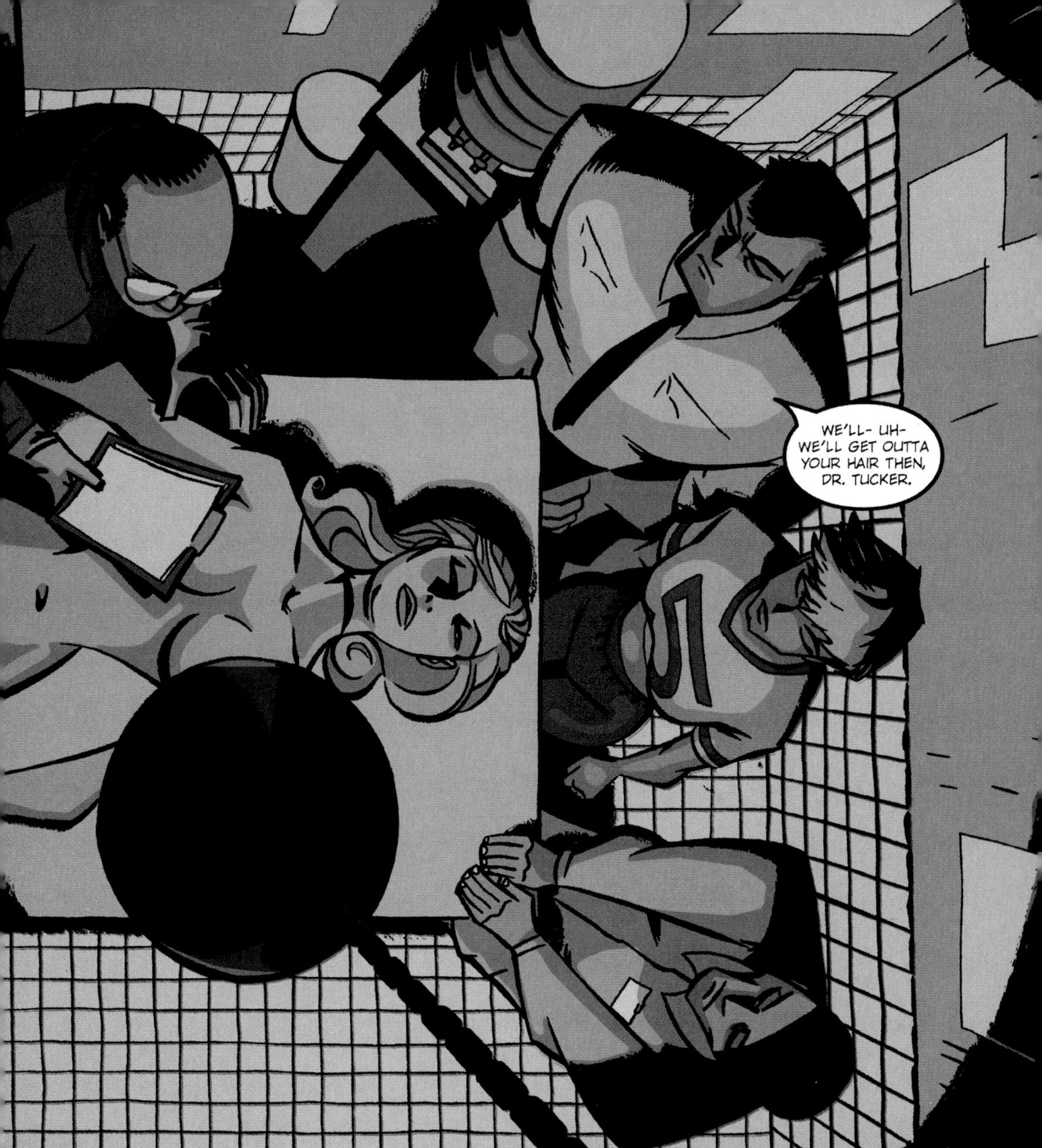
WE'LL- UH- WE'LL GET OUTTA YOUR HAIR THEN, DR. TUCKER.

T WAS JUST UNDER THREE HOURS AGO, EASTERN STANDARD TIME, THAT WE RECEIVED WORD THAT THE ALLEN BODY OF RETRO GIRL VAS FOUND LYING DEAD ON THE PLAYGROUND OF MORRISON ELEMENTARY.

THESE EXCLUSIVE IMAGES WHERE TAKEN JUST MOMENTS BEFORE POLICE ARRIVED, CLOSING BOTH THE PLAYGROUND AND THE SCHOOL TO THE PUBLIC.

THE CAUSE AND INCIDENT OF HER DEATH REMAINS A MYSTERY. WAS IT AN ACCIDENT THAT BEFELL ONE OF OUR NATION'S MOST BELOVED AND REVERED HEROES?

OR DID SHE BECOME YET ANOTHER VICTIM OF THE VIOLENT WORLD THAT SHE HAD SO BOLDLY SWORN TO PROTECT?

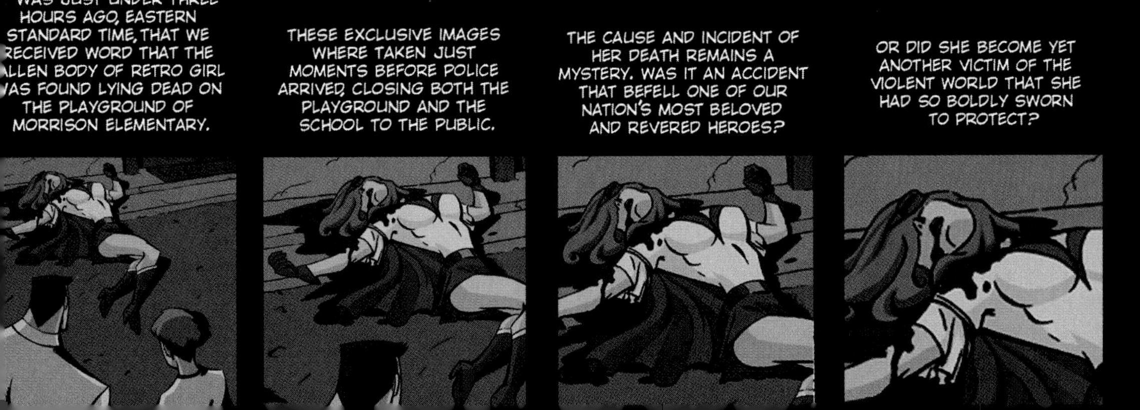

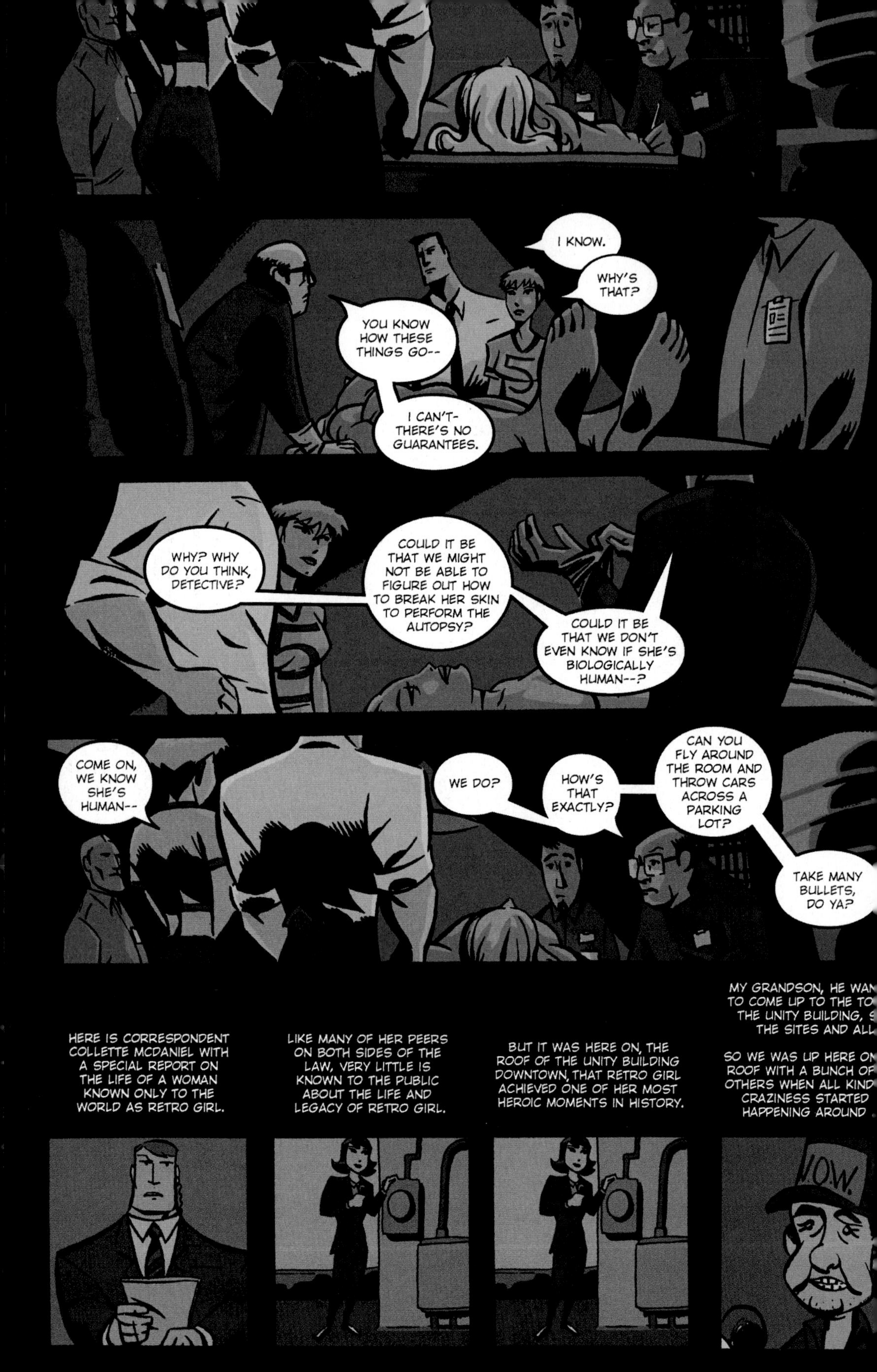

I KNOW.
WHY'S THAT?
YOU KNOW HOW THESE THINGS GO--
I CAN'T- THERE'S NO GUARANTEES.
WHY? WHY DO YOU THINK, DETECTIVE?
COULD IT BE THAT WE MIGHT NOT BE ABLE TO FIGURE OUT HOW TO BREAK HER SKIN TO PERFORM THE AUTOPSY?
COULD IT BE THAT WE DON'T EVEN KNOW IF SHE'S BIOLOGICALLY HUMAN--?
COME ON, WE KNOW SHE'S HUMAN--
WE DO?
HOW'S THAT EXACTLY?
CAN YOU FLY AROUND THE ROOM AND THROW CARS ACROSS A PARKING LOT?
TAKE MANY BULLETS, DO YA?
HERE IS CORRESPONDENT COLLETTE MCDANIEL WITH A SPECIAL REPORT ON THE LIFE OF A WOMAN KNOWN ONLY TO THE WORLD AS RETRO GIRL.
LIKE MANY OF HER PEERS ON BOTH SIDES OF THE LAW, VERY LITTLE IS KNOWN TO THE PUBLIC ABOUT THE LIFE AND LEGACY OF RETRO GIRL.
BUT IT WAS HERE ON, THE ROOF OF THE UNITY BUILDING DOWNTOWN, THAT RETRO GIRL ACHIEVED ONE OF HER MOST HEROIC MOMENTS IN HISTORY.
MY GRANDSON, HE WAN TO COME UP TO THE TO THE UNITY BUILDING, THE SITES AND ALL
SO WE WAS UP HERE ON ROOF WITH A BUNCH OF OTHERS WHEN ALL KIND CRAZINESS STARTED HAPPENING AROUND
V.O.W.

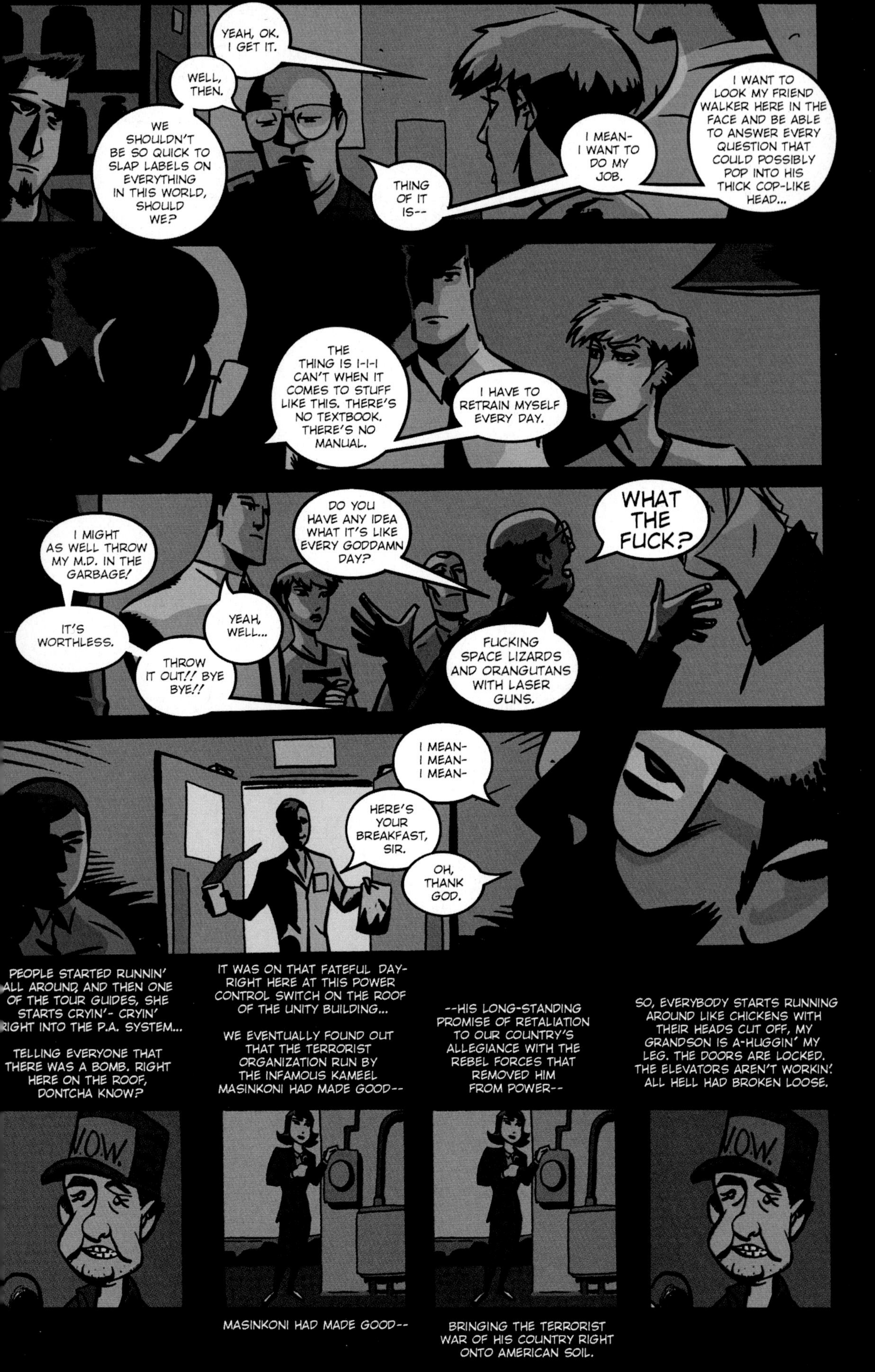
YEAH, OK. I GET IT.
WELL, THEN.
WE SHOULDN'T BE SO QUICK TO SLAP LABELS ON EVERYTHING IN THIS WORLD, SHOULD WE?
THING OF IT IS--
I MEAN- I WANT TO DO MY JOB.
I WANT TO LOOK MY FRIEND WALKER HERE IN THE FACE AND BE ABLE TO ANSWER EVERY QUESTION THAT COULD POSSIBLY POP INTO HIS THICK COP-LIKE HEAD...
THE THING IS I-I-I CAN'T WHEN IT COMES TO STUFF LIKE THIS. THERE'S NO TEXTBOOK. THERE'S NO MANUAL.
I HAVE TO RETRAIN MYSELF EVERY DAY.
I MIGHT AS WELL THROW MY M.D. IN THE GARBAGE!
IT'S WORTHLESS.
THROW IT OUT!! BYE BYE!!
YEAH, WELL...
DO YOU HAVE ANY IDEA WHAT IT'S LIKE EVERY GODDAMN DAY?
WHAT THE FUCK?
FUCKING SPACE LIZARDS AND ORANGUTANS WITH LASER GUNS.
I MEAN- I MEAN- I MEAN-
HERE'S YOUR BREAKFAST, SIR.
OH, THANK GOD.
PEOPLE STARTED RUNNIN' ALL AROUND, AND THEN ONE OF THE TOUR GUIDES, SHE STARTS CRYIN'- CRYIN' RIGHT INTO THE P.A. SYSTEM...
TELLING EVERYONE THAT THERE WAS A BOMB. RIGHT HERE ON THE ROOF, DONTCHA KNOW?
V.O.W.
IT WAS ON THAT FATEFUL DAY- RIGHT HERE AT THIS POWER CONTROL SWITCH ON THE ROOF OF THE UNITY BUILDING...
WE EVENTUALLY FOUND OUT THAT THE TERRORIST ORGANIZATION RUN BY THE INFAMOUS KAMEEL MASINKONI HAD MADE GOOD--
MASINKONI HAD MADE GOOD--
--HIS LONG-STANDING PROMISE OF RETALIATION TO OUR COUNTRY'S ALLEGIANCE WITH THE REBEL FORCES THAT REMOVED HIM FROM POWER--
BRINGING THE TERRORIST WAR OF HIS COUNTRY RIGHT ONTO AMERICAN SOIL.
SO, EVERYBODY STARTS RUNNING AROUND LIKE CHICKENS WITH THEIR HEADS CUT OFF, MY GRANDSON IS A-HUGGIN' MY LEG. THE DOORS ARE LOCKED. THE ELEVATORS AREN'T WORKIN'. ALL HELL HAD BROKEN LOOSE.
V.O.W.

AAAAHHH! MAMA LUCIOUSEN!

WHAT WAS I SAYING?

'ORANGUTANS WITH LASER GUNS...'

OH YEAH. OH- NEVER MIND ABOUT THAT--

I HAVE TO GET TO WORK.

I'LL SEE WHAT I CAN DO ABOUT OUR FALLEN HERO.

GREAT.

THIS IS DEENA PILGRIM. SHE'S WORKING WITH ME, IT SEEMS.

THIS IS HER FIRST...

I DIDN'T GET YOUR NAME--

WELL, VERY NICE TO MEET YOU. I GUESS WE'LL BE TALKING OFTEN.

GREAT.

O.T.R.

NO SHIT.

I MEAN, HAVE YOU EVER SEEN HER IN PERSON?

SHE'S- SHE'S QUITE A HANDSOME LITTLE WOMAN. EVEN WITH ALL THE RUCKUS AND THE BOMB AND ALL. I COULDN'T HELP BUT NOTICE.

AND I MEAN, AS FAST AS YOU CAN SAY FANG DANG DOODLE- SHE RIPPED THE GODDAMN CONTRAPTION OR WHATEVER IT WAS OFF THE WALL AND FLEW WAY UP INTO THE SKY WITH IT.

--AND THAT'S- THAT'S WHEN I FIRST SAW HER.

AND THEN...BLOOEY!

AMATUER VIDEO FOOTAGE

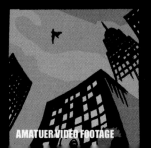

AMATUER VIDEO FOOTAGE

AMATUER VIDEO FOOTAGE

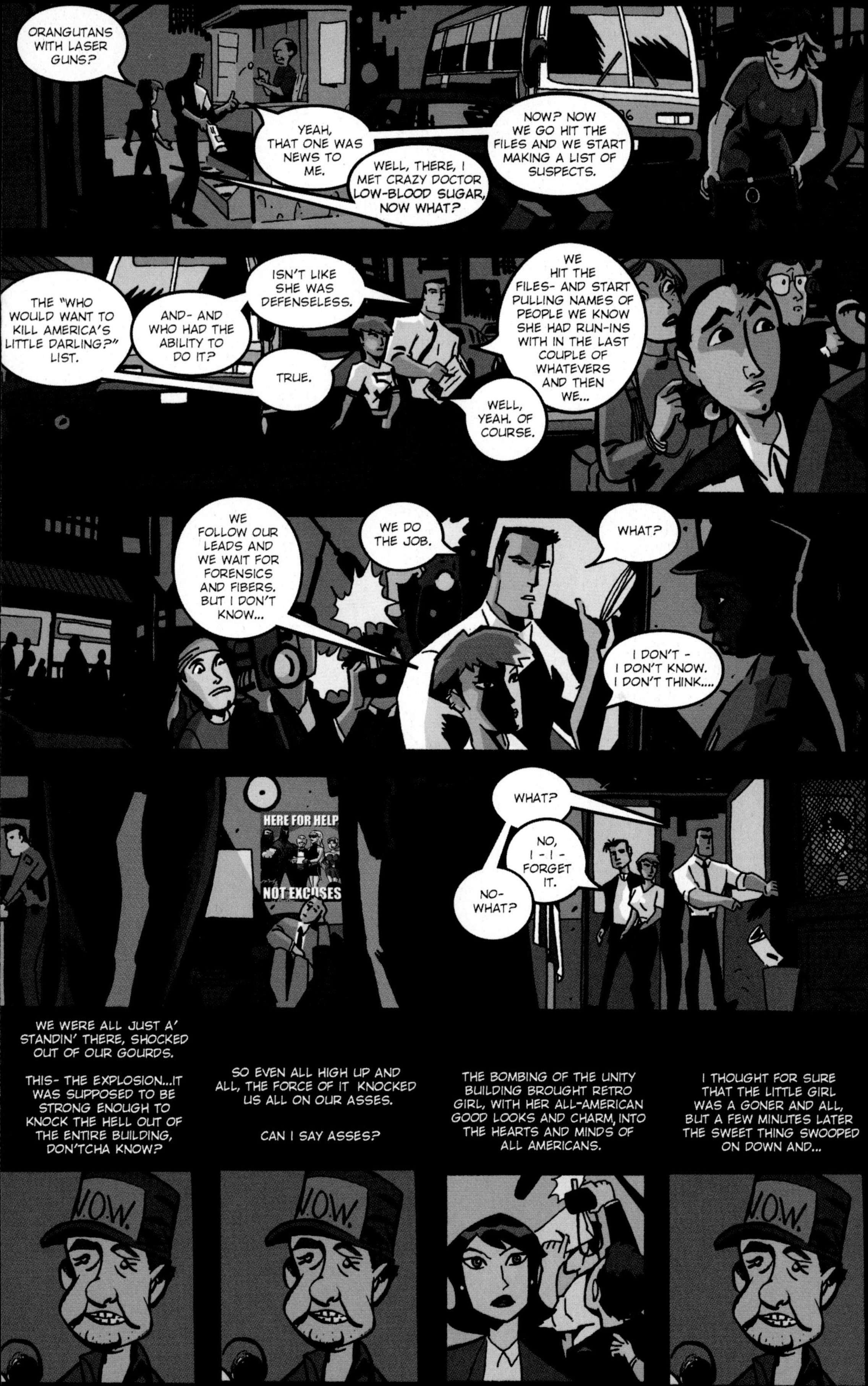
ORANGUTANS WITH LASER GUNS?
YEAH, THAT ONE WAS NEWS TO ME.
WELL, THERE, I MET CRAZY DOCTOR LOW-BLOOD SUGAR, NOW WHAT?
NOW? NOW WE GO HIT THE FILES AND WE START MAKING A LIST OF SUSPECTS.
THE "WHO WOULD WANT TO KILL AMERICA'S LITTLE DARLING?" LIST.
AND- AND WHO HAD THE ABILITY TO DO IT?
ISN'T LIKE SHE WAS DEFENSELESS.
TRUE.
WE HIT THE FILES- AND START PULLING NAMES OF PEOPLE WE KNOW SHE HAD RUN-INS WITH IN THE LAST COUPLE OF WHATEVERS AND THEN WE...
WELL, YEAH. OF COURSE.
WE FOLLOW OUR LEADS AND WE WAIT FOR FORENSICS AND FIBERS. BUT I DON'T KNOW...
WE DO THE JOB.
WHAT?
I DON'T - I DON'T KNOW. I DON'T THINK....
HERE FOR HELP
NOT EXCUSES
WHAT?
NO, I - I - FORGET IT.
NO- WHAT?
WE WERE ALL JUST A' STANDIN' THERE, SHOCKED OUT OF OUR GOURDS.
THIS- THE EXPLOSION...IT WAS SUPPOSED TO BE STRONG ENOUGH TO KNOCK THE HELL OUT OF THE ENTIRE BUILDING, DON'TCHA KNOW?
SO EVEN ALL HIGH UP AND ALL, THE FORCE OF IT KNOCKED US ALL ON OUR ASSES.
CAN I SAY ASSES?
THE BOMBING OF THE UNITY BUILDING BROUGHT RETRO GIRL, WITH HER ALL-AMERICAN GOOD LOOKS AND CHARM, INTO THE HEARTS AND MINDS OF ALL AMERICANS.
I THOUGHT FOR SURE THAT THE LITTLE GIRL WAS A GONER AND ALL, BUT A FEW MINUTES LATER THE SWEET THING SWOOPED ON DOWN AND...
V.O.W.

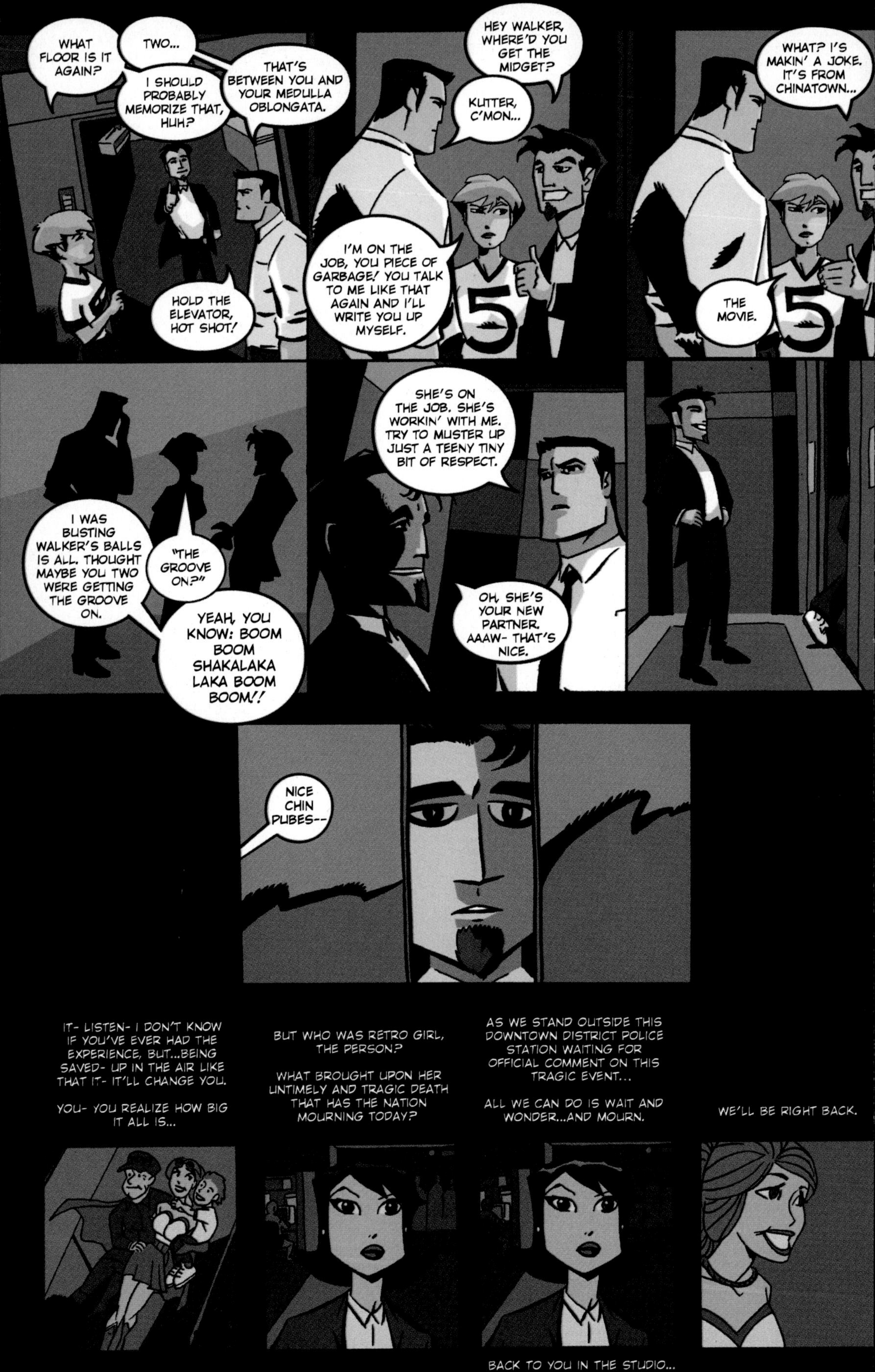
WHAT FLOOR IS IT AGAIN?
TWO...
I SHOULD PROBABLY MEMORIZE THAT, HUH?
THAT'S BETWEEN YOU AND YOUR MEDULLA OBLONGATA.
HOLD THE ELEVATOR, HOT SHOT!
HEY WALKER, WHERE'D YOU GET THE MIDGET?
KUTTER, C'MON...
I'M ON THE JOB, YOU PIECE OF GARBAGE! YOU TALK TO ME LIKE THAT AGAIN AND I'LL WRITE YOU UP MYSELF.
WHAT? I'S MAKIN' A JOKE. IT'S FROM CHINATOWN...
THE MOVIE.
I WAS BUSTING WALKER'S BALLS IS ALL. THOUGHT MAYBE YOU TWO WERE GETTING THE GROOVE ON.
"THE GROOVE ON?"
YEAH, YOU KNOW: BOOM BOOM SHAKALAKA LAKA BOOM BOOM!!
SHE'S ON THE JOB. SHE'S WORKIN' WITH ME. TRY TO MUSTER UP JUST A TEENY TINY BIT OF RESPECT.
OH, SHE'S YOUR NEW PARTNER. AAAW- THAT'S NICE.
NICE CHIN PUBES--
IT- LISTEN- I DON'T KNOW IF YOU'VE EVER HAD THE EXPERIENCE, BUT...BEING SAVED- UP IN THE AIR LIKE THAT IT- IT'LL CHANGE YOU.
YOU- YOU REALIZE HOW BIG IT ALL IS...
BUT WHO WAS RETRO GIRL, THE PERSON?
WHAT BROUGHT UPON HER UNTIMELY AND TRAGIC DEATH THAT HAS THE NATION MOURNING TODAY?
AS WE STAND OUTSIDE THIS DOWNTOWN DISTRICT POLICE STATION WAITING FOR OFFICIAL COMMENT ON THIS TRAGIC EVENT...
ALL WE CAN DO IS WAIT AND WONDER...AND MOURN.
WE'LL BE RIGHT BACK.
BACK TO YOU IN THE STUDIO...

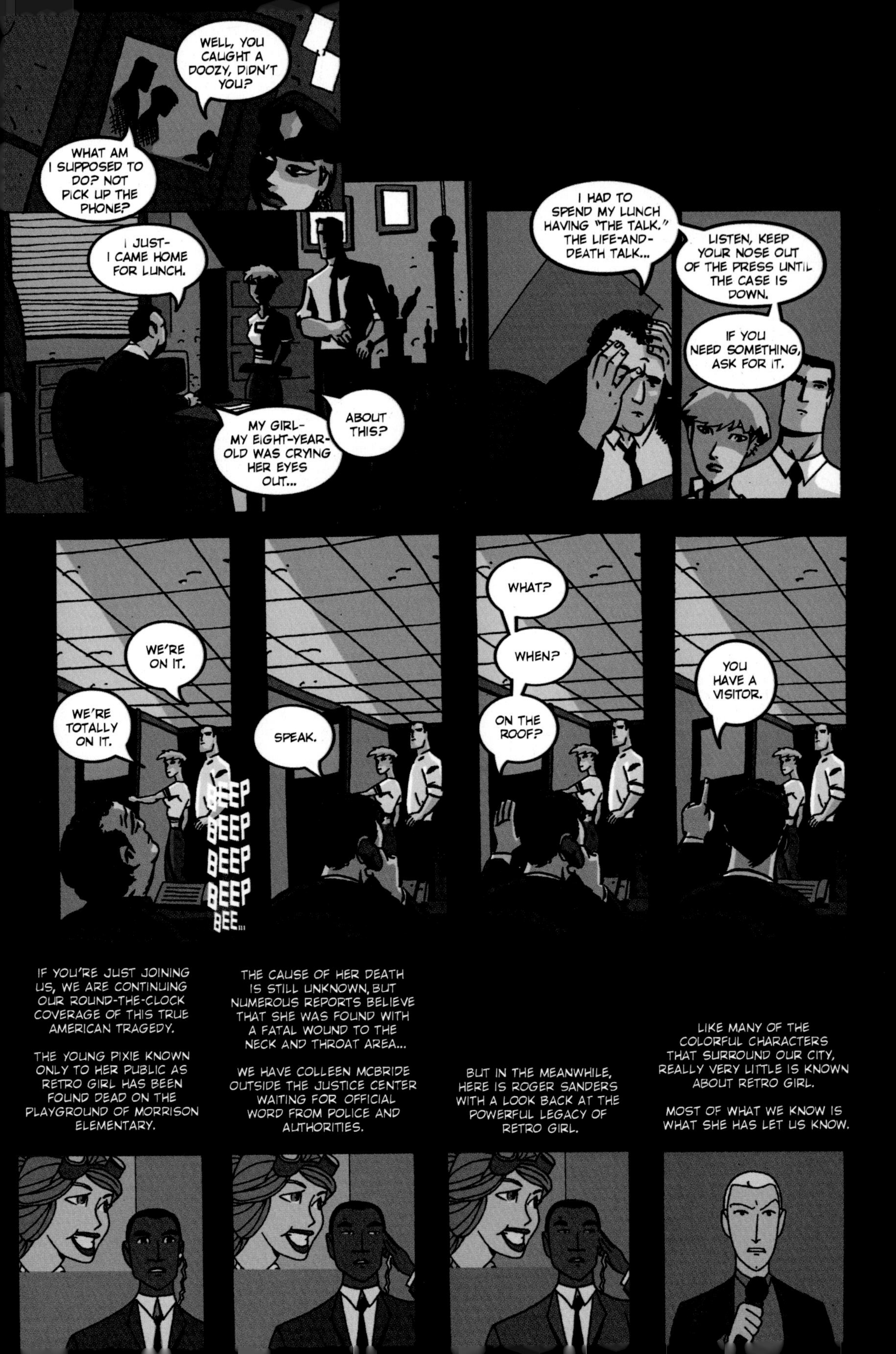
WELL, YOU CAUGHT A DOOZY, DIDN'T YOU?
WHAT AM I SUPPOSED TO DO? NOT PICK UP THE PHONE?
I JUST- I CAME HOME FOR LUNCH.
MY GIRL- MY EIGHT-YEAR-OLD WAS CRYING HER EYES OUT...
ABOUT THIS?
I HAD TO SPEND MY LUNCH HAVING "THE TALK." THE LIFE-AND-DEATH TALK...
LISTEN, KEEP YOUR NOSE OUT OF THE PRESS UNTIL THE CASE IS DOWN.
IF YOU NEED SOMETHING, ASK FOR IT.
WE'RE ON IT.
WE'RE TOTALLY ON IT.
BEEP BEEP BEEP BEEP BEE...
SPEAK.
WHAT?
WHEN?
ON THE ROOF?
YOU HAVE A VISITOR.
IF YOU'RE JUST JOINING US, WE ARE CONTINUING OUR ROUND-THE-CLOCK COVERAGE OF THIS TRUE AMERICAN TRAGEDY.
THE YOUNG PIXIE KNOWN ONLY TO HER PUBLIC AS RETRO GIRL HAS BEEN FOUND DEAD ON THE PLAYGROUND OF MORRISON ELEMENTARY.
THE CAUSE OF HER DEATH IS STILL UNKNOWN, BUT NUMEROUS REPORTS BELIEVE THAT SHE WAS FOUND WITH A FATAL WOUND TO THE NECK AND THROAT AREA...
WE HAVE COLLEEN MCBRIDE OUTSIDE THE JUSTICE CENTER WAITING FOR OFFICIAL WORD FROM POLICE AND AUTHORITIES.
BUT IN THE MEANWHILE, HERE IS ROGER SANDERS WITH A LOOK BACK AT THE POWERFUL LEGACY OF RETRO GIRL.
LIKE MANY OF THE COLORFUL CHARACTERS THAT SURROUND OUR CITY, REALLY VERY LITTLE IS KNOWN ABOUT RETRO GIRL.
MOST OF WHAT WE KNOW IS WHAT SHE HAS LET US KNOW.

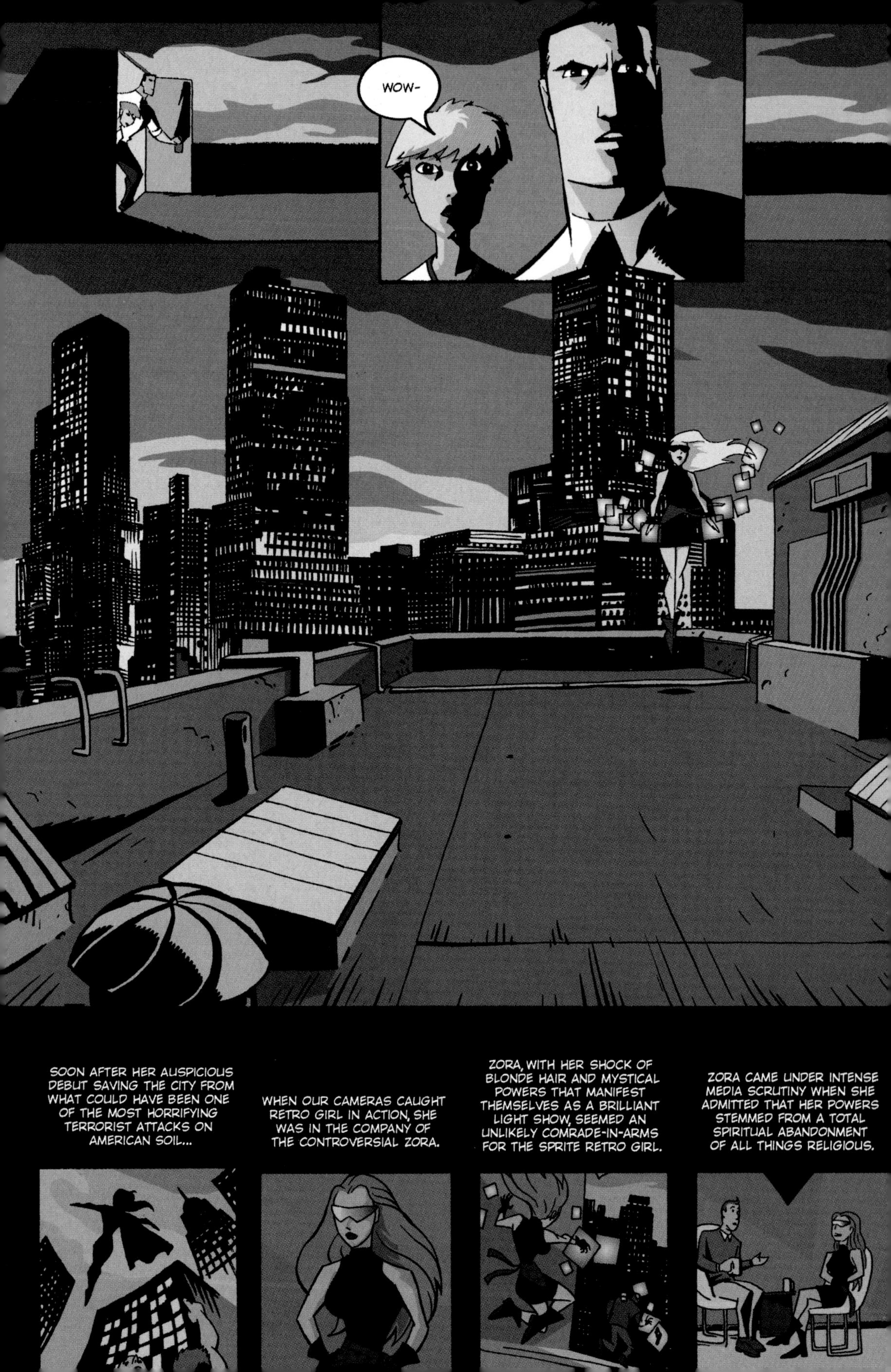

WOW-
SOON AFTER HER AUSPICIOUS DEBUT SAVING THE CITY FROM WHAT COULD HAVE BEEN ONE OF THE MOST HORRIFYING TERRORIST ATTACKS ON AMERICAN SOIL...
WHEN OUR CAMERAS CAUGHT RETRO GIRL IN ACTION, SHE WAS IN THE COMPANY OF THE CONTROVERSIAL ZORA.
ZORA, WITH HER SHOCK OF BLONDE HAIR AND MYSTICAL POWERS THAT MANIFEST THEMSELVES AS A BRILLIANT LIGHT SHOW, SEEMED AN UNLIKELY COMRADE-IN-ARMS FOR THE SPRITE RETRO GIRL.
ZORA CAME UNDER INTENSE MEDIA SCRUTINY WHEN SHE ADMITTED THAT HER POWERS STEMMED FROM A TOTAL SPIRITUAL ABANDONMENT OF ALL THINGS RELIGIOUS.

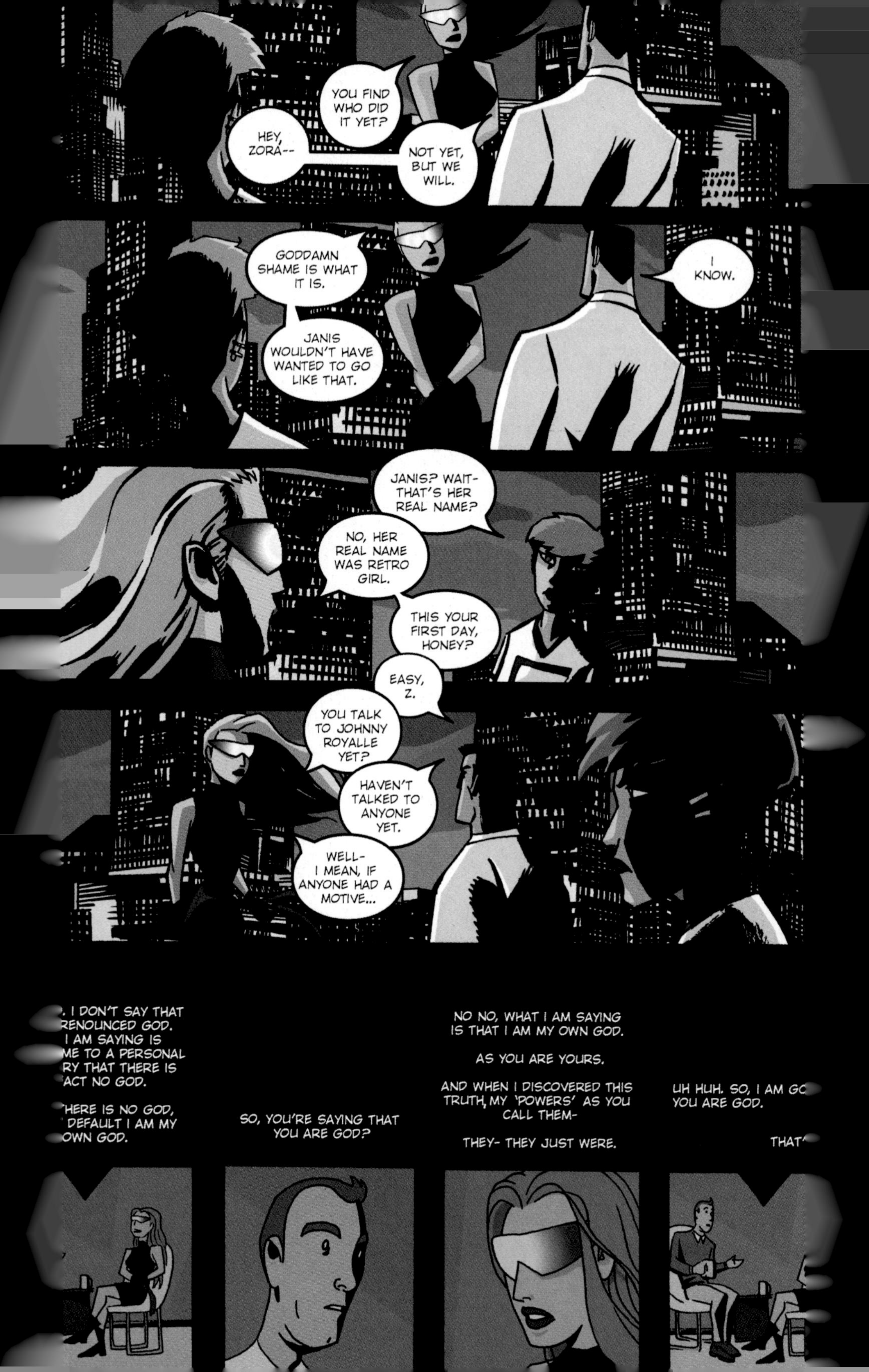

HEY, ZORA--
YOU FIND WHO DID IT YET?
NOT YET, BUT WE WILL.
GODDAMN SHAME IS WHAT IT IS.
JANIS WOULDN'T HAVE WANTED TO GO LIKE THAT.
I KNOW.
JANIS? WAIT- THAT'S HER REAL NAME?
NO, HER REAL NAME WAS RETRO GIRL.
THIS YOUR FIRST DAY, HONEY?
EASY, Z.
YOU TALK TO JOHNNY ROYALLE YET?
HAVEN'T TALKED TO ANYONE YET.
WELL- I MEAN, IF ANYONE HAD A MOTIVE...
I DON'T SAY THAT RENOUNCED GOD. I AM SAYING IS ME TO A PERSONAL RY THAT THERE IS ACT NO GOD.
HERE IS NO GOD, DEFAULT I AM MY OWN GOD.
SO, YOU'RE SAYING THAT YOU ARE GOD?
NO NO, WHAT I AM SAYING IS THAT I AM MY OWN GOD.
AS YOU ARE YOURS.
AND WHEN I DISCOVERED THIS TRUTH, MY 'POWERS' AS YOU CALL THEM-
THEY- THEY JUST WERE.
UH HUH. SO, I AM GO YOU ARE GOD.

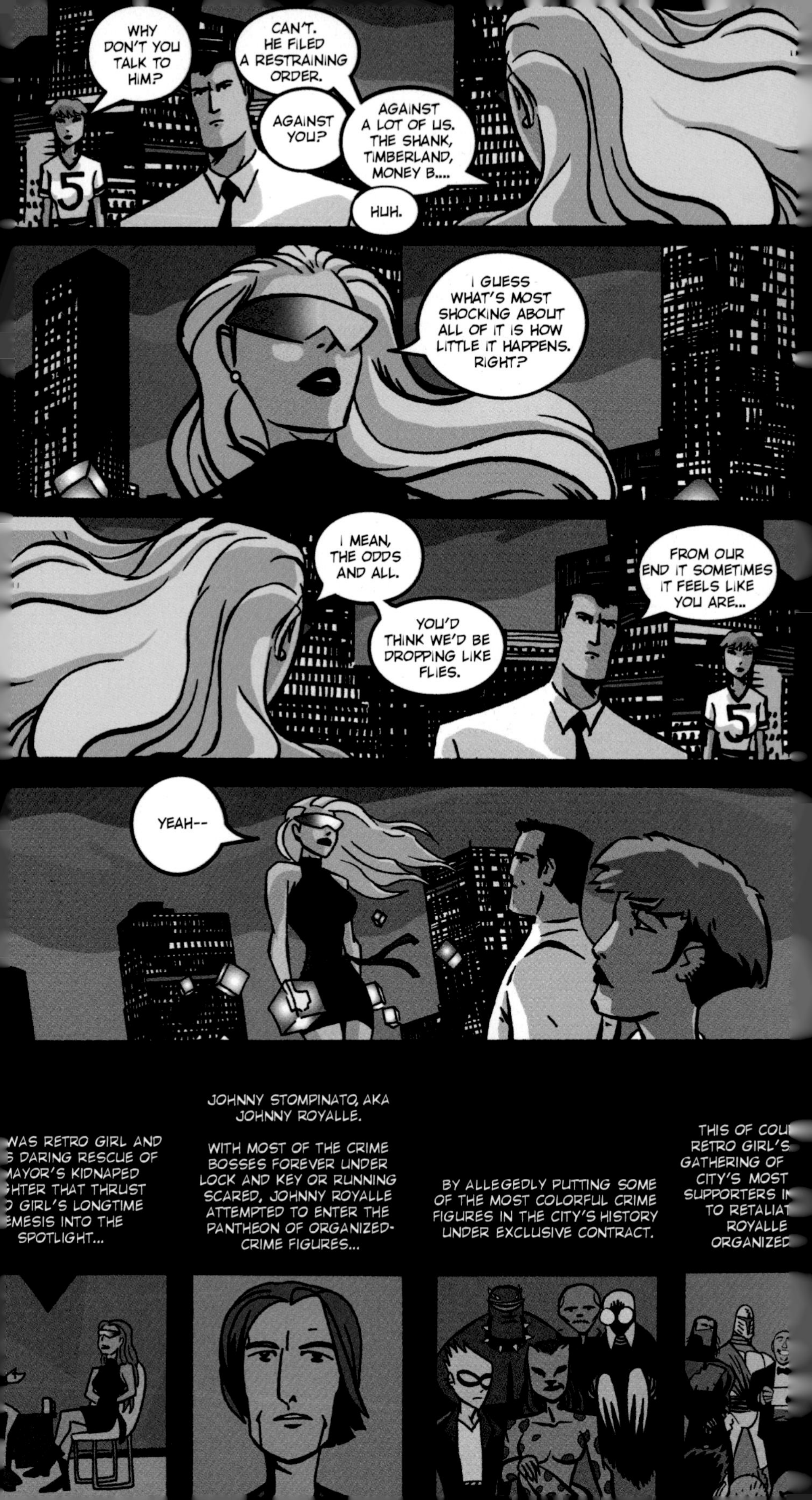
WHY DON'T YOU TALK TO HIM?
CAN'T. HE FILED A RESTRAINING ORDER.
AGAINST YOU?
AGAINST A LOT OF US. THE SHANK, TIMBERLAND, MONEY B....
HUH.
I GUESS WHAT'S MOST SHOCKING ABOUT ALL OF IT IS HOW LITTLE IT HAPPENS. RIGHT?
I MEAN, THE ODDS AND ALL.
YOU'D THINK WE'D BE DROPPING LIKE FLIES.
FROM OUR END IT SOMETIMES IT FEELS LIKE YOU ARE...
YEAH--
WAS RETRO GIRL AND
S DARING RESCUE OF
MAYOR'S KIDNAPED
GHTER THAT THRUST
O GIRL'S LONGTIME
EMESIS INTO THE
SPOTLIGHT...
JOHNNY STOMPINATO, AKA JOHNNY ROYALLE.
WITH MOST OF THE CRIME BOSSES FOREVER UNDER LOCK AND KEY OR RUNNING SCARED, JOHNNY ROYALLE ATTEMPTED TO ENTER THE PANTHEON OF ORGANIZED-CRIME FIGURES...
BY ALLEGEDLY PUTTING SOME OF THE MOST COLORFUL CRIME FIGURES IN THE CITY'S HISTORY UNDER EXCLUSIVE CONTRACT.
THIS OF COU
RETRO GIRL'S
GATHERING OF
CITY'S MOST
SUPPORTERS IN
TO RETALIAT
ROYALLE
ORGANIZED

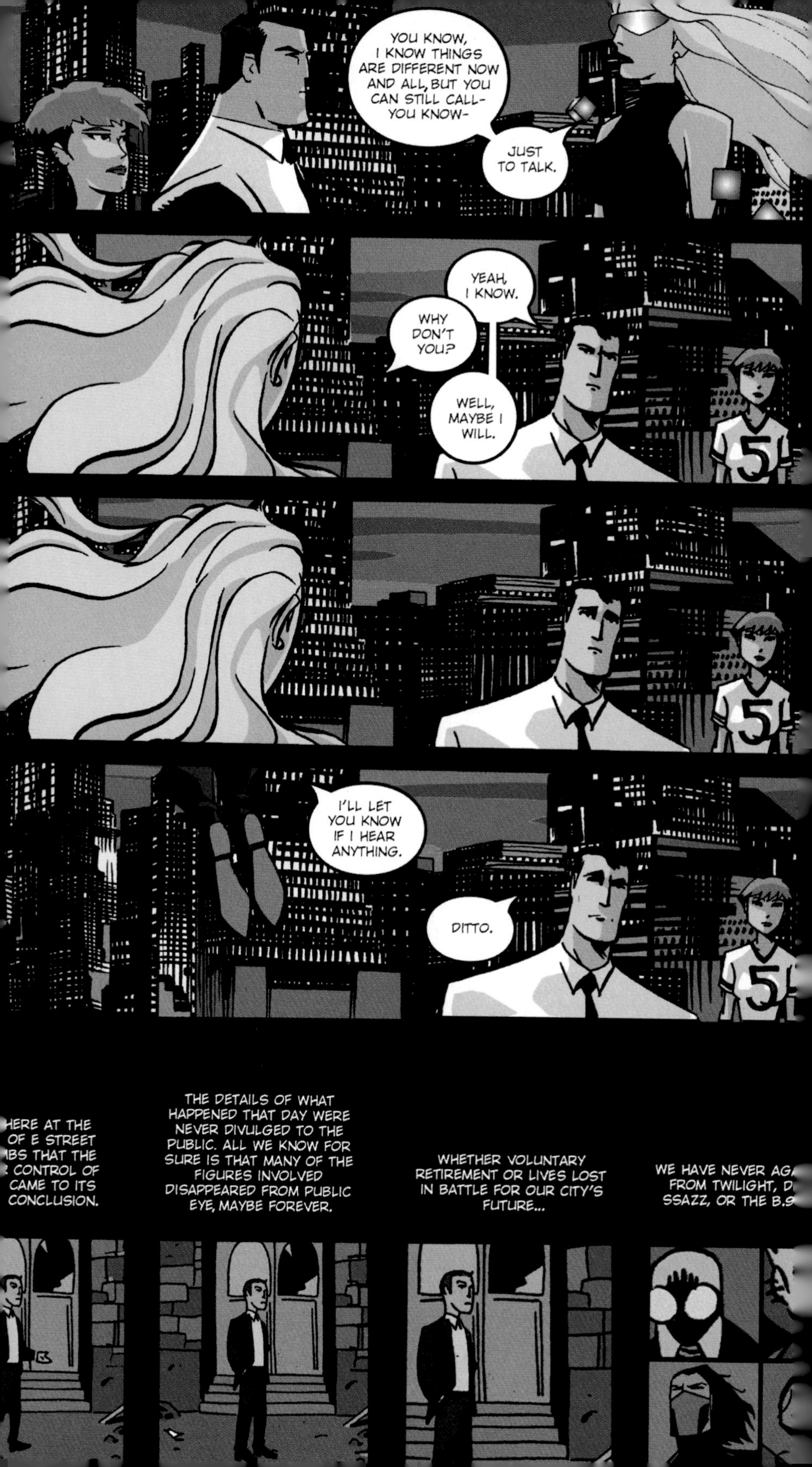
YOU KNOW, I KNOW THINGS ARE DIFFERENT NOW AND ALL, BUT YOU CAN STILL CALL- YOU KNOW-
JUST TO TALK.
YEAH, I KNOW.
WHY DON'T YOU?
WELL, MAYBE I WILL.
I'LL LET YOU KNOW IF I HEAR ANYTHING.
DITTO.
HERE AT THE
OF E STREET
THAT THE
CONTROL OF
CAME TO ITS
CONCLUSION.
THE DETAILS OF WHAT HAPPENED THAT DAY WERE NEVER DIVULGED TO THE PUBLIC. ALL WE KNOW FOR SURE IS THAT MANY OF THE FIGURES INVOLVED DISAPPEARED FROM PUBLIC EYE, MAYBE FOREVER.
WHETHER VOLUNTARY RETIREMENT OR LIVES LOST IN BATTLE FOR OUR CITY'S FUTURE...
WE HAVE NEVER
FROM TWILIGHT,
SSAZZ, OR THE

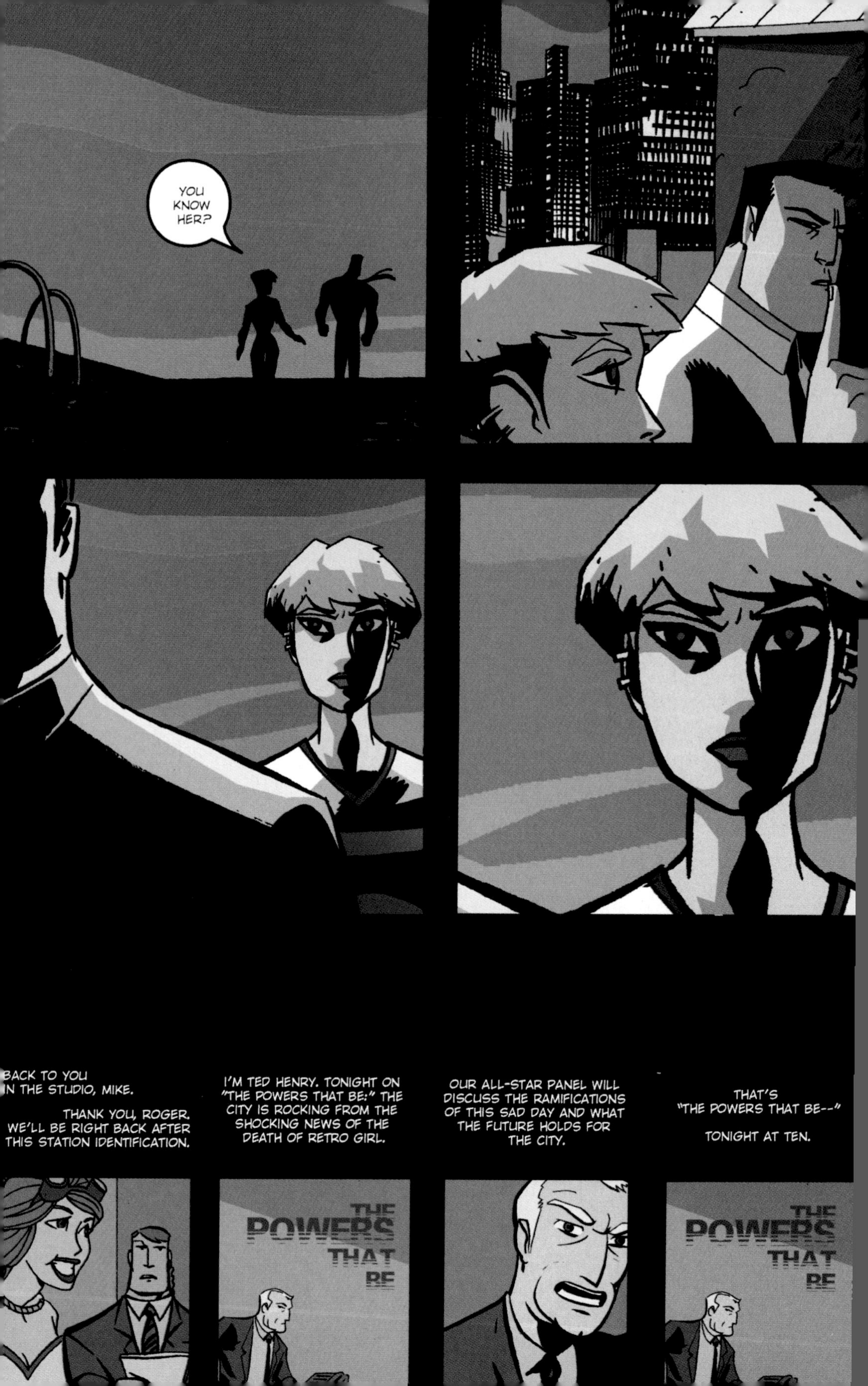
YOU KNOW HER?
BACK TO YOU IN THE STUDIO, MIKE.
THANK YOU, ROGER. WE'LL BE RIGHT BACK AFTER THIS STATION IDENTIFICATION.
I'M TED HENRY. TONIGHT ON "THE POWERS THAT BE:" THE CITY IS ROCKING FROM THE SHOCKING NEWS OF THE DEATH OF RETRO GIRL.
OUR ALL-STAR PANEL WILL DISCUSS THE RAMIFICATIONS OF THIS SAD DAY AND WHAT THE FUTURE HOLDS FOR THE CITY.
THAT'S "THE POWERS THAT BE--"
TONIGHT AT TEN.
THE POWERS THAT BE
THE POWERS THAT BE

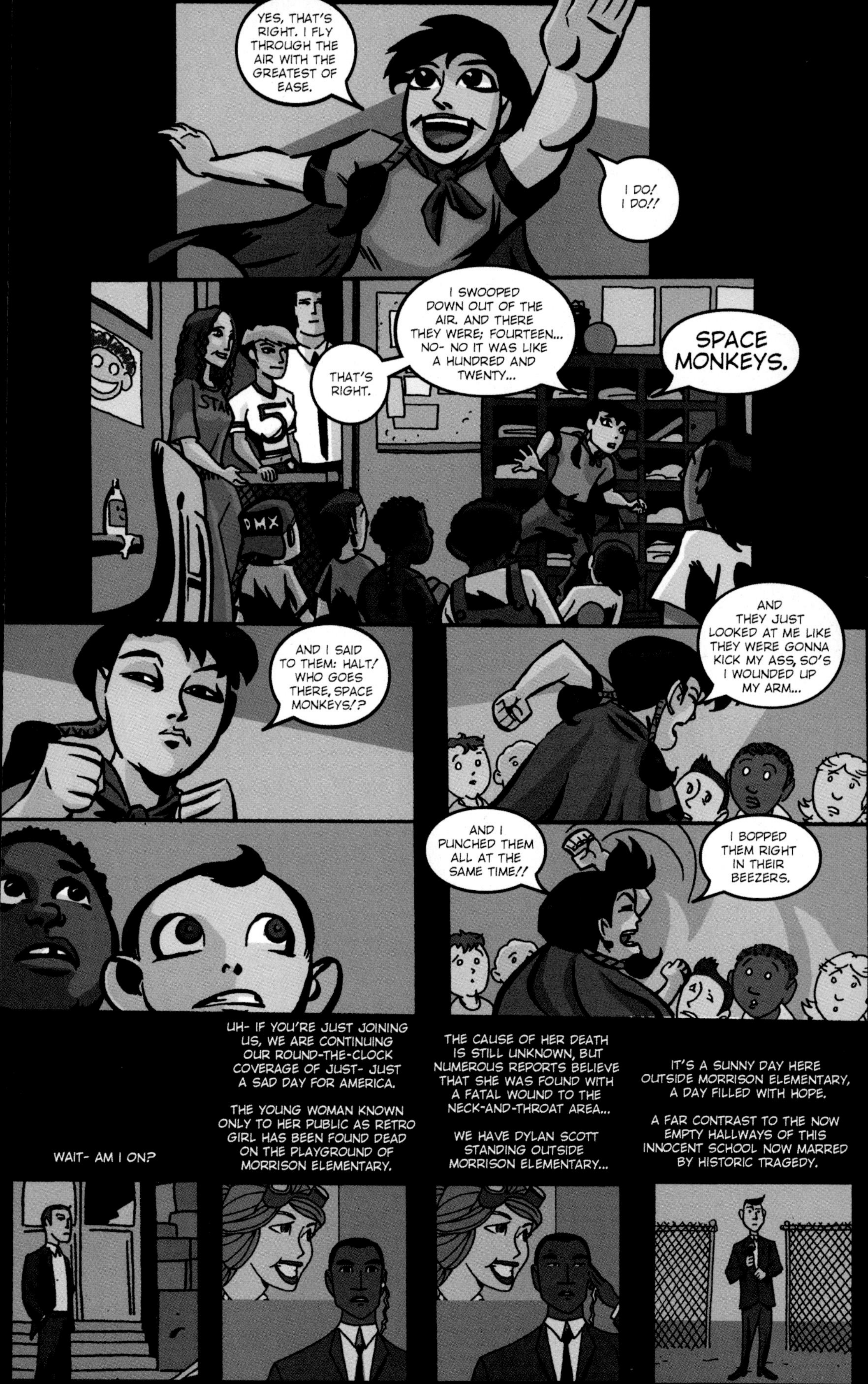
YES, THAT'S RIGHT. I FLY THROUGH THE AIR WITH THE GREATEST OF EASE.
I DO! I DO!!
THAT'S RIGHT.
I SWOOPED DOWN OUT OF THE AIR. AND THERE THEY WERE; FOURTEEN... NO- NO IT WAS LIKE A HUNDRED AND TWENTY...
SPACE MONKEYS.
AND I SAID TO THEM: HALT! WHO GOES THERE, SPACE MONKEYS!?
AND THEY JUST LOOKED AT ME LIKE THEY WERE GONNA KICK MY ASS, SO'S I WOUNDED UP MY ARM...
AND I PUNCHED THEM ALL AT THE SAME TIME!!
I BOPPED THEM RIGHT IN THEIR BEEZERS.
WAIT- AM I ON?
UH- IF YOU'RE JUST JOINING US, WE ARE CONTINUING OUR ROUND-THE-CLOCK COVERAGE OF JUST- JUST A SAD DAY FOR AMERICA.
THE YOUNG WOMAN KNOWN ONLY TO HER PUBLIC AS RETRO GIRL HAS BEEN FOUND DEAD ON THE PLAYGROUND OF MORRISON ELEMENTARY.
THE CAUSE OF HER DEATH IS STILL UNKNOWN, BUT NUMEROUS REPORTS BELIEVE THAT SHE WAS FOUND WITH A FATAL WOUND TO THE NECK-AND-THROAT AREA...
WE HAVE DYLAN SCOTT STANDING OUTSIDE MORRISON ELEMENTARY...
IT'S A SUNNY DAY HERE OUTSIDE MORRISON ELEMENTARY, A DAY FILLED WITH HOPE.
A FAR CONTRAST TO THE NOW EMPTY HALLWAYS OF THIS INNOCENT SCHOOL NOW MARRED BY HISTORIC TRAGEDY.

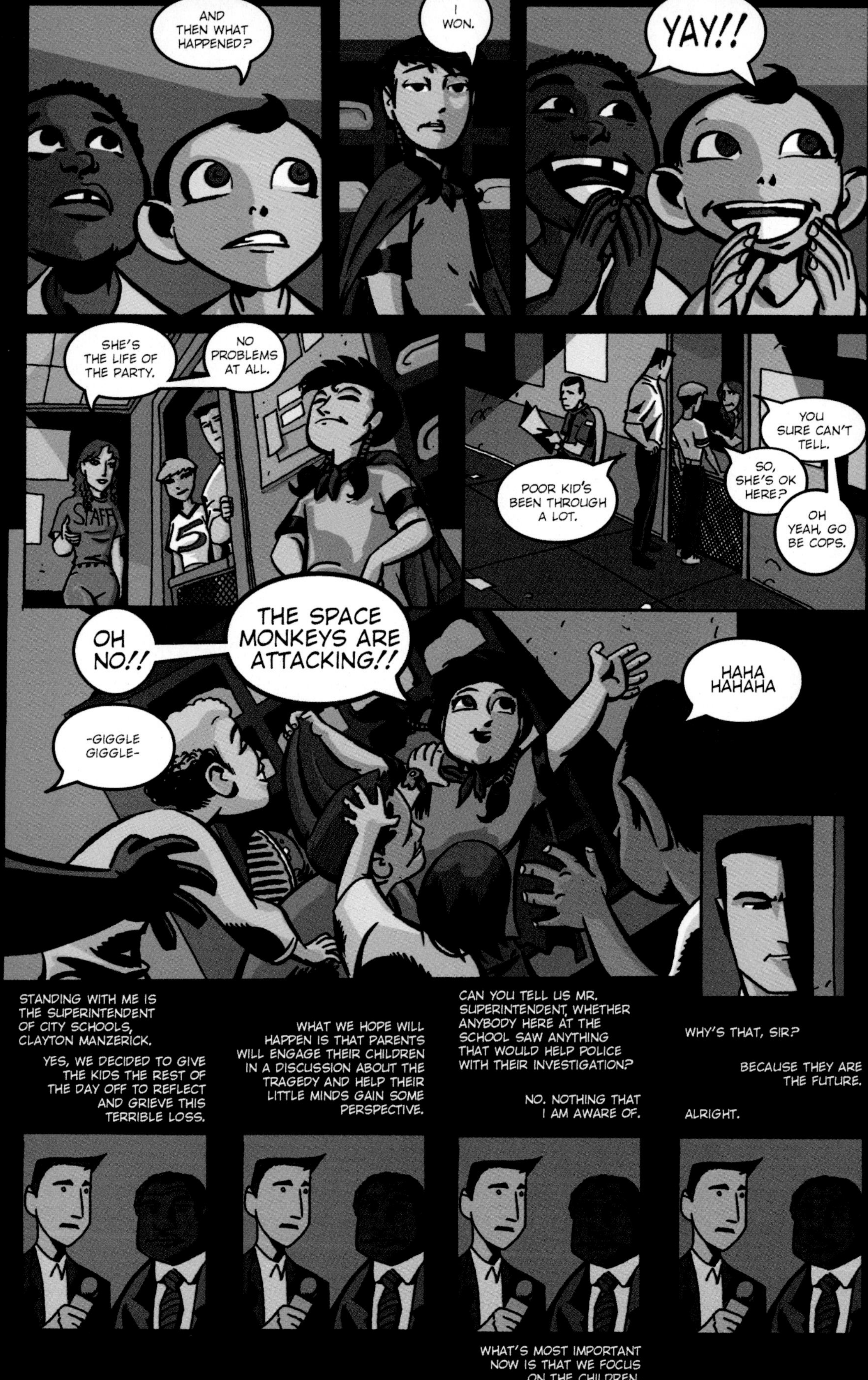
AND THEN WHAT HAPPENED?
I WON.
YAY!!
SHE'S THE LIFE OF THE PARTY.
NO PROBLEMS AT ALL.
STAFF
5
POOR KID'S BEEN THROUGH A LOT.
YOU SURE CAN'T TELL.
SO, SHE'S OK HERE?
OH YEAH, GO BE COPS.
OH NO!!
THE SPACE MONKEYS ARE ATTACKING!!
HAHA HAHAHA
-GIGGLE GIGGLE-
STANDING WITH ME IS THE SUPERINTENDENT OF CITY SCHOOLS, CLAYTON MANZERICK.
YES, WE DECIDED TO GIVE THE KIDS THE REST OF THE DAY OFF TO REFLECT AND GRIEVE THIS TERRIBLE LOSS.
WHAT WE HOPE WILL HAPPEN IS THAT PARENTS WILL ENGAGE THEIR CHILDREN IN A DISCUSSION ABOUT THE TRAGEDY AND HELP THEIR LITTLE MINDS GAIN SOME PERSPECTIVE.
CAN YOU TELL US MR. SUPERINTENDENT, WHETHER ANYBODY HERE AT THE SCHOOL SAW ANYTHING THAT WOULD HELP POLICE WITH THEIR INVESTIGATION?
NO. NOTHING THAT I AM AWARE OF.
WHAT'S MOST IMPORTANT NOW IS THAT WE FOCUS ON THE CHILDREN.
WHY'S THAT, SIR?
BECAUSE THEY ARE THE FUTURE.
ALRIGHT.

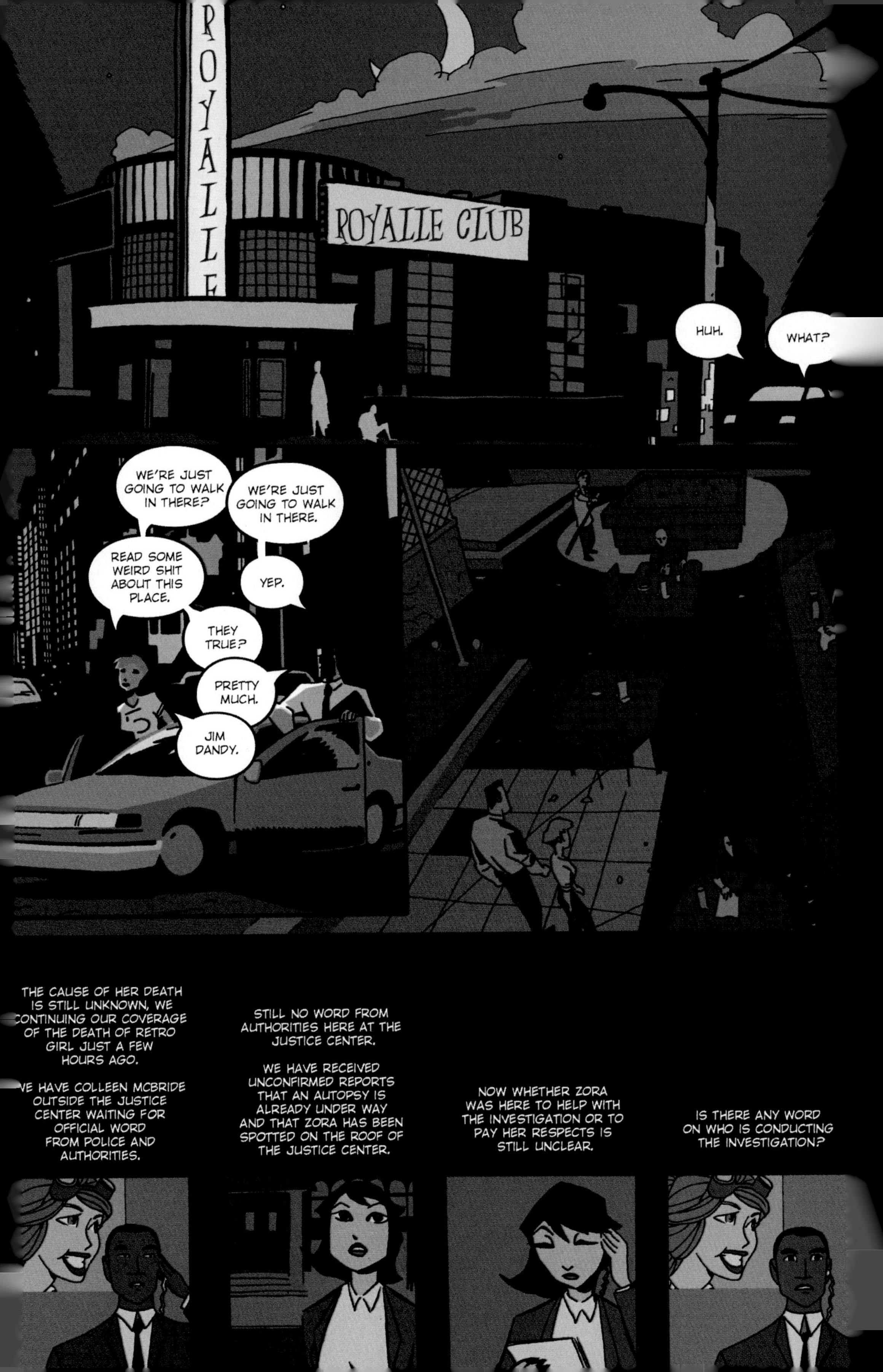
ROYALLE CLUB
HUH.
WHAT?
WE'RE JUST GOING TO WALK IN THERE?
WE'RE JUST GOING TO WALK IN THERE.
READ SOME WEIRD SHIT ABOUT THIS PLACE.
YEP.
THEY TRUE?
PRETTY MUCH.
JIM DANDY.
THE CAUSE OF HER DEATH IS STILL UNKNOWN, WE CONTINUING OUR COVERAGE OF THE DEATH OF RETRO GIRL JUST A FEW HOURS AGO.
WE HAVE COLLEEN MCBRIDE OUTSIDE THE JUSTICE CENTER WAITING FOR OFFICIAL WORD FROM POLICE AND AUTHORITIES.
STILL NO WORD FROM AUTHORITIES HERE AT THE JUSTICE CENTER.
WE HAVE RECEIVED UNCONFIRMED REPORTS THAT AN AUTOPSY IS ALREADY UNDER WAY AND THAT ZORA HAS BEEN SPOTTED ON THE ROOF OF THE JUSTICE CENTER.
NOW WHETHER ZORA WAS HERE TO HELP WITH THE INVESTIGATION OR TO PAY HER RESPECTS IS STILL UNCLEAR.
IS THERE ANY WORD ON WHO IS CONDUCTING THE INVESTIGATION?

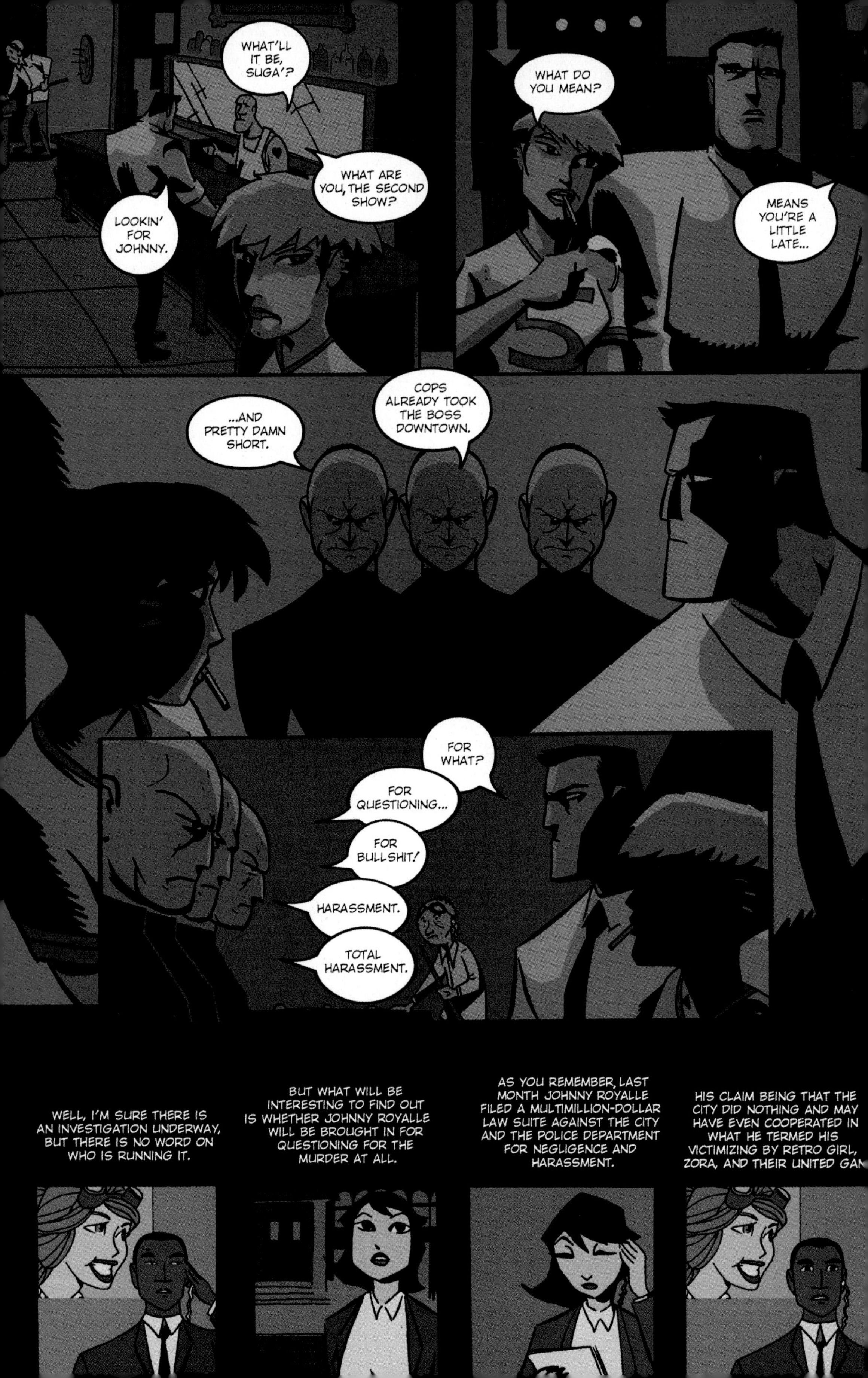
WHAT'LL IT BE, SUGA'?
LOOKIN' FOR JOHNNY.
WHAT ARE YOU, THE SECOND SHOW?
WHAT DO YOU MEAN?
MEANS YOU'RE A LITTLE LATE...
...AND PRETTY DAMN SHORT.
COPS ALREADY TOOK THE BOSS DOWNTOWN.
FOR WHAT?
FOR QUESTIONING...
FOR BULLSHIT!
HARASSMENT.
TOTAL HARASSMENT.
WELL, I'M SURE THERE IS AN INVESTIGATION UNDERWAY, BUT THERE IS NO WORD ON WHO IS RUNNING IT.
BUT WHAT WILL BE INTERESTING TO FIND OUT IS WHETHER JOHNNY ROYALLE WILL BE BROUGHT IN FOR QUESTIONING FOR THE MURDER AT ALL.
AS YOU REMEMBER, LAST MONTH JOHNNY ROYALLE FILED A MULTIMILLION-DOLLAR LAW SUITE AGAINST THE CITY AND THE POLICE DEPARTMENT FOR NEGLIGENCE AND HARASSMENT.
HIS CLAIM BEING THAT THE CITY DID NOTHING AND MAY HAVE EVEN COOPERATED IN WHAT HE TERMED HIS VICTIMIZING BY RETRO GIRL, ZORA, AND THEIR UNITED GA

SO- WHAT'S YOUR GUYS' SHTICK?

YOU JUST HAVE THE POWER TO BE PLAIN OL' CREEPY?

SO- WHO PICKED JOHNNY UP?

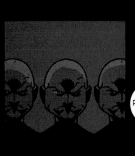

Y'KNOW- I HAVE HAD JUST ABOUT MY DAILY LIMIT FOR BULLSHIT LIKE THIS.

WHO PICKED HIM UP?

HOLD THIS, IF YOU WILL.

WE ACTUALLY HAVE SOME FOOTAGE OF THE PRESS CONFERENCE BY ROYALLE'S LAWYERS.

MAYBE WE SHOULD SHOW THAT NOW IF...

I'M SORRY, HOLD ON A MOMENT, DAN....

CAN YOU TELL US WHAT'S GOING ON, COLLETTE?

THERE'S SOME COMMOTION HERE NOW...

I CAN'T MAKE OUT WHAT IT IS JUST YET...

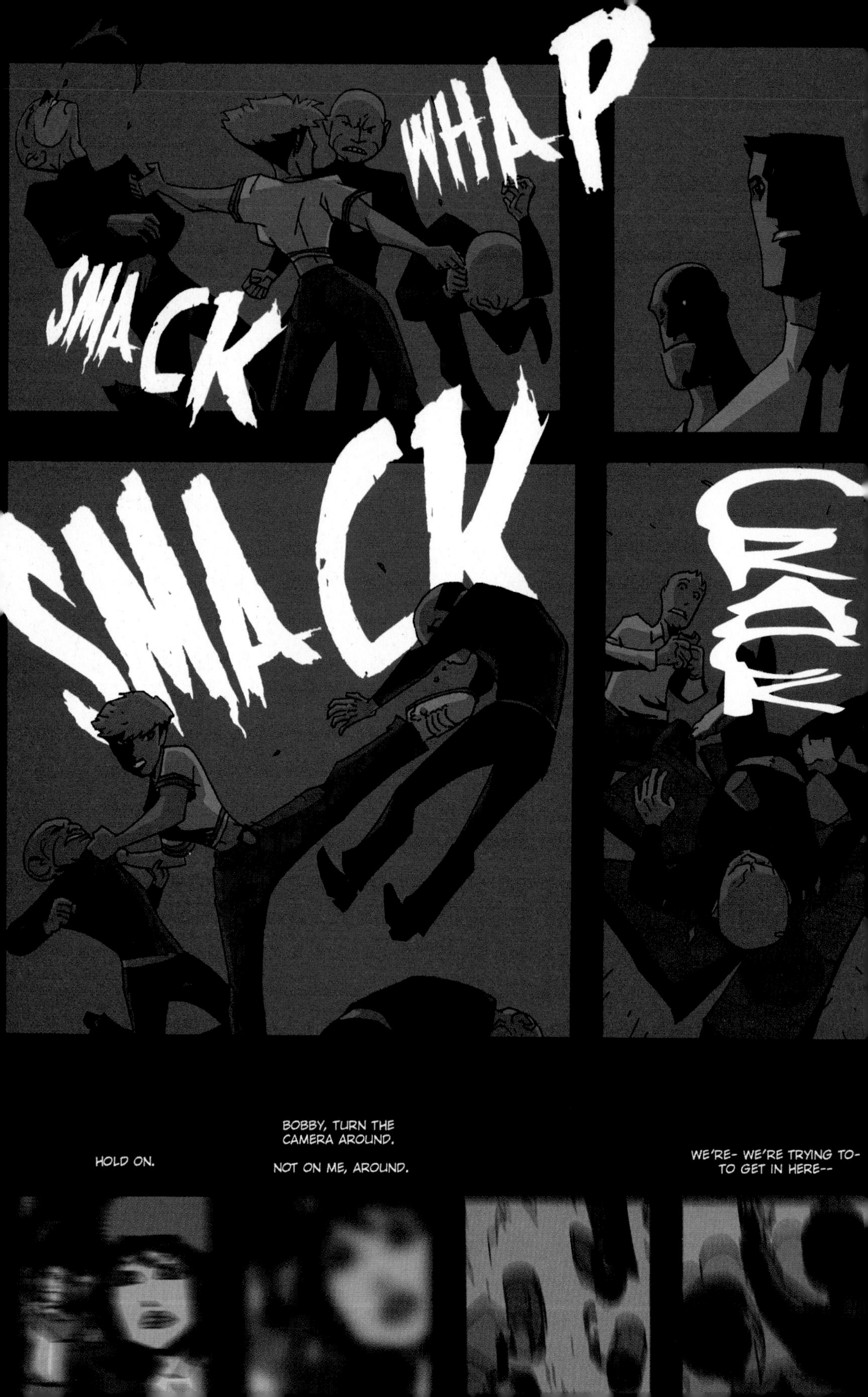
SMACK
WHAP
SMACK
HOLD ON.
BOBBY, TURN THE CAMERA AROUND.
NOT ON ME, AROUND.
WE'RE- WE'RE TRYING TO- TO GET IN HERE--

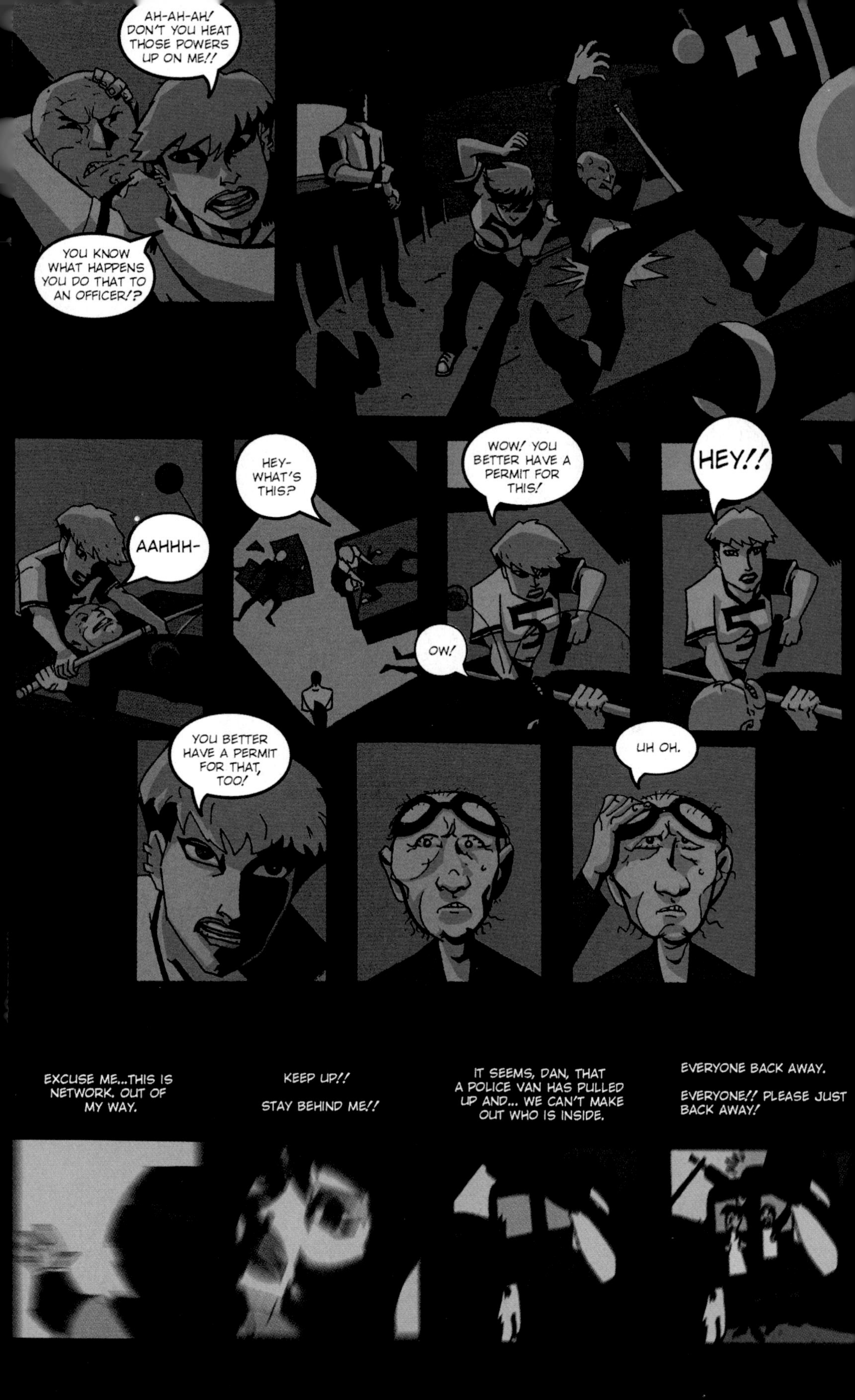
AH-AH-AH! DON'T YOU HEAT THOSE POWERS UP ON ME!!
YOU KNOW WHAT HAPPENS YOU DO THAT TO AN OFFICER!?
AAHHH-
HEY- WHAT'S THIS?
WOW! YOU BETTER HAVE A PERMIT FOR THIS!
OW!
HEY!!
YOU BETTER HAVE A PERMIT FOR THAT, TOO!
UH OH.
EXCUSE ME...THIS IS NETWORK. OUT OF MY WAY.
KEEP UP!!
STAY BEHIND ME!!
IT SEEMS, DAN, THAT A POLICE VAN HAS PULLED UP AND... WE CAN'T MAKE OUT WHO IS INSIDE.
EVERYONE BACK AWAY.
EVERYONE!! PLEASE JUST BACK AWAY!

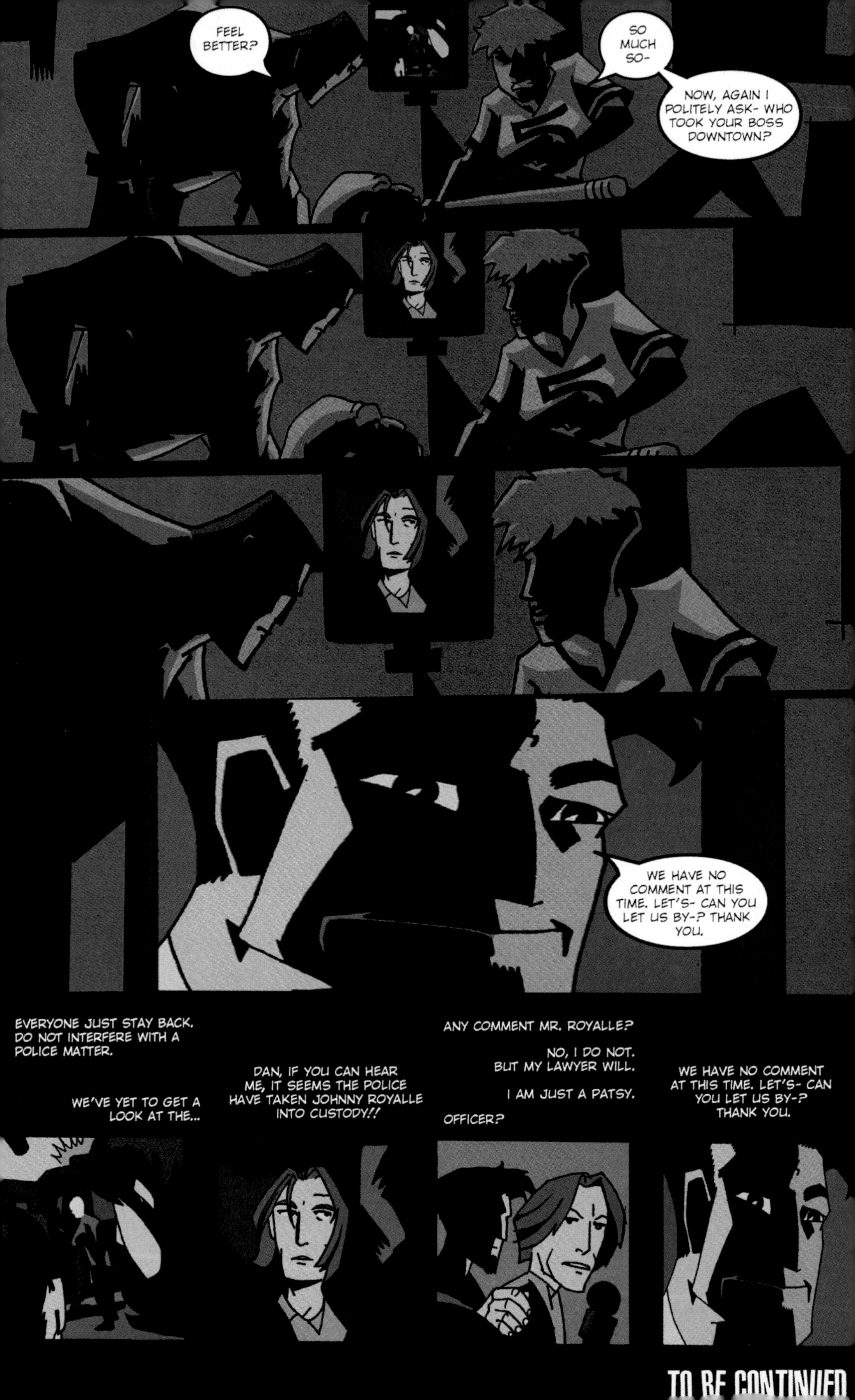
FEEL BETTER?
SO MUCH SO-
NOW, AGAIN I POLITELY ASK- WHO TOOK YOUR BOSS DOWNTOWN?
WE HAVE NO COMMENT AT THIS TIME. LET'S- CAN YOU LET US BY-? THANK YOU.
EVERYONE JUST STAY BACK. DO NOT INTERFERE WITH A POLICE MATTER.
WE'VE YET TO GET A LOOK AT THE...
DAN, IF YOU CAN HEAR ME, IT SEEMS THE POLICE HAVE TAKEN JOHNNY ROYALLE INTO CUSTODY!!
ANY COMMENT MR. ROYALLE?
NO, I DO NOT. BUT MY LAWYER WILL.
I AM JUST A PATSY.
OFFICER?
WE HAVE NO COMMENT AT THIS TIME. LET'S- CAN YOU LET US BY-? THANK YOU.
TO BE CONTINUED

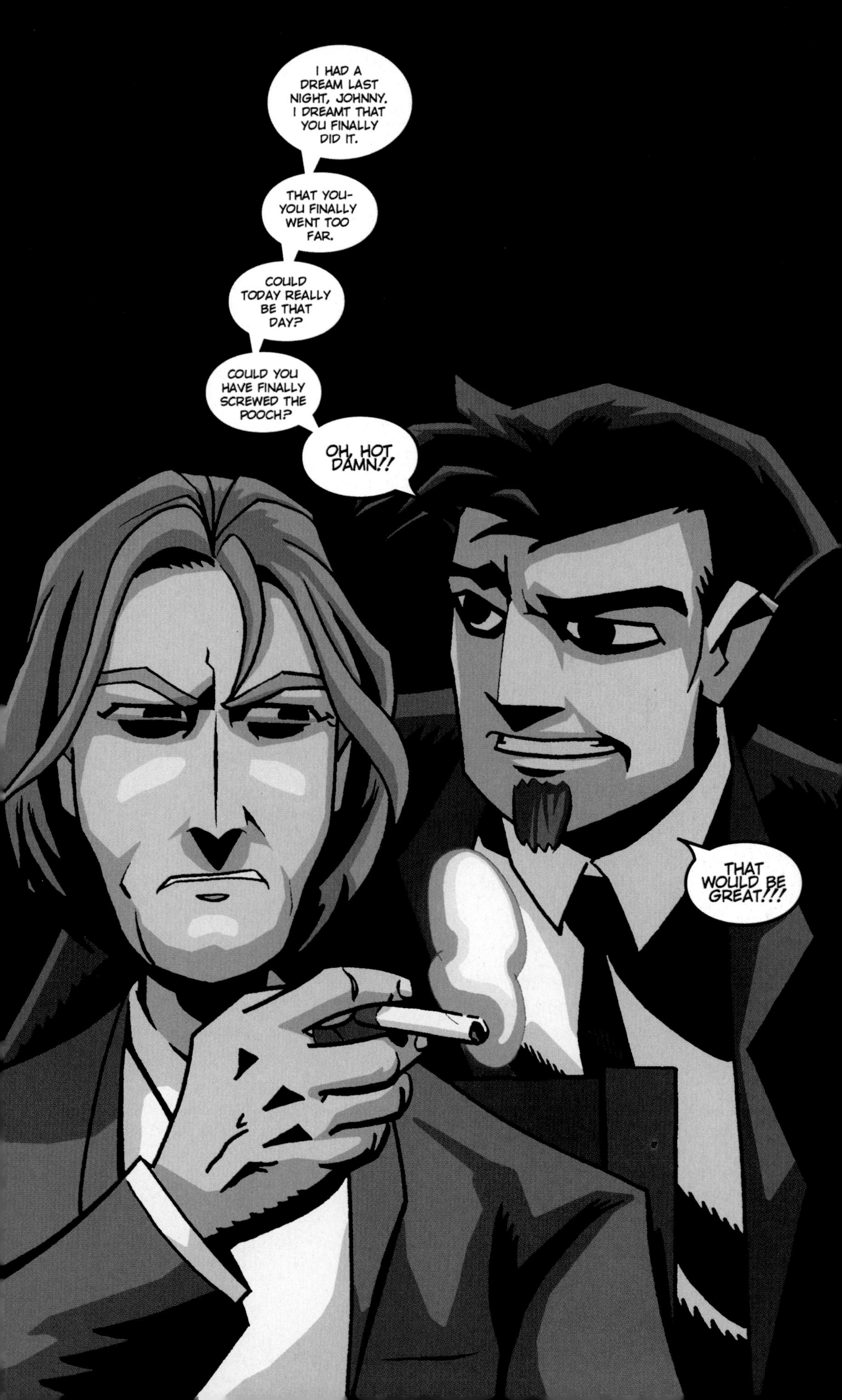
I HAD A DREAM LAST NIGHT, JOHNNY. I DREAMT THAT YOU FINALLY DID IT.
THAT YOU-- YOU FINALLY WENT TOO FAR.
COULD TODAY REALLY BE THAT DAY?
COULD YOU HAVE FINALLY SCREWED THE POOCH?
OH, HOT DAMN!!
THAT WOULD BE GREAT!!!

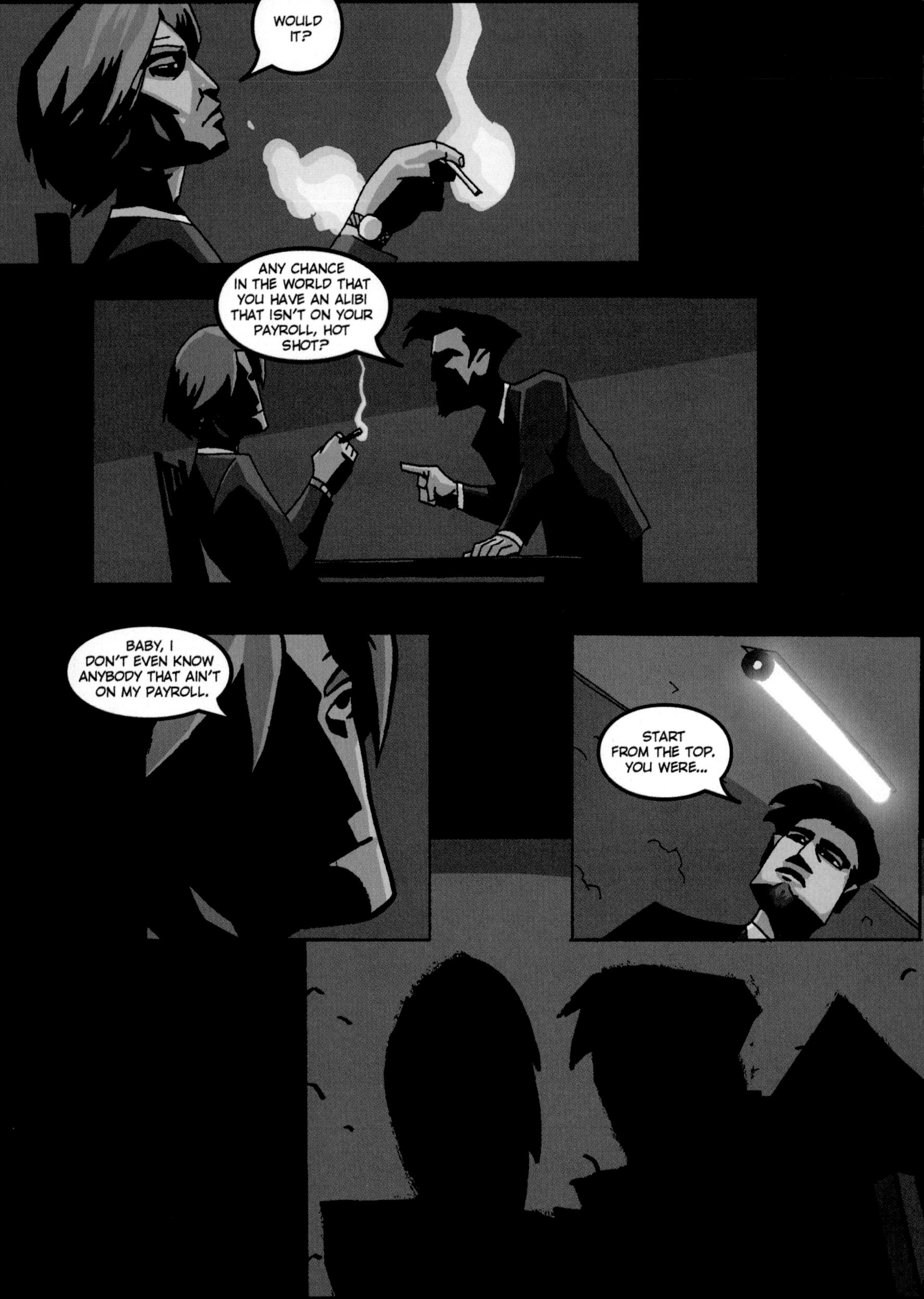
WOULD IT?
ANY CHANCE IN THE WORLD THAT YOU HAVE AN ALIBI THAT ISN'T ON YOUR PAYROLL, HOT SHOT?
BABY, I DON'T EVEN KNOW ANYBODY THAT AIN'T ON MY PAYROLL.
START FROM THE TOP. YOU WERE...

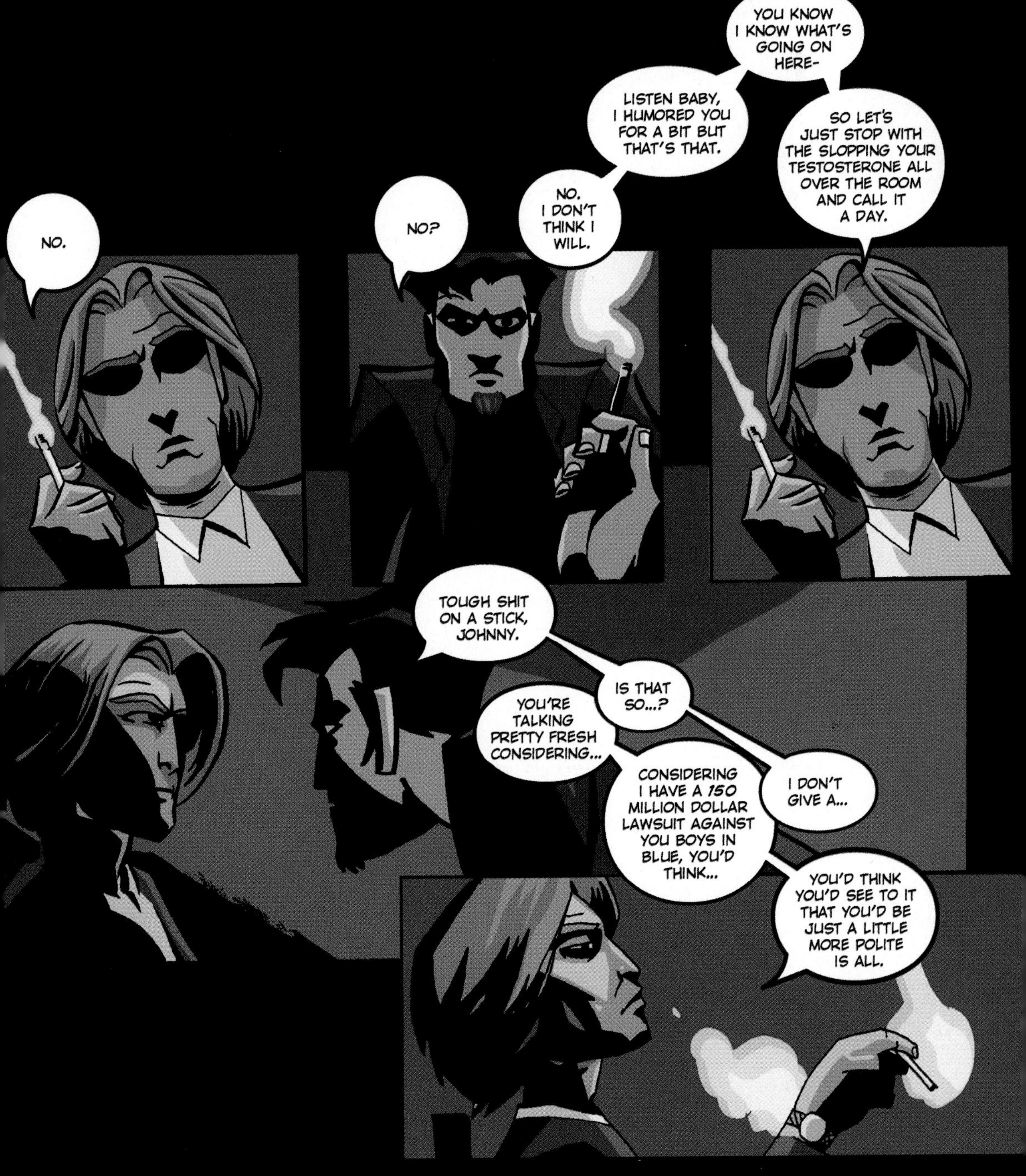
NO.
NO?
NO. I DON'T THINK I WILL.
LISTEN BABY, I HUMORED YOU FOR A BIT BUT THAT'S THAT.
YOU KNOW I KNOW WHAT'S GOING ON HERE-
SO LET'S JUST STOP WITH THE SLOPPING YOUR TESTOSTERONE ALL OVER THE ROOM AND CALL IT A DAY.
TOUGH SHIT ON A STICK, JOHNNY.
IS THAT SO...?
YOU'RE TALKING PRETTY FRESH CONSIDERING...
I DON'T GIVE A...
CONSIDERING I HAVE A 150 MILLION DOLLAR LAWSUIT AGAINST YOU BOYS IN BLUE, YOU'D THINK...
YOU'D THINK YOU'D SEE TO IT THAT YOU'D BE JUST A LITTLE MORE POLITE IS ALL.

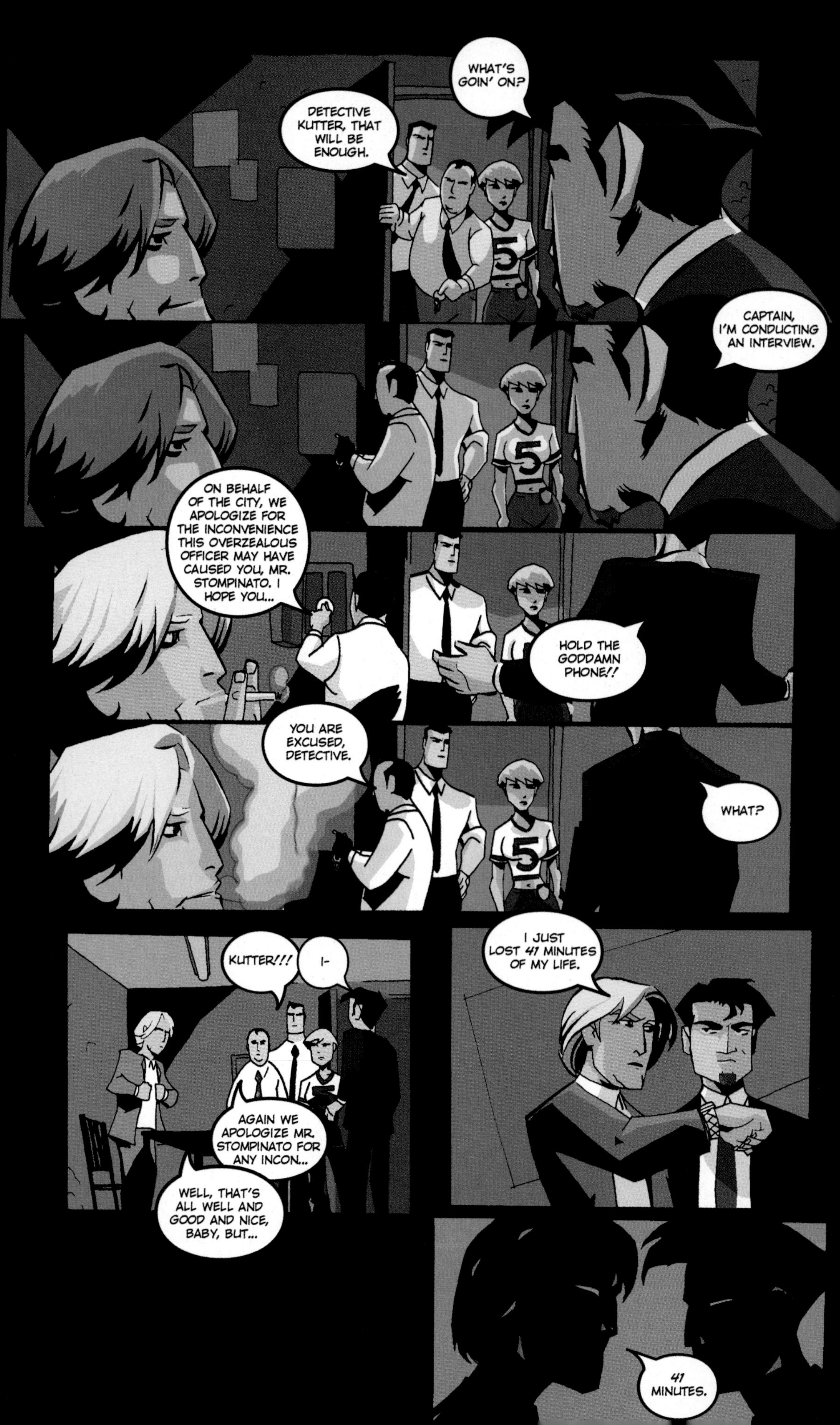
DETECTIVE KUTTER, THAT WILL BE ENOUGH.
WHAT'S GOIN' ON?
CAPTAIN, I'M CONDUCTING AN INTERVIEW.
ON BEHALF OF THE CITY, WE APOLOGIZE FOR THE INCONVENIENCE THIS OVERZEALOUS OFFICER MAY HAVE CAUSED YOU, MR. STOMPINATO. I HOPE YOU...
HOLD THE GODDAMN PHONE!!
YOU ARE EXCUSED, DETECTIVE.
WHAT?
KUTTER!!!
I-
AGAIN WE APOLOGIZE MR. STOMPINATO FOR ANY INCON...
WELL, THAT'S ALL WELL AND GOOD AND NICE, BABY, BUT...
I JUST LOST 41 MINUTES OF MY LIFE.
41 MINUTES.

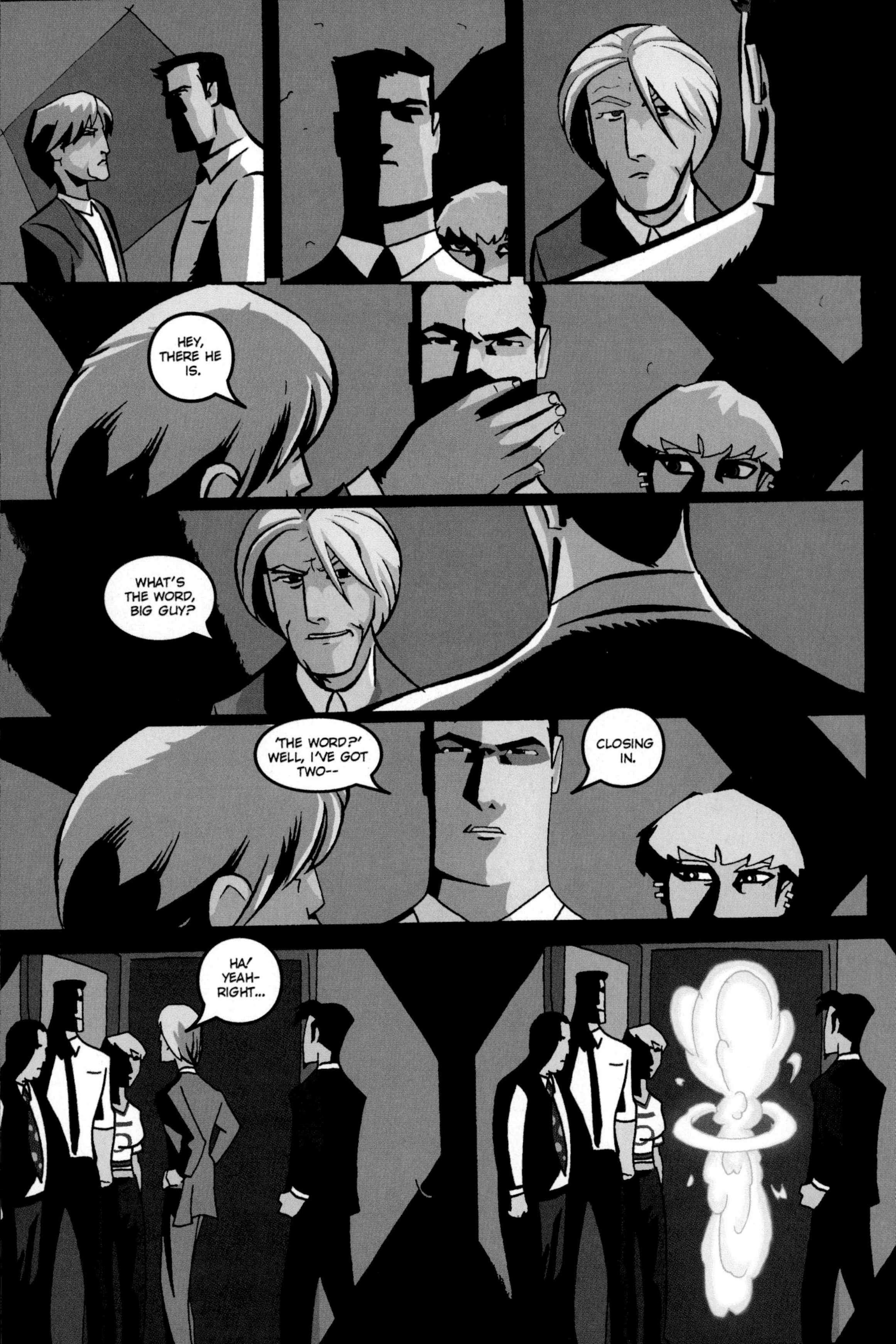
HEY, THERE HE IS.
WHAT'S THE WORD, BIG GUY?
'THE WORD?' WELL, I'VE GOT TWO--
CLOSING IN.
HA! YEAH-RIGHT...

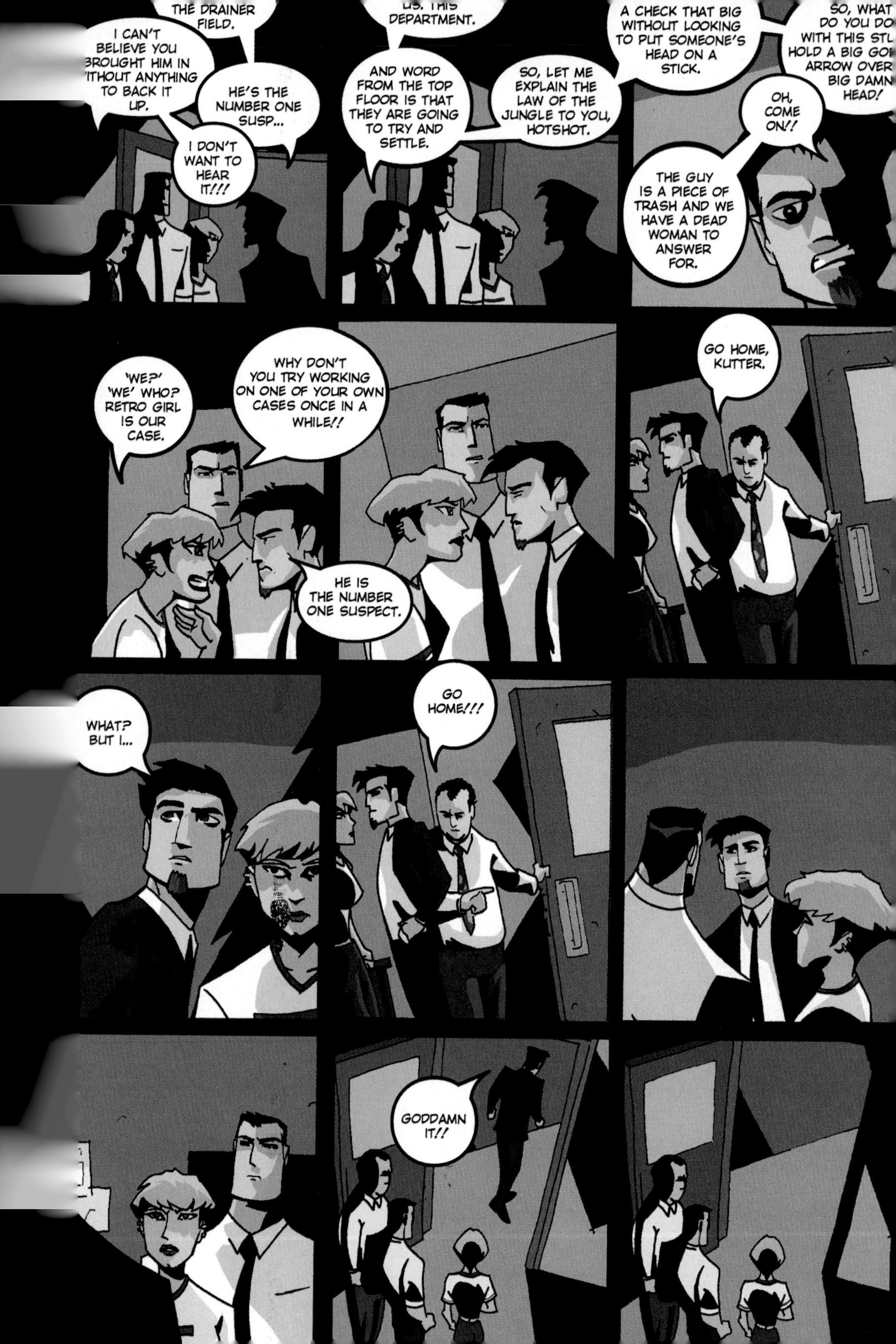
THE DRAINER FIELD.
I CAN'T BELIEVE YOU ROUGHT HIM IN ITHOUT ANYTHING TO BACK IT UP.
HE'S THE NUMBER ONE SUSP...
I DON'T WANT TO HEAR IT!!!
US. THIS DEPARTMENT.
AND WORD FROM THE TOP FLOOR IS THAT THEY ARE GOING TO TRY AND SETTLE.
SO, LET ME EXPLAIN THE LAW OF THE JUNGLE TO YOU, HOTSHOT.
A CHECK THAT BIG WITHOUT LOOKING TO PUT SOMEONE'S HEAD ON A STICK.
SO, WHAT DO YOU DO WITH THIS STU HOLD A BIG GO ARROW OVER BIG DAMN HEAD!
OH, COME ON!!
THE GUY IS A PIECE OF TRASH AND WE HAVE A DEAD WOMAN TO ANSWER FOR.
'WE?' 'WE' WHO? RETRO GIRL IS OUR CASE.
WHY DON'T YOU TRY WORKING ON ONE OF YOUR OWN CASES ONCE IN A WHILE!!
HE IS THE NUMBER ONE SUSPECT.
GO HOME, KUTTER.
WHAT? BUT I...
GO HOME!!!
GODDAMN IT!!

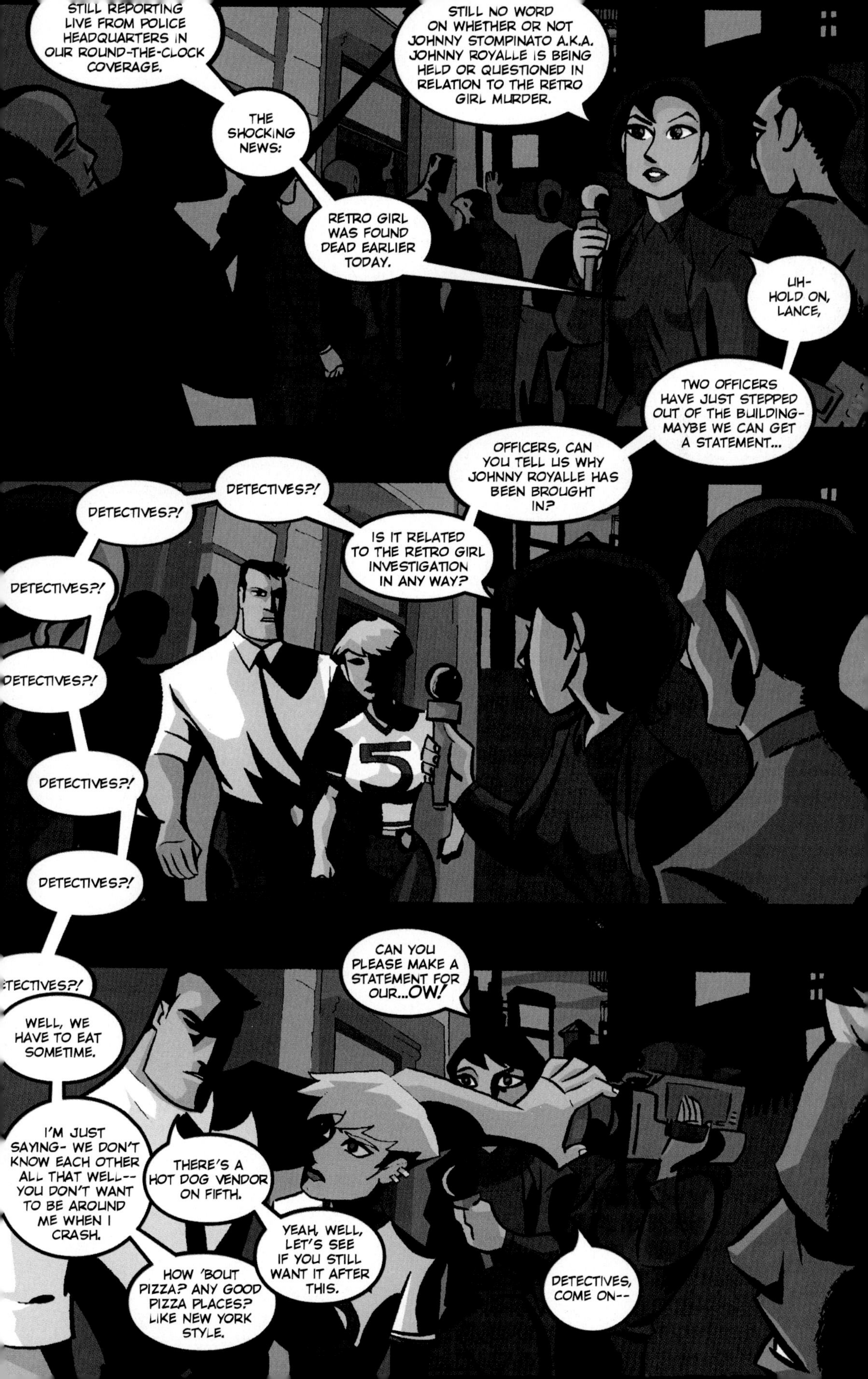

STILL REPORTING LIVE FROM POLICE HEADQUARTERS IN OUR ROUND-THE-CLOCK COVERAGE.
THE SHOCKING NEWS:
RETRO GIRL WAS FOUND DEAD EARLIER TODAY.
STILL NO WORD ON WHETHER OR NOT JOHNNY STOMPINATO A.K.A. JOHNNY ROYALLE IS BEING HELD OR QUESTIONED IN RELATION TO THE RETRO GIRL MURDER.
UH- HOLD ON, LANCE,
TWO OFFICERS HAVE JUST STEPPED OUT OF THE BUILDING- MAYBE WE CAN GET A STATEMENT...
OFFICERS, CAN YOU TELL US WHY JOHNNY ROYALLE HAS BEEN BROUGHT IN?
IS IT RELATED TO THE RETRO GIRL INVESTIGATION IN ANY WAY?
DETECTIVES?!
DETECTIVES?!
DETECTIVES?!
DETECTIVES?!
DETECTIVES?!
DETECTIVES?!
TECTIVES?!
CAN YOU PLEASE MAKE A STATEMENT FOR OUR...OW!
WELL, WE HAVE TO EAT SOMETIME.
I'M JUST SAYING- WE DON'T KNOW EACH OTHER ALL THAT WELL-- YOU DON'T WANT TO BE AROUND ME WHEN I CRASH.
THERE'S A HOT DOG VENDOR ON FIFTH.
HOW 'BOUT PIZZA? ANY GOOD PIZZA PLACES? LIKE NEW YORK STYLE.
YEAH, WELL, LET'S SEE IF YOU STILL WANT IT AFTER THIS.
DETECTIVES, COME ON--

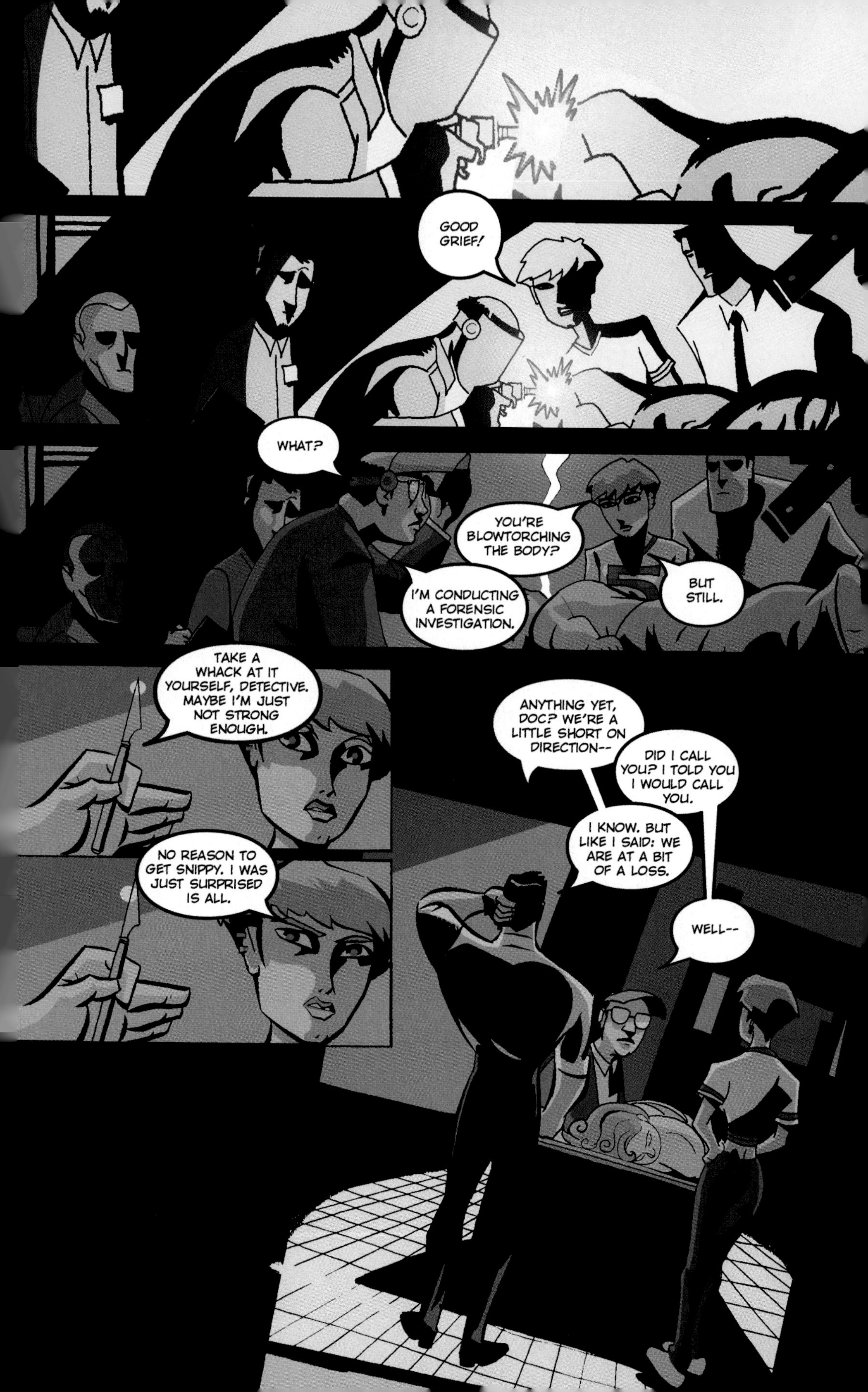
GOOD GRIEF!
WHAT?
YOU'RE BLOWTORCHING THE BODY?
I'M CONDUCTING A FORENSIC INVESTIGATION.
BUT STILL.
TAKE A WHACK AT IT YOURSELF, DETECTIVE. MAYBE I'M JUST NOT STRONG ENOUGH.
NO REASON TO GET SNIPPY. I WAS JUST SURPRISED IS ALL.
ANYTHING YET, DOC? WE'RE A LITTLE SHORT ON DIRECTION--
DID I CALL YOU? I TOLD YOU I WOULD CALL YOU.
I KNOW. BUT LIKE I SAID: WE ARE AT A BIT OF A LOSS.
WELL--

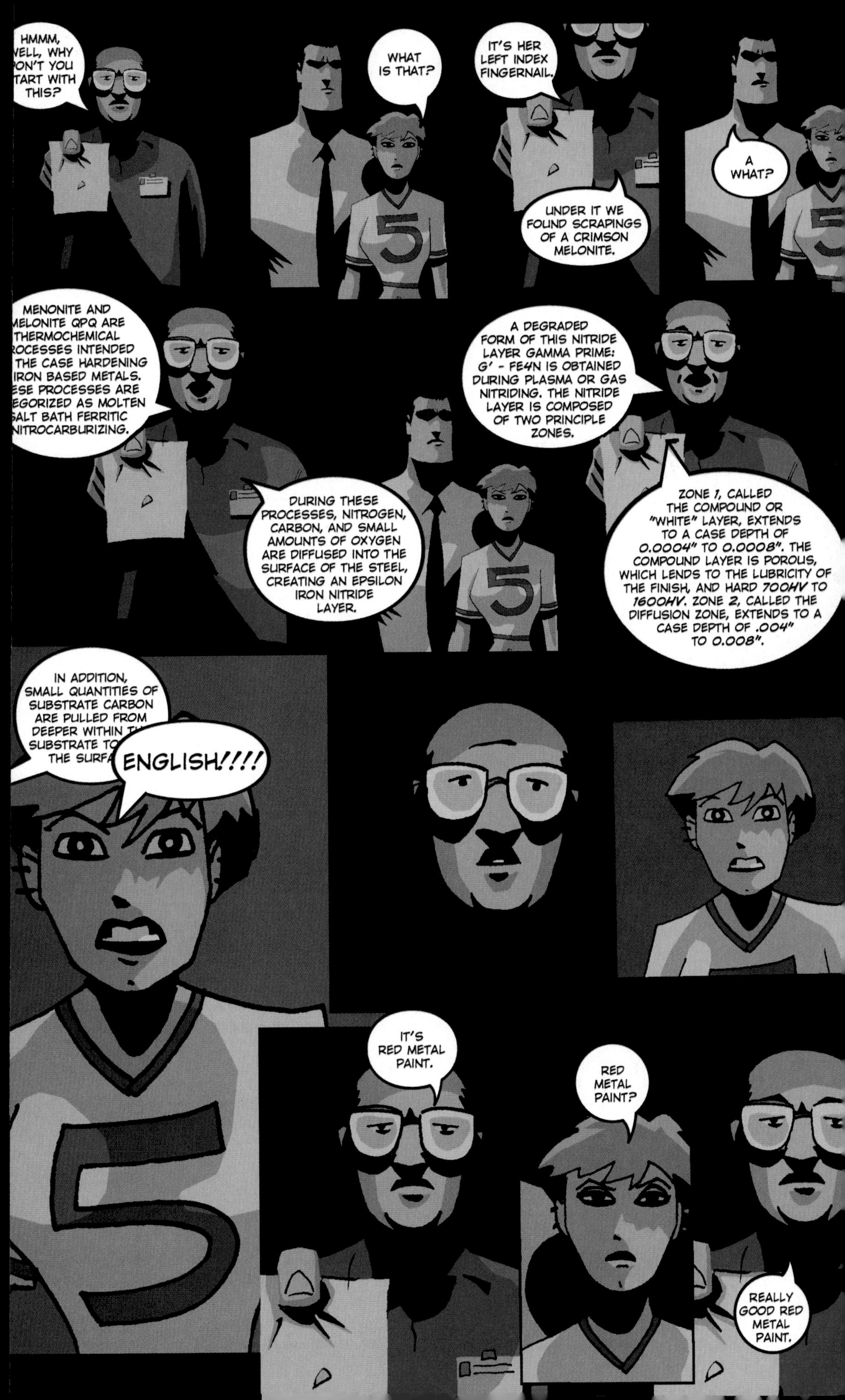
HMMM, WELL, WHY DON'T YOU START WITH THIS?
WHAT IS THAT?
IT'S HER LEFT INDEX FINGERNAIL.
UNDER IT WE FOUND SCRAPINGS OF A CRIMSON MELONITE.
A WHAT?
MENONITE AND MELONITE QPQ ARE THERMOCHEMICAL PROCESSES INTENDED THE CASE HARDENING IRON BASED METALS. ESE PROCESSES ARE EGORIZED AS MOLTEN SALT BATH FERRITIC NITROCARBURIZING.
DURING THESE PROCESSES, NITROGEN, CARBON, AND SMALL AMOUNTS OF OXYGEN ARE DIFFUSED INTO THE SURFACE OF THE STEEL, CREATING AN EPSILON IRON NITRIDE LAYER.
A DEGRADED FORM OF THIS NITRIDE LAYER GAMMA PRIME: G' - FE4N IS OBTAINED DURING PLASMA OR GAS NITRIDING. THE NITRIDE LAYER IS COMPOSED OF TWO PRINCIPLE ZONES.
ZONE 1, CALLED THE COMPOUND OR "WHITE" LAYER, EXTENDS TO A CASE DEPTH OF 0.0004" TO 0.0008". THE COMPOUND LAYER IS POROUS, WHICH LENDS TO THE LUBRICITY OF THE FINISH, AND HARD 700HV TO 1600HV. ZONE 2, CALLED THE DIFFUSION ZONE, EXTENDS TO A CASE DEPTH OF .004" TO 0.008".
IN ADDITION, SMALL QUANTITIES OF SUBSTRATE CARBON ARE PULLED FROM DEEPER WITHIN TH SUBSTRATE TO THE SURFA
ENGLISH!!!!
IT'S RED METAL PAINT.
RED METAL PAINT?
REALLY GOOD RED METAL PAINT.

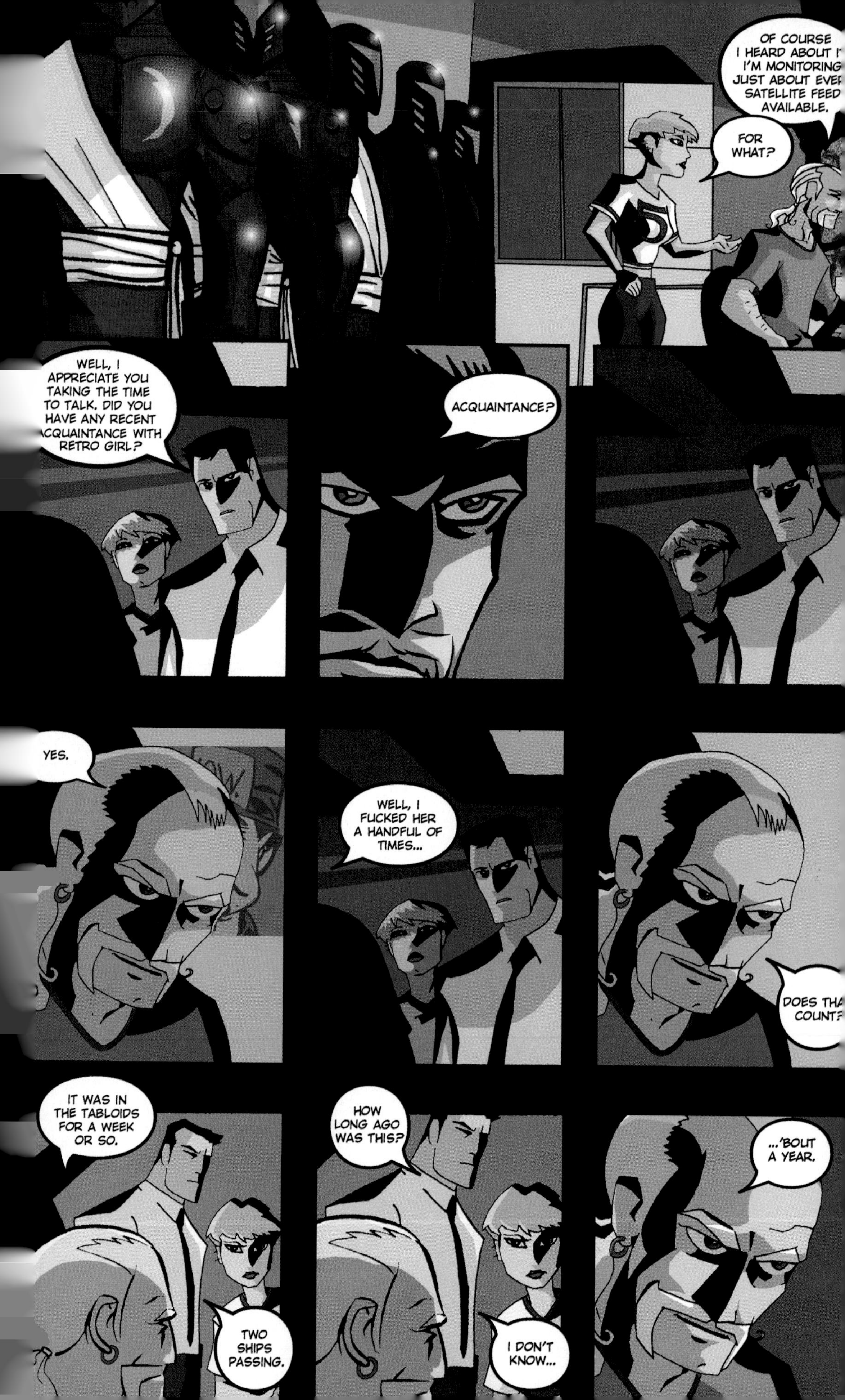
OF COURSE I HEARD ABOUT I' I'M MONITORING JUST ABOUT EVER SATELLITE FEED AVAILABLE.
FOR WHAT?
WELL, I APPRECIATE YOU TAKING THE TIME TO TALK. DID YOU HAVE ANY RECENT ACQUAINTANCE WITH RETRO GIRL?
ACQUAINTANCE?
YES.
WELL, I FUCKED HER A HANDFUL OF TIMES...
DOES THA COUNT?
IT WAS IN THE TABLOIDS FOR A WEEK OR SO.
TWO SHIPS PASSING.
HOW LONG AGO WAS THIS?
I DON'T KNOW...
...'BOUT A YEAR.

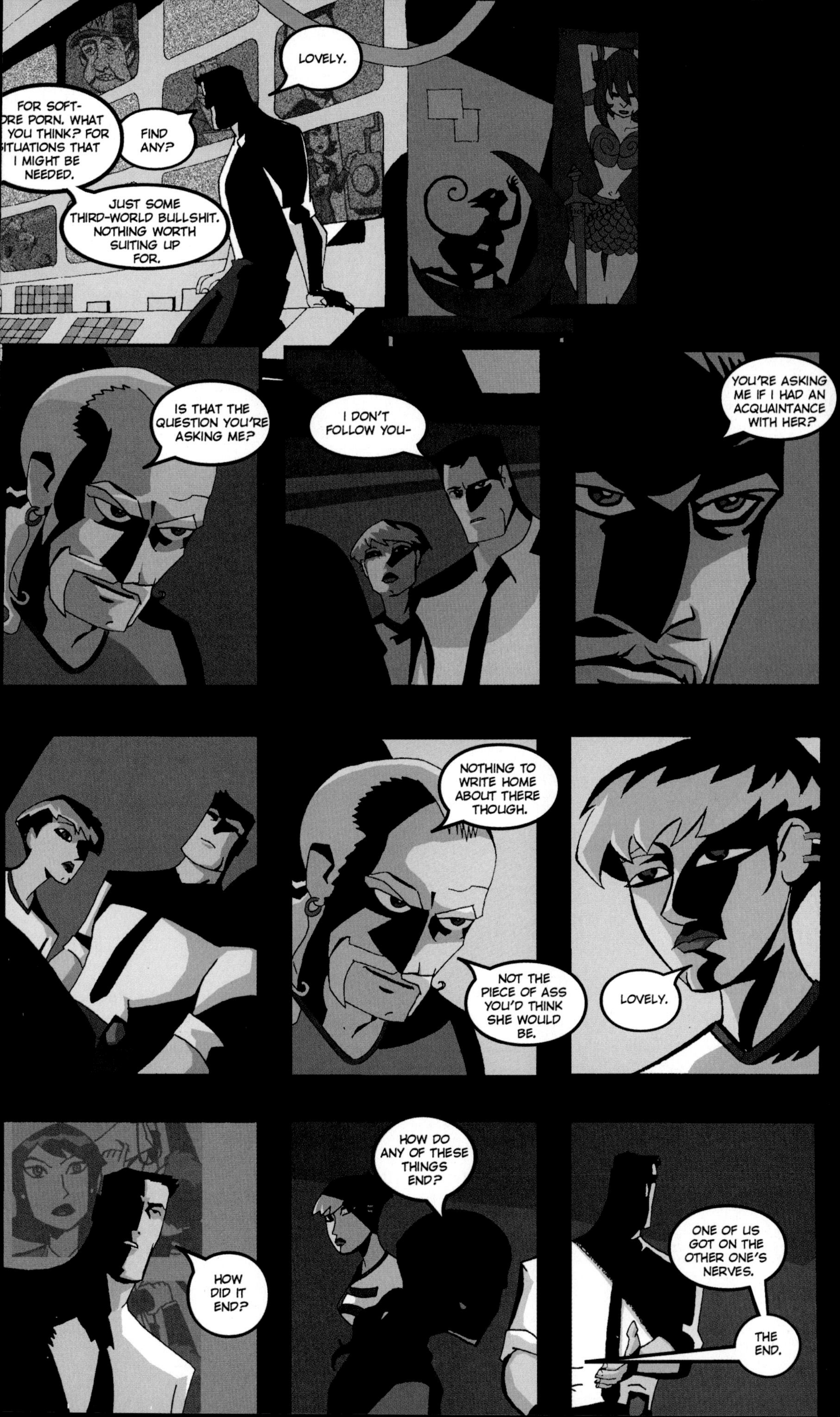
LOVELY.
FIND ANY?
FOR SOFT-
ORE PORN. WHAT
YOU THINK? FOR
SITUATIONS THAT
I MIGHT BE
NEEDED.
JUST SOME THIRD-WORLD BULLSHIT. NOTHING WORTH SUITING UP FOR.
IS THAT THE QUESTION YOU'RE ASKING ME?
I DON'T FOLLOW YOU-
YOU'RE ASKING ME IF I HAD AN ACQUAINTANCE WITH HER?
NOTHING TO WRITE HOME ABOUT THERE THOUGH.
NOT THE PIECE OF ASS YOU'D THINK SHE WOULD BE.
LOVELY.
HOW DID IT END?
HOW DO ANY OF THESE THINGS END?
ONE OF US GOT ON THE OTHER ONE'S NERVES.
THE END.

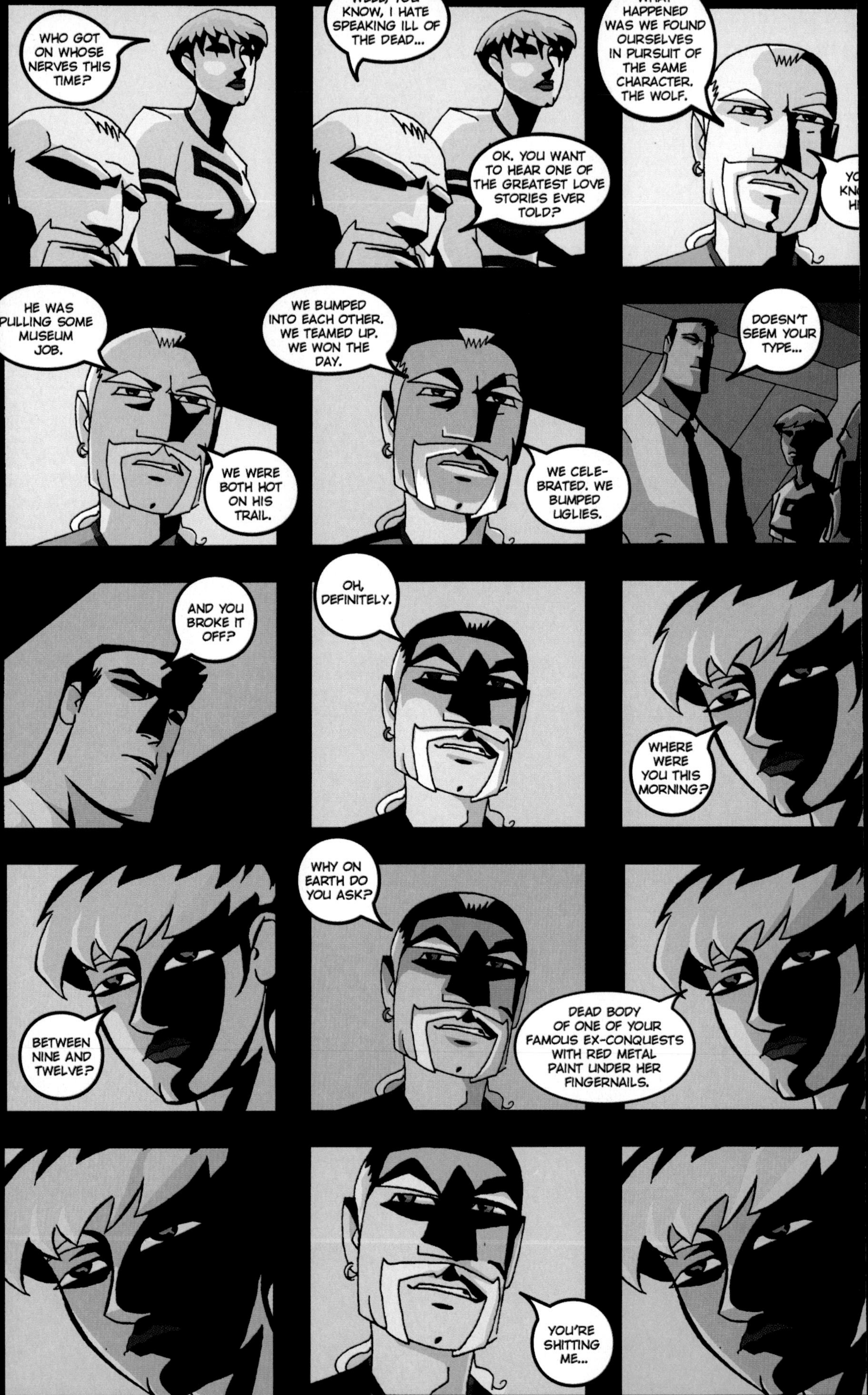
WHO GOT ON WHOSE NERVES THIS TIME?
WELL, YOU KNOW, I HATE SPEAKING ILL OF THE DEAD...
OK. YOU WANT TO HEAR ONE OF THE GREATEST LOVE STORIES EVER TOLD?
WHAT HAPPENED WAS WE FOUND OURSELVES IN PURSUIT OF THE SAME CHARACTER. THE WOLF.
HE WAS PULLING SOME MUSEUM JOB.
WE WERE BOTH HOT ON HIS TRAIL.
WE BUMPED INTO EACH OTHER. WE TEAMED UP. WE WON THE DAY.
WE CELE-BRATED. WE BUMPED UGLIES.
DOESN'T SEEM YOUR TYPE...
AND YOU BROKE IT OFF?
OH, DEFINITELY.
WHERE WERE YOU THIS MORNING?
BETWEEN NINE AND TWELVE?
WHY ON EARTH DO YOU ASK?
DEAD BODY OF ONE OF YOUR FAMOUS EX-CONQUESTS WITH RED METAL PAINT UNDER HER FINGERNAILS.
YOU'RE SHITTING ME...

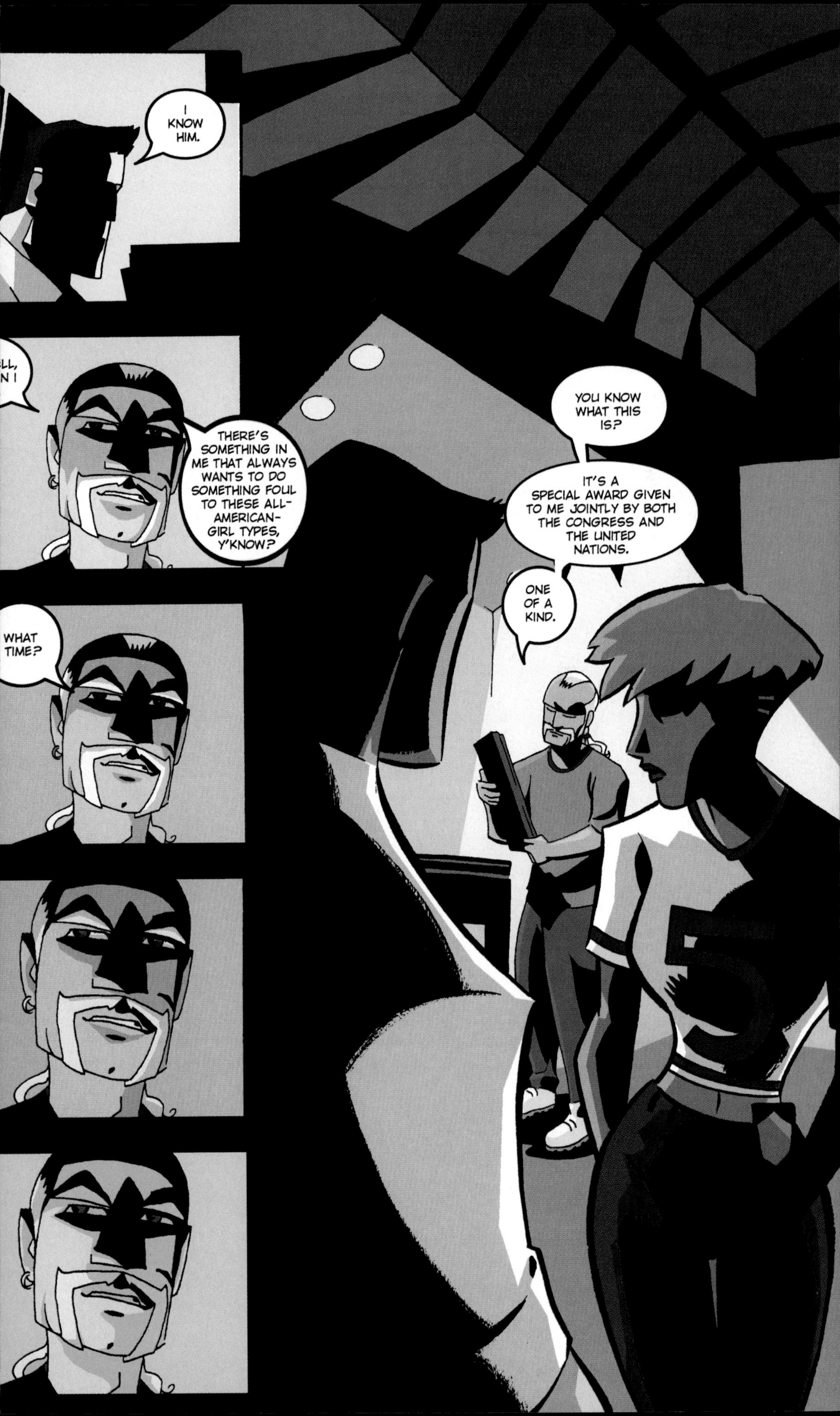
I KNOW HIM.
THERE'S SOMETHING IN ME THAT ALWAYS WANTS TO DO SOMETHING FOUL TO THESE ALL-AMERICAN-GIRL TYPES, Y'KNOW?
WHAT TIME?
YOU KNOW WHAT THIS IS?
IT'S A SPECIAL AWARD GIVEN TO ME JOINTLY BY BOTH THE CONGRESS AND THE UNITED NATIONS.
ONE OF A KIND.

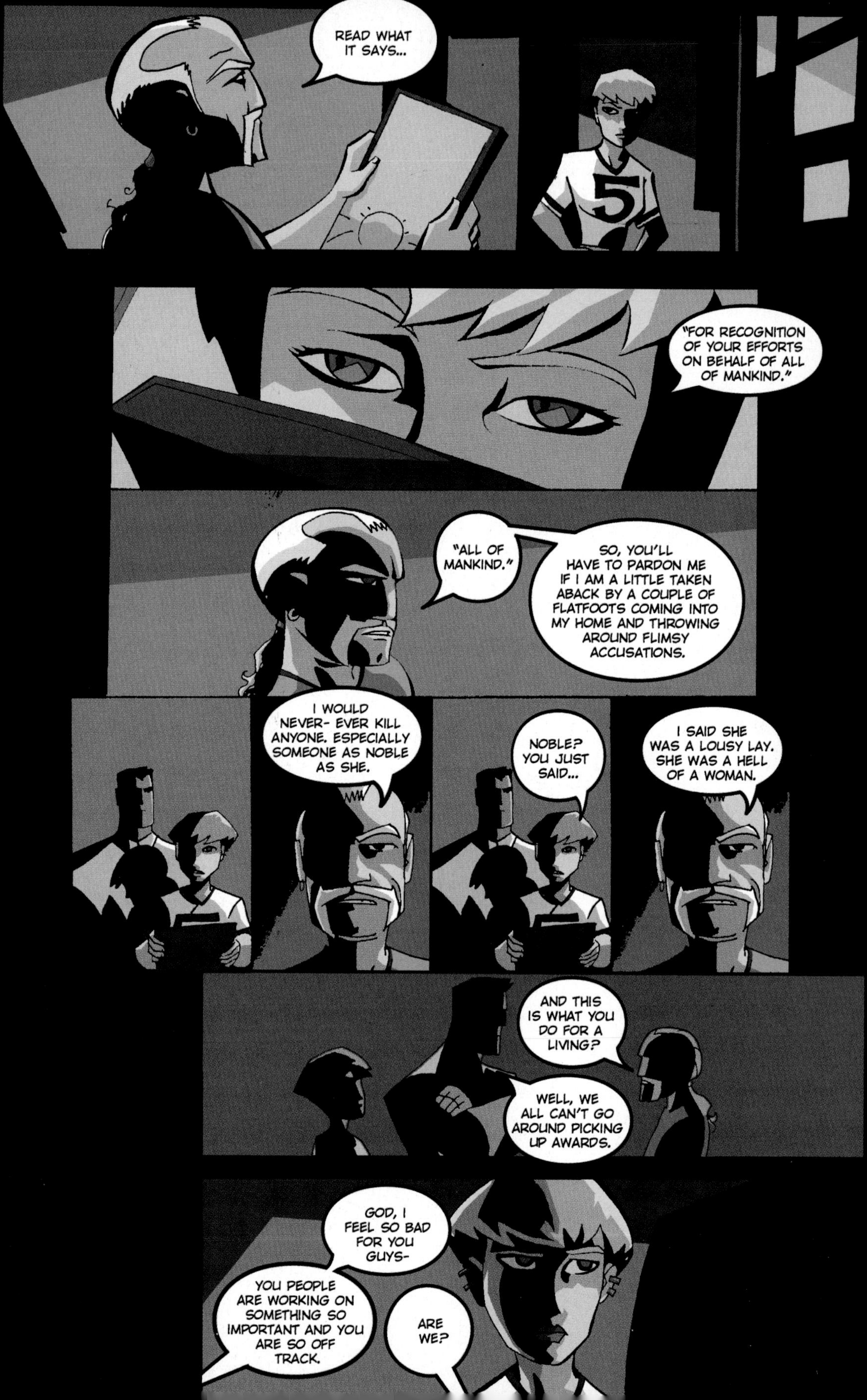
READ WHAT IT SAYS...
"FOR RECOGNITION OF YOUR EFFORTS ON BEHALF OF ALL OF MANKIND."
"ALL OF MANKIND."
SO, YOU'LL HAVE TO PARDON ME IF I AM A LITTLE TAKEN ABACK BY A COUPLE OF FLATFOOTS COMING INTO MY HOME AND THROWING AROUND FLIMSY ACCUSATIONS.
I WOULD NEVER- EVER KILL ANYONE. ESPECIALLY SOMEONE AS NOBLE AS SHE.
NOBLE? YOU JUST SAID...
I SAID SHE WAS A LOUSY LAY. SHE WAS A HELL OF A WOMAN.
AND THIS IS WHAT YOU DO FOR A LIVING?
WELL, WE ALL CAN'T GO AROUND PICKING UP AWARDS.
GOD, I FEEL SO BAD FOR YOU GUYS-
YOU PEOPLE ARE WORKING ON SOMETHING SO IMPORTANT AND YOU ARE SO OFF TRACK.
ARE WE?

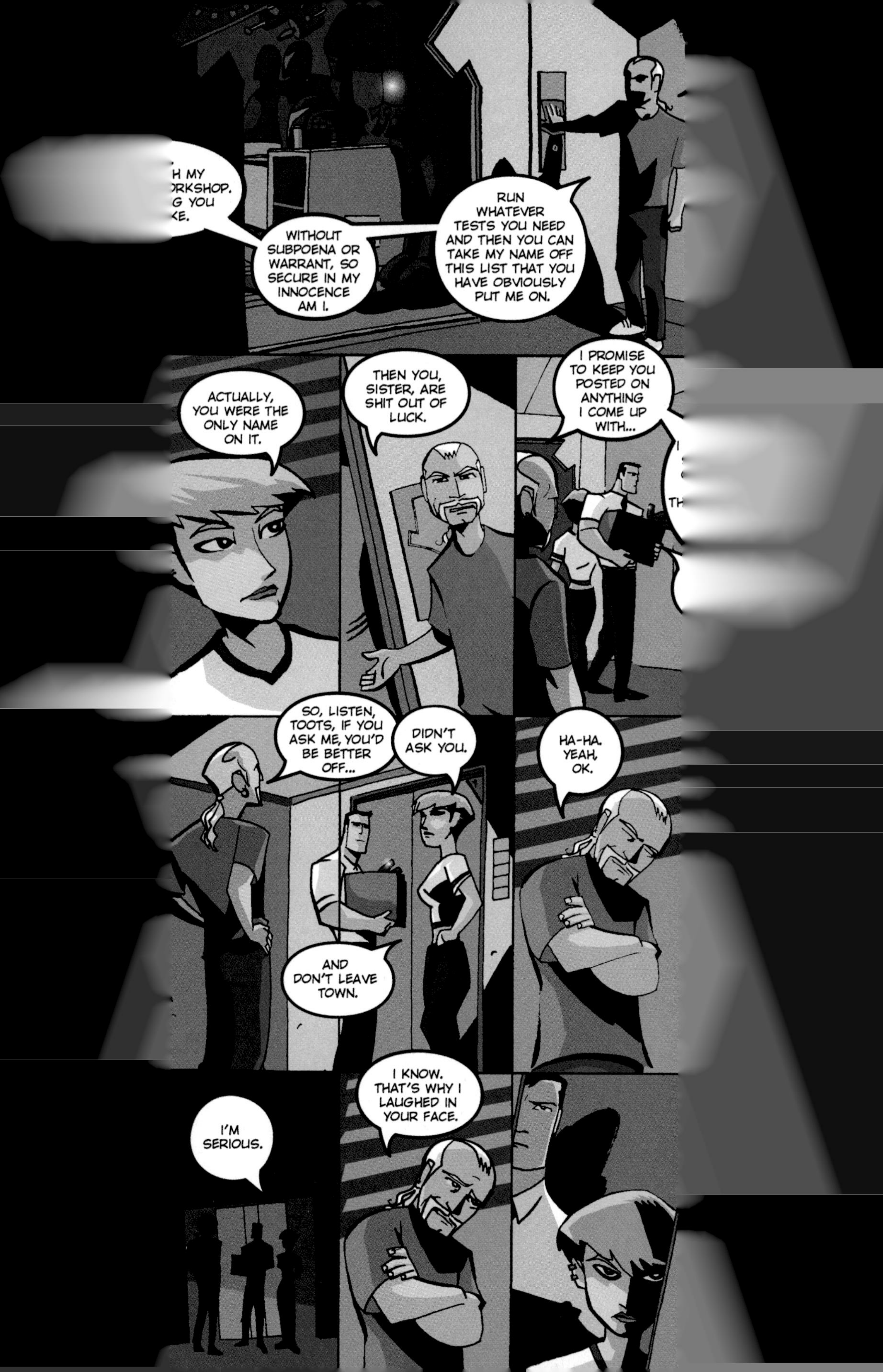

H MY
ORKSHOP.
G YOU
KE.
WITHOUT SUBPOENA OR WARRANT, SO SECURE IN MY INNOCENCE AM I.
RUN WHATEVER TESTS YOU NEED AND THEN YOU CAN TAKE MY NAME OFF THIS LIST THAT YOU HAVE OBVIOUSLY PUT ME ON.
ACTUALLY, YOU WERE THE ONLY NAME ON IT.
THEN YOU, SISTER, ARE SHIT OUT OF LUCK.
I PROMISE TO KEEP YOU POSTED ON ANYTHING I COME UP WITH...
SO, LISTEN, TOOTS, IF YOU ASK ME, YOU'D BE BETTER OFF...
DIDN'T ASK YOU.
HA-HA. YEAH, OK.
AND DON'T LEAVE TOWN.
I'M SERIOUS.
I KNOW. THAT'S WHY I LAUGHED IN YOUR FACE.

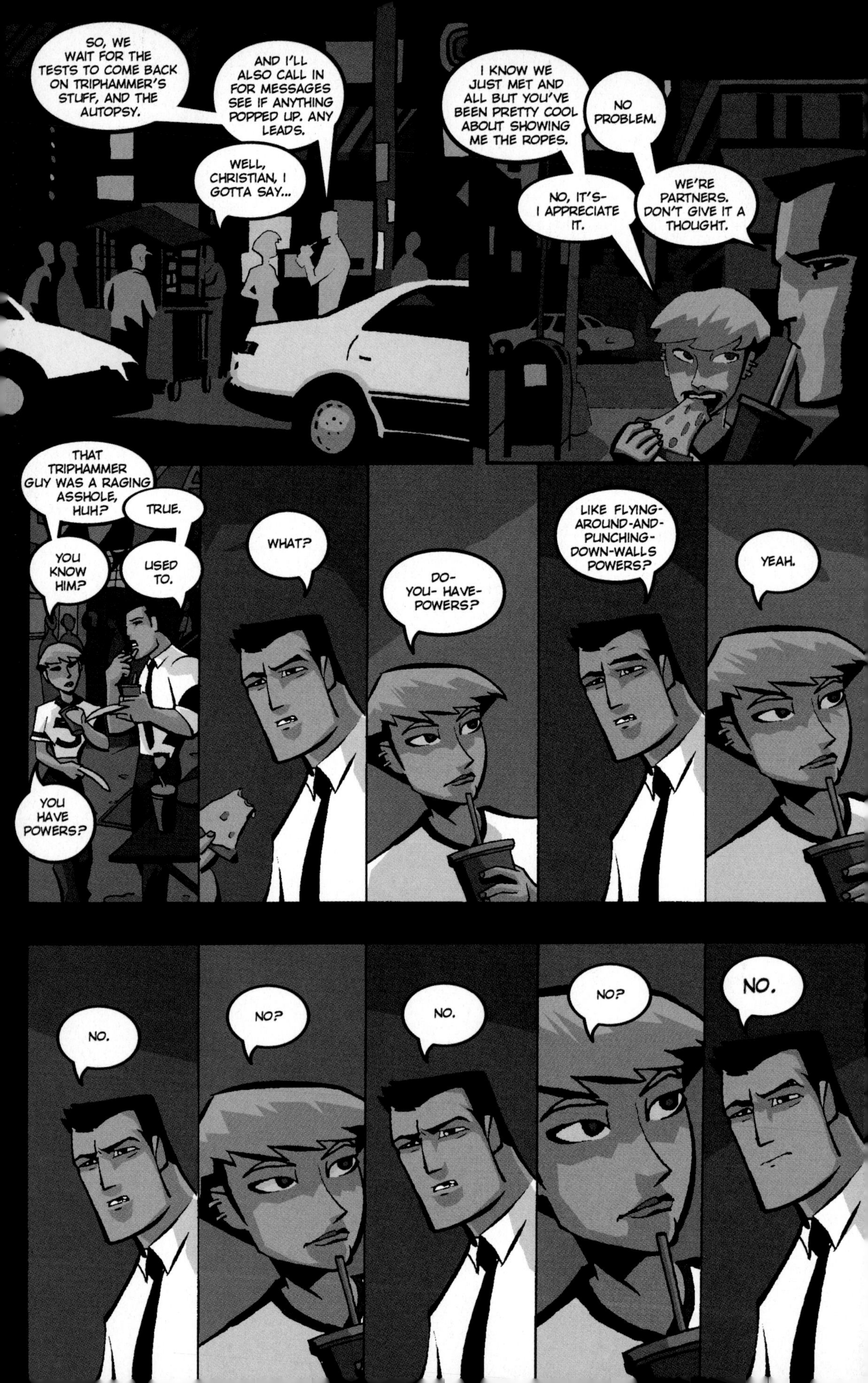
SO, WE WAIT FOR THE TESTS TO COME BACK ON TRIPHAMMER'S STUFF, AND THE AUTOPSY.
AND I'LL ALSO CALL IN FOR MESSAGES SEE IF ANYTHING POPPED UP. ANY LEADS.
WELL, CHRISTIAN, I GOTTA SAY...
I KNOW WE JUST MET AND ALL BUT YOU'VE BEEN PRETTY COOL ABOUT SHOWING ME THE ROPES.
NO PROBLEM.
NO, IT'S- I APPRECIATE IT.
WE'RE PARTNERS. DON'T GIVE IT A THOUGHT.
THAT TRIPHAMMER GUY WAS A RAGING ASSHOLE, HUH?
TRUE.
YOU KNOW HIM?
USED TO.
YOU HAVE POWERS?
WHAT?
DO- YOU- HAVE- POWERS?
LIKE FLYING-AROUND-AND-PUNCHING-DOWN-WALLS POWERS?
YEAH.
NO.
NO?
NO.
NO?
NO.

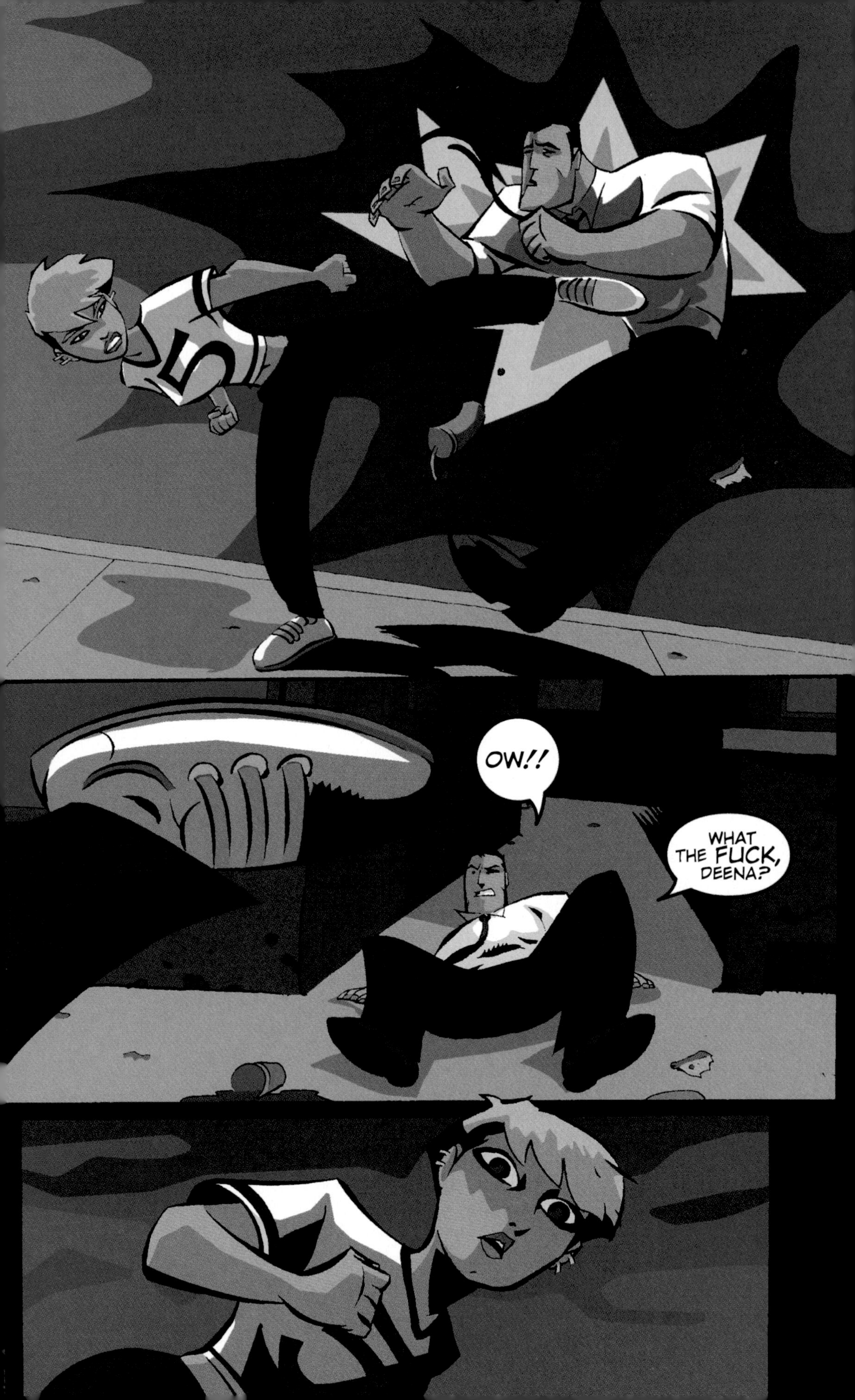
OW!!
WHAT THE FUCK, DEENA?

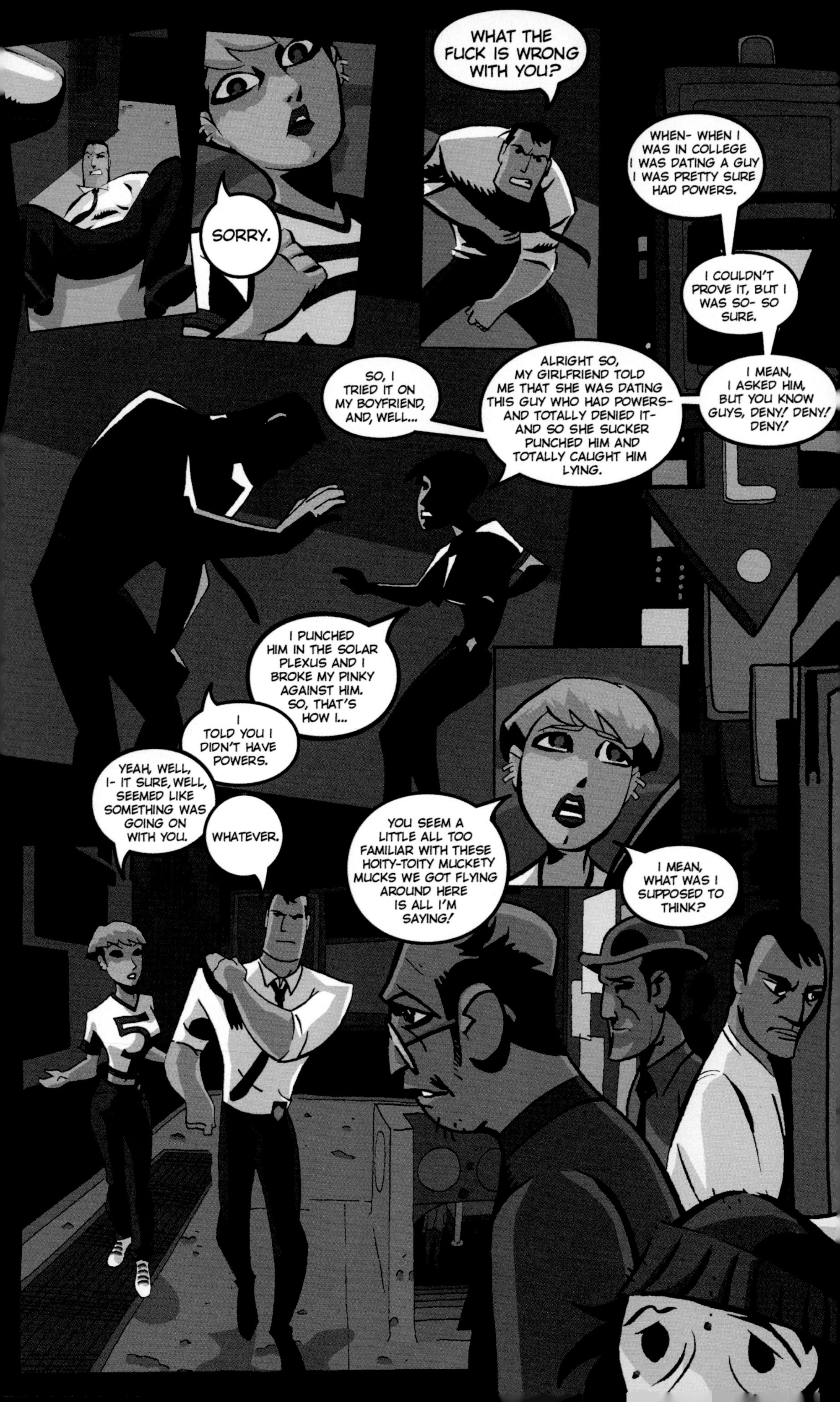
SORRY.
WHAT THE FUCK IS WRONG WITH YOU?
WHEN- WHEN I WAS IN COLLEGE I WAS DATING A GUY I WAS PRETTY SURE HAD POWERS.
I COULDN'T PROVE IT, BUT I WAS SO- SO SURE.
I MEAN, I ASKED HIM, BUT YOU KNOW GUYS, DENY! DENY! DENY!
ALRIGHT SO, MY GIRLFRIEND TOLD ME THAT SHE WAS DATING THIS GUY WHO HAD POWERS- AND TOTALLY DENIED IT- AND SO SHE SUCKER PUNCHED HIM AND TOTALLY CAUGHT HIM LYING.
SO, I TRIED IT ON MY BOYFRIEND, AND, WELL...
I PUNCHED HIM IN THE SOLAR PLEXUS AND I BROKE MY PINKY AGAINST HIM. SO, THAT'S HOW I...
I TOLD YOU I DIDN'T HAVE POWERS.
YEAH, WELL, I- IT SURE, WELL, SEEMED LIKE SOMETHING WAS GOING ON WITH YOU.
WHATEVER.
YOU SEEM A LITTLE ALL TOO FAMILIAR WITH THESE HOITY-TOITY MUCKETY MUCKS WE GOT FLYING AROUND HERE IS ALL I'M SAYING!
I MEAN, WHAT WAS I SUPPOSED TO THINK?

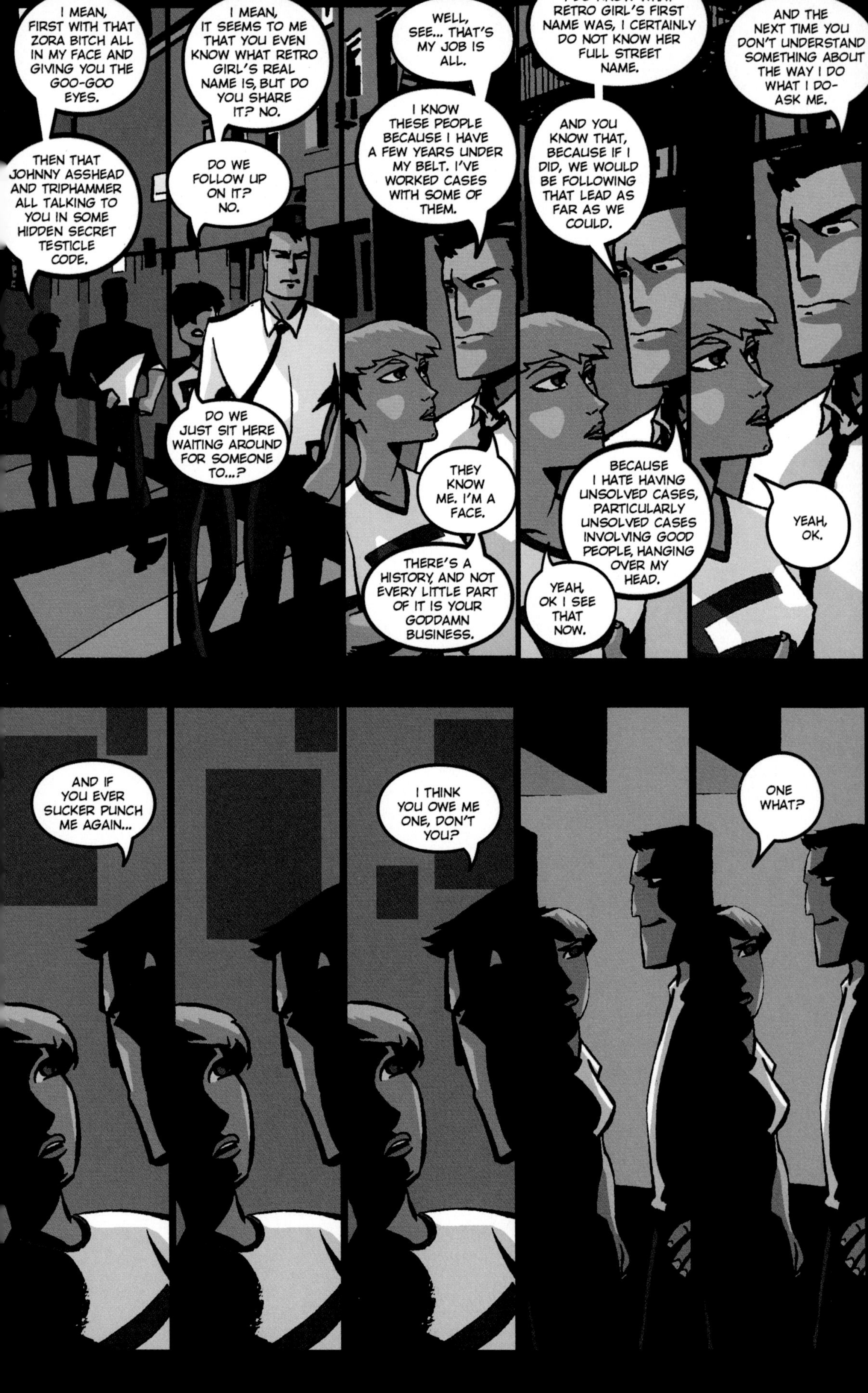
I MEAN, FIRST WITH THAT ZORA BITCH ALL IN MY FACE AND GIVING YOU THE GOO-GOO EYES.
THEN THAT JOHNNY ASSHEAD AND TRIPHAMMER ALL TALKING TO YOU IN SOME HIDDEN SECRET TESTICLE CODE.
I MEAN, IT SEEMS TO ME THAT YOU EVEN KNOW WHAT RETRO GIRL'S REAL NAME IS, BUT DO YOU SHARE IT? NO.
DO WE FOLLOW UP ON IT? NO.
DO WE JUST SIT HERE WAITING AROUND FOR SOMEONE TO...?
WELL, SEE... THAT'S MY JOB IS ALL.
I KNOW THESE PEOPLE BECAUSE I HAVE A FEW YEARS UNDER MY BELT. I'VE WORKED CASES WITH SOME OF THEM.
THEY KNOW ME. I'M A FACE.
THERE'S A HISTORY, AND NOT EVERY LITTLE PART OF IT IS YOUR GODDAMN BUSINESS.
AND THOUGH I DO KNOW WHAT RETRO GIRL'S FIRST NAME WAS, I CERTAINLY DO NOT KNOW HER FULL STREET NAME.
AND YOU KNOW THAT, BECAUSE IF I DID, WE WOULD BE FOLLOWING THAT LEAD AS FAR AS WE COULD.
BECAUSE I HATE HAVING UNSOLVED CASES, PARTICULARLY UNSOLVED CASES INVOLVING GOOD PEOPLE, HANGING OVER MY HEAD.
YEAH, OK I SEE THAT NOW.
AND THE NEXT TIME YOU DON'T UNDERSTAND SOMETHING ABOUT THE WAY I DO WHAT I DO- ASK ME.
YEAH, OK.
AND IF YOU EVER SUCKER PUNCH ME AGAIN...
I THINK YOU OWE ME ONE, DON'T YOU?
ONE WHAT?

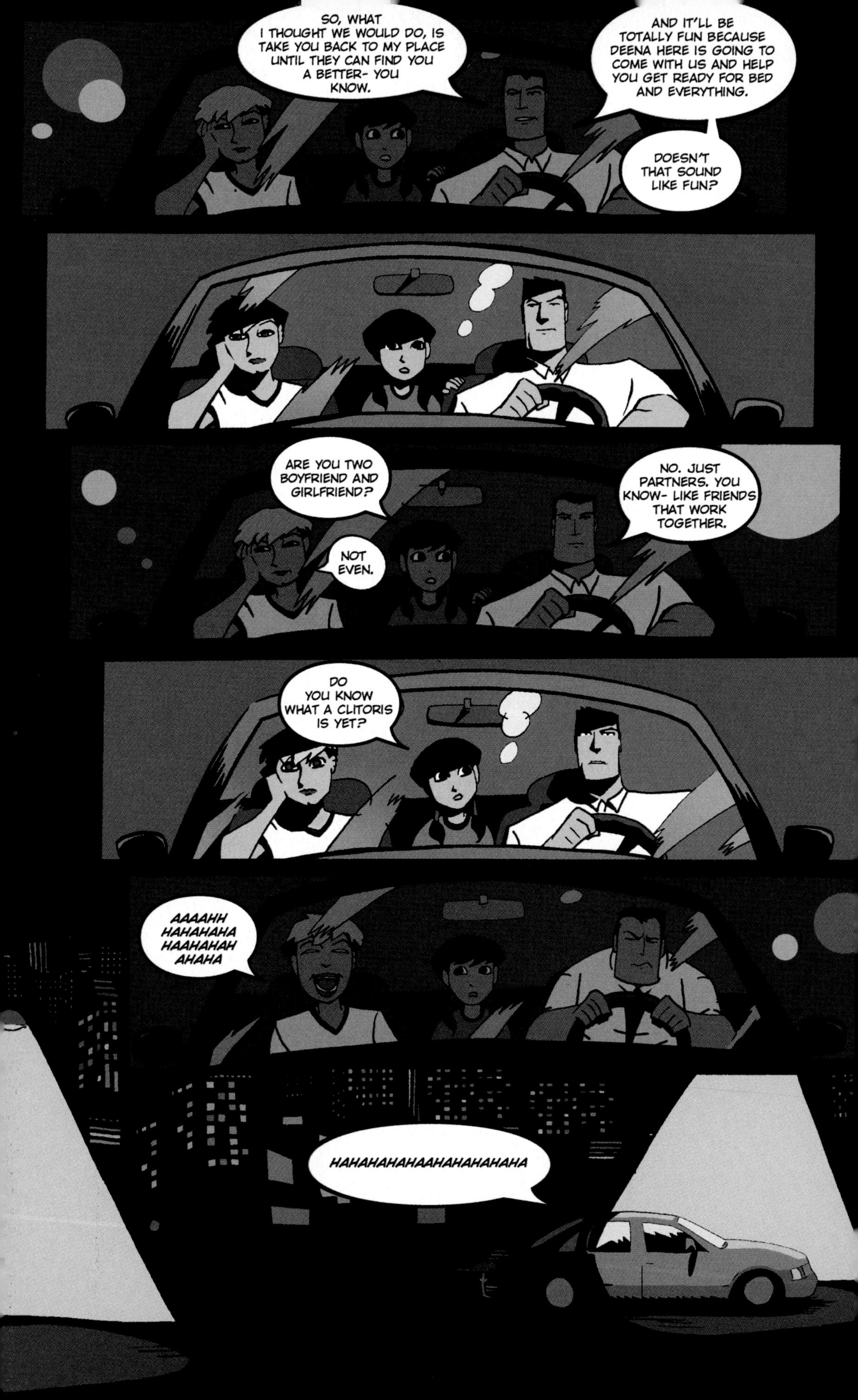
SO, WHAT I THOUGHT WE WOULD DO, IS TAKE YOU BACK TO MY PLACE UNTIL THEY CAN FIND YOU A BETTER- YOU KNOW.
AND IT'LL BE TOTALLY FUN BECAUSE DEENA HERE IS GOING TO COME WITH US AND HELP YOU GET READY FOR BED AND EVERYTHING.
DOESN'T THAT SOUND LIKE FUN?
ARE YOU TWO BOYFRIEND AND GIRLFRIEND?
NO. JUST PARTNERS. YOU KNOW- LIKE FRIENDS THAT WORK TOGETHER.
NOT EVEN.
DO YOU KNOW WHAT A CLITORIS IS YET?
AAAAHH HAHAHAHA HAAHAHAH AHAHA
HAHAHAHAHAAHAHAHAHAHA

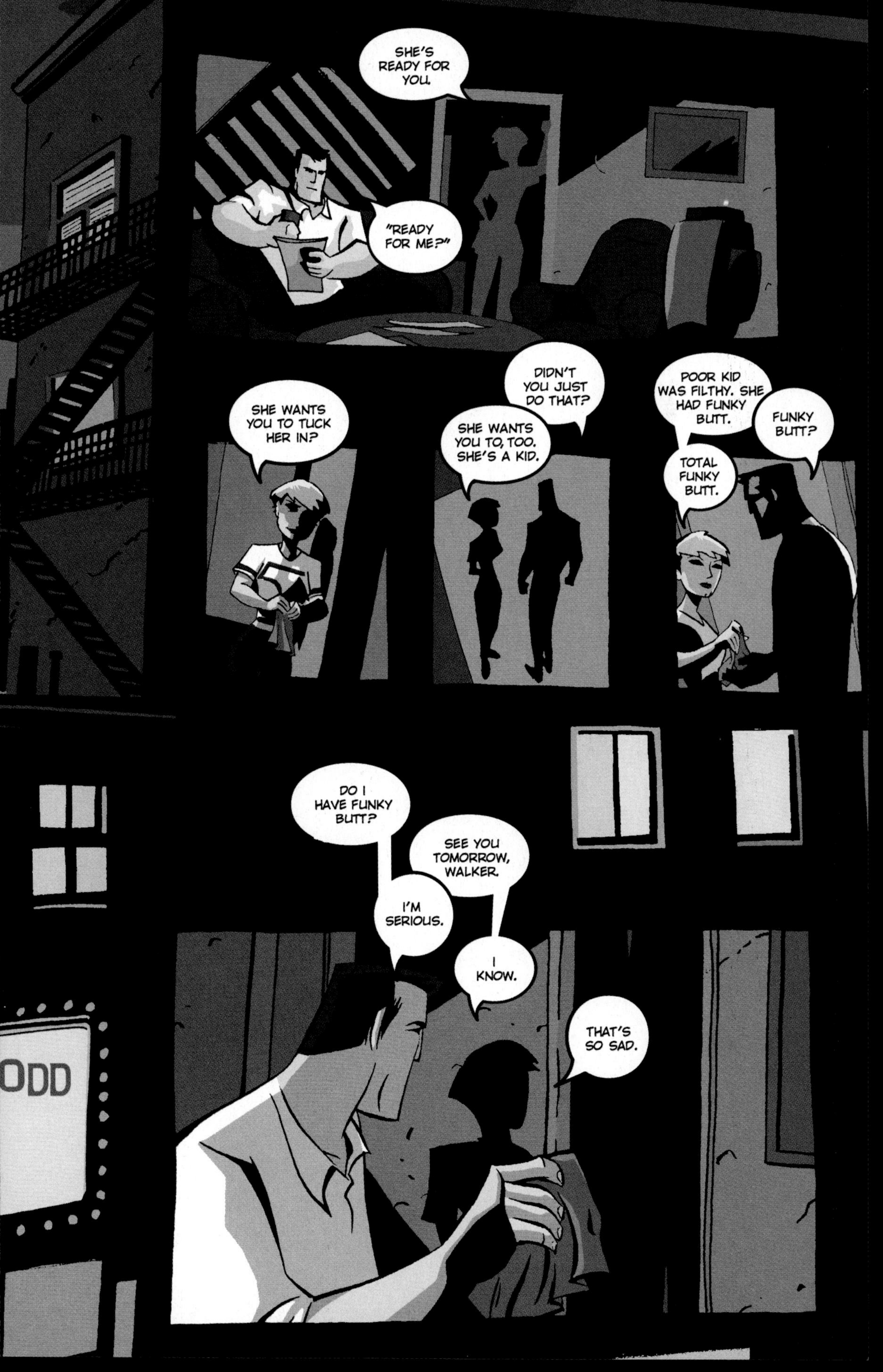
SHE'S READY FOR YOU.
"READY FOR ME?"
SHE WANTS YOU TO TUCK HER IN?
DIDN'T YOU JUST DO THAT?
SHE WANTS YOU TO, TOO. SHE'S A KID.
POOR KID WAS FILTHY. SHE HAD FUNKY BUTT.
FUNKY BUTT?
TOTAL FUNKY BUTT.
DO I HAVE FUNKY BUTT?
SEE YOU TOMORROW, WALKER.
I'M SERIOUS.
I KNOW.
THAT'S SO SAD.
ODD

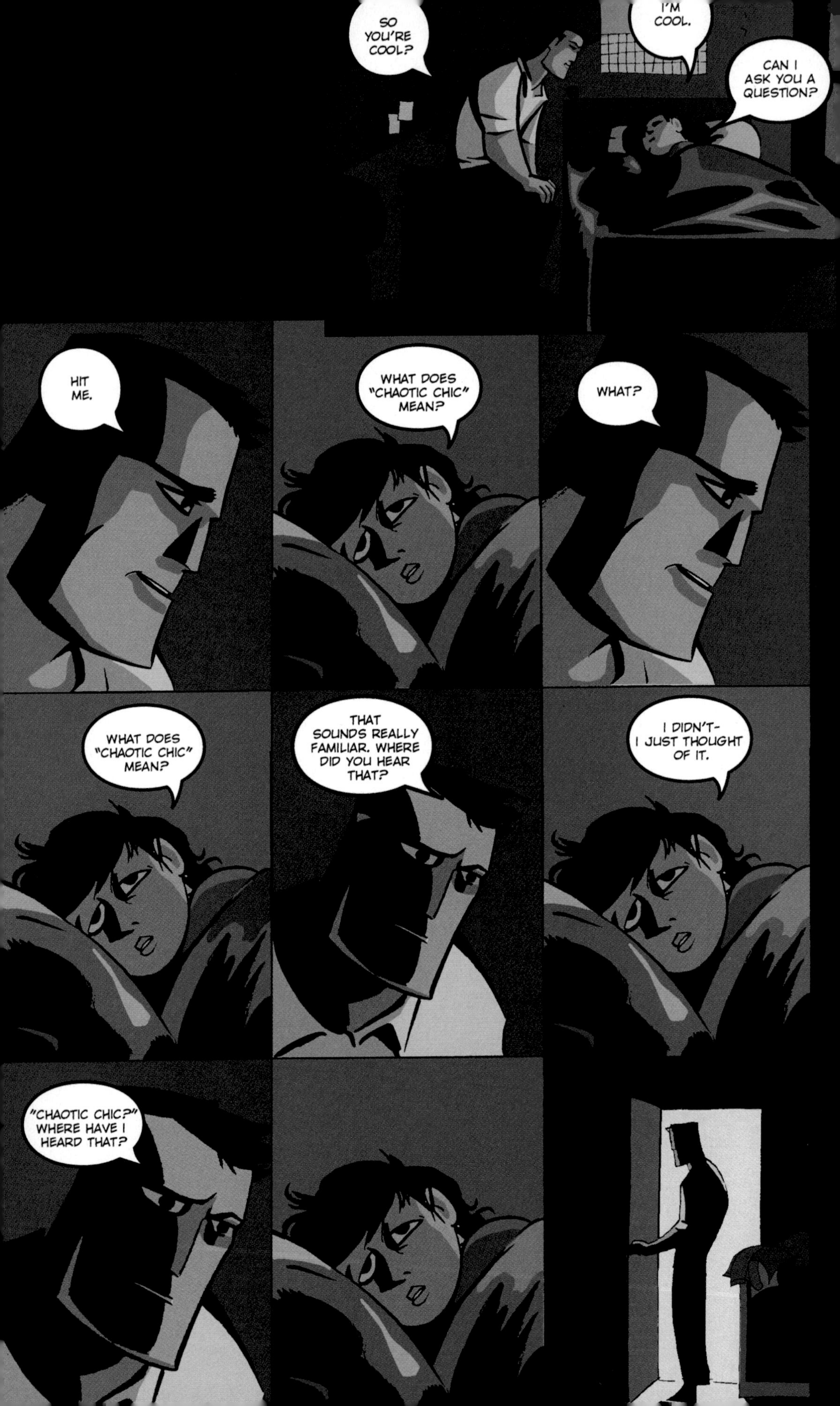
SO YOU'RE COOL?
I'M COOL.
CAN I ASK YOU A QUESTION?
HIT ME.
WHAT DOES "CHAOTIC CHIC" MEAN?
WHAT?
WHAT DOES "CHAOTIC CHIC" MEAN?
THAT SOUNDS REALLY FAMILIAR. WHERE DID YOU HEAR THAT?
I DIDN'T- I JUST THOUGHT OF IT.
"CHAOTIC CHIC?" WHERE HAVE I HEARD THAT?

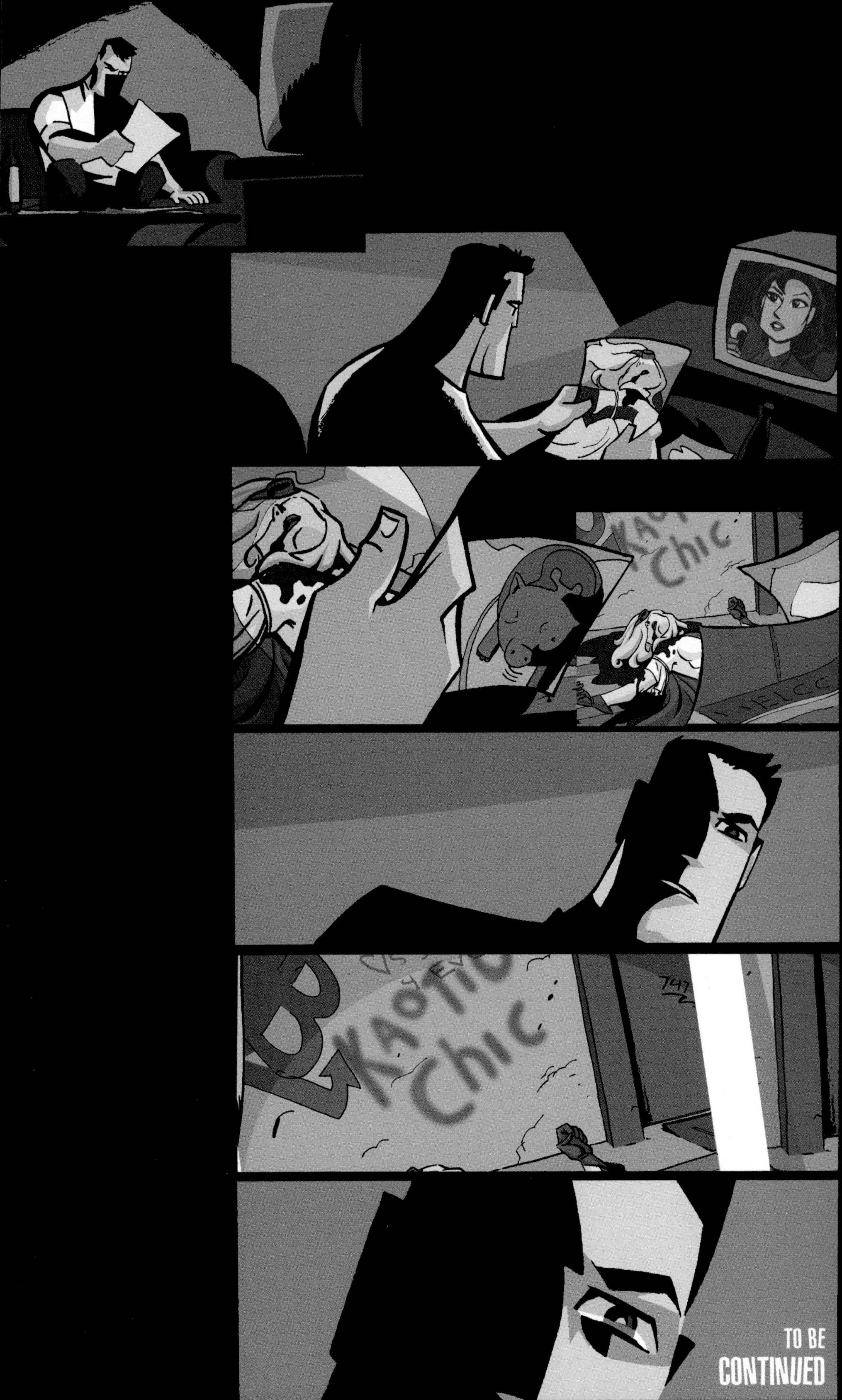
Chic
TO BE
CONTINUED

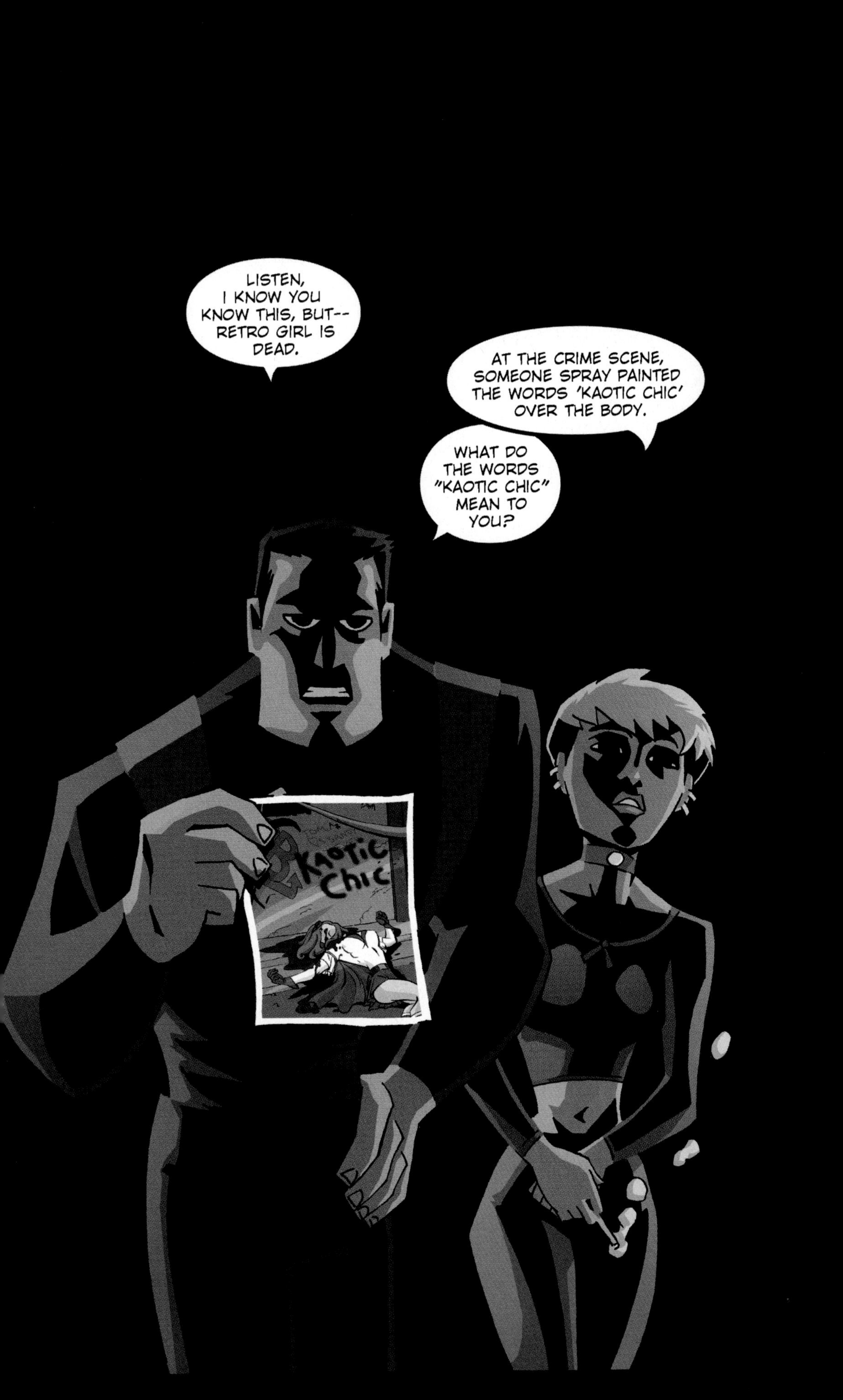

LISTEN, I KNOW YOU KNOW THIS, BUT-- RETRO GIRL IS DEAD.
AT THE CRIME SCENE, SOMEONE SPRAY PAINTED THE WORDS 'KAOTIC CHIC' OVER THE BODY.
WHAT DO THE WORDS "KAOTIC CHIC" MEAN TO YOU?
KAOTIC CHIC

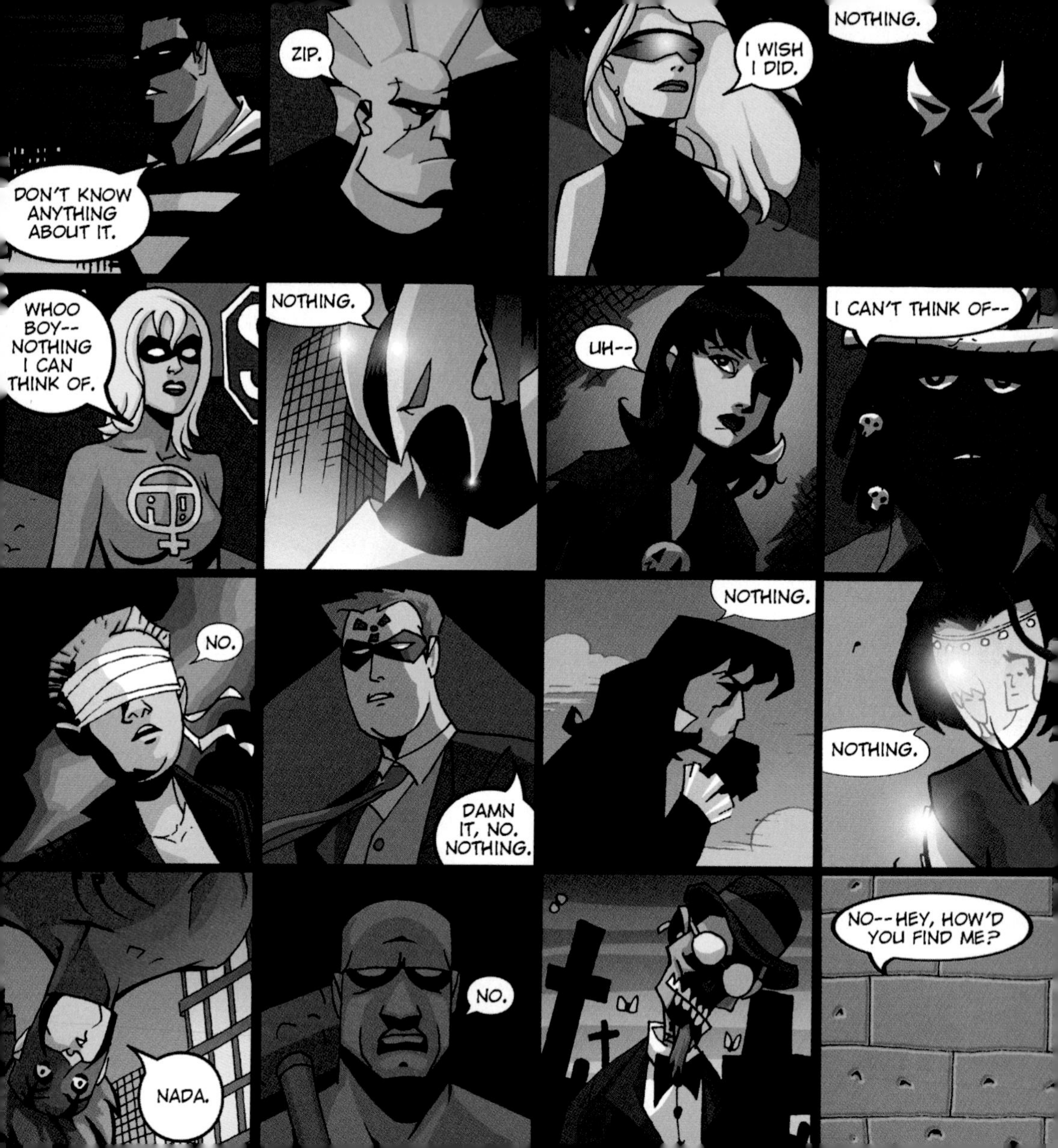
DON'T KNOW ANYTHING ABOUT IT.
ZIP.
I WISH I DID.
NOTHING.
WHOO BOY-- NOTHING I CAN THINK OF.
NOTHING.
UH--
I CAN'T THINK OF--
NO.
DAMN IT, NO. NOTHING.
NOTHING.
NOTHING.
NADA.
NO.
NO--HEY, HOW'D YOU FIND ME?

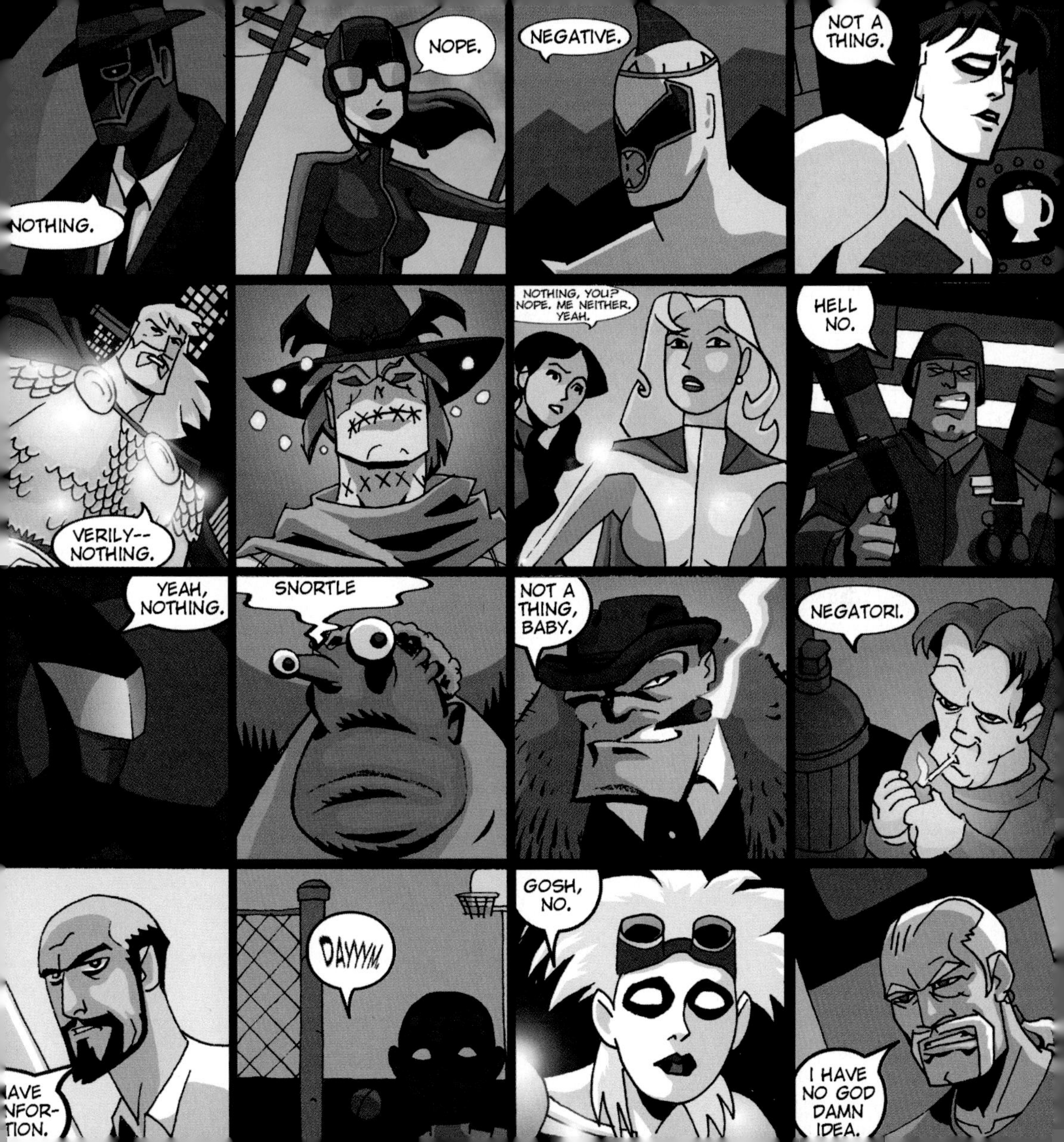
NOTHING.
NOPE.
NEGATIVE.
NOT A THING.
VERILY--NOTHING.
NOTHING, YOU? NOPE. ME NEITHER. YEAH.
HELL NO.
YEAH, NOTHING.
SNORTLE
NOT A THING, BABY.
NEGATORI.
AVE
NFOR-
TION.
DAYYYM.
GOSH, NO.
I HAVE NO GOD DAMN IDEA.

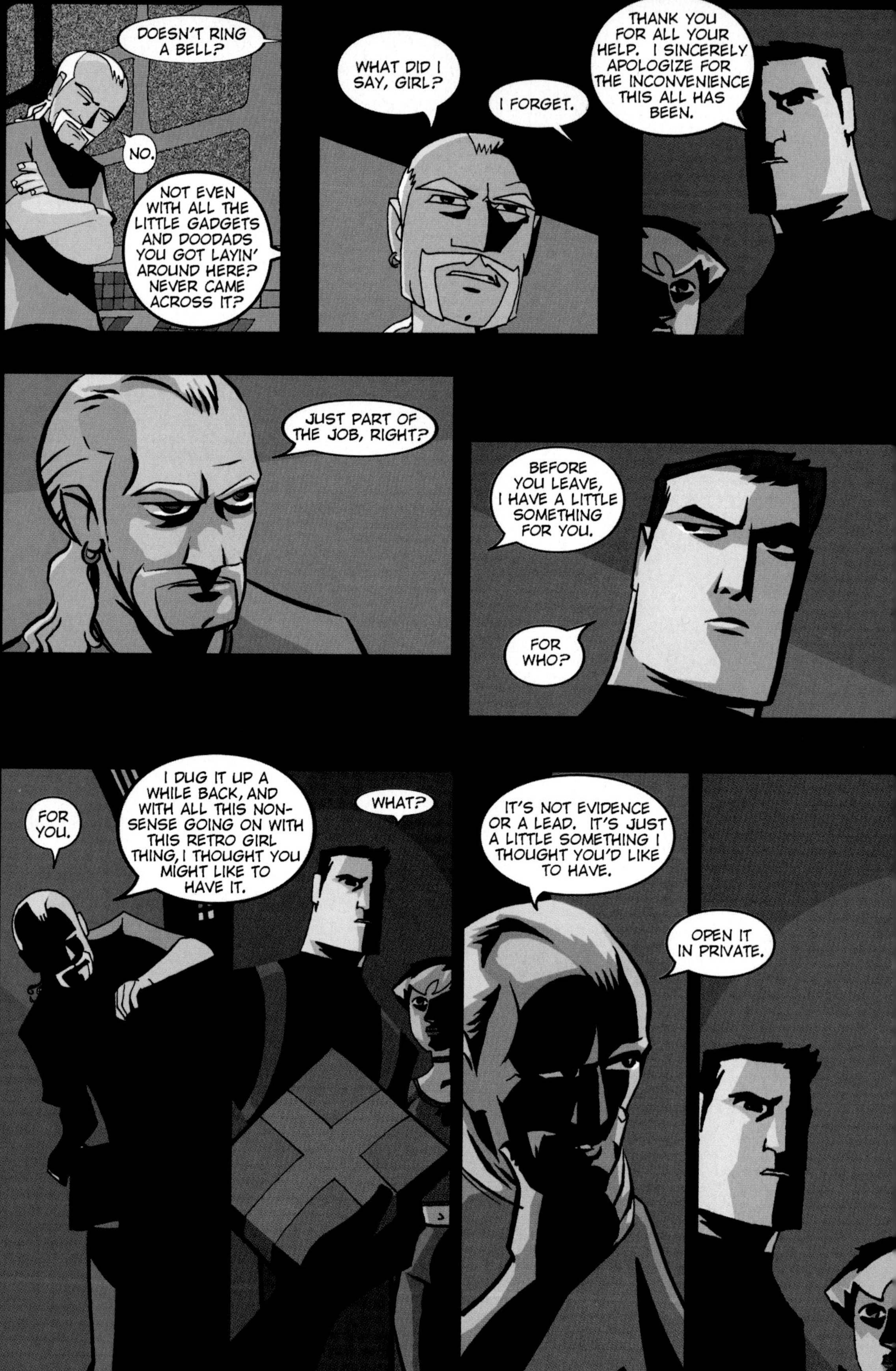
DOESN'T RING A BELL?
NO.
NOT EVEN WITH ALL THE LITTLE GADGETS AND DOODADS YOU GOT LAYIN' AROUND HERE? NEVER CAME ACROSS IT?
WHAT DID I SAY, GIRL?
I FORGET.
THANK YOU FOR ALL YOUR HELP. I SINCERELY APOLOGIZE FOR THE INCONVENIENCE THIS ALL HAS BEEN.
JUST PART OF THE JOB, RIGHT?
BEFORE YOU LEAVE, I HAVE A LITTLE SOMETHING FOR YOU.
FOR WHO?
FOR YOU.
I DUG IT UP A WHILE BACK, AND WITH ALL THIS NON-SENSE GOING ON WITH THIS RETRO GIRL THING, I THOUGHT YOU MIGHT LIKE TO HAVE IT.
WHAT?
IT'S NOT EVIDENCE OR A LEAD. IT'S JUST A LITTLE SOMETHING I THOUGHT YOU'D LIKE TO HAVE.
OPEN IT IN PRIVATE.

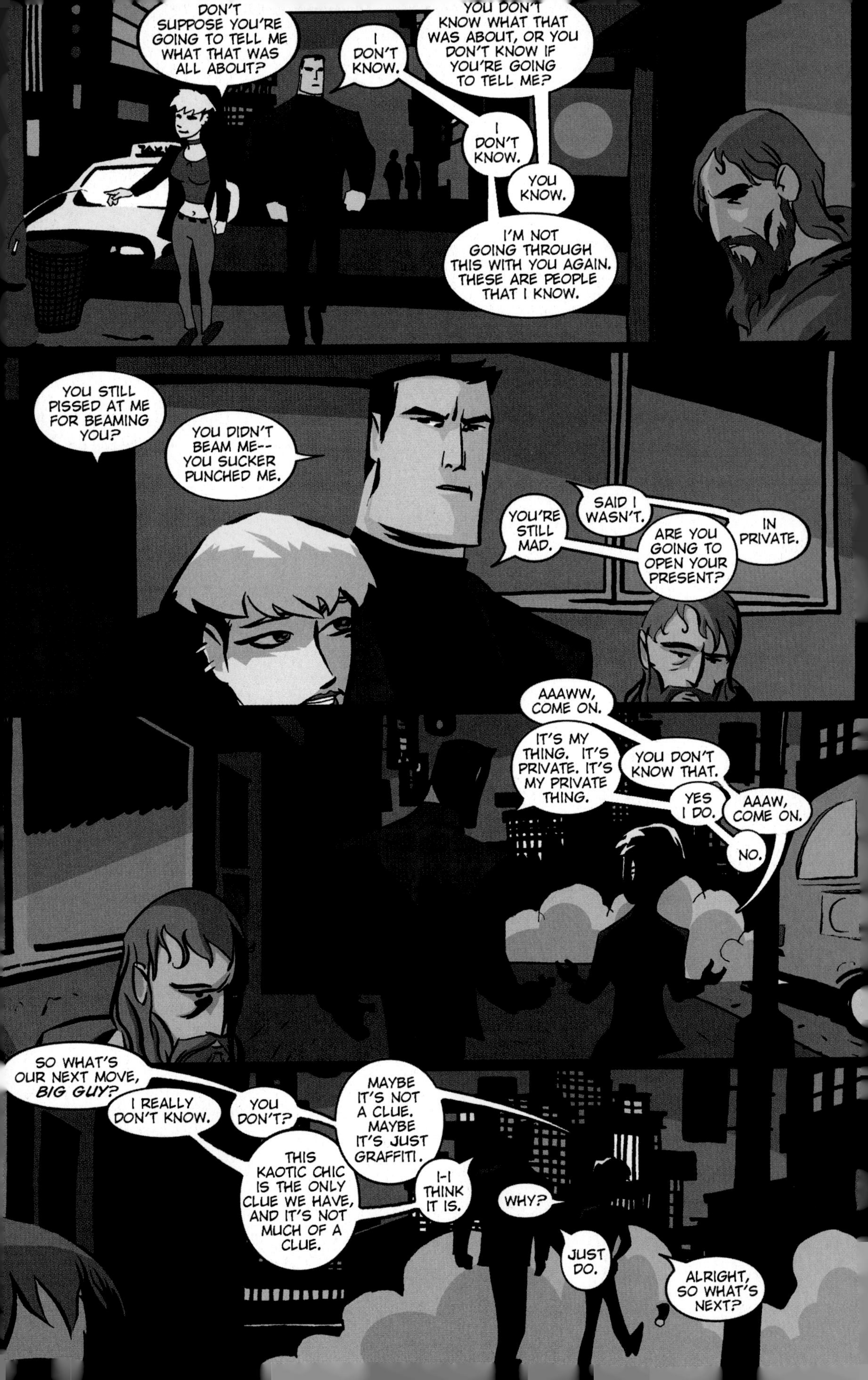
DON'T SUPPOSE YOU'RE GOING TO TELL ME WHAT THAT WAS ALL ABOUT?
I DON'T KNOW.
YOU DON'T KNOW WHAT THAT WAS ABOUT, OR YOU DON'T KNOW IF YOU'RE GOING TO TELL ME?
I DON'T KNOW.
YOU KNOW.
I'M NOT GOING THROUGH THIS WITH YOU AGAIN. THESE ARE PEOPLE THAT I KNOW.
YOU STILL PISSED AT ME FOR BEAMING YOU?
YOU DIDN'T BEAM ME-- YOU SUCKER PUNCHED ME.
YOU'RE STILL MAD.
SAID I WASN'T.
ARE YOU GOING TO OPEN YOUR PRESENT?
IN PRIVATE.
AAAWW, COME ON.
IT'S MY THING. IT'S PRIVATE. IT'S MY PRIVATE THING.
YOU DON'T KNOW THAT.
YES I DO.
AAAW, COME ON.
NO.
SO WHAT'S OUR NEXT MOVE, *BIG GUY?*
I REALLY DON'T KNOW.
YOU DON'T?
THIS KAOTIC CHIC IS THE ONLY CLUE WE HAVE, AND IT'S NOT MUCH OF A CLUE.
MAYBE IT'S NOT A CLUE. MAYBE IT'S JUST GRAFFITI.
I-I THINK IT IS.
WHY?
JUST DO.
ALRIGHT, SO WHAT'S NEXT?

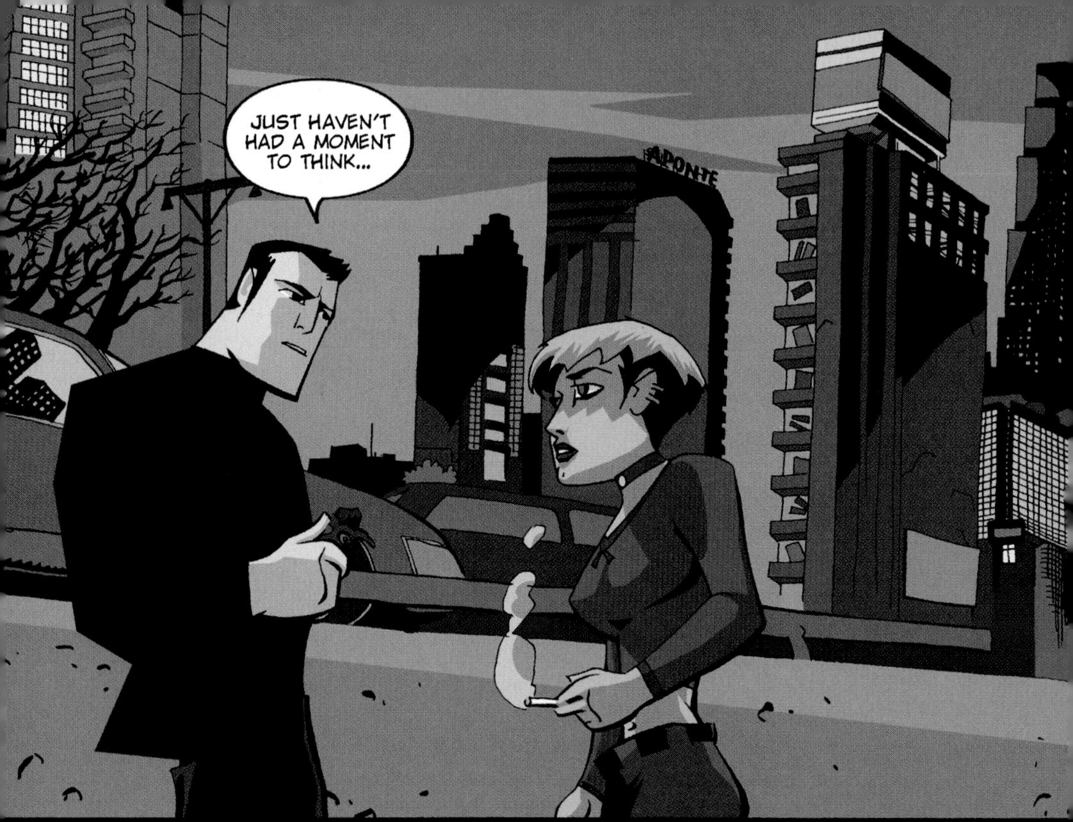
JUST HAVEN'T HAD A MOMENT TO THINK...
APONTE

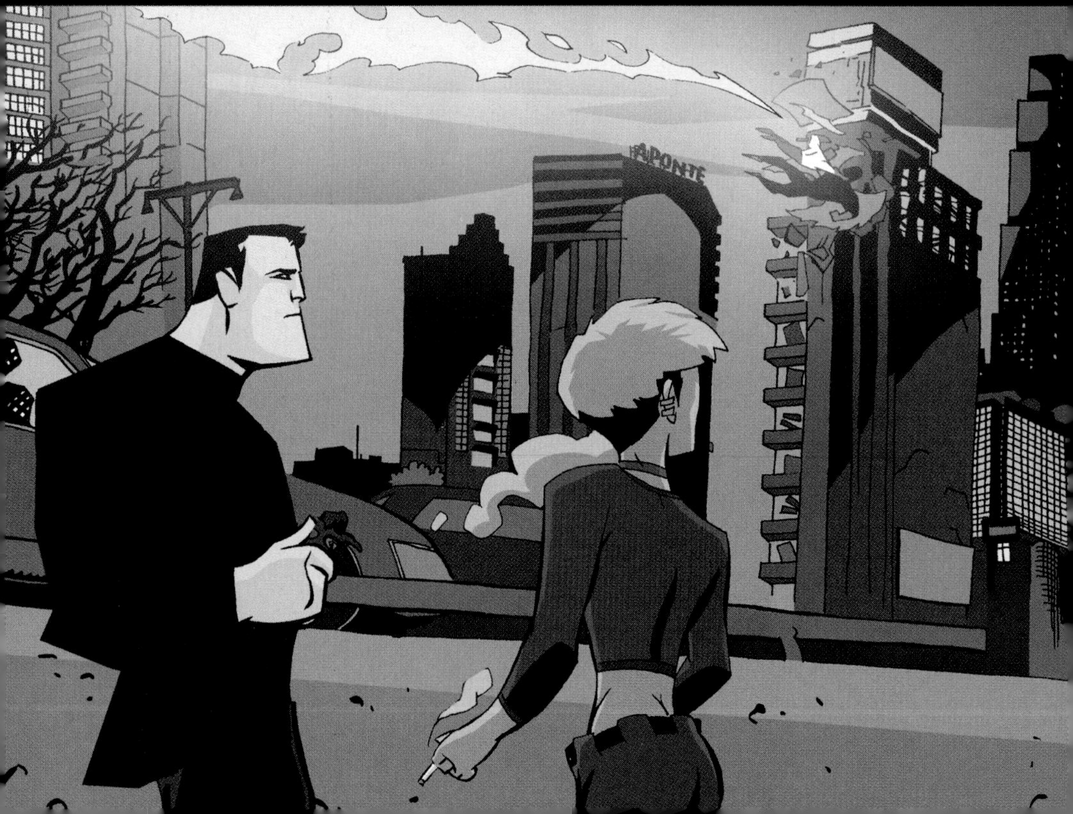
APONTE

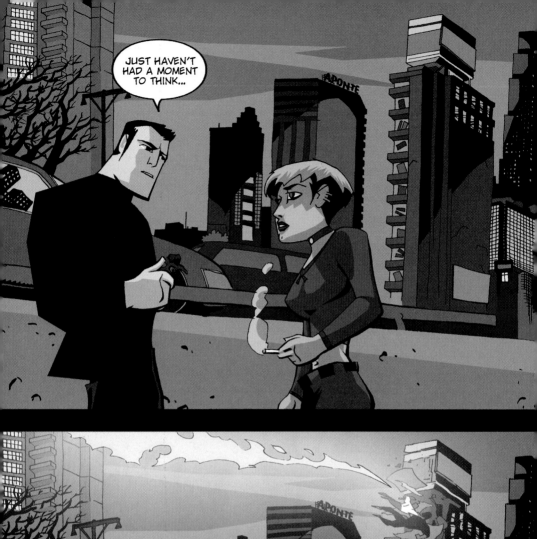

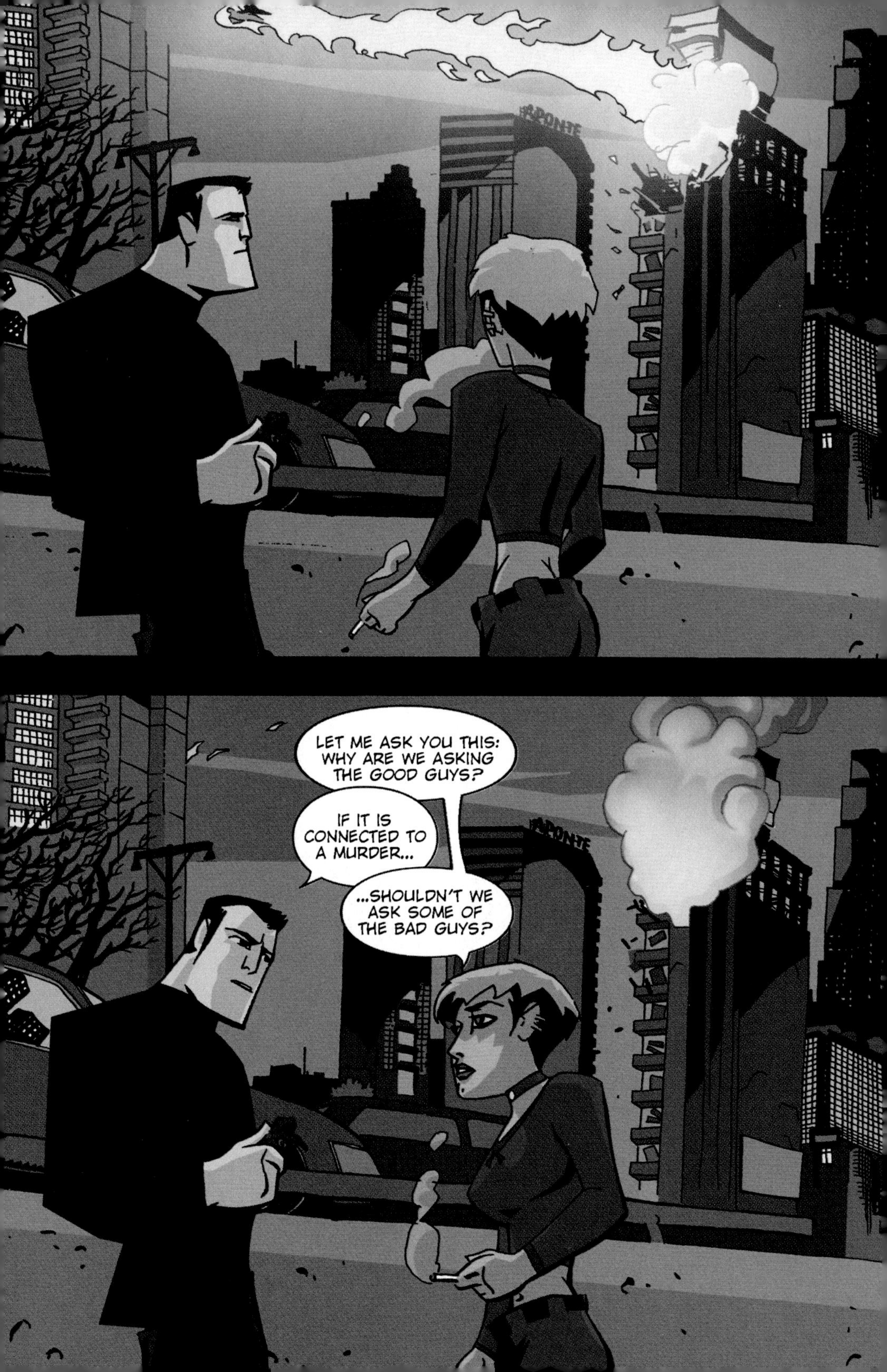
LET ME ASK YOU THIS: WHY ARE WE ASKING THE GOOD GUYS?
IF IT IS CONNECTED TO A MURDER...
...SHOULDN'T WE ASK SOME OF THE BAD GUYS?

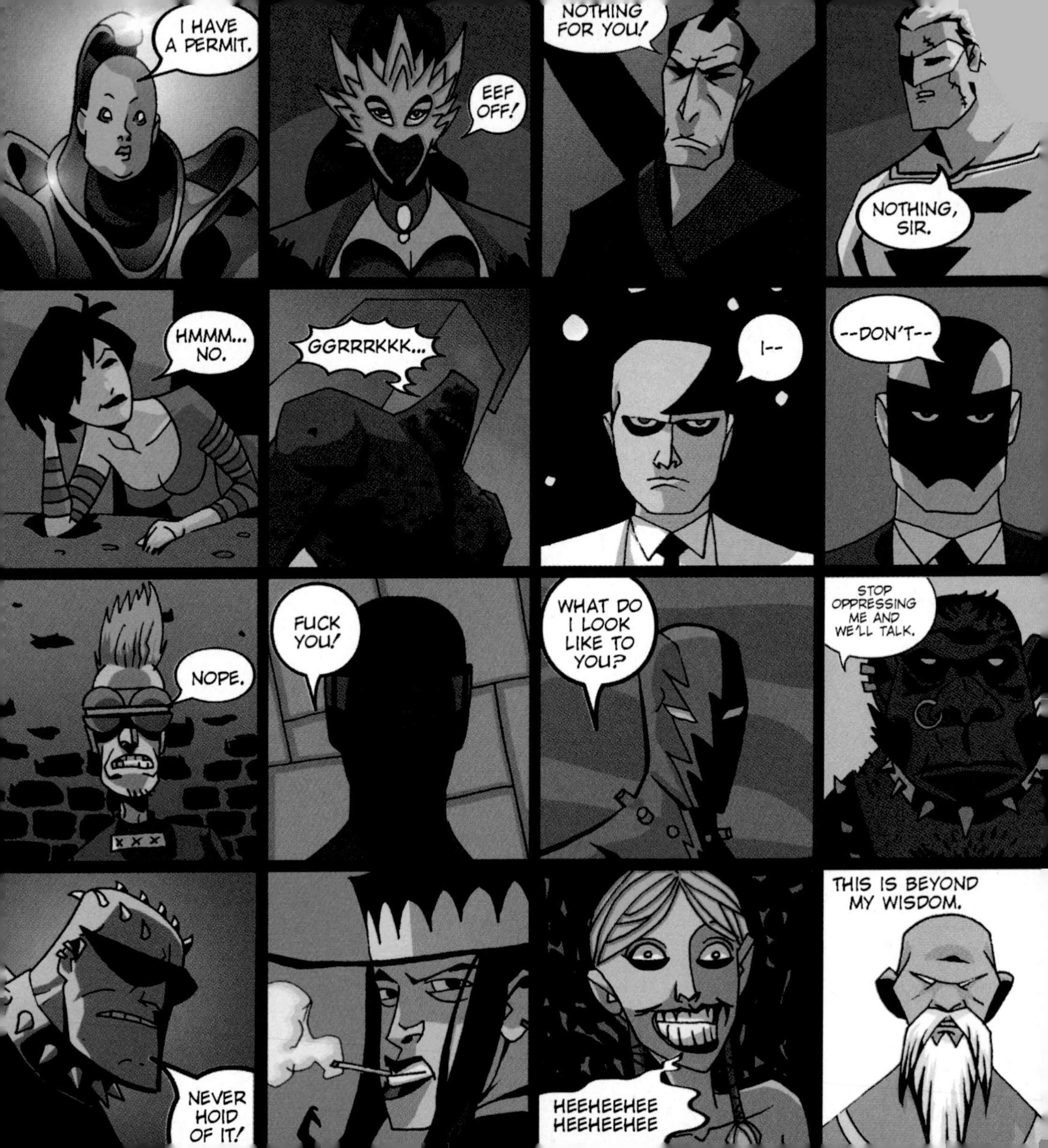
I HAVE A PERMIT.
EEF OFF!
NOTHING FOR YOU!
NOTHING, SIR.
HMMM... NO.
GGRRRKKK...
I--
--DON'T--
NOPE.
FUCK YOU!
WHAT DO I LOOK LIKE TO YOU?
STOP OPPRESSING ME AND WE'LL TALK.
NEVER HOID OF IT!
HEEHEEHEE HEEHEEHEE
THIS IS BEYOND MY WISDOM.

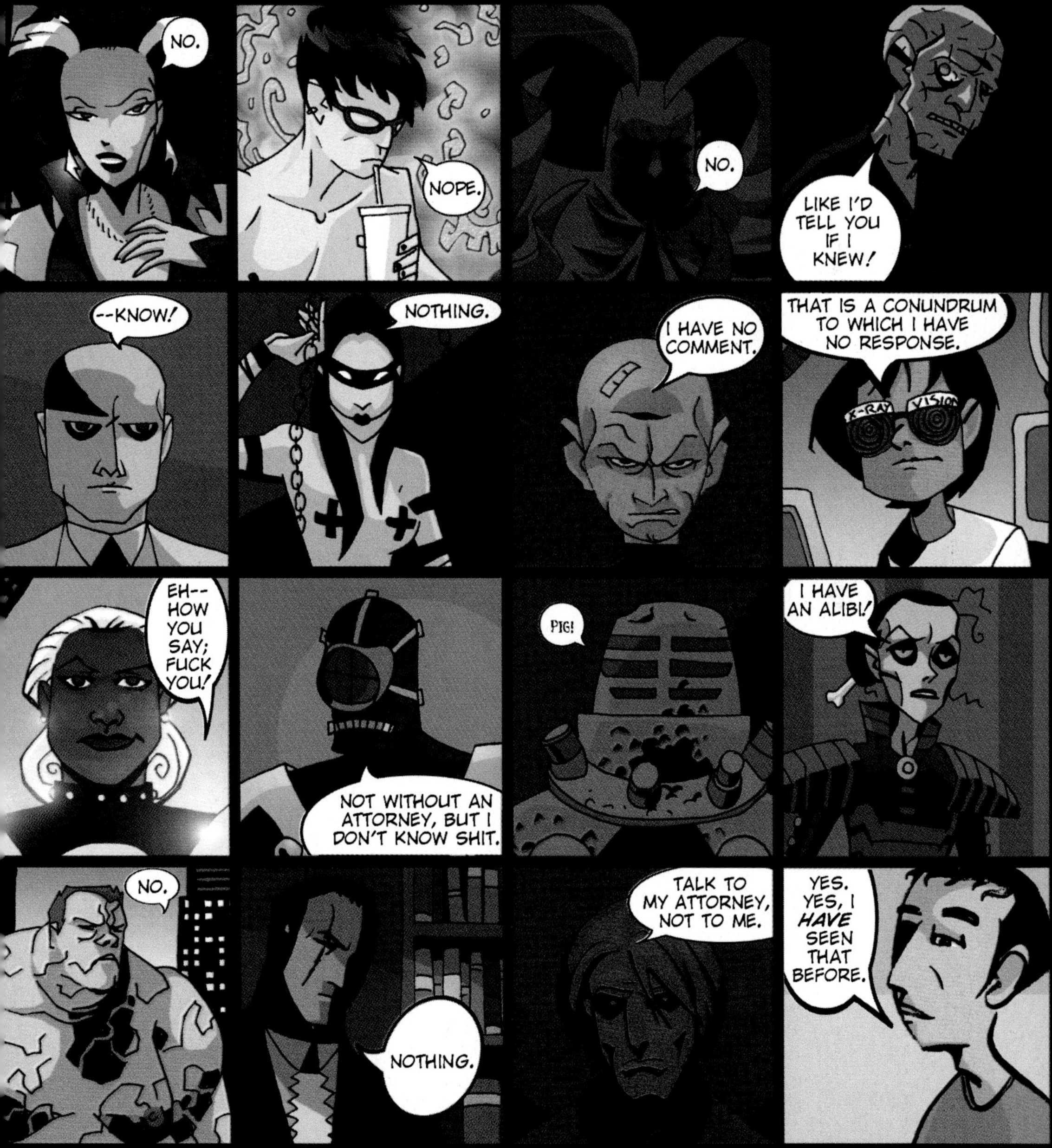
NO.
NOPE.
NO.
LIKE I'D TELL YOU IF I KNEW!
--KNOW!
NOTHING.
I HAVE NO COMMENT.
THAT IS A CONUNDRUM TO WHICH I HAVE NO RESPONSE.
X-RAY VISION
EH-- HOW YOU SAY; FUCK YOU!
NOT WITHOUT AN ATTORNEY, BUT I DON'T KNOW SHIT.
PIG!
I HAVE AN ALIBI!
NO.
NOTHING.
TALK TO MY ATTORNEY, NOT TO ME.
YES. YES, I *HAVE* SEEN THAT BEFORE.

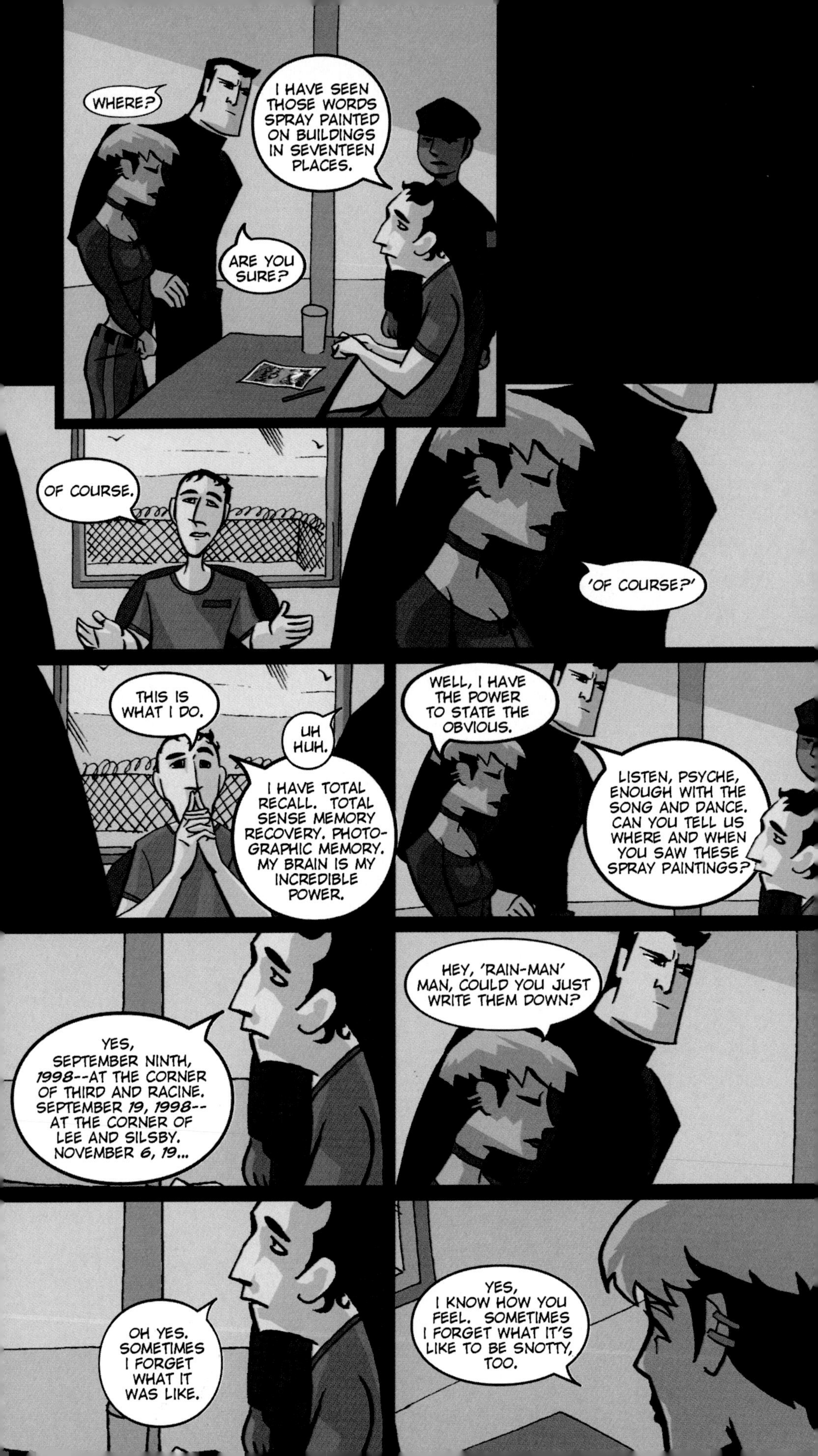

WHERE?
I HAVE SEEN THOSE WORDS SPRAY PAINTED ON BUILDINGS IN SEVENTEEN PLACES.
ARE YOU SURE?
OF COURSE.
'OF COURSE?'
THIS IS WHAT I DO.
UH HUH.
I HAVE TOTAL RECALL. TOTAL SENSE MEMORY RECOVERY. PHOTO-GRAPHIC MEMORY. MY BRAIN IS MY INCREDIBLE POWER.
WELL, I HAVE THE POWER TO STATE THE OBVIOUS.
LISTEN, PSYCHE, ENOUGH WITH THE SONG AND DANCE. CAN YOU TELL US WHERE AND WHEN YOU SAW THESE SPRAY PAINTINGS?
YES, SEPTEMBER NINTH, 1998--AT THE CORNER OF THIRD AND RACINE. SEPTEMBER 19, 1998--AT THE CORNER OF LEE AND SILSBY. NOVEMBER 6, 19...
HEY, 'RAIN-MAN' MAN, COULD YOU JUST WRITE THEM DOWN?
OH YES. SOMETIMES I FORGET WHAT IT WAS LIKE.
YES, I KNOW HOW YOU FEEL. SOMETIMES I FORGET WHAT IT'S LIKE TO BE SNOTTY, TOO.

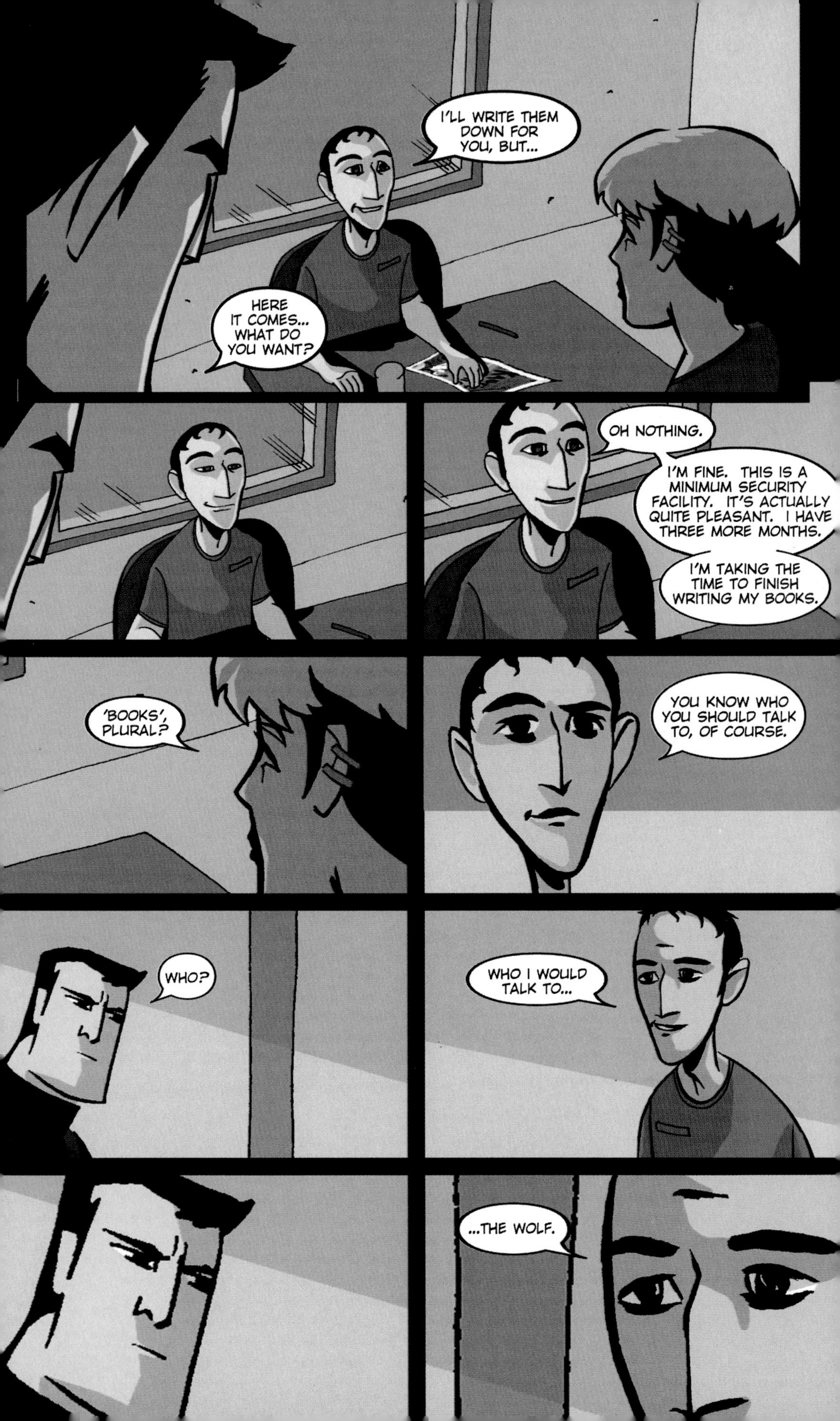
I'LL WRITE THEM DOWN FOR YOU, BUT...
HERE IT COMES... WHAT DO YOU WANT?
OH NOTHING.
I'M FINE. THIS IS A MINIMUM SECURITY FACILITY. IT'S ACTUALLY QUITE PLEASANT. I HAVE THREE MORE MONTHS.
I'M TAKING THE TIME TO FINISH WRITING MY BOOKS.
'BOOKS', PLURAL?
YOU KNOW WHO YOU SHOULD TALK TO, OF COURSE.
WHO?
WHO I WOULD TALK TO...
...THE WOLF.

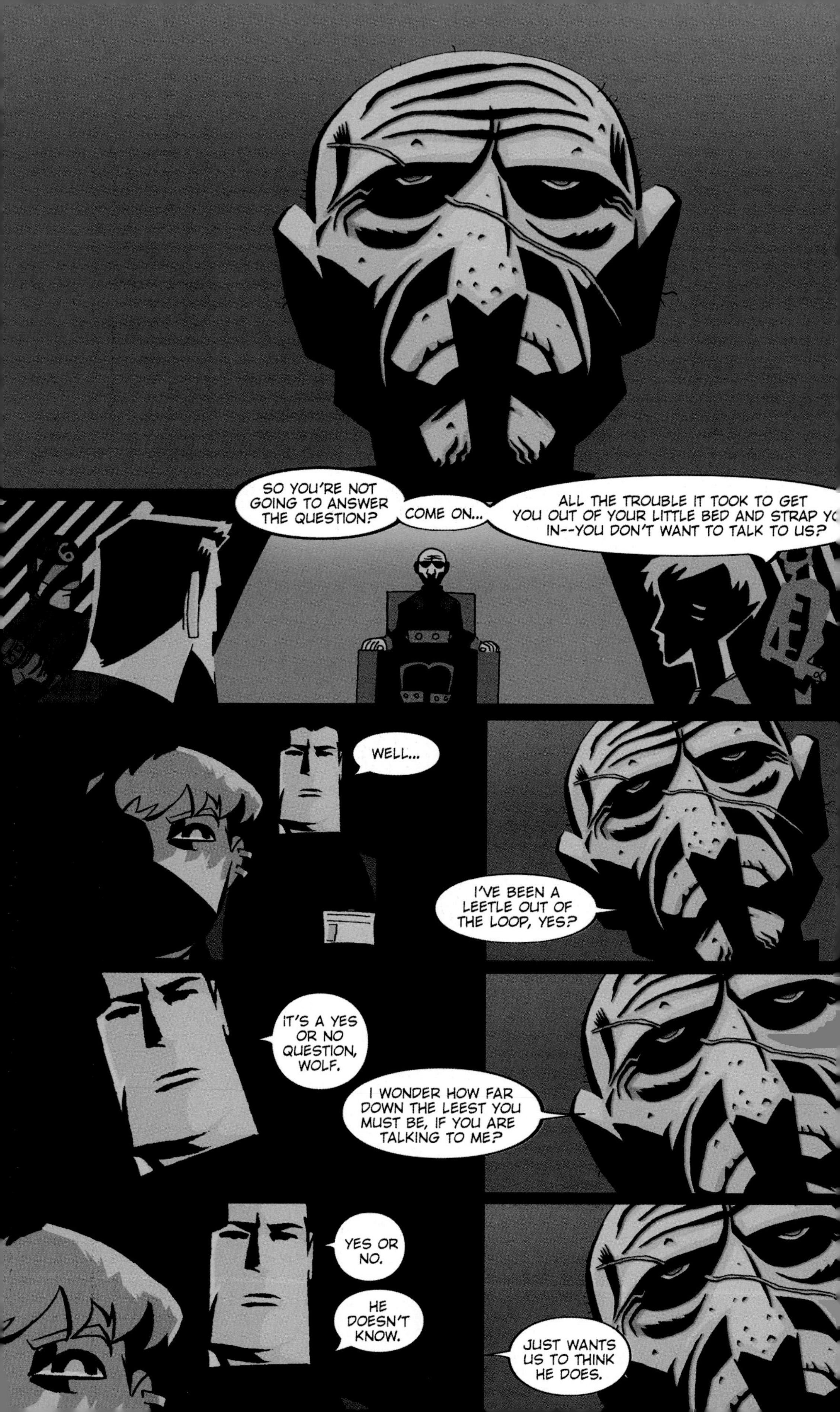
SO YOU'RE NOT GOING TO ANSWER THE QUESTION?
COME ON...
ALL THE TROUBLE IT TOOK TO GET YOU OUT OF YOUR LITTLE BED AND STRAP YO IN--YOU DON'T WANT TO TALK TO US?
WELL...
I'VE BEEN A LEETLE OUT OF THE LOOP, YES?
IT'S A YES OR NO QUESTION, WOLF.
I WONDER HOW FAR DOWN THE LEEST YOU MUST BE, IF YOU ARE TALKING TO ME?
YES OR NO.
HE DOESN'T KNOW.
JUST WANTS US TO THINK HE DOES.

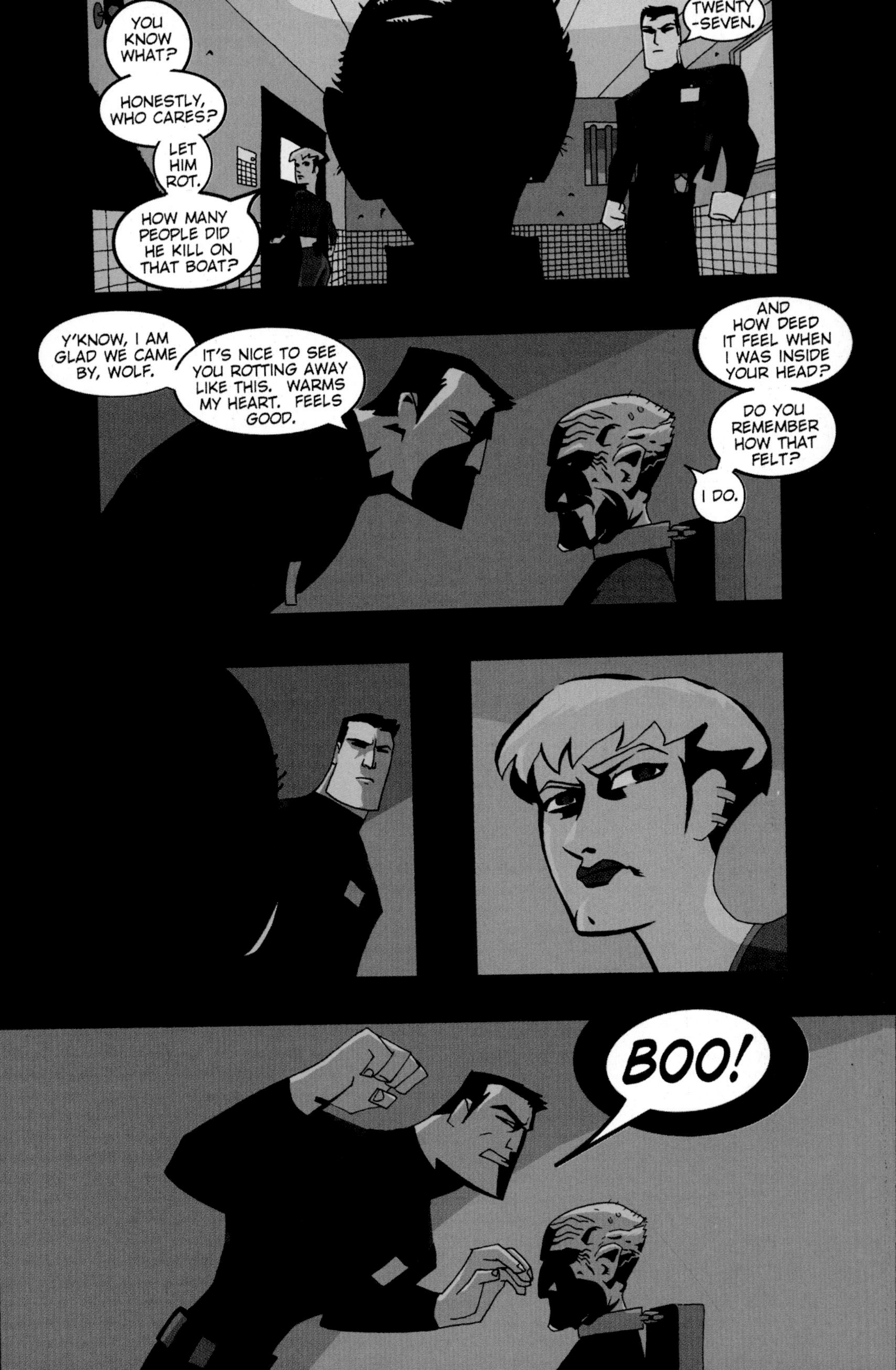
YOU KNOW WHAT?
HONESTLY, WHO CARES?
LET HIM ROT.
HOW MANY PEOPLE DID HE KILL ON THAT BOAT?
TWENTY -SEVEN.
Y'KNOW, I AM GLAD WE CAME BY, WOLF.
IT'S NICE TO SEE YOU ROTTING AWAY LIKE THIS. WARMS MY HEART. FEELS GOOD.
AND HOW DEED IT FEEL WHEN I WAS INSIDE YOUR HEAD?
DO YOU REMEMBER HOW THAT FELT?
I DO.
BOO!

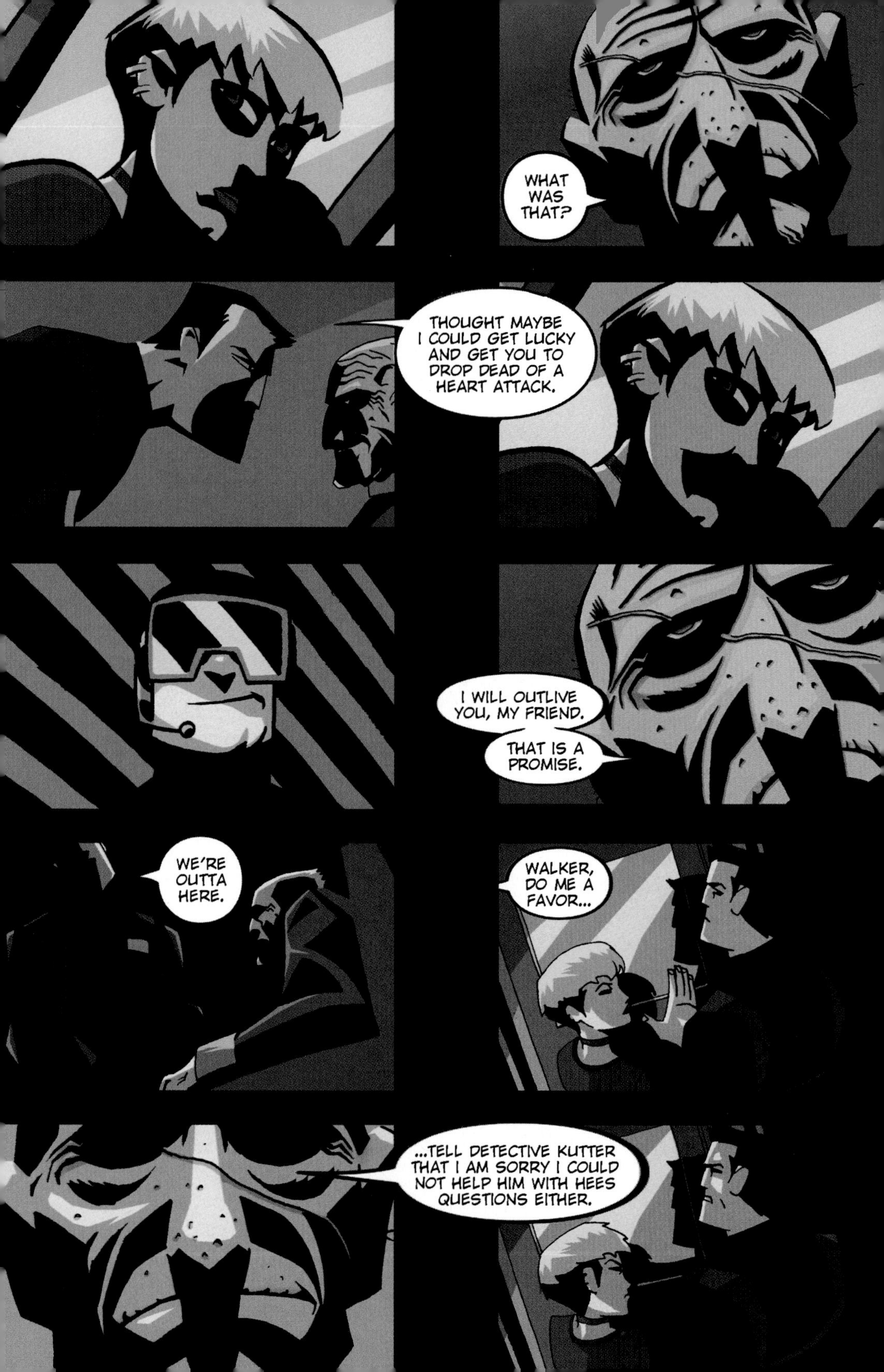
WHAT WAS THAT?
THOUGHT MAYBE I COULD GET LUCKY AND GET YOU TO DROP DEAD OF A HEART ATTACK.
I WILL OUTLIVE YOU, MY FRIEND.
THAT IS A PROMISE.
WE'RE OUTTA HERE.
WALKER, DO ME A FAVOR...
...TELL DETECTIVE KUTTER THAT I AM SORRY I COULD NOT HELP HIM WITH HEES QUESTIONS EITHER.

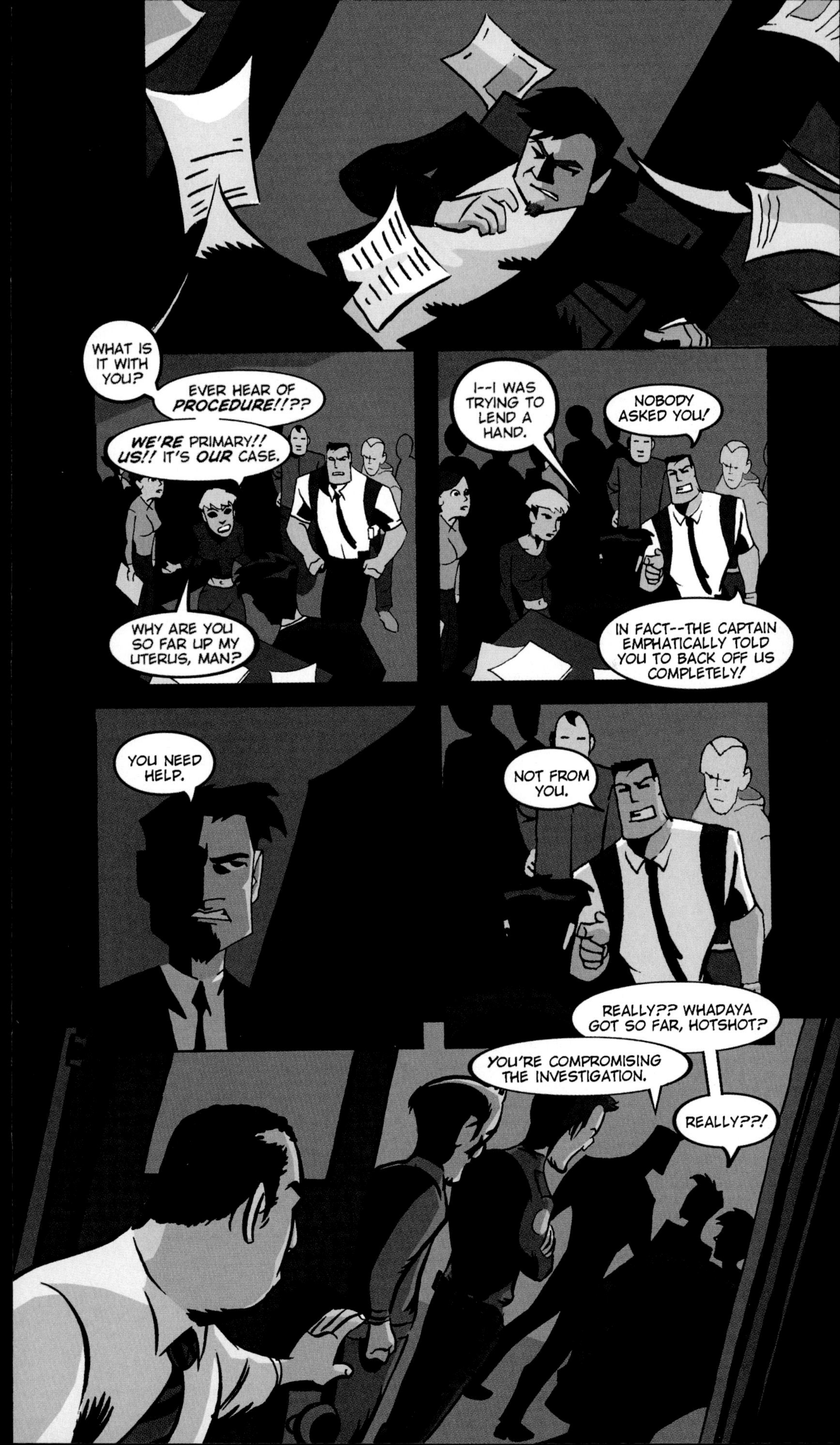
WHAT IS IT WITH YOU?
EVER HEAR OF PROCEDURE!!??
WE'RE PRIMARY!! US!! IT'S OUR CASE.
WHY ARE YOU SO FAR UP MY UTERUS, MAN?
I--I WAS TRYING TO LEND A HAND.
NOBODY ASKED YOU!
IN FACT--THE CAPTAIN EMPHATICALLY TOLD YOU TO BACK OFF US COMPLETELY!
YOU NEED HELP.
NOT FROM YOU.
YOU'RE COMPROMISING THE INVESTIGATION.
REALLY?? WHADAYA GOT SO FAR, HOTSHOT?
REALLY??!

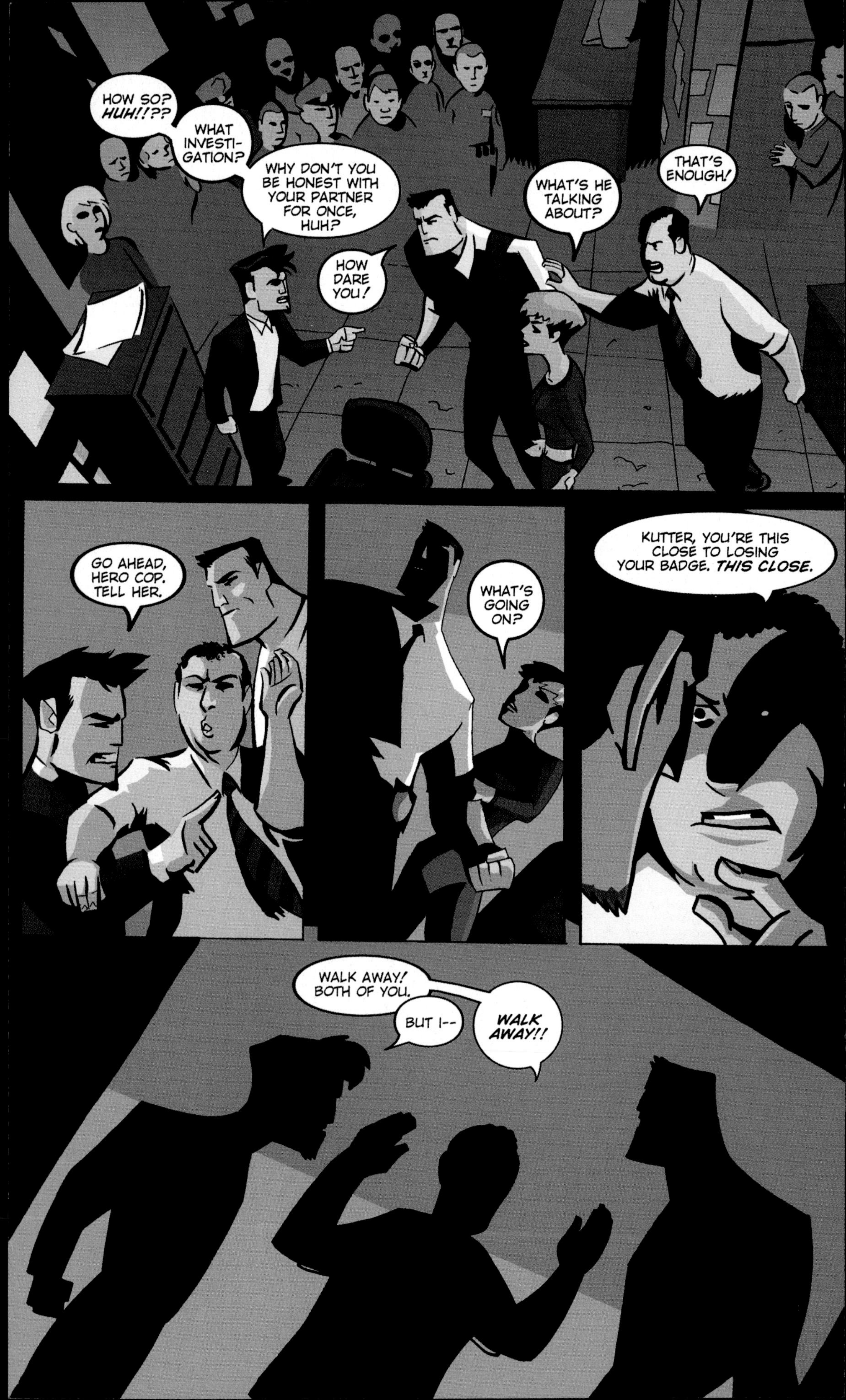
HOW SO? *HUH!!??*
WHAT INVESTI-GATION?
WHY DON'T YOU BE HONEST WITH YOUR PARTNER FOR ONCE, HUH?
HOW DARE YOU!
WHAT'S HE TALKING ABOUT?
THAT'S ENOUGH!
GO AHEAD, HERO COP. TELL HER.
WHAT'S GOING ON?
KUTTER, YOU'RE THIS CLOSE TO LOSING YOUR BADGE. *THIS CLOSE.*
WALK AWAY! BOTH OF YOU.
BUT I--
WALK AWAY!!

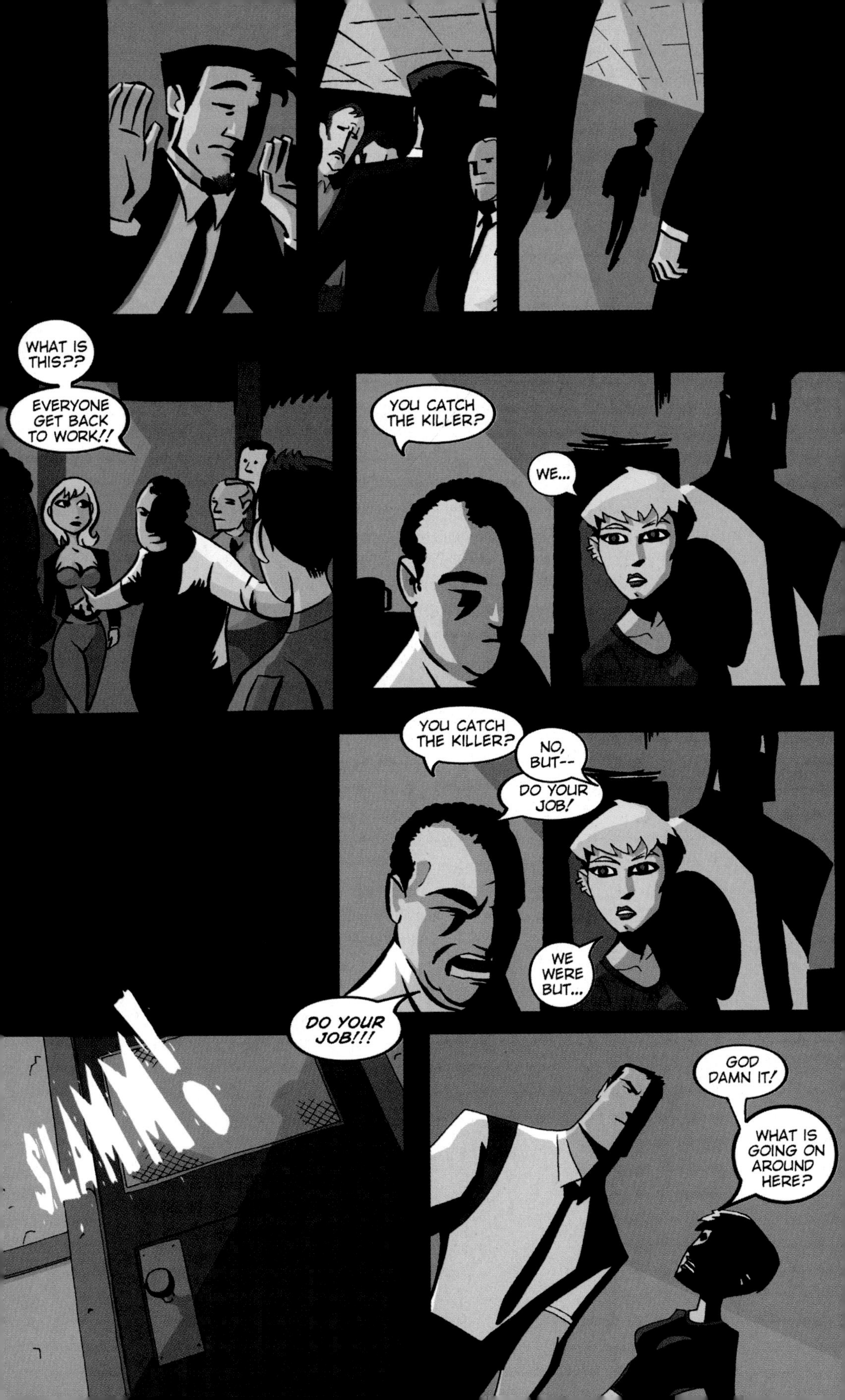
WHAT IS THIS??
EVERYONE GET BACK TO WORK!!
YOU CATCH THE KILLER?
WE...
YOU CATCH THE KILLER?
NO, BUT--
DO YOUR JOB!
WE WERE BUT...
DO YOUR JOB!!!
SLAMM!
GOD DAMN IT!
WHAT IS GOING ON AROUND HERE?

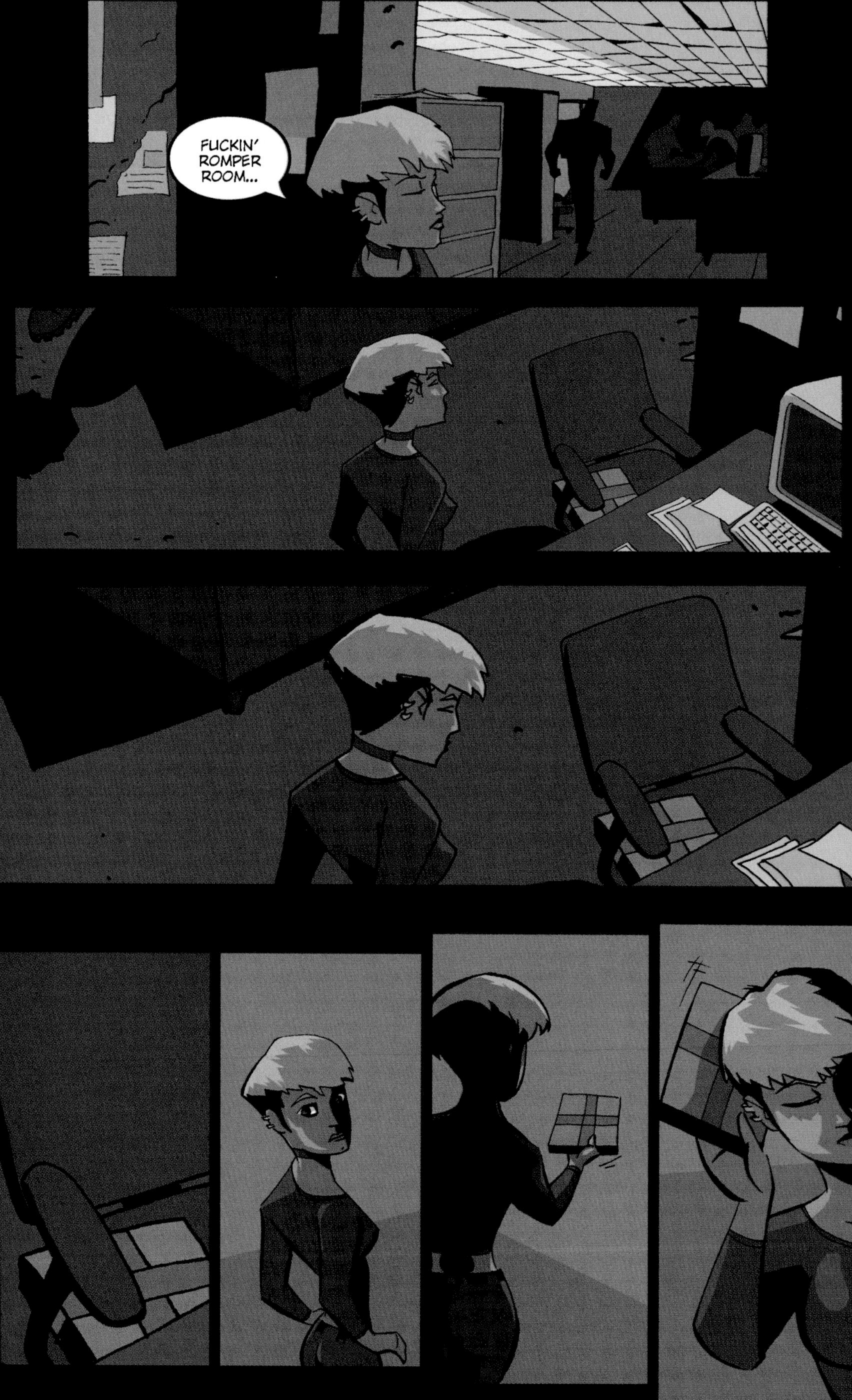
FUCKIN' ROMPER ROOM...

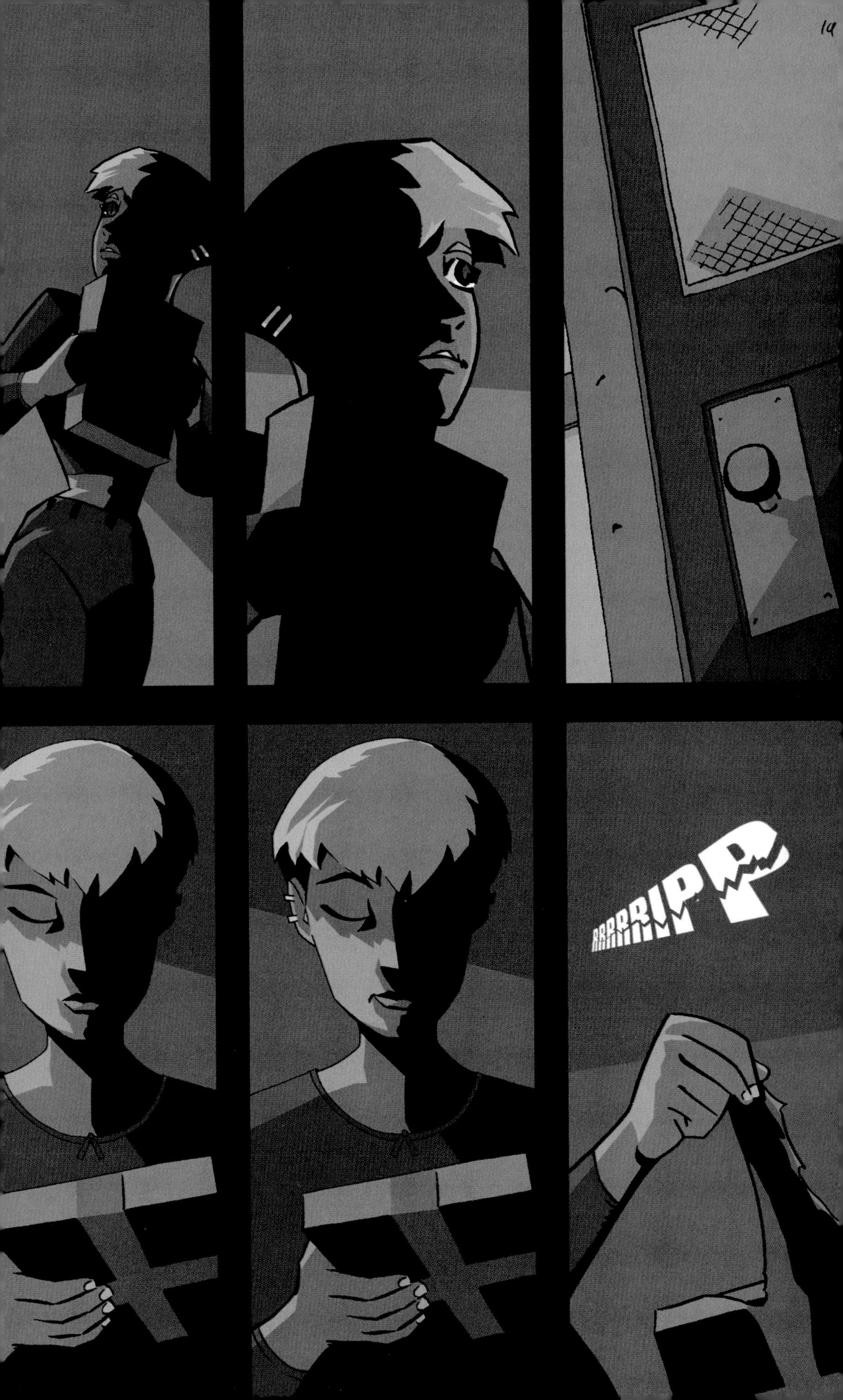
RRRRRIPP

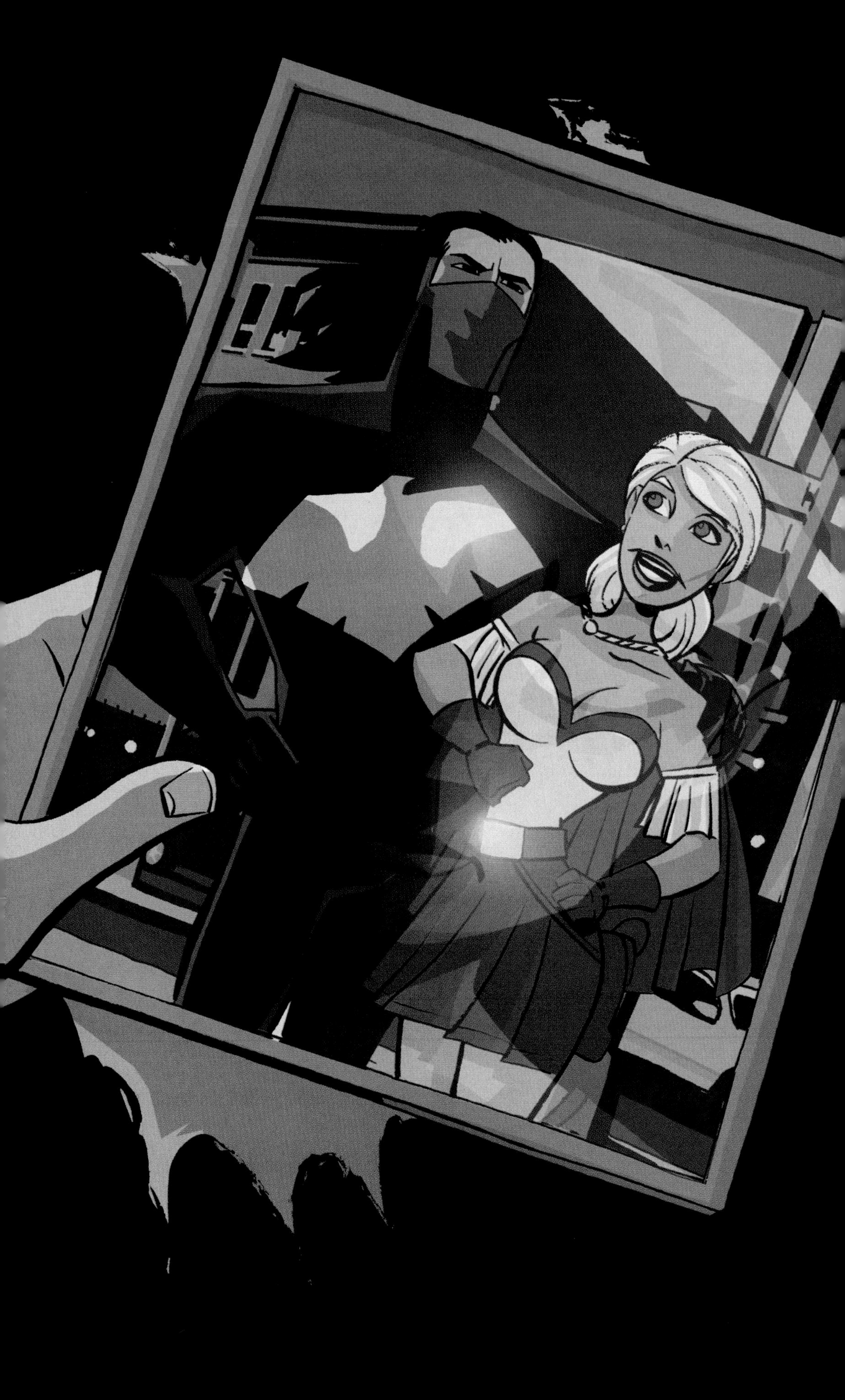

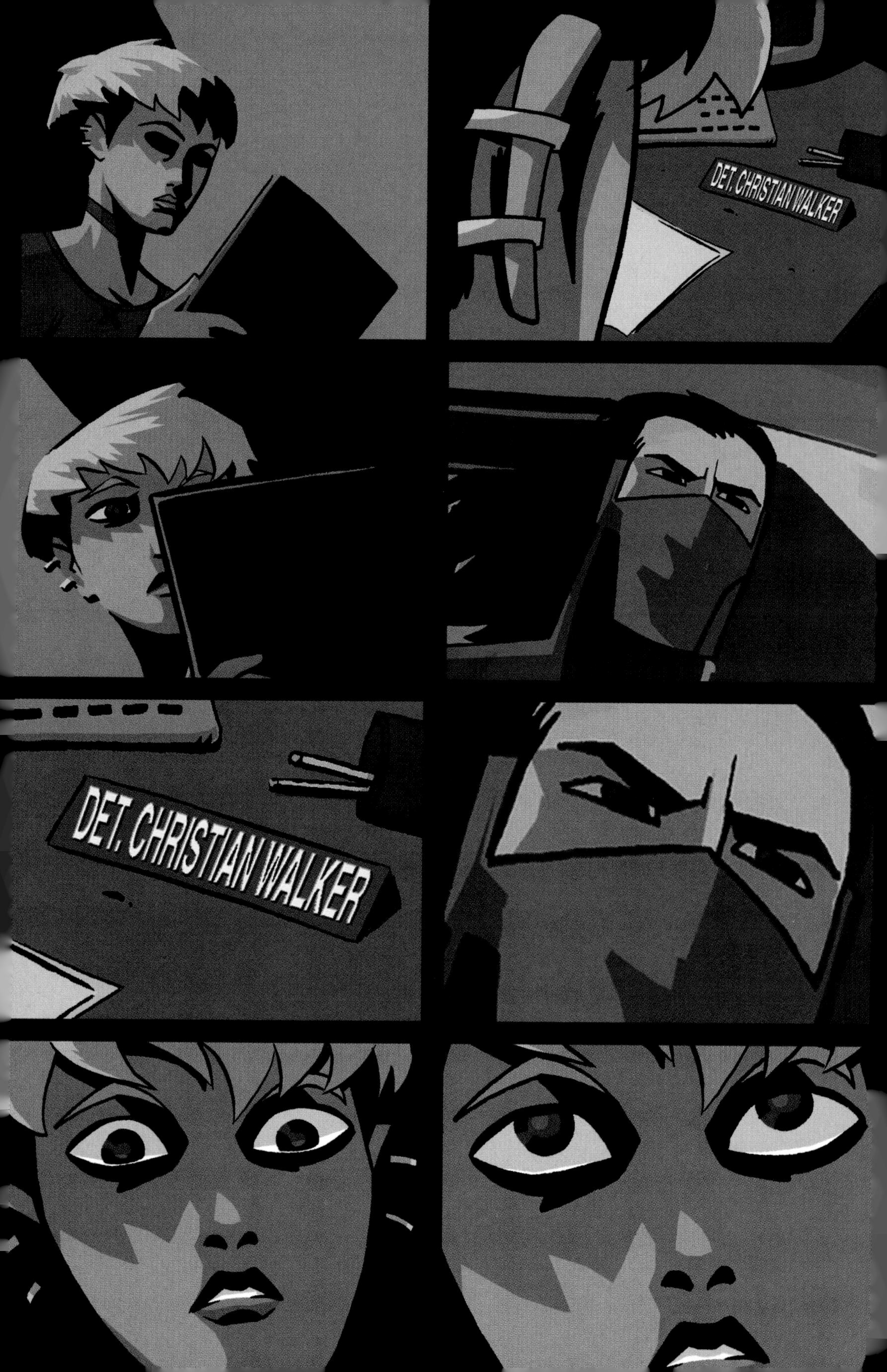
DET. CHRISTIAN WALKER
DET. CHRISTIAN WALKER

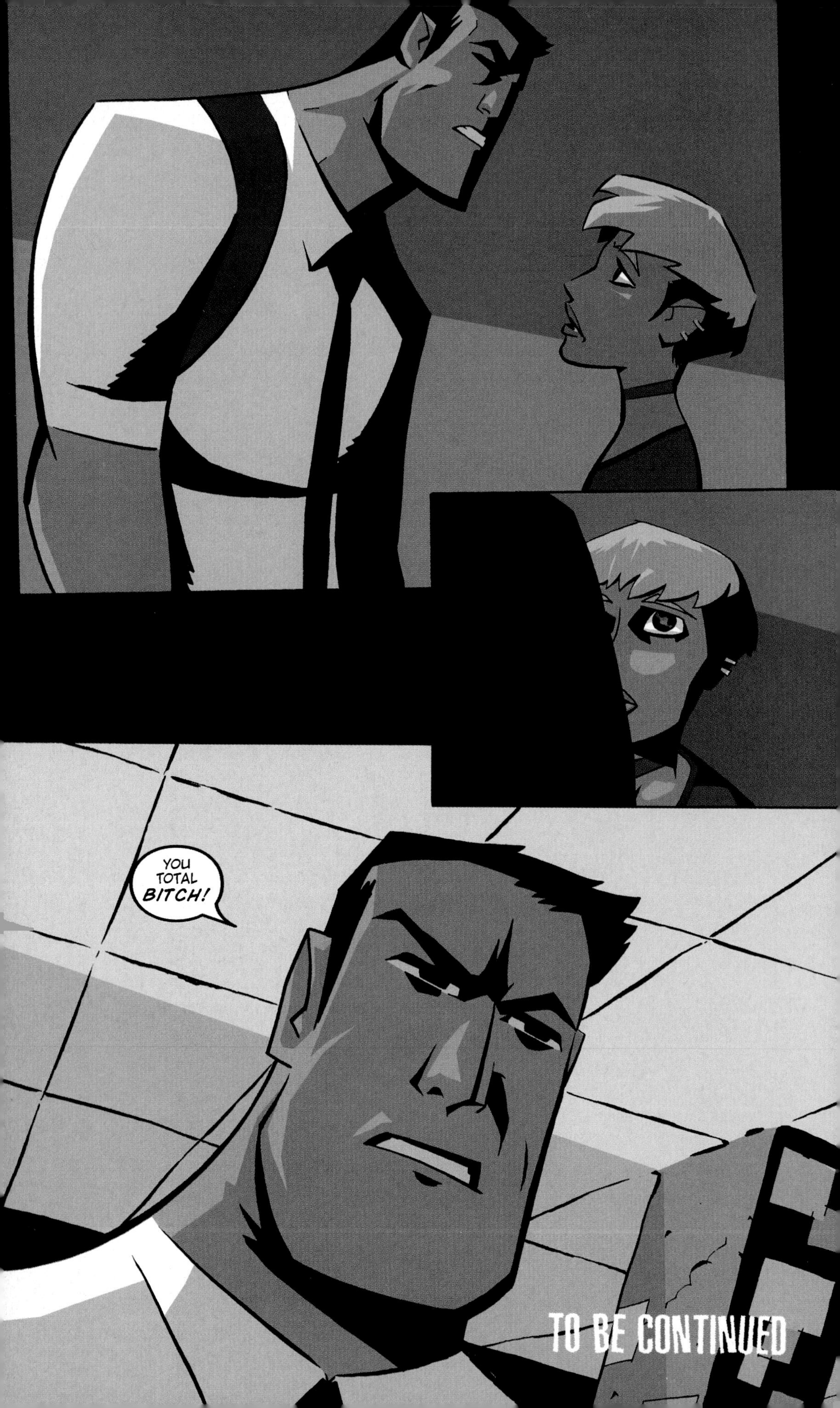
YOU TOTAL BITCH!
TO BE CONTINUED

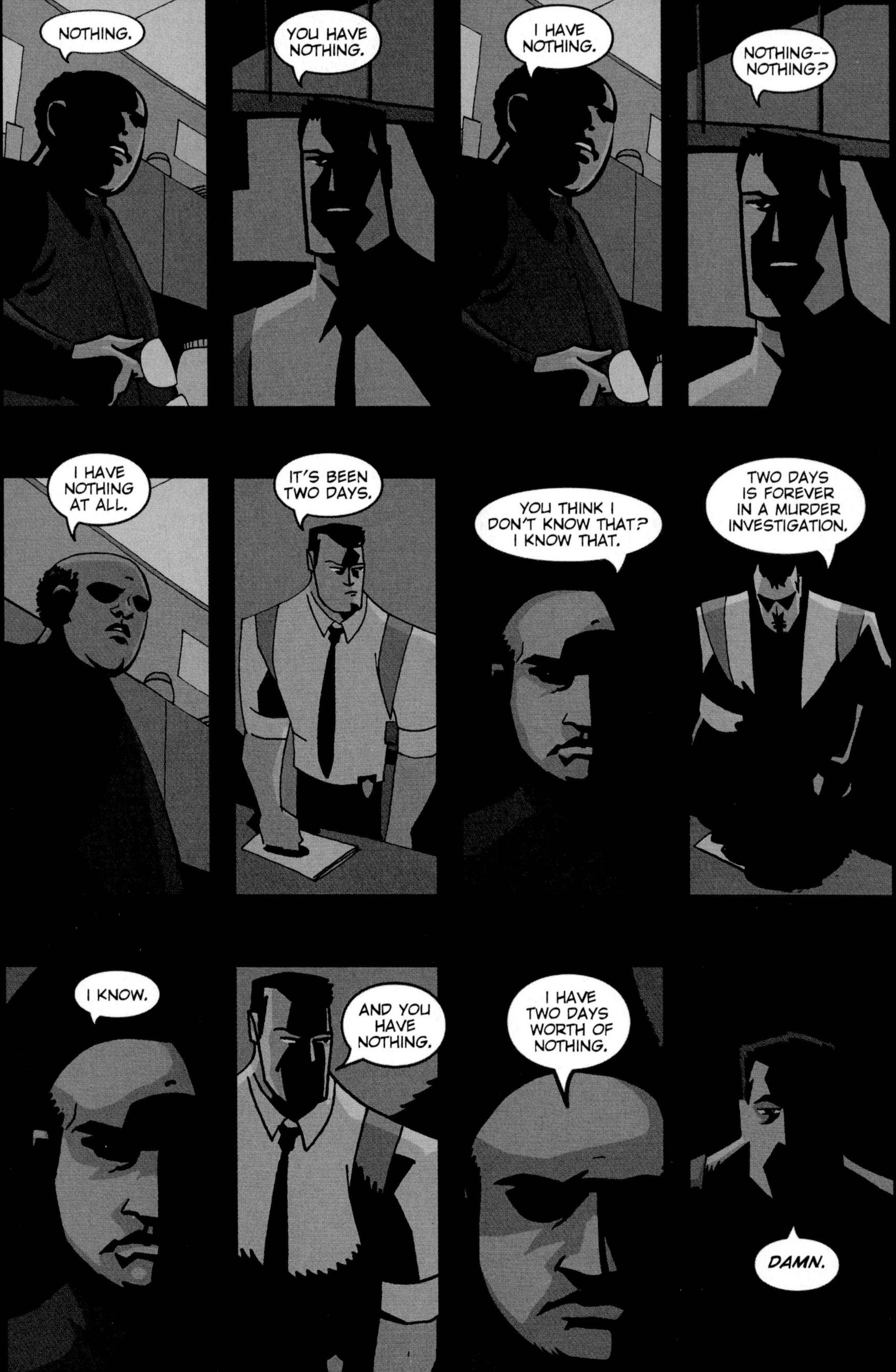
NOTHING.
YOU HAVE NOTHING.
I HAVE NOTHING.
NOTHING-- NOTHING?
I HAVE NOTHING AT ALL.
IT'S BEEN TWO DAYS.
YOU THINK I DON'T KNOW THAT? I KNOW THAT.
TWO DAYS IS FOREVER IN A MURDER INVESTIGATION.
I KNOW.
AND YOU HAVE NOTHING.
I HAVE TWO DAYS WORTH OF NOTHING.
DAMN.

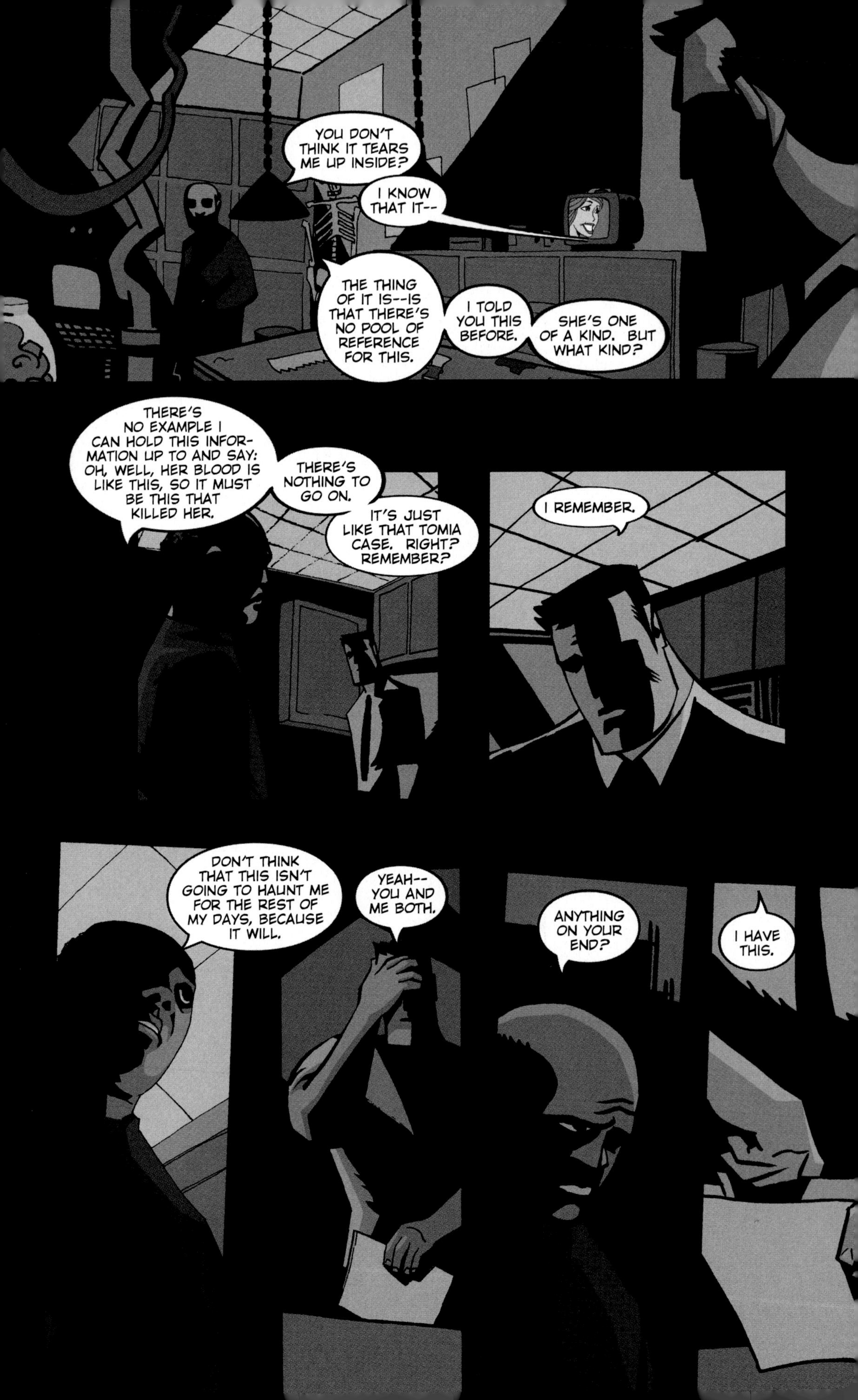
YOU DON'T THINK IT TEARS ME UP INSIDE?
I KNOW THAT IT--
THE THING OF IT IS--IS THAT THERE'S NO POOL OF REFERENCE FOR THIS.
I TOLD YOU THIS BEFORE.
SHE'S ONE OF A KIND. BUT WHAT KIND?
THERE'S NO EXAMPLE I CAN HOLD THIS INFORMATION UP TO AND SAY: OH, WELL, HER BLOOD IS LIKE THIS, SO IT MUST BE THIS THAT KILLED HER.
THERE'S NOTHING TO GO ON.
IT'S JUST LIKE THAT TOMIA CASE. RIGHT? REMEMBER?
I REMEMBER.
DON'T THINK THAT THIS ISN'T GOING TO HAUNT ME FOR THE REST OF MY DAYS, BECAUSE IT WILL.
YEAH-- YOU AND ME BOTH.
ANYTHING ON YOUR END?
I HAVE THIS.

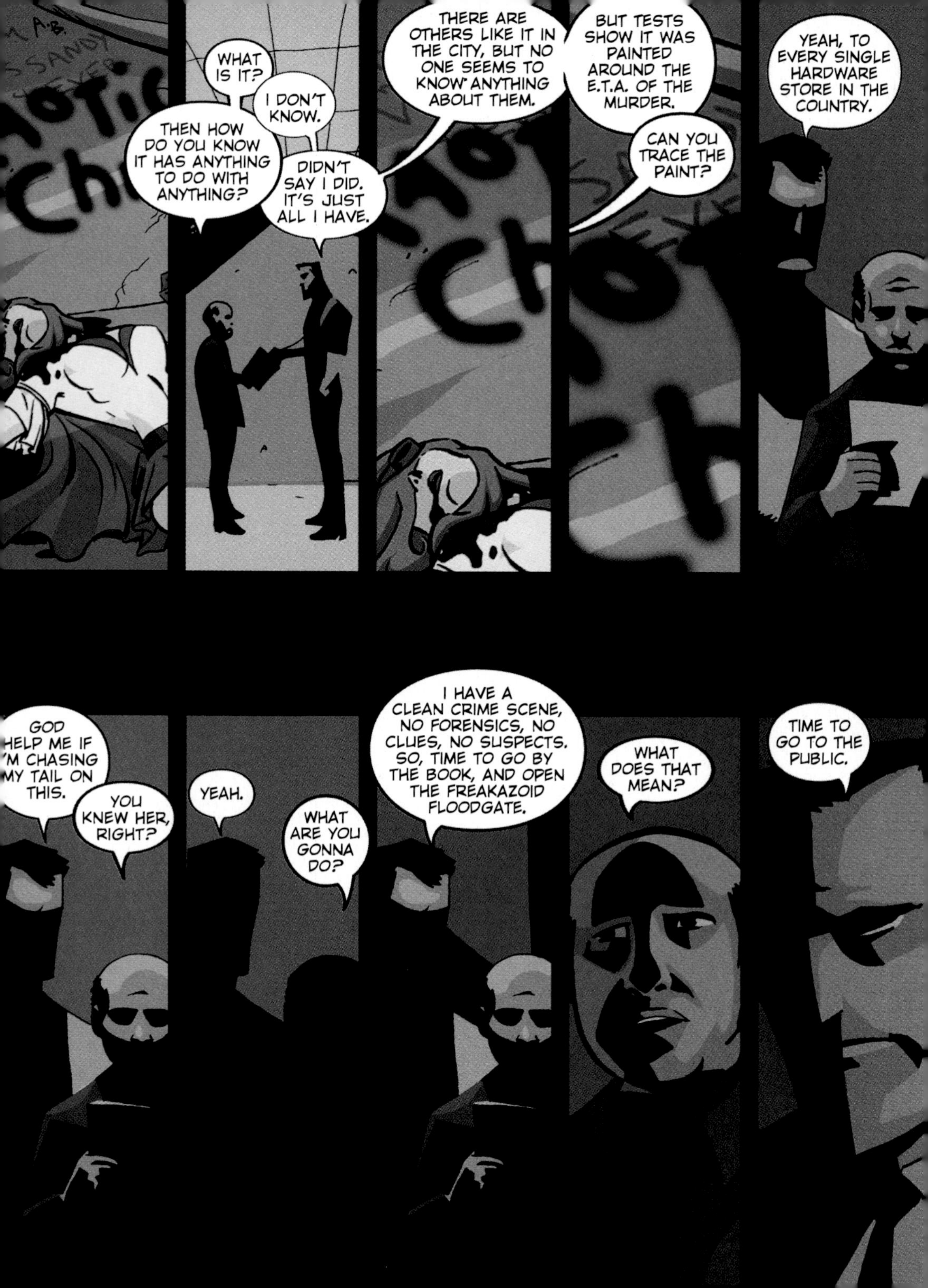
WHAT IS IT?
I DON'T KNOW.
THEN HOW DO YOU KNOW IT HAS ANYTHING TO DO WITH ANYTHING?
DIDN'T SAY I DID. IT'S JUST ALL I HAVE.
THERE ARE OTHERS LIKE IT IN THE CITY, BUT NO ONE SEEMS TO KNOW ANYTHING ABOUT THEM.
BUT TESTS SHOW IT WAS PAINTED AROUND THE E.T.A. OF THE MURDER.
CAN YOU TRACE THE PAINT?
YEAH, TO EVERY SINGLE HARDWARE STORE IN THE COUNTRY.
GOD HELP ME IF 'M CHASING MY TAIL ON THIS.
YOU KNEW HER, RIGHT?
YEAH.
WHAT ARE YOU GONNA DO?
I HAVE A CLEAN CRIME SCENE, NO FORENSICS, NO CLUES, NO SUSPECTS. SO, TIME TO GO BY THE BOOK, AND OPEN THE FREAKAZOID FLOODGATE.
WHAT DOES THAT MEAN?
TIME TO GO TO THE PUBLIC.

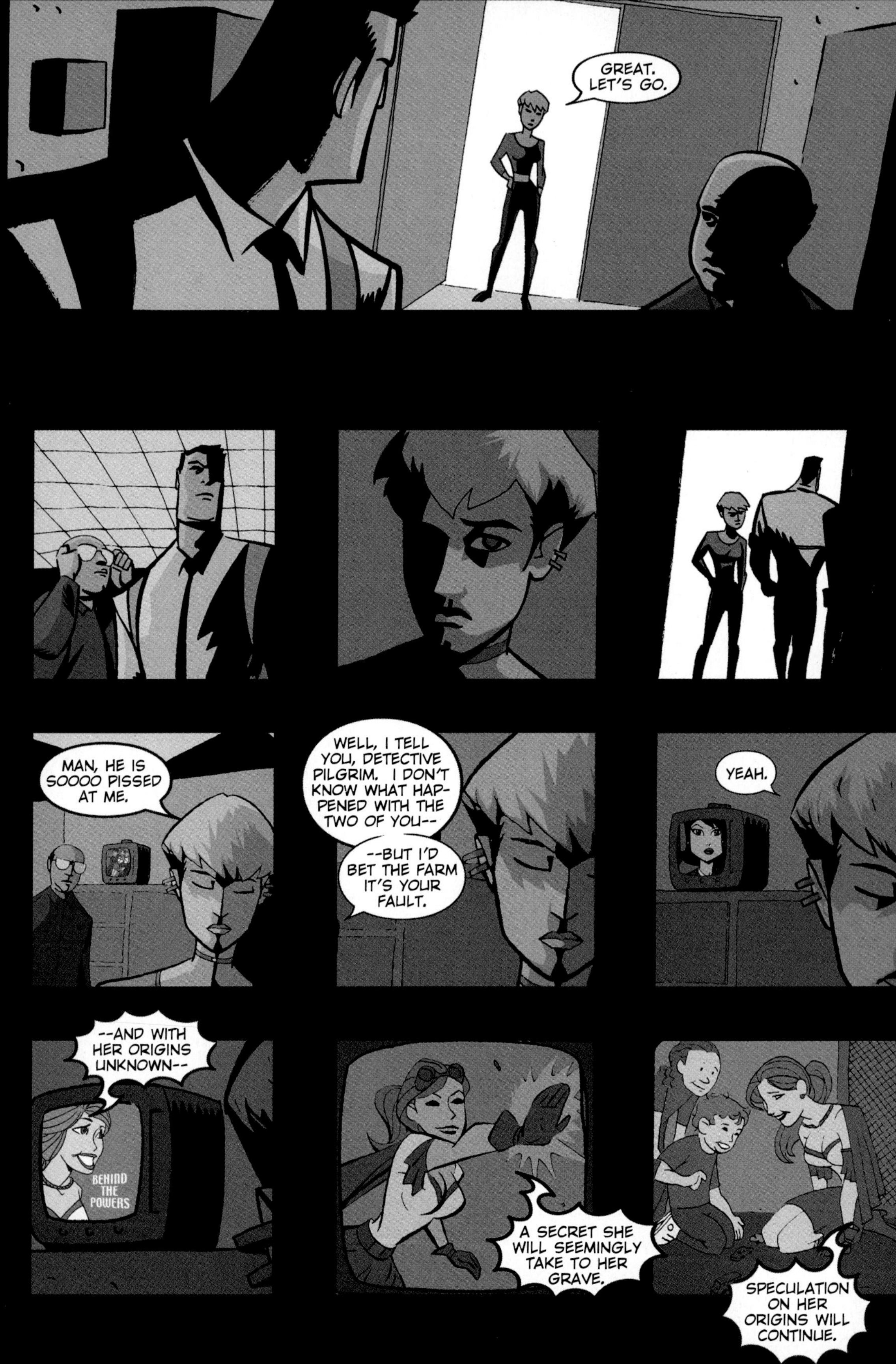
GREAT. LET'S GO.
MAN, HE IS SOOOO PISSED AT ME.
WELL, I TELL YOU, DETECTIVE PILGRIM. I DON'T KNOW WHAT HAPPENED WITH THE TWO OF YOU--
--BUT I'D BET THE FARM IT'S YOUR FAULT.
YEAH.
--AND WITH HER ORIGINS UNKNOWN--
BEHIND THE POWERS
A SECRET SHE WILL SEEMINGLY TAKE TO HER GRAVE.
SPECULATION ON HER ORIGINS WILL CONTINUE.

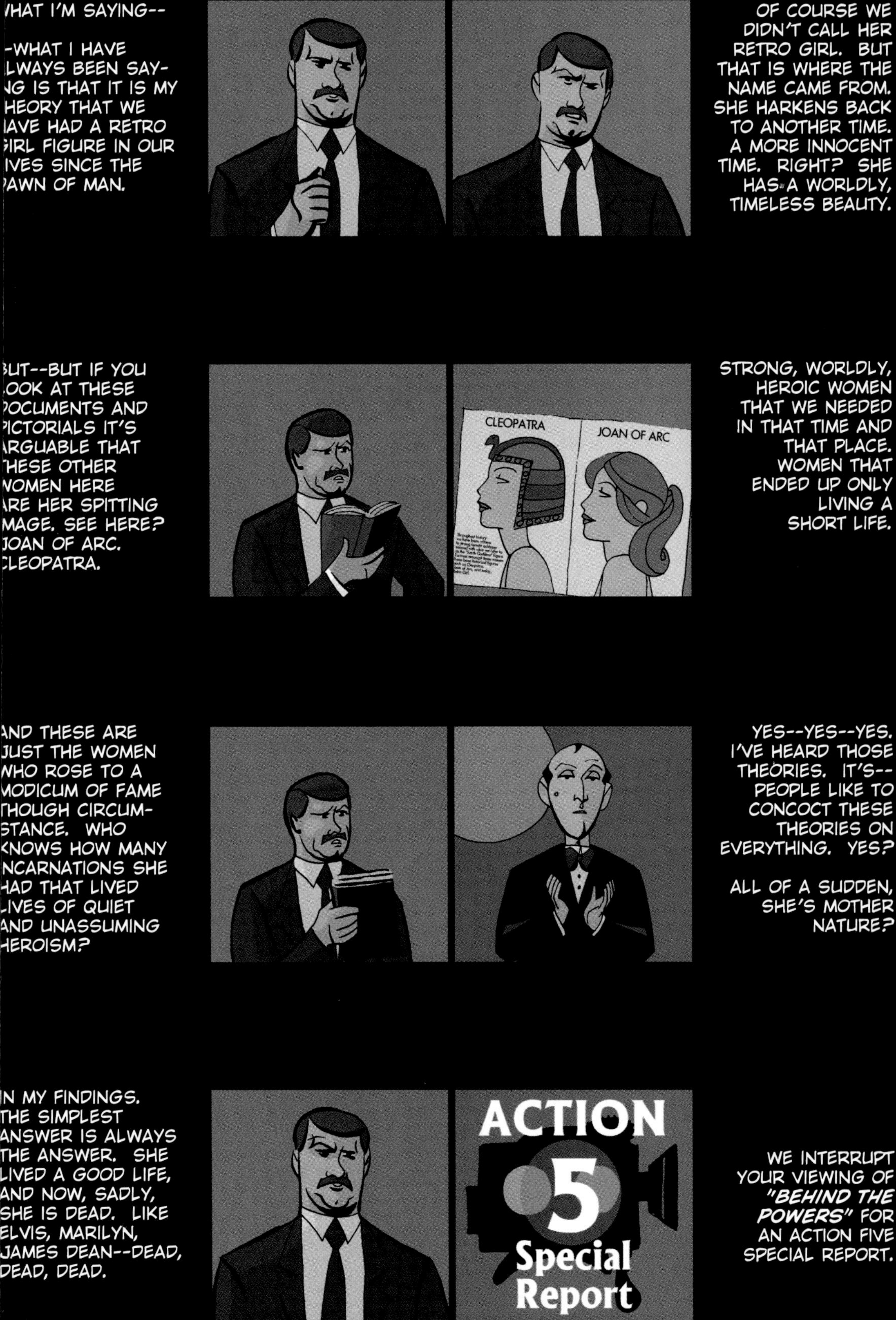

VHAT I'M SAYING--

-WHAT I HAVE ALWAYS BEEN SAYING IS THAT IT IS MY THEORY THAT WE HAVE HAD A RETRO GIRL FIGURE IN OUR LIVES SINCE THE DAWN OF MAN.

OF COURSE WE DIDN'T CALL HER RETRO GIRL. BUT THAT IS WHERE THE NAME CAME FROM. SHE HARKENS BACK TO ANOTHER TIME. A MORE INNOCENT TIME. RIGHT? SHE HAS A WORLDLY, TIMELESS BEAUTY.

BUT--BUT IF YOU LOOK AT THESE DOCUMENTS AND PICTORIALS IT'S ARGUABLE THAT THESE OTHER WOMEN HERE ARE HER SPITTING IMAGE. SEE HERE? JOAN OF ARC. CLEOPATRA.

CLEOPATRA   JOAN OF ARC

STRONG, WORLDLY, HEROIC WOMEN THAT WE NEEDED IN THAT TIME AND THAT PLACE. WOMEN THAT ENDED UP ONLY LIVING A SHORT LIFE.

AND THESE ARE JUST THE WOMEN WHO ROSE TO A MODICUM OF FAME THOUGH CIRCUMSTANCE. WHO KNOWS HOW MANY INCARNATIONS SHE HAD THAT LIVED LIVES OF QUIET AND UNASSUMING HEROISM?

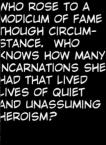

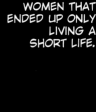

YES--YES--YES. I'VE HEARD THOSE THEORIES. IT'S-- PEOPLE LIKE TO CONCOCT THESE THEORIES ON EVERYTHING. YES?

ALL OF A SUDDEN, SHE'S MOTHER NATURE?

IN MY FINDINGS. THE SIMPLEST ANSWER IS ALWAYS THE ANSWER. SHE LIVED A GOOD LIFE, AND NOW, SADLY, SHE IS DEAD. LIKE ELVIS, MARILYN, JAMES DEAN--DEAD, DEAD, DEAD.

ACTION
5
Special Report

WE INTERRUPT YOUR VIEWING OF *"BEHIND THE POWERS"* FOR AN ACTION FIVE SPECIAL REPORT.

THIS IS AN ACTION FIVE SPECIAL REPORT.

WE NOW BRING YOU LIVE INSIDE THE CITY JUSTICE CENTER WHERE COLLETTE MCDANIEL IS REPORTING LIVE. COLLETTE?

ACTION
5
Special
Report

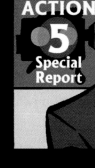

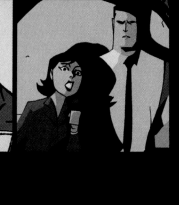

THIS IS COLLETTE MCDANIEL. I AM HERE INSIDE THE HOMICIDE UNIT OF DISTRICT 55.

STANDING WITH ME IS DETECTIVE CHRISTIAN WALKER.

DETECTIVE WALKER IS THE PRIMARY DETECTIVE FOR THE RETRO GIRL MURDER INVESTIGATION--THE HORRIBLE RETRO GIRL TRADGEDY THAT HAS GRIPPED OUR CITY IN MOURNING.

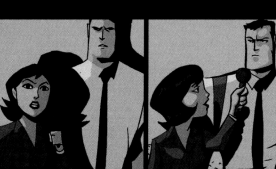

DETECTIVE, WHAT CAN YOU TELL US ABOUT YOUR PROGRESS ON THE INVESTIGATION SO FAR?

WELL, MA'AM, MOST OF THAT INFORMATION IS CLASSIFIED UNTIL THE CASE IS OFFICIALLY CLOSED, WHICH AT THIS TIME IS NOT THE CASE.

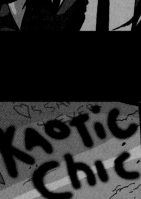

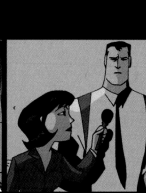

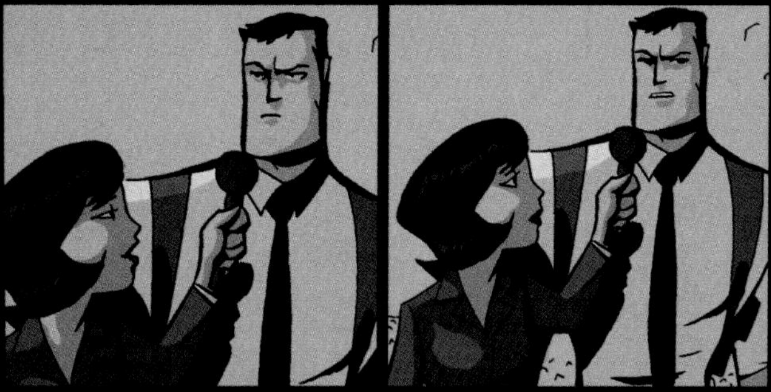

WE ARE ASKING THE PUBLIC'S HELP WITH INFORMATION IN REGARD TO THE MURDER, SPECIFICALLY TO A PIECE OF GRAFFITI THAT WE HAVE AT THE CRIME SCENE. I BELIEVE WE HA--

YES, IT'S UP NOW.

ANY INFORMATION THAT ANYONE HAS ABOUT THIS OR ANYTHING THAT CAN HELP US IN OUR INVESTIGATION --ANY INFORMATION ABOUT THE MEANING OF THE WORDS OF THE PERSON OR PERSONS RESPONSIBLE FOR THE GRAFFITI-- PLEASE CALL OUR HOTLINE AT 1-888-333-6665.

Kaotic
Chic

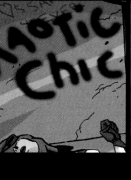

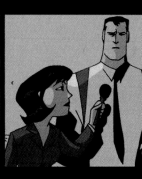

OBVIOUSLY THIS MATTER IS OF THE HIGHEST IMPORTANCE--ANYONE CALLING WITH PURPOSELY FALSE OR PRANK INFORMATION WILL BE TRACED AND PROSECUTED FOR OBSTRUCTION OF JUSTICE.

DETECTIVE, ANY WORD ON WHY JOHNNY ROYALLE WAS BROUGHT INTO THE STATION YESTERDAY?

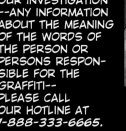

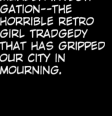

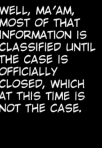

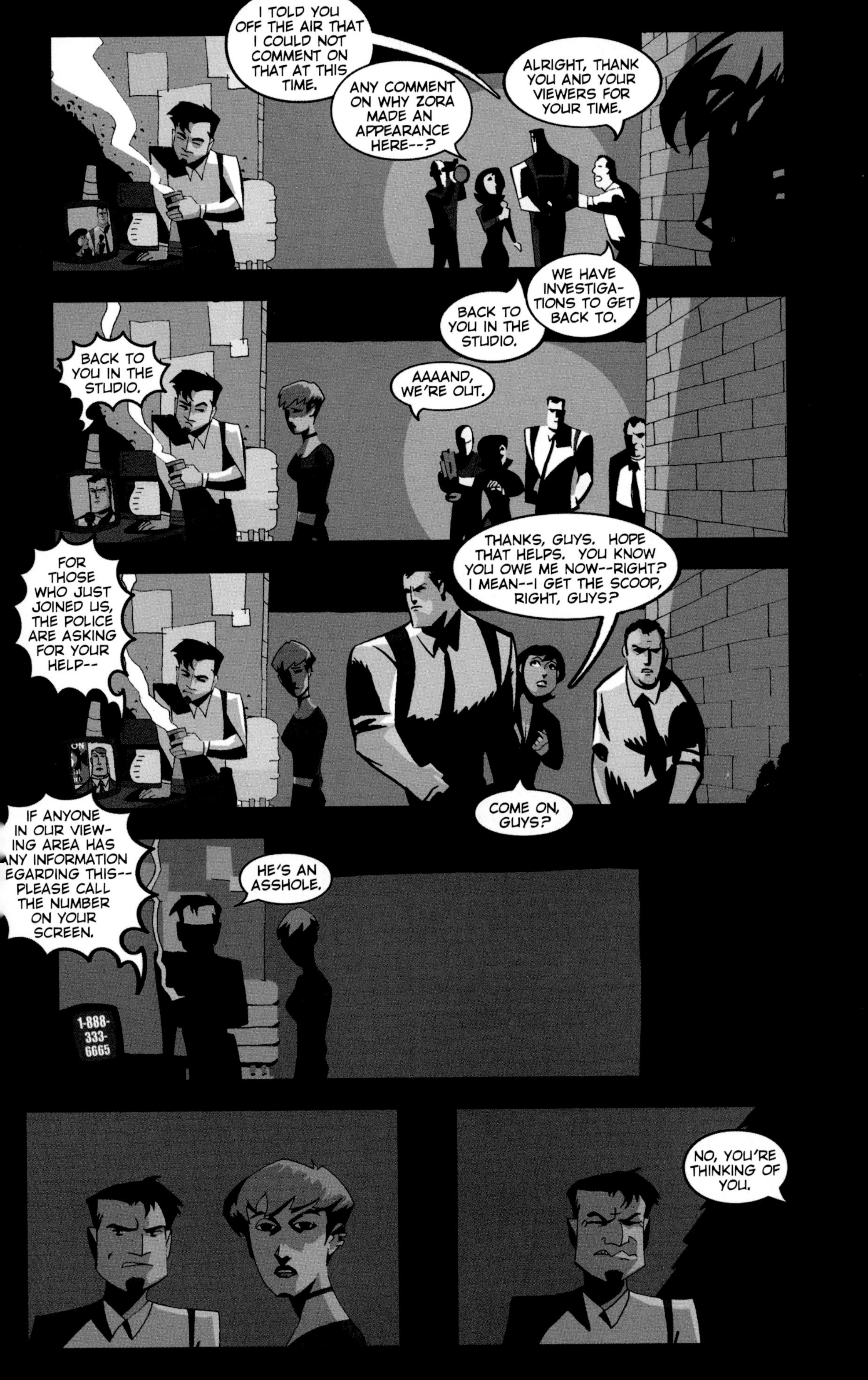
I TOLD YOU OFF THE AIR THAT I COULD NOT COMMENT ON THAT AT THIS TIME.
ANY COMMENT ON WHY ZORA MADE AN APPEARANCE HERE--?
ALRIGHT, THANK YOU AND YOUR VIEWERS FOR YOUR TIME.
WE HAVE INVESTIGATIONS TO GET BACK TO.
BACK TO YOU IN THE STUDIO.
BACK TO YOU IN THE STUDIO.
AAAAND, WE'RE OUT.
FOR THOSE WHO JUST JOINED US, THE POLICE ARE ASKING FOR YOUR HELP--
THANKS, GUYS. HOPE THAT HELPS. YOU KNOW YOU OWE ME NOW--RIGHT? I MEAN--I GET THE SCOOP, RIGHT, GUYS?
COME ON, GUYS?
IF ANYONE IN OUR VIEWING AREA HAS ANY INFORMATION EGARDING THIS--PLEASE CALL THE NUMBER ON YOUR SCREEN.
HE'S AN ASSHOLE.
1-888-333-6665
NO, YOU'RE THINKING OF YOU.

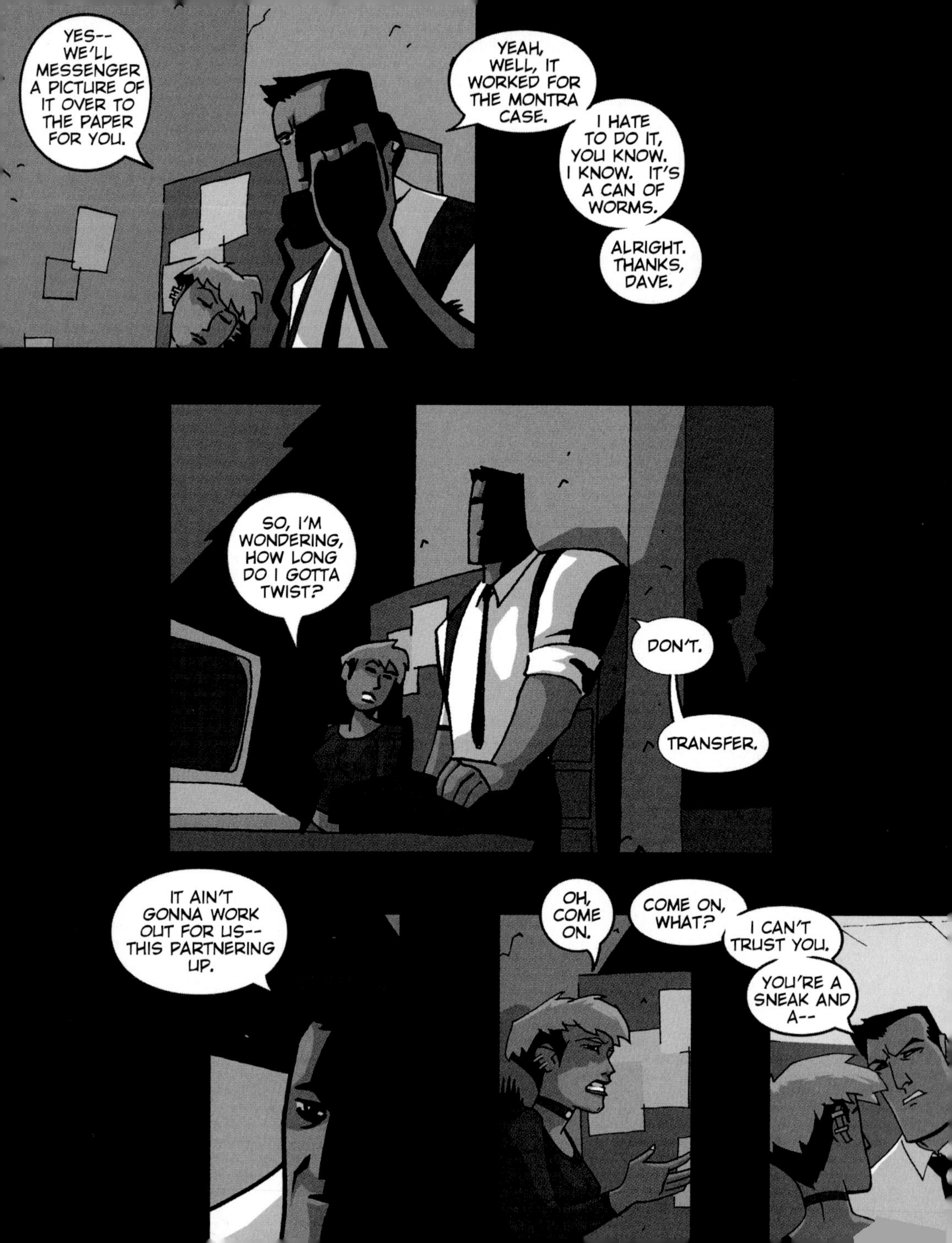
YES-- WE'LL MESSENGER A PICTURE OF IT OVER TO THE PAPER FOR YOU.
YEAH, WELL, IT WORKED FOR THE MONTRA CASE.
I HATE TO DO IT, YOU KNOW. I KNOW. IT'S A CAN OF WORMS.
ALRIGHT. THANKS, DAVE.
SO, I'M WONDERING, HOW LONG DO I GOTTA TWIST?
DON'T.
TRANSFER.
IT AIN'T GONNA WORK OUT FOR US-- THIS PARTNERING UP.
OH, COME ON.
COME ON, WHAT?
I CAN'T TRUST YOU.
YOU'RE A SNEAK AND A--

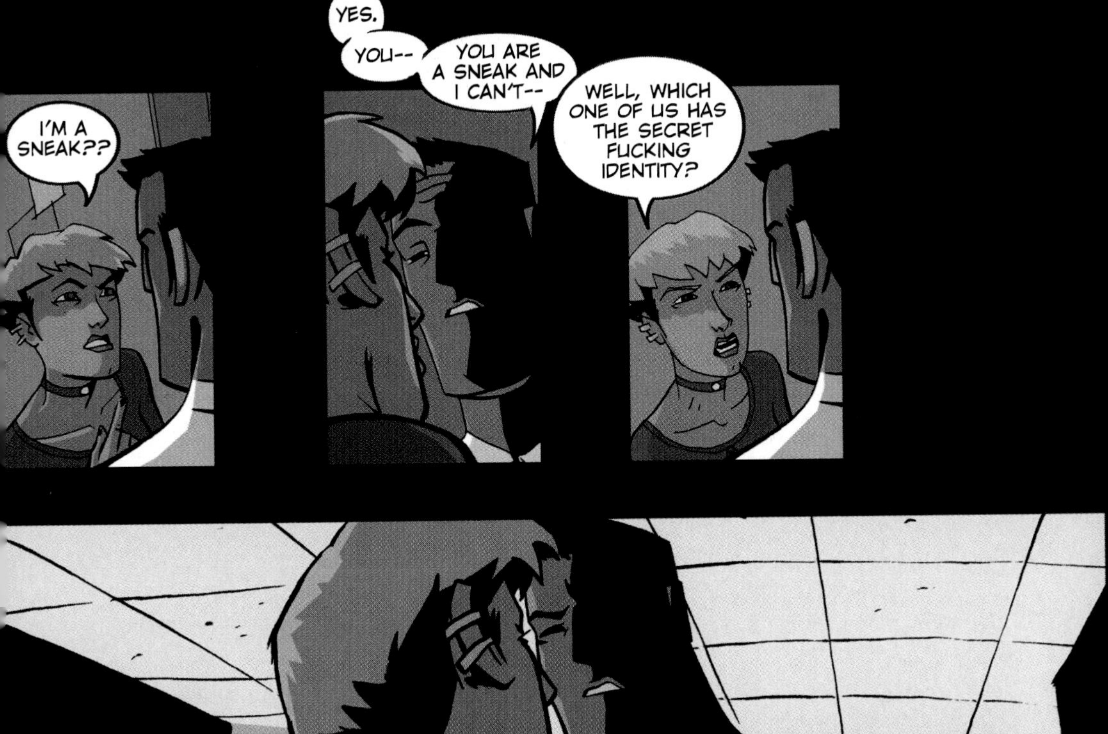
I'M A SNEAK??
YES.
YOU--
YOU ARE A SNEAK AND I CAN'T--
WELL, WHICH ONE OF US HAS THE SECRET FUCKING IDENTITY?

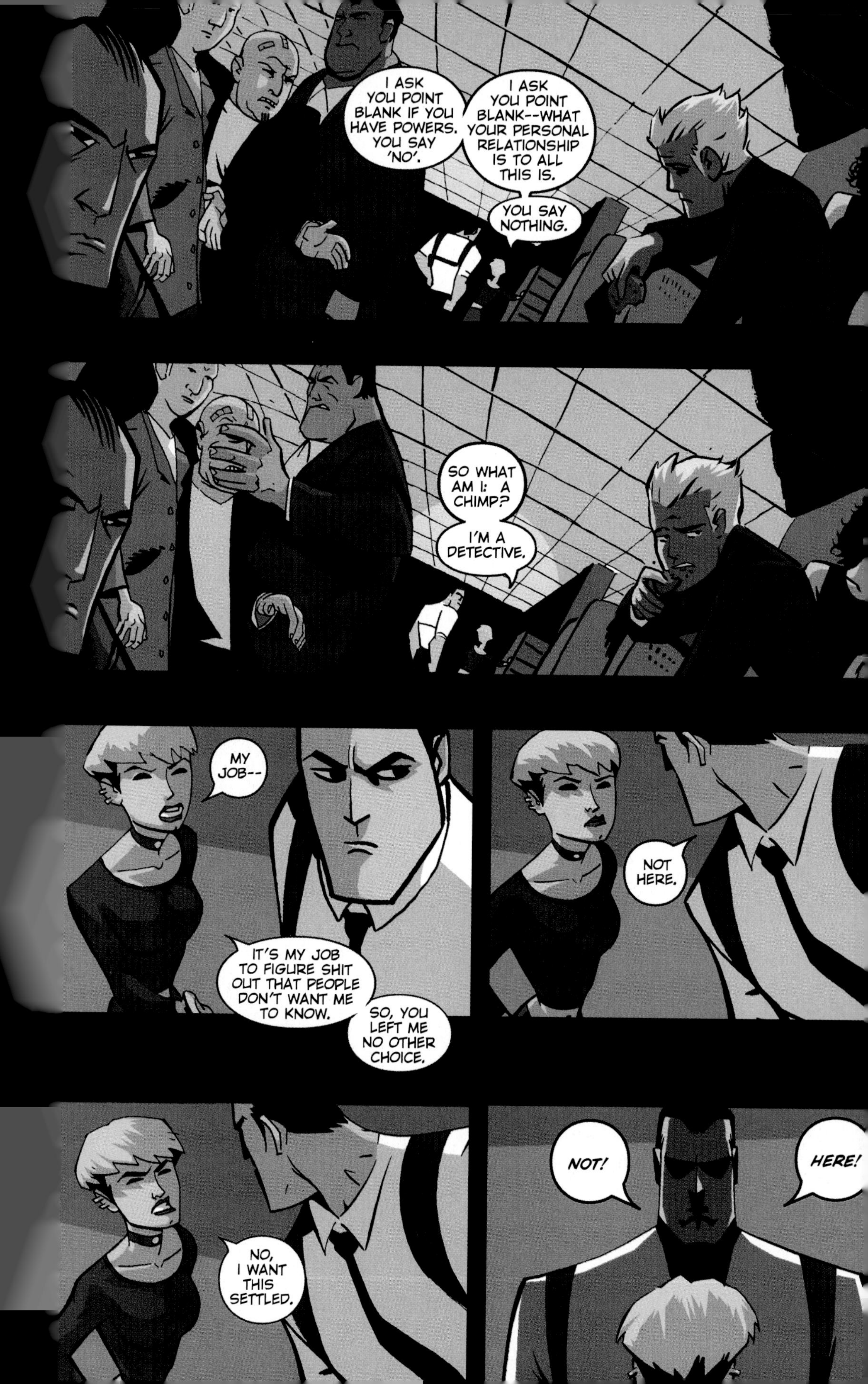
I ASK YOU POINT BLANK IF YOU HAVE POWERS. YOU SAY 'NO'.
I ASK YOU POINT BLANK--WHAT YOUR PERSONAL RELATIONSHIP IS TO ALL THIS IS.
YOU SAY NOTHING.
SO WHAT AM I: A CHIMP?
I'M A DETECTIVE.
MY JOB--
IT'S MY JOB TO FIGURE SHIT OUT THAT PEOPLE DON'T WANT ME TO KNOW.
SO, YOU LEFT ME NO OTHER CHOICE.
NOT HERE.
NO, I WANT THIS SETTLED.
NOT!
HERE!

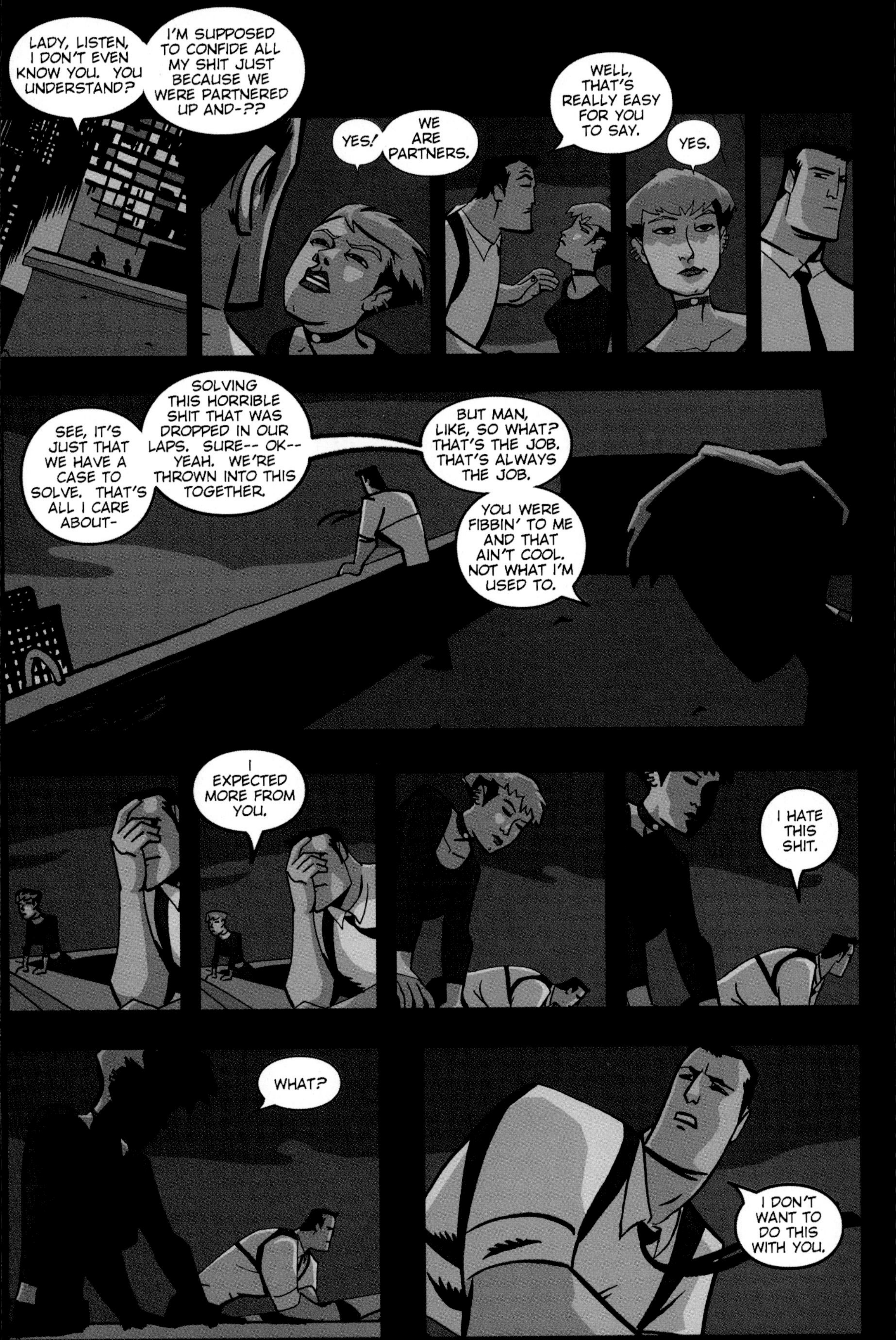
LADY, LISTEN, I DON'T EVEN KNOW YOU. YOU UNDERSTAND?
I'M SUPPOSED TO CONFIDE ALL MY SHIT JUST BECAUSE WE WERE PARTNERED UP AND-??
YES!
WE ARE PARTNERS.
WELL, THAT'S REALLY EASY FOR YOU TO SAY.
YES.
SEE, IT'S JUST THAT WE HAVE A CASE TO SOLVE. THAT'S ALL I CARE ABOUT-
SOLVING THIS HORRIBLE SHIT THAT WAS DROPPED IN OUR LAPS. SURE-- OK-- YEAH. WE'RE THROWN INTO THIS TOGETHER.
BUT MAN, LIKE, SO WHAT? THAT'S THE JOB. THAT'S ALWAYS THE JOB.
YOU WERE FIBBIN' TO ME AND THAT AIN'T COOL. NOT WHAT I'M USED TO.
I EXPECTED MORE FROM YOU.
I HATE THIS SHIT.
WHAT?
I DON'T WANT TO DO THIS WITH YOU.

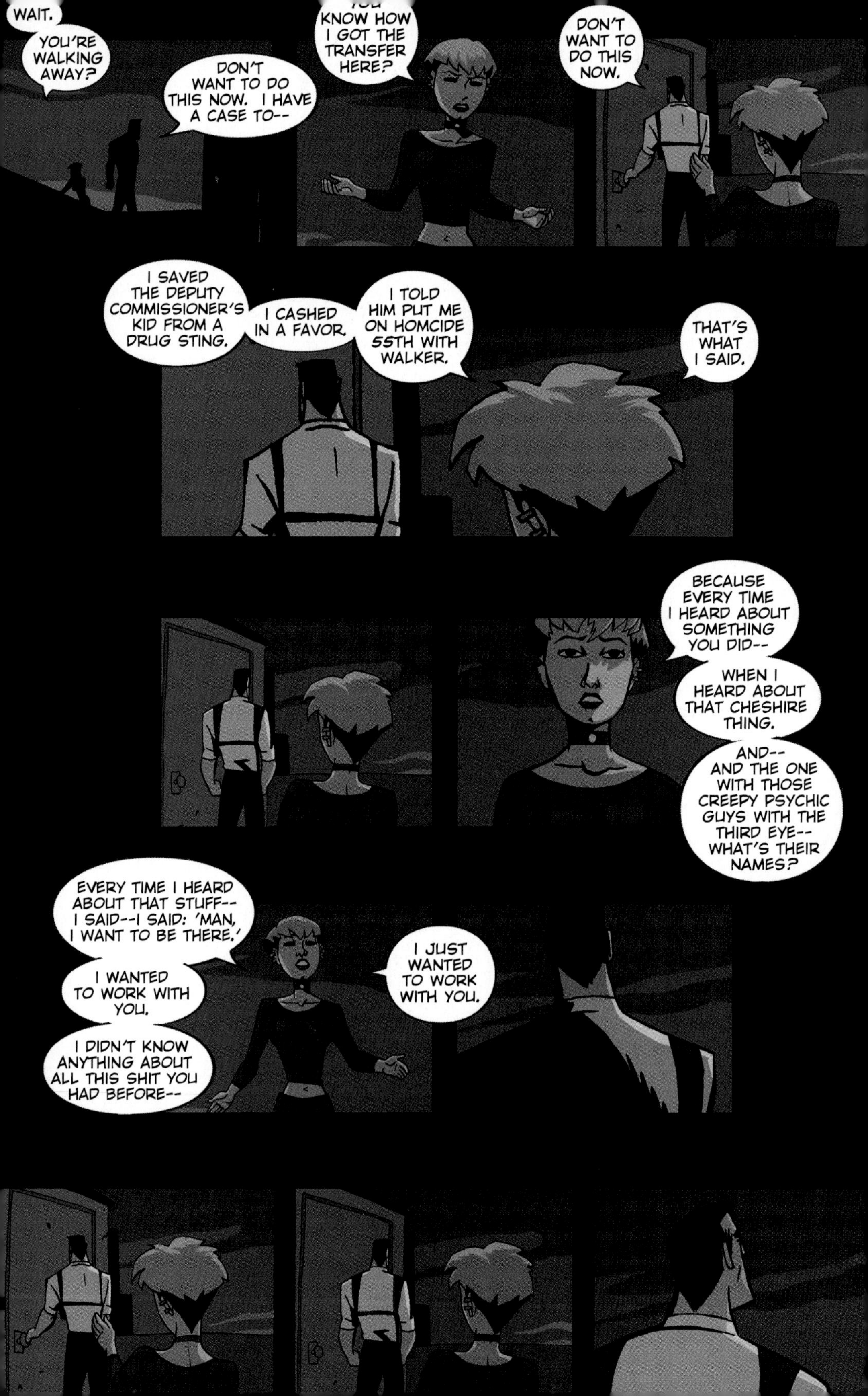
WAIT.
YOU'RE WALKING AWAY?
DON'T WANT TO DO THIS NOW. I HAVE A CASE TO--
KNOW HOW I GOT THE TRANSFER HERE?
DON'T WANT TO DO THIS NOW.
I SAVED THE DEPUTY COMMISSIONER'S KID FROM A DRUG STING.
I CASHED IN A FAVOR.
I TOLD HIM PUT ME ON HOMCIDE 55TH WITH WALKER.
THAT'S WHAT I SAID.
BECAUSE EVERY TIME I HEARD ABOUT SOMETHING YOU DID--
WHEN I HEARD ABOUT THAT CHESHIRE THING.
AND-- AND THE ONE WITH THOSE CREEPY PSYCHIC GUYS WITH THE THIRD EYE-- WHAT'S THEIR NAMES?
EVERY TIME I HEARD ABOUT THAT STUFF-- I SAID--I SAID: 'MAN, I WANT TO BE THERE.'
I WANTED TO WORK WITH YOU.
I DIDN'T KNOW ANYTHING ABOUT ALL THIS SHIT YOU HAD BEFORE--
I JUST WANTED TO WORK WITH YOU.

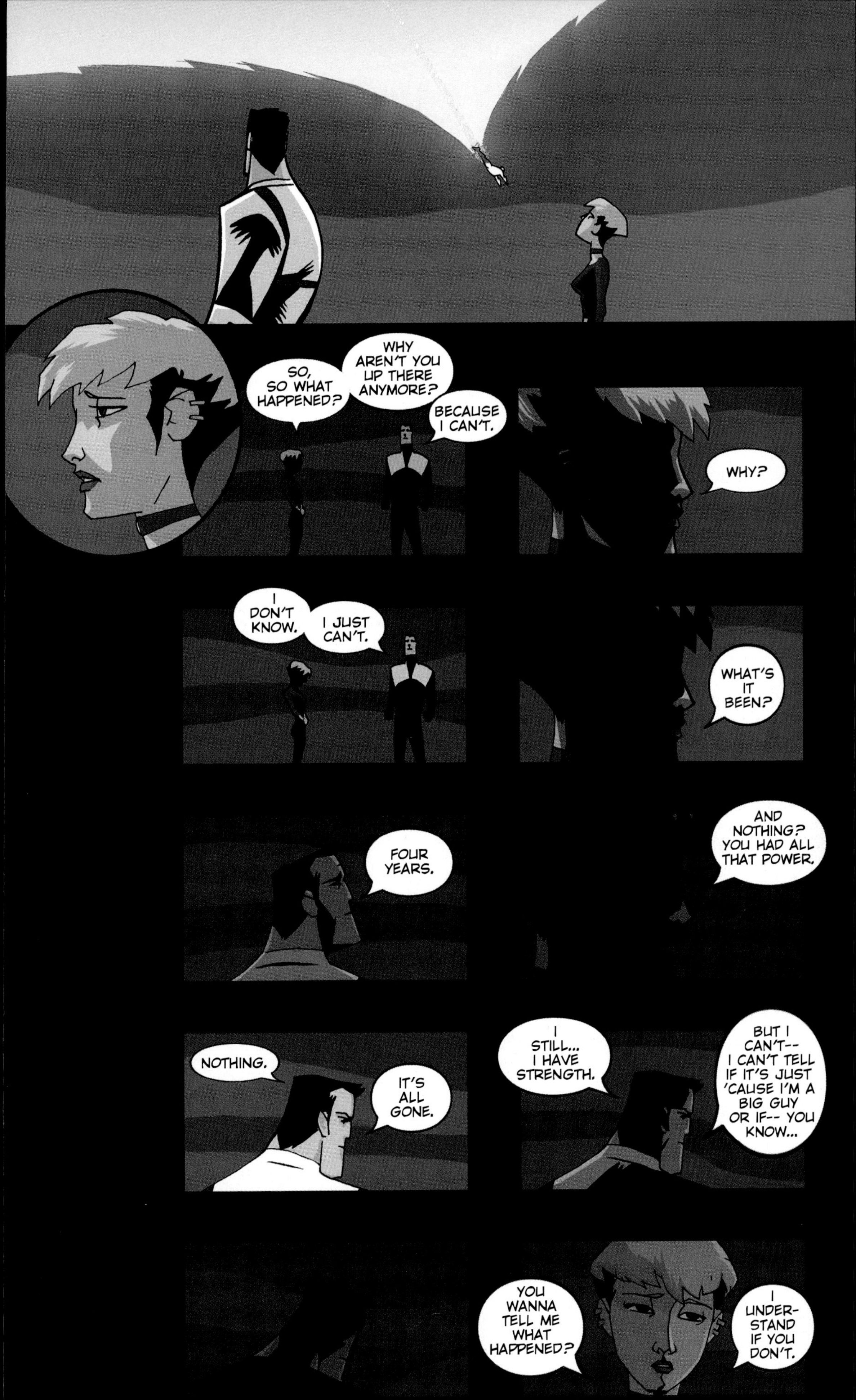
SO, SO WHAT HAPPENED?
WHY AREN'T YOU UP THERE ANYMORE?
BECAUSE I CAN'T.
WHY?
I DON'T KNOW.
I JUST CAN'T.
WHAT'S IT BEEN?
FOUR YEARS.
AND NOTHING? YOU HAD ALL THAT POWER.
NOTHING.
IT'S ALL GONE.
I STILL... I HAVE STRENGTH.
BUT I CAN'T-- I CAN'T TELL IF IT'S JUST 'CAUSE I'M A BIG GUY OR IF-- YOU KNOW...
YOU WANNA TELL ME WHAT HAPPENED?
I UNDER-STAND IF YOU DON'T.

WELL Y'SEE, I--I REALLY HAVE
NO DAMN IDEA WHAT HAPPENED.
JUST WHEN--IT WAS DURING
THE WHOLE TERRIBLE INCIDENT
WITH THE JOHNNY ROYALLE
GANG.

OH YEAH--THAT'S THE LAST
ANYONE EVER SAW OR HEARD
FROM YOU--LIKE THAT. AS
DIAMOND.

YEAH. WE WERE--WE WERE
GOING AT IT PRETTY TOUGH,
YOU KNOW. I MEAN--ALL THE
FIGHTS ARE TOUGH--BUT THIS
ONE--THIS ONE--THERE WAS
SOMETHING JUST OFF ABOUT IT.
IT WAS VERY CARNAL. VERY
ANIMAL-LIKE. IT WAS ME AND
TRIPHAMMER, WHO YOU'VE
MET, AND ZORA AND RETRO
GIRL AGAINST ALL THESE
WACKOS. I MEAN, I DON'T
EVEN REMEMBER HOW IT
STARTED. SOME STUPID
SCHEME OR SOMETHING.

SHIT! THAT FREAKY B.9.
FOM-FOM DUDE WAS THERE.

YEAH--YEAH THAT'S RIGHT.
AND CHESHIRE, AND TWILIGHT,
BUT I WAS FIGHTING SSAZZ.
AGAIN! HE'S SOME KIND OF
MUTATION OR SOMETHING. ONE
OF THOSE GENETIC MISHAPS
WITH A HARD-ON FOR EVERY-
THING. AND HE SMELLS SO--
SO BAD. WE HAD FOUGHT
BEFORE, Y'SEE, AND OF
COURSE I BEAT THE HOLY
CRAP OUT OF HIM. BUT THIS
TIME HE HAD SOME KIND OF--
SOME KIND OF ENHANCEMENT
ON HIM OR SOMETHING.

LIKE A POWER ENHANCER?

YEAH.

I READ ABOUT THOSE IN
SCIENTIFIC AMERI--

AND--AND I'M DOING EVERY-
THING I CAN JUST TO END
THE FIGHT. JUST END THE
FIGHTING. JUST STOP IT.
I GET, LIKE, THIS SUDDEN
BURST OF ADRENALINE OR
WHATNOT, LIKE A BURST
OF ENERGY. NEVER HAPPENED
BEFORE. BUT, WHAM!, AND
I WAS WINNING THE DAY. AND
THEN--AND THEN--*POOF!*

POOF?

POOF.

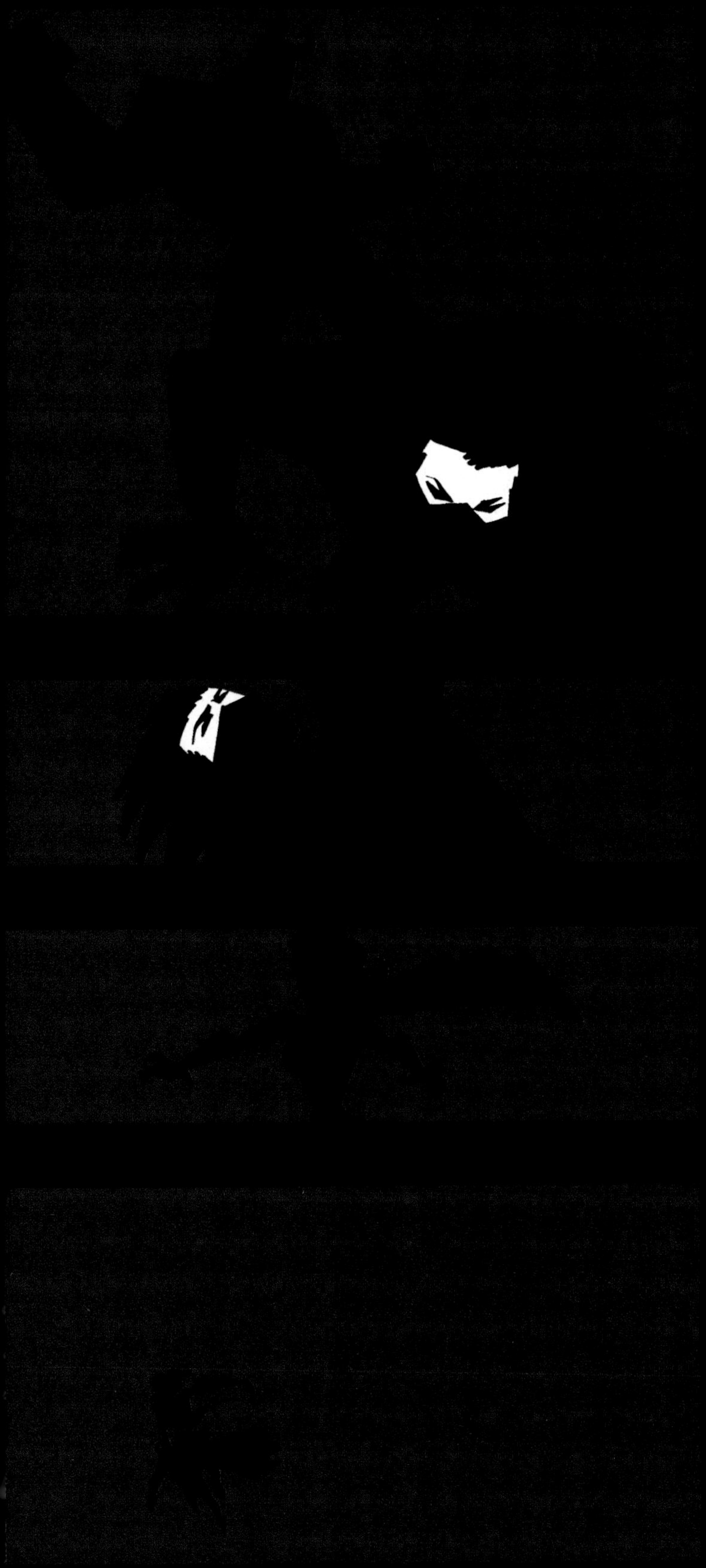

THAT'S IT?

THAT'S IT. BUT I WAS RIGHT IN THE MIDDLE OF IT. THE FRAY. Y'SEE? I MEAN. HERE I AM--AND NOW I'M JUST A GUY IN AN OUTFIT. AND ON TOP OF IT, I'M CONFUSED AND DISORIENTED. AND I HAVE NO WAY TO DEFEND MYSELF, AND I DON'T KNOW WHAT THE FUCK HAS HAPPENED TO ME.

DO YOU THINK IT'S SOMETHING THAT SSAZZ GUY DID TO YOU?

NO, ACTUALLY. BECAUSE WHEN GUYS LIKE THAT DO SOMETHING LIKE THAT--THEY NEVER SHUT UP ABOUT IT. I DON'T THINK HE EVEN FIGURED IT OUT. JUST THOUGHT HE WAS PUTTING A BEATING ON ME.

HOW'D YOU GET OUT OF THERE?

WELL, I WAS GETTING BEATEN ON PRETTY BAD. AND SSAZZ--HE WAS ABOUT TO BASICALLY ELECTROCUTE ME, WHEN--WHEN JANIS--***RETRO GIRL***--SHE SAVED MY LIFE. SHE FLEW ME OUT OF THERE.

SHE STOPPED--***HA***--SHE STOPPED TO KISS THE BOO BOO I HAD ON MY FOREHEAD. AND SHE FLEW BACK TO FINISH THE FIGHT. THAT'S ACTUALLY THE LAST TIME I EVER SAW HER.

BUT WEREN'T YOU GUYS FRIENDS?

SEE, YOU KEEP MISSING THE POINT ON THAT.

WERE YOU OR WEREN'T YOU?

WELL, YES AND NO. WE--WE WORKED TOGETHER ON OCCASION IS ALL. WE--WE DIDN'T MAKE A HABIT OF GETTING INTO EACH OTHER'S PERSONAL LIVES. WE DIDN'T HAVE A CLUB HOUSE. JUST--

WE UNDERSTOOD THIS--IT WAS AN UNWRITTEN RULE TO SUPPORT EACH OTHER IN PUBLIC AND NOT TO GET INTO EACH OTHER'S BUSINESS.

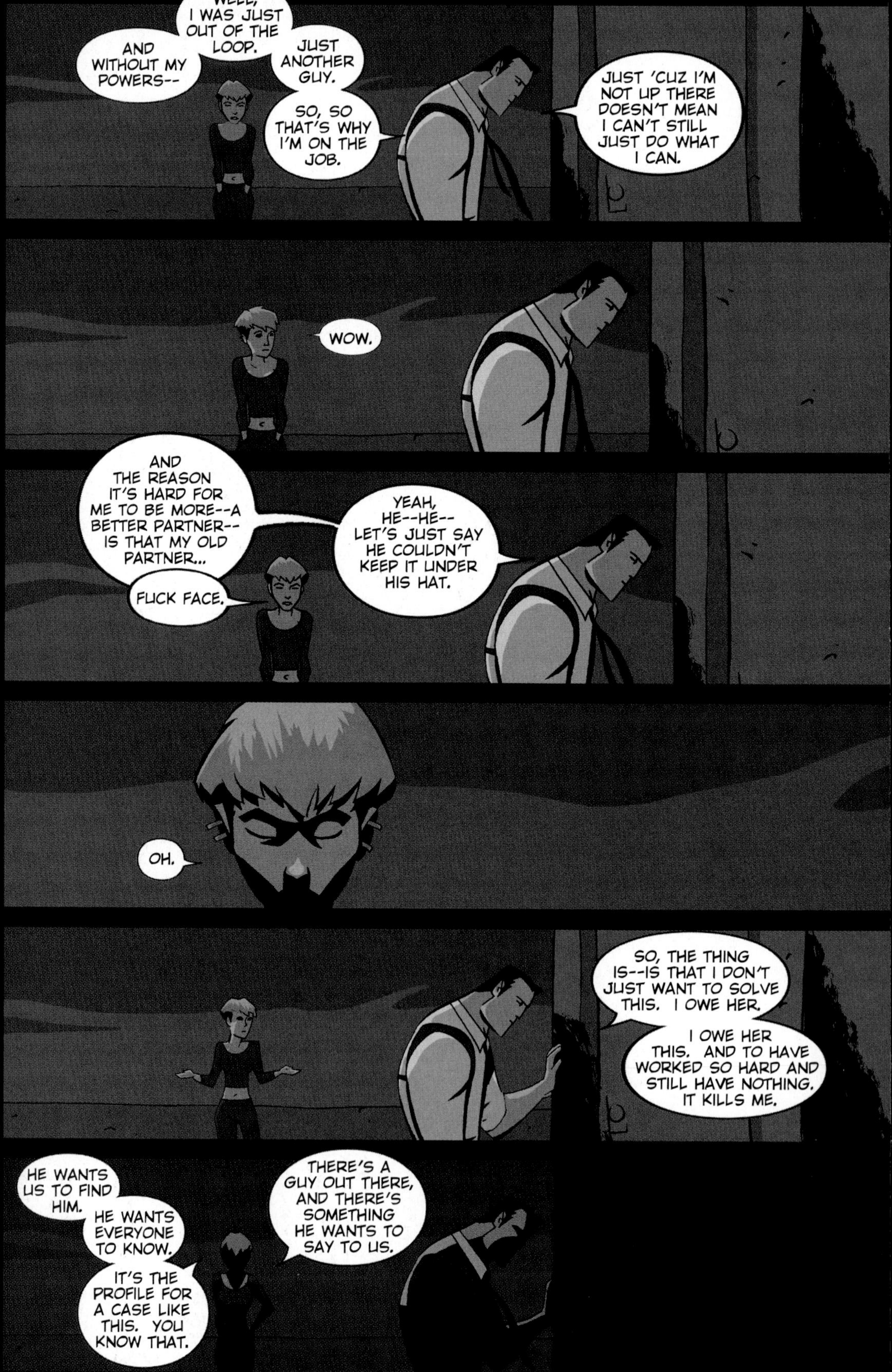
WELL, I WAS JUST OUT OF THE LOOP.
AND WITHOUT MY POWERS--
JUST ANOTHER GUY.
SO, SO THAT'S WHY I'M ON THE JOB.
JUST 'CUZ I'M NOT UP THERE DOESN'T MEAN I CAN'T STILL JUST DO WHAT I CAN.
WOW.
AND THE REASON IT'S HARD FOR ME TO BE MORE--A BETTER PARTNER--IS THAT MY OLD PARTNER...
FUCK FACE.
YEAH, HE--HE--LET'S JUST SAY HE COULDN'T KEEP IT UNDER HIS HAT.
OH.
SO, THE THING IS--IS THAT I DON'T JUST WANT TO SOLVE THIS. I OWE HER.
I OWE HER THIS. AND TO HAVE WORKED SO HARD AND STILL HAVE NOTHING. IT KILLS ME.
HE WANTS US TO FIND HIM.
HE WANTS EVERYONE TO KNOW.
IT'S THE PROFILE FOR A CASE LIKE THIS. YOU KNOW THAT.
THERE'S A GUY OUT THERE, AND THERE'S SOMETHING HE WANTS TO SAY TO US.

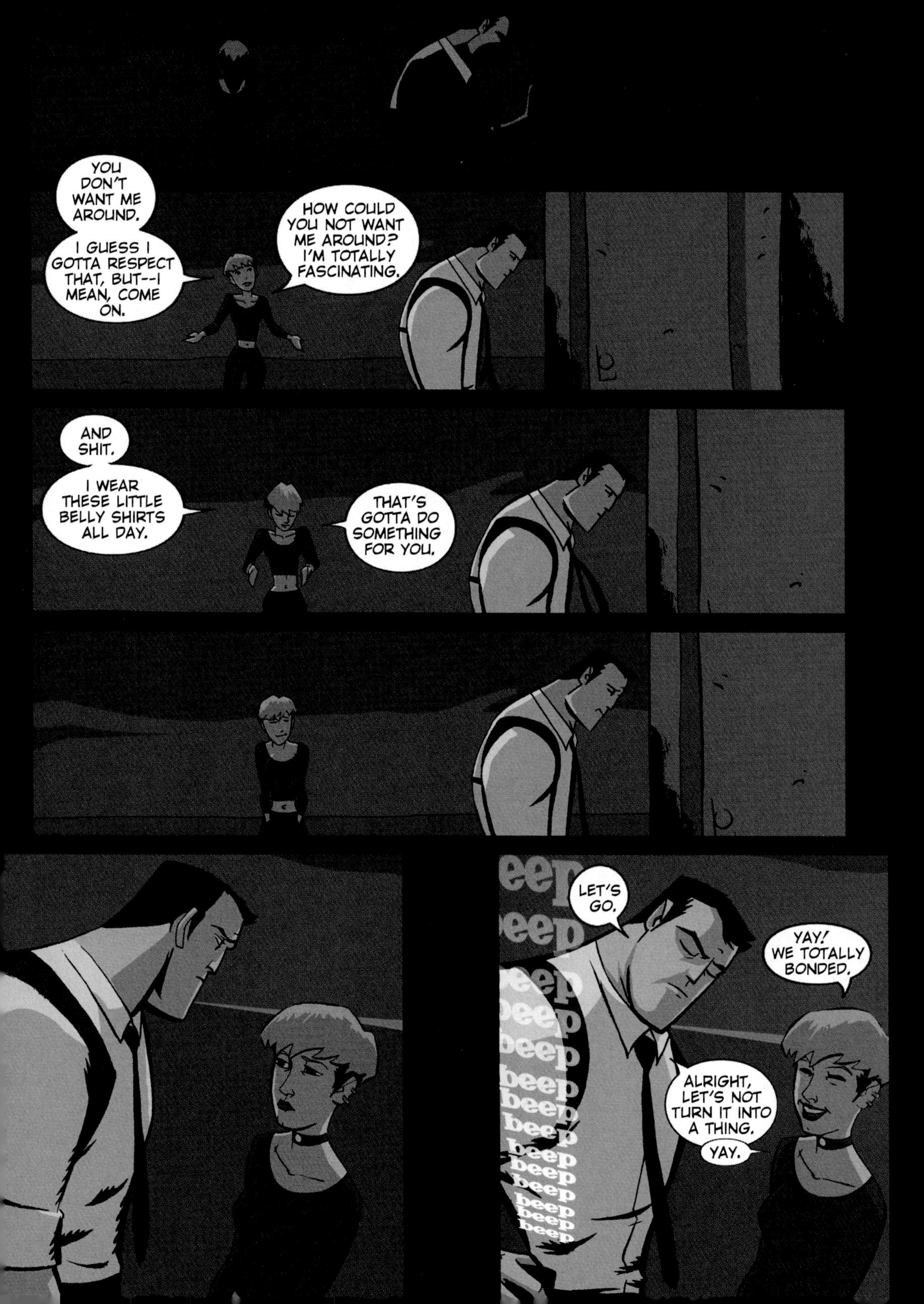
YOU DON'T WANT ME AROUND.
I GUESS I GOTTA RESPECT THAT, BUT--I MEAN, COME ON.
HOW COULD YOU NOT WANT ME AROUND? I'M TOTALLY FASCINATING.
AND SHIT.
I WEAR THESE LITTLE BELLY SHIRTS ALL DAY.
THAT'S GOTTA DO SOMETHING FOR YOU.
beep beep beep beep beep beep beep beep beep beep beep beep beep
LET'S GO.
YAY! WE TOTALLY BONDED.
ALRIGHT, LET'S NOT TURN IT INTO A THING.
YAY.

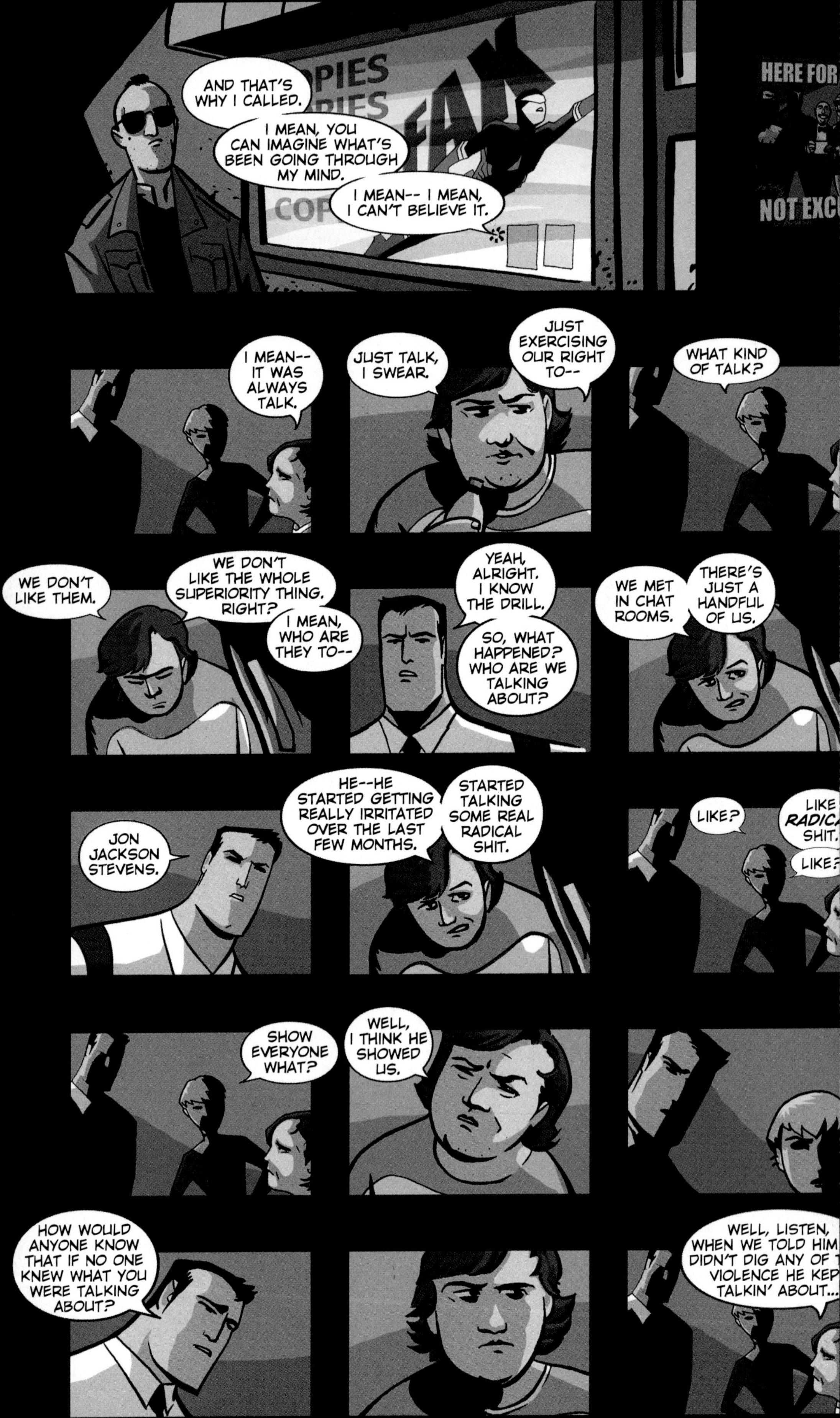
COPIES
HERE FOR
NOT EXC
AND THAT'S WHY I CALLED.
I MEAN, YOU CAN IMAGINE WHAT'S BEEN GOING THROUGH MY MIND.
I MEAN-- I MEAN, I CAN'T BELIEVE IT.
I MEAN-- IT WAS ALWAYS TALK.
JUST TALK, I SWEAR.
JUST EXERCISING OUR RIGHT TO--
WHAT KIND OF TALK?
WE DON'T LIKE THEM.
WE DON'T LIKE THE WHOLE SUPERIORITY THING. RIGHT?
I MEAN, WHO ARE THEY TO--
YEAH, ALRIGHT. I KNOW THE DRILL.
SO, WHAT HAPPENED? WHO ARE WE TALKING ABOUT?
WE MET IN CHAT ROOMS.
THERE'S JUST A HANDFUL OF US.
JON JACKSON STEVENS.
HE--HE STARTED GETTING REALLY IRRITATED OVER THE LAST FEW MONTHS.
STARTED TALKING SOME REAL RADICAL SHIT.
LIKE?
LIKE *RADICA* SHIT.
LIKE?
SHOW EVERYONE WHAT?
WELL, I THINK HE SHOWED US.
HOW WOULD ANYONE KNOW THAT IF NO ONE KNEW WHAT YOU WERE TALKING ABOUT?
WELL, LISTEN, WHEN WE TOLD HIM DIDN'T DIG ANY OF T VIOLENCE HE KEP TALKIN' ABOUT...

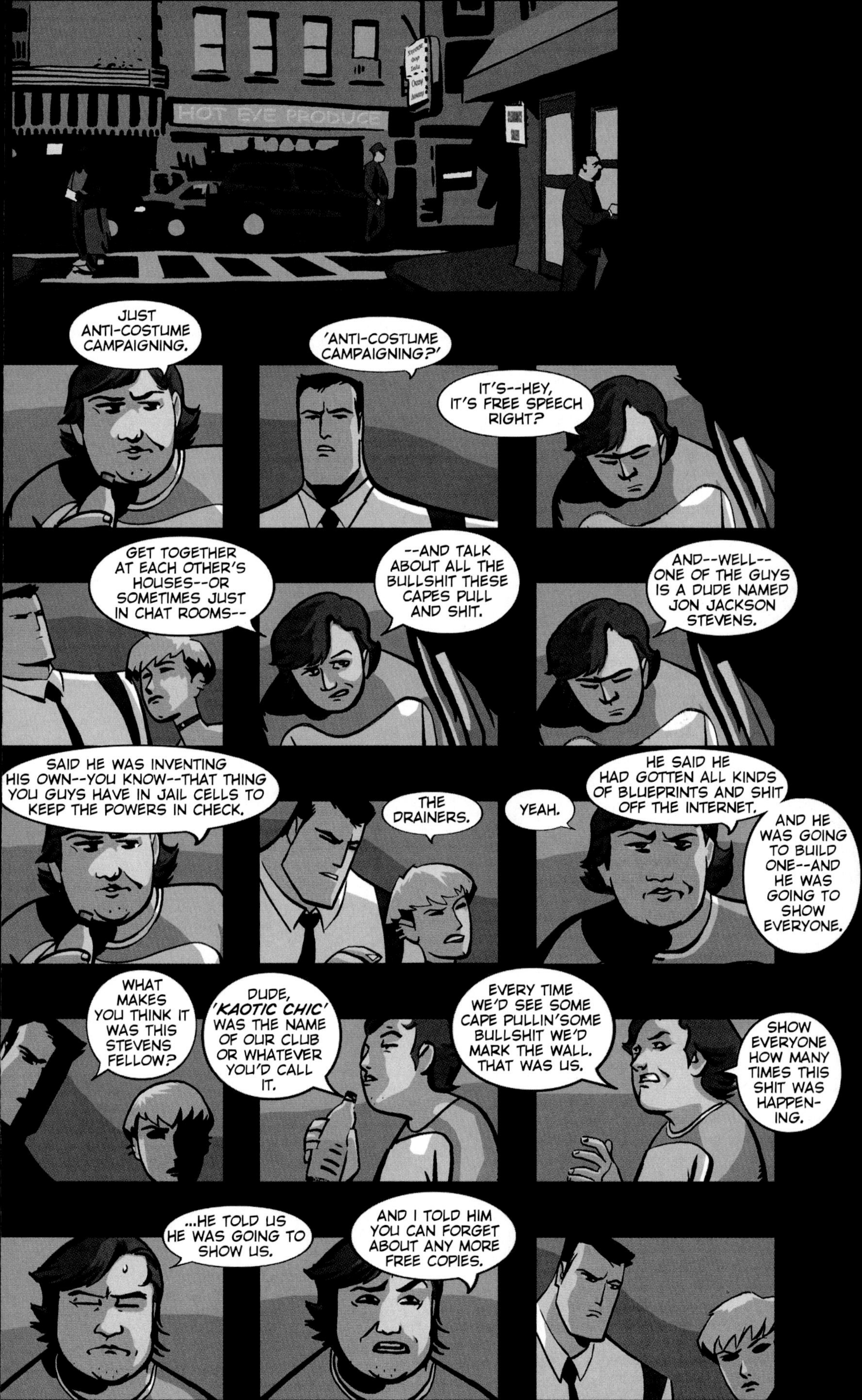
HOT EYE PRODUCE
JUST ANTI-COSTUME CAMPAIGNING.
'ANTI-COSTUME CAMPAIGNING?'
IT'S--HEY, IT'S FREE SPEECH RIGHT?
GET TOGETHER AT EACH OTHER'S HOUSES--OR SOMETIMES JUST IN CHAT ROOMS--
--AND TALK ABOUT ALL THE BULLSHIT THESE CAPES PULL AND SHIT.
AND--WELL--ONE OF THE GUYS IS A DUDE NAMED JON JACKSON STEVENS.
SAID HE WAS INVENTING HIS OWN--YOU KNOW--THAT THING YOU GUYS HAVE IN JAIL CELLS TO KEEP THE POWERS IN CHECK.
THE DRAINERS.
YEAH.
HE SAID HE HAD GOTTEN ALL KINDS OF BLUEPRINTS AND SHIT OFF THE INTERNET.
AND HE WAS GOING TO BUILD ONE--AND HE WAS GOING TO SHOW EVERYONE.
WHAT MAKES YOU THINK IT WAS THIS STEVENS FELLOW?
DUDE, *'KAOTIC CHIC'* WAS THE NAME OF OUR CLUB OR WHATEVER YOU'D CALL IT.
EVERY TIME WE'D SEE SOME CAPE PULLIN'SOME BULLSHIT WE'D MARK THE WALL. THAT WAS US.
SHOW EVERYONE HOW MANY TIMES THIS SHIT WAS HAPPEN-ING.
...HE TOLD US HE WAS GOING TO SHOW US.
AND I TOLD HIM YOU CAN FORGET ABOUT ANY MORE FREE COPIES.

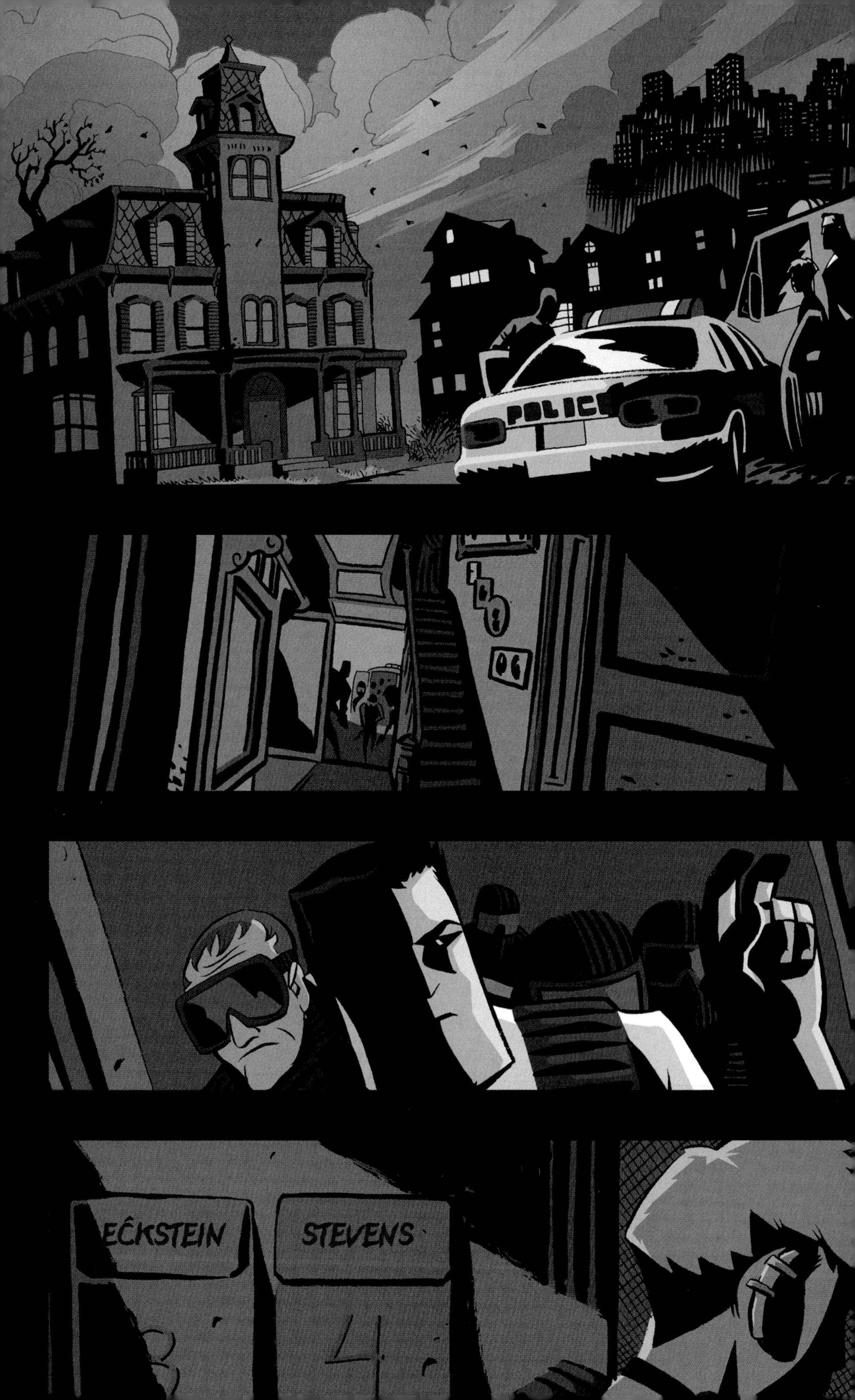
ECKSTEIN
STEVENS
4

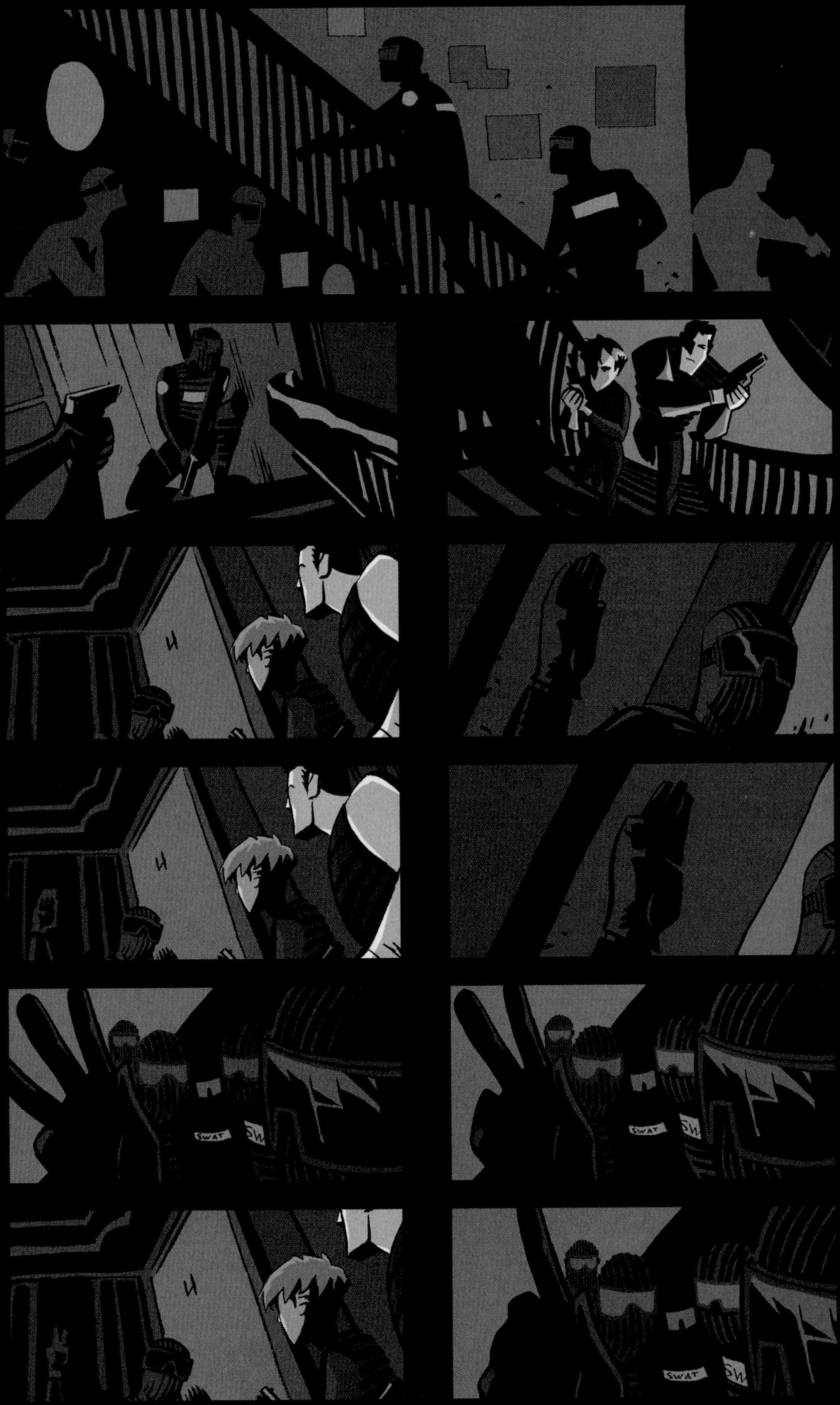
SWAT
SWAT
SWAT

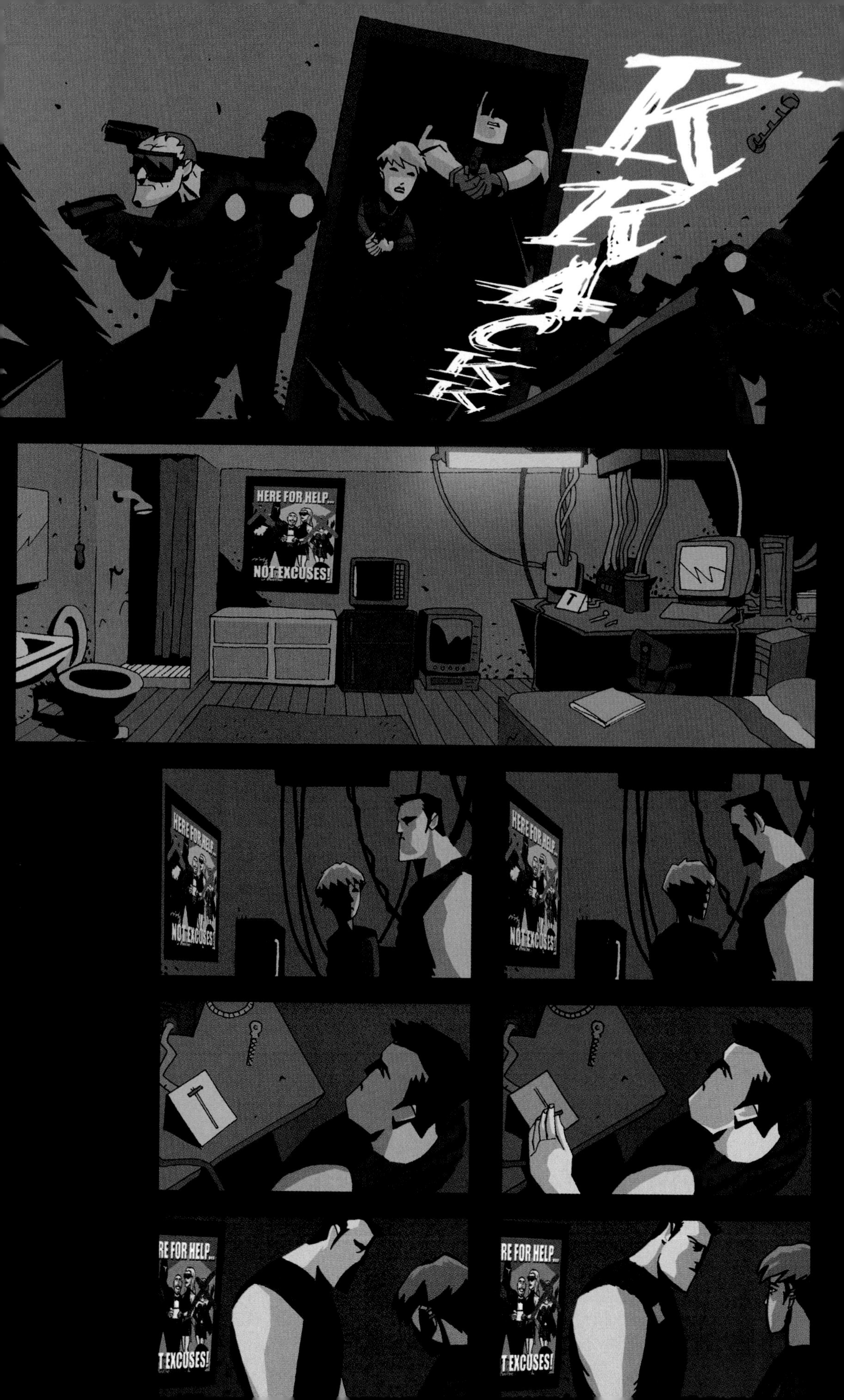
KRAACK
HERE FOR HELP...
NOT EXCUSES!

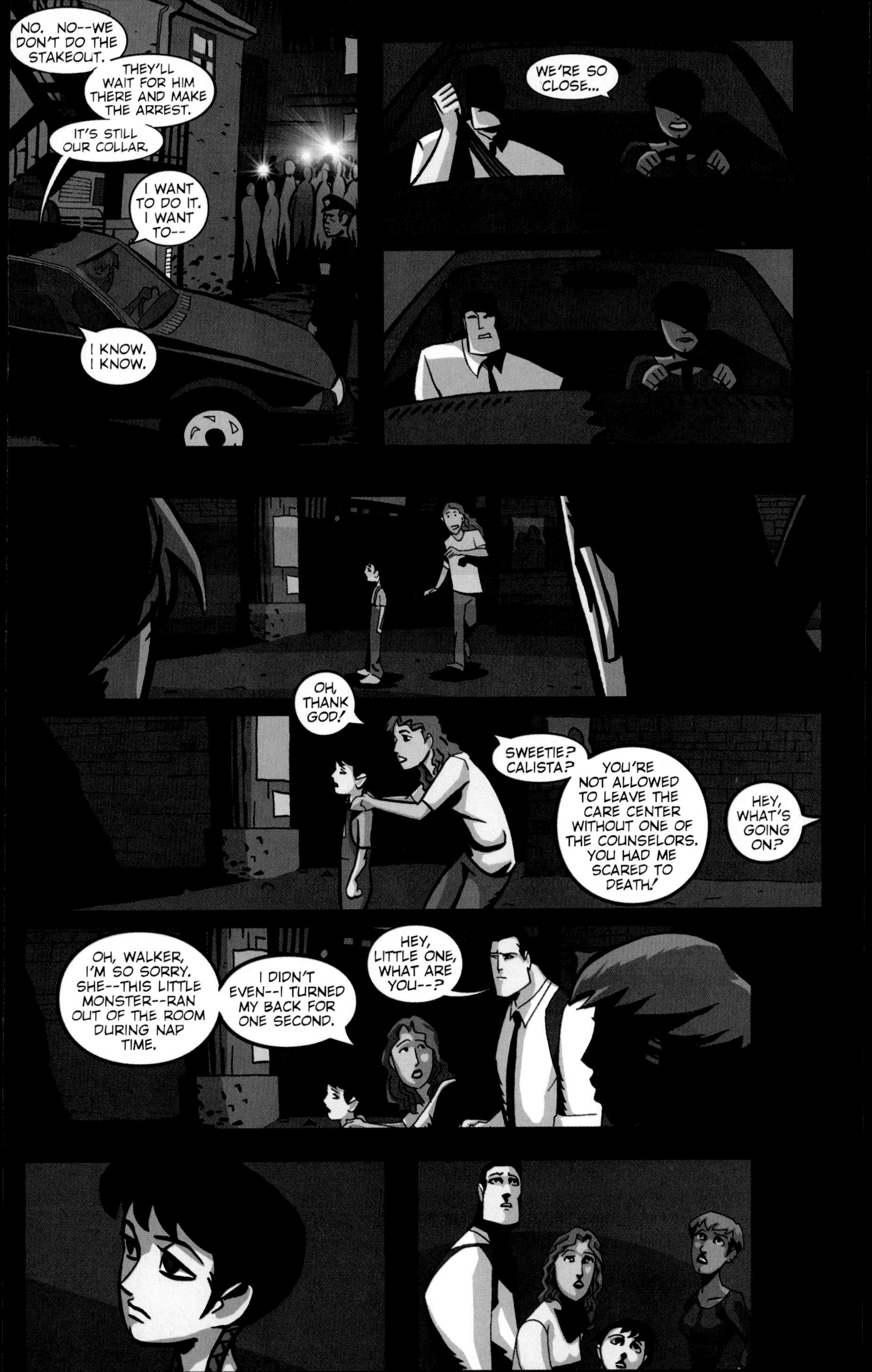
NO. NO--WE DON'T DO THE STAKEOUT.
THEY'LL WAIT FOR HIM THERE AND MAKE THE ARREST.
IT'S STILL OUR COLLAR.
I WANT TO DO IT. I WANT TO--
I KNOW. I KNOW.
WE'RE SO CLOSE...
OH, THANK GOD!
SWEETIE? CALISTA?
YOU'RE NOT ALLOWED TO LEAVE THE CARE CENTER WITHOUT ONE OF THE COUNSELORS. YOU HAD ME SCARED TO DEATH!
HEY, WHAT'S GOING ON?
OH, WALKER, I'M SO SORRY. SHE--THIS LITTLE MONSTER--RAN OUT OF THE ROOM DURING NAP TIME.
I DIDN'T EVEN--I TURNED MY BACK FOR ONE SECOND.
HEY, LITTLE ONE, WHAT ARE YOU--?

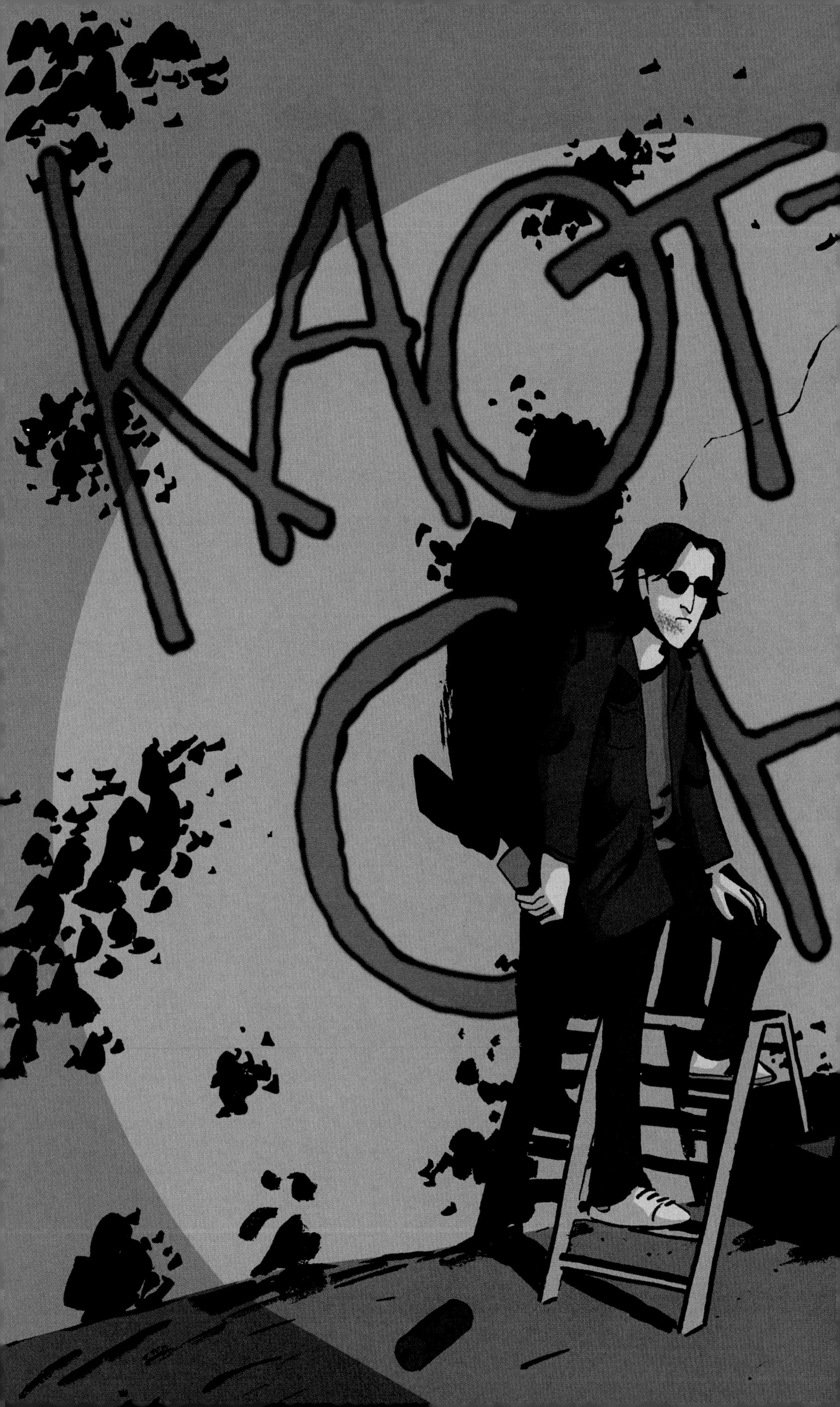

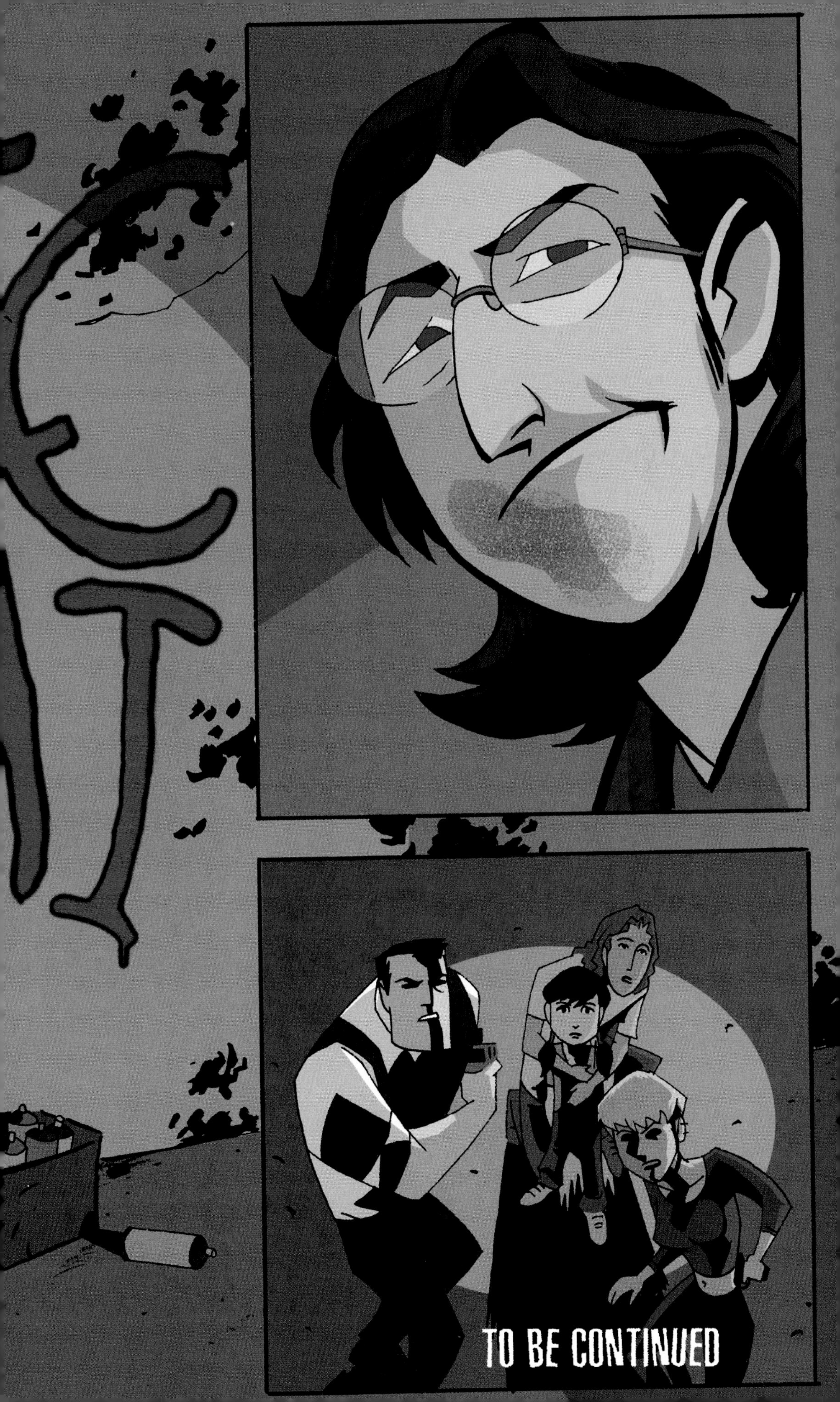
TO BE CONTINUED

AM I ON?
WELL, HOW LONG
WILL IT--?
HELLO??

OH MY! AHEM--
THIS IS COLLETTE
MCDANIEL. IT WAS
RIGHT HERE, ON THE
SOUTH SIDE OF THE
POLICE DEPARTMENT
ENTRANCE AT THE
THE DOWNTOWN
JUSTICE CENTER

THAT--
JUST MOMENTS
AGO--DETECTIVE
CHRISTIAN WALKER
AND RELATIVE
NEWCOMER TO
THE HOMICIDE
DEPARTMENT
DETECTIVE
DEENA PILGRIM
BROUGHT AN
UNKNOWN
MAN INTO
CUSTODY

HE MAN WAS
APPREHENDED
WHILE DEFACING
POLICE PROPERTY
WITH THIS GRAFFITI,
JUST A FEW FEET
AND AROUND THE
CORNER FROM THE
VERITABLE THRONG
OF MEDIA THAT
HAS BEEN CAMPED
OUT HERE SINCE
THIS TRAGEDY
BEGAN.

IF ANYONE AT
ALL KNOWS
ANYTHING ABOUT
THIS--

KAOTIC CHIC--
THIS ODD GRAFFITI
MATCHES THE GRAFFITI
FOUND AT THE *RETRO
GIRL* CRIME SCENE. IT
WAS RIGHT HERE ON
LIVE AT FIVE
EARLIER TODAY, THAT
DETECTIVE WALKER
PLEADED WITH OUR
VIEWERSHIP FOR
INFORMATION RELATED
TO THE CRYPTIC
MESSAGE.

OUR CAMERAS
CAUGHT ONLY A
GLIMPSE OF THE
MAN. THERE HAS
BEEN NO WORD AS
YET TO THE IDENTITY
OF THE MAN OR IF
HE HAS IN FACT
BEEN CHARGED IN
THE RETRO GIRL
MURDER.

WE WILL STAY
ON THE AIR
WITH ROUND-THE-
CLOCK COVERAGE
UNTIL THE BLUE CODE
OF SILENCE LIFTS
HERE AT POLICE
HEADQUARTERS.

WE CAN ONLY
WAIT AND HOPE
THAT THIS
HORRIBLE
TRAGEDY
IS NEAR
AN END.

BACK TO
YOU IN THE
STUDIO.

THANK YOU
COLLETTE.

FOR THOSE JUST
JOINING US, THIS IS
DAY TWO IN OUR
WALL-TO-WALL
LIVE COVERAGE OF...
*THE MURDER OF
RETRO GIRL*

WE'LL BE RIGHT BACK
AFTER THIS STATION
IDENTIFICATION.

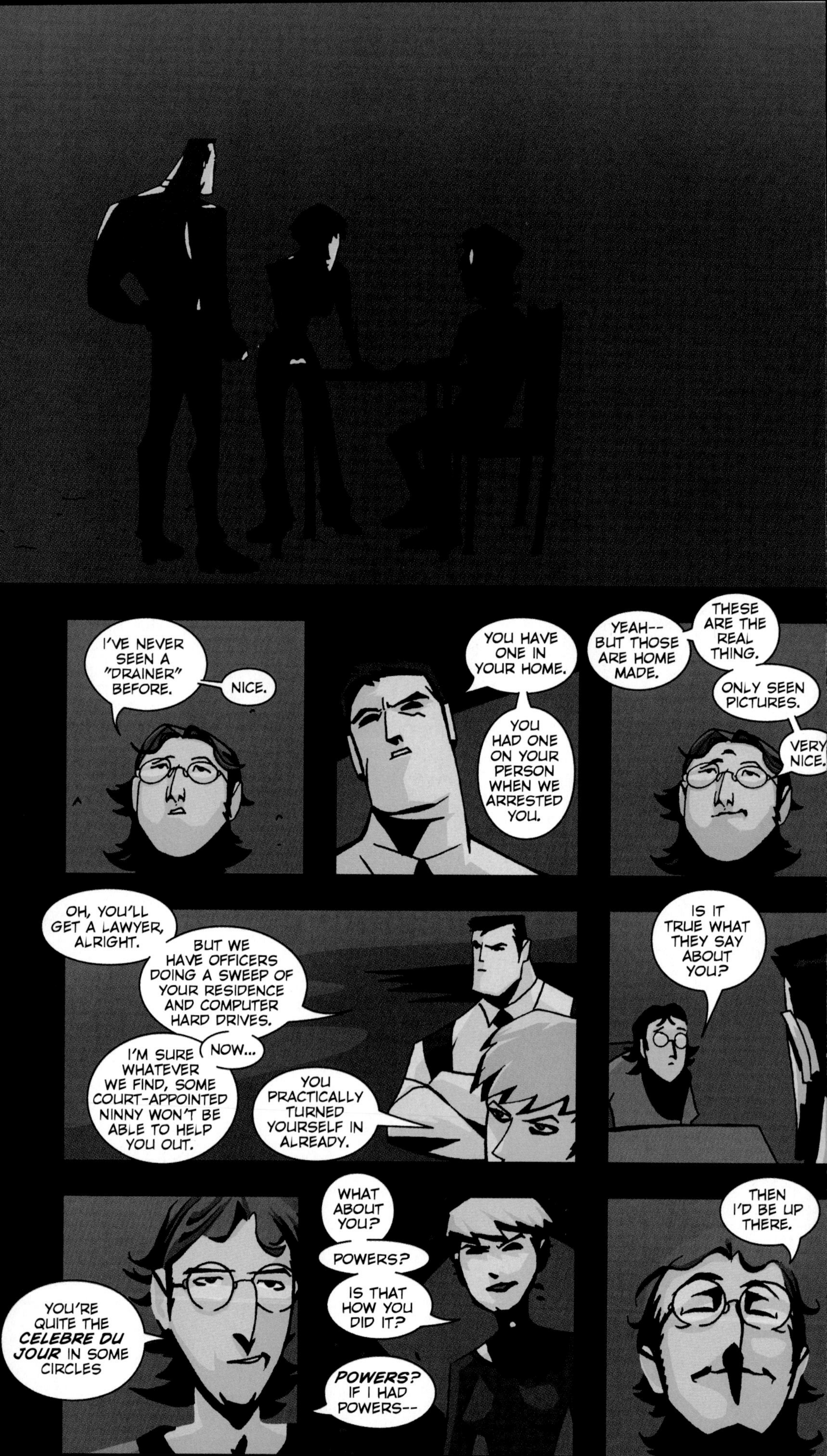
I'VE NEVER SEEN A "DRAINER" BEFORE.
NICE.
YOU HAVE ONE IN YOUR HOME.
YOU HAD ONE ON YOUR PERSON WHEN WE ARRESTED YOU.
YEAH-- BUT THOSE ARE HOME MADE.
THESE ARE THE REAL THING.
ONLY SEEN PICTURES.
VERY NICE.
OH, YOU'LL GET A LAWYER, ALRIGHT.
BUT WE HAVE OFFICERS DOING A SWEEP OF YOUR RESIDENCE AND COMPUTER HARD DRIVES.
I'M SURE WHATEVER WE FIND, SOME COURT-APPOINTED NINNY WON'T BE ABLE TO HELP YOU OUT.
NOW...
YOU PRACTICALLY TURNED YOURSELF IN ALREADY.
IS IT TRUE WHAT THEY SAY ABOUT YOU?
YOU'RE QUITE THE ***CELEBRE DU JOUR*** IN SOME CIRCLES
WHAT ABOUT YOU?
POWERS?
IS THAT HOW YOU DID IT?
POWERS? IF I HAD POWERS--
THEN I'D BE UP THERE.

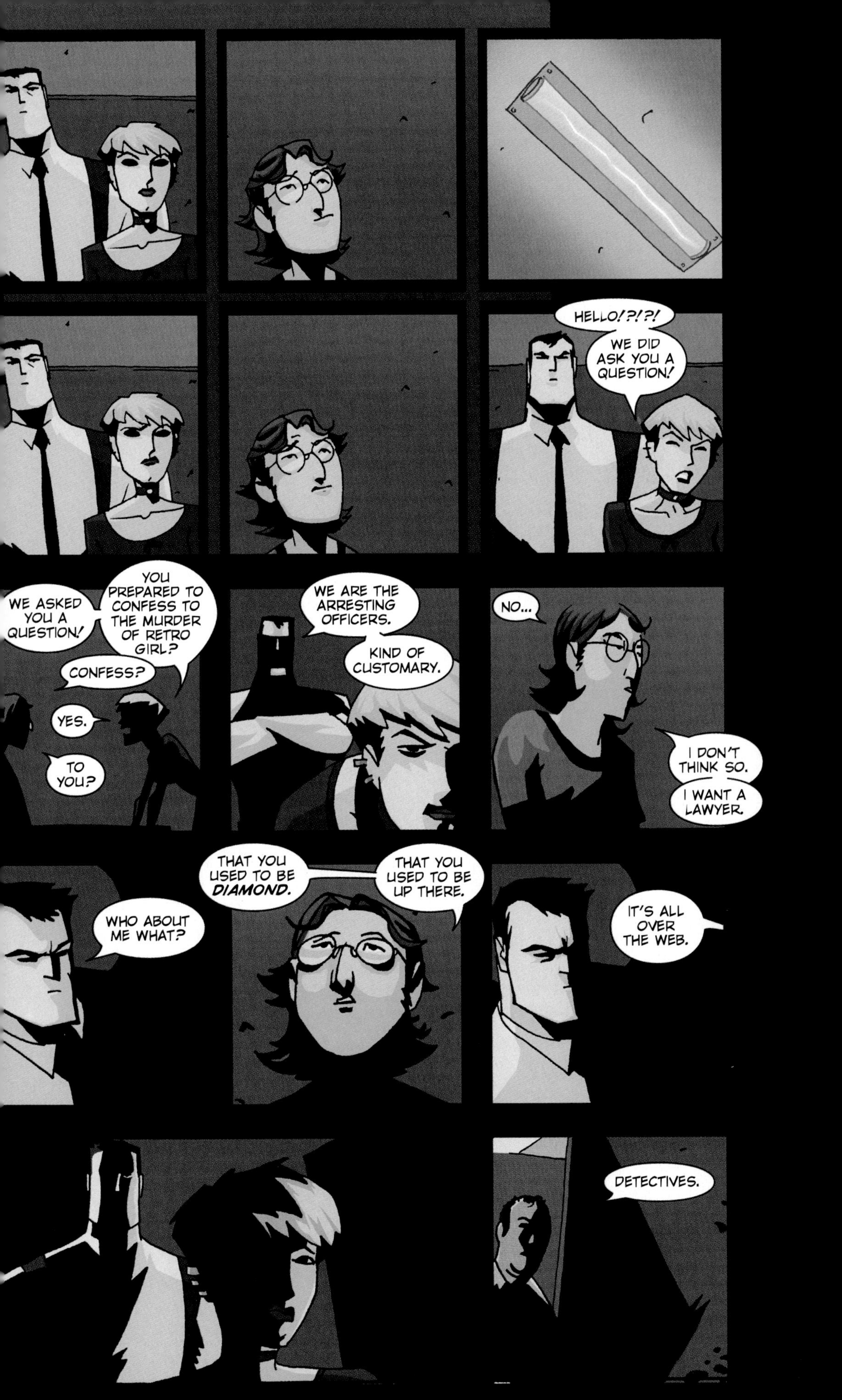
HELLO!?!?!
WE DID ASK YOU A QUESTION!
WE ASKED YOU A QUESTION!
YOU PREPARED TO CONFESS TO THE MURDER OF RETRO GIRL?
CONFESS?
YES.
TO YOU?
WE ARE THE ARRESTING OFFICERS.
KIND OF CUSTOMARY.
NO...
I DON'T THINK SO.
I WANT A LAWYER.
WHO ABOUT ME WHAT?
THAT YOU USED TO BE *DIAMOND.*
THAT YOU USED TO BE UP THERE.
IT'S ALL OVER THE WEB.
DETECTIVES.

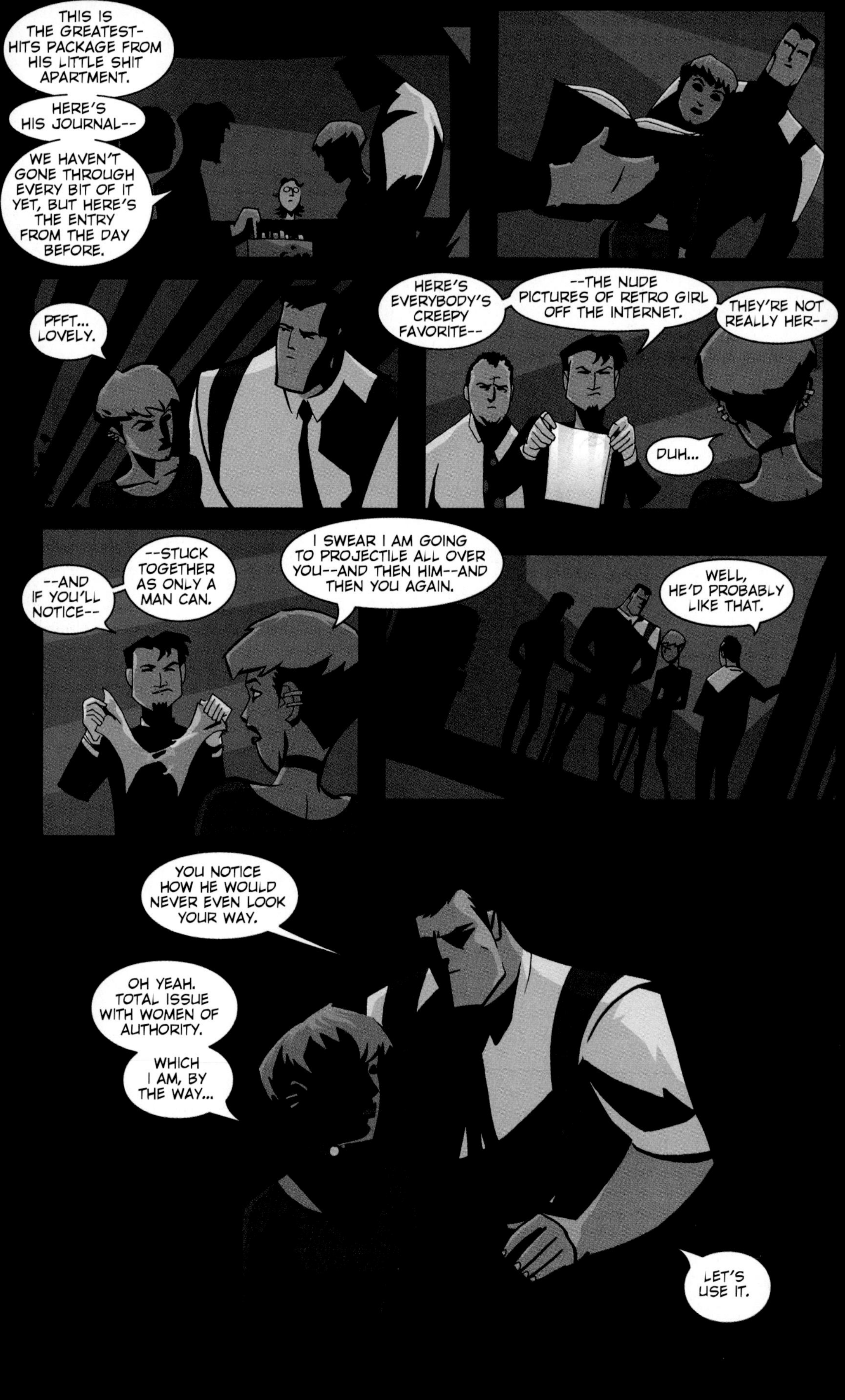
THIS IS THE GREATEST-HITS PACKAGE FROM HIS LITTLE SHIT APARTMENT.
HERE'S HIS JOURNAL--
WE HAVEN'T GONE THROUGH EVERY BIT OF IT YET, BUT HERE'S THE ENTRY FROM THE DAY BEFORE.
PFFT... LOVELY.
HERE'S EVERYBODY'S CREEPY FAVORITE--
--THE NUDE PICTURES OF RETRO GIRL OFF THE INTERNET.
THEY'RE NOT REALLY HER--
DUH...
--AND IF YOU'LL NOTICE--
--STUCK TOGETHER AS ONLY A MAN CAN.
I SWEAR I AM GOING TO PROJECTILE ALL OVER YOU--AND THEN HIM--AND THEN YOU AGAIN.
WELL, HE'D PROBABLY LIKE THAT.
YOU NOTICE HOW HE WOULD NEVER EVEN LOOK YOUR WAY.
OH YEAH. TOTAL ISSUE WITH WOMEN OF AUTHORITY.
WHICH I AM, BY THE WAY...
LET'S USE IT.

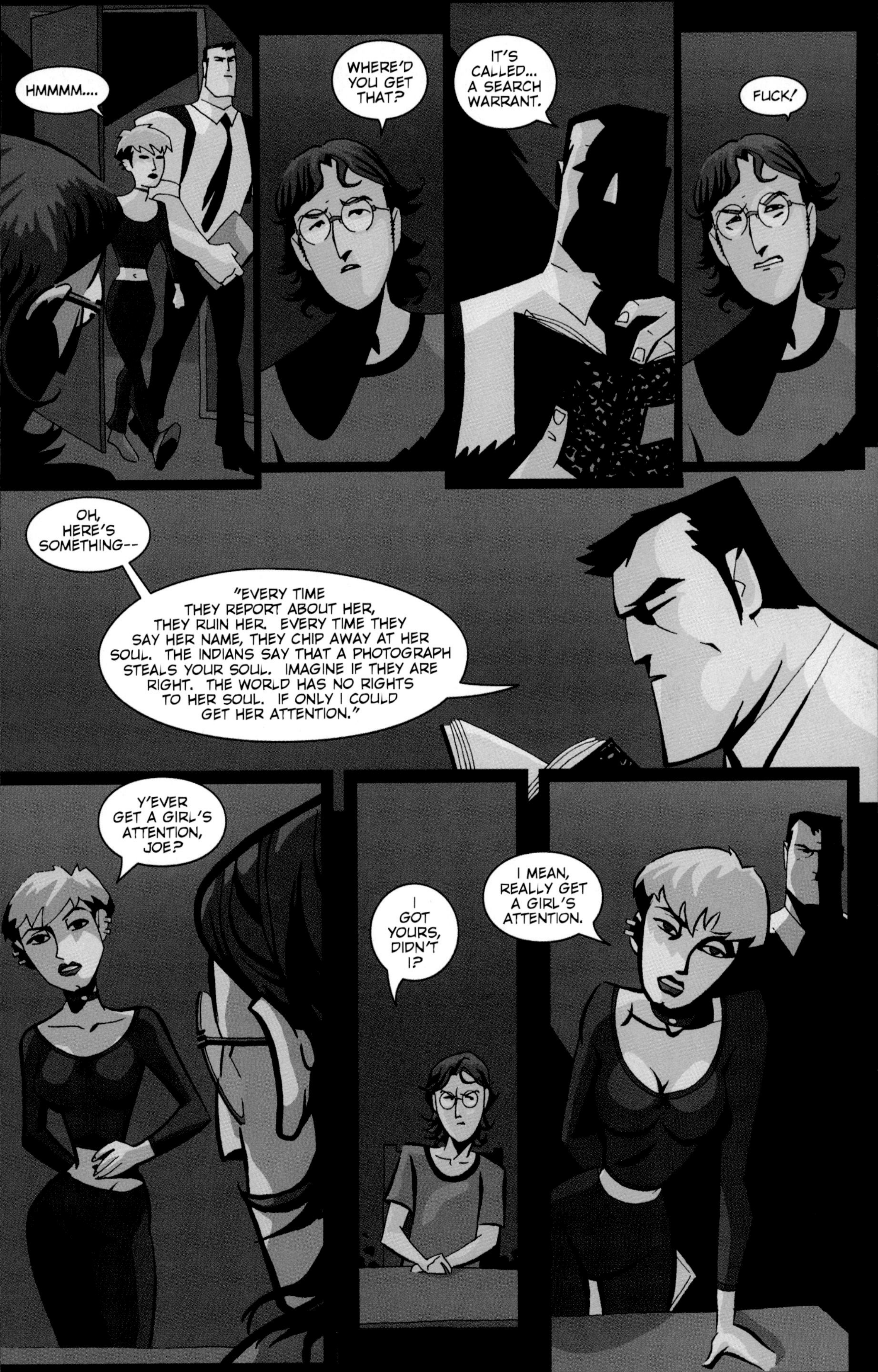
HMMMM....
WHERE'D YOU GET THAT?
IT'S CALLED... A SEARCH WARRANT.
FUCK!
OH, HERE'S SOMETHING--
"EVERY TIME THEY REPORT ABOUT HER, THEY RUIN HER. EVERY TIME THEY SAY HER NAME, THEY CHIP AWAY AT HER SOUL. THE INDIANS SAY THAT A PHOTOGRAPH STEALS YOUR SOUL. IMAGINE IF THEY ARE RIGHT. THE WORLD HAS NO RIGHTS TO HER SOUL. IF ONLY I COULD GET HER ATTENTION."
Y'EVER GET A GIRL'S ATTENTION, JOE?
I GOT YOURS, DIDN'T I?
I MEAN, REALLY GET A GIRL'S ATTENTION.

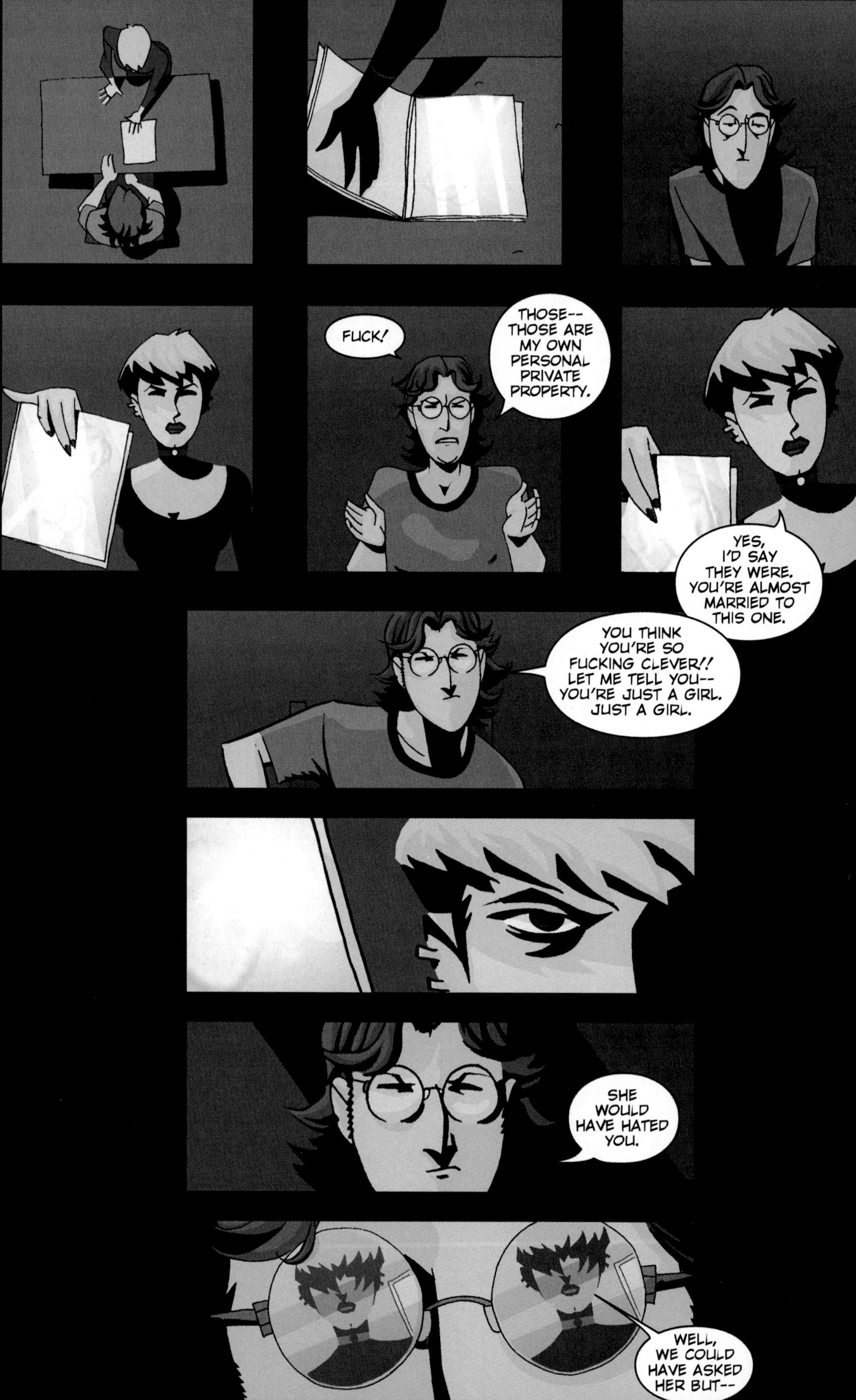
FUCK!
THOSE-- THOSE ARE MY OWN PERSONAL PRIVATE PROPERTY.
YES, I'D SAY THEY WERE. YOU'RE ALMOST MARRIED TO THIS ONE.
YOU THINK YOU'RE SO FUCKING CLEVER!! LET ME TELL YOU-- YOU'RE JUST A GIRL. JUST A GIRL.
SHE WOULD HAVE HATED YOU.
WELL, WE COULD HAVE ASKED HER BUT--

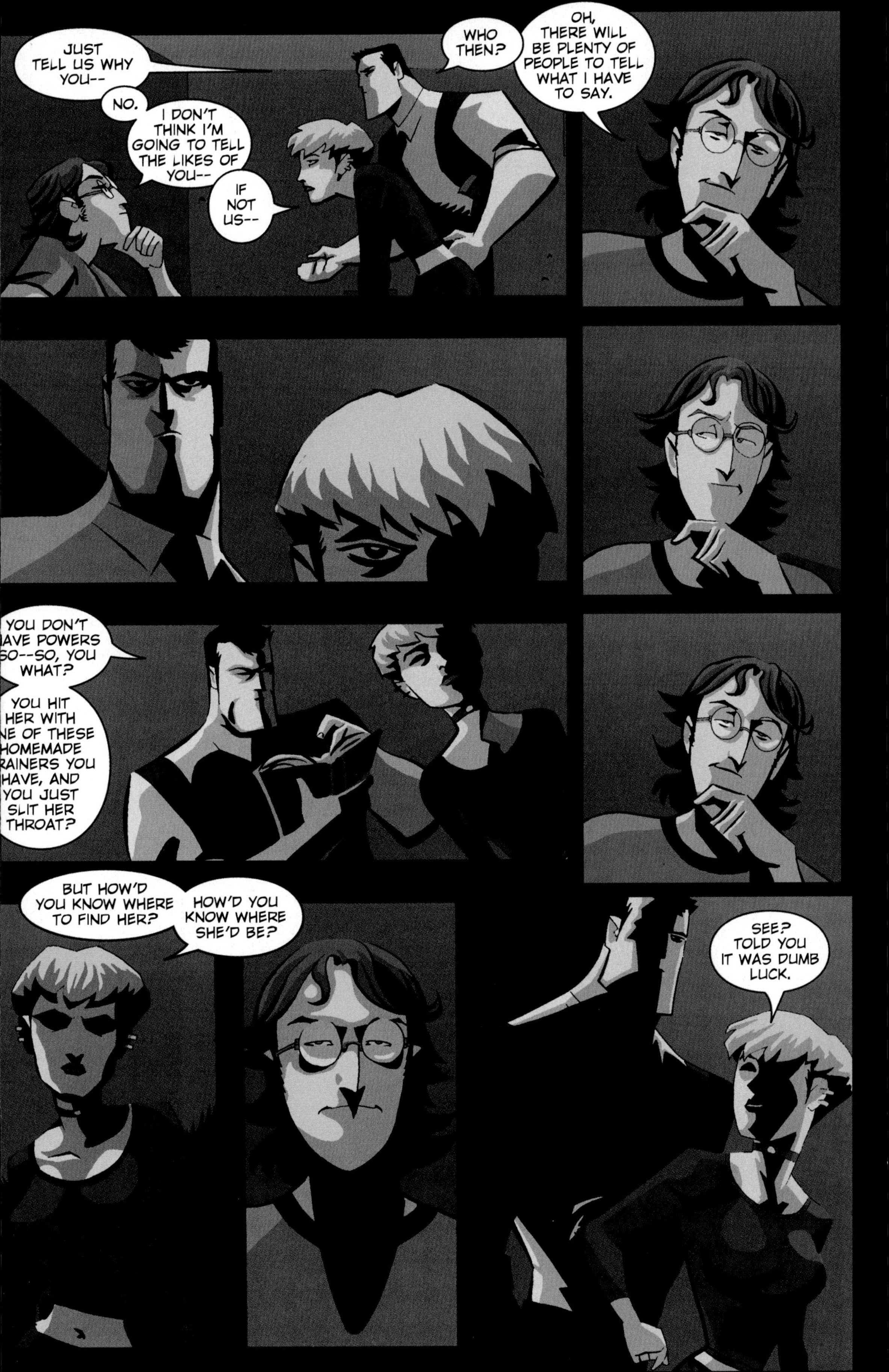
JUST TELL US WHY YOU--
NO.
I DON'T THINK I'M GOING TO TELL THE LIKES OF YOU--
IF NOT US--
WHO THEN?
OH, THERE WILL BE PLENTY OF PEOPLE TO TELL WHAT I HAVE TO SAY.
YOU DON'T AVE POWERS O--SO, YOU WHAT?
YOU HIT HER WITH E OF THESE OMEMADE AINERS YOU HAVE, AND YOU JUST SLIT HER THROAT?
BUT HOW'D YOU KNOW WHERE TO FIND HER?
HOW'D YOU KNOW WHERE SHE'D BE?
SEE? TOLD YOU IT WAS DUMB LUCK.

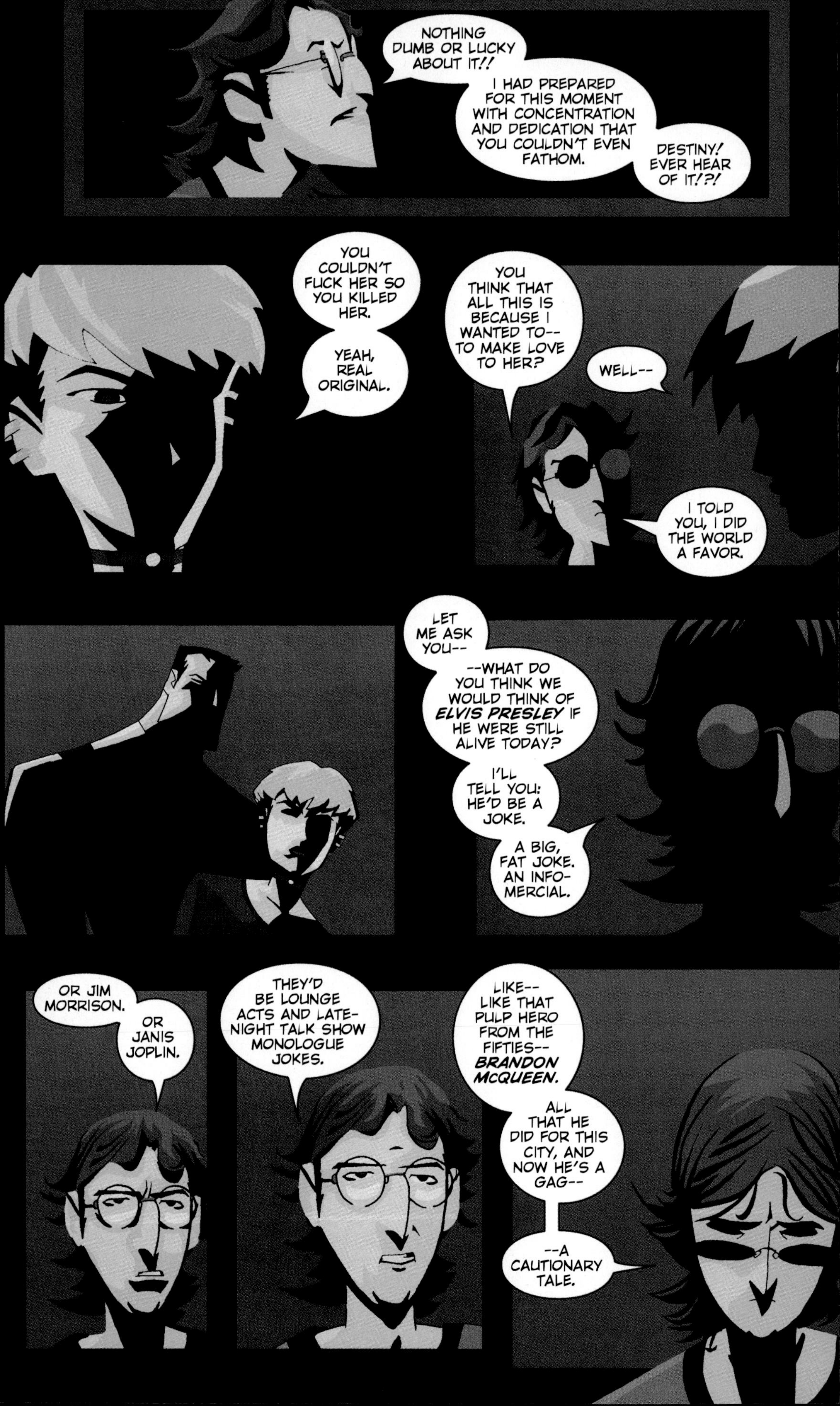
NOTHING DUMB OR LUCKY ABOUT IT!!
I HAD PREPARED FOR THIS MOMENT WITH CONCENTRATION AND DEDICATION THAT YOU COULDN'T EVEN FATHOM.
DESTINY! EVER HEAR OF IT!?!
YOU COULDN'T FUCK HER SO YOU KILLED HER.
YEAH, REAL ORIGINAL.
YOU THINK THAT ALL THIS IS BECAUSE I WANTED TO-- TO MAKE LOVE TO HER?
WELL--
I TOLD YOU, I DID THE WORLD A FAVOR.
LET ME ASK YOU--
--WHAT DO YOU THINK WE WOULD THINK OF ELVIS PRESLEY IF HE WERE STILL ALIVE TODAY?
I'LL TELL YOU: HE'D BE A JOKE.
A BIG, FAT JOKE. AN INFO-MERCIAL.
OR JIM MORRISON.
OR JANIS JOPLIN.
THEY'D BE LOUNGE ACTS AND LATE-NIGHT TALK SHOW MONOLOGUE JOKES.
LIKE-- LIKE THAT PULP HERO FROM THE FIFTIES-- BRANDON McQUEEN.
ALL THAT HE DID FOR THIS CITY, AND NOW HE'S A GAG--
--A CAUTIONARY TALE.

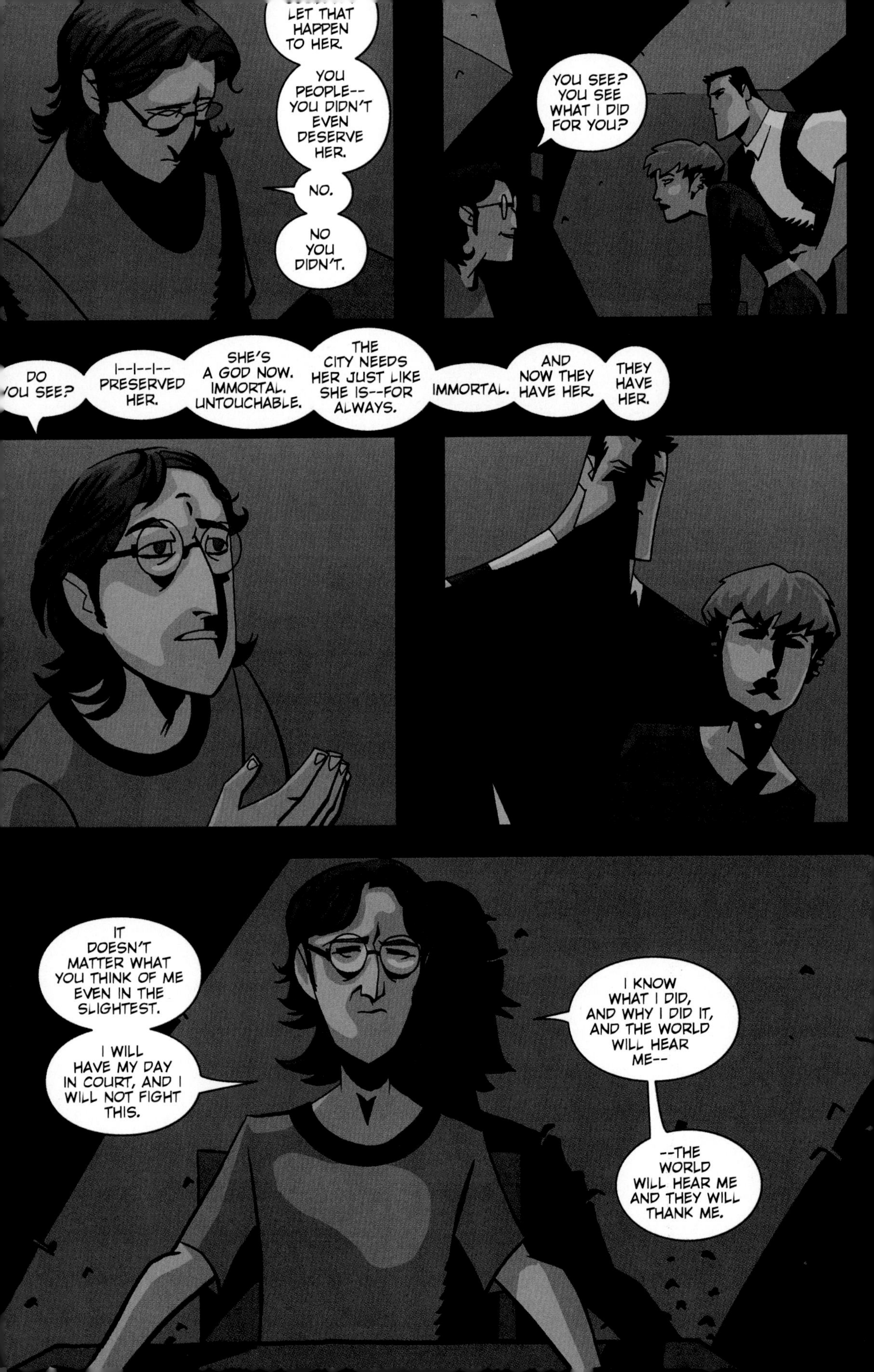
LET THAT HAPPEN TO HER.
YOU PEOPLE--YOU DIDN'T EVEN DESERVE HER.
NO.
NO YOU DIDN'T.
YOU SEE? YOU SEE WHAT I DID FOR YOU?
DO YOU SEE?
I--I--I--PRESERVED HER.
SHE'S A GOD NOW. IMMORTAL. UNTOUCHABLE.
THE CITY NEEDS HER JUST LIKE SHE IS--FOR ALWAYS.
IMMORTAL.
AND NOW THEY HAVE HER.
THEY HAVE HER.
IT DOESN'T MATTER WHAT YOU THINK OF ME EVEN IN THE SLIGHTEST.
I WILL HAVE MY DAY IN COURT, AND I WILL NOT FIGHT THIS.
I KNOW WHAT I DID, AND WHY I DID IT, AND THE WORLD WILL HEAR ME--
--THE WORLD WILL HEAR ME AND THEY WILL THANK ME.

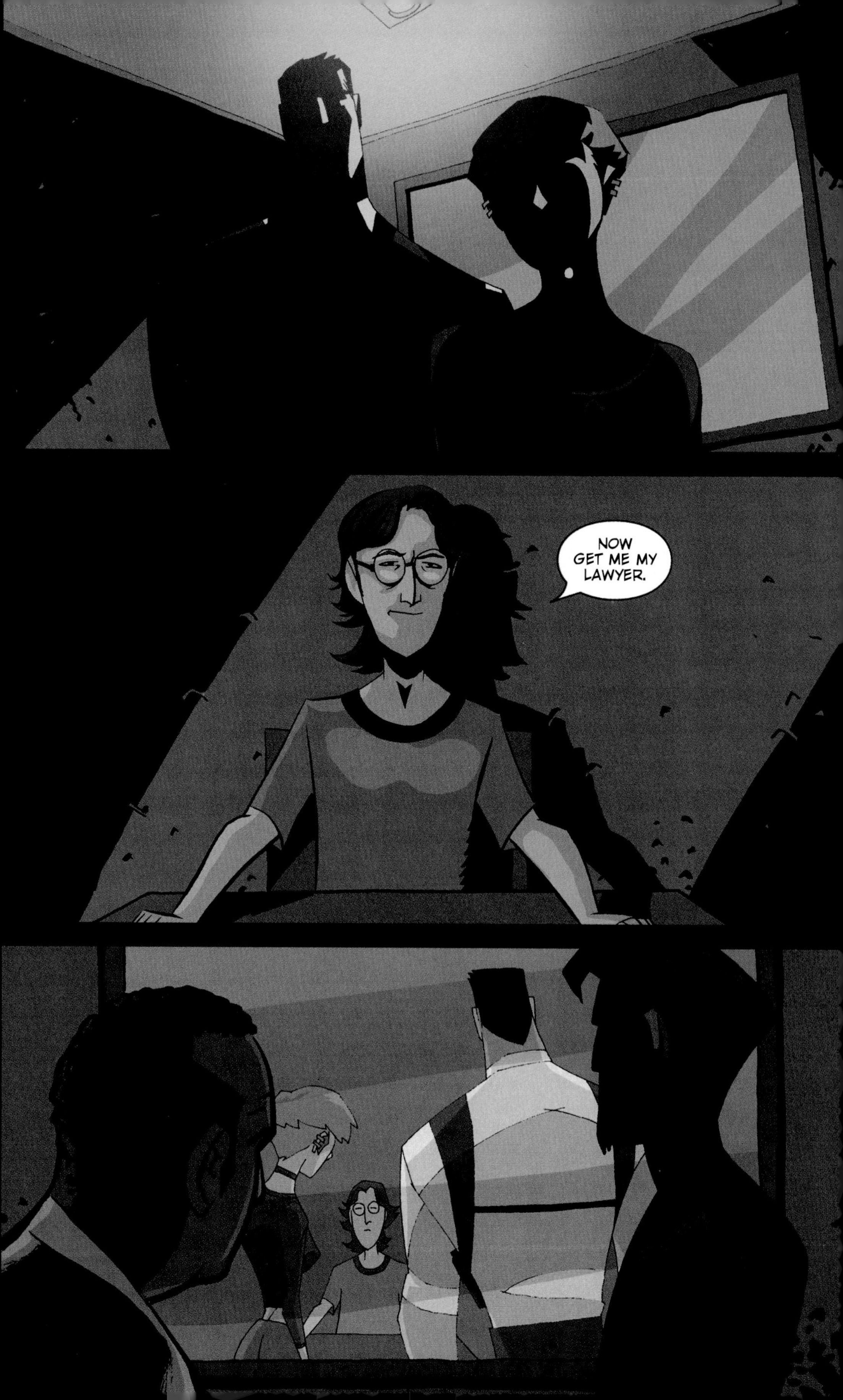
NOW GET ME MY LAWYER.

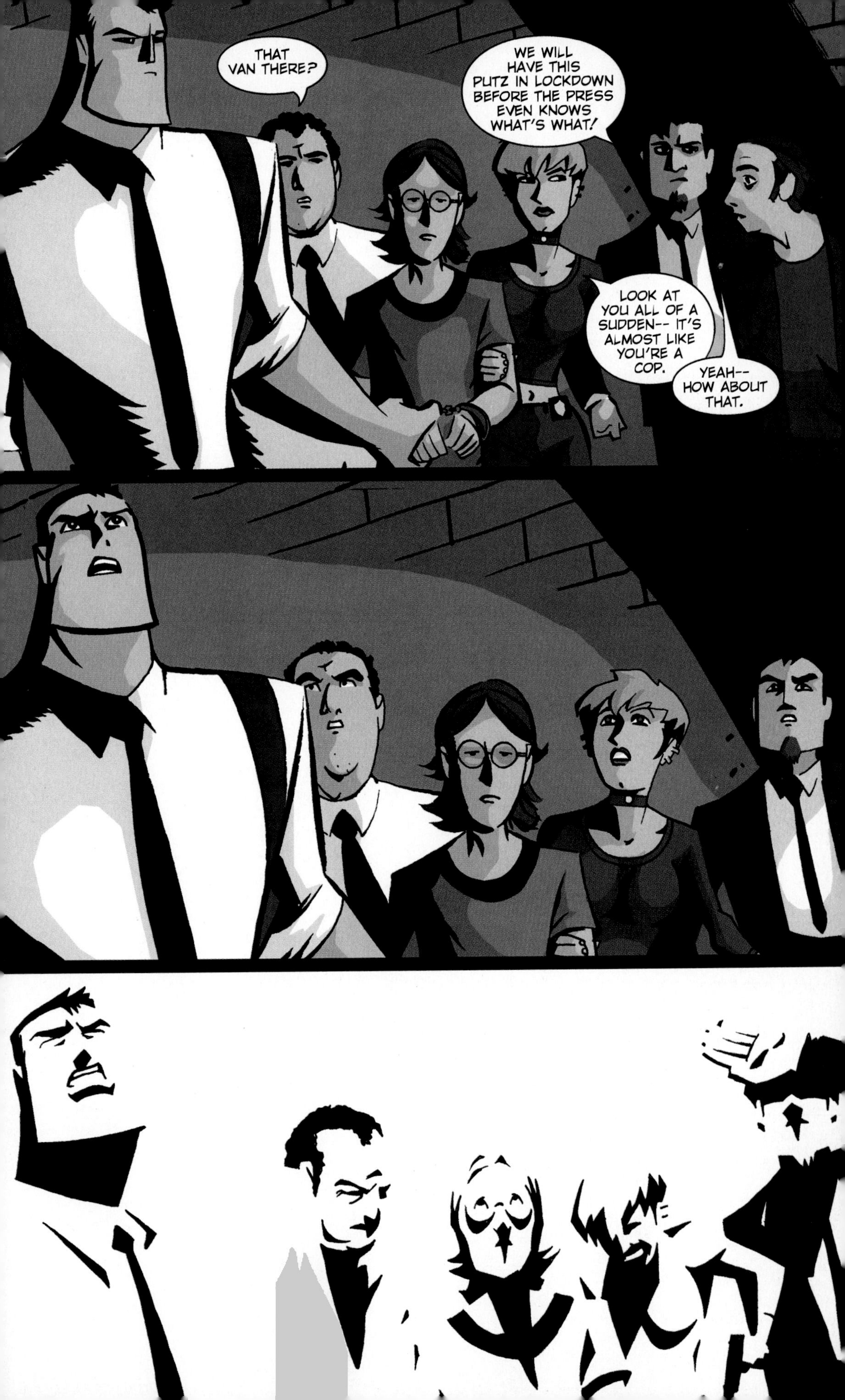
THAT VAN THERE?
WE WILL HAVE THIS PUTZ IN LOCKDOWN BEFORE THE PRESS EVEN KNOWS WHAT'S WHAT!
LOOK AT YOU ALL OF A SUDDEN-- IT'S ALMOST LIKE YOU'RE A COP.
YEAH-- HOW ABOUT THAT.

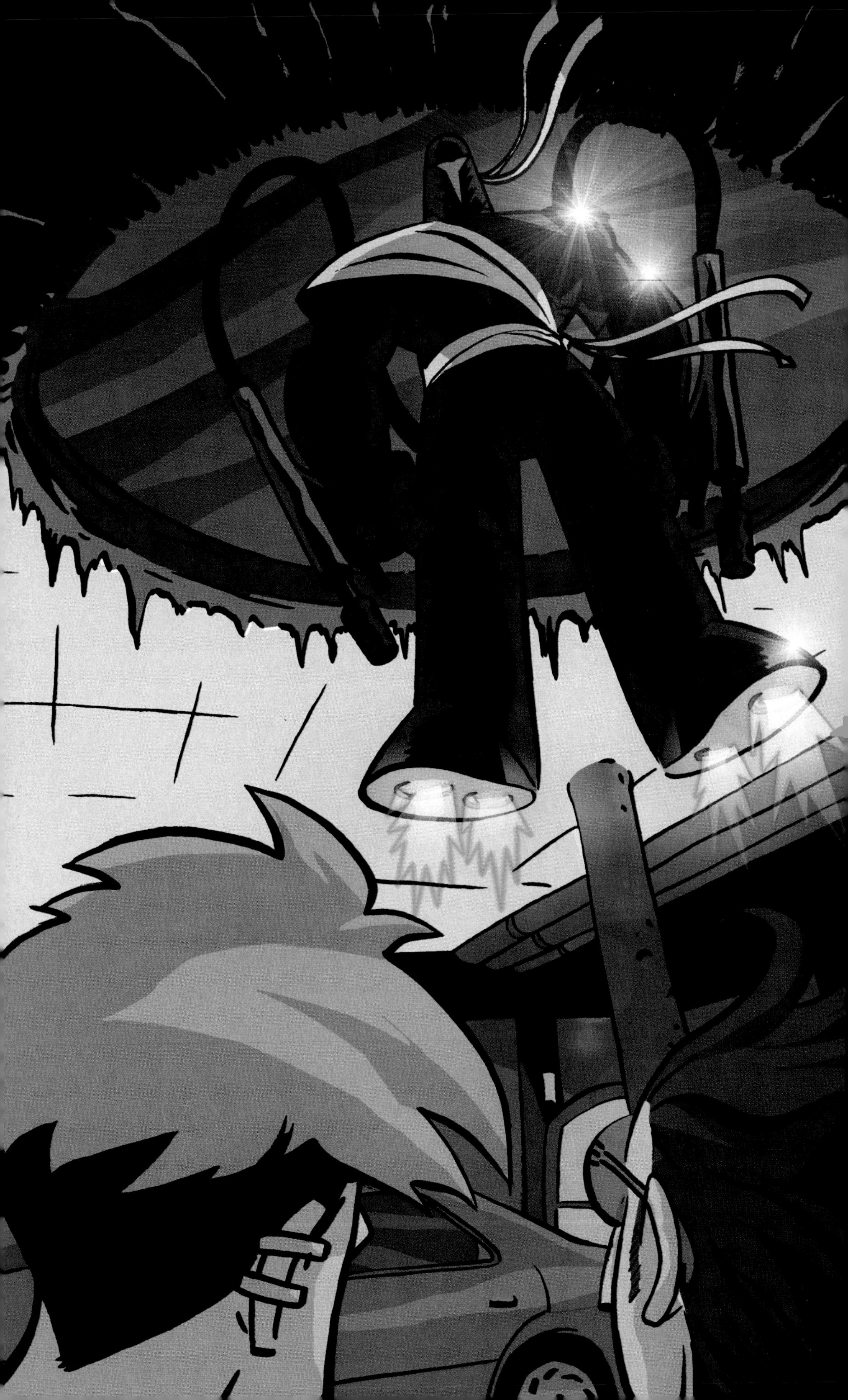

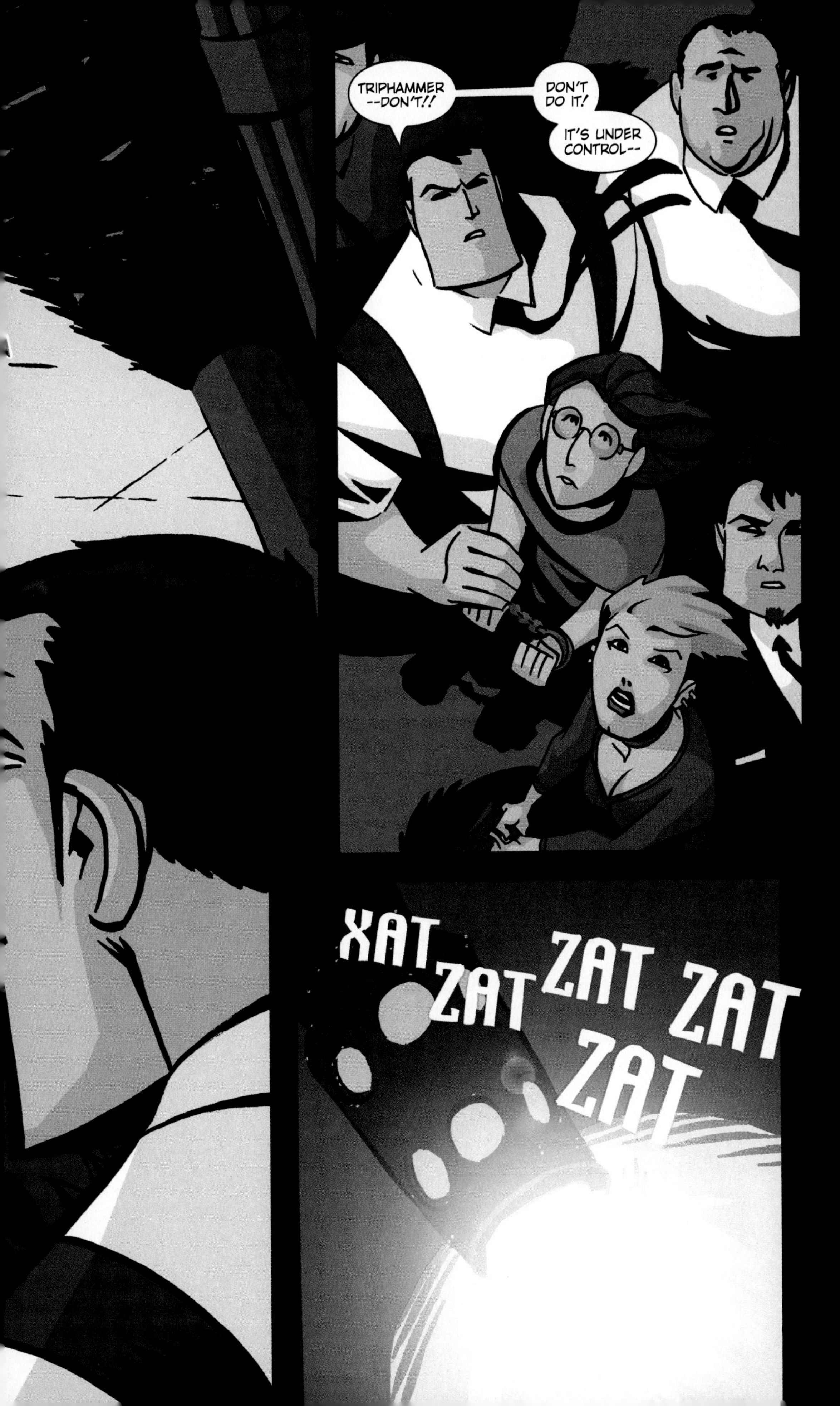
TRIPHAMMER
--DON'T!!
DON'T
DO IT!
IT'S UNDER
CONTROL--
XAT
ZAT
ZAT ZAT
ZAT

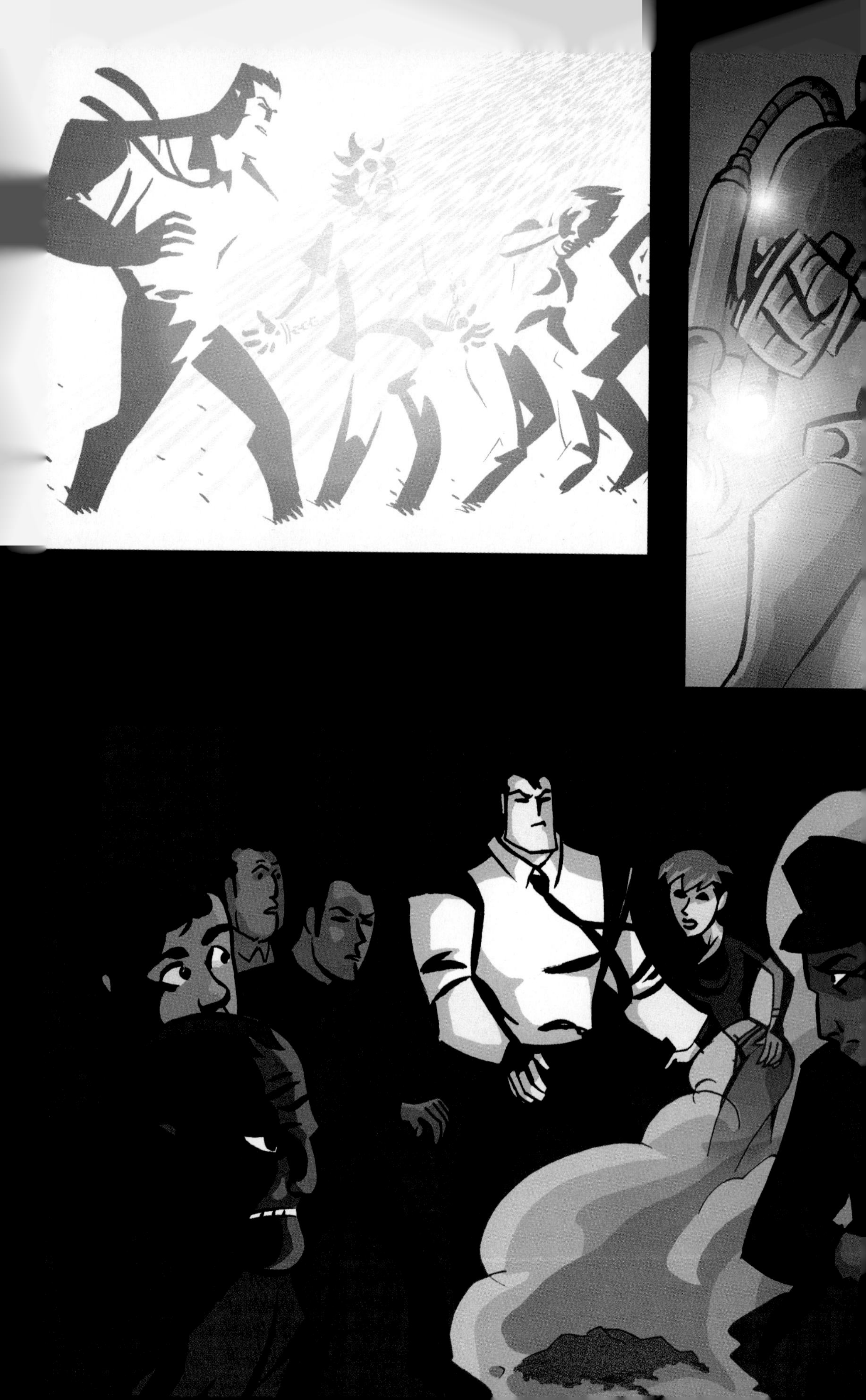

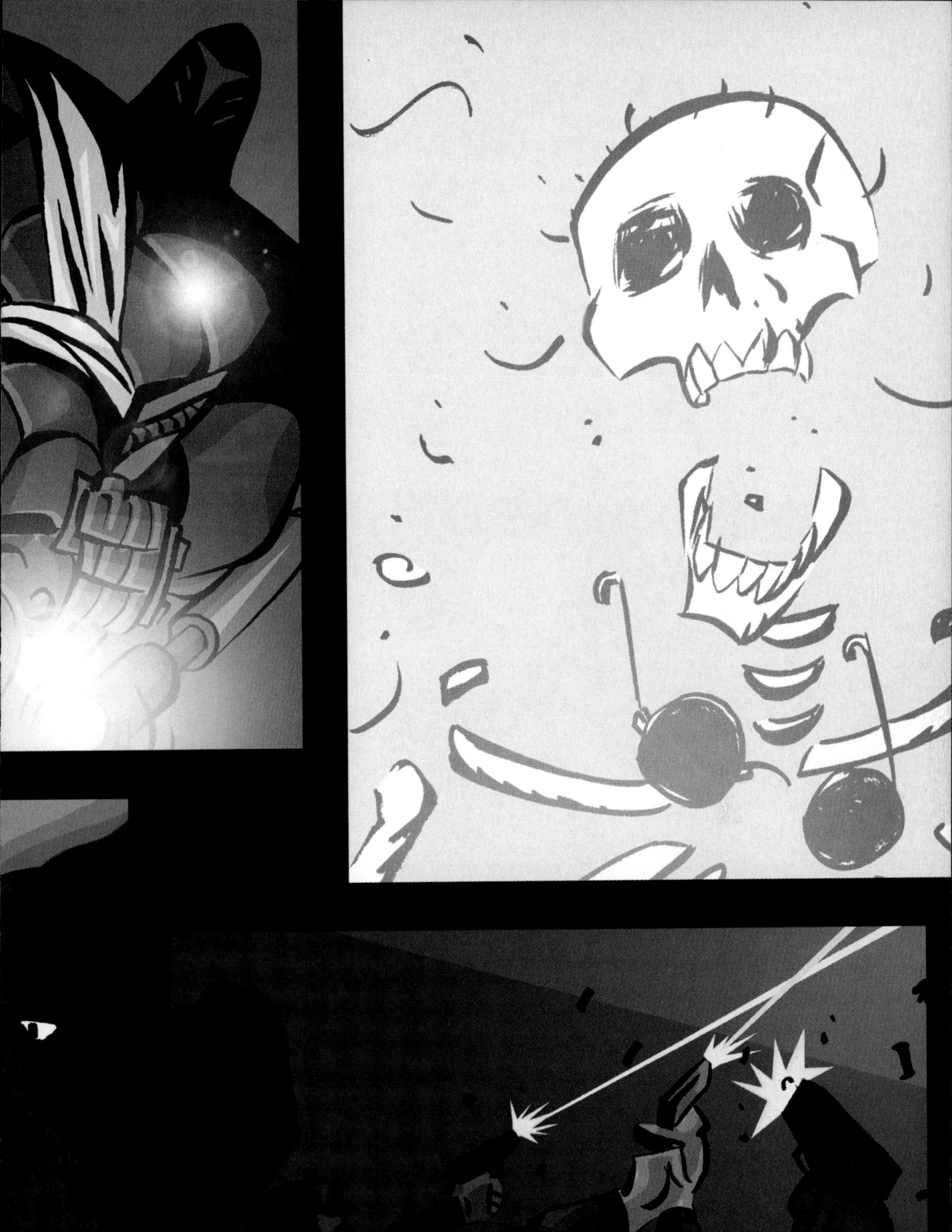

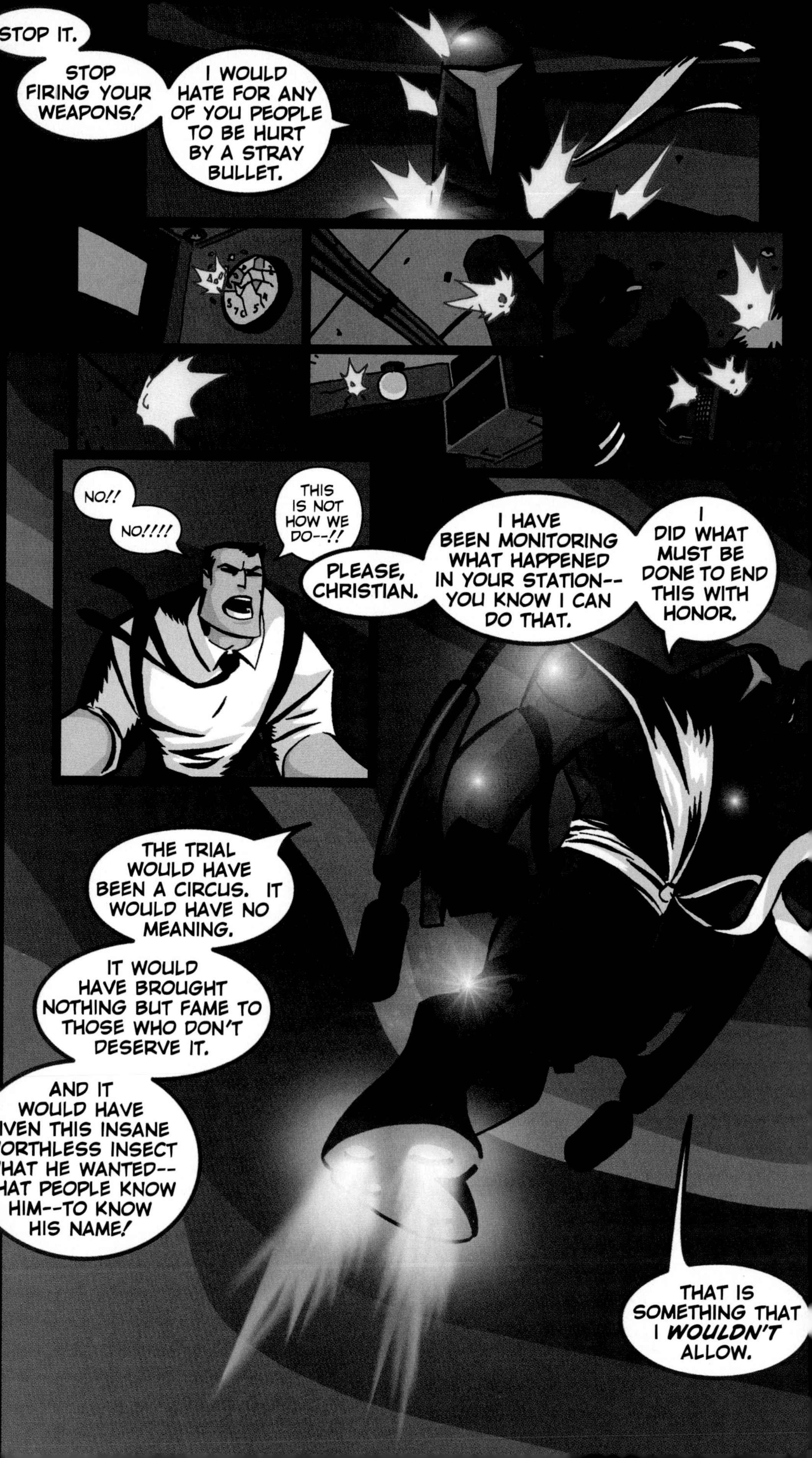
STOP IT.
STOP FIRING YOUR WEAPONS!
I WOULD HATE FOR ANY OF YOU PEOPLE TO BE HURT BY A STRAY BULLET.
NO!!
NO!!!!
THIS IS NOT HOW WE DO--!!
PLEASE, CHRISTIAN.
I HAVE BEEN MONITORING WHAT HAPPENED IN YOUR STATION-- YOU KNOW I CAN DO THAT.
I DID WHAT MUST BE DONE TO END THIS WITH HONOR.
THE TRIAL WOULD HAVE BEEN A CIRCUS. IT WOULD HAVE NO MEANING.
IT WOULD HAVE BROUGHT NOTHING BUT FAME TO THOSE WHO DON'T DESERVE IT.
AND IT WOULD HAVE GIVEN THIS INSANE WORTHLESS INSECT WHAT HE WANTED-- THAT PEOPLE KNOW HIM--TO KNOW HIS NAME!
THAT IS SOMETHING THAT I *WOULDN'T* ALLOW.

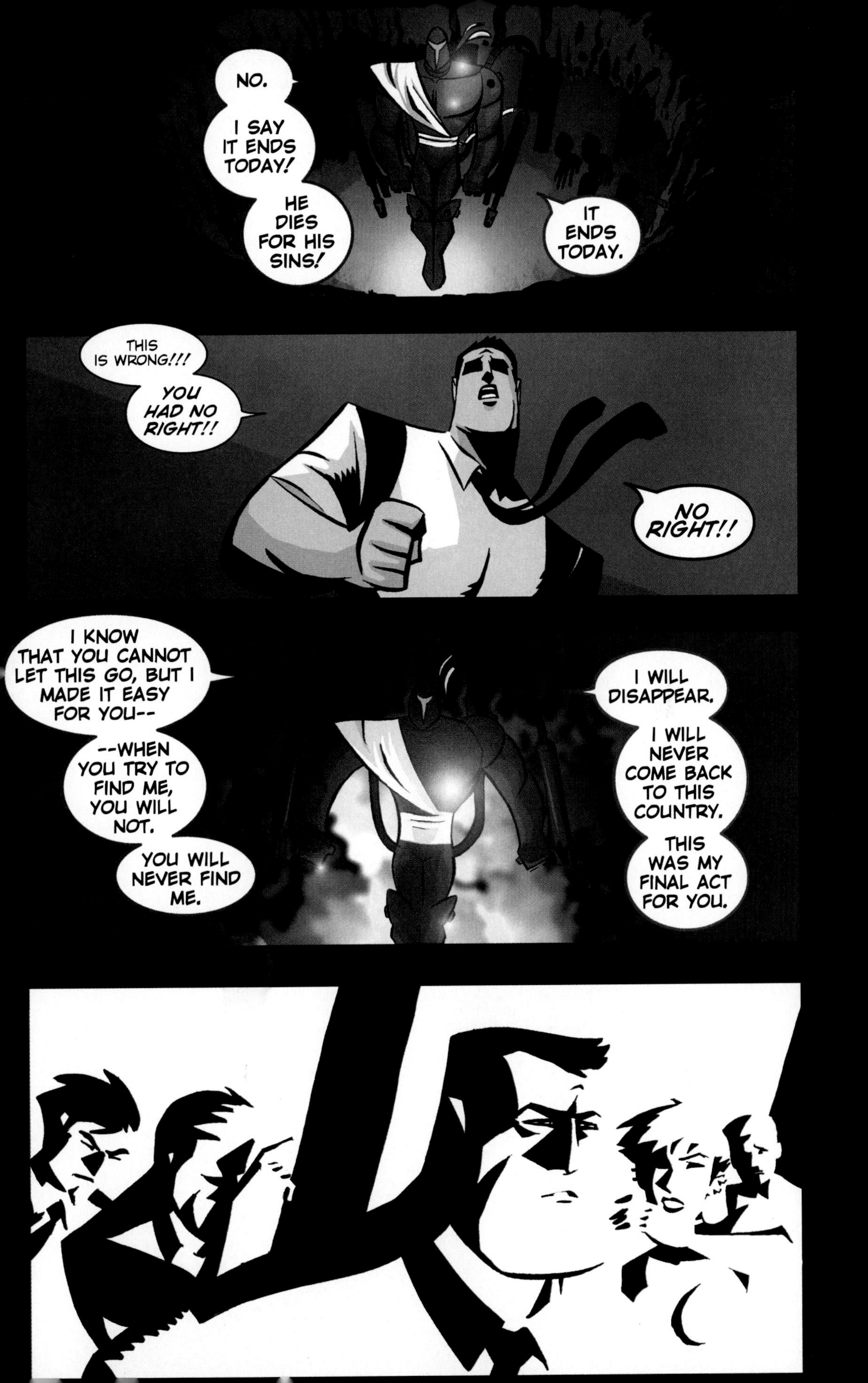
NO.
I SAY IT ENDS TODAY!
HE DIES FOR HIS SINS!
IT ENDS TODAY.
THIS IS WRONG!!!
YOU HAD NO RIGHT!!
NO RIGHT!!
I KNOW THAT YOU CANNOT LET THIS GO, BUT I MADE IT EASY FOR YOU--
--WHEN YOU TRY TO FIND ME, YOU WILL NOT.
YOU WILL NEVER FIND ME.
I WILL DISAPPEAR.
I WILL NEVER COME BACK TO THIS COUNTRY.
THIS WAS MY FINAL ACT FOR YOU.

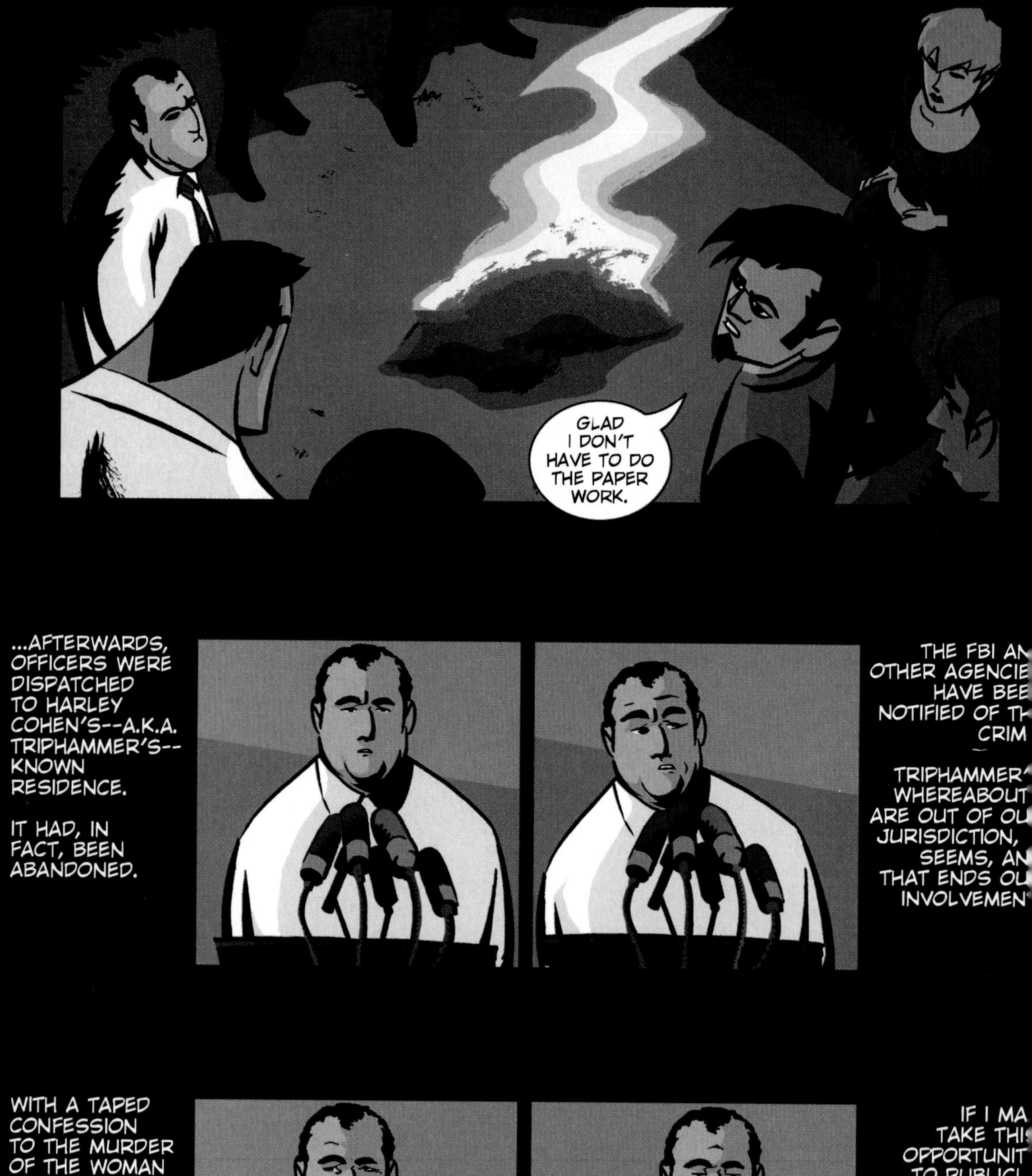
GLAD I DON'T HAVE TO DO THE PAPER WORK.
...AFTERWARDS, OFFICERS WERE DISPATCHED TO HARLEY COHEN'S--A.K.A. TRIPHAMMER'S--KNOWN RESIDENCE.
IT HAD, IN FACT, BEEN ABANDONED.
THE FBI AN OTHER AGENCIE HAVE BEE NOTIFIED OF TH CRIM
TRIPHAMMER' WHEREABOUT ARE OUT OF OU JURISDICTION, SEEMS, AN THAT ENDS OU INVOLVEMEN
WITH A TAPED CONFESSION TO THE MURDER OF THE WOMAN KNOWN AS RETRO GIRL BY JON JACKSON STEVENS, AND THE PHYSICAL EVIDENCE FOUND AT HIS RESIDENCE--WE CAN ANNOUNCE TO YOU, THE PEOPLE OF THE CITY, THAT THIS CASE IS CLOSED.
IF I MA TAKE THI OPPORTUNIT TO PUBLICL ACKNOWLEDG THE TIRELES EFFORTS O DETECTIVE CHRISTIA WALKE AND DEEN PILGRIM-

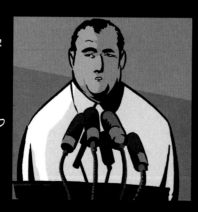

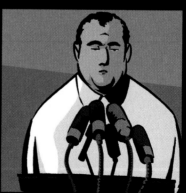

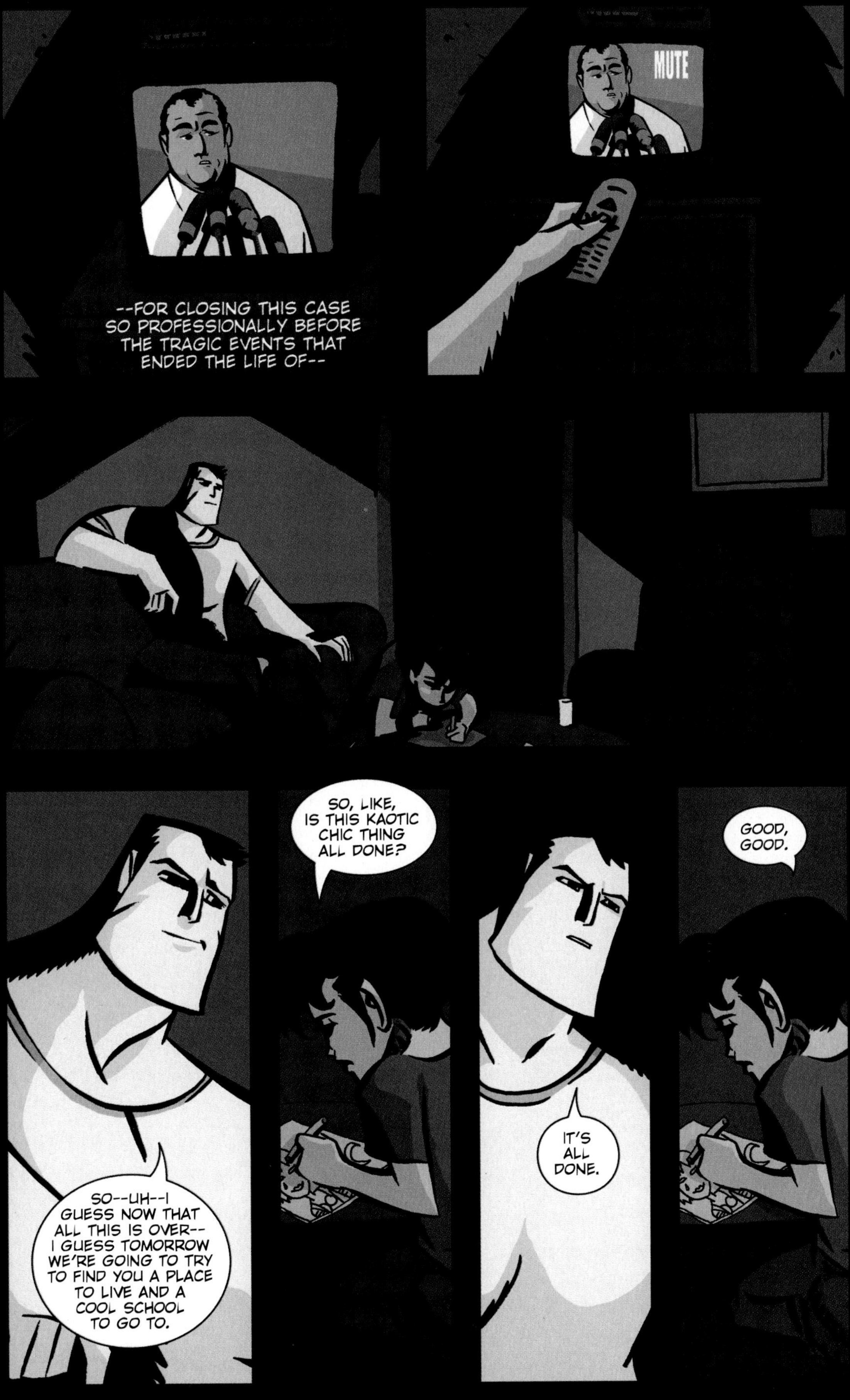
MUTE
--FOR CLOSING THIS CASE SO PROFESSIONALLY BEFORE THE TRAGIC EVENTS THAT ENDED THE LIFE OF--
SO--UH--I GUESS NOW THAT ALL THIS IS OVER-- I GUESS TOMORROW WE'RE GOING TO TRY TO FIND YOU A PLACE TO LIVE AND A COOL SCHOOL TO GO TO.
SO, LIKE, IS THIS KAOTIC CHIC THING ALL DONE?
IT'S ALL DONE.
GOOD, GOOD.

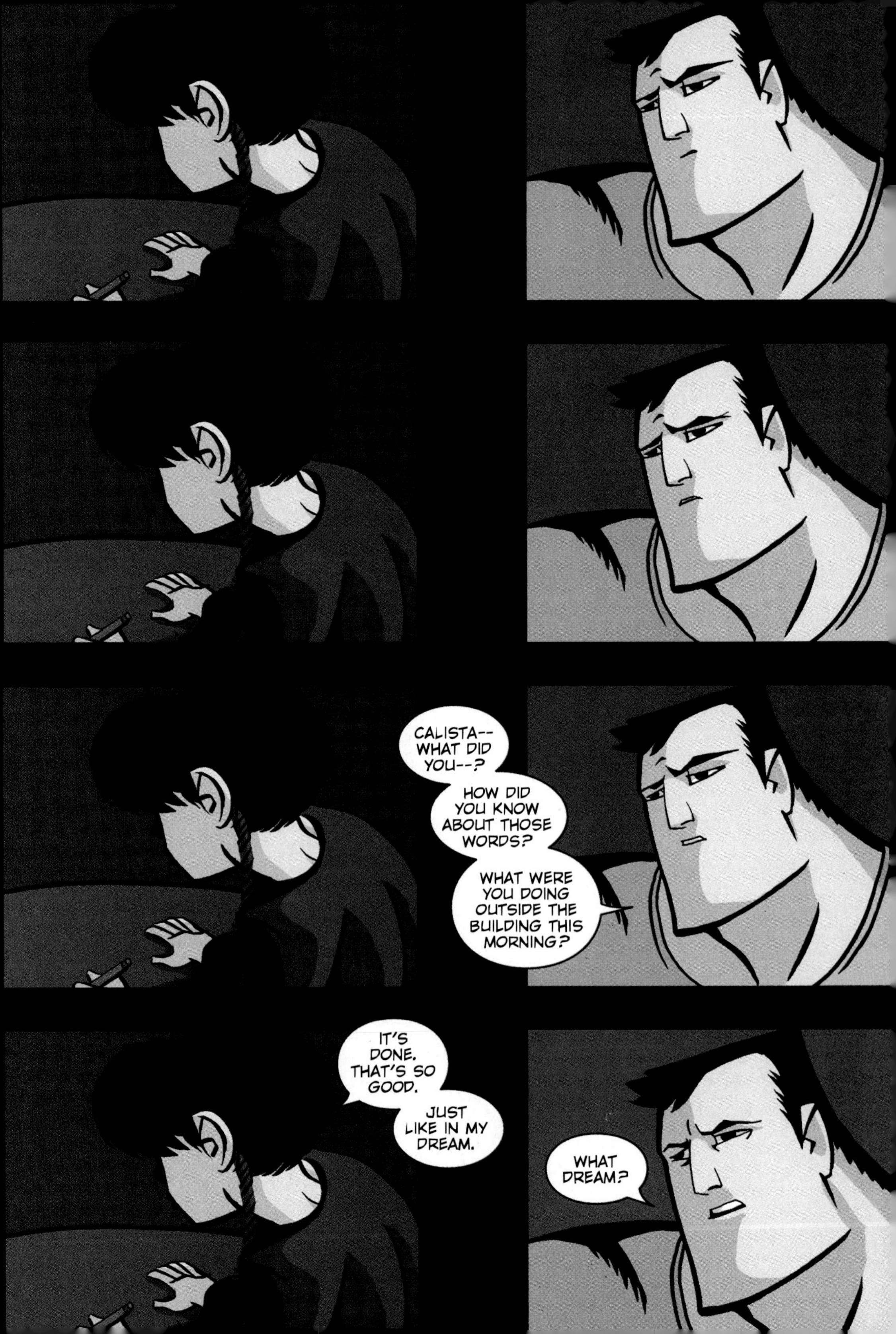
CALISTA-- WHAT DID YOU--?
HOW DID YOU KNOW ABOUT THOSE WORDS?
WHAT WERE YOU DOING OUTSIDE THE BUILDING THIS MORNING?
IT'S DONE. THAT'S SO GOOD.
JUST LIKE IN MY DREAM.
WHAT DREAM?

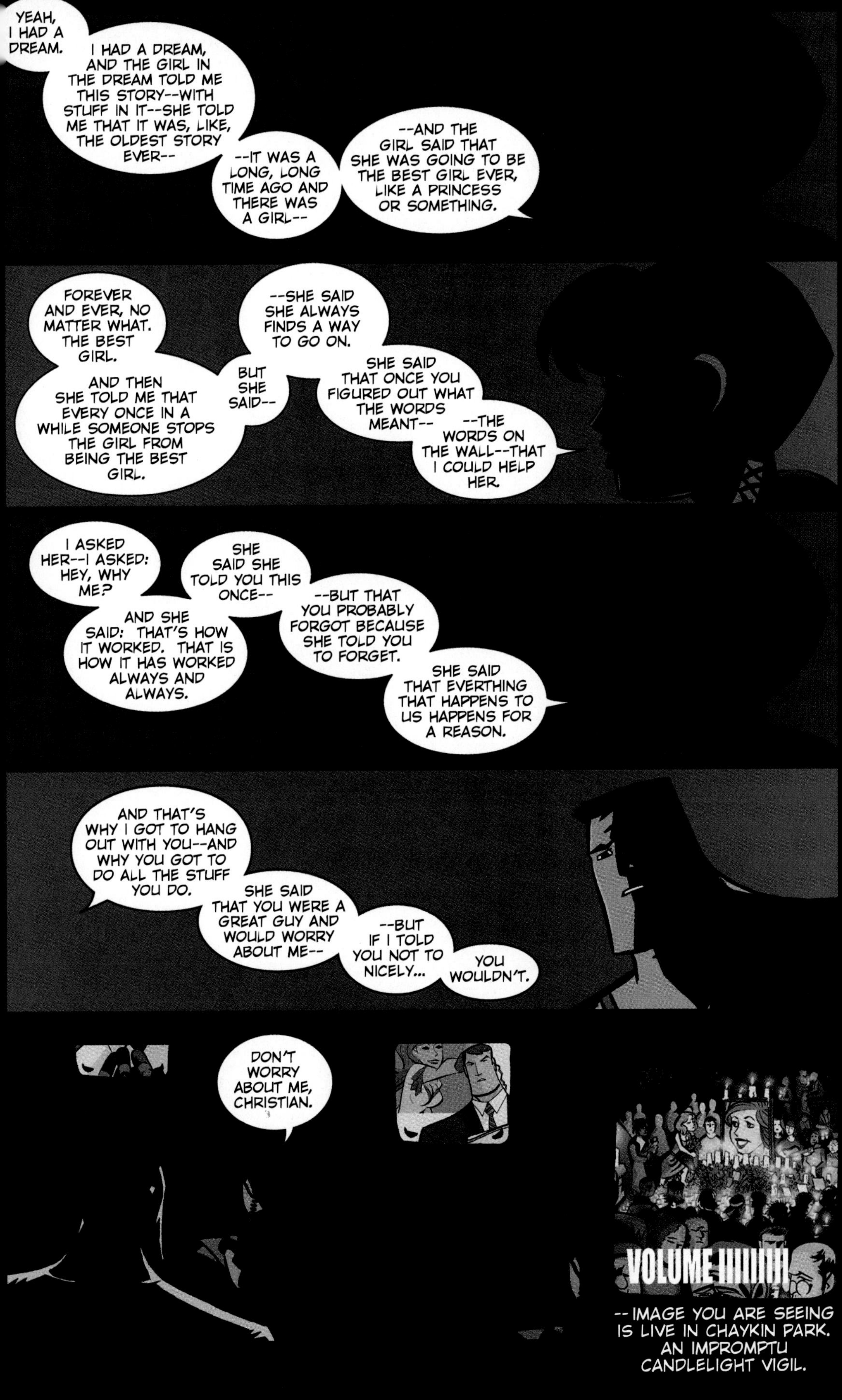
YEAH, I HAD A DREAM.
I HAD A DREAM, AND THE GIRL IN THE DREAM TOLD ME THIS STORY--WITH STUFF IN IT--SHE TOLD ME THAT IT WAS, LIKE, THE OLDEST STORY EVER--
--IT WAS A LONG, LONG TIME AGO AND THERE WAS A GIRL--
--AND THE GIRL SAID THAT SHE WAS GOING TO BE THE BEST GIRL EVER, LIKE A PRINCESS OR SOMETHING.
FOREVER AND EVER, NO MATTER WHAT. THE BEST GIRL.
AND THEN SHE TOLD ME THAT EVERY ONCE IN A WHILE SOMEONE STOPS THE GIRL FROM BEING THE BEST GIRL.
BUT SHE SAID--
--SHE SAID SHE ALWAYS FINDS A WAY TO GO ON.
SHE SAID THAT ONCE YOU FIGURED OUT WHAT THE WORDS MEANT--
--THE WORDS ON THE WALL--THAT I COULD HELP HER.
I ASKED HER--I ASKED: HEY, WHY ME?
AND SHE SAID: THAT'S HOW IT WORKED. THAT IS HOW IT HAS WORKED ALWAYS AND ALWAYS.
SHE SAID SHE TOLD YOU THIS ONCE--
--BUT THAT YOU PROBABLY FORGOT BECAUSE SHE TOLD YOU TO FORGET.
SHE SAID THAT EVERTHING THAT HAPPENS TO US HAPPENS FOR A REASON.
AND THAT'S WHY I GOT TO HANG OUT WITH YOU--AND WHY YOU GOT TO DO ALL THE STUFF YOU DO.
SHE SAID THAT YOU WERE A GREAT GUY AND WOULD WORRY ABOUT ME--
--BUT IF I TOLD YOU NOT TO NICELY...
YOU WOULDN'T.
DON'T WORRY ABOUT ME, CHRISTIAN.
VOLUME IIIIIIIII
--IMAGE YOU ARE SEEING IS LIVE IN CHAYKIN PARK. AN IMPROMPTU CANDLELIGHT VIGIL.

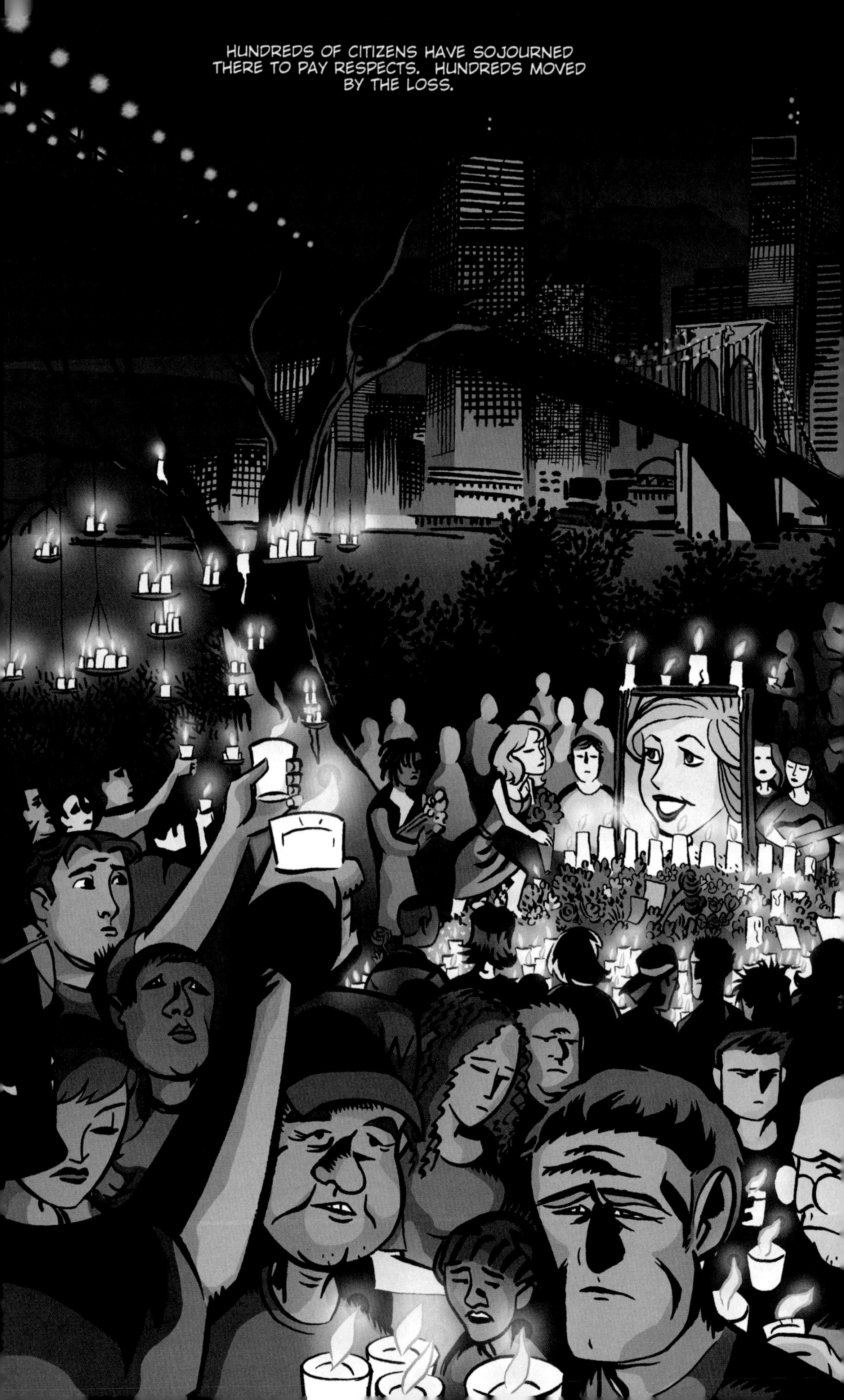
HUNDREDS OF CITIZENS HAVE SOJOURNED THERE TO PAY RESPECTS. HUNDREDS MOVED BY THE LOSS.

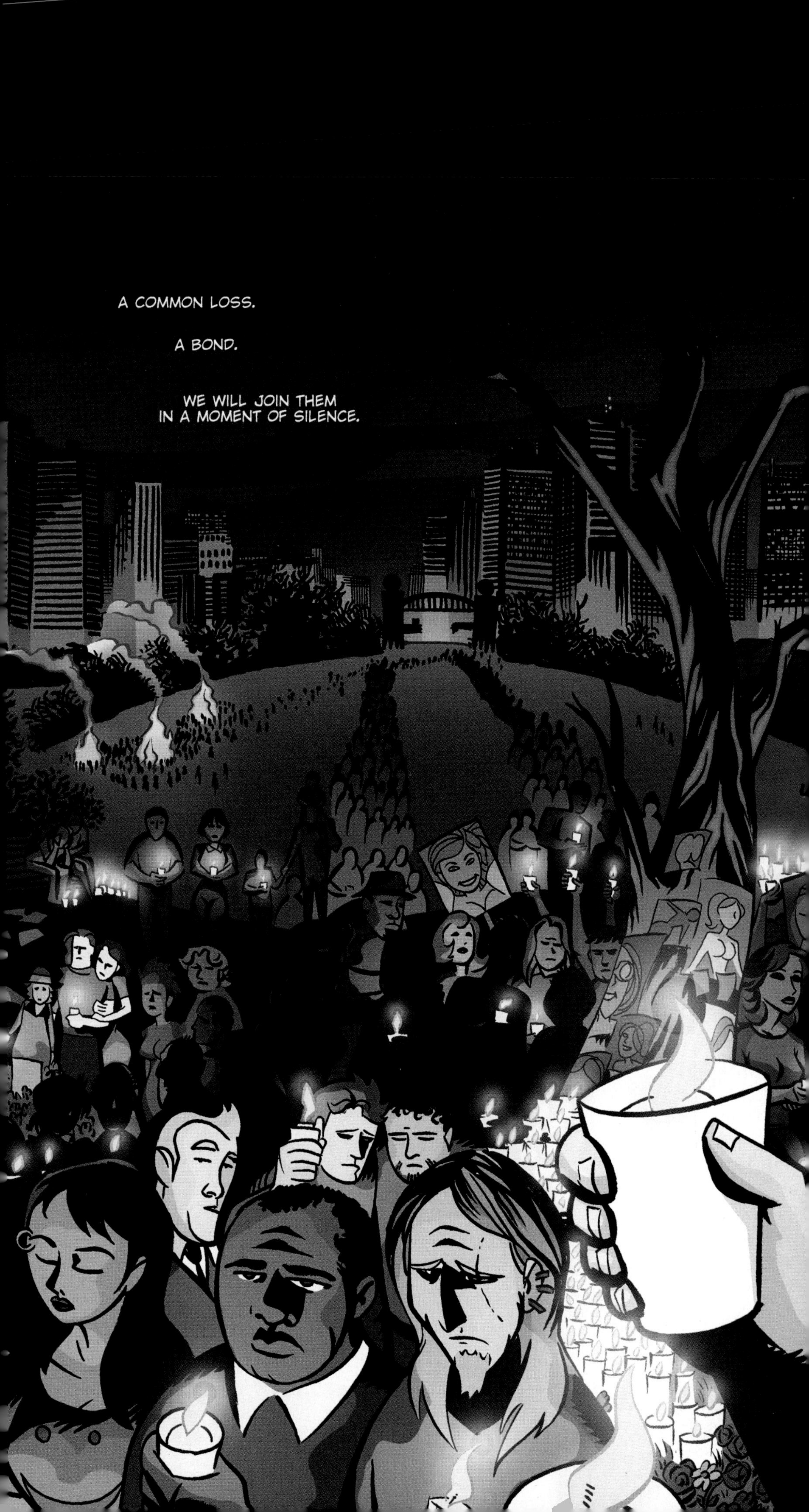
A COMMON LOSS.
A BOND.
WE WILL JOIN THEM IN A MOMENT OF SILENCE.

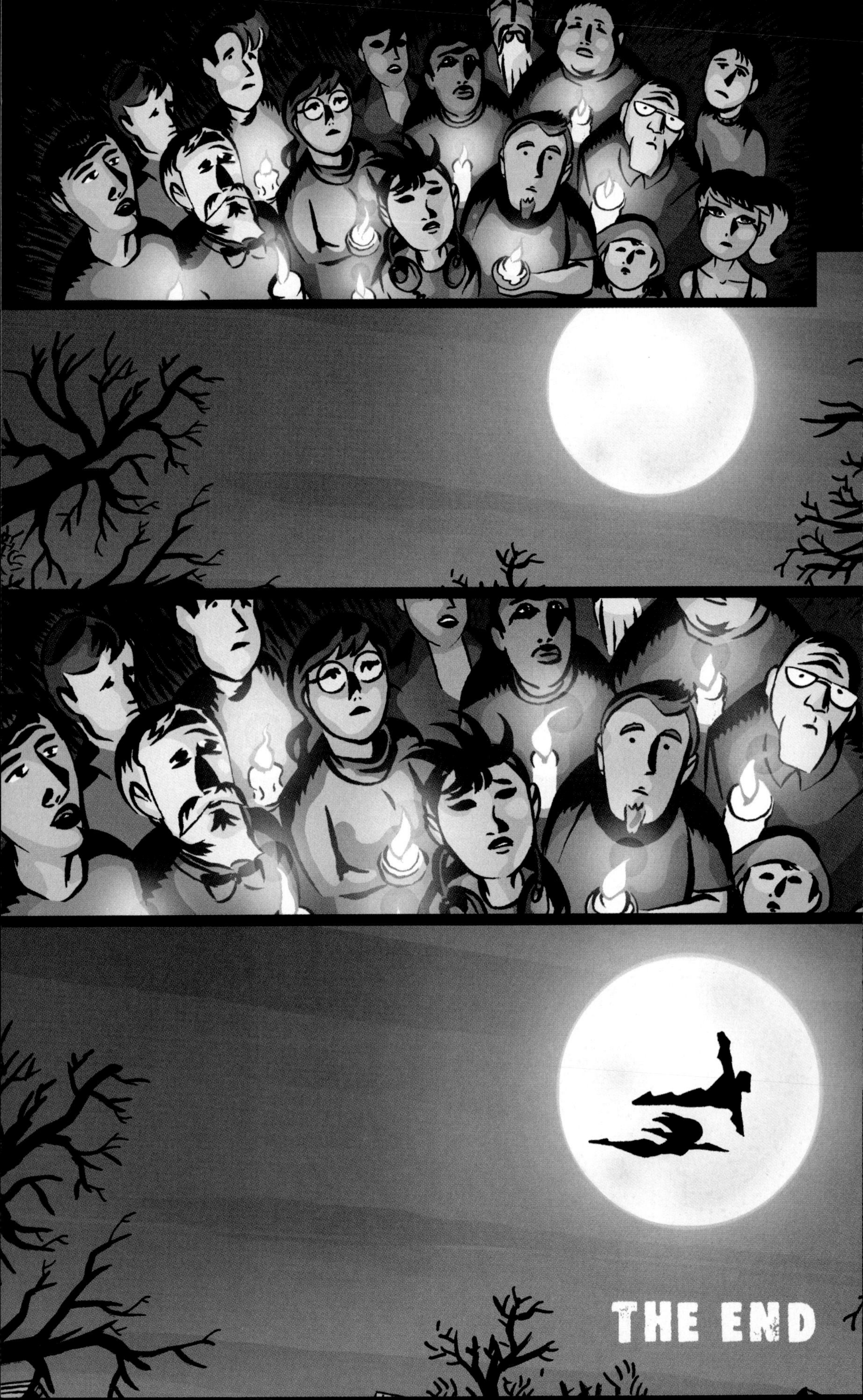
THE END

POWERS SUPPLEMENTAL MATERIAL

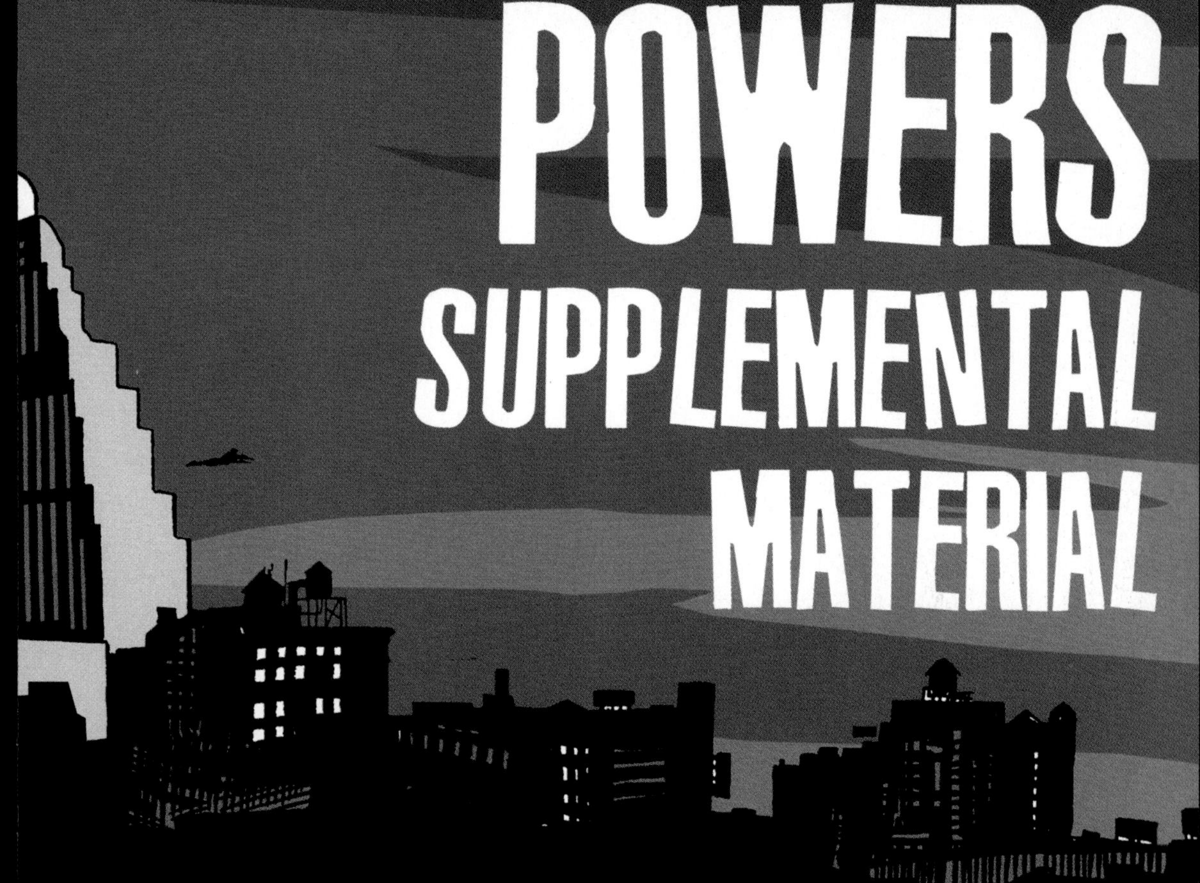

Hi! Powers writer Brian Michael Bendis with you.

Let me be your tour guide through this bonus material section, which has been prepared specifically for this collection.

Creating this work has turned into one of the most creatively vibrant times of our lives and you may view this section as a diary of this experience.

THE POWERS COMIC SHOP NEWS STRIPS

Cliff Biggers and Ward Batty, long time supporters of my career, were kind enough to offer us the opportunity to preview our new series in strips that ran in the pages of their excellent periodical Comic Shop News.

This is the first time these strips have been printed in any comic book publication. The coloring and lettering were done by me because this was pre- Pat.

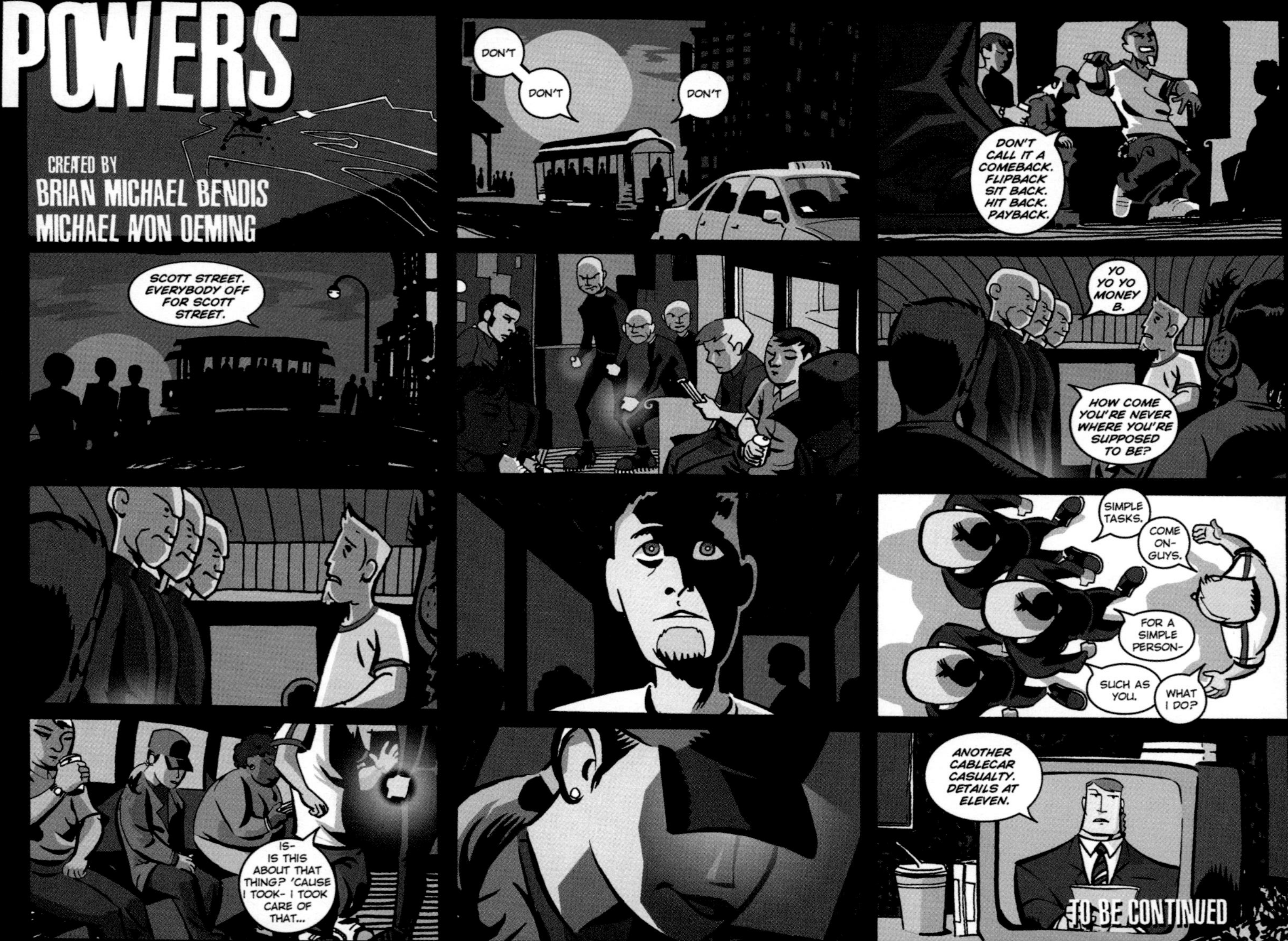
POWERS
CREATED BY
BRIAN MICHAEL BENDIS
MICHAEL AVON OEMING
DON'T
DON'T
DON'T
DON'T CALL IT A COMEBACK. FLIPBACK SIT BACK. HIT BACK. PAYBACK.
SCOTT STREET. EVERYBODY OFF FOR SCOTT STREET.
YO YO YO MONEY B.
HOW COME YOU'RE NEVER WHERE YOU'RE SUPPOSED TO BE?
SIMPLE TASKS.
COME ON- GUYS.
FOR A SIMPLE PERSON-
SUCH AS YOU.
WHAT I DO?
IS- IS THIS ABOUT THAT THING? 'CAUSE I TOOK- I TOOK CARE OF THAT...
ANOTHER CABLECAR CASUALTY. DETAILS AT ELEVEN.
TO BE CONTINUED

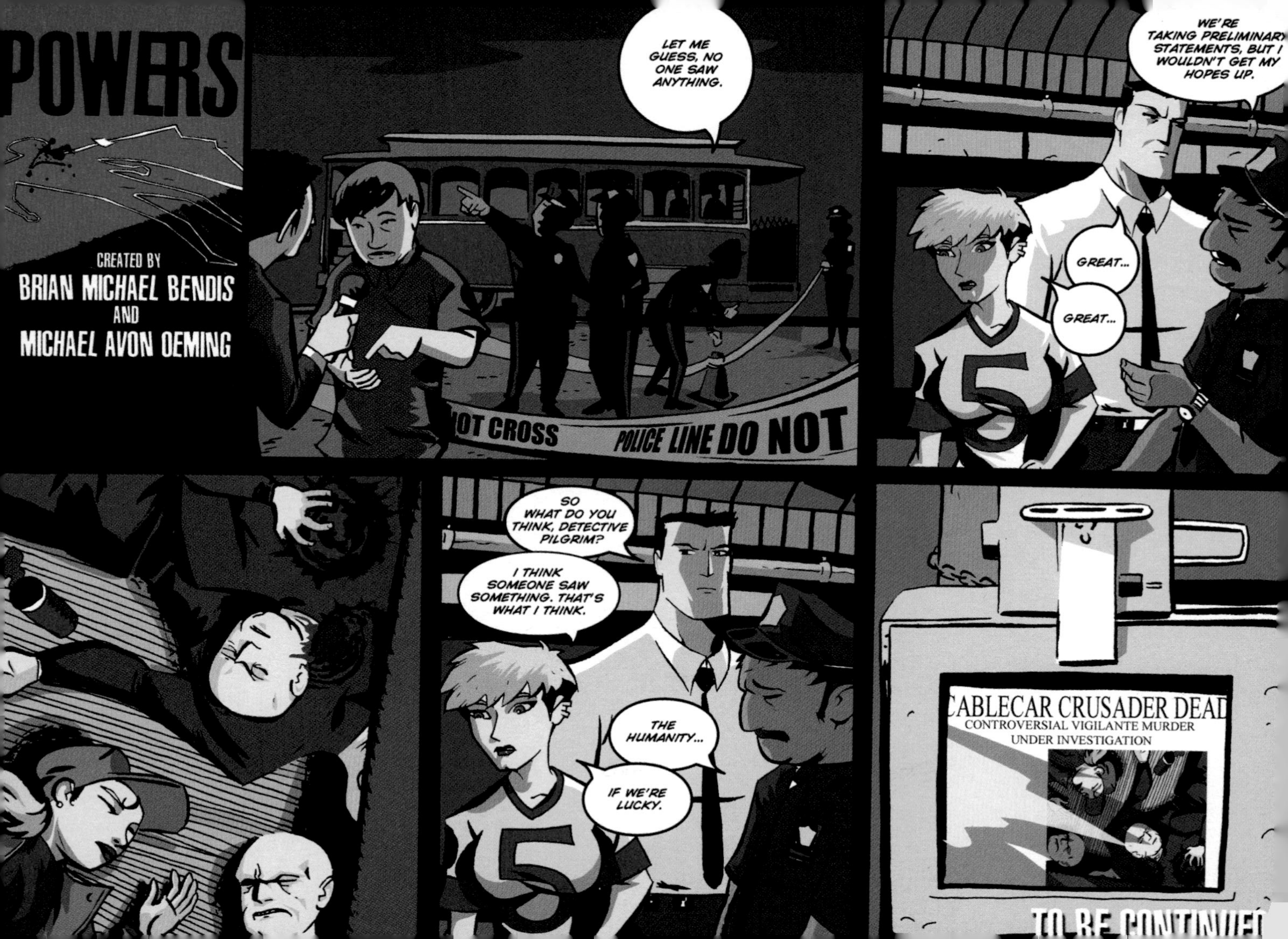
POWERS
CREATED BY
BRIAN MICHAEL BENDIS
AND
MICHAEL AVON OEMING
LET ME GUESS, NO ONE SAW ANYTHING.
OT CROSS
POLICE LINE DO NOT
WE'RE TAKING PRELIMINARY STATEMENTS, BUT I WOULDN'T GET MY HOPES UP.
GREAT...
GREAT...
SO WHAT DO YOU THINK, DETECTIVE PILGRIM?
I THINK SOMEONE SAW SOMETHING. THAT'S WHAT I THINK.
THE HUMANITY...
IF WE'RE LUCKY.
CABLECAR CRUSADER DEAD
CONTROVERSIAL VIGILANTE MURDER
UNDER INVESTIGATION
TO BE CONTINUED

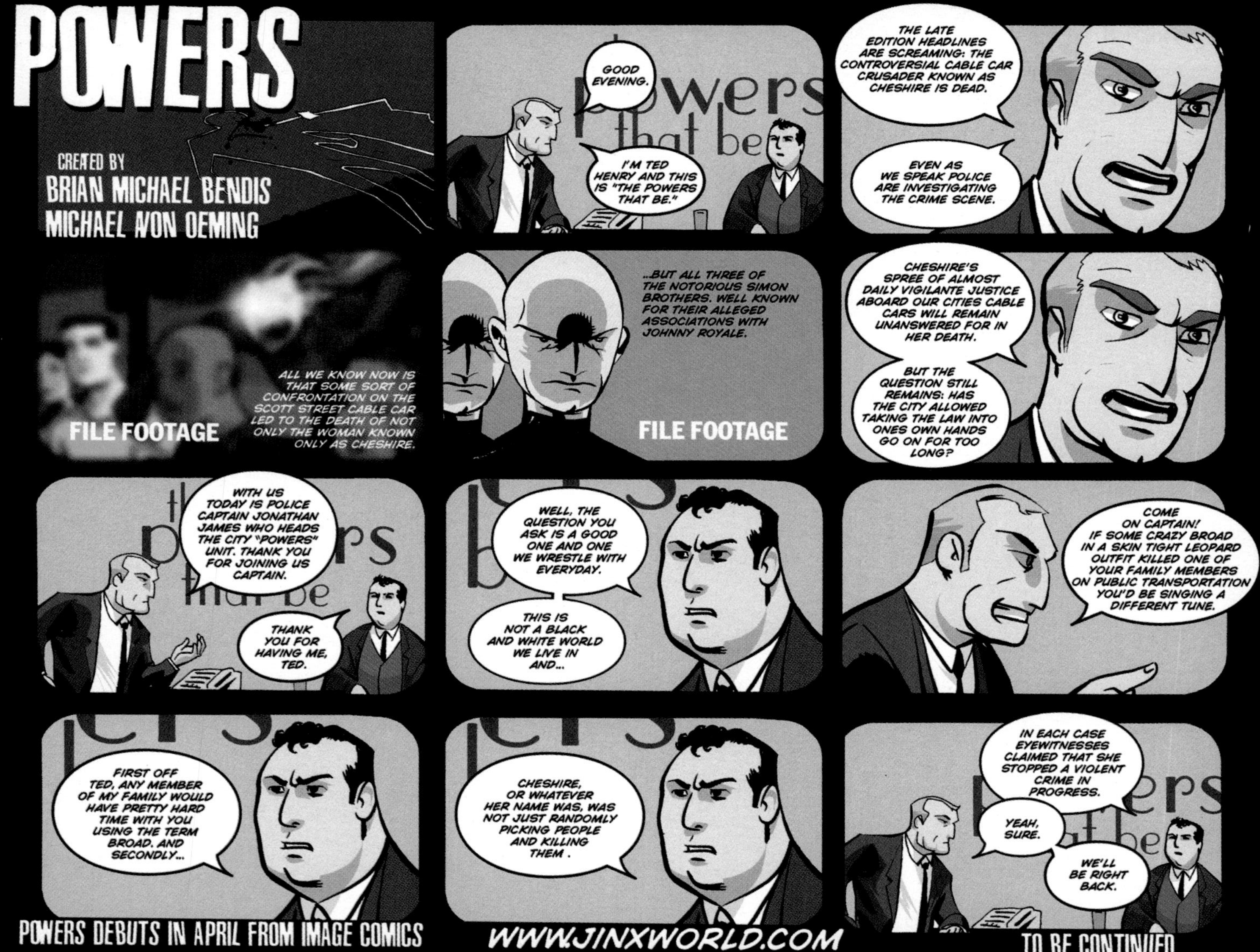
POWERS
CREATED BY
BRIAN MICHAEL BENDIS
MICHAEL AVON OEMING
GOOD EVENING.
I'M TED HENRY AND THIS IS "THE POWERS THAT BE."
powers that be
THE LATE EDITION HEADLINES ARE SCREAMING: THE CONTROVERSIAL CABLE CAR CRUSADER KNOWN AS CHESHIRE IS DEAD.
EVEN AS WE SPEAK POLICE ARE INVESTIGATING THE CRIME SCENE.
ALL WE KNOW NOW IS THAT SOME SORT OF CONFRONTATION ON THE SCOTT STREET CABLE CAR LED TO THE DEATH OF NOT ONLY THE WOMAN KNOWN ONLY AS CHESHIRE.
FILE FOOTAGE
...BUT ALL THREE OF THE NOTORIOUS SIMON BROTHERS. WELL KNOWN FOR THEIR ALLEGED ASSOCIATIONS WITH JOHNNY ROYALE.
FILE FOOTAGE
CHESHIRE'S SPREE OF ALMOST DAILY VIGILANTE JUSTICE ABOARD OUR CITIES CABLE CARS WILL REMAIN UNANSWERED FOR IN HER DEATH.
BUT THE QUESTION STILL REMAINS: HAS THE CITY ALLOWED TAKING THE LAW INTO ONES OWN HANDS GO ON FOR TOO LONG?
WITH US TODAY IS POLICE CAPTAIN JONATHAN JAMES WHO HEADS THE CITY "POWERS" UNIT. THANK YOU FOR JOINING US CAPTAIN.
THANK YOU FOR HAVING ME, TED.
WELL, THE QUESTION YOU ASK IS A GOOD ONE AND ONE WE WRESTLE WITH EVERYDAY.
THIS IS NOT A BLACK AND WHITE WORLD WE LIVE IN AND...
COME ON CAPTAIN! IF SOME CRAZY BROAD IN A SKIN TIGHT LEOPARD OUTFIT KILLED ONE OF YOUR FAMILY MEMBERS ON PUBLIC TRANSPORTATION YOU'D BE SINGING A DIFFERENT TUNE.
FIRST OFF TED, ANY MEMBER OF MY FAMILY WOULD HAVE PRETTY HARD TIME WITH YOU USING THE TERM BROAD. AND SECONDLY...
CHESHIRE, OR WHATEVER HER NAME WAS, WAS NOT JUST RANDOMLY PICKING PEOPLE AND KILLING THEM .
IN EACH CASE EYEWITNESSES CLAIMED THAT SHE STOPPED A VIOLENT CRIME IN PROGRESS.
YEAH, SURE.
WE'LL BE RIGHT BACK.
POWERS DEBUTS IN APRIL FROM IMAGE COMICS
WWW.JINXWORLD.COM
TO BE CONTINUED

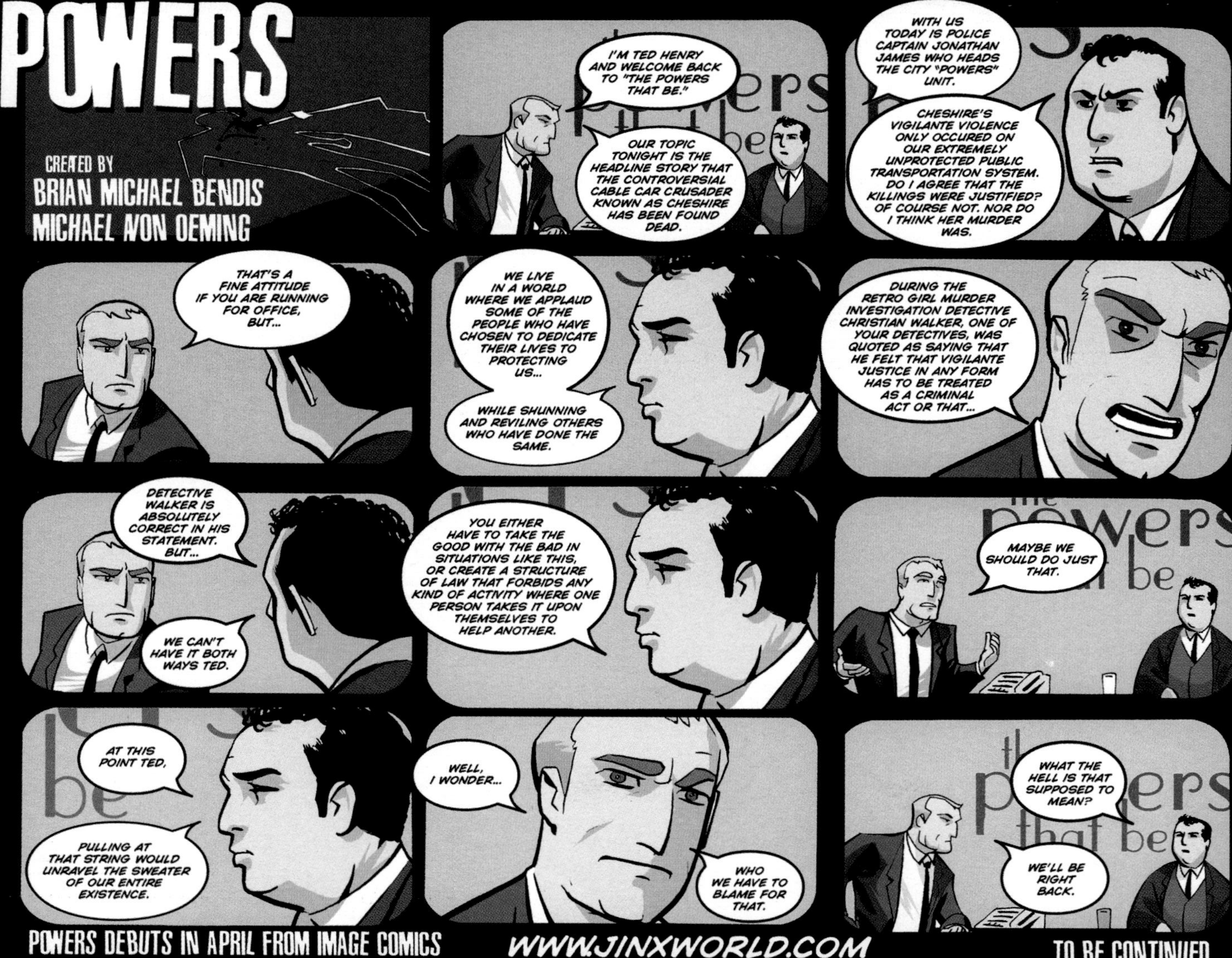
POWERS
CREATED BY
BRIAN MICHAEL BENDIS
MICHAEL AVON OEMING
I'M TED HENRY AND WELCOME BACK TO "THE POWERS THAT BE."
OUR TOPIC TONIGHT IS THE HEADLINE STORY THAT THE CONTROVERSIAL CABLE CAR CRUSADER KNOWN AS CHESHIRE HAS BEEN FOUND DEAD.
WITH US TODAY IS POLICE CAPTAIN JONATHAN JAMES WHO HEADS THE CITY "POWERS" UNIT.
CHESHIRE'S VIGILANTE VIOLENCE ONLY OCCURED ON OUR EXTREMELY UNPROTECTED PUBLIC TRANSPORTATION SYSTEM. DO I AGREE THAT THE KILLINGS WERE JUSTIFIED? OF COURSE NOT. NOR DO I THINK HER MURDER WAS.
THAT'S A FINE ATTITUDE IF YOU ARE RUNNING FOR OFFICE, BUT...
WE LIVE IN A WORLD WHERE WE APPLAUD SOME OF THE PEOPLE WHO HAVE CHOSEN TO DEDICATE THEIR LIVES TO PROTECTING US...
WHILE SHUNNING AND REVILING OTHERS WHO HAVE DONE THE SAME.
DURING THE RETRO GIRL MURDER INVESTIGATION DETECTIVE CHRISTIAN WALKER, ONE OF YOUR DETECTIVES, WAS QUOTED AS SAYING THAT HE FELT THAT VIGILANTE JUSTICE IN ANY FORM HAS TO BE TREATED AS A CRIMINAL ACT OR THAT...
DETECTIVE WALKER IS ABSOLUTELY CORRECT IN HIS STATEMENT. BUT...
WE CAN'T HAVE IT BOTH WAYS TED.
YOU EITHER HAVE TO TAKE THE GOOD WITH THE BAD IN SITUATIONS LIKE THIS, OR CREATE A STRUCTURE OF LAW THAT FORBIDS ANY KIND OF ACTIVITY WHERE ONE PERSON TAKES IT UPON THEMSELVES TO HELP ANOTHER.
MAYBE WE SHOULD DO JUST THAT.
AT THIS POINT TED.
PULLING AT THAT STRING WOULD UNRAVEL THE SWEATER OF OUR ENTIRE EXISTENCE.
WELL, I WONDER...
WHO WE HAVE TO BLAME FOR THAT.
WHAT THE HELL IS THAT SUPPOSED TO MEAN?
WE'LL BE RIGHT BACK.
POWERS DEBUTS IN APRIL FROM IMAGE COMICS
WWW.JINXWORLD.COM
TO BE CONTINUED

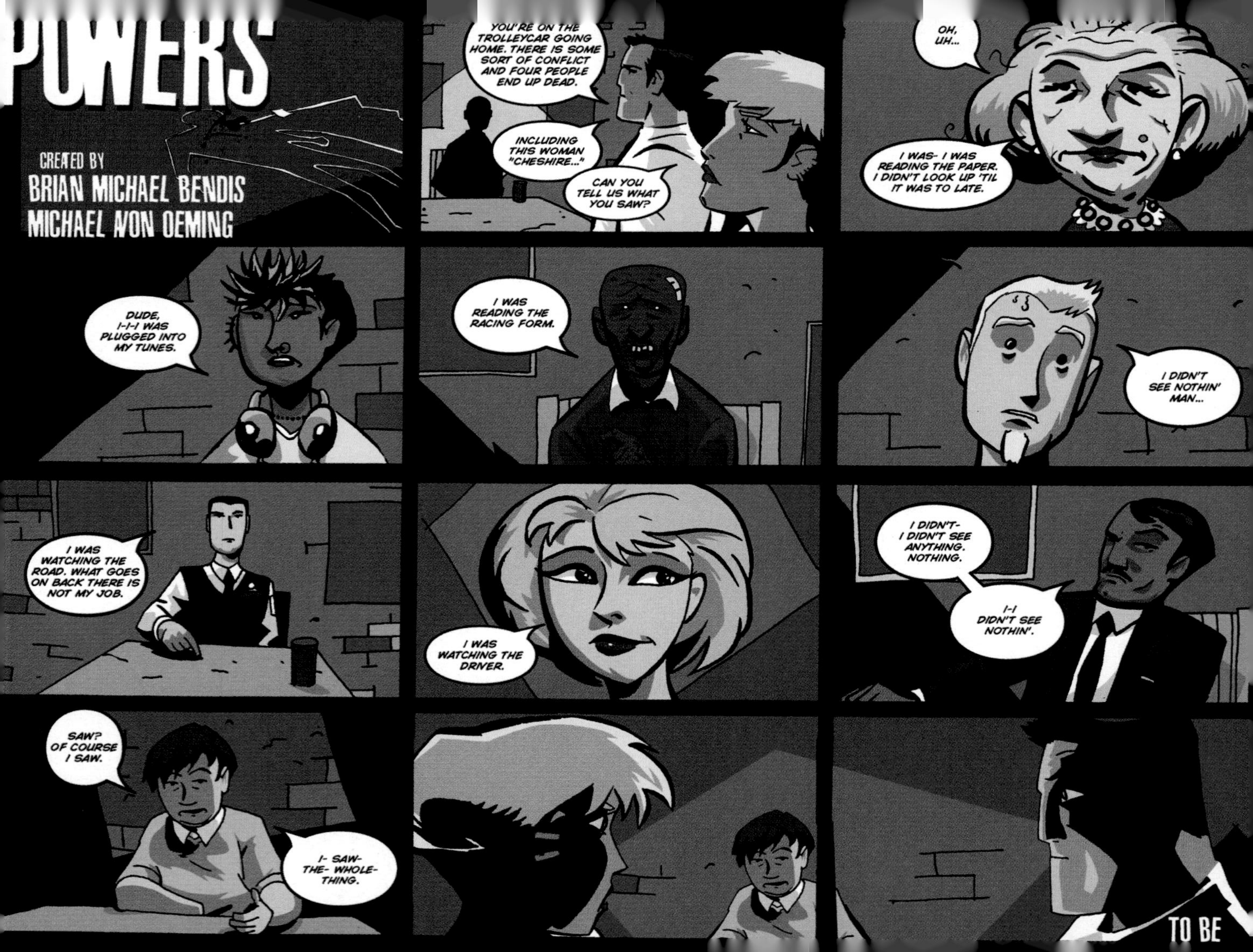
POWERS
CREATED BY
BRIAN MICHAEL BENDIS
MICHAEL AVON OEMING
YOU'RE ON THE TROLLEYCAR GOING HOME. THERE IS SOME SORT OF CONFLICT AND FOUR PEOPLE END UP DEAD.
INCLUDING THIS WOMAN "CHESHIRE..."
CAN YOU TELL US WHAT YOU SAW?
OH, UH...
I WAS- I WAS READING THE PAPER. I DIDN'T LOOK UP 'TIL IT WAS TO LATE.
DUDE, I-I-I WAS PLUGGED INTO MY TUNES.
I WAS READING THE RACING FORM.
I DIDN'T SEE NOTHIN' MAN...
I WAS WATCHING THE ROAD. WHAT GOES ON BACK THERE IS NOT MY JOB.
I WAS WATCHING THE DRIVER.
I DIDN'T- I DIDN'T SEE ANYTHING. NOTHING.
I-I DIDN'T SEE NOTHIN'.
SAW? OF COURSE I SAW.
I- SAW- THE- WHOLE- THING.
TO BE

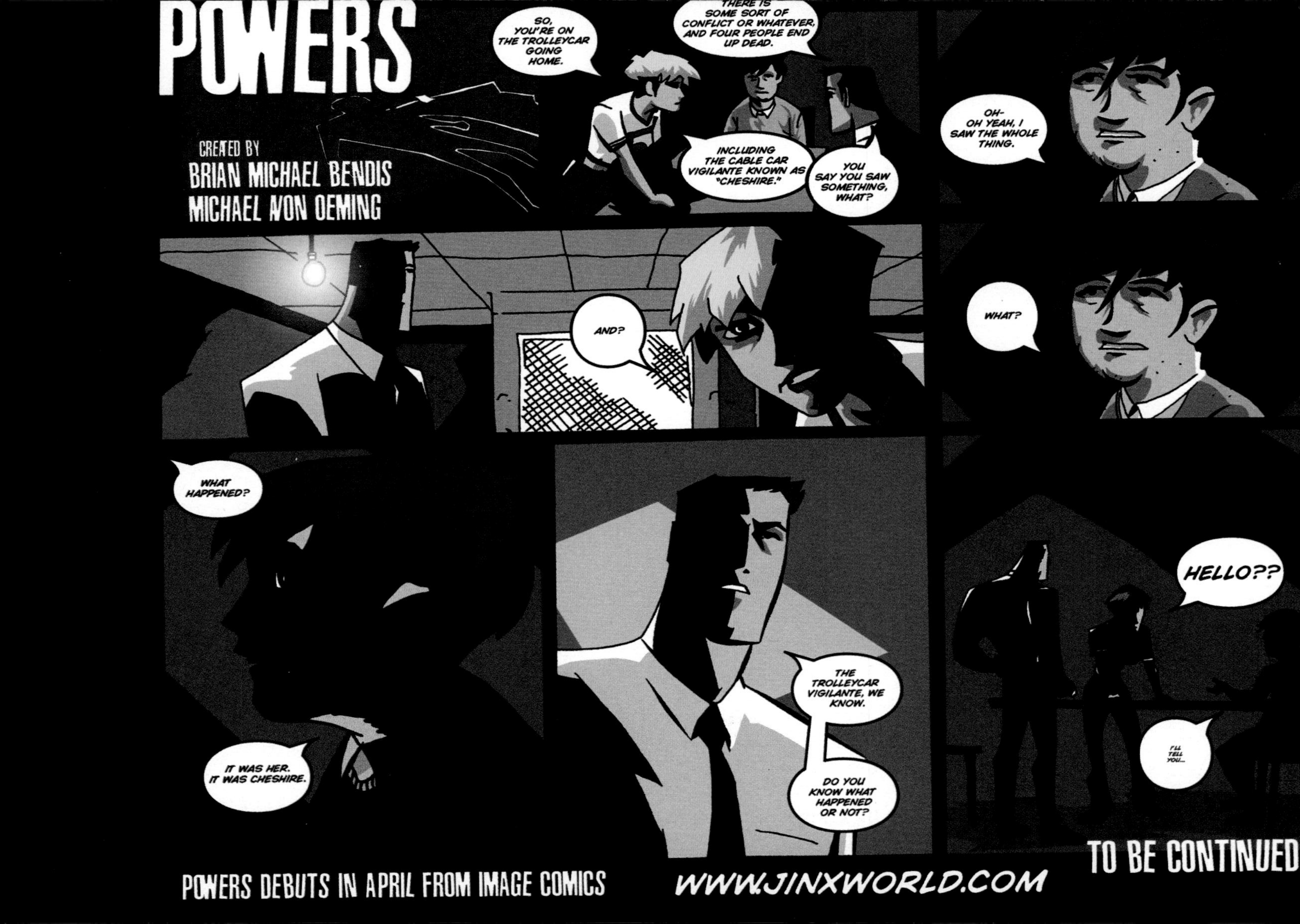
POWERS
CREATED BY
BRIAN MICHAEL BENDIS
MICHAEL AVON OEMING
SO, YOU'RE ON THE TROLLEYCAR GOING HOME.
THERE IS SOME SORT OF CONFLICT OR WHATEVER, AND FOUR PEOPLE END UP DEAD.
INCLUDING THE CABLE CAR VIGILANTE KNOWN AS "CHESHIRE."
YOU SAY YOU SAW SOMETHING, WHAT?
OH- OH YEAH, I SAW THE WHOLE THING.
AND?
WHAT?
WHAT HAPPENED?
IT WAS HER. IT WAS CHESHIRE.
THE TROLLEYCAR VIGILANTE, WE KNOW.
DO YOU KNOW WHAT HAPPENED OR NOT?
HELLO??
I'LL TELL YOU...
TO BE CONTINUED
POWERS DEBUTS IN APRIL FROM IMAGE COMICS
WWW.JINXWORLD.COM

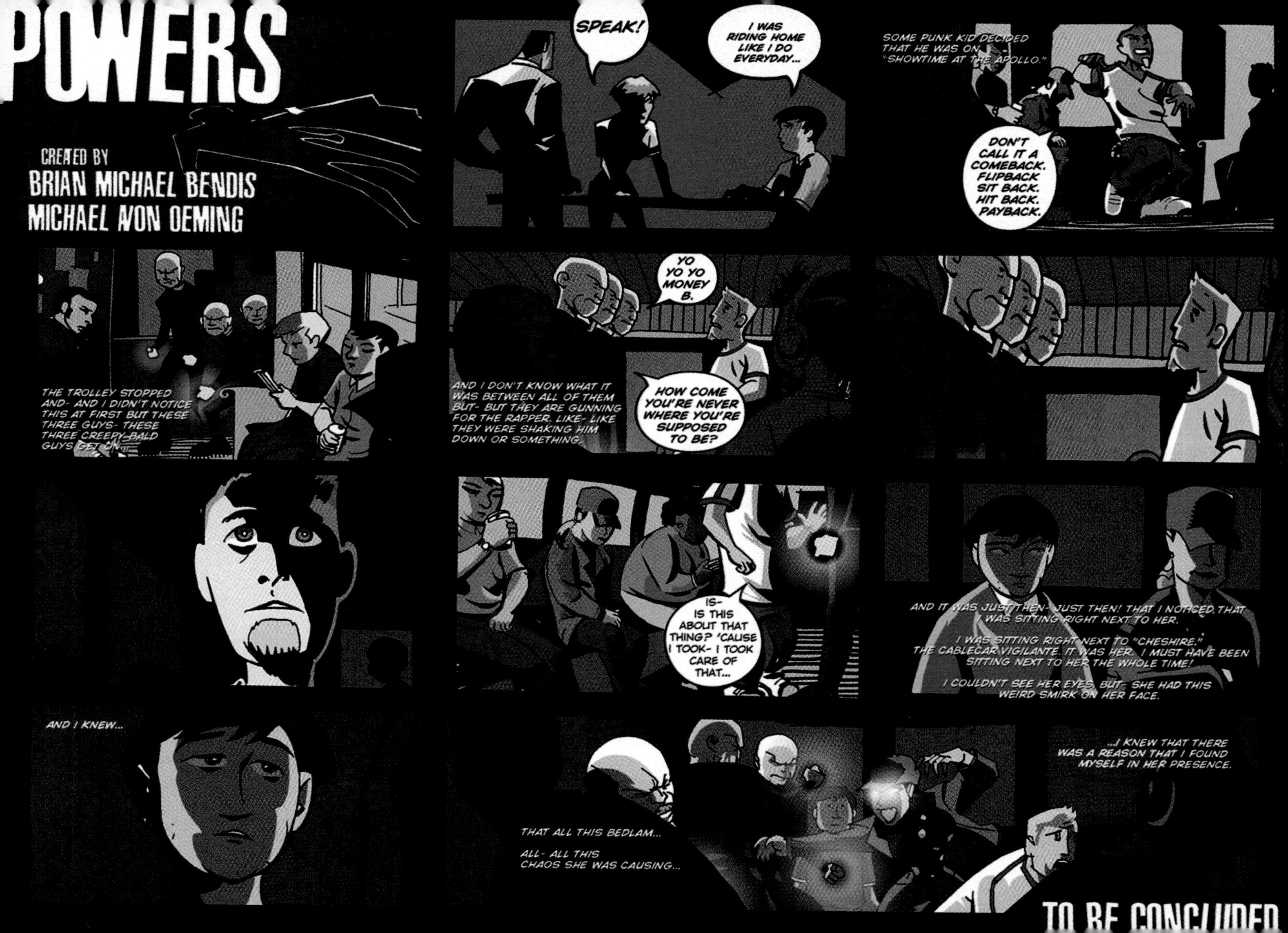
POWERS
CREATED BY
BRIAN MICHAEL BENDIS
MICHAEL AVON OEMING
SPEAK!
I WAS RIDING HOME LIKE I DO EVERYDAY...
SOME PUNK KID DECIDED THAT HE WAS ON "SHOWTIME AT THE APOLLO."
DON'T CALL IT A COMEBACK. FLIPBACK SIT BACK. HIT BACK. PAYBACK.
THE TROLLEY STOPPED AND- AND I DIDN'T NOTICE THIS AT FIRST BUT THESE THREE GUYS- THESE THREE CREEPY BALD GUYS GET ON...
AND I DON'T KNOW WHAT IT WAS BETWEEN ALL OF THEM BUT- BUT THEY ARE GUNNING FOR THE RAPPER. LIKE- LIKE THEY WERE SHAKING HIM DOWN OR SOMETHING.
YO YO YO MONEY B.
HOW COME YOU'RE NEVER WHERE YOU'RE SUPPOSED TO BE?
IS- IS THIS ABOUT THAT THING? 'CAUSE I TOOK- I TOOK CARE OF THAT...
AND IT WAS JUST THEN- JUST THEN! THAT I NOTICED THAT I WAS SITTING RIGHT NEXT TO HER.
I WAS SITTING RIGHT NEXT TO "CHESHIRE." THE CABLECAR VIGILANTE. IT WAS HER. I MUST HAVE BEEN SITTING NEXT TO HER THE WHOLE TIME!
I COULDN'T SEE HER EYES, BUT- SHE HAD THIS WEIRD SMIRK ON HER FACE.
AND I KNEW...
THAT ALL THIS BEDLAM...
ALL- ALL THIS CHAOS SHE WAS CAUSING...
...I KNEW THAT THERE WAS A REASON THAT I FOUND MYSELF IN HER PRESENCE.
TO BE CONCLUDED

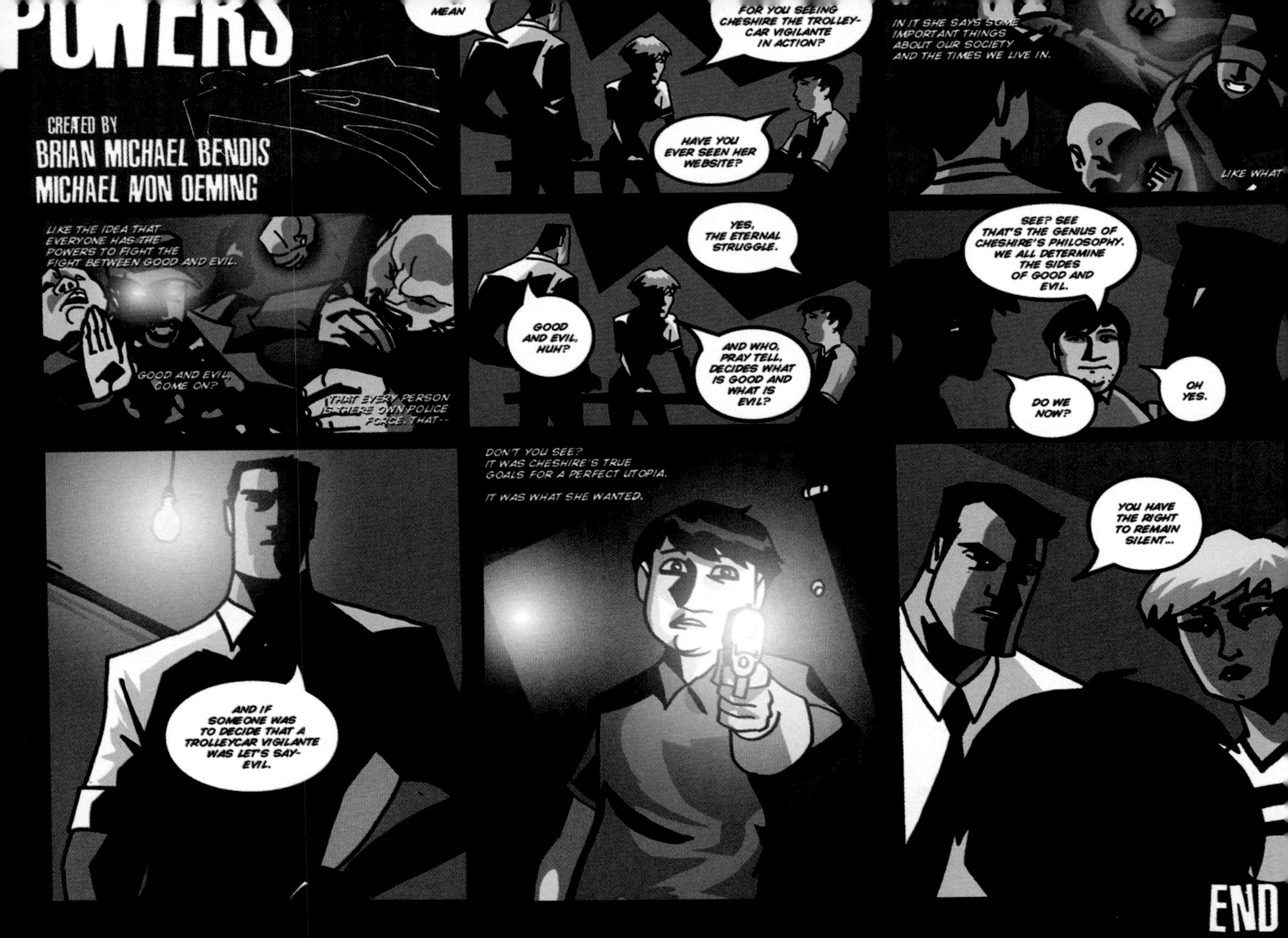
POWERS
CREATED BY
BRIAN MICHAEL BENDIS
MICHAEL AVON OEMING
MEAN
FOR YOU SEEING CHESHIRE THE TROLLEY-CAR VIGILANTE IN ACTION?
HAVE YOU EVER SEEN HER WEBSITE?
IN IT SHE SAYS SOME IMPORTANT THINGS ABOUT OUR SOCIETY AND THE TIMES WE LIVE IN.
LIKE WHAT
LIKE THE IDEA THAT EVERYONE HAS THE POWERS TO FIGHT THE FIGHT BETWEEN GOOD AND EVIL.
GOOD AND EVIL. COME ON?
THAT EVERY PERSON IS THERE OWN POLICE FORCE. THAT--
YES, THE ETERNAL STRUGGLE.
GOOD AND EVIL, HUH?
AND WHO, PRAY TELL, DECIDES WHAT IS GOOD AND WHAT IS EVIL?
SEE? SEE THAT'S THE GENIUS OF CHESHIRE'S PHILOSOPHY. WE ALL DETERMINE THE SIDES OF GOOD AND EVIL.
DO WE NOW?
OH YES.
AND IF SOMEONE WAS TO DECIDE THAT A TROLLEYCAR VIGILANTE WAS LET'S SAY- EVIL.
DON'T YOU SEE? IT WAS CHESHIRE'S TRUE GOALS FOR A PERFECT UTOPIA.
IT WAS WHAT SHE WANTED.
YOU HAVE THE RIGHT TO REMAIN SILENT...
END

POWERS ISSUE ONE THE FULL SCRIPT

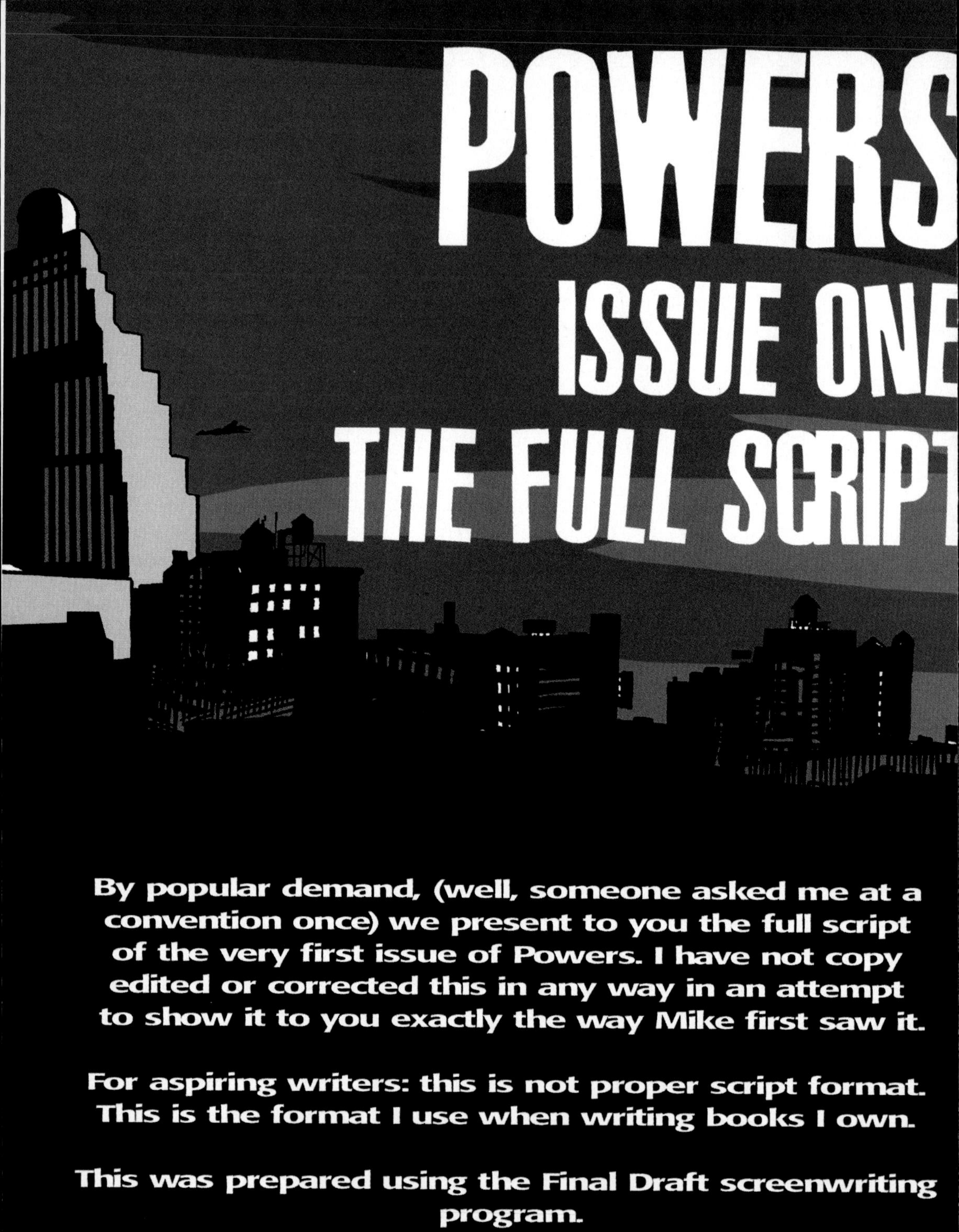

By popular demand, (well, someone asked me at a convention once) we present to you the full script of the very first issue of Powers. I have not copy edited or corrected this in any way in an attempt to show it to you exactly the way Mike first saw it.

For aspiring writers: this is not proper script format. This is the format I use when writing books I own.

This was prepared using the Final Draft screenwriting program.

WERS

O KILLED RETRO GIRL?

SUE ONE

BRIAN MICHAEL BENDIS FOR MIKE AVON OEMING

GE IFC & 1-

REE EQUAL SIZED PAGE LONG PANELS.

NEL 1- THE SKY LINE OF OUR NAMELESS CITY. SILHOUETTE TOWERS
ERCE A GRAY BLUE NIGHT SKY.

KE: THIS IS OUR WORLD AND WE MAKE THE RULES , BUT WHATEVER
LES WE MAKE HERE WE HAVE TO STICK TO.

IIS CITY IS AN EQUAL CHARACTER TO EVERY LEAD IN THE BOOK. IT
S TO SMELL AND BREATHE AND TASTE LIKE IT.

- TIGHTER ON A INDISCRIMINATE BLOCK OF BUILDINGS. EACH HAS
S OWN DISTINCT CHARACTERS.

- A SLIGHT WORM'S EYE OF A CITY STREET CORNER BELOW. IT'S A
STAGE CRIME SCENE OUTSIDE A SEMI- RUNDOWN APARTMENT
ILDING. GO AHEAD AND FIND PHOTO REFERENCE FOR IT.

LICE CARS, EMERGENCY VEHICLES. YELLOW POLICE TAPE IS UP
EPING THE CASUAL SMATTERING OF A CROWD AT BAY.

COUPLE OF NEWS VANS ARE PARKED AS CLOSE AS THEY CAN GET.

PS MILL ABOUT. THIS HAS BEEN GOING ON FOR QUITE A WHILE.

NONDESCRIPT WHITE CAR HAS MADE ITS WAY TO THE FRONT OF THE
ENE.

AGE 2-

IVE EQUAL SIZED PAGE LONG PANELS.

ACH PANEL IS THE SAME SHOT- ITS THE SAME CRIME SCENE THE
AME MOMENT AS THE LAST PANEL, BUT FROM THE TOP OF THE STAIRS
F THE APARTMENT BUILDING LOOKING DOWN ONTO THE STREET.

(CONTINUED

CONTINUED:

1- THE WHITE CAR HAS STOPPED DEAD-CENTER OF THE PANEL.
GETTING OUT OF THE CAR IS DETECTIVE CHRISTIAN WALKER WHO IS
IMMEDIATELY SURROUNDED BY THE TOP COPS WHO WERE ALREADY ON
THE SCENE.

THEY FOLLOW HIM AS THEY TALK.

                    CAPTAIN
          WALKER.

                    WALKER
          CAPTAIN...

                    CAPTAIN
          WE BEEN CALLING...

                    WALKER
          I WAS AT THE MOVIES.

                    CAPTAIN
          WE BEEN CALLING IS ALL...

                    WALKER
          YEAH, WELL--
          WHAT IS THIS?
          I'M HOMICIDE.

                    CAPTAIN
          YOU'RE A COP,
          AND THE GUY INSIDE WANTS YOU.

                    WALKER
          WHO? WILLIAMS?

                    WILLIAMS
              (THE NEGOTIATOR)
          NO- HEY WALKER- NO, I SCREWED THE POOCH.

                    CAPTAIN
          YOU COULDN'T NEGOTIATE SUPER-SIZING A
          HAPPY MEAL, YOU PIECE OF--!!!

                    WILLIAMS
          COME ON...

                    CAPTAIN
          I'M GOING TO DEAL WITH YOUR INCOMPETENT
          ASS LATER.

          NO, THE GUY HOLDING THE PLACE, HE ASKED
          FOR YOU.

                                        (CONTINUED

                    WALKER
     THE GUY INSIDE?

     HE ASKED FOR ME?

                    CAPTAIN
     AND YOU ONLY?

                    WALKER
     HE ASKED FOR ME? WHO IS IT?

                    CAPTAIN
     SOME SHMUCK...

     GOES BY THE NAME OF- OF FINCH.

     FINCH.

                    WALKER
     FINCH?

                    CAPTAIN
     FINCH. WEARS A GREEN THING WITH A THING
     ON HIS BACK.

                    WALKER
     FINCH?

                    CAPTAIN
     HE'S GOT A LITTLE GIRL IN THERE.
     USED TO DATE THE MOM.

     HE CAME OVER THEY GOT INTO A DOMESTIC...

     HE THREW HER OUT THE SECOND STORY WINDOW
     AND BOARDED HIMSELF UP IN THERE.

                    WALKER
     THE WOMAN? THE MOM?

                    CAPTAIN
     TOOK HER DOWN TO MERCY? SHE WAS ALERT
     ENOUGH TO CALL US.

                    WALKER
     FINCH? I DON'T KNOW A FINCH.

                    CAPTAIN
     THEN THE DOCTORS AT THE HOSPITAL LEFT HER
     ALONE FOR SOMETHING LIKE TWO SECONDS AND
     SHE VANISHED.

                                        (CONTINUED

CONTINUED: (3)

                    WALKER
          VANISHED?

                    CAPTAIN
          NO ONE SAW, NO ONE KNOWS.

          THE GUY INSIDE- THE GUYS GOT ONE OF THOSE
          BACK PACK THINGS. GOT PINCHED ON A COUPLE
          OF DEPARTMENT STORE HOLD UPS...

                    WALKER
          DOESN'T HELP ME...

                    CAPTAIN
          WELL, HE KNOWS YOU AND HE'S GOT A GOD
          DAMN SEVEN YEAR OLD GIRL IN THERE.

          GUYS BEEN CRYING LIKE A BABY FOR OVER AND
          HOUR.

                    WALKER
          THE GIRL OR THE GUY?

                    CAPTAIN
          THE GUY.

          AND I'M NOT GOING TO HAVE THIS LOSER
          PSYCHO POP A GIRL ON THE SIX O CLOCK!!
          NOT TODAY. NOT ANY DAY.

                    WALKER
          YEAH...WELL, COULD YA-

          LET'S TRY TO MODULATE THE VOLUME, OK?

PAGE 3-

1-WALKER IS AT THE DOOR TO THE APARTMENT WITH HIS GUN OUT OF
THE HOLSTER. THERE ARE SWAT GUYS ALL AROUND. ONE IN
PARTICULAR IS HUGGING THE OTHER SIDE OF THE DOOR.

VARIANTS OF THIS SHOT IS REPEATED OVER AND OVER UNTIL THE
SCENE IS OVER.

                    SETZER
          HEY WALKER...

                                        (CONTINUED

                    WALKER
          HEY, OH HEY SETZER. WHAT'S GOING ON?

                    SETZER
          WHERE YOU BEEN?

                    WALKER
          MOVIES.

                    SETZER
          WHAT YOU SEE?

                    WALKER
          THE TRAILERS.

                    SETZER
          WELL THIS SUCKS, THIS GUY IN HERE SUCKS.
          FUCK THIS GUY.

          GUY'S GOING TO DO THE DUTCH IS ALL.

          THE KID'S WATCHING CARTOONS.
          HE KEEPS CRYIN' LIKE A...

                    WALKER
          --LIKE A BABY. I HEARD.

- PAUSE AS THEY LISTEN TO THE GUYS FAINT RAMBLING.

-

                    WALKER (CONT'D)
               (TO THE DOOR)
          FINCH. IT'S DETECTIVE WALKER.

- PAUSE.

-

                    WALKER (CONT'D)
          FINCH? WHAT DID YOU CALL ME DOWN HERE
          FOR?

                    FLINCH
          OOOOOH!!! EFF YOU WEAR YOU LIVE, WALKER!!
          YOU SHITHEEL!!!

                    WALKER
          DO I KNOW YOU?

                    FLINCH
          ITS FLINCH!! NOT FINCH, FLINCH!!! YOU
          EFFIN' ASSHOLES!!!

                                        (CONTINUED

                        WALKER
        OH!!! FLINCH!!! DUDE! I'M SORRY MAN.

        THESE ASSHOLES DON'T KNOW ANYTHING OUT
        HERE.

PAGE 4-

1- SETZER LOOKS TO HIM AS IF TO SAY: "YOU KNOW THIS GUY."

WALKER LOOKS BACK AS IF TO SAY: "I HAVE NO FUCKING IDEA WHO
THIS IS."

                        FLINCH
        YEAH, WELL. I'VE HAD TO LISTEN TO THEIR
        BULLSHIT ALL DAY!!! STUPID, STUPID
        BULLSHIT!!

                        WALKER
        YEAH WELL, EVERYONE'S SORTA OUTTA SORTS
        TODAY-- SEEING AS YOU GOT A KID IN THERE.

2- PAUSE.

3-

                        WALKER (CONT'D)
        NO MORE BULLSHIT, FLINCH. THIS IS THE
        GOODS-- IF YOU SEND THE KID OUT OF THERE
        WE CAN HAVE A TALK.

                        FLINCH
        MOTHER'S A BITCH!!!

                        WALKER
        PROBABLY IS FLINCH, DOESN'T HAVE A THING
        TO DO WITH THE KID.

4- PAUSE

5-

                        WALKER (CONT'D)
        RIGHT?

                        FLINCH
        BITCH TOOK ALL MY MONEY!!

                                        (CONTINUED

CONTINUED: (6)

                    WALKER
        SHE DID?

                    FLINCH
        I WAS SAVING THAT MONEY TO FINISH MY GOD
        DAMN PROJECT AND NOW I'M GOING
        TO....AAAARRGGHH!!!

        IT'S ALL RUINED. DO YOU KNOW WALKER? DO
        YOU KNOW? YOU DON'T KNOW.

                    WALKER
        I KNOW THAT THE GIRL IN THERE IS NOT THE
        ANSWER TO YOUR PROBLEMS.

        AND I CAN'T EVEN THINK ABOUT HELPING YOU
        UNTIL YOU GIVE ME THE GIRL AND START
        TALKING TO ME MAN TO MAN.

        FACE TO FACE.

PAGE 5-

- PAUSE.

- SAME SHOT, BUT IT IS GETTING SLIGHTLY TIGHTER ON WALKER

                    WALKER (CONT'D)
        TODAY'S A SHIT DAY, FLINCH.

        I SWEAR TO YOU- I SWEAR TO YOU I KNOW
        THAT KIND OF DAY.

        BUT YOU GOTTA LOOK AT IT ANOTHER WAY. A
        DAY LIKE THIS- A DAY LIKE THIS IS WHEN
        YOU FIND OUT WHAT YOUR MADE OF. RIGHT?

        ANY ASSHOLE CAN KEEP THEIR SHIT TOGETHER
        ON THE GOOD DAYS.

        BUT THE SHIT DAY?

        THAT'S WHEN YOU SHOW YOUR CHARACTER.
        TODAY'S THE DAY YOU SHOW EVERYONE WHAT
        YOU'RE REALLY MADE OF.

- SAME BUT EVEN TIGHTER.

(CONTINUED

                    WALKER (CONT'D)
AND I DAMN WELL KNOW YOU'RE MADE OF
BETTER THAN THIS, RIGHT FLINCH?

YOU'RE GONNA LET A GIRL DRIVE YOU NUTS
LIKE THIS?

ROLL IT OFF AND BE A MAN.

ALL YOU DONE IN YOUR LIFE- ALL THE STUFF
THAT MADE YOU, YOU--

--AND YOU WANNA BE REMEMBERED AS SOME
SHMUCK HELD A LITTLE GIRL?

HELL, NO. AM I RIGHT? THIS IS SILLY SHIT.

I SAY- I SAY WE FORGET THIS SILLY SHIT
TODAY, YOU OPEN THE DOOR, THEN ME AND
YOU, WHAT ARE WE GONNA DO?

WE'LL FIND THAT BITCH AND GET YOUR MONEY
BACK IS WHAT.

4- PAUSE. SAME EVEN TIGHTER

5- SAME EVEN TIGHTER. THIS IS NOW A CLOSE UP ON WALKERS
DETERMINED FACE. JUST ONE BEAD OF SWEAT.

                    FLINCH
AH DAMN IT... THIS IS JUST...

                    WALKER
YEAH, LET'S JUST OPEN THE DOOR AND...

PAGE 6-

1- BIG PANEL- HALF A PAGE

SPX: BOOM!!

WIDER SHOT OF HALLWAY. THE NOISE KNOCKS WALKER AND THE SWAT
TEAM OFF THEIR FEET FOR A SECOND.

2- IN A FURY OF ACTIVITY, LIKE A WELL OILED MACHINE, POWERS
DIVES OUT OF THE WAY SO THE SWAT TEAM CAN BURST THE DOOR
DOWN.

                                        (CONTINUED

CONTINUED: (8)

PX: CRACK!!

- FROM POWERS P.O.V. POWER'S GUN IS OUT IN THE FOREGROUND.
N THE LIVING ROOM OF A TYPICAL CHEAP APARTMENT. RUBBLE IS
ALLING DOWN IN THE CENTER OF THE ROOM. SWAT TEAM IS RUNNING
LL OVER THE APARTMENT.

- HE POINTS HIS GUN TO A GIANT HOLE IN THE CEILING.

- THEN POINTS DOWN TO THE FLOOR WHERE THE FALLING RUBBLE
ANDS.

- THEN POINTS TO THE RIGHT, NOTHING BUT HALLWAY AND SWAT.

- THEN TO THE LEFT, A CUTE SEVEN YEAR OLD GIRL, CALISTA IS
ATING PEANUT BUTTER OUT OF A JAR AND WATCHING A CARTOON
APE. SHE IS JUST NOW, BROKEN FROM HER INTENSE TELEVISION
ATCHING TO SEE THE LARGE GROUP OF MEN COMING INTO THE ROOM.

- SAME. TIGHT ON WALKER LOOKING AT THE GIRL. SHES OK.

PAGE 7-

EQUAL HALF PAGE PANELS

- WALKER AND A COUPLE OF SWAT LOOK UP THROUGH THE HOLE IN
THE CEILING. ALL WE CAN SEE IS A DOT WITH A SMOKE TRAIL.

- A HIGH BIRD'S EYE LOOK DOWN AT WALKER AND A COUPLE OF SWAT
TARING UP AT THE SKY. THEY LOOK LIKE LITTLE KIDS LOOKING UP
T A KITE.

                    SETZER
          TOTAL ASSHOLE!

                    WALKER
          WELL, HE FOUND ANOTHER WAY OUT.

                    SETZER
          HE COULDN'T DO THAT THREE HOURS AGO? I
          MISSED THE GAME.

(CONTINUED

CONTINUED: (9)

PAGES 8- 9

DOUBLE PAGE SPREAD

PANELS 1-3 ARE PAGE LONG SLANTED SHOTS.

A STREET LEVEL WORM'S EYE VIEW OF WALKER AND SOME OF THE SWAT
TEAM COMING OUT THE FRONT DOOR OF THE APARTMENT BUILDING.
THEY ARE LOOKING UP TOWARDS THE DOT AND SMOKE TRAIL THAT
POPPED OUT OF THE ROOF OF THE APARTMENT. IT IS A LITTLE
BIGGER NOW.

3- SAME. WE ARE FOLLOWING WALKER AND THE COPS AS THEY FOLLOW
FLINCH LIKE HE IS A KITE IN THE AIR. THEY ARE NOW DOWN THE
STAIRS IN THE MIDDLE OF THE STREET.

THERE ARE MANY GUNS TRAINED ON THE DOT AND TRAIL AS IT IS NOW
COMING TOWARDS THEM. WALKER HAS TURNED TOWARDS THE READER BUT
IS LOOKING ANNOYED AT THE OTHER COPS.

                    WALKER
              WHOAH WHOAH WHOAH!
              DO NOT SHOOT!!

                    SETZER
              WHAT?

                    WALKER
              WHO KNOWS WHAT HE- HE COULD HAVE A
              NUCLEAR DEVISE STRAPPED TO HIS BACK FOR
              ALL WE KNOW!! CHRIST SAKE!!

4- SAME. THE GUNS ARE STILL TRAINED ON FLINCH, WHO WE CAN
CLEARLY SEE. HE IS HEADING TOWARDS THE GROUND. FEET FIRST.

FLINCH IS A SKINNY LOSER IN A GREEN JUMP SUIT WITH A CRAPPY
VERSION OF THE ROCKETEER BACK PACK STRAPPED TO HIS BACK.

HIS BACK PACK IS PUTTING...

SPX:PUT PUT PUT

THIS IS SLOWING FLINCH'S DESCENT DOWN, BUT HE ISN'T IN
CONTROL OF HIS LANDING.

                    FLINCH
              OW...OW...OW...OH NO...

5- WORM'S EYE VIEW OF WALKER, THE COPS AND THE PRESS. THEY
ALL FLINCH AS FLINCH HITS THE GROUND WITH A THUD.

SPX: THUD.

                                        (CONTINUED

CONTINUED: (10)

- THE BILL MURRAY I HAVE BEEN SLIMED SHOT FROM GHOSTBUSTERS.
FLINCH IS LAYING ON HIS BACK PACK, IN PAIN

>   FLINCH (CONT'D)
>   SERIOUSLY...OW.

PAGE 10-

- THE EDDIE MURPHY "IS THERE A PROBLEM OFFICER'S?" SHOT FROM
TRADING PLACES. TIGHT ON FLINCH'S FACE WHICH NOW HAS EIGHT
GUNS TO IT.

- WIDE SHOT. THE STREET IS A CHAOS OF ACTIVITY. IN THE
FOREGROUND FLINCH IS BEING PUT INTO AN AMBULANCE. WALKER HAS
CAUGHT UP JUST BEFORE THEY SLIDE HIM IN. IN THE BACKGROUND WE
CAN SEE A COUPLE OF SPECIAL SWAT TEAM MEMBERS PUTTING HIS
BACK PACK INTO A TRANSPARENT HIGH TECH CONTAINER. THE PRESS
IS EATING IT ALL UP.

>   WALKER
>   HOLD ON. HOLD ON.

- TWO SHOT OF WALKER. HE IS IN FLINCH'S FACE.

>   WALKER (CONT'D)
>   HEY ASSHOLE, WHAT'S WITH YOU, MAN?

>   FLINCH
>   WHAT?

>   WALKER
>   I'VE NEVER SEEN YOU BEFORE IN MY LIFE?
>   WHAT IS WITH YOU CALLING ME DOWN HERE TO
>   DEAL WITH ALL YOUR BULLSHIT?

4- TIGHT ON FLINCH, IN PAIN AND A LITTLE SCARED. WALKER IS
CASTING A SHADOW OVER HIM.

>   FLINCH
>   IT WAS- IT WAS WOLFE...HE...

5- WALKER FROM FLINCH'S P.O.V.

>   WALKER
>   WHAT?

6- SAME AS FOUR.

>   (CONTINUED

CONTINUED: (11)

                        FLINCH
          IT WAS WOLFE HE- HE SAID...WHEN I WAS
          HOLD UP IN BLAIR GREEN WITH WOLFE AND
          THOSE GUYS...

          HE SAID- HE SAID IF THE SHIT EVER GOT TO
          THICK WE SHOULD ALWAYS ASK FOR YOU-D-D-D-
          DETECTIVE CHRISTIAN WALKER...

7- SAME AS FIVE.

                        WALKER
          WHY?

8- SAME AS FOUR.

                        FLINCH
          HE SAID YOU WERE SOFT- SOFT ON GUYS WITH
          POWERS.

9- SAME AS FIVE. WALKER IS REALLY MIFFED AT THIS.

PAGE 11-

1- SAME AS PANEL 2 OF LAST PAGE. A TWO SHOT OF FLINCH AND
WALKER. BUT WALKER IS GRABBING FLINCH BY THE COLLAR AND IS
READY TO HIT HIM. THE OTHER PEOPLE REACT, TRYING TO STOP HIM.

                        WALKER
          WELL, YOU TELL WOLFE THAT WHEN HE'S UP
          FOR PAROLE IN 4 YEARS AND 3 MONTHS!!

          YOU TELL HIM THAT I'LL BE THERE AT THE
          HEARING AND HE'LL SEE HOW SOFT I AM!!

                        FLINCH
          PLEASE- NO DON'T.

                        AMBULANCE DRIVER
          DETECTIVE PLEASE!!

                        CAPTAIN
          WHAT'S GOING ON HERE?

2- MID SHOT OF WALKER. HE HAS COMPOSED HIMSELF AND NOW HE IS
A LITTLE ASHAMED OF HIMSELF. HIS CAPTAIN IS STANDING BEHIND
HIM.

                                        (CONTINUED

CONTINUED: (12)

                    CAPTAIN (CONT'D)
          WALKER, WHAT'S WRONG WITH YOU?

          THE PRESS IS ALL OVER THIS.

                    WALKER
          IT'S DONE. LET'S NOT MAKE A THING OF IT.

                    CAPTAIN
          A THING? I'LL SEE YOU BACK AT THE
          STATION.

3- WALKER IS WATCHING HIS CAPTAIN KISS THE MEDIA'S ASS AS HE
GOES TO LEAVE THE OTHER COPS TO CLEAN UP THE MESS.

IN THE BACKGROUND IS THE FRONT OF THE APARTMENT BUILDING. A
SWAT TEAM MEMBER IS HOLDING THE GIRL.

                    SWAT 1
          WALKER...

4- THE SWAT TEAM MEMBER HOLDING THE GIRL COMES UP TO WALKER.

                    SWAT 1 (CONT'D)
          HAPPY BIRTHDAY!

                    WALKER
          WHAT IS THIS?

                    SWAT 1
          LIEUTENANT SAYS SHE'S YOURS...

                    WALKER
          HOW SO?

                    SWAT 1
          YOUR COLLAR. DEMS THE RULES...

5- TIGHT ON CALISTA'S ADORABLE FACE. SHE IS SAD AND CONFUSED.

6- HER POINT OF VIEW, WALKER LOOKS DOWN AT HER.

(CONTINUED

CONTINUED: (13)

PAGE 12-

1- EXTERIOR SHOT OF THE POLICE STATION. AN OLD FASHIONED
BUILDING ON THE OUTSIDE. SOMETHING OUT OF A 50'S CRIME MOVIE.
THE LIT BALL LIGHT OUTSIDE THAT SAYS POLICE STATION.

>   WALKER
>   YES HELLO? I'VE BEEN ON HOLD FOR--
>
>   LISTEN THIS IS DETECTIVE CHRISTIAN
>   WALKER... HOMI- HOMICIDE. YES.
>
>   WHAT? NO, I NEED YOUR HELP. I- WHAT? NO.
>   IS THIS SOCIAL SERVICES? WELL, I HAVE A
>   YOUNG-- WHAT?
>
>   NO. NO I DIDN'T HEAR. NO.

2- THE INSIDE OF A THE HOMICIDE SQUAD ROOM. ITS A HUSTLE AND
A BUSTLE. ITS A TYPICAL STATION HOUSE, GO GET YOUR PHOT
REFERENCE YOU LAZY FUCKER.

PEOPLE HUSTLE ABOUT, BUT....

BIG BUT.

THERE IS SOMETHING A LITTLE OFF ABOUT IT. WE CAN TELL THAT
PEOPLE WITH SUPERPOWERS EFFECT EVERY PART OF THE STATION.

THERE ARE BULLETPROOF GLASS CAGES AND SOME PEOPLE HAVE WEIRD
ARMOR ON. THERE ARE POSTERS ON THE WALL. ONE OF THEM IS RETRO
GIRL SAYING TO BUCKLE YOUR SEAT BELT. THIS BROUGHT TO YOU BY
RETRO GIRL INC. AND CITY COUNCIL FOR A BETTER TOMORROW.

I DON'T WANT THIS TO BE A HIGH TECH PLACE OR FILLED WITH
SUPERPOWERED PEOPLE. THAT WOULD BE SILLY AND ITS BEEN DONE,
THIS IS MORE SUBTLE.

WANTED POSTERS AND A SPECIAL WEAPONS WALL IS ENOUGH.

THINK THE SQUAD ROOM OF HOMICIDE LIFE ON THE STREET...
PLAYING EVERY NIGHT ON COURT TV.

>   WALKER (CONT'D)
>   WHEN DID THIS HAPPEN? NO, I HAVEN'T SEEN
>   THE NEWS. NO, I DIDN'T-- WERE PEOPLE
>   HURT?
>
>   GONE, GONE?
>
>   THE BUILDING IS JUST- ITS GONE.
>
>   (MORE)

CONTINUED: (14)

                    WALKER (CONT'D)
          FIREBALL? FIREBALL- GOOD LORD! YEAH, I
          THOUGHT THAT GUY WAS...NO.

          OK. WELL, I AM REALLY SORRY TO- THAT'S
          HORRIBLE. IT...

          WELL, I HAVE THIS LITTLE GIRL AND...

          HOW IS THAT GOING TO? WELL, I CAN'T. I
          UNDERSTAND THERE'S NOBODY THERE.

           YES, I UNDERSTAND THAT THERE IS NO THERE
          ANYMORE.

          HEY, I SAID I- YES I DO.

          I AM A HOMICIDE DETECTIVE AND I AM IN THE
          MIDDLE OF FIFTEEN OPEN- NO I CAN'T.

3- TIGHTER ON WALKER. HE IS LOSING HIS BATTLE ON THE PHONE.

                    WALKER (CONT'D)
          NO- NO I CAN'T.

          'CAUSE YOU'RE SUPPOSED TO- CAN'T YOU SEE
          I AM TRYING TO DO THE BEST THING FOR THE--

          DAMN.

4- THE CONVERSATION HAS OBVIOUSLY ENDED.

5- RUBBING HIS FACE IN FRUSTRATION WITH ONE HAND, WALKER
DANGLES THE PHONE OVER THE RECEIVER.

6- THEN HANGS IT UP.

7- TIGHT ON THE GIRL LOOKING AT THE PHONE

8- THEN AT WALKER.

9- WALKER IS INTERNALLY CONFUSED AS TO WHAT TO DO NOW.

(CONTINUED

CONTINUED: (15)

PAGE 13-

1- HE LOOKS AT THE GIRL.

2- SHE LOOKS BACK. INNOCENT EYES. CHILDLIKE EXPRESSION OF
CURIOSITY.

                    CALISTA
          WHAT'S A CLITORIS?

3- WALKER JUST STARES AT HER BLANKLY.

4- SAME.

                    WALKER
          UH- I DON'T KNOW.

5- CALISTA LOOKING AT THE FLOOR. TALKING TO HERSELF.

                    CALISTA
          HOW COME NOBODY KNOWS THAT?

          I ASK EVERYONE AND NOBODY HAS A CLUE.

PAGE 14-15

DOUBLE PAGE SPREAD.

A ROW OF LITTLE PANELS ON TOP. A LONG DOUBLE PAGE SPREAD OF
THE ROOM IN THE MIDDLE AND A ANOTHER ROW OF LITTLE PANELS ON
THE BOTTOM.

1- WALKER.

                    WALKER
          YOU HUNGRY?

2- WALKER REACHES INTO HIS DESK AND PULLS OUT A BOWL.

                    CALISTA
          TOTALLY. LAST NIGHT MY MOM MADE THESE
          PORK CHOPS LIKE SHE SAW ON THE FOOD
          CHANNEL,

3- THEN ANOTHER. THEN SILVERWARE.

                                        (CONTINUED

CONTINUED: (16)

CALISTA (CONT'D)
BUT SHE LIKE TOTALLY BURNED THE SHIT OUT
OF THEM. AND I HATE PEAS. YOU LIKE PEAS?

- THEN A BIG BOX OF FRUITY CHOCO CRUNCHIES SERIAL.

WALKER
I DO NOT LIKE PEAS.

- CALISTA AMAZED.

CALISTA
YOU KEEP CEREAL IN YOUR DESK?

- WALKER OPENS THE BOX AND POURS THE DRY CEREAL IN.

WALKER
YEP.

- CALISTA IMPRESSED.

CALISTA
THAT IS THE COOLEST THING I'VE EVER SEEN
IN MY LIFE.

- WALKER HANDS HER BOWL OF DRY CEREAL AND HOLDS HIS.

WALKER
WELL, YOU'RE YOUNG.

- BIG PANEL!!- WALKER AND THE GIRL WALK THROUGH HOMICIDE
DEPARTMENT. A WAIST LEVEL LOOK AROUND THIS UNIQUE DEPARTMENT.

CALISTA
HEY, YOU KNOW WHAT?

WALKER
WHAT?

CALISTA
MY MOMMY SAYS THAT I CAN EXPRENTIATE
MYSELF ANY WAY I WANT.

WALKER
EXPRENTIATE?

CALISTA
SHE SAYS HER DADDY- HE USED TO LIKE SMACK
HER EVERY TIME SHE TALKED AND THAT I CAN
TALK ABOUT WHATEVER I WANT BECAUSE SHE
SAID HE WAS AN ASSHOLE.

(CONTINUED

CONTINUED: (17)

>   WALKER
> YOU DON'T SAY?

>   CALISTA
> DO YOU KNOW HIM?

>   WALKER
> WHO?

LITTLE PANELS.

10- WALKER AND CALISTA AT THE VENDING MACHINES.

>   CALISTA
> MY MOM'S DAD?

>   WALKER
> DO I KNOW HIM? NO.

>   CALISTA
> OH. I THINK HE KILLED SOMEBODY OR
> SOMETHING,

> THAT'S WHY I ASKED IS ALL.

11- WALKER LOOKS DOWN PUZZLED AT HER. HE HAS A MILK.

>   WALKER
> HE DID?

>   CALISTA
> I THINK. OR SOMEBODY KILLED HIM OR
> SOMETHING, I DON'T KNOW.

>   WALKER
> YOU'RE TOO LITTLE TO BE THINKING ABOUT
> THINGS LIKE THAT.

12- CALISTA LOOKS AT HER BOWL OF DRY CEREAL.

>   CALISTA
> YOU WATCH CARTOONS?

>   WALKER
> USED TO.

13- CALISTA LOOKS UP.

(CONTINUED

CONTINUED: (18)

                    CALISTA
          DO YOU SEE THIS THING THAT SOMETIMES THE
          BACKGROUNDS AND THE PEOPLE DON'T LOOK
          RIGHT?

14- WALKER IS LOOKING ACROSS THE STATION HOUSE. THERE IS
COMMOTION.

PAGE 16-

ALL THE KUTTER SHOTS ARE WIDE. FROM WALKER'S POV.

KUTTER, 20'S, IS A YOUNG, SEVERELY AMBITIOUS ROOKIE DETECTIVE
WHOSE IDEALS AND ALLEGIANCES MAY OR MAY NOT BE ON THE UP AND
UP.

HE LOOKS JUST LIKE BENJAMIN BRATT FROM LAW AND ORDER

1- HE HAS BROUGHT IN A VILLAIN...YOUR CHOICE MIKE.

                    VILLAIN
          YOU ONLY THINK YOU CAN HOLD ME!! DO YOU
          UNDERSTAND? DO YOU? YOUR PLAIN OF
          EXISTENCE IS ONLY ONE OF...

                    KUTTER
          CALM DOWN BIG TIME!

          IT'S OVER. YOU KNOW IT'S OVER. I KNOW ITS
          OVER. EVERYBODY KNOWS IT'S OVER. SUCK IT
          UP.

2- WALKER IS WATCHING.

                    WALKER
          HOW SO?

                    CALISTA
          SOMETIMES THE BACKGROUNDS ARE ALL COOL
          LOOKING AND NICELY COLORED IN OR
          SOMETHING. BUT THE PEOPLE AREN'T. THEY-
          THEY ARE JUST FLAT LOOKING. SUCKY.

3- THE VILLAIN TRIES TO ESCAPE AND THEY HIT HIM WITH
SOMETHING THAT IS SIMILAR TO A CATTLEPROD.

                                        (CONTINUED

CONTINUED: (19)

                    VILLAIN
          YOU WILL NEVER LEARN!! YOU WILL
          NEVER...!!

4- WALKER IS WATCHING THIS AND NOT THE GIRL.

                    WALKER
          NEVER NOTICED.

5- THEY THROW HIM IN THE TANK.

                    CALISTA
          NEVER NOTICED? IT DRIVES ME UP THE DAMN
          WALL IS ALL. WHY DO THEY DO THAT?? WHY
          CAN'T THEY PAINT THE PEOPLE AS NICE AS
          THEY PAINT THE SKY?

                    COP
          KUTTER, CAN YOU KEEP IT UNDER CONTROL
          OVER THERE, I'M TRYING TO READ!!

                    KUTTER
          GOOD LUCK, HOT SHOT.

6- KUTTER SEES THAT WALKER IS WATCHING HIM.

                    WALKER
          YEAH, I DON'T - I DON'T KNOW.

7- KUTTER SMILES THERE IS SOMETHING BAD BETWEEN THE TWO.

PAGE 17-

1- WALKER IS FOCUSED BACK ON THE GIRL. THEY ARE WALKING BACK
TO THE DESK.

                    WALKER (CONT'D)
          HEY, WHY DO YOU HAVE TO SWEAR EVERY
          THIRTY SECONDS?

                    CALISTA
          SWEAR?

                    WALKER
          YOU KNOW...

                                        (CONTINUED

ONTINUED: (20)

                    CALISTA
          I TOLD YOU, MY MOM...

                    WALKER
          YOUR MOM DOESN'T LET YOU TALK THAT WAY,
          YOU AIN'T FOOLIN' ME.

- THEY ARE BACK AT THE DESK. CALISTA SITTING IN HER LITTLE
HAIR.

                    CALISTA
          SHE AIN'T COMIN BACK TO GET ME IS SHE?

- WALKER IN HIS SEAT. SERIOUS.

                    WALKER
          I DON'T KNOW.

- SHE LOOKS AT HER CEREAL.

                    CALISTA
          DAMN SUCKY CARTOONS.

- TIGHT ON THE BOWL FULL OF LITTLE 'R'S FLOATING IN MILK.

AGE 18-

IX PAGE LONG PANELS

VERY TIGHT CLOSE UP OF DEENA PILGRIM. SHE IS TELLING AN
NECDOTE.

HE SHOT EVENTUALLY PULLS OUT TO A WIDE SHOT OF THE CAPTAIN'S
FFICE. HE LISTENS INTENTLY.

-

                    DEENA
          HA! YEAH--THAT'S A FUNNY STORY ACTUALLY.

          I WAS ON SWAT FOR I DON'T KNOW- LIKE A
          WEEK.

          THERE WAS THIS GUY HOLD- HE HOLD HIMSELF
          UP IN SOME GOVERNMENT OFFICE.

                                        (CONTINUED

CONTINUED: (21)

     CAPTAIN
DID HE HAVE..?

     DEENA
WHAT? NO. JUST A GUY.

GUY WITH A BEEF. GUY WITH A SCREW LOOSE
HOLDS HIMSELF UP IN A BUILDING. HIS MOMMY
DIDN'T SPANK HIM ENOUGH AS A KID, I DON'T
KNOW.

BUT HE HOLDS HIMSELF UP IN THERE SO LONG
WE HAD TO BE RELIEVED FOR A SECOND SHIFT.

     CAPTAIN
THAT'S A LONG..

     DEENA
TOTALLY. SO, THE SHIFTS OVER. WE DROP OUR
GEAR IN THE VAN AND WE ALL HEAD OVER TO
THIS THAI PLACE THAT WE HAD BEEN STARING
AT FROM ACROSS THE STREET FOR THE LAST
BILLION HOURS STRAIGHT.

2-

     DEENA (CONT'D)
NOW THE WHOLE RESTAURANT IS FILLED WITH
SWAT TEAM GUYS. SO WE'RE EATIN' OUR
APPETIZERS AND KICKIN' BACK WHEN MY
PARTNER DAVE...

HE POINTS OUT THE WINDOW TO THE PAYPHONE.

THE GUY- THE GUY WE WERE WAITIN' ON-

THE GUY THE NEGOTIATOR HAD SPENT LIKE A
BILLION HOURS TRYING TO TALK OUT OF THE
BUILDING UNTIL HE STOPPED TALKING...

THE GUY IS RIGHT THERE MAKIN' A PHONE
CALL.

     CAPTAIN
YOU RECOGNIZED THE GUY?

     DEENA
WELL, WE ALL DID ONCE WE SEEN HIM.

THEY HAD A PIC THEY PASSED AROUND SO WE
KNEW WHO TO TAKE DOWN IF IT CAME TO THAT.

    (MORE)

CONTINUED: (22)

                    DEENA (cont'd)
SO LIKE- LIKE THE WHOLE RESTAURANT JUST
STARES AT HIM IN DISBELIEF AND THEN ALL
AT ONCE- LIKE ALL AT THE SAME TIME...WE
POUR OUT-

THE WHOLE RESTAURANT POURS OUT ONTO THE
STREET AND CIRCLES THE PHONE BOOTH.

3-

                    DEENA (CONT'D)
WE ALL HAVE OUR GUNS OUT. WE'RE READY.
WE'RE READY FOR FREDDY.

THE GUY- THE GUY DOESN'T EVEN NOTICE US.
HE JUST KEEPS ON TALKING.

FIFTY GUNS AT HIS HEAD HE'S TOTALLY
OBLIVIOUS.

                    CAPTAIN
'S FUNNY...

                    DEENA
NOT THE END OF IT.

SO ONE OF THE GUYS, JOEY, HE LIGHTLY TAPS
ON THE GLASS TO GET HIS ATTENTION.

THE GUY DOES ONE OF THESE MOVES WHERE HE
JUST TURNS AWAY FROM THE DOOR HOLDING HIS
HAND TO HIS EAR.

SO JOEY TAPS ON THE GLASS AGAIN, NOW THE
PERP TURNS REAL SHARP AND BARKS: "DO YOU
SEE I'M ON THE...."

AND NOW HE SEES WHAT'S WHAT. SO FUCKING
FUNNY. THE GUY SHAT HIMSELF I SWEAR
TOO...PRICELESS.

                    CAPTAIN
GOOD ONE...

4-

                    DEENA
YEAH...

SO THE GUY HE - HE GOES FOR IT.

                    CAPTAIN
NO...

                                        (CONTINUED

CONTINUED: (23)

                        DEENA
          YEAH.

                        CAPTAIN
          SO...

                        DEENA
          SO, HE'S RIDDLED IN A SECOND. DOWN FOR
          THE COUNT. ITS OVER. POPPED.

                        CAPTAIN
          JEEZ...

                        DEENA
          THAT'S THE WAY IT WENT DOWN.

          BUT THE PHONE- BUT THE PHONE IS STILL
          DANGING OFF THE HOOK.

          STILL IN ONE PIECE.

          WHOEVER WAS ON THE OTHER LINE, THEY HEARD
          THE WHOLE THING. CAN YOU IMAGINE?

          SO- SO DAVE HE- HE PICKS UP THE PHONE AND
          HE SAYS INTO THE RECEIVER:

          "I'M SORRY, YOUR FRIEND HERE HAS BEEN
          DISCONNECTED."

          AND WE- WE COULDN'T HELP IT, WE ALL BURST
          OUT LAUGHING AT THIS CRAZY FUCKING THING
          HE JUST SAID.

6-

                        CAPTAIN
          HE SAID THAT? THAT'S...

                        DEENA
          YEAH, THING OF IT IS THOUGH...THE PERSON
          ON THE OTHER END WAS THE GUY'S MOM.

                        CAPTAIN
          OY..

                        DEENA
          CAN YOU IMAGINE?

          SO - SO THAT'S WHAT HAPPENED TO MY OLD
          PARTNER.

                        (MORE)

(CONTINUED

CONTINUED: (24)

>>>>DEENA (cont'd)
I THINK HE'S WORKING AT BORDERS NOW
SOMEONE TOLD ME.

PAGE 19-

1- SAME AS SIX FROM LAST PAGE. WALKER BARGES IN.

>>>>WALKER
RED ALERT.

>>>>CAPTAIN
WALKER...

>>>>WALKER
I GOT SIDELINED WITH THE LITTLE GIRL FROM
THIS AFTERNOON'S BULLSHIT--
>>>>(TO DEENA)
HI
>>>>(TO CAPTAIN)
AND SOCIAL SERVICES...

>>>>CAPTAIN
IS NO MORE. I KNOW.

>>>>WALKER
I DIDN'T. I CAN'T - I DON'T KNOW WHAT TO
DO WITH...

2- SAME BUT TIGHTER. WALKER IS A LITTLE FRAZZED COMPARED TO
THE OTHER TWO'S LAID BACK MEETING.

>>>>DEENA
WHAT HAPPENED TO SOCIAL SERVICES?

>>>>CAPTAIN
A BLAST I HEARD...

>>>>WALKER
FIREBALL IS WHAT...

>>>>CAPTAIN
I'LL PUT IN A CALL TO GEAUGA COUNTY BUT
FOR THE MEANTIME YOU'RE GOING TO HAVE TO
BABY-SIT, I...

>>>>WALKER
BUT I HAVE CASES.

(CONTINUED

                  CAPTAIN
THIS IS TRUE.

                  WALKER
I HAVE CASES.

                  CAPTAIN
WE ALL HAVE CASES.

                  WALKER
BUT I HAVE CASES.

                  CAPTAIN
AND THAT'S WHY WE HAVE DAY CARE.

DROP HER OFF WITH BABS FOR THE SHIFT AND
WE WILL SEE WHAT WE CAN DO.

3- SAME BUT TIGHTER ONTO DEENA AND WALKER.

                  DEENA
HOW OLD IS SHE?

                  WALKER
WHAT? I DON'T I- I DON'T KNOW SIX OR- HOW
CAN YOU TELL?

                  DEENA
YOU COULD ASK.

                  WALKER
YEAH, WELL IT'S A- I'M SORRY, WHO ARE...?

                  DEENA
OH, I'M DEENA PILGRIM. I'VE JUST BEEN
REASSIGNED.

                  WALKER
OH- UH- CONGRATS I GUESS. PULL THE SHORT
END OF THE...

                  DEENA
NOPE, REQUESTED.

                  WALKER
SERIOUSLY?

                  DEENA
TOTALLY.

                  WALKER
HUH.

                    (CONTINUED

CONTINUED: (26)

                    DEENA
          SO DID YOU, RIGHT?

- WALKER JUST STARES AT HER.

- WALKER BACK TO THE CAPTAIN

                    WALKER
               (TO CAPTAIN)
          SO, WHAT FLOOR IS DAY CARE?

                    CAPTAIN
          THIRD. 309. TAKE YOUR NEW PARTNER WITH
          YOU.

- WALKER JUST STARES AT HER AGAIN.

                    WALKER
          HUH.

                    DEENA
          HUH, YOURSELF.

                    WALKER
          NO I...

                    DEENA
          COME ON.

PAGE 20-

- CALISTA LOOKING AROUND THE SQUAD ROOM. SHE SEES A COUPLE
OF COPS ARGUING.

                    COP 1
          HOW COULD YOU EVEN SAY THAT, THE GUY HAD
          A...

                    COP 2
          YOU KNOW!! YOU KNOW WHAT HE WAS GOING
          TO....

                    COP 1
          IT'S A 314. WHAT DO YOU DO IN A 314?

                                        (CONTINUED

CONTINUED: (27)

2- CALISTA WATCHES A COP PICK UP THE PHONE.

                    COP 3
          HOMICIDE. 4TH. THIS IS BERMAN...

3- CALISTA LOOKS TO THE PHONE ON WALKER'S DESK AS IT RINGS.

4- AND RINGS.

5- AND RINGS, CALISTA IS LOOKING TO SEE IF SOMEONE IS GOING
TO PICK IT UP.

6- CALISTA PICKS IT UP.

                    CALISTA
          HOMICIDE. 4TH. THIS IS CALISTA.

          WHAT?

          EEWW!!

          THAT'S SO GROSS- WHAT?

7- BIGGER PANEL. WALKER, PILGRIM BEHIND HIM, GRABS THE PHONE
AWAY FROM HER.

                    WALKER
          HOMICIDE, WAL- WHAT?

8- WALKER LOOKS LIKE HE SAW A GHOST.

9- DEENA LOOKS AT HIS REACTION.

                    DEENA
          WE ON THE MOVE?

10- SAME AS 8

                    WALKER
          WE'RE ON THE MOVE.

PAGE 21-

1- BIG PANEL. WALKER AND PILGRIM PULL UP TO A CRIME SCENE.

THIS ONE IS A BARRICADED ALLY. THE COPS ARE FENDING OFF AN
EXTREMELY LARGE GATHERING CROWD.

                                        (CONTINUED

CONTINUED: (28)

THE PRESS BEAT THEM TO IT BUT CAN'T GET NEAR THE SCENE.

2- DEENA AND WALKER IN THE CAR.

                    DEENA
          WELL- WELL, THIS IS A FUCKING CIRCUS.

                    WALKER
          THREE RING. GET USED TO IT.

3- THESE SHOTS ARE FROM THE P.O.V. OF THE CORPSE WE ARE
LOOKING UP AT WALKER AND PILGRIM AND A UNIFORM YOUNG
POLICEMAN.

BUILDING TOWER INTO PERSPECTIVE IN THE BACKGROUND

                    WALKER (CONT'D)
          WHO CALLED IT IN?

                    COP
          ANONYMOUS.

                    WALKER
          IT'S A LONG SHOT- BUT RUN A TAP ANYHOW.

                    DEENA
          COULD IT BE? THERE'S NO WAY IT'S HER.

                    WALKER
          IT'S HER.

                    DEENA
          COULD BE A LOOK-A-LIKE...

5- SAME, WALKER IS VERY SERIOUS.

                    WALKER
          COULD BE. BUT IT ISN'T.

                    DEENA
          BUT- HOW DO YOU KNOW?

                    WALKER
          MET HER.

                    DEENA
          STILL...

                    WALKER
          TRUST ME.

          SHES NOT-

(CONTINUED

CONTINUED: (29)

6- WALKER

                    WALKER (CONT'D)
          YOU DON'T FORGET HER.

          IT'S HER.

PAGE 22-

BIG PAGE SHOT OVER THEIR SHOULDERS DOWN TO THE GROUND OF THE
ALLEY.

IT IS A DEAD GIRL IN A HIP AND TASTEFUL WONDER GIRL STYLE
SUPERHERO OUTFIT AND SHORT SKIRT AND GO- GO BOOTS.

ITS RETRO GIRL.

AND SHE IS DEAD. HER THROAT CUT. A POOL OF ALMOST BLACK
BLOOD.

ON THE ALLEY WALL. MORE GRAFFITI LIKE IN THE FIRST SCENE.

THE PHRASE KAOTIC CHIC IS SPRAY PAINTED ON THE WALL WITH SOME
OTHER STUFF.

                    DEENA
          BUT SHE'S- SHE'S...

                    WALKER
          WHO COULD HAVE KILLED RETRO GIRL?

                    DEENA
          SHIT OL' MIGHTY, CAN I PICK EM.

NEXT ISSUE: WHO KILLED RETRO GIRL?

POWERS
THE SKETCHBOOK

In this section you will see one of Michael Avon Oeming's true strengths as an artist. Every gesture, every character design, every brushstroke looks so simple- so effortless- but in reality it is a laborious process. This is an intense decision making process that defines everything about the book.

For every sketch revealed here, there are literally dozens more. Mike is a fountain of ideas and images. For months prior to working on the actual pages I would receive daily faxes of these ideas and images. What a rush.

I hope you get even half the thrill from these that I do.

THE CHARACTERS

Here is a smattering of images that explore how many ways any of the characters could have gone.

WALKER

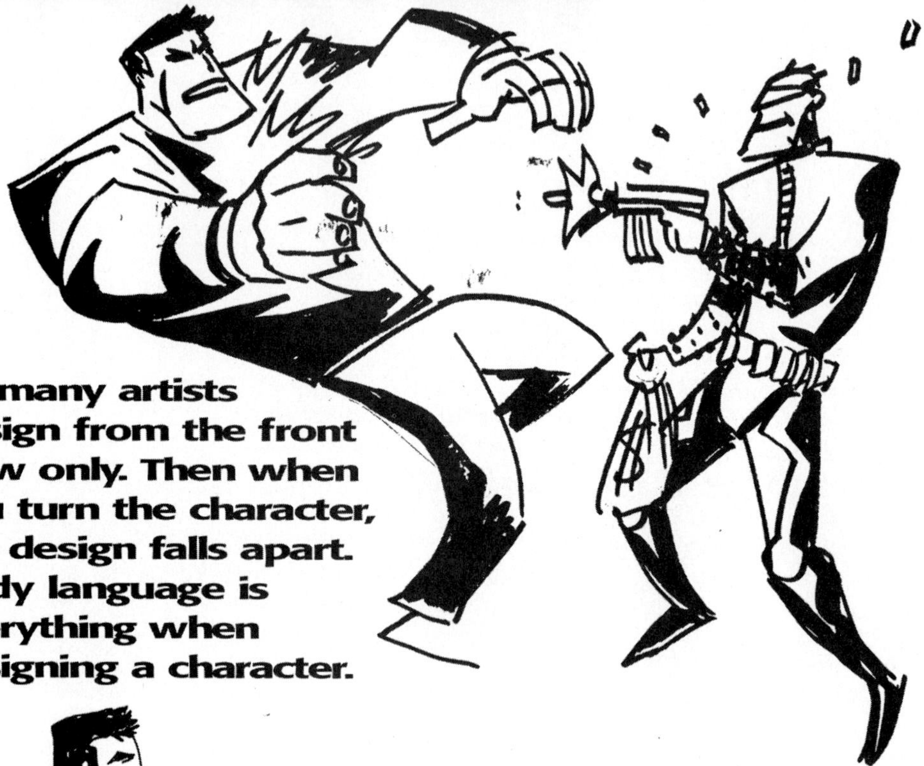

So many artists design from the front view only. Then when you turn the character, the design falls apart. Body language is everything when designing a character.

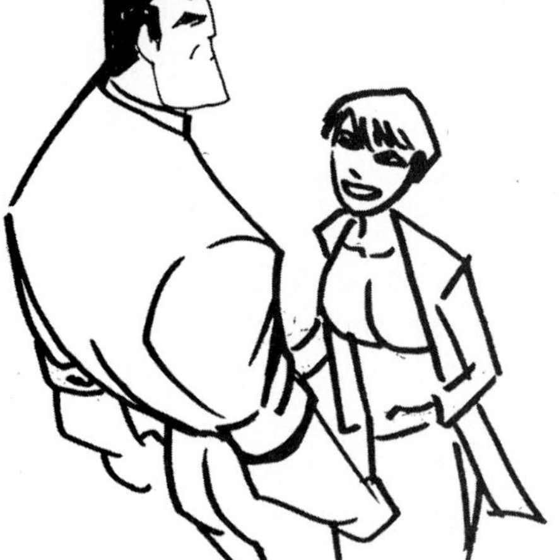

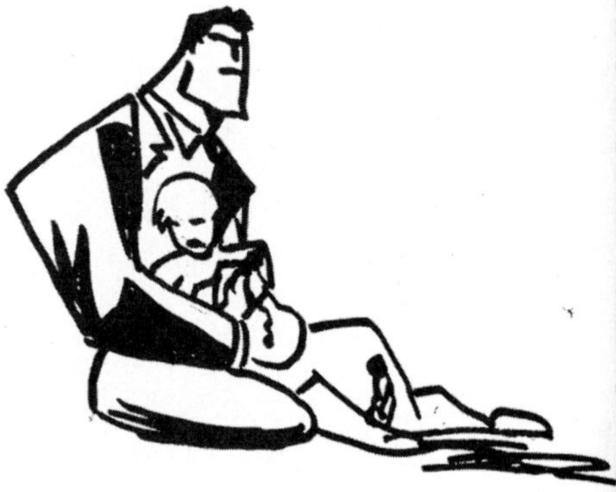

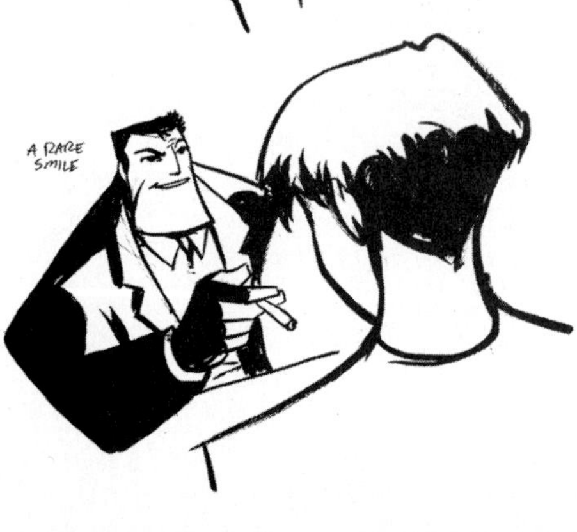
A RARE SMILE

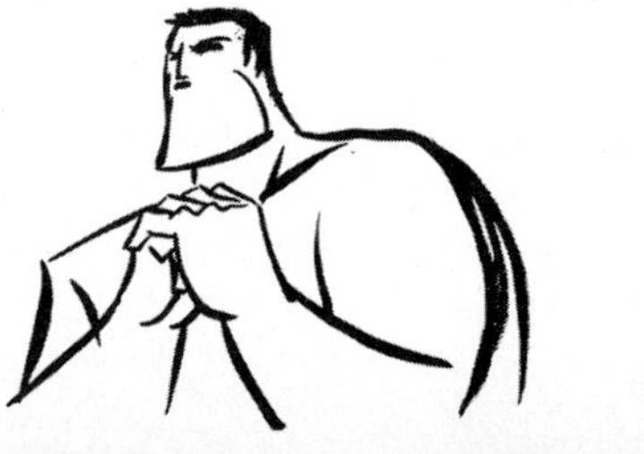

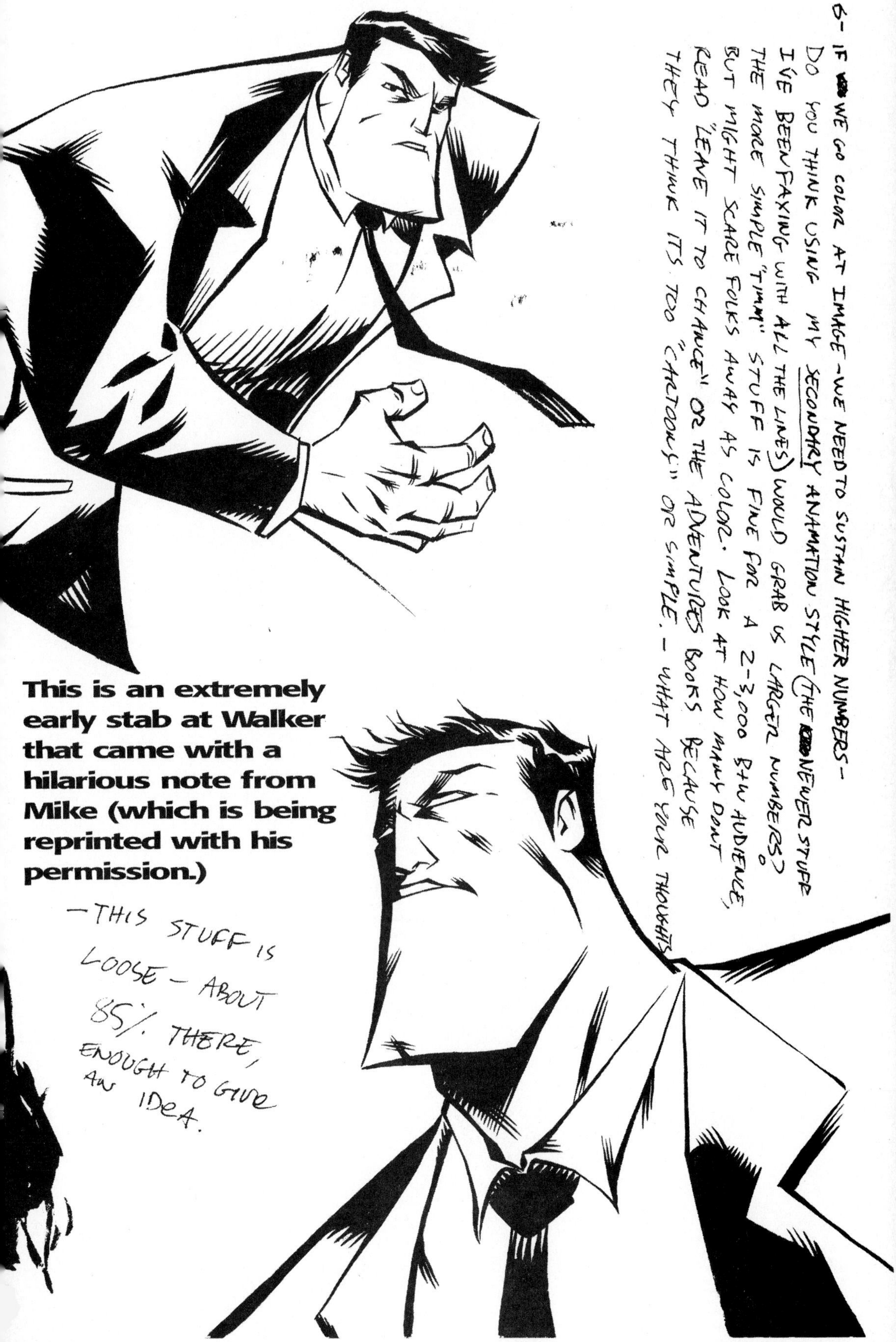
6- IF WE GO COLOR AT IMAGE - WE NEED TO SUSTAIN HIGHER NUMBERS -
DO YOU THINK USING MY SECONDARY ANAMATION STYLE (THE NEWER STUFF
I'VE BEEN FAXING WITH ALL THE LINES) WOULD GRAB US LARGER NUMBERS?
THE MORE SIMPLE "TIMM" STUFF IS FINE FOR A 2-3,000 B+W AUDIENCE,
BUT MIGHT SCARE FOLKS AWAY AS COLOR. LOOK AT HOW MANY DON'T
READ "LEAVE IT TO CHANCE" OR THE ADVENTURES BOOKS BECAUSE
THEY THINK ITS TOO "CARTOONS" OR SIMPLE. - WHAT ARE YOUR THOUGHTS
-THIS STUFF IS LOOSE - ABOUT 85%. THERE, ENOUGH TO GIVE AN IDEA.

This is an extremely early stab at Walker that came with a hilarious note from Mike (which is being reprinted with his permission.)

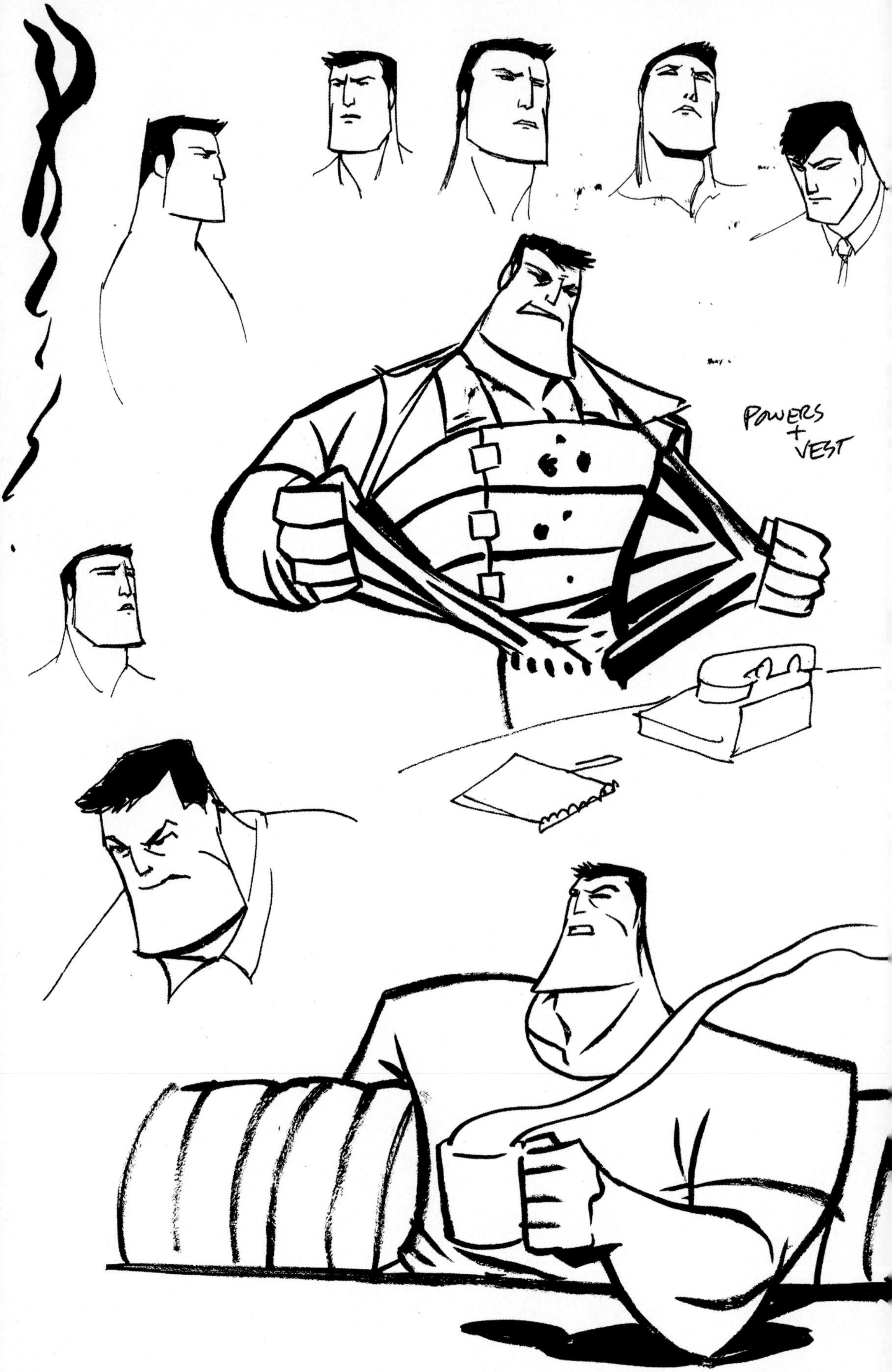
POWERS
+
VEST

elow: early model sheets for
Valker and Pilgrim. Notice that
ınky Leno chin.

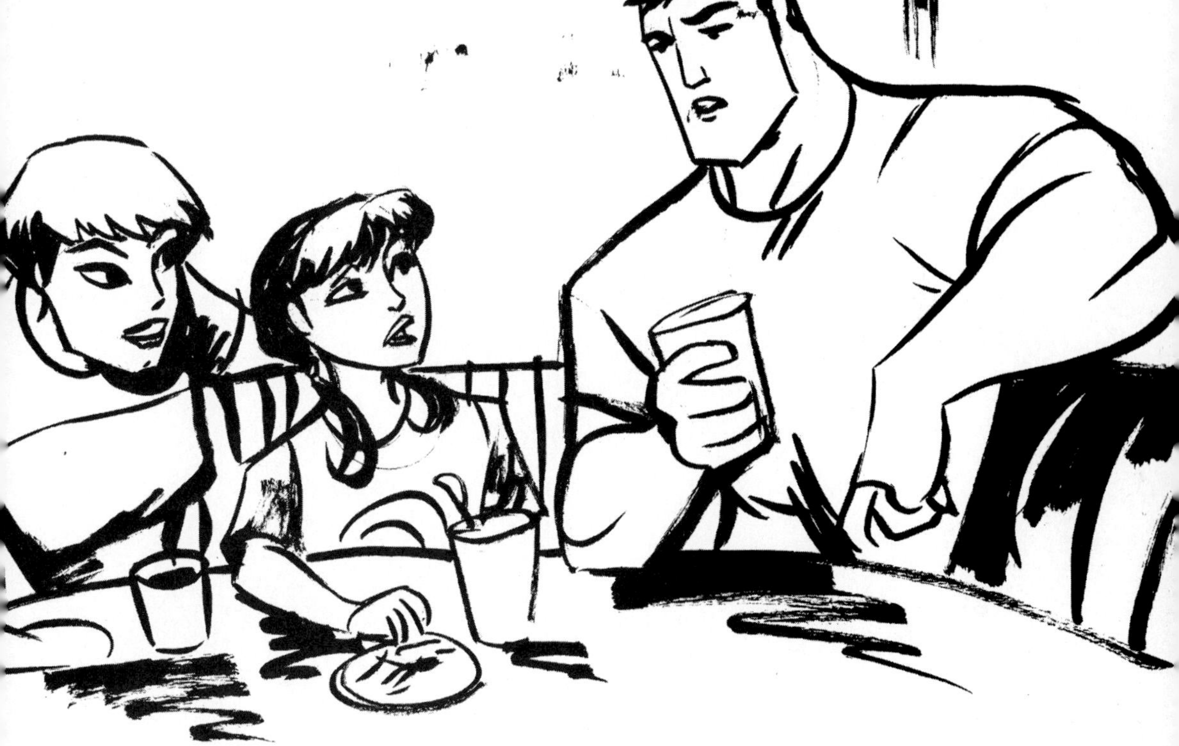

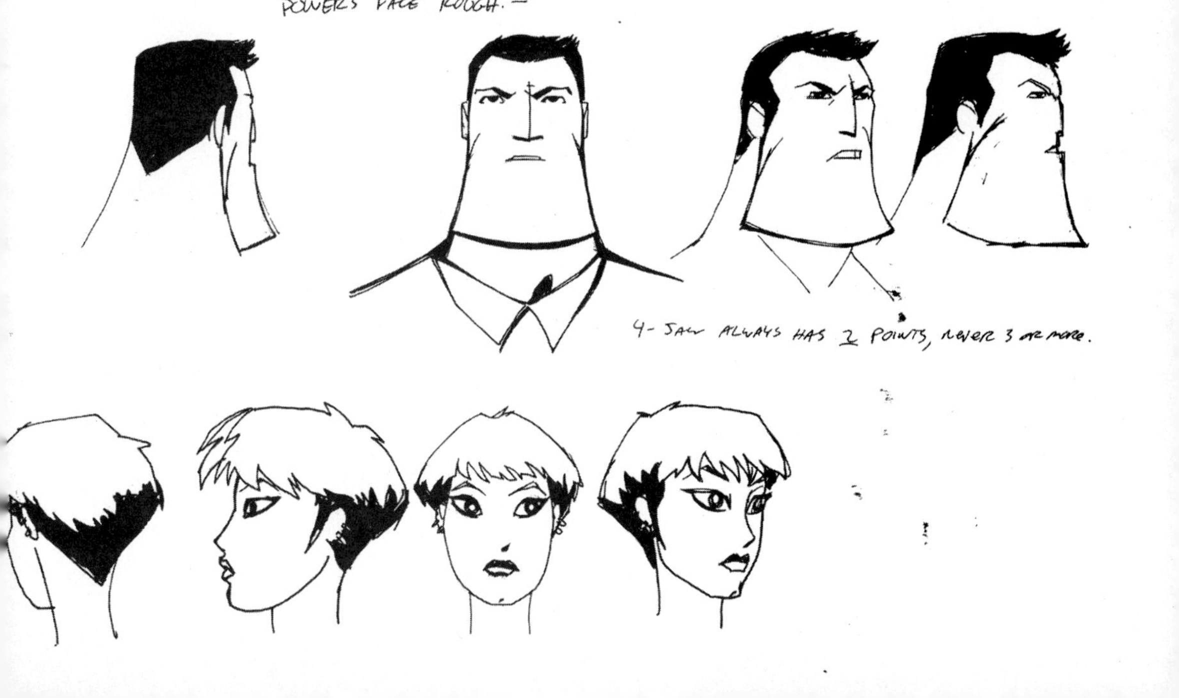
EYE OR NOSE
3-NOSE BRIDGE IS CURVED, NOT SHARP.
POWERS FACE ROUGH.—
4- JAW ALWAYS HAS 2 POINTS, NEVER 3 OR MORE.

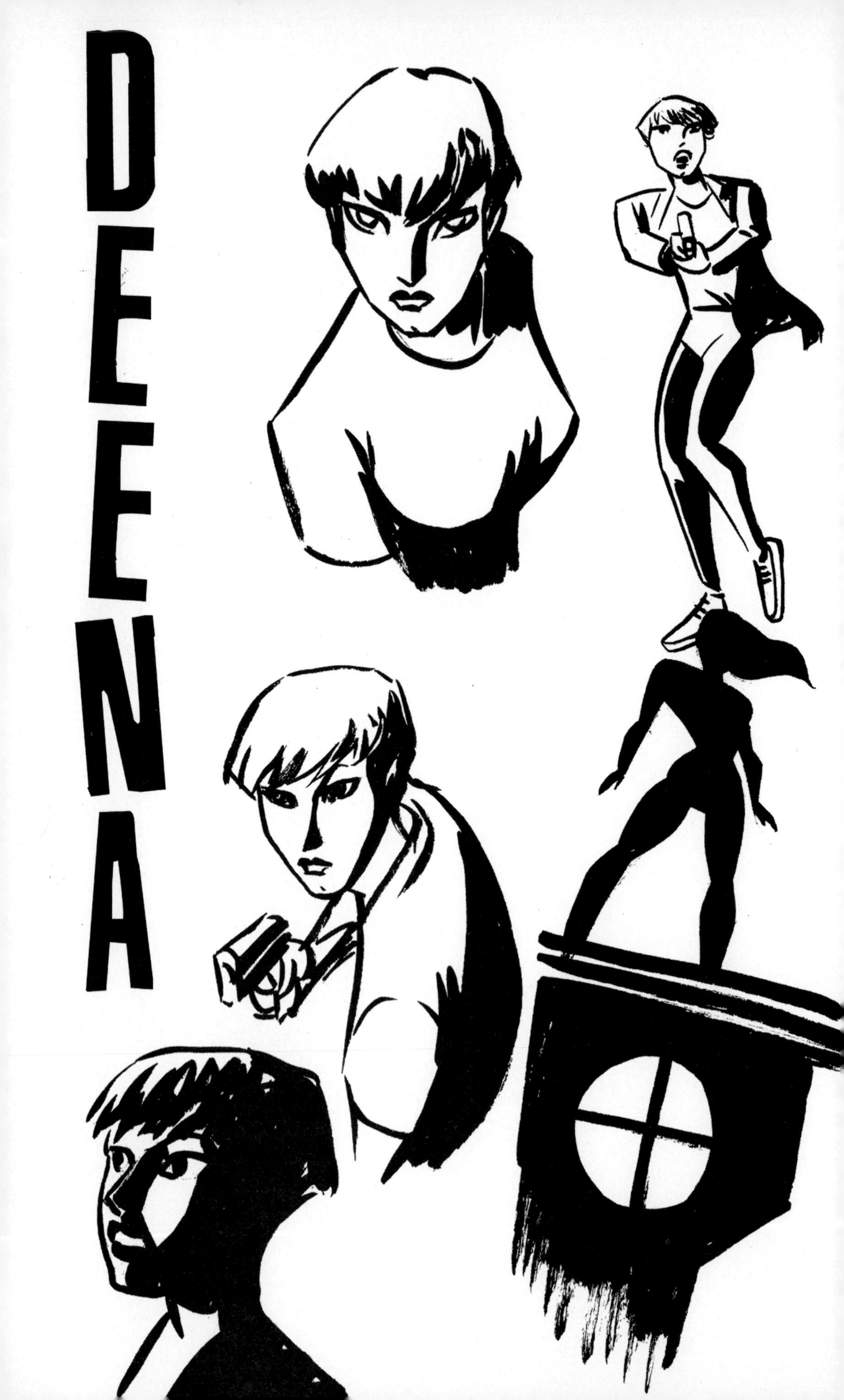
DEENA

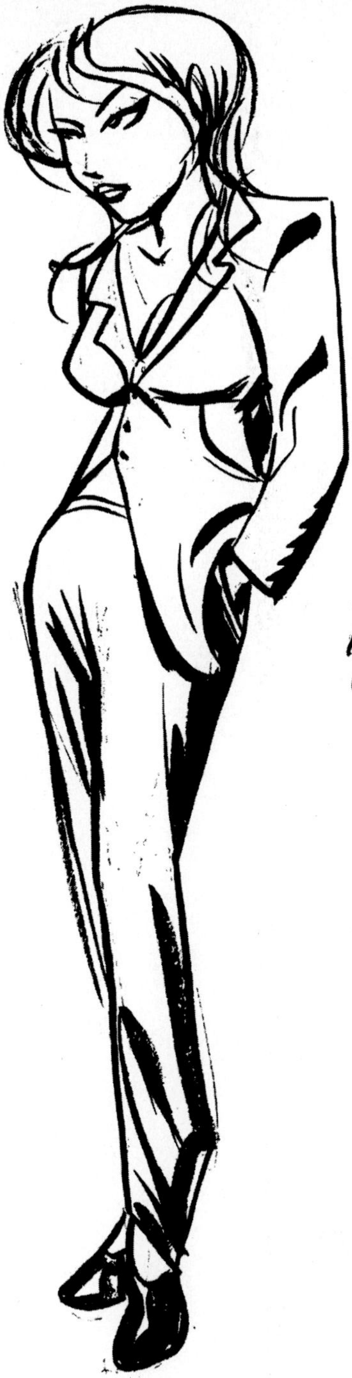

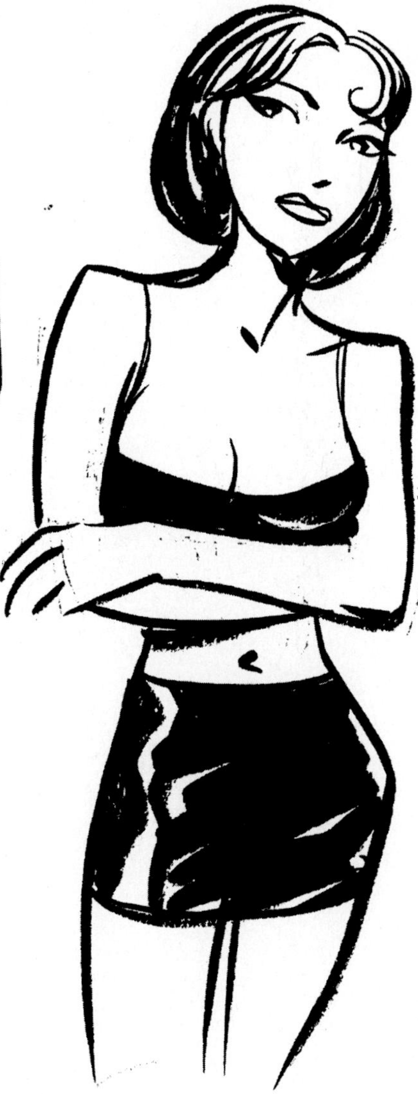

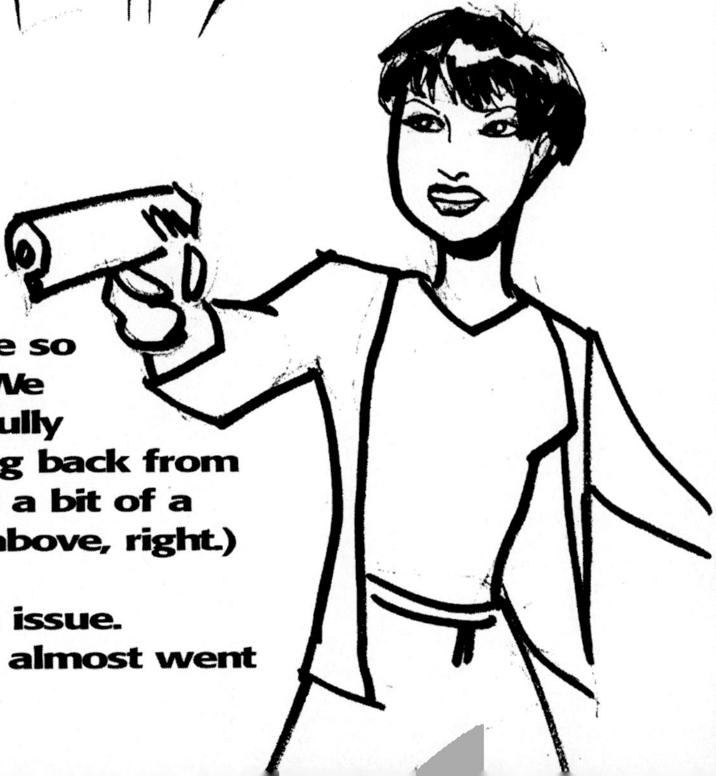

Deena could have gone so many different ways. We almost went with a Scully (seen above) but pulling back from that look put Deena in a bit of a danceclub look (seen above, right.)

Even hair color was an issue. A brunette Deena? We almost went that way. (See right.)

CALISTA

Little Calista. What age do we make Calista? We resisted the cute little kid look, but really when it came down to it...she's a cute little kid.

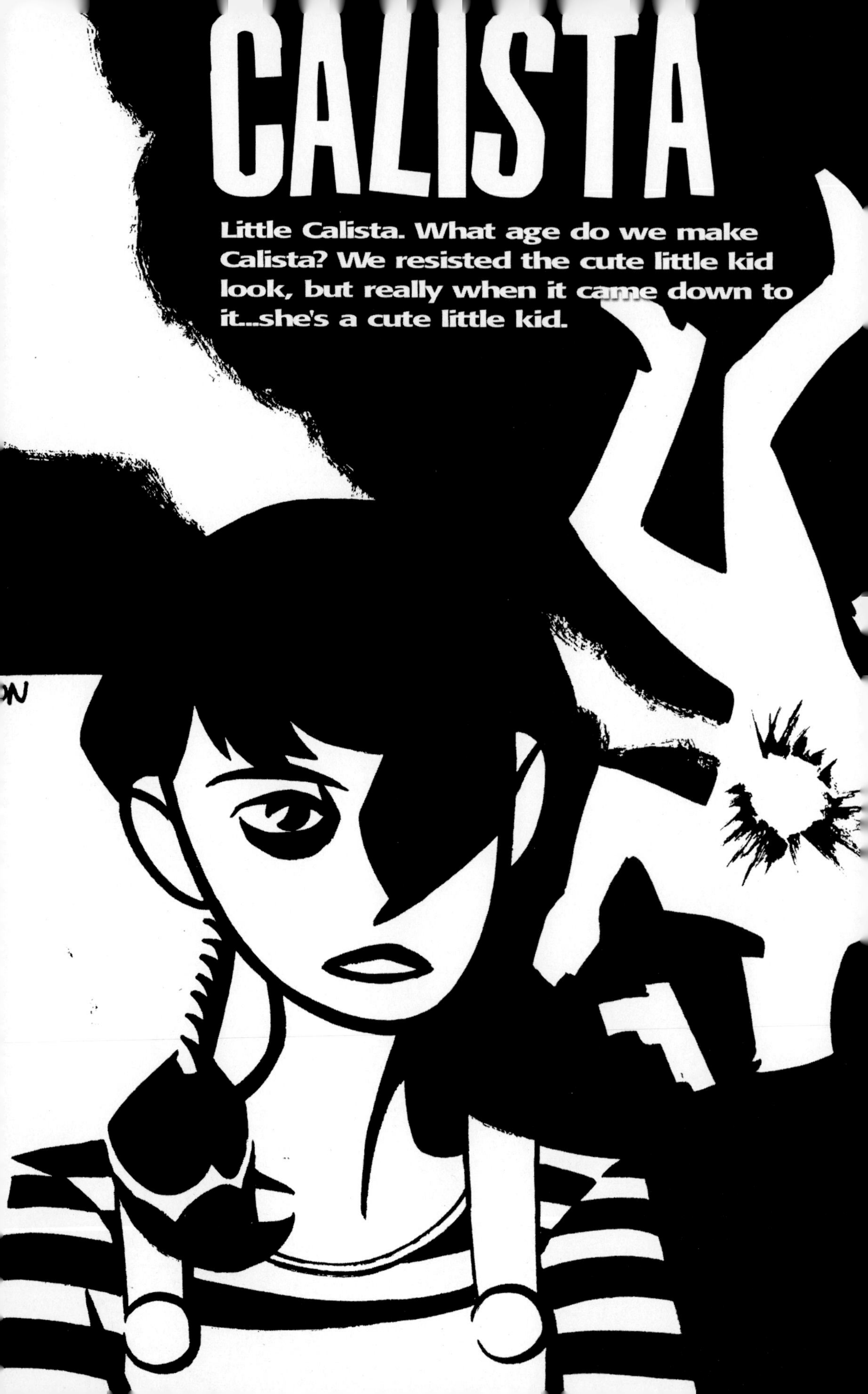

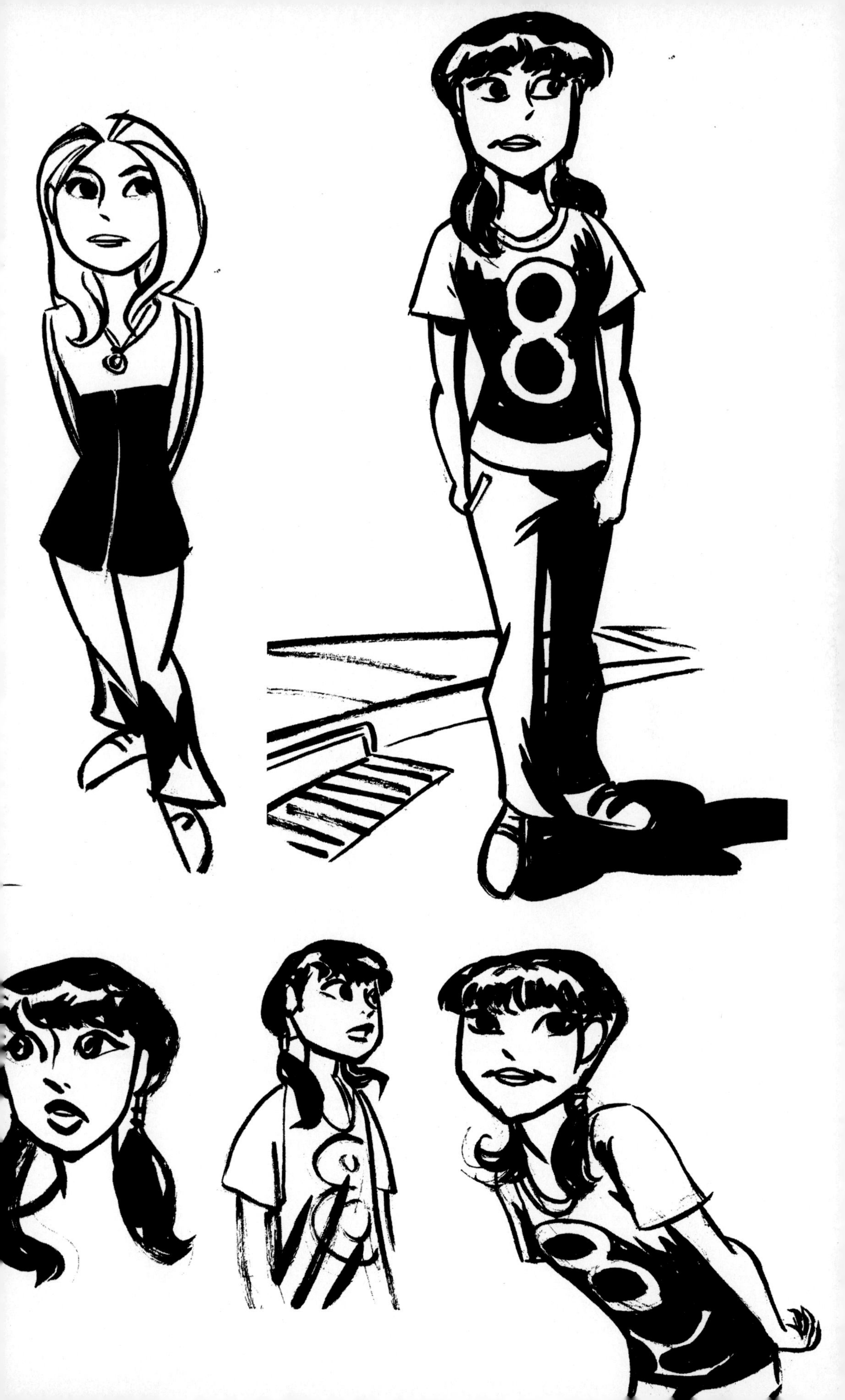

The sketch on the left is by far my all time favorite. I just adore it.

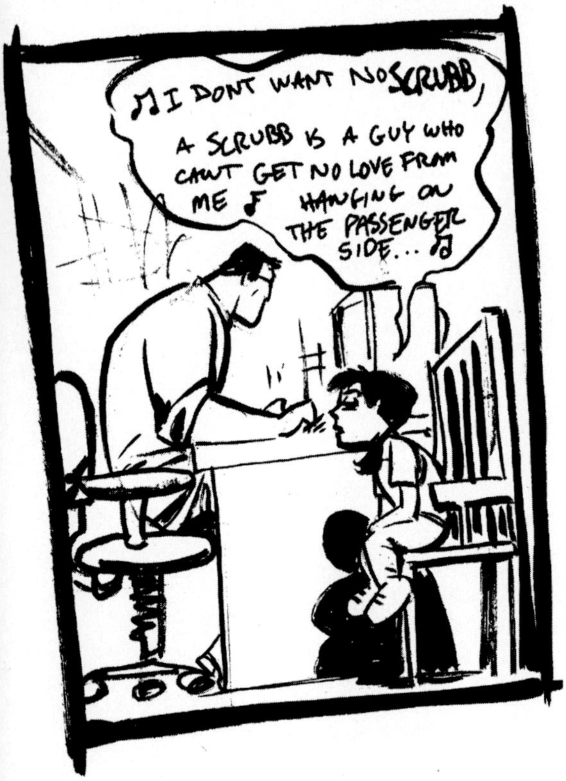

I DONT WANT NO SCRUBB,
A SCRUBB IS A GUY WHO CANT GET NO LOVE FROM ME HANGING ON THE PASSENGER SIDE...

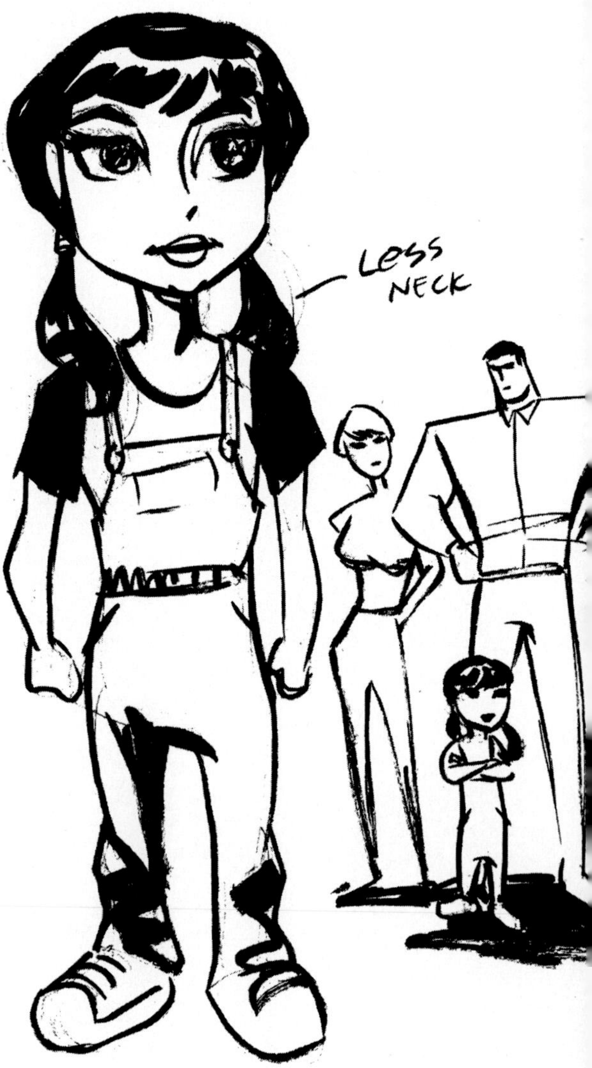

LESS NECK

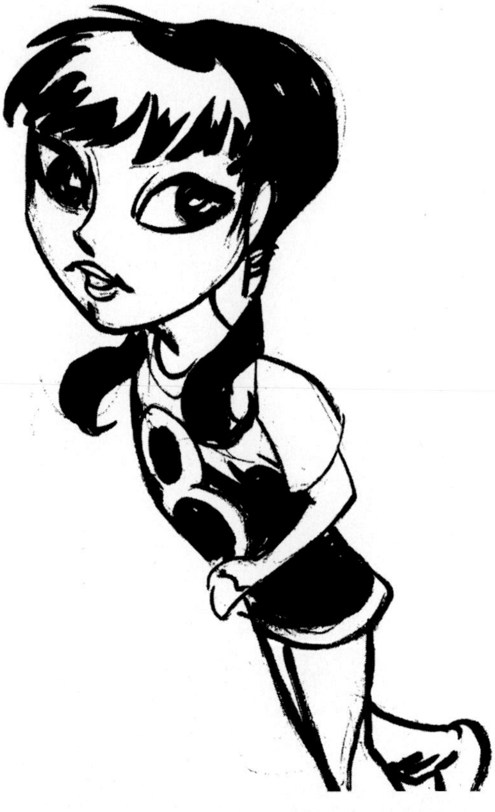

Retro Girl is probably the single most important character design. The design has to say everything about the character. It has to give across all of her traits and attributes. It has to tell her entire story on a subliminal level without coming off as silly or trite. And I think these do.

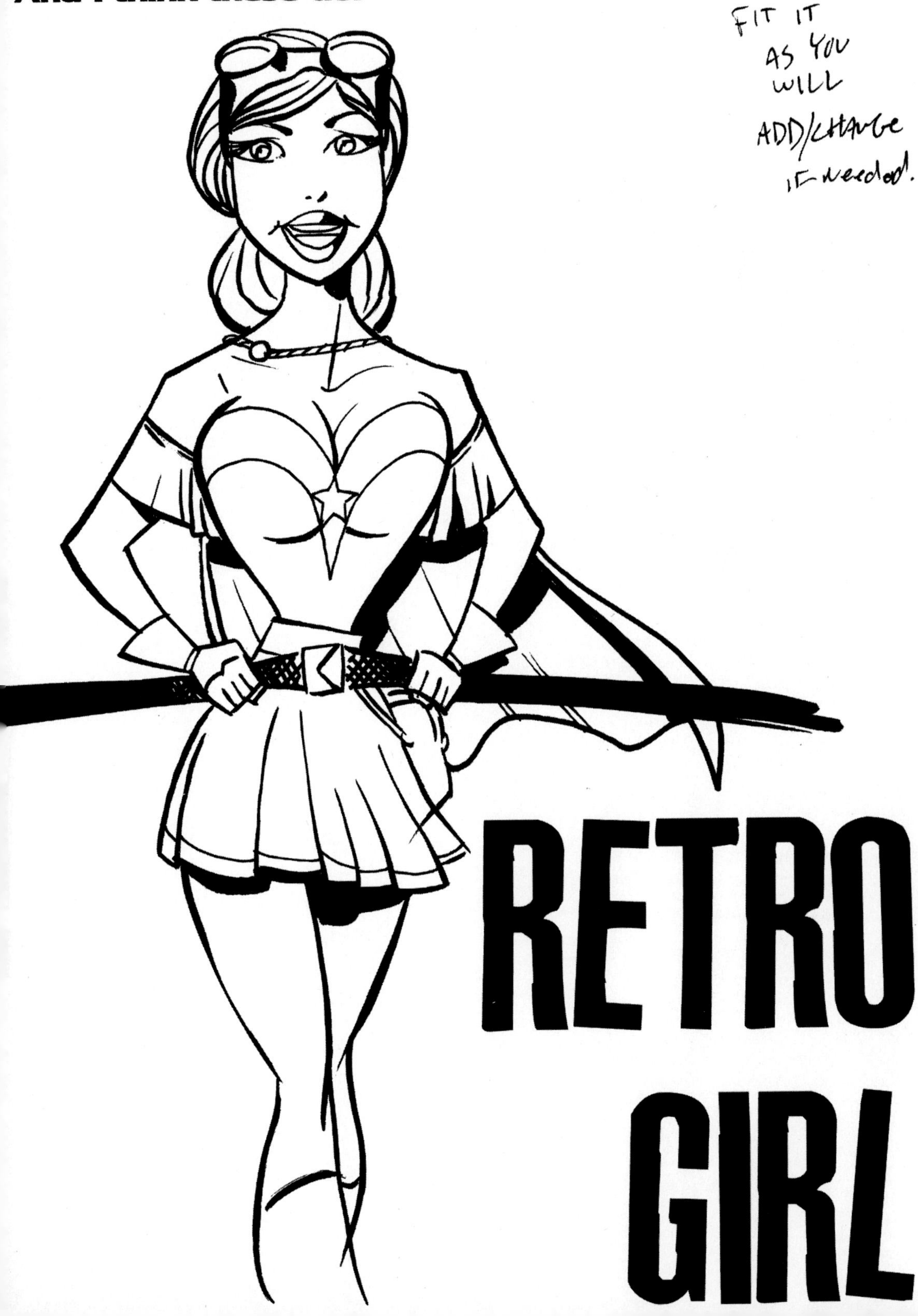
FIT IT AS YOU WILL
ADD/CHANGE IF needed!
RETRO GIRL

RETRO- FIRST TRY-

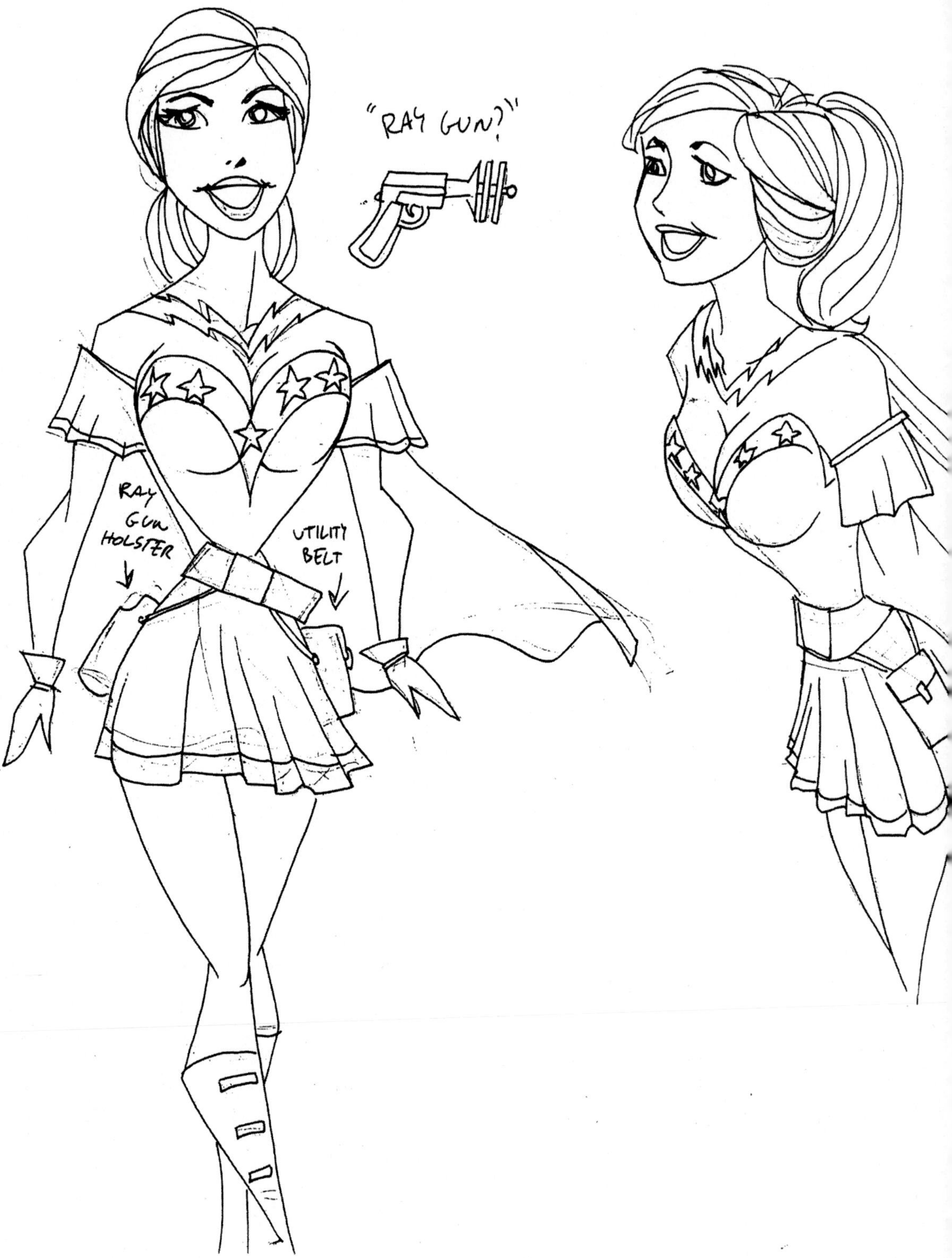
"RAY GUN?"
RAY GUN HOLSTER
UTILITY BELT

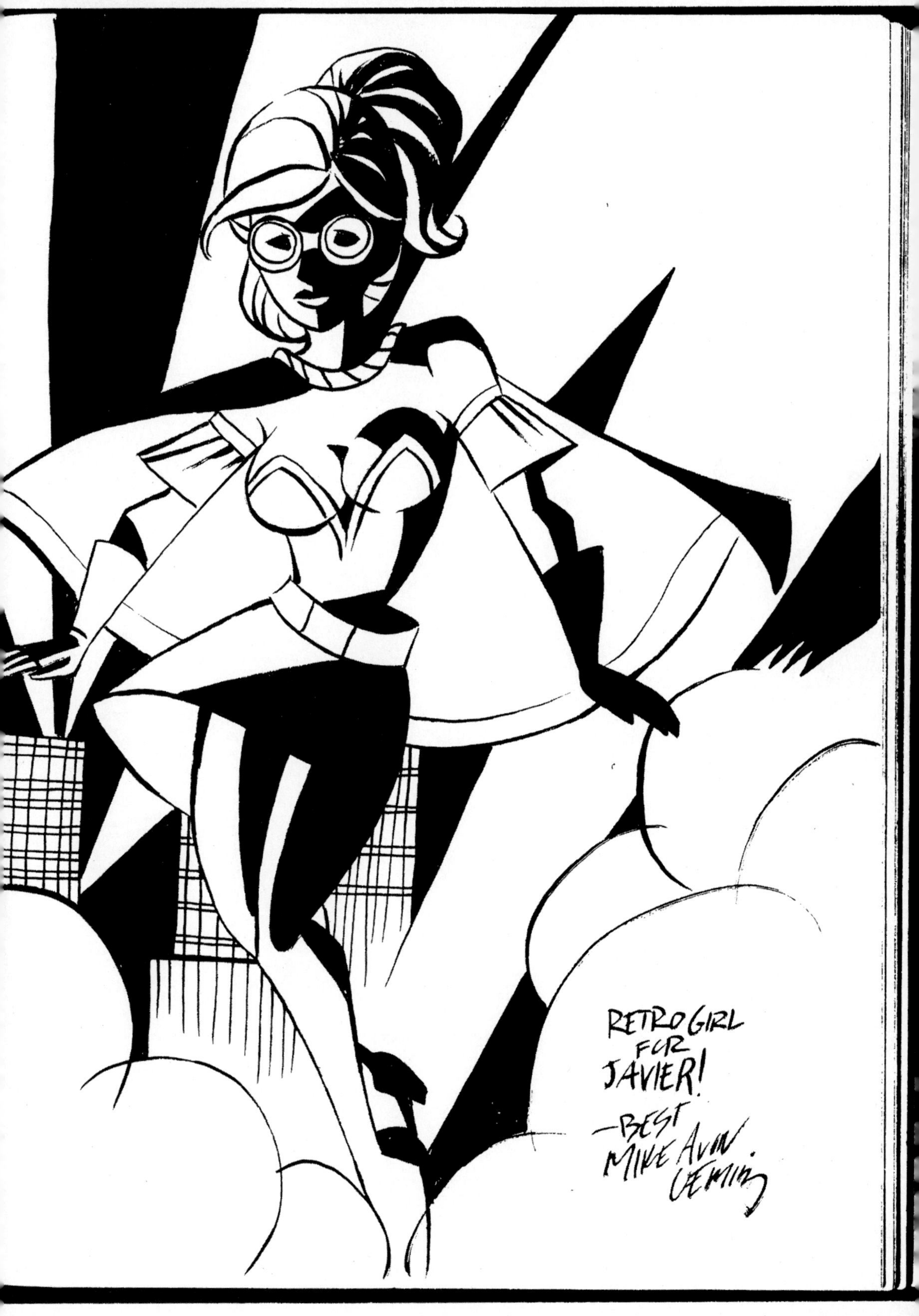
RETRO GIRL
FOR
JAVIER!
—BEST
MIKE AVON
OEMING

Retro Girl is Mike's most requested commission sketch. The following two pages are reproductions of a couple of my favorite pieces that Mike has done for a couple of lucky readers of the monthly book.

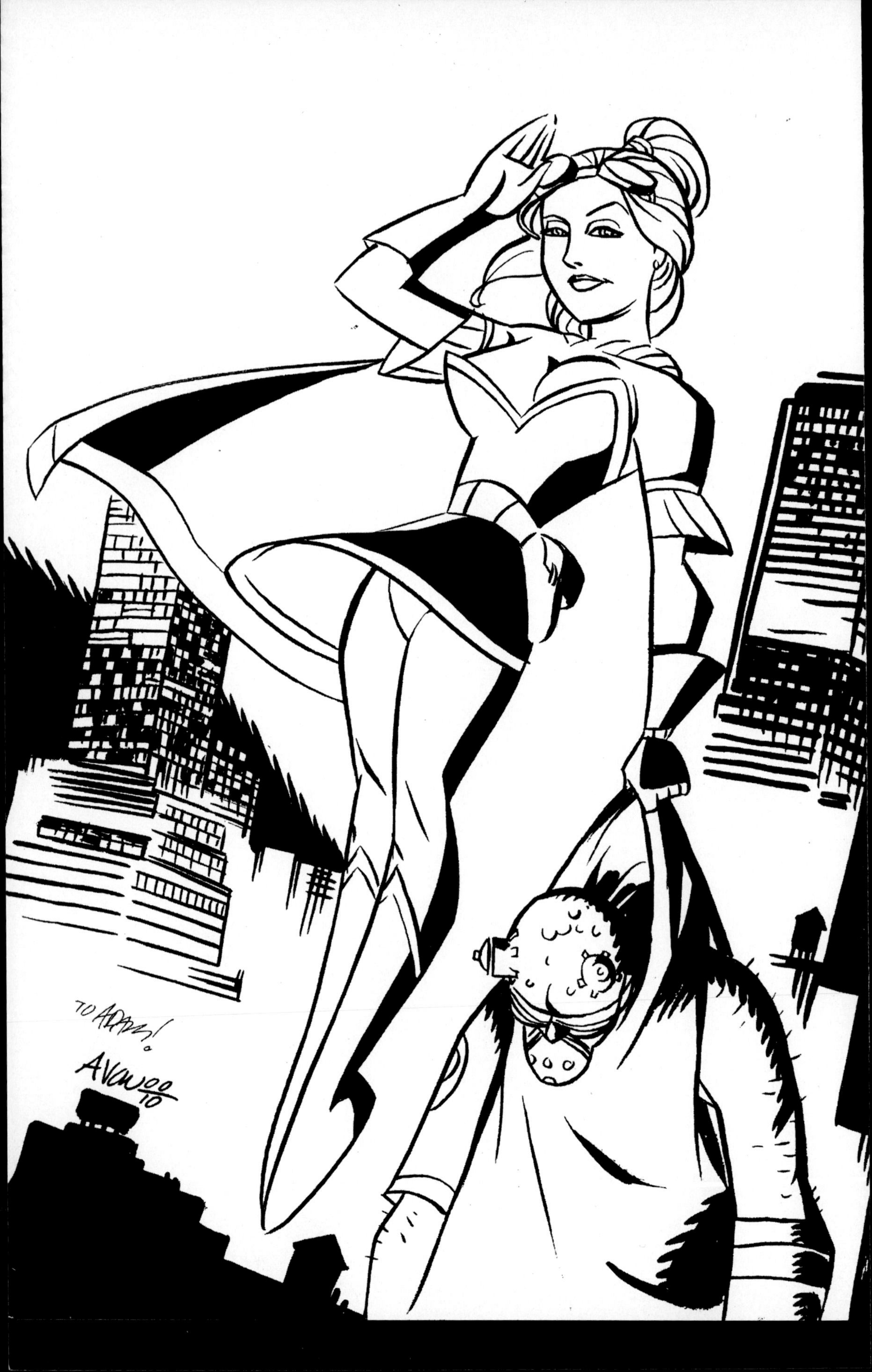

–
e 12
H HEROES
– keys TO
?

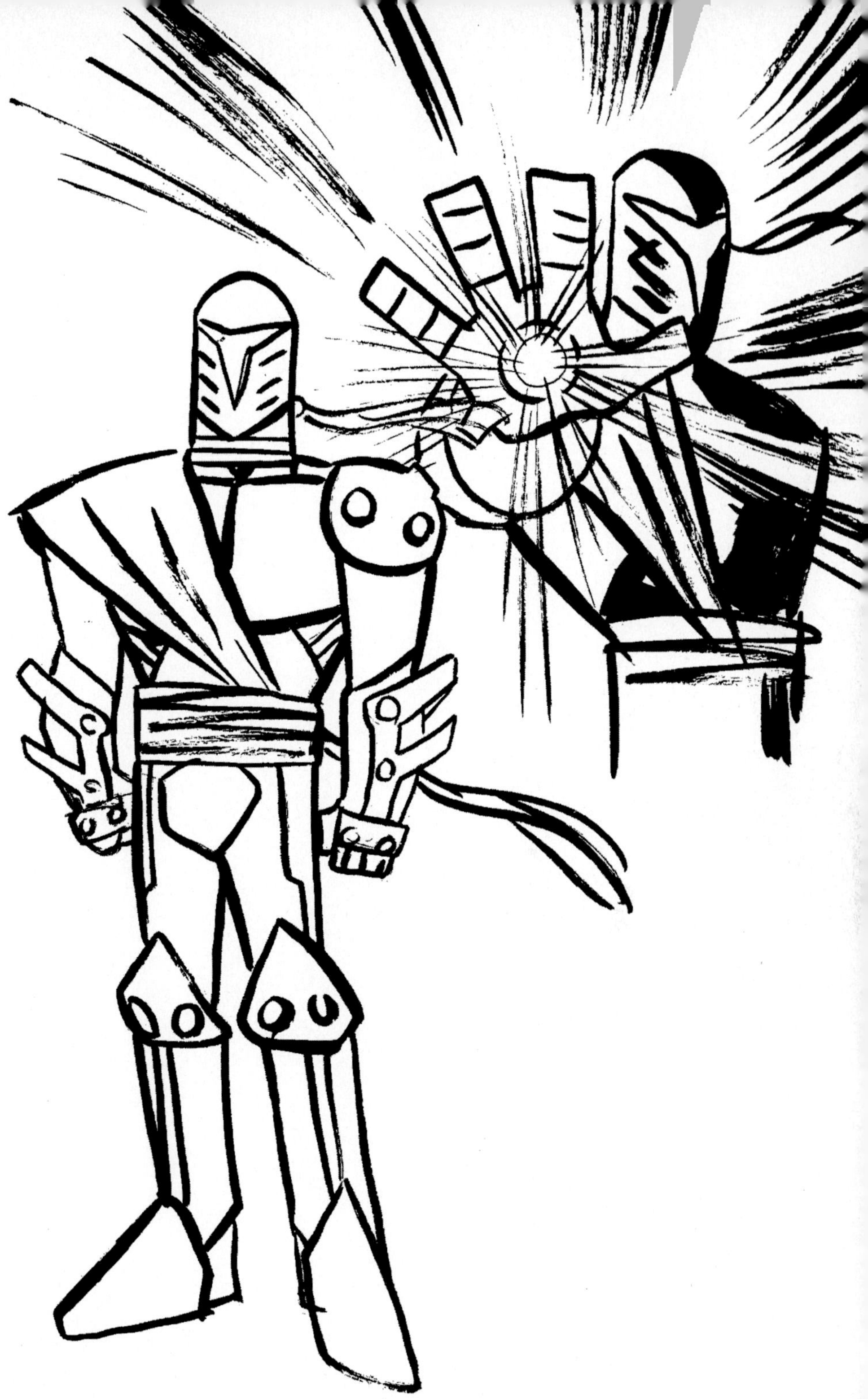

TRIPHAMMER

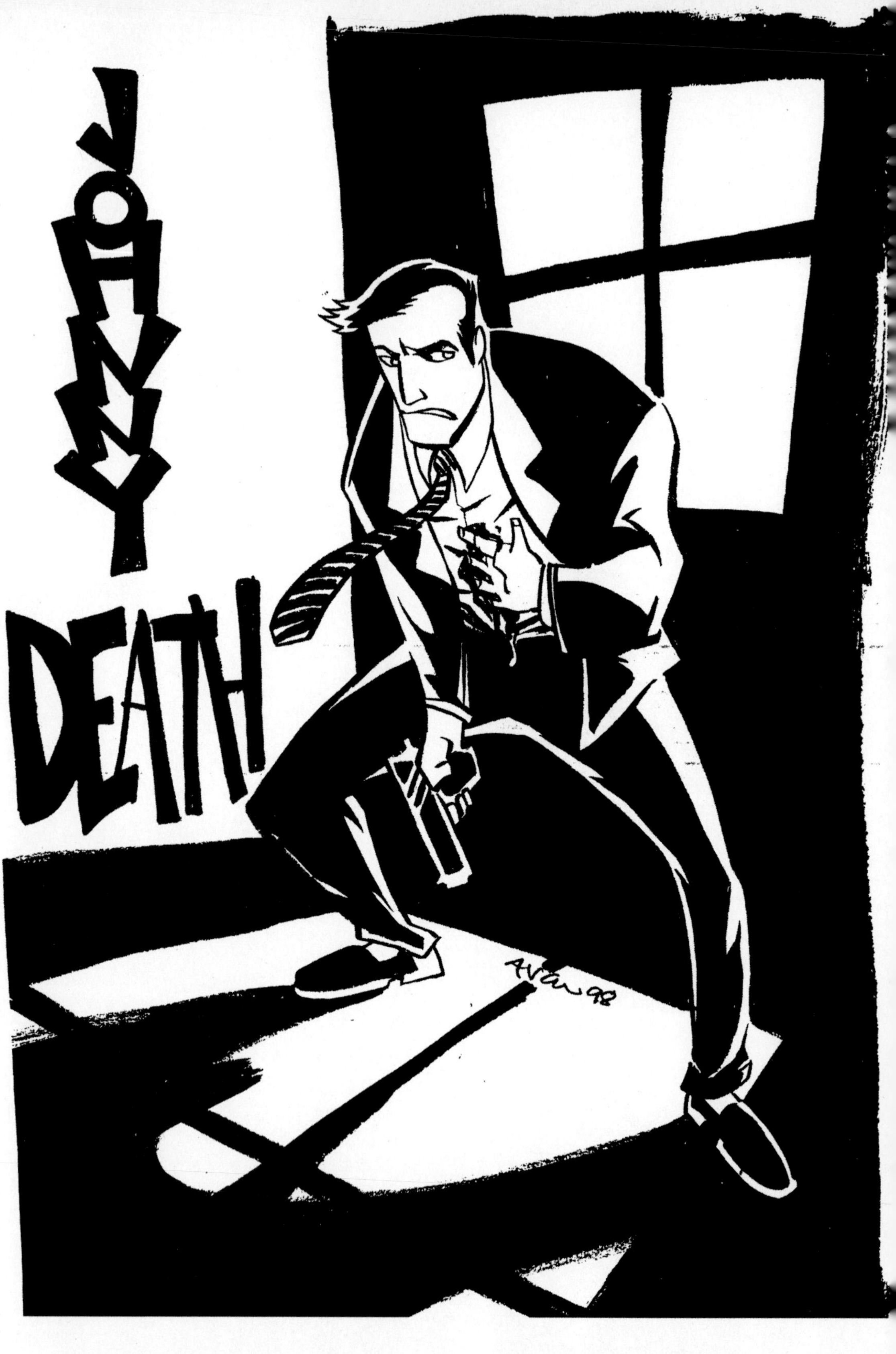
JOHNNY
DEATH

JOHNNY ROYALE

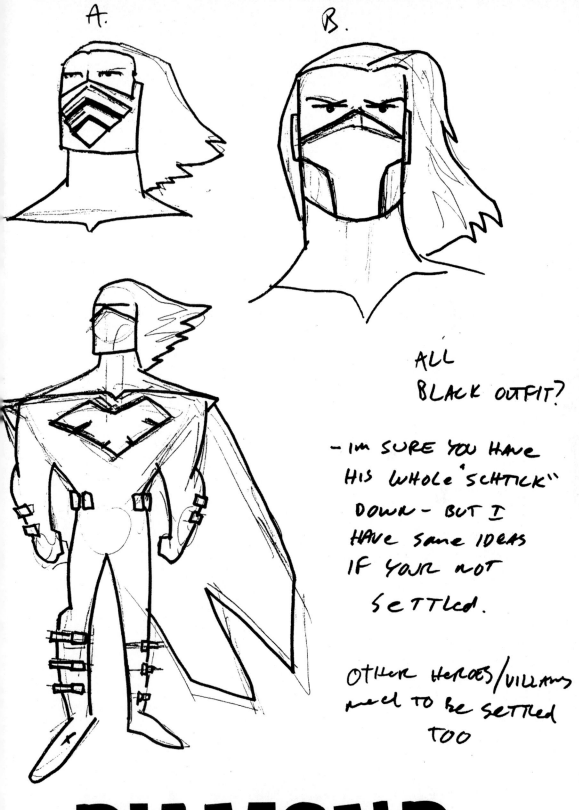

A.

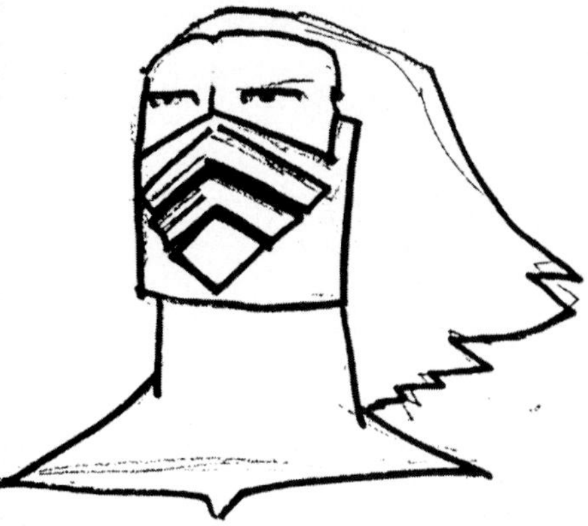

B.

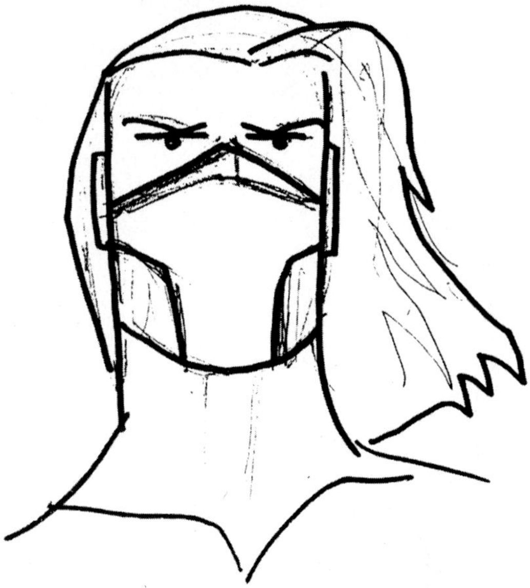

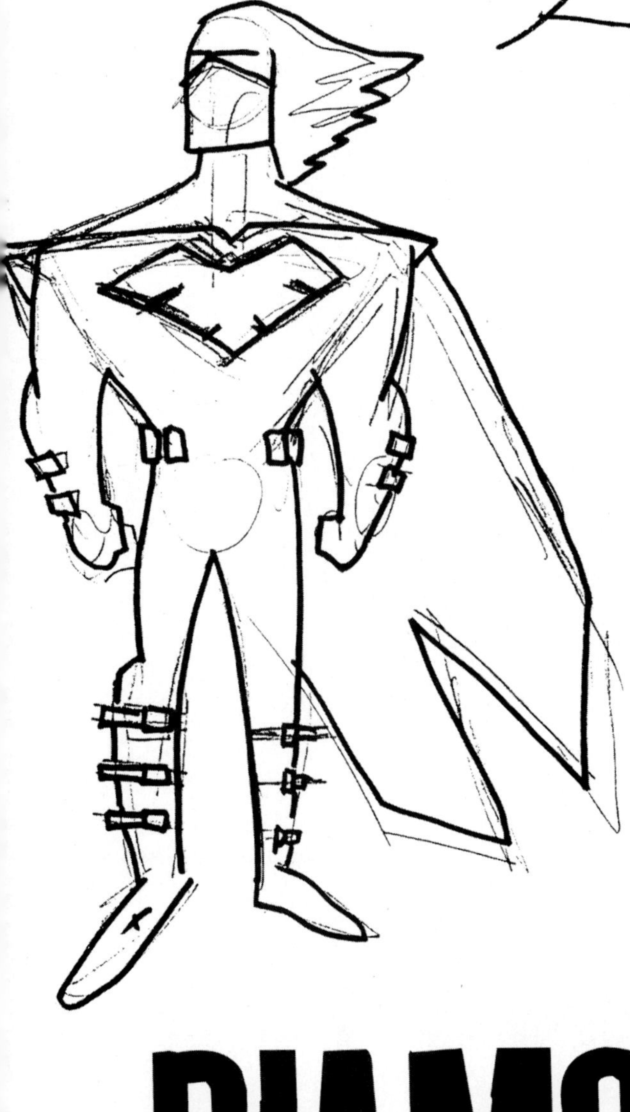

ALL BLACK OUTFIT?

- IM SURE YOU HAVE HIS WHOLE "SCHTICK" DOWN - BUT I HAVE SOME IDEAS IF YOUR NOT SETTLED.

OTHER HEROES/VILLAINS NEED TO BE SETTLED TOO

DIAMOND

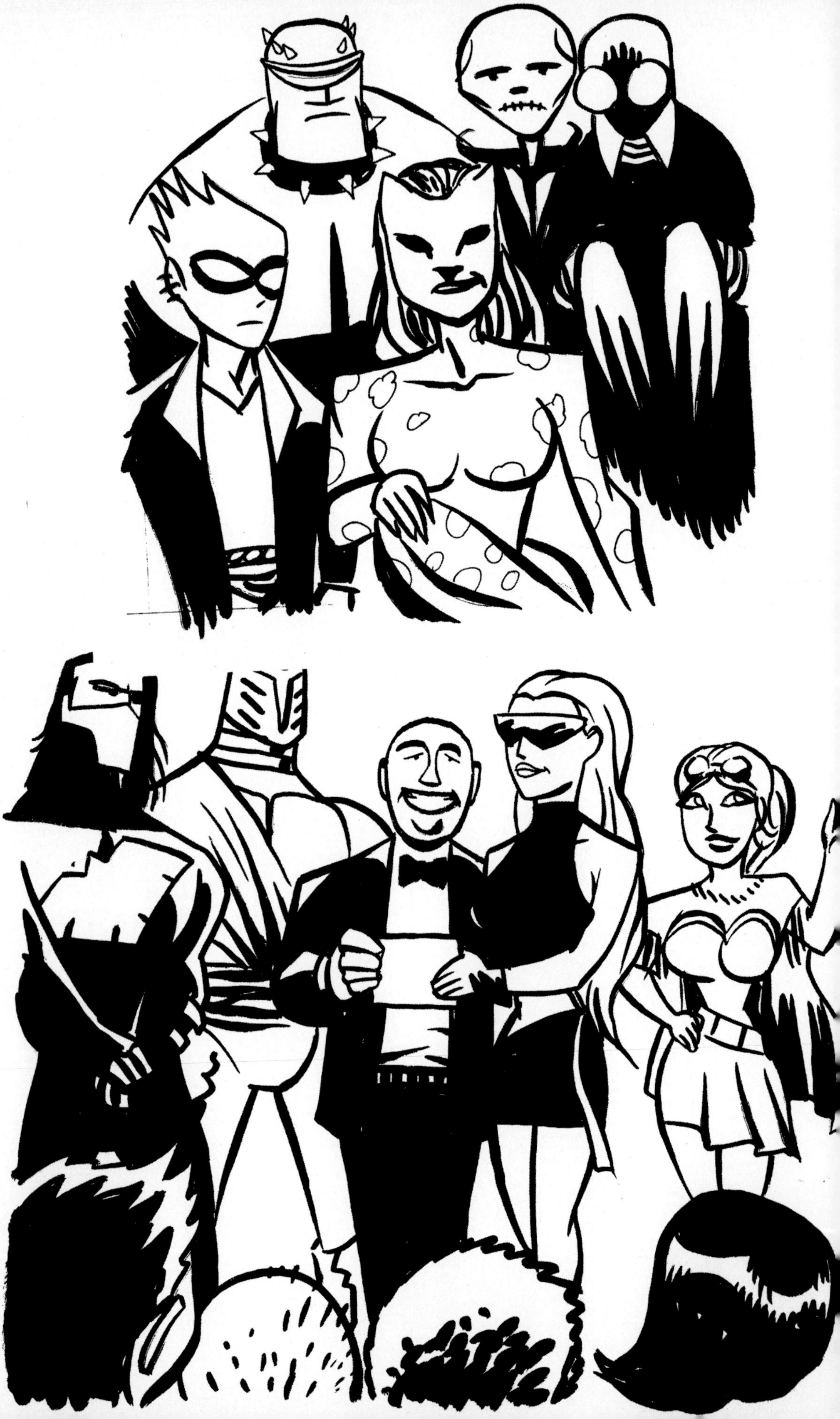

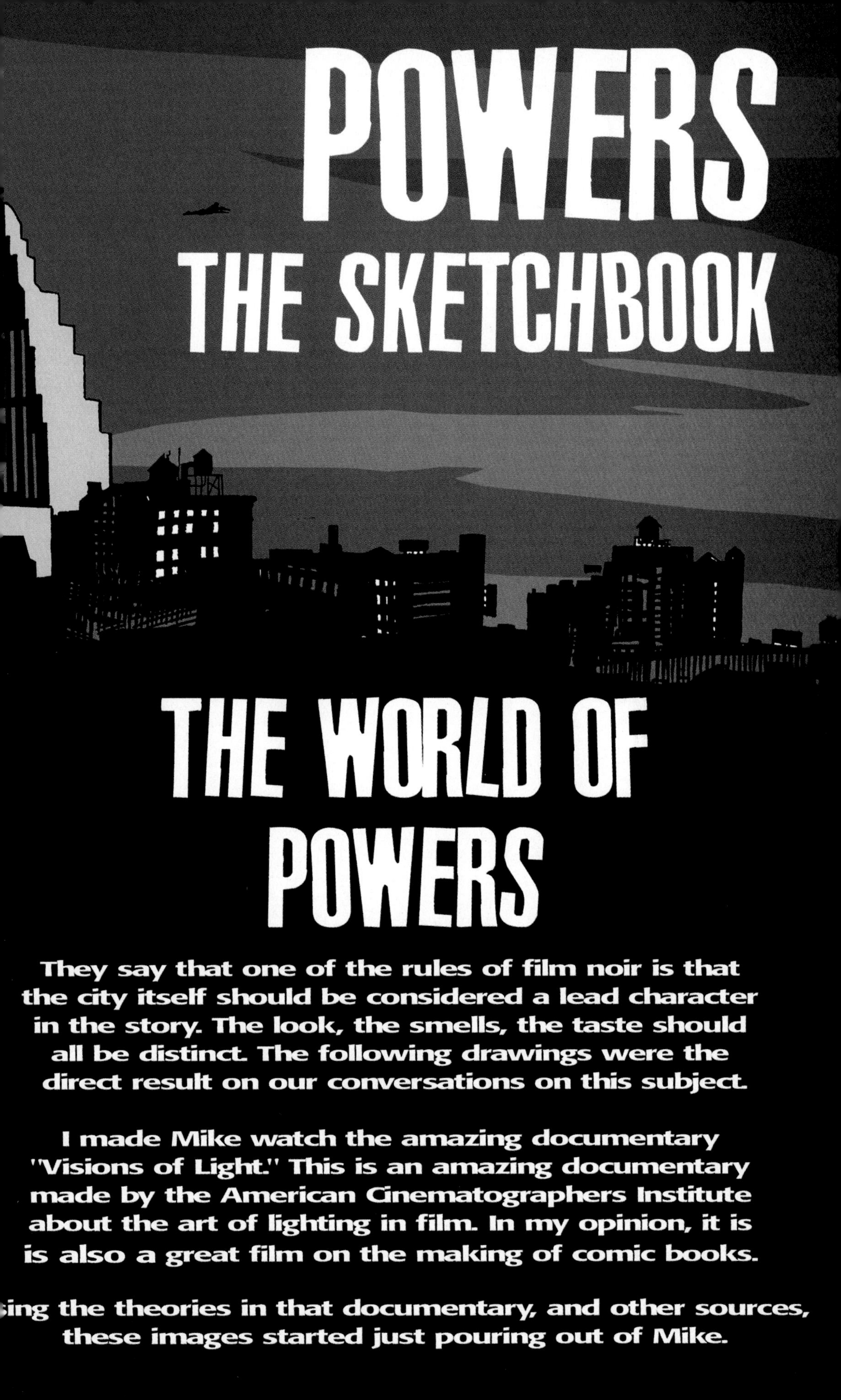

POWERS
THE SKETCHBOOK

THE WORLD OF POWERS

They say that one of the rules of film noir is that the city itself should be considered a lead character in the story. The look, the smells, the taste should all be distinct. The following drawings were the direct result on our conversations on this subject.

I made Mike watch the amazing documentary "Visions of Light." This is an amazing documentary made by the American Cinematographers Institute about the art of lighting in film. In my opinion, it is is also a great film on the making of comic books.

sing the theories in that documentary, and other sources, these images started just pouring out of Mike.

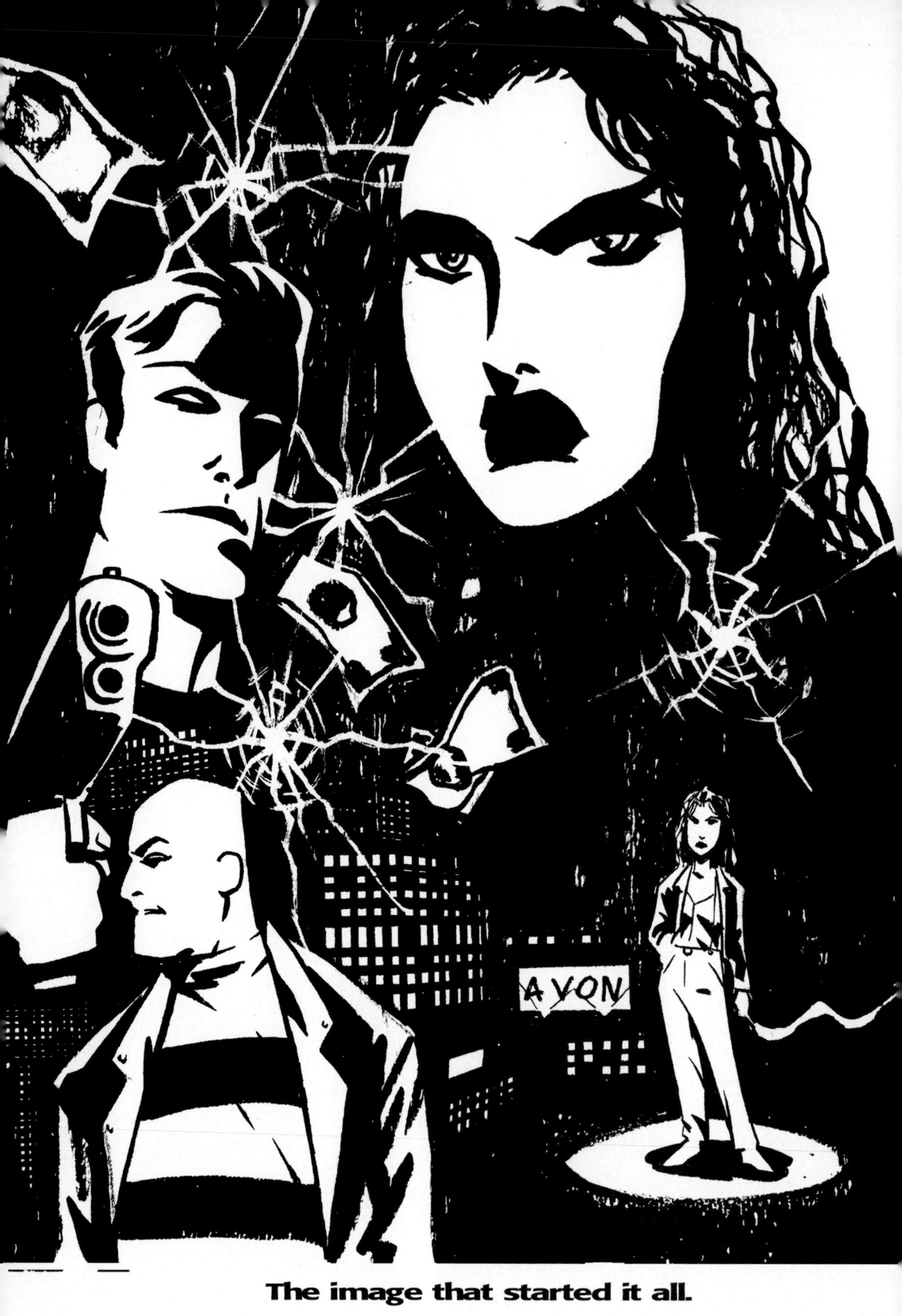
AVON

The image that started it all.

Years ago, Mike, did a pin up of my comic book series Jin (above) and one of David Mack's comic book series Kabu in a style he was working with... just for fun. It is now referred to as his Powers' style. This single image inspire everything in this book.

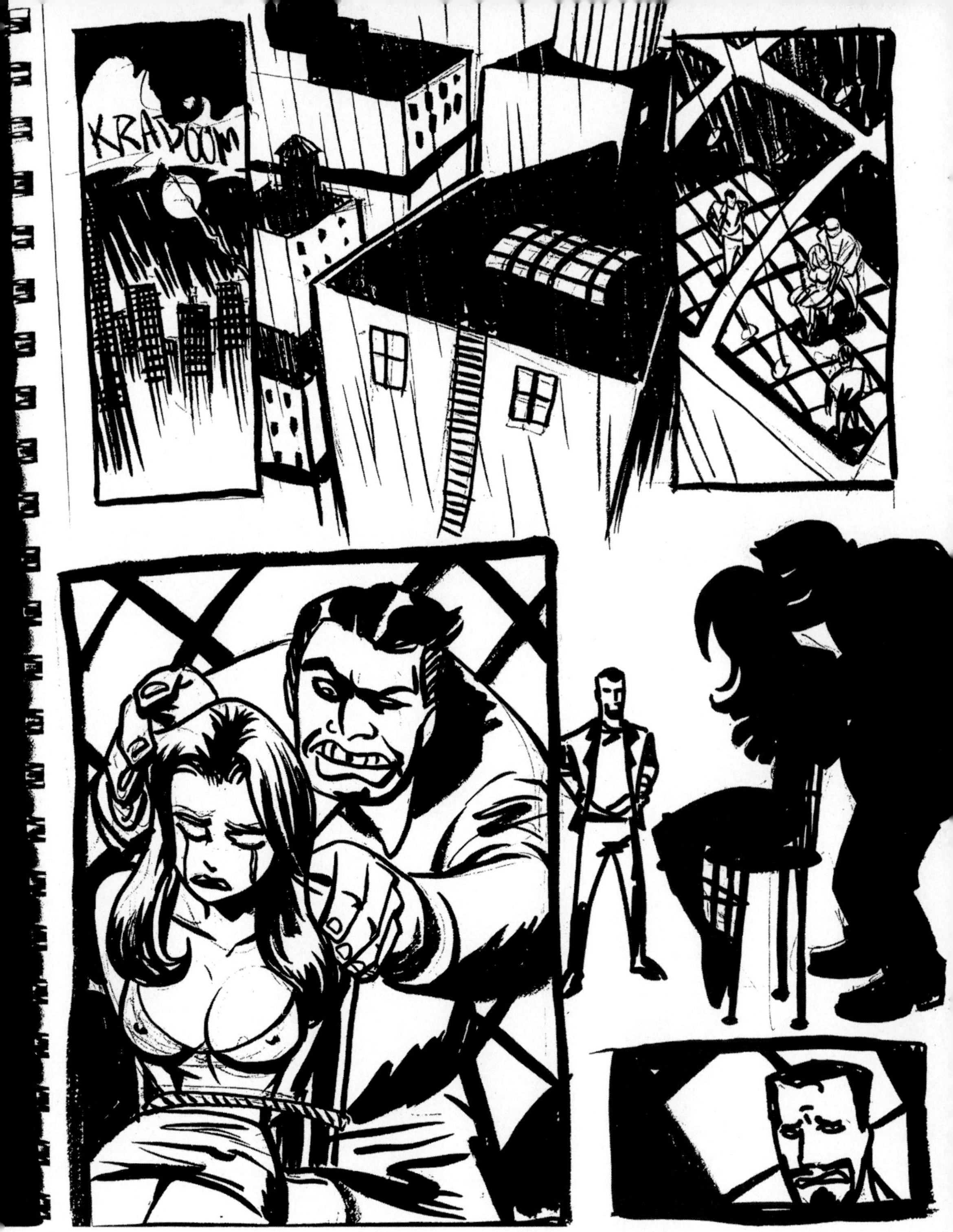
KRADOOM

Even before there was a script, Mike started doing practice pages so he could get a handle on how this style would feel "in use."

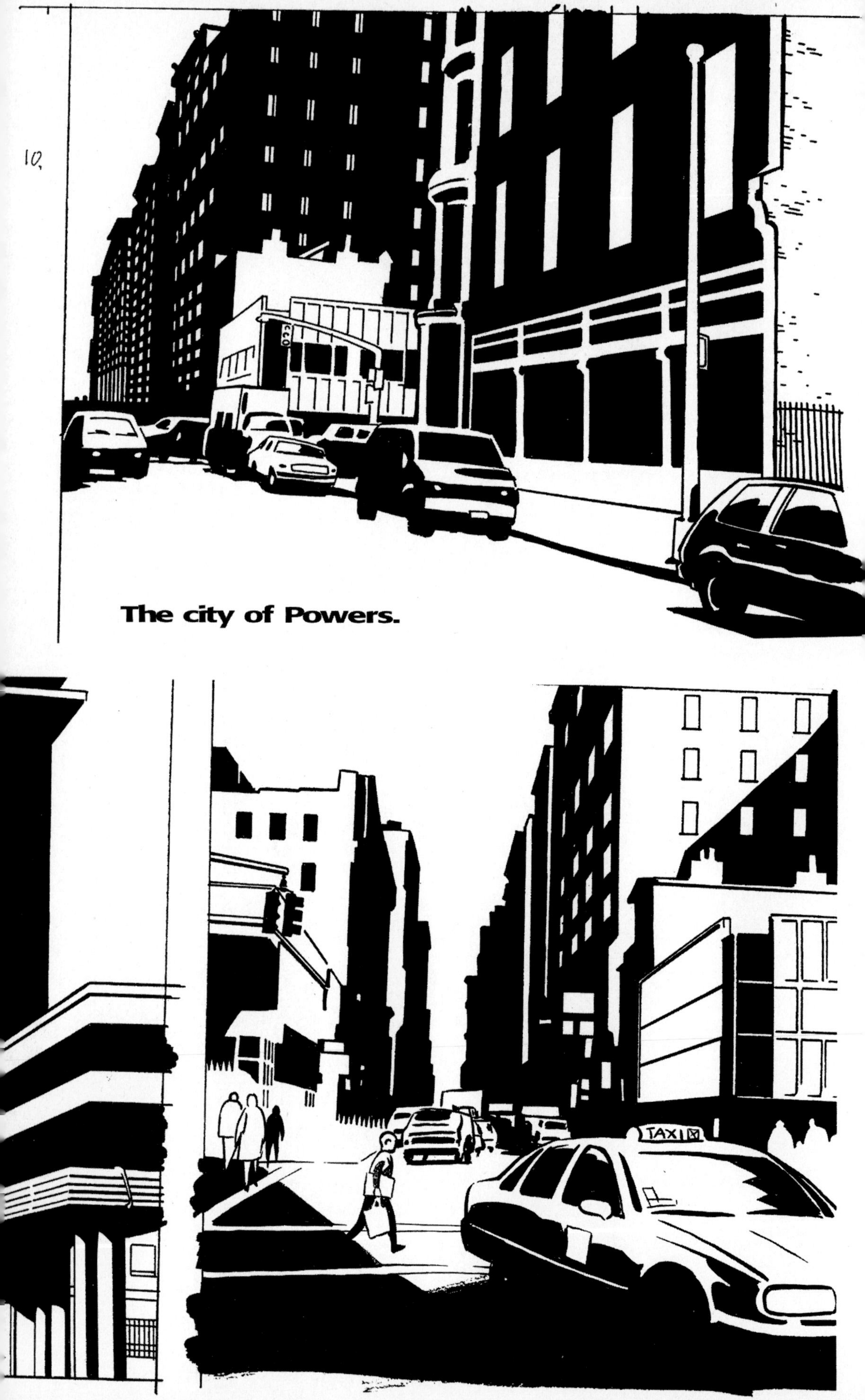
The city of Powers.
TAXI

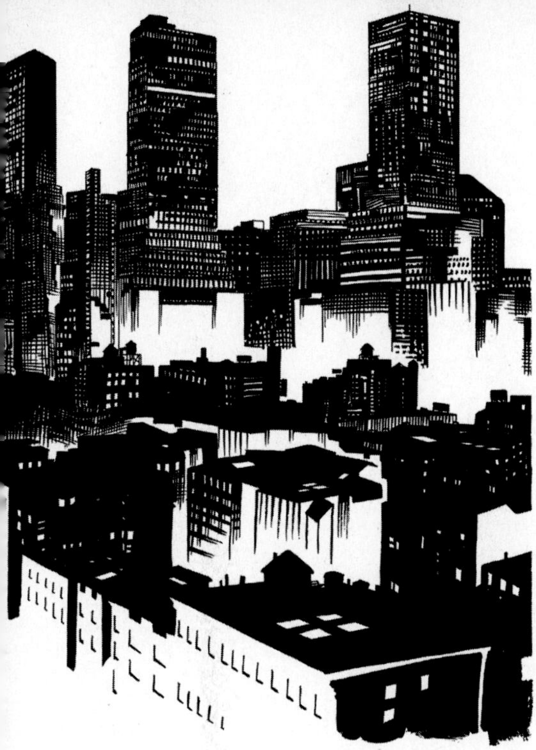

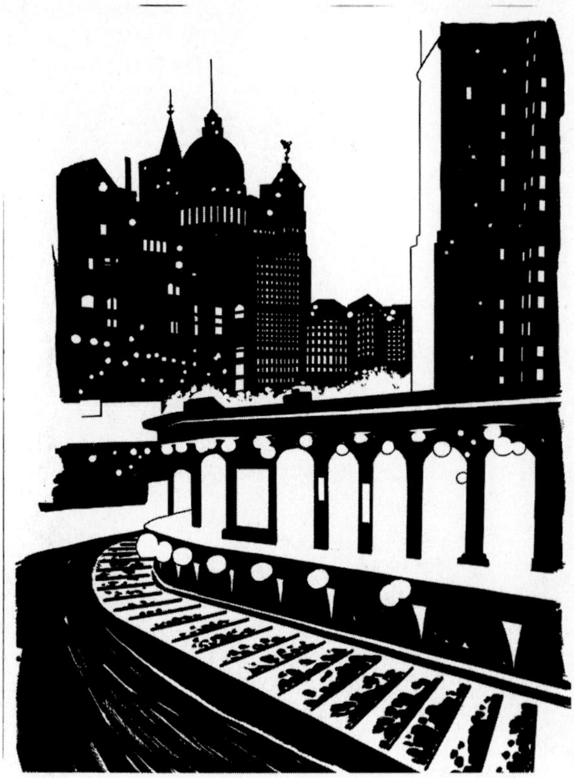

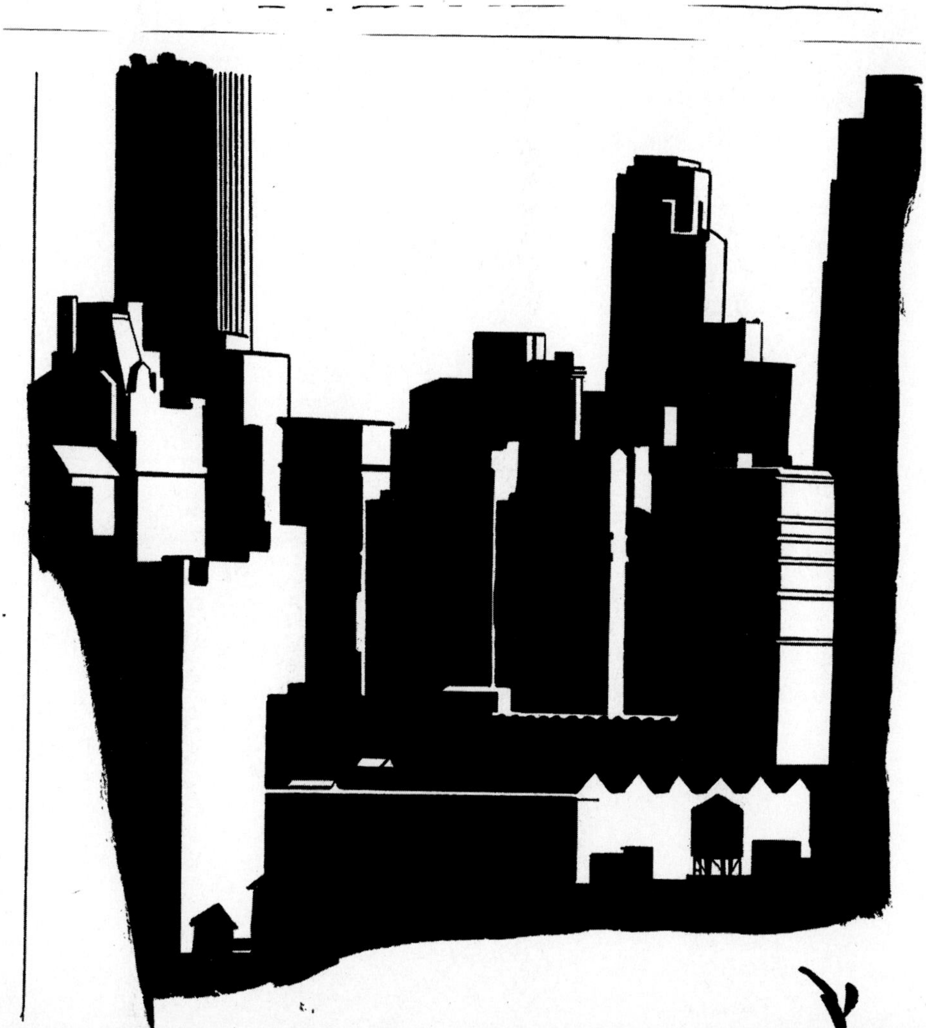

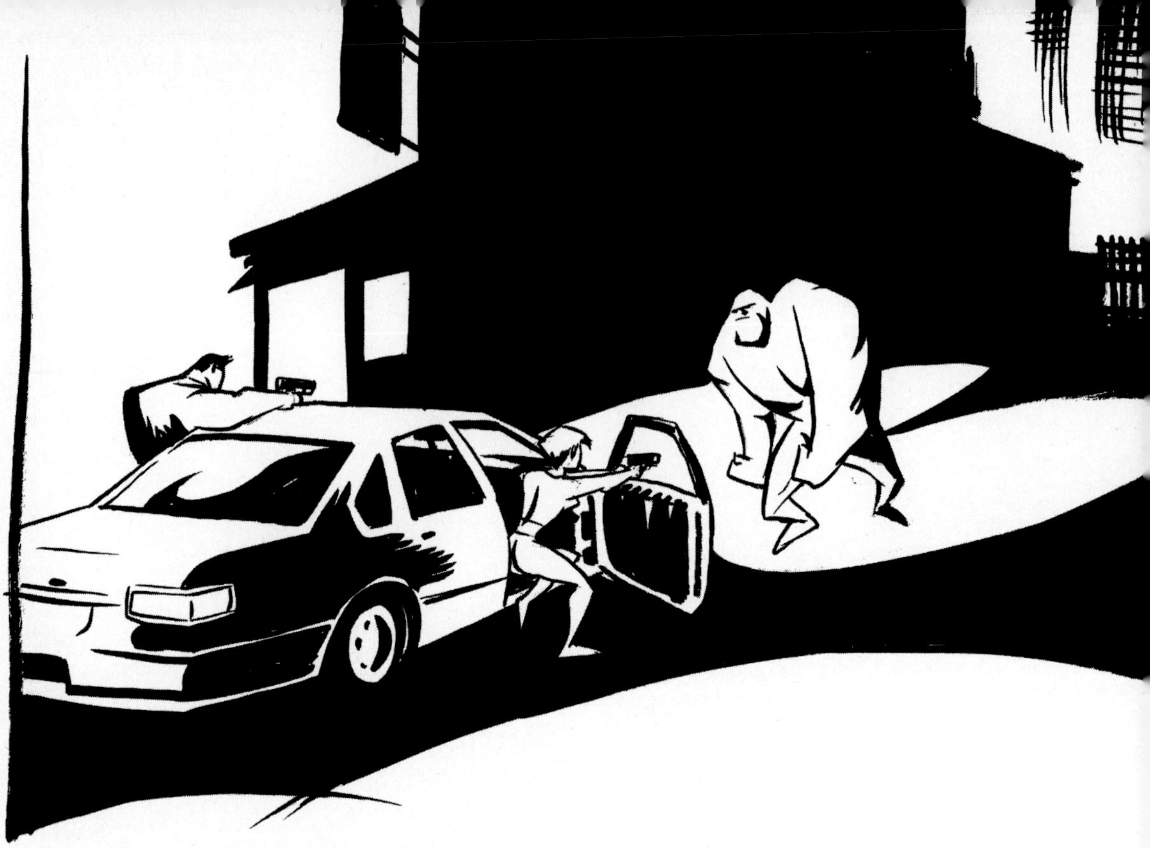

One of the key elements to the visuals of Powers is the juxtaposition of noir and superhero images. These are some of the ideas Mike was toying with while thinking about this juxtaposition.

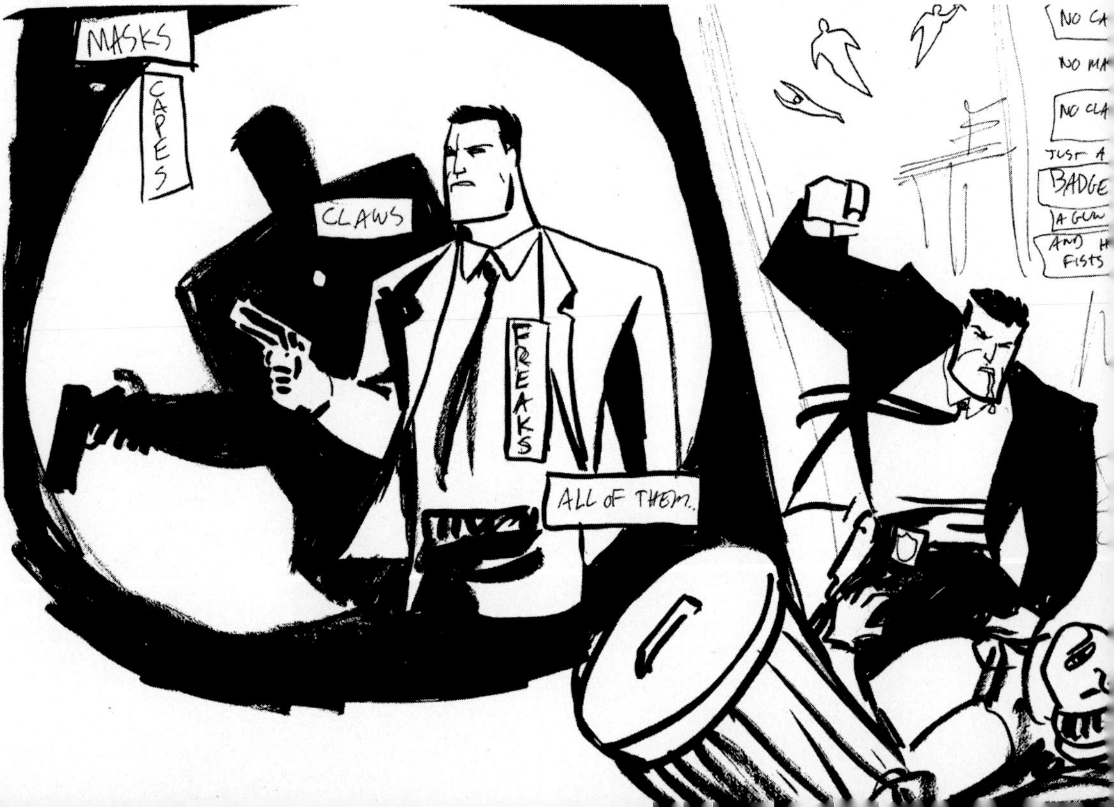
MASKS
CAPES
CLAWS
FREAKS
ALL OF THEM.
BADGE
FISTS

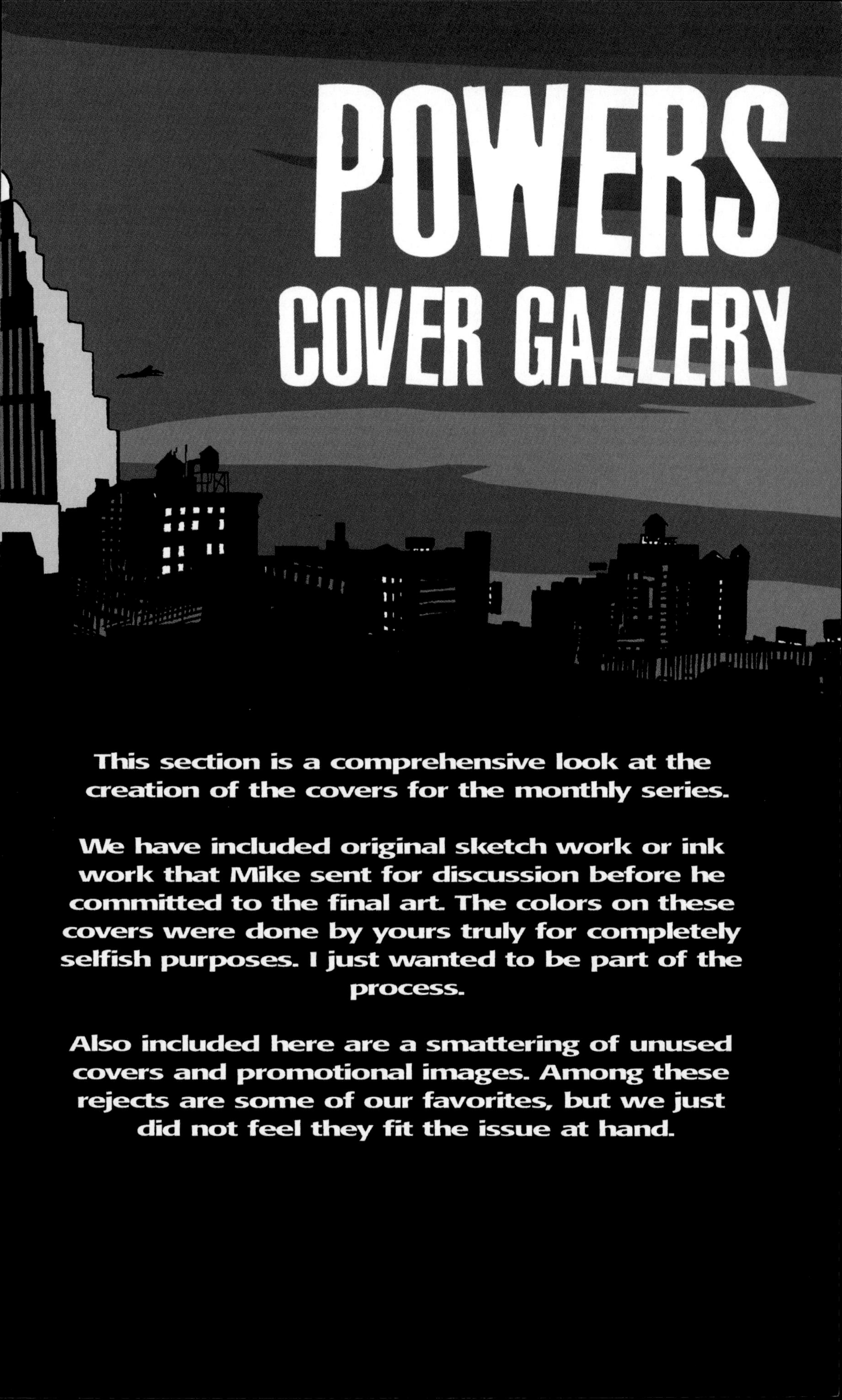
POWERS
COVER GALLERY

This section is a comprehensive look at the creation of the covers for the monthly series.

We have included original sketch work or ink work that Mike sent for discussion before he committed to the final art. The colors on these covers were done by yours truly for completely selfish purposes. I just wanted to be part of the process.

Also included here are a smattering of unused covers and promotional images. Among these rejects are some of our favorites, but we just did not feel they fit the issue at hand.

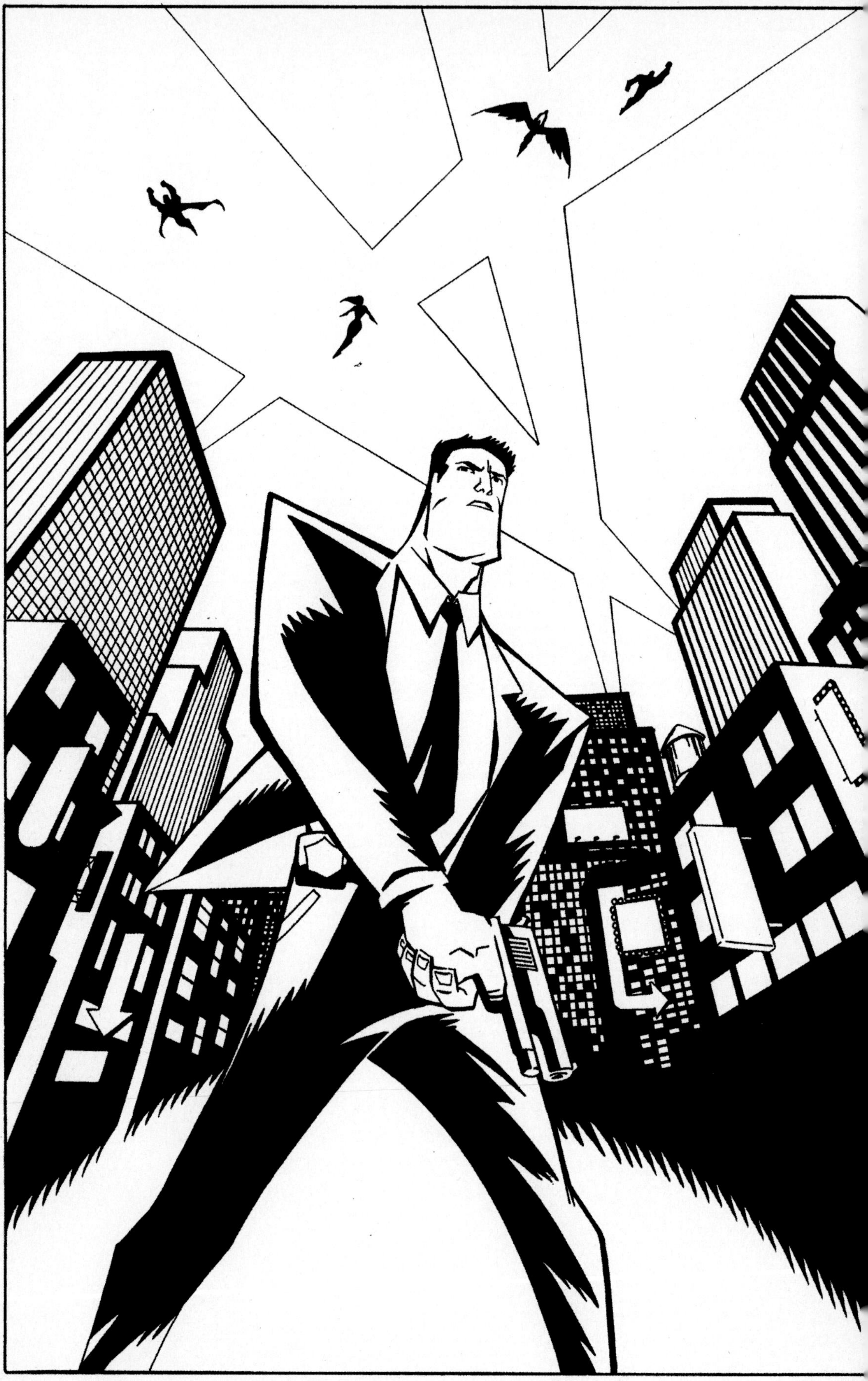

Mike's first full Powers drawing- right on the mone

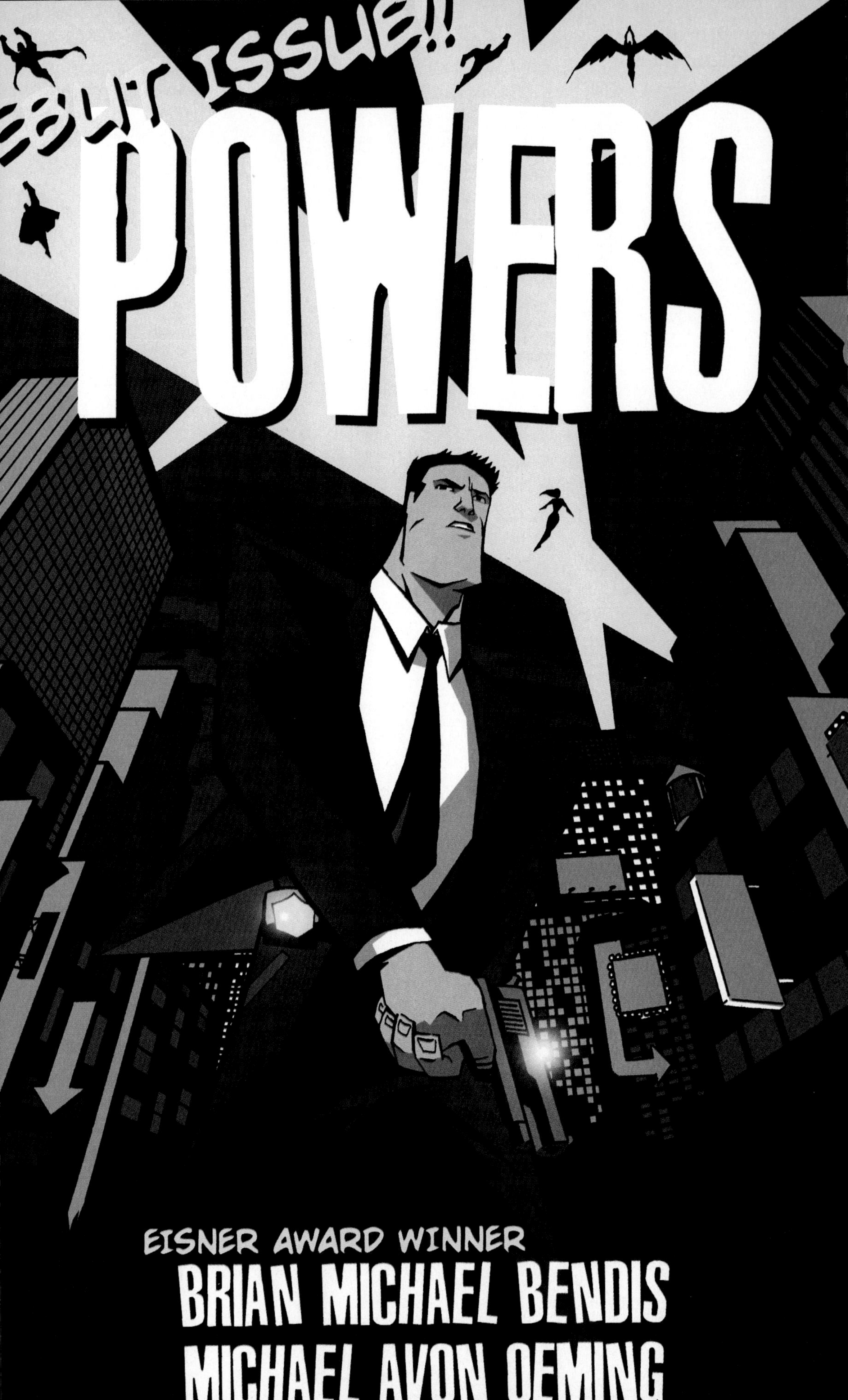
ISSUE!!
POWERS
EISNER AWARD WINNER
BRIAN MICHAEL BENDIS
MICHAEL AVON OEMING

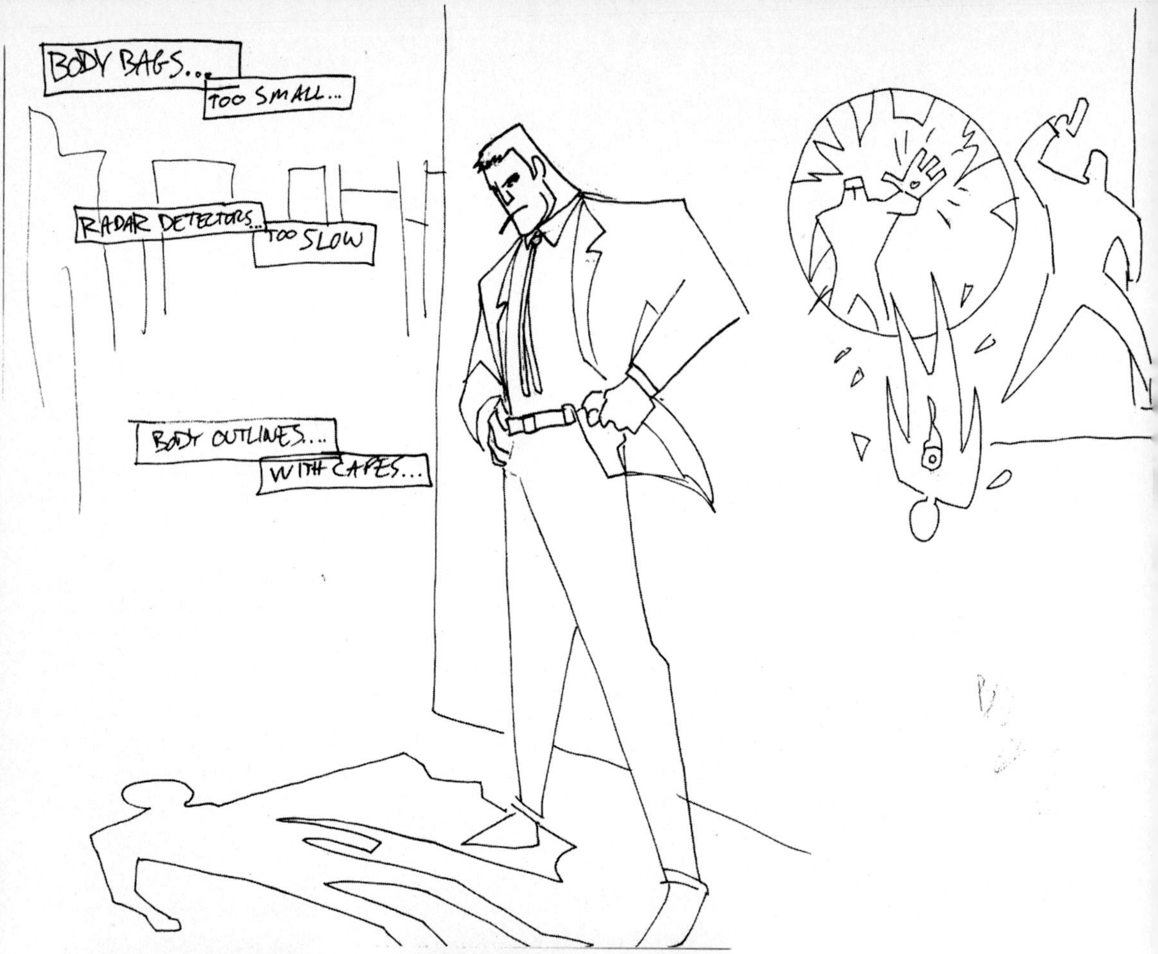
BODY BAGS...
TOO SMALL...
RADAR DETECTORS...
TOO SLOW
BODY OUTLINES...
WITH CAPES...

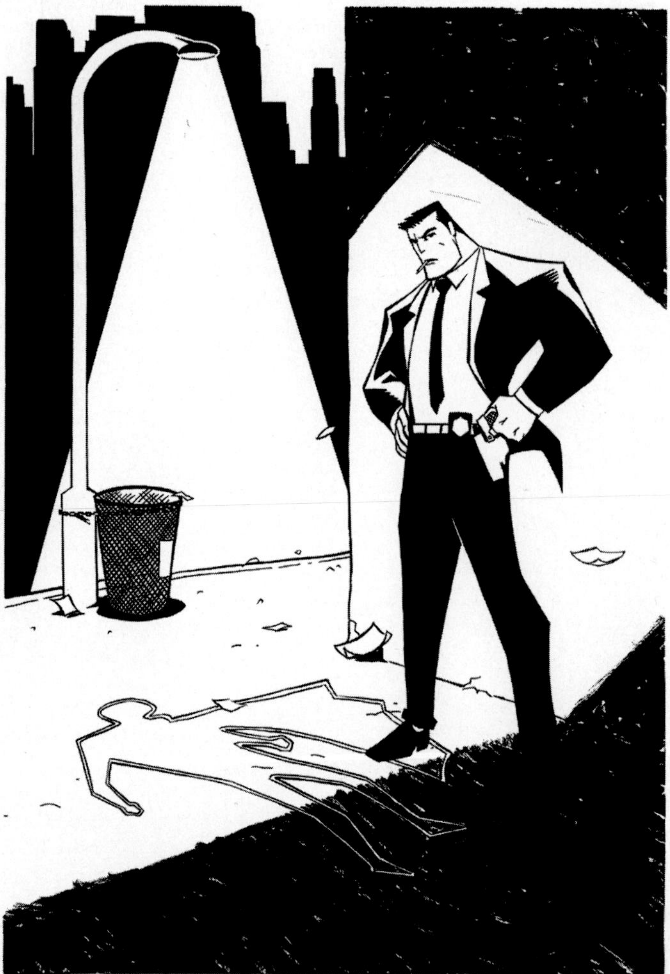

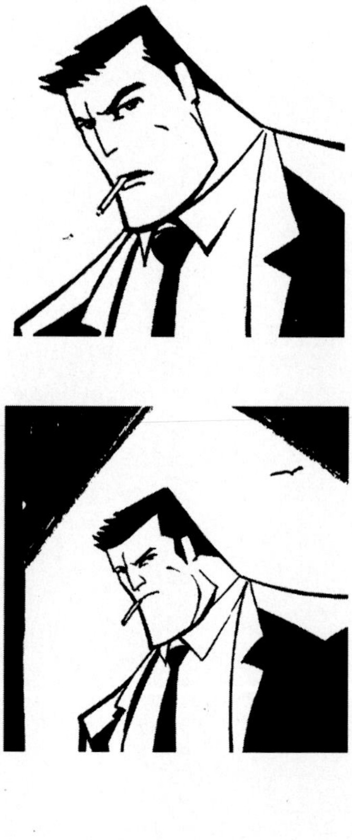

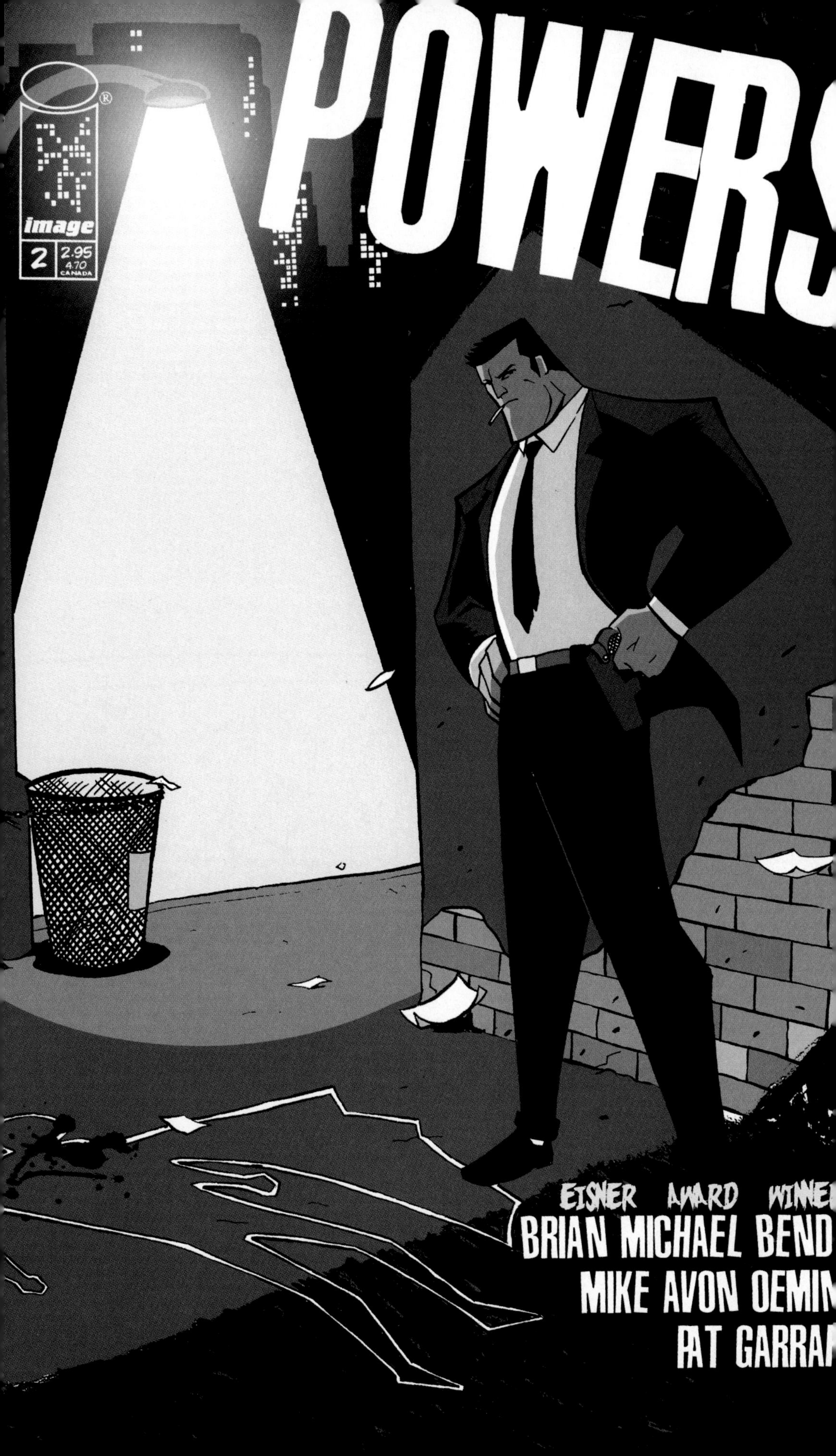

POWERS
image
2
2.95
4.70 CANADA
EISNER AWARD WINNE
BRIAN MICHAEL BEND
MIKE AVON OEMIN
PAT GARRA

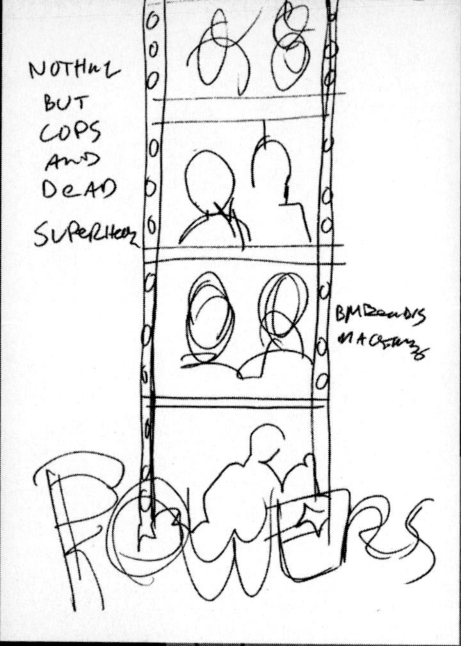
NOTHING
BUT
COPS
AND
DEAD
SUPERHEROES
POWERS

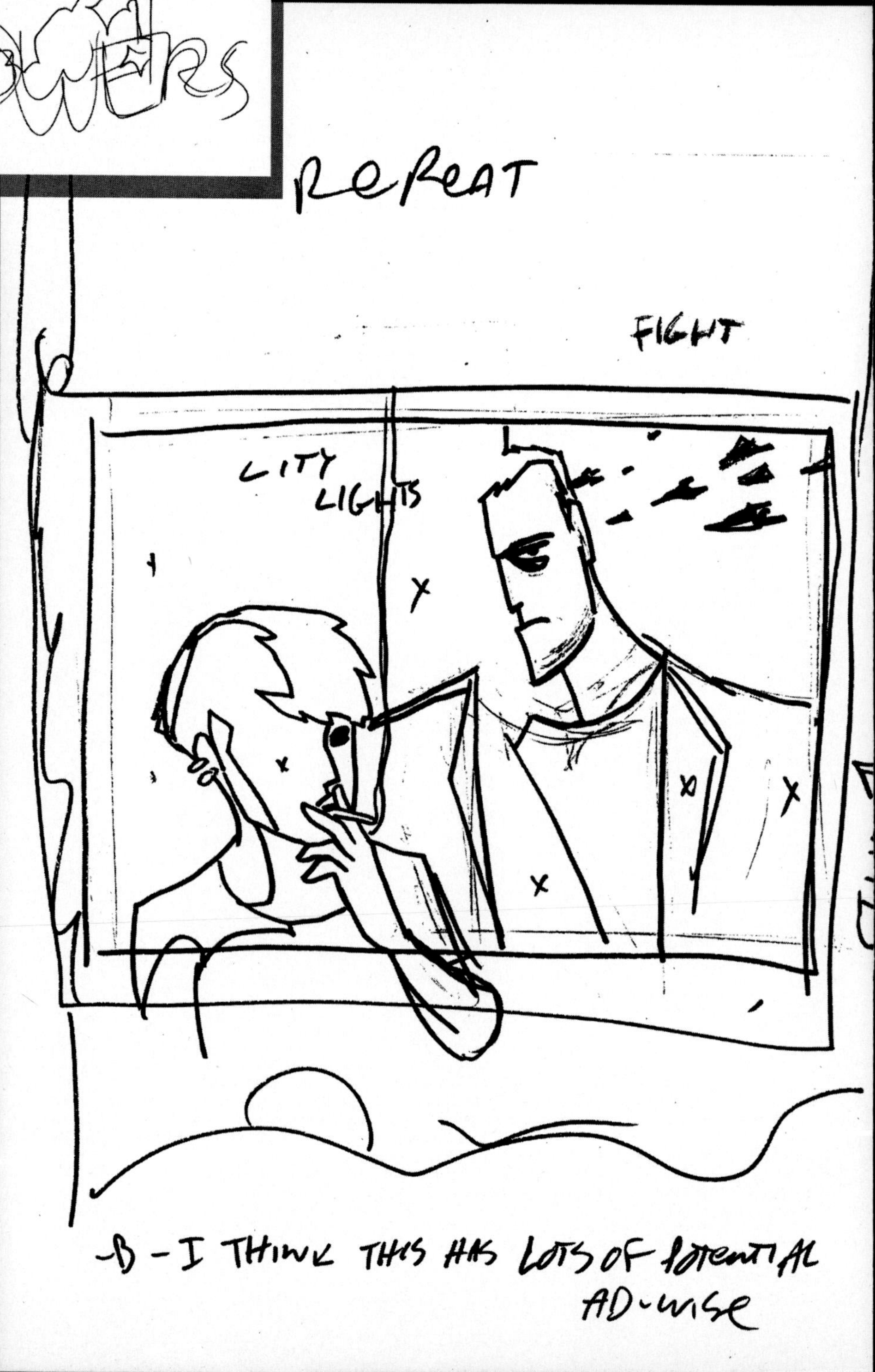
REPEAT
FIGHT
CITY
LIGHTS
-B- I THINK THIS HAS LOTS OF POTENTIAL
AD-WISE

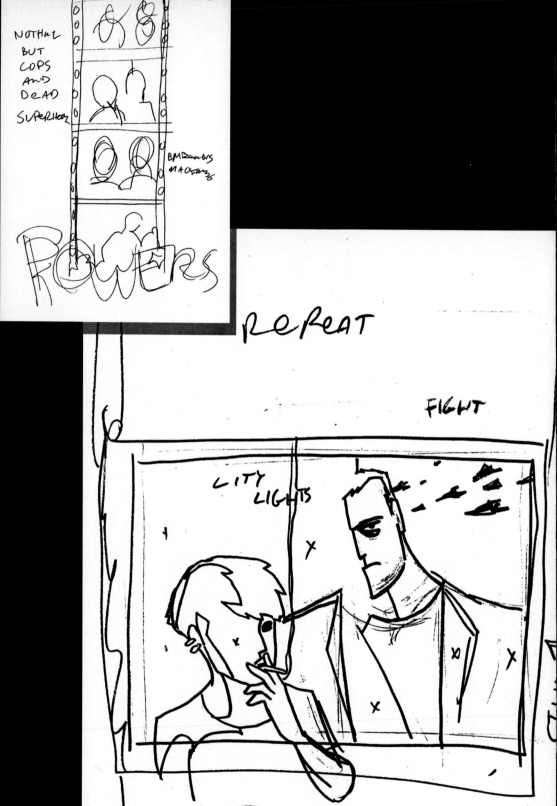

the biggest case of their careers...

POWERS

brian michael bendis
michael avon oeming

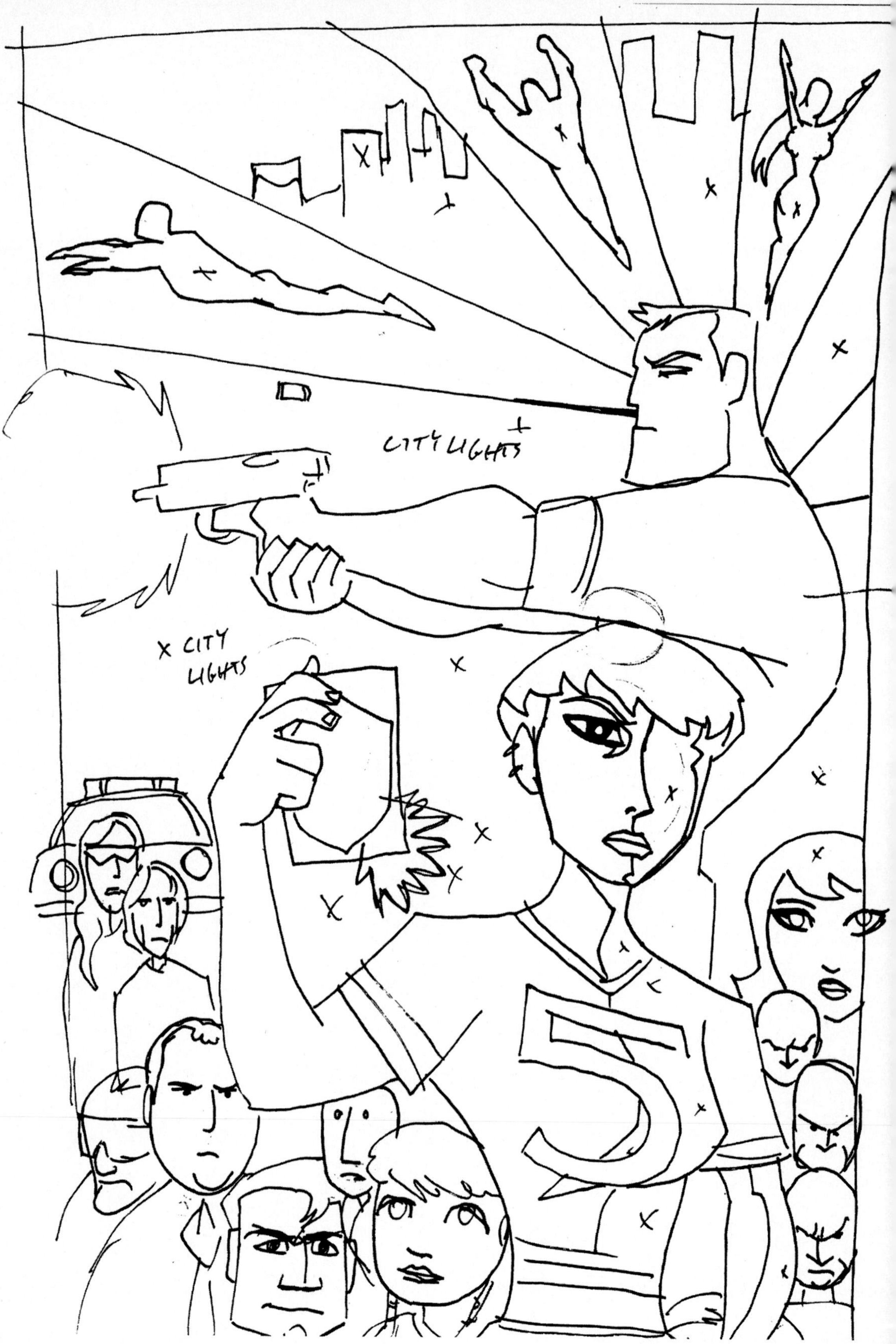

CITY LIGHTS
CITY LIGHTS
5

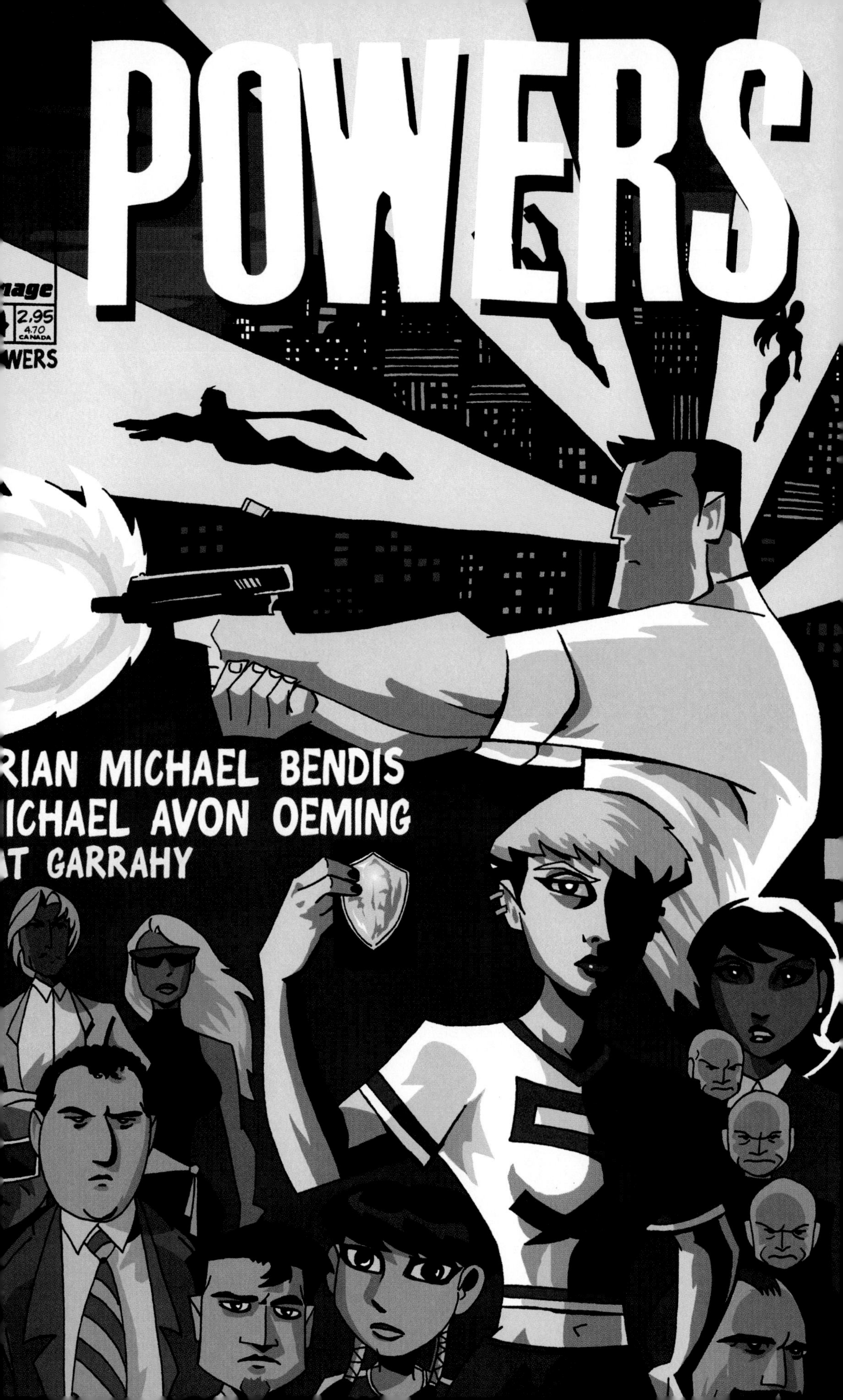
POWERS
mage
2.95
4.70
CANADA
WERS
RIAN MICHAEL BENDIS
ICHAEL AVON OEMING
T GARRAHY

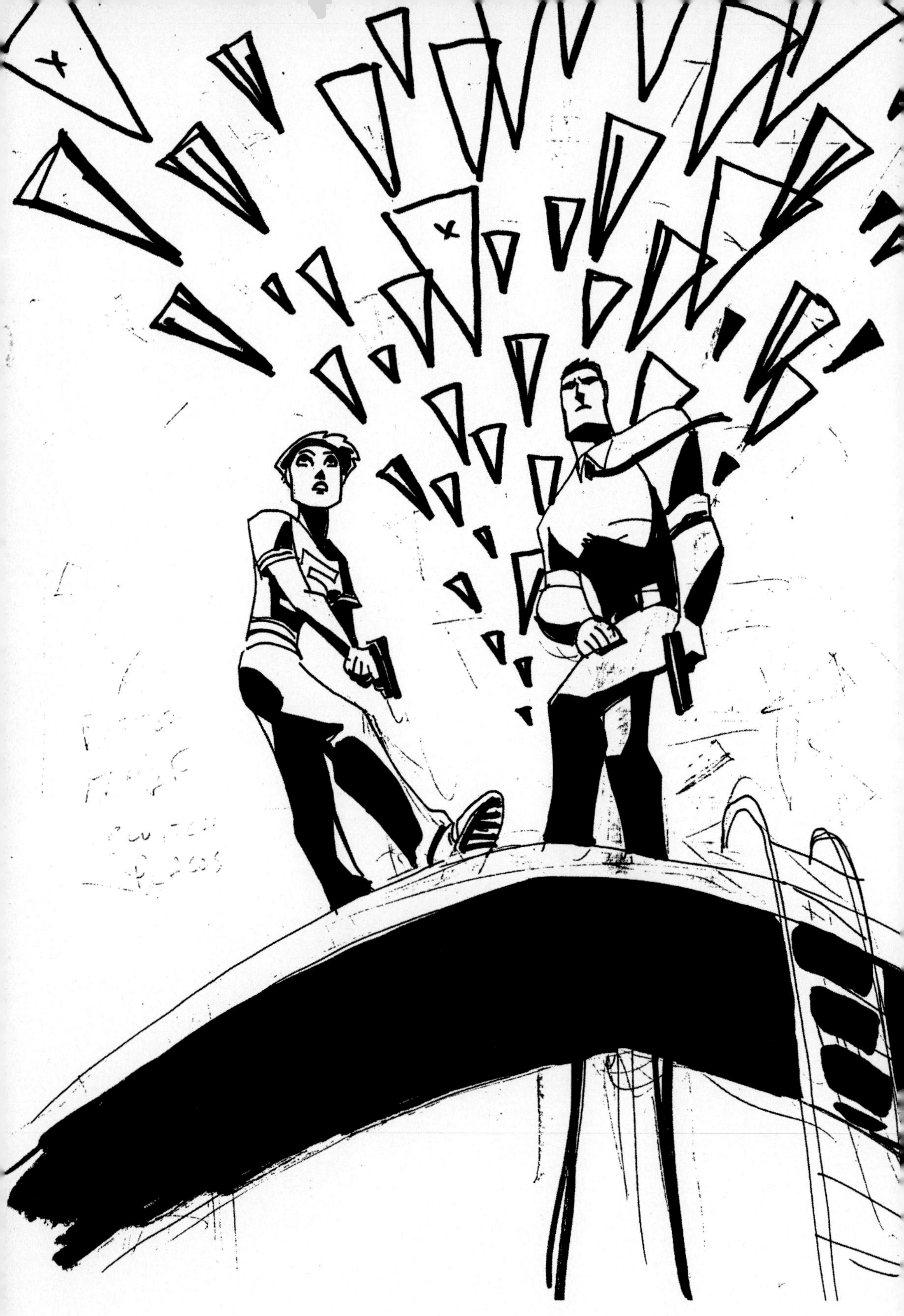

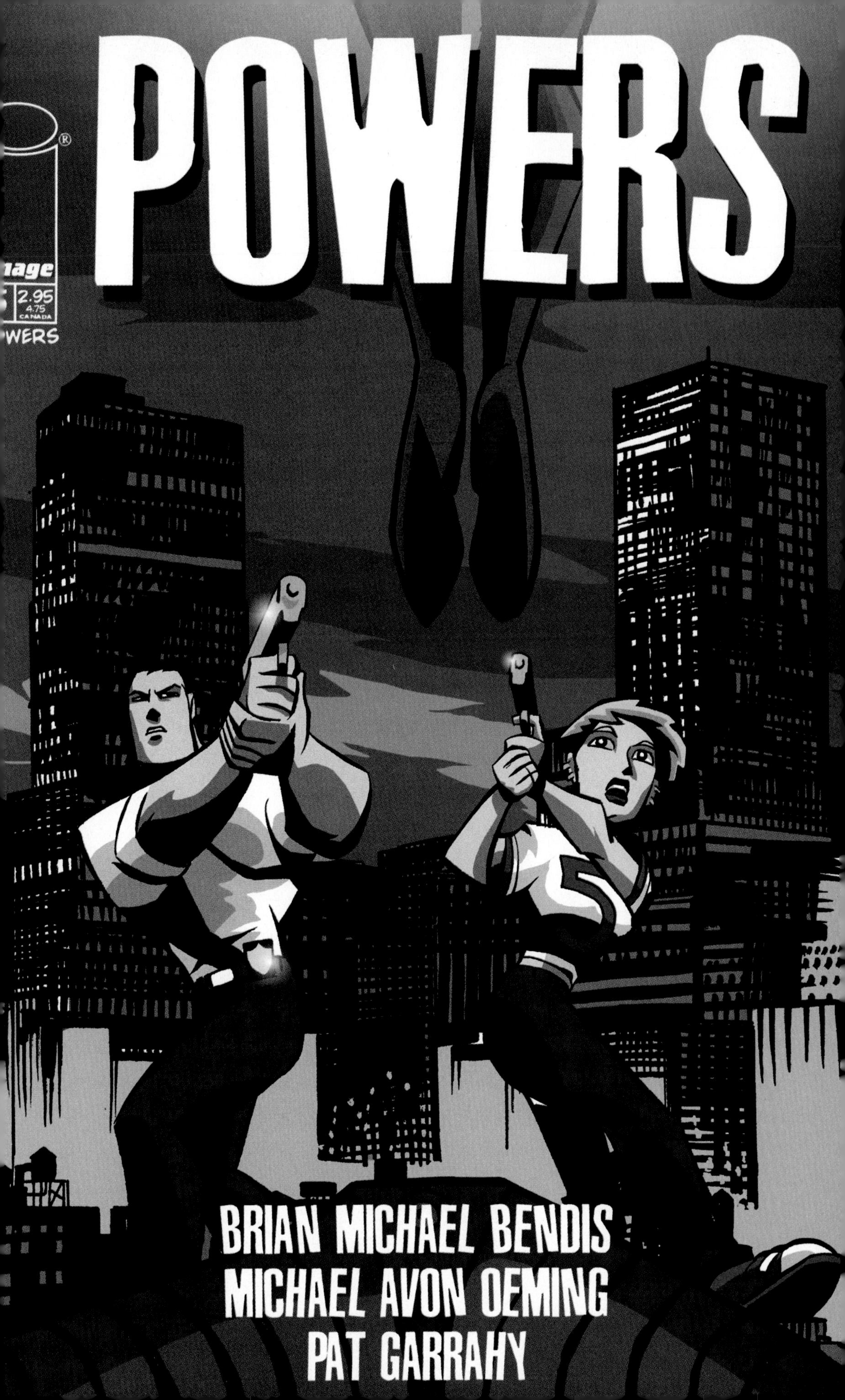
POWERS
2.95
4.75 CANADA
BRIAN MICHAEL BENDIS
MICHAEL AVON OEMING
PAT GARRAHY

Unused layout and cover for issue six.

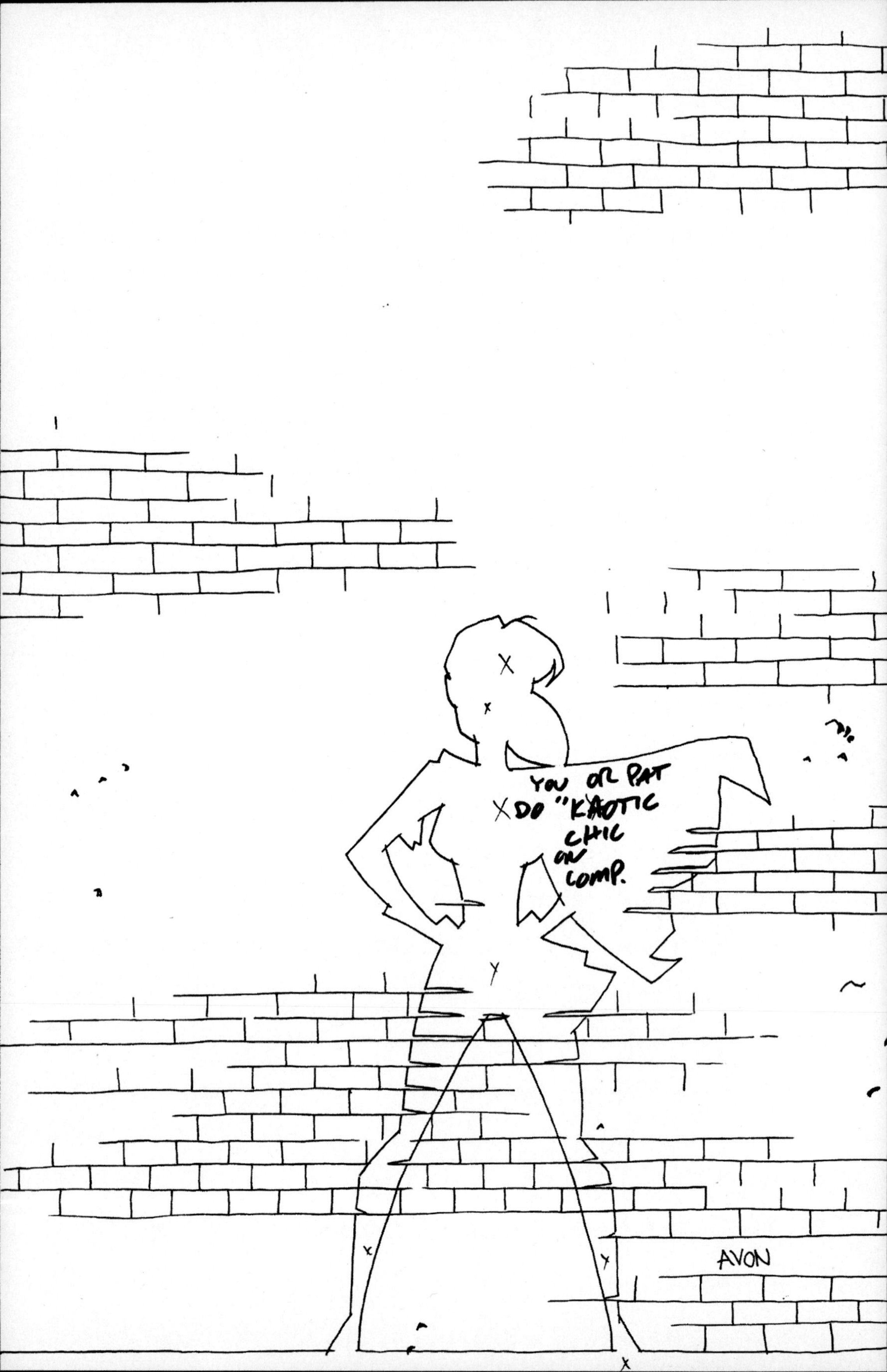

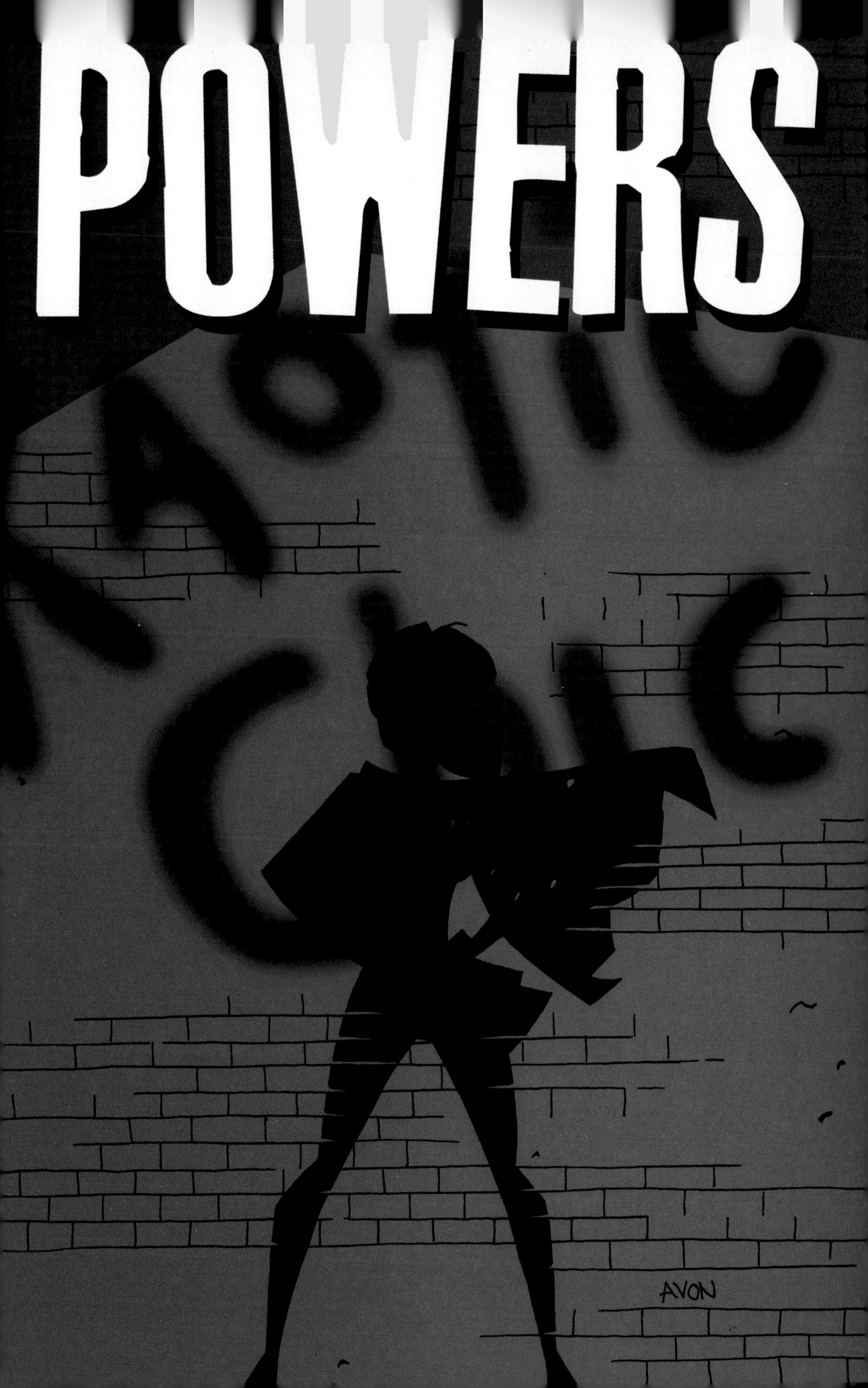
POWERS
AVON

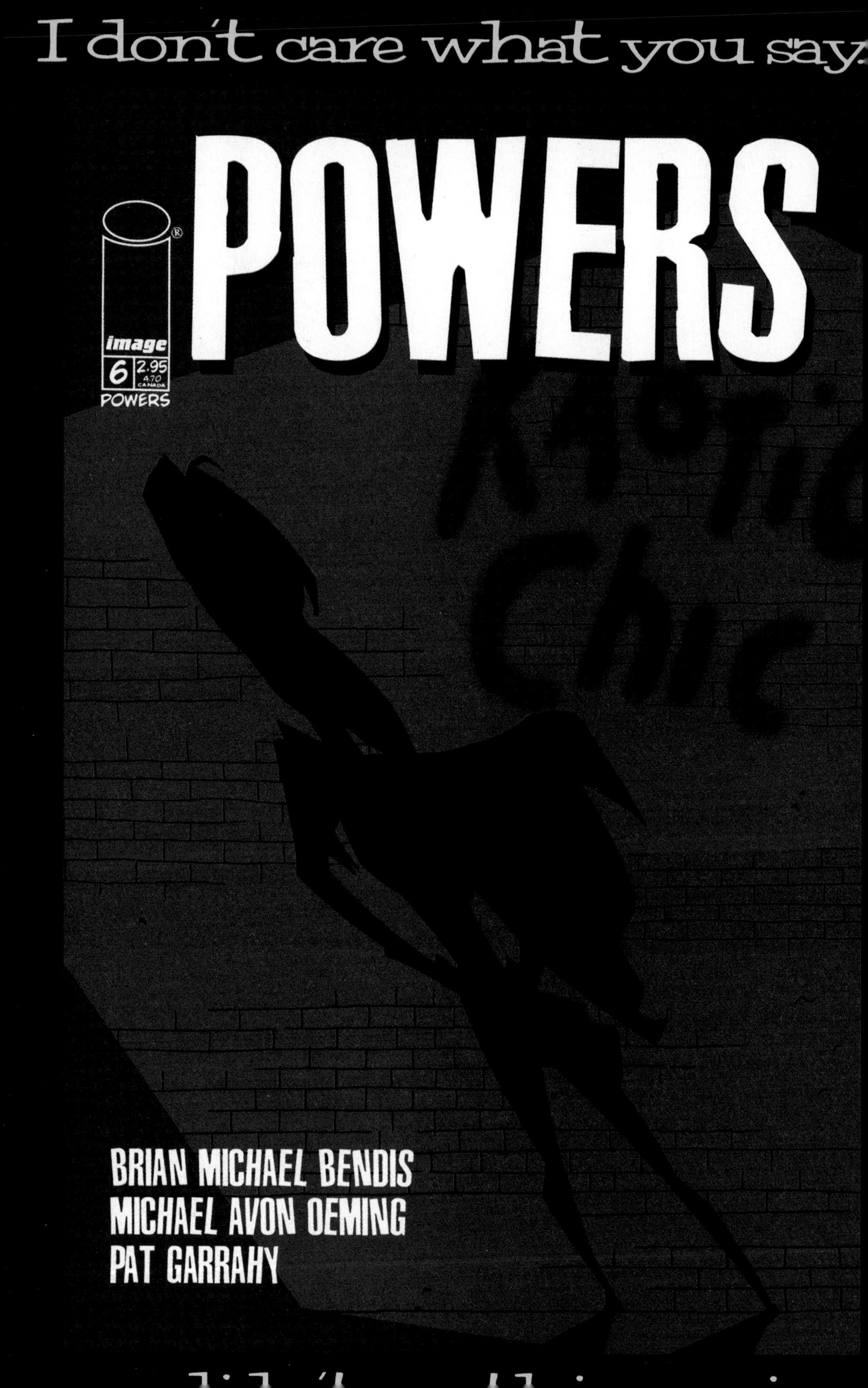
I don't care what you say:
POWERS
image
6
2.95
4.70 CANADA
POWERS
BRIAN MICHAEL BENDIS
MICHAEL AVON OEMING
PAT GARRAHY

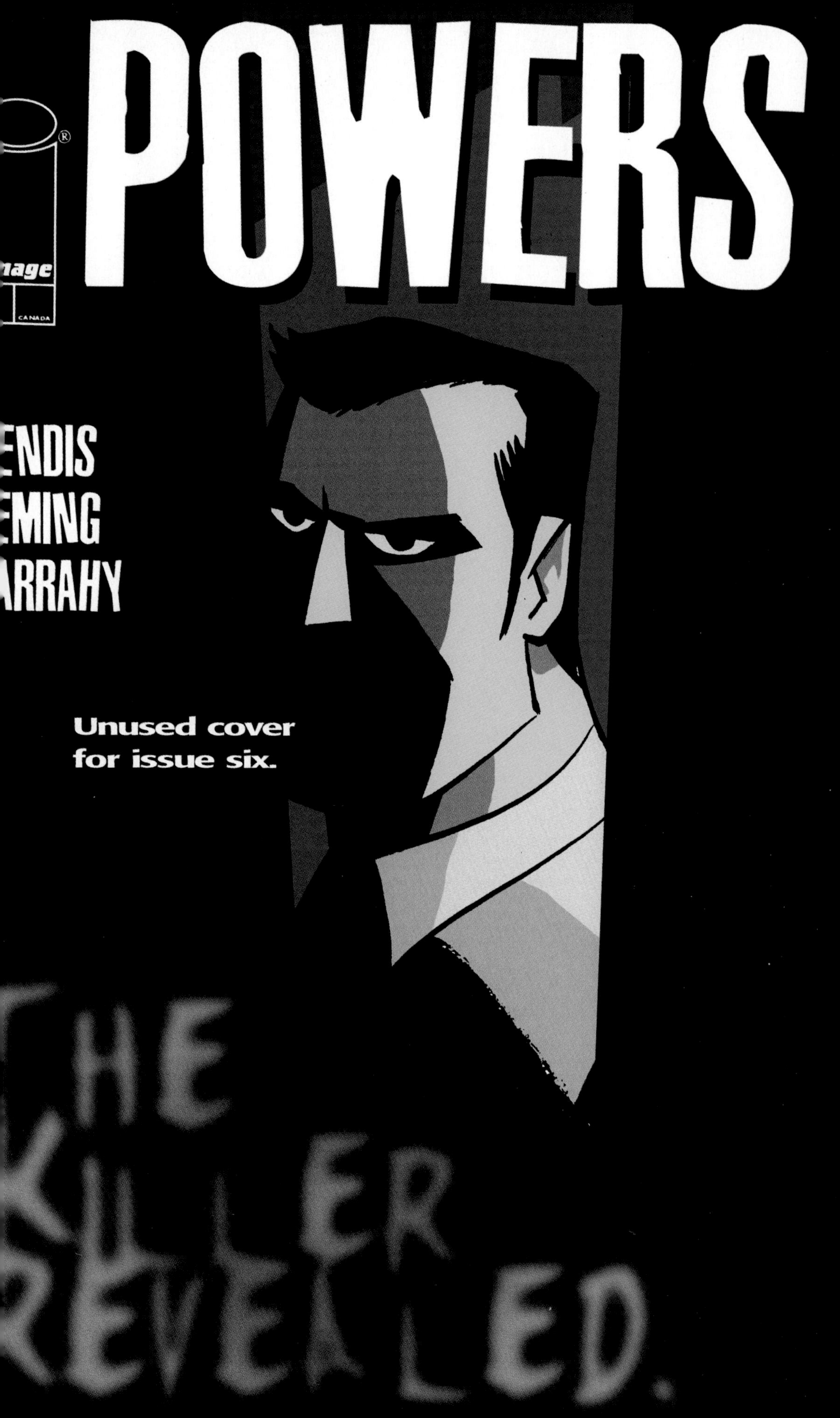

Unused cover
for issue six.

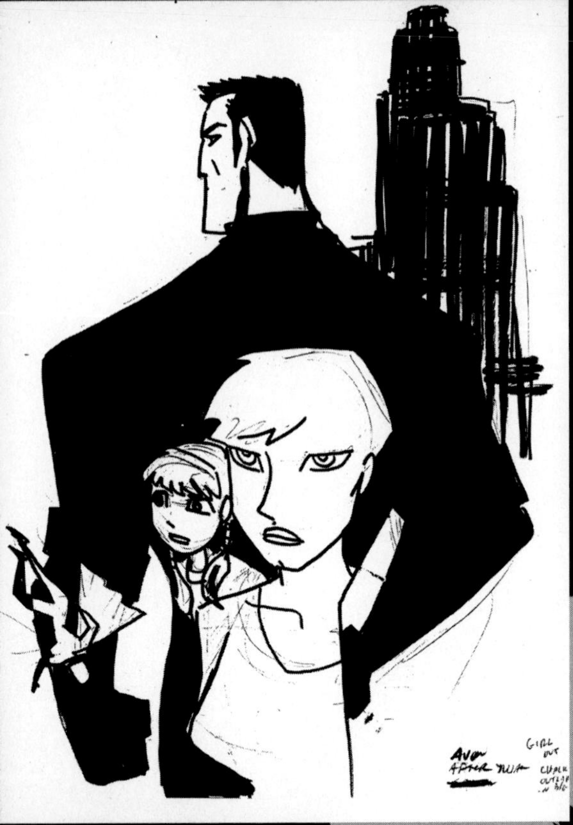
AVON
GIRL

Unused layout and cover for issue three.

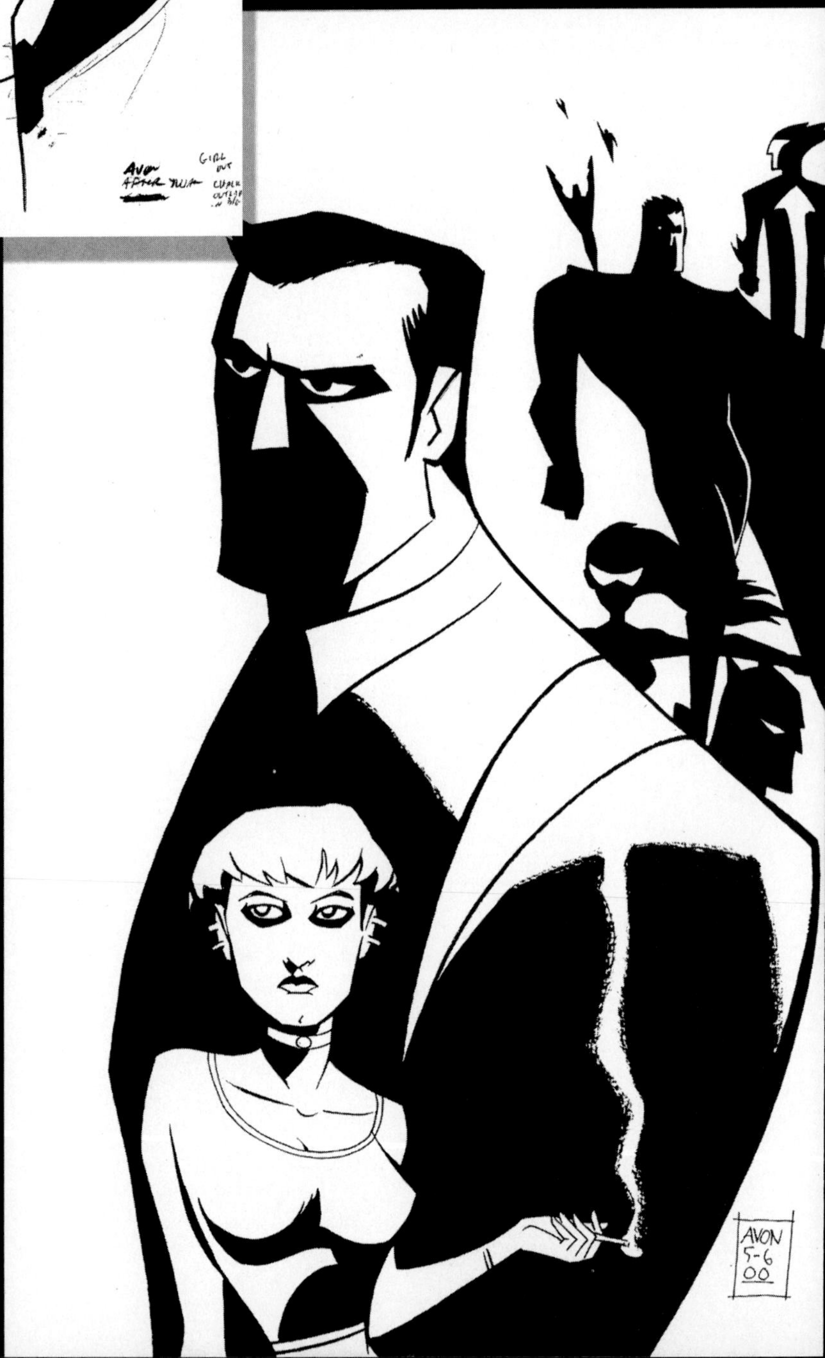
AVON
5-6
00

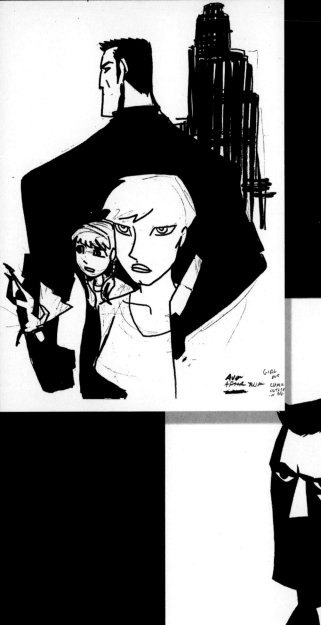

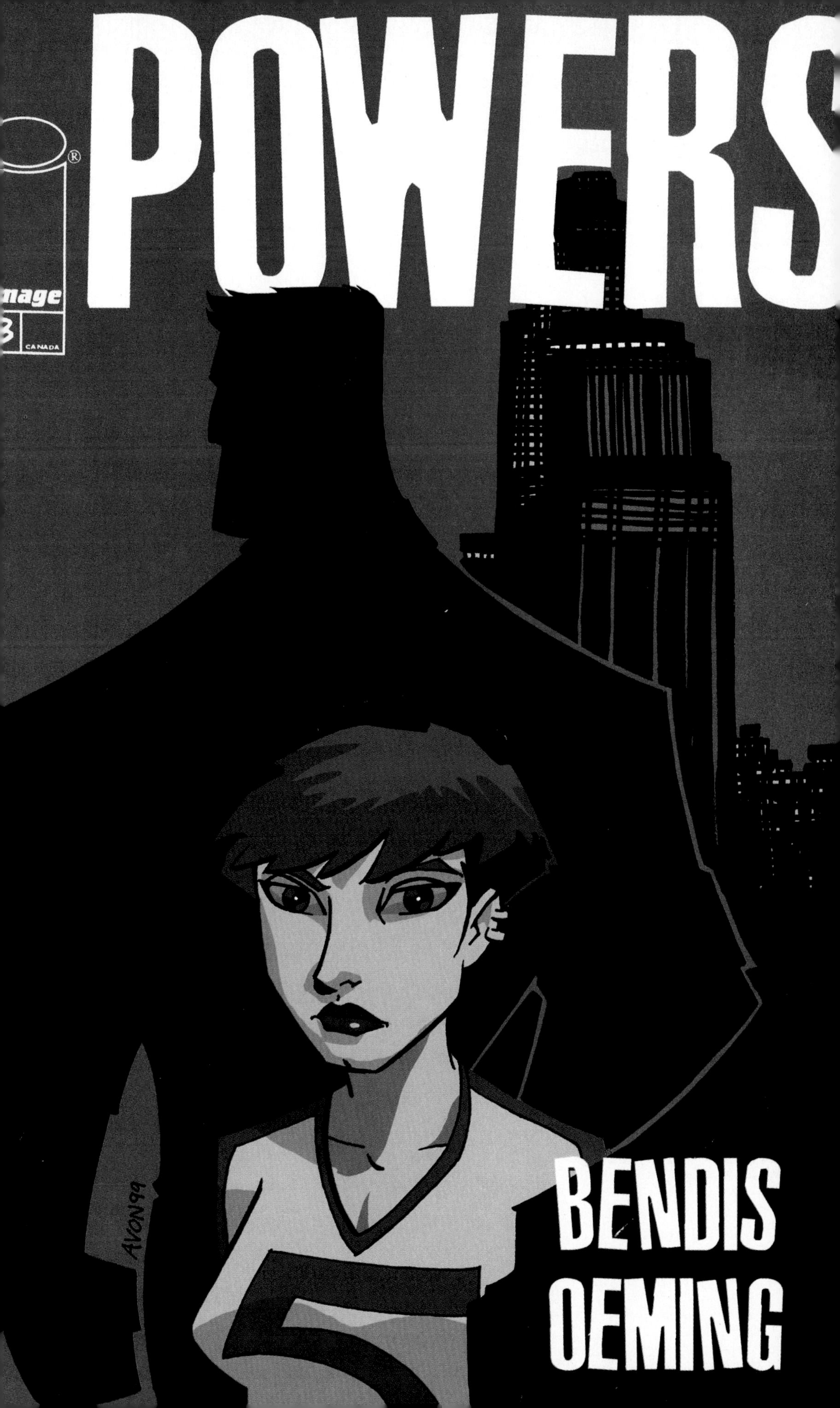

POWERS
image
CANADA
AVON99
BENDIS
OEMING

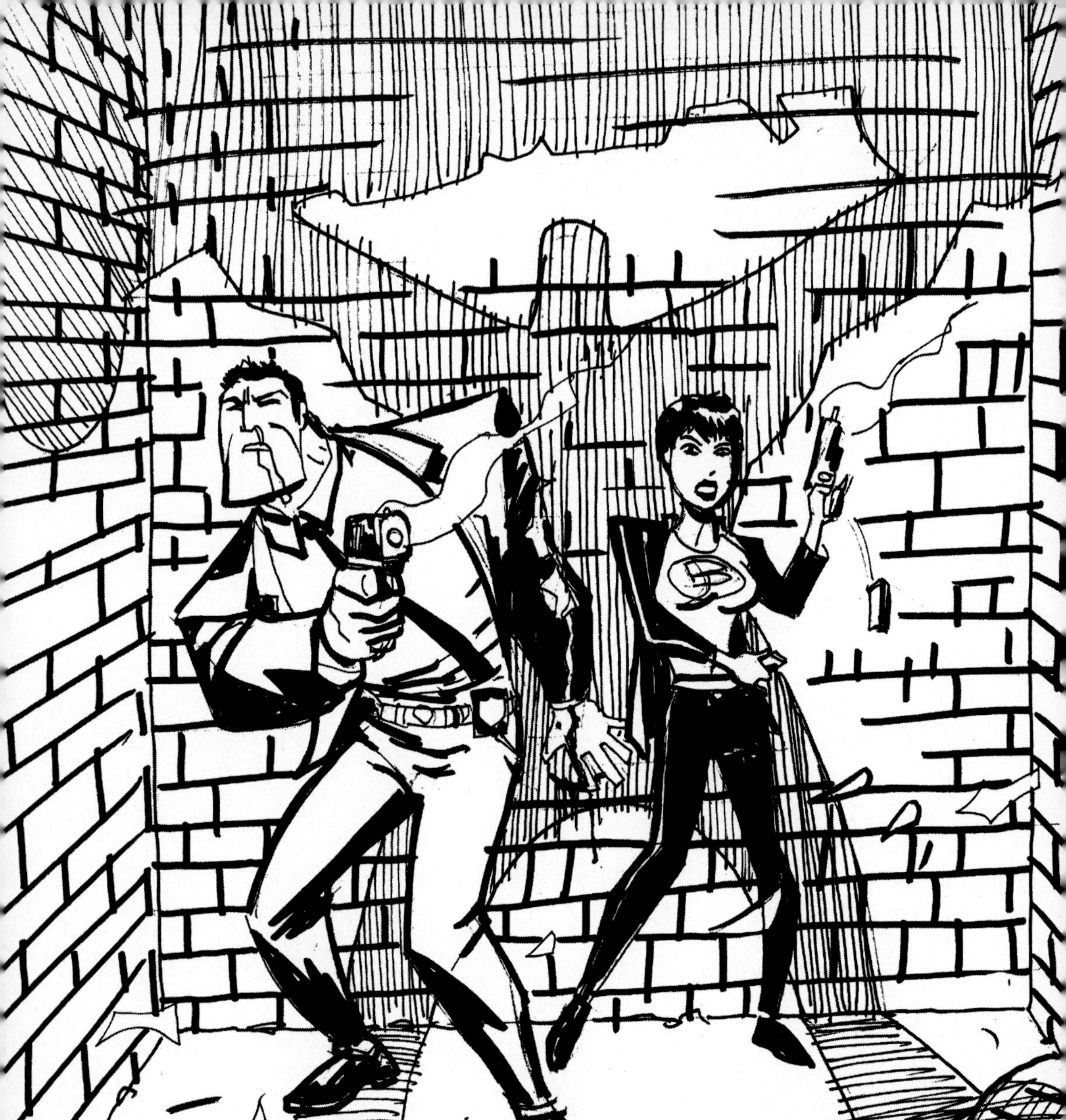

Unused layout and cover for issue three.

It ended up being the cover to the Mid-Ohio Convention program book.

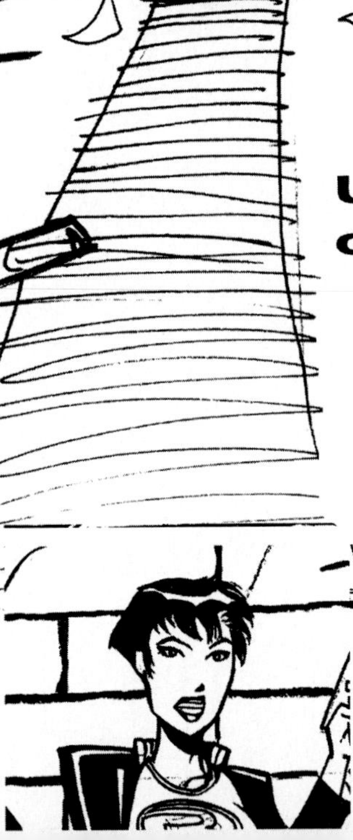

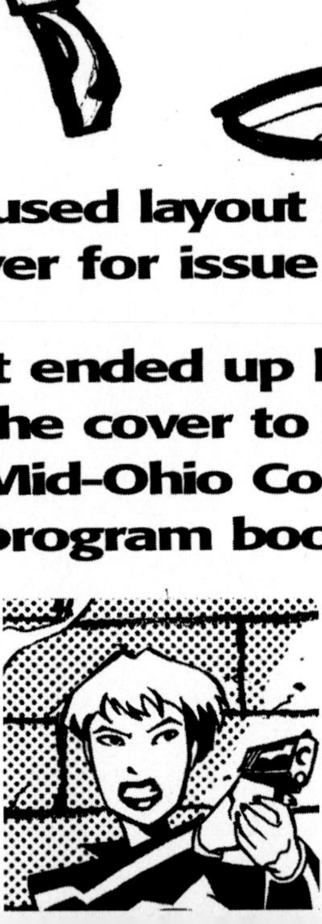

The ongoing sa
of Deena's hair.

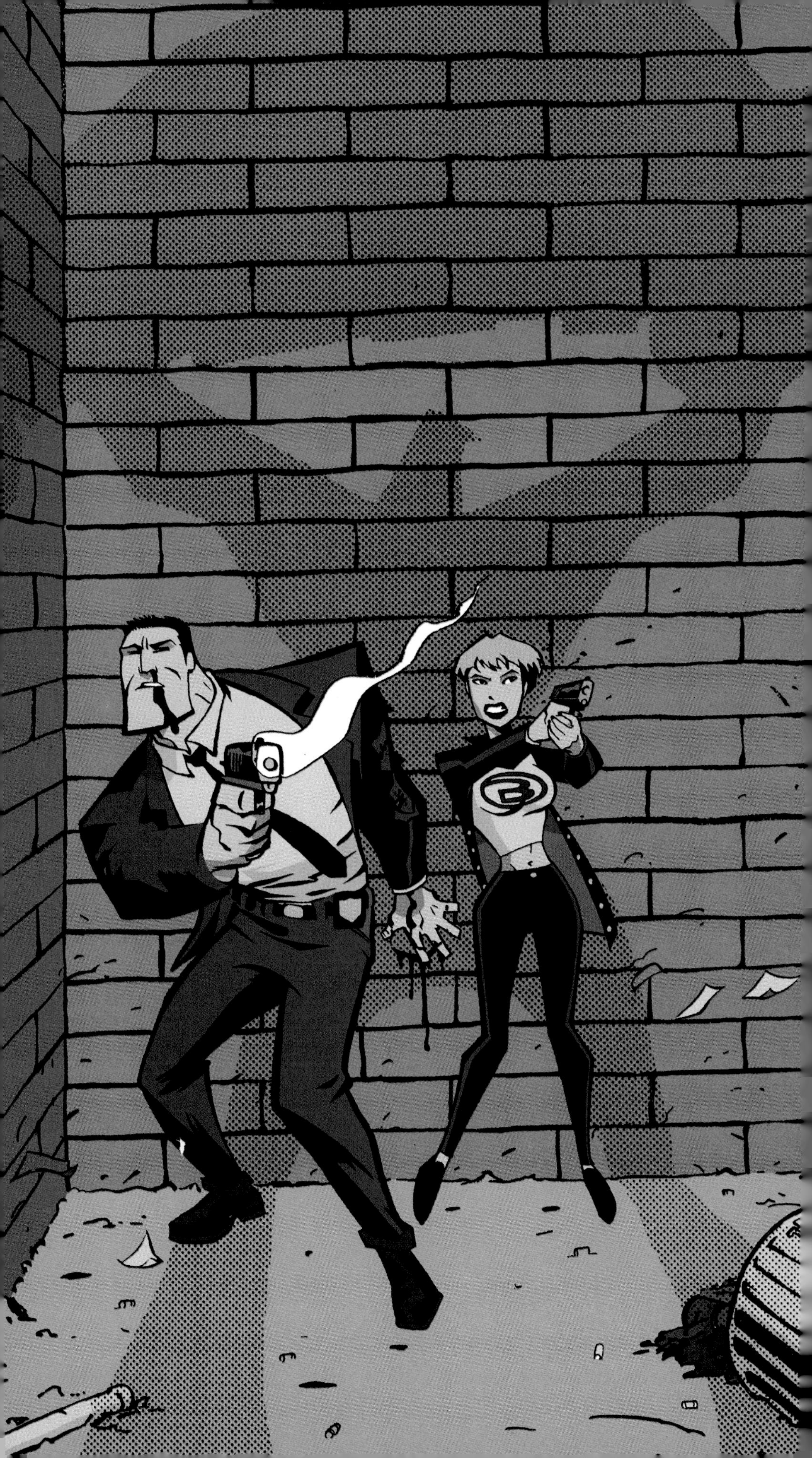

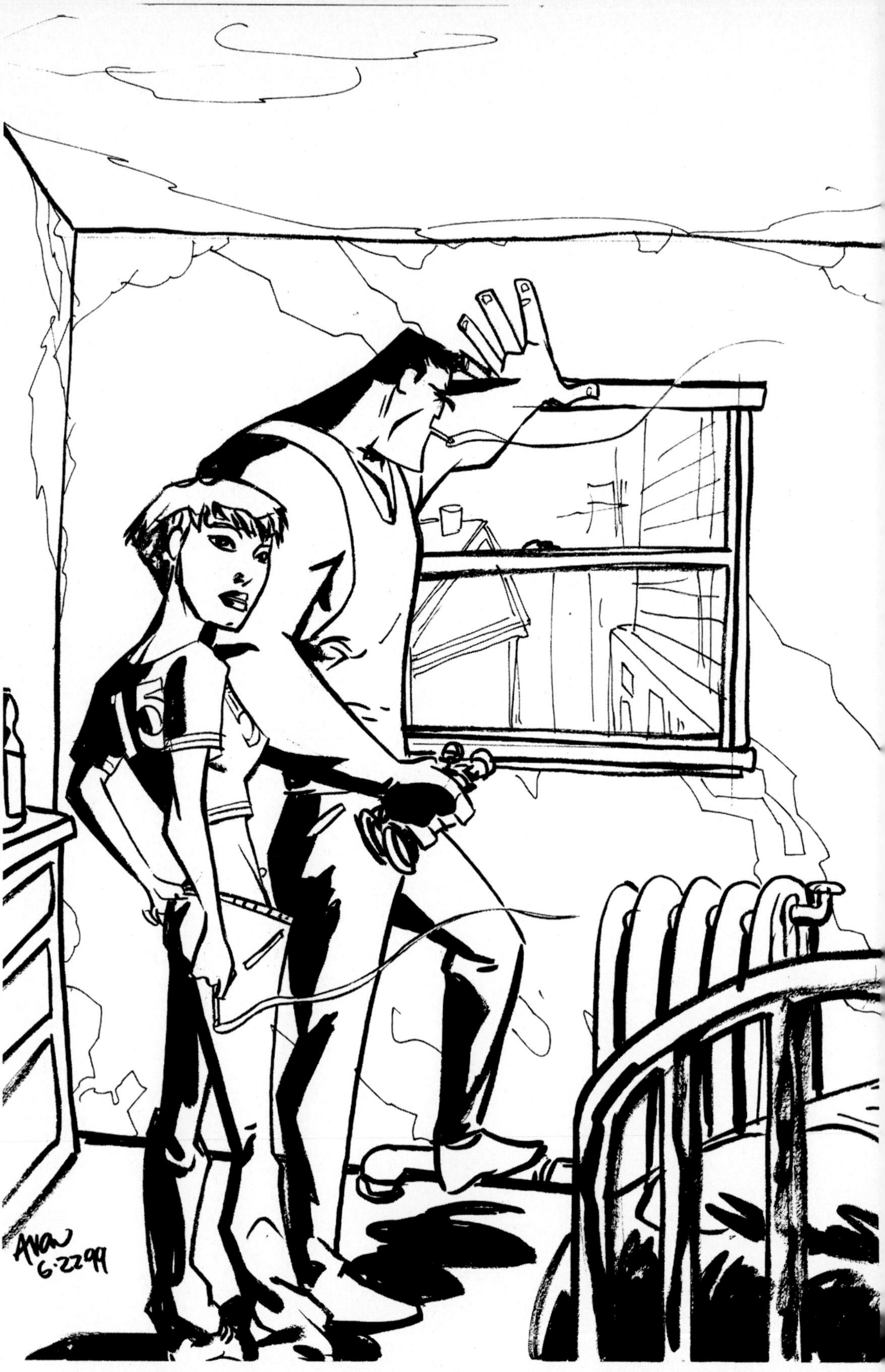
6.22.99

Unused cover idea- but one of my faves.
It will be used as part of a Wizard promotion.

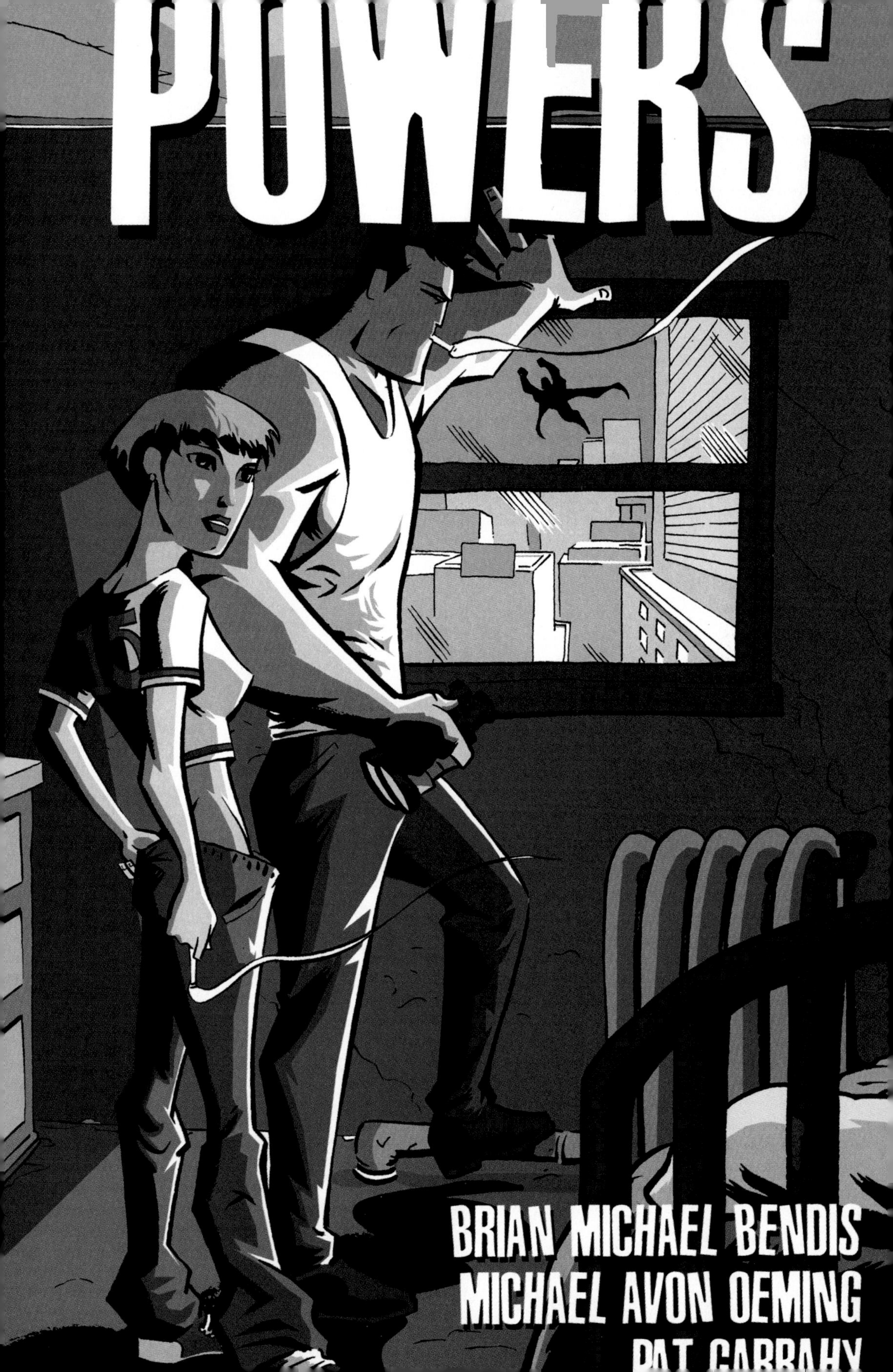
POWERS
BRIAN MICHAEL BENDIS
MICHAEL AVON OEMING
PAT GARRAHY

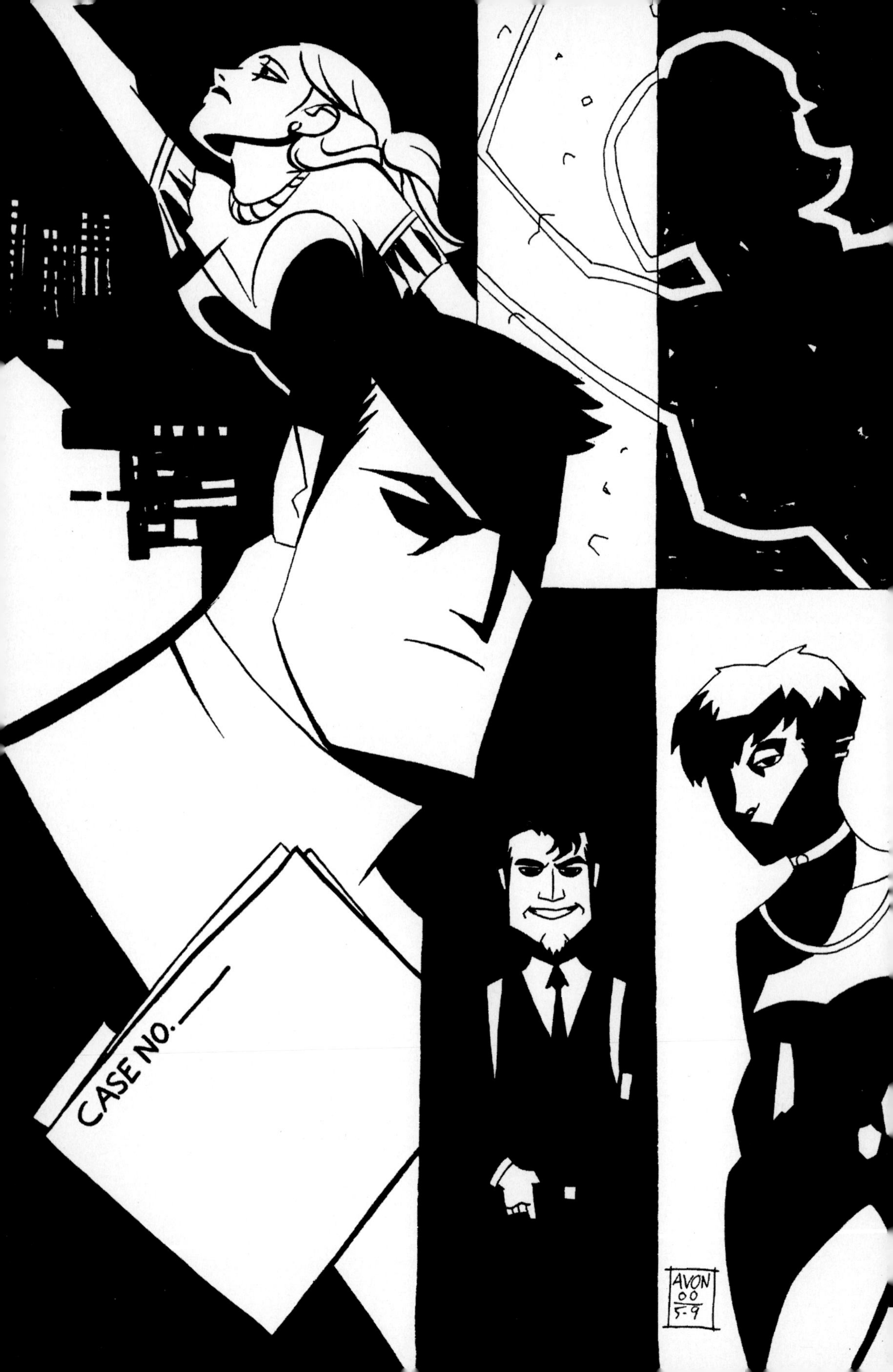
CASE NO.
AVON 00 5-9

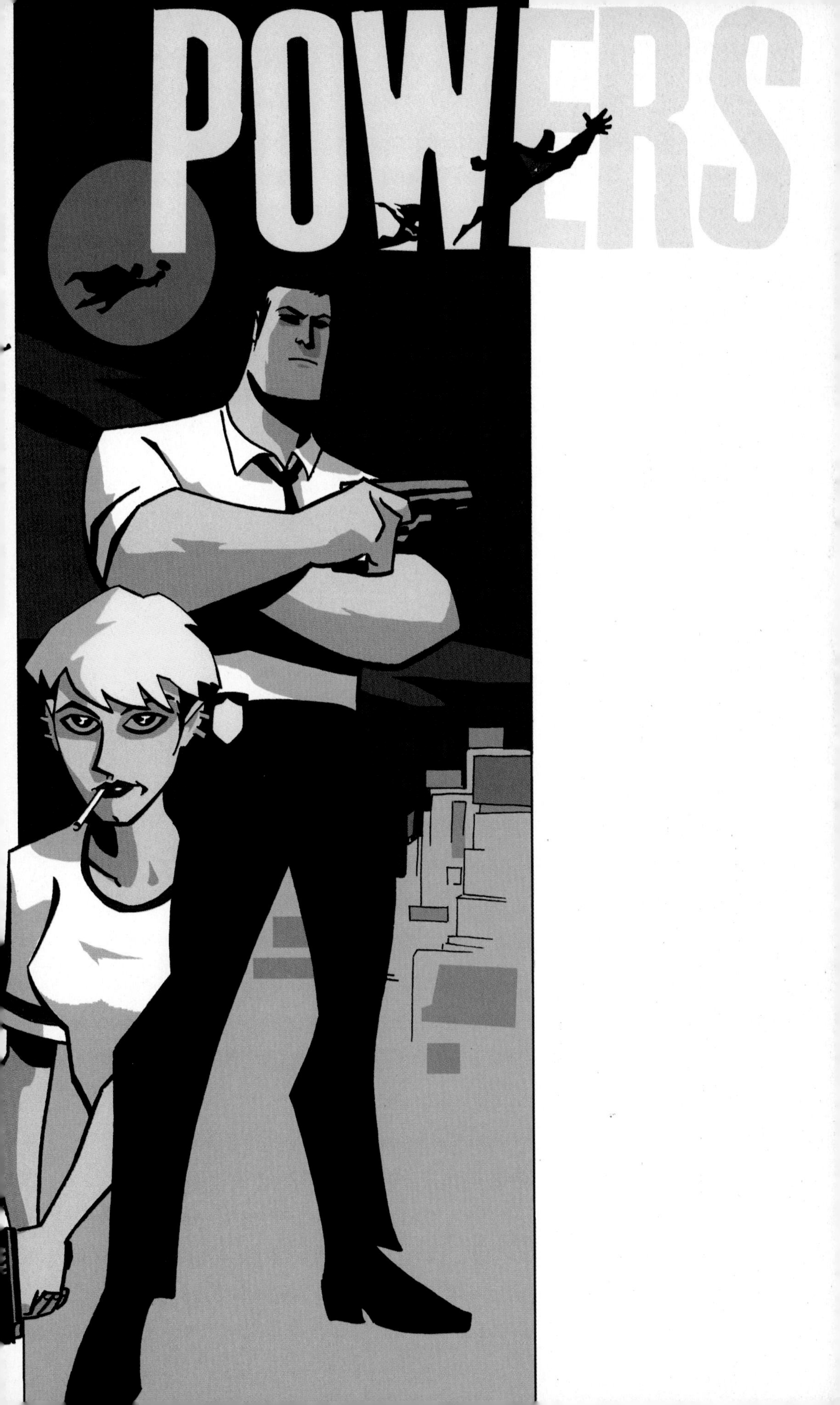
POWERS

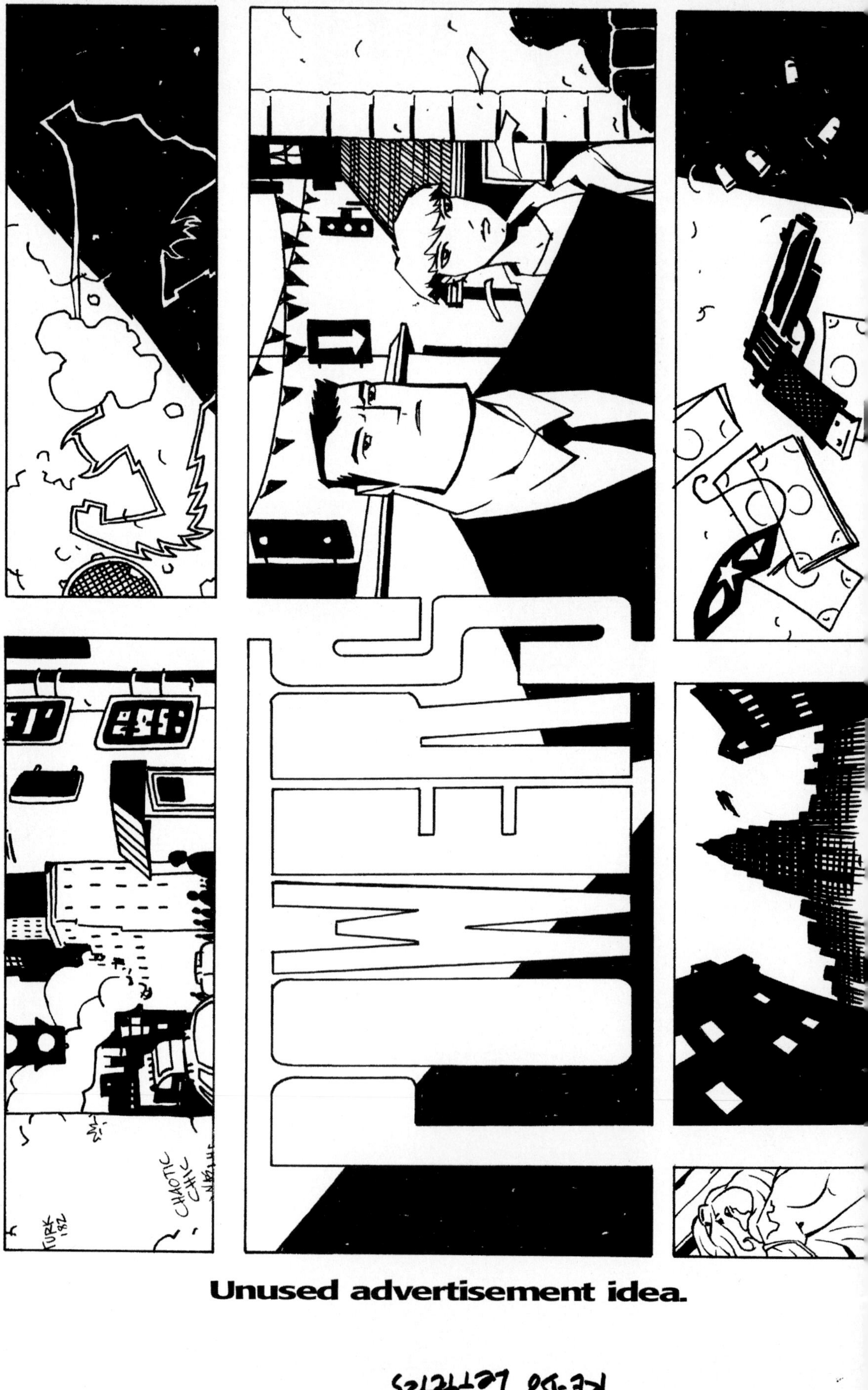
POWERS
TURK 182
CHAOTIC CHIC

Unused advertisement idea.

8- SQUEEZED OUT ANOTHER, YOU MAY WANT TO RE-DO LETTERS

A Mike Oeming Commision sketch

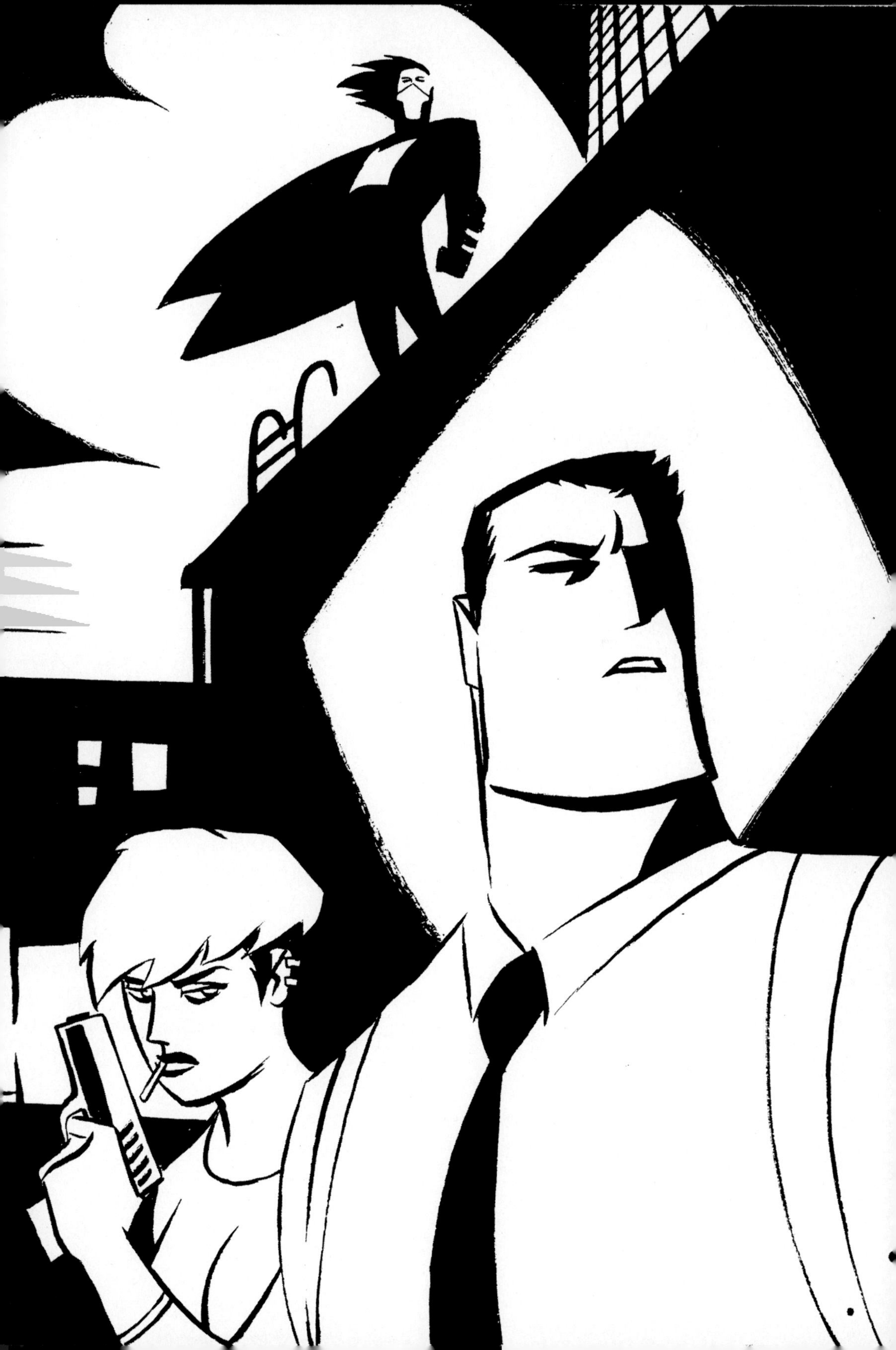

POWERS
THE CAMEOS

One of the best ideas we came up with for this book, and by 'best' I mean 'logistic nightmares,' was to ask well-known comic book creator friends of ours to lend us brand new super hero and villain creations to fill our cityscape.

This added an extra layer of fun to the whole thing. Many big name talents, talents people don't usually think of in this genre, were extremely generous by lending us their babies.

So, here on the following pages, for the first time, is a key to the identities of all the characters and their creators. Each character is copyright the creator named here. If no name is listed, that character is copyright Mike and myself and will be featured in an upcoming Powers storyarc.

We thank them all for being friends and pros.

DREI
DAVE JOHNSON

TWIGHLIGHT

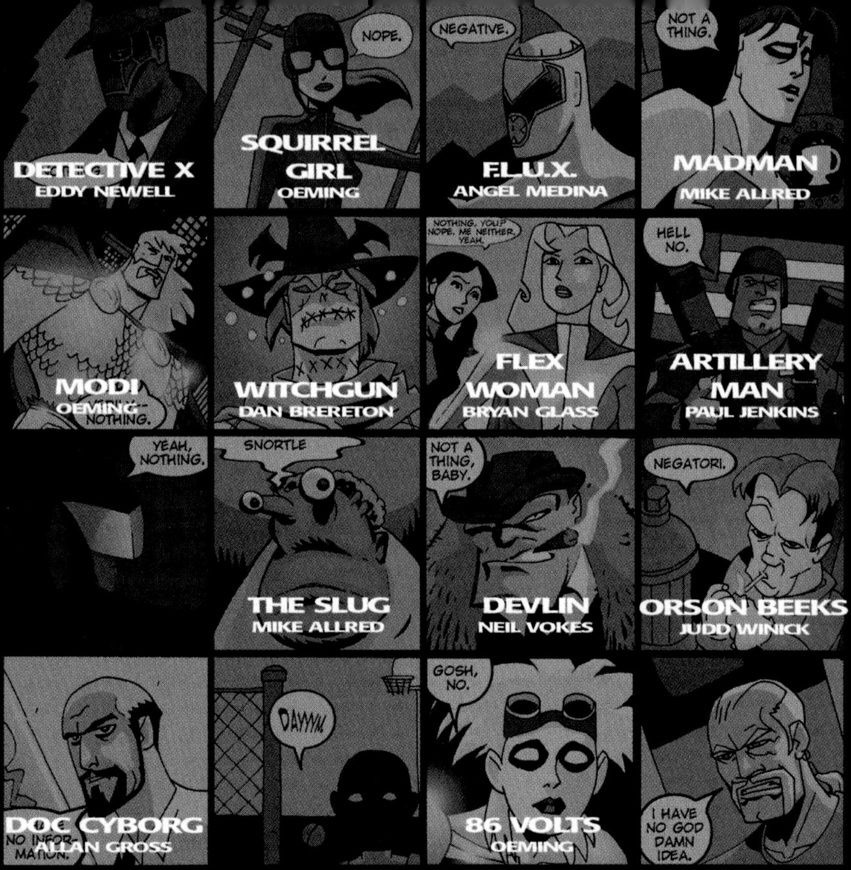
DETECTIVE X
EDDY NEWELL
NOPE.
SQUIRREL GIRL
OEMING
NEGATIVE.
F.L.U.X.
ANGEL MEDINA
NOT A THING.
MADMAN
MIKE ALLRED
MODI
OEMING
NOTHING.
WITCHGUN
DAN BRERETON
NOTHING. YOU? NOPE. ME NEITHER. YEAH.
FLEX WOMAN
BRYAN GLASS
HELL NO.
ARTILLERY MAN
PAUL JENKINS
YEAH, NOTHING.
SNORTLE
THE SLUG
MIKE ALLRED
NOT A THING, BABY.
DEVLIN
NEIL VOKES
NEGATORI.
ORSON BEEKS
JUDD WINICK
DOC CYBORG
ALLAN GROSS
NO INFOR-MATION.
DAYYYM
GOSH, NO.
86 VOLTS
OEMING
I HAVE NO GOD DAMN IDEA.

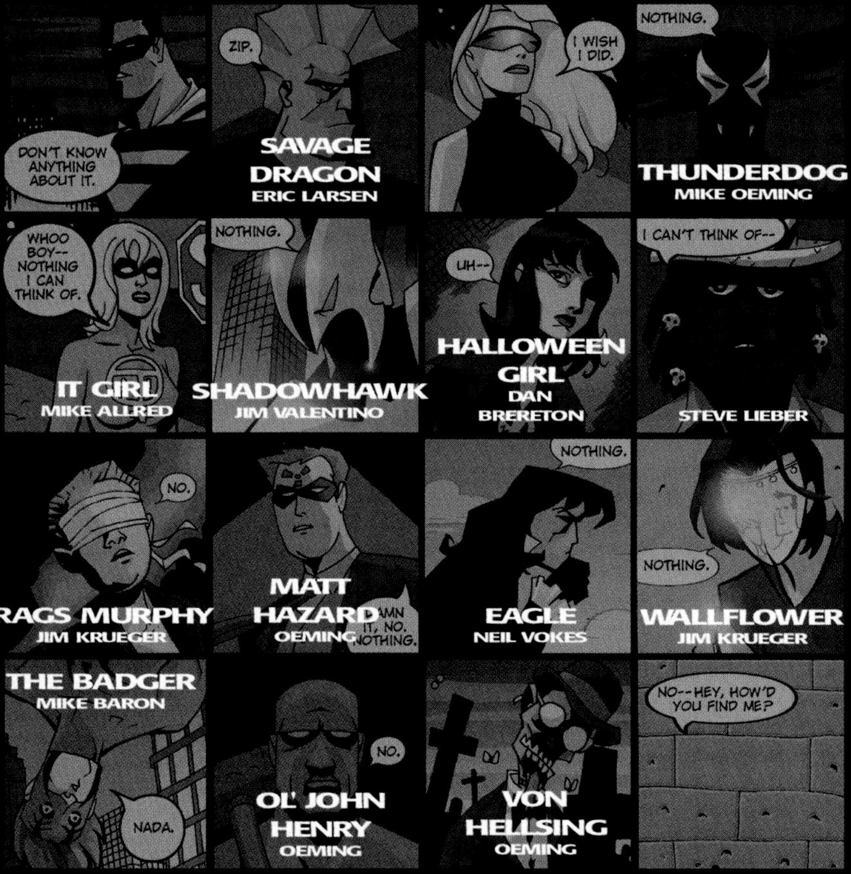
DON'T KNOW ANYTHING ABOUT IT.
ZIP.
SAVAGE DRAGON
ERIC LARSEN
I WISH I DID.
NOTHING.
THUNDERDOG
MIKE OEMING
WHOO BOY-- NOTHING I CAN THINK OF.
IT GIRL
MIKE ALLRED
NOTHING.
SHADOWHAWK
JIM VALENTINO
UH--
HALLOWEEN GIRL
DAN BRERETON
I CAN'T THINK OF--
STEVE LIEBER
NO.
RAGS MURPHY
JIM KRUEGER
MATT HAZARD
OEMING
DAMN IT, NO. NOTHING.
NOTHING.
EAGLE
NEIL VOKES
NOTHING.
WALLFLOWER
JIM KRUEGER
THE BADGER
MIKE BARON
NADA.
NO.
OL' JOHN HENRY
OEMING
VON HELLSING
OEMING
NO--HEY, HOW'D YOU FIND ME?

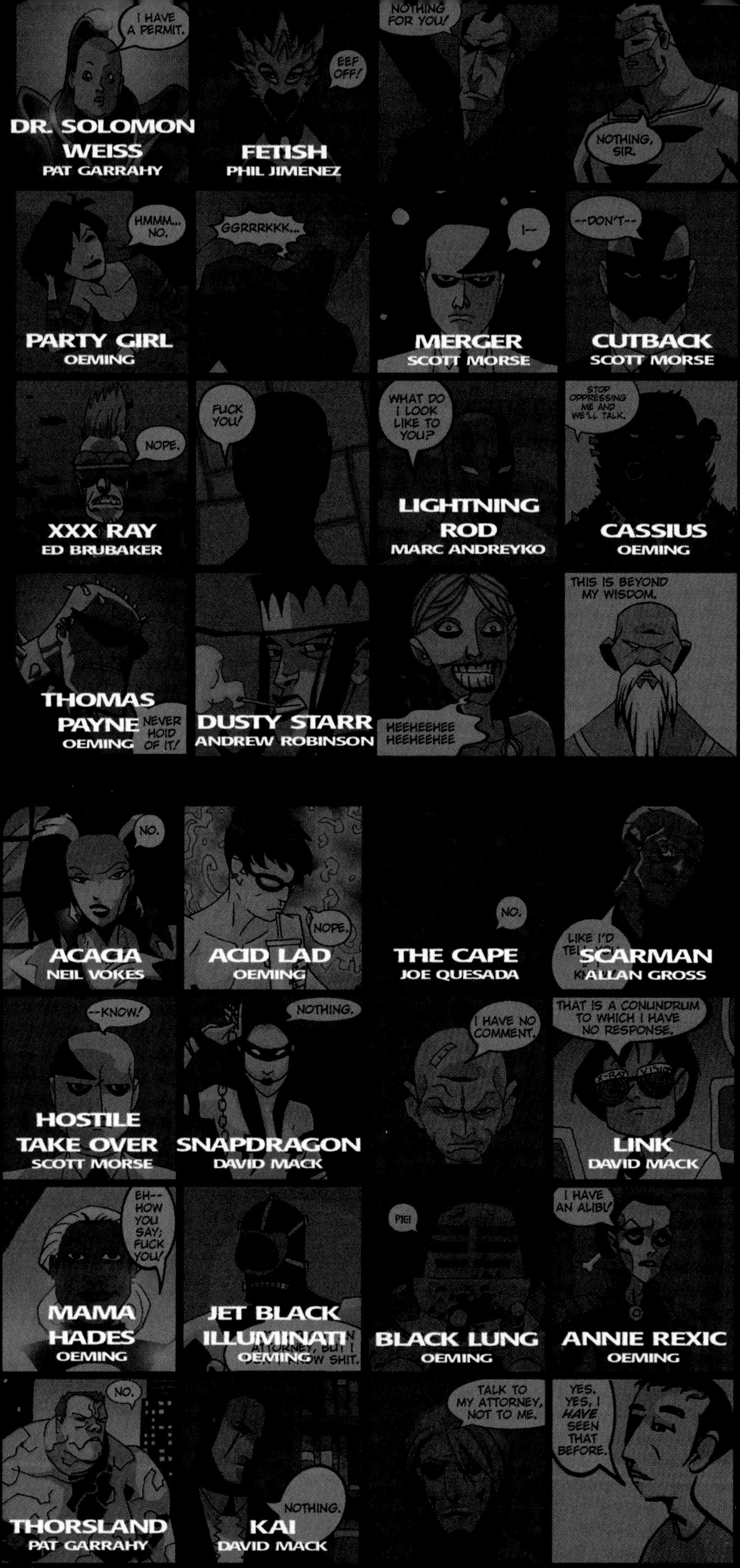
I HAVE A PERMIT.
DR. SOLOMON WEISS
PAT GARRAHY
EEF OFF!
FETISH
PHIL JIMENEZ
NOTHING FOR YOU!
NOTHING, SIR.
HMMM... NO.
PARTY GIRL
OEMING
GGRRRKKK...
I--
MERGER
SCOTT MORSE
--DON'T--
CUTBACK
SCOTT MORSE
NOPE.
XXX RAY
ED BRUBAKER
FUCK YOU!
WHAT DO I LOOK LIKE TO YOU?
LIGHTNING ROD
MARC ANDREYKO
STOP OPPRESSING ME AND WE'LL TALK.
CASSIUS
OEMING
THOMAS PAYNE
OEMING
NEVER HOID OF IT!
DUSTY STARR
ANDREW ROBINSON
HEEHEEHEE HEEHEEHEE
THIS IS BEYOND MY WISDOM.
NO.
ACACIA
NEIL VOKES
NOPE.
ACID LAD
OEMING
NO.
THE CAPE
JOE QUESADA
SCARMAN
ALLAN GROSS
--KNOW!
HOSTILE TAKE OVER
SCOTT MORSE
NOTHING.
SNAPDRAGON
DAVID MACK
I HAVE NO COMMENT.
THAT IS A CONUNDRUM TO WHICH I HAVE NO RESPONSE.
X-RAY VISION
LINK
DAVID MACK
EH-- HOW YOU SAY; FUCK YOU!
MAMA HADES
OEMING
JET BLACK ILLUMINATI
OEMING
PIG!
BLACK LUNG
OEMING
I HAVE AN ALIBI!
ANNIE REXIC
OEMING
NO.
THORSLAND
PAT GARRAHY
NOTHING.
KAI
DAVID MACK
TALK TO MY ATTORNEY, NOT TO ME.
YES, YES, I HAVE SEEN THAT BEFORE.

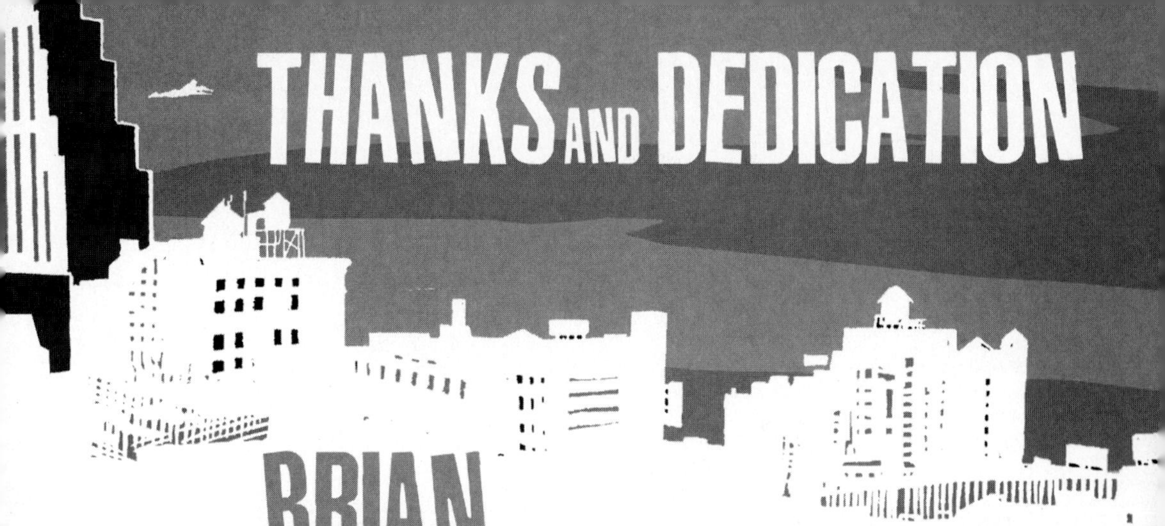

THANKS AND DEDICATION

BRIAN

avid Engel, Jim Valentino, Anthony Bozzi, Mace Neufeld, rent Braun, Traci Hale, Joe Quesada, Bill Jemas, Kel Symons, ug Belgrad, Jim McLaughlin, Randy Lander, Don lcphereson, Jason Prichett, Justin Silvera, Chris Silberman, ohn Skrtic, Cliff Biggers, Ward Batty, Chris Lawrence, Warren llis, David Mack, James S. Rich, Joe Nozemack, Michael Doran, latt Brady, Joel Meadows, Jared Bendis, Pat, K.C., Mike, Alisa, nd the JINXWORLD messageboard.

MIKE

or Melissa and Ethan, the center of my world. Special hanks to Mom, Aunt Carol, Uncle Larry, Neil Vokes, the endis Board Posters and the Bordentown Police Depart-nent for all the support and help!

PAT

d like to thank the OCPStudios gents--Marshall Johnson, osh Read, Mike Smith, James Dean Conklin, Tony Stocco, en Chang, and Scott Helmer. And I'd like to make sure o thank both my parents, 'cause I don't think I have hanked them previously in print.

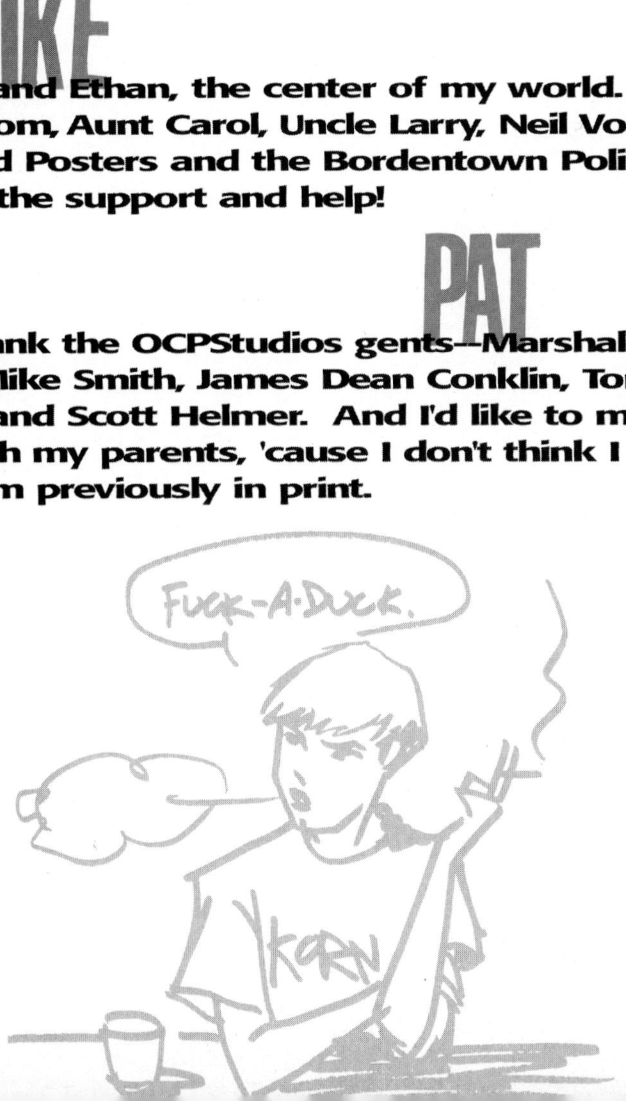
FUCK-A-DUCK.
KORN

MORE GREAT BOOKS FROM IMAGE COMICS

POWERS
Who Killed Retro Girl?
BRIAN MICHAEL BENDIS
MICHAEL AVON OEMING

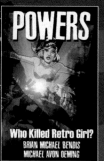

POWERS, VOL. 1: WHO KILLED RETRO GIRL? TP
ISBN# 1-58240-669-3
$21.99

POWERS
ROLEPLAY
BRIAN MICHAEL BENDIS
MICHAEL AVON OEMING

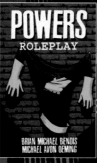

POWERS, VOL. 2: ROLEPLAY TP
ISBN# 1-58240-695-2
$13.99

COSTUMED CONSPIRACIES TAKE FLIGHT
POWERS

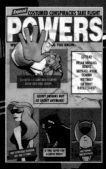

POWERS, VOL. 3: LITTLE DEATHS TP
ISBN# 1-58240-670-7
$19.99

POWERS
SUPERGROUP
BRIAN MICHAEL BENDIS
MICHAEL AVON OEMING

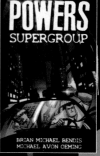

POWERS, VOL. 4: SUPERGROUP TP
ISBN# 1-58240-671-5
$21.99

POWERS
ANARCHY

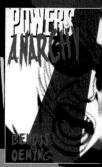

POWERS, VOL. 5: ANARCHY TP
ISBN# 1-58240-331-7
$14.95

goldfish
a crime graphic novel
by brian michael bendis

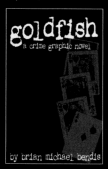

GOLDFISH: THE DEFINITIVE COLLECTION TP
ISBN# 1-58240-195-0
$19.95

jinx
brian michael bendis

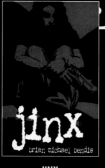

JINX: THE DEFINITIVE COLLECTION TP
ISBN# 1-58240-179-9
$24.95

fire
a spy graphic novel
brian michael bendis

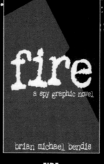

FIRE: THE DEFINITIVE COLLECTION TP
ISBN# 1-58240-071-7
$9.95

torso
a true crime graphic novel
brian michael bendis
marc andreyko

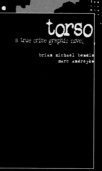

TORSO: THE DEFINITIVE COLLECTION TP
ISBN# 1-58240-174-8
$21.95

BRIAN MICHAEL BENDIS
TOTAL SELL OUT

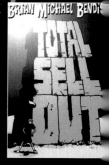

TOTAL SELL OUT TP
ISBN# 1-58240-287-6
$14.95

ALSO AVAILABLE

40 OZ. COLLECTED TP
ISBN# 1-58240-329-5
$9.95

BAD IDEAS: COLLECTED! TP
ISBN# 1-58240-531-X
$12.99

CLASSIC 40 OZ.: TALES FROM THE BROWN BAG TP
ISBN# 1-58240-438-0
$14.95

DIORAMAS, A LOVE STORY GN
ISBN# 1-58240-359-7
$12.95

BLOOD RIVER GN
ISBN# 1-58240-509-3
$7.99

WINGS OF ANASI GN
$6.99

KABUKI

VOL. 1: CIRCLE OF BLOOD TP
ISBN# 1-88727-980-6
$19.95

VOL. 2: DREAMS TP
ISBN# 1-58240-277-9
$12.95

VOL. 3: MASKS OF NOH TP
ISBN# 1-58240-108-X
$12.95

VOL. 4: SKIN DEEP TP
ISBN# 1-58240-000-8
$12.95

VOL. 5: METAMORPHOSIS TP
ISBN# 1-58240-203-5
$24.99

VOL. 6: SCARAB TP
ISBN# 1-58240-258-2
$19.95

NIGHT TRIPPERS GN
ISBN# 1-58240-606-5
$16.99

NOWHERESVILLE TP
ISBN# 1-58240-241-8
$14.95

THE FURTHER ADVENTURES OF ONE PAGE FILLER MAN TP
ISBN# 1-58240-535-2
$11.99

GIRLS

VOL. 1: CONCEPTION TP
ISBN# 1-58240-529-8
$14.99

VOL. 2: EMERGENCE TP
ISBN# 1-58240-608-1
$14.99

GRRL SCOUTS

VOL. 1: TP
ISBN# 1-58240-316-3
$12.95

VOL. 2: WORK SUCKS TP
ISBN# 1-58240-343-0
$12.95

HAMMER OF THE GODS, VOL. 1: MORTAL ENEMY TP
ISBN# 1-58240-271-X
$18.95

POWERS SCRIPTBOOK
ISBN# 1-58240-233-7
$19.95

PUTTIN THE BACKBONE BACK TP
ISBN# 1-58240-402-X
$9.95

QUIXOTE NOVEL
ISBN# 1-58240-434-8
$9.95

SAN AND TWITCH: THE BRIAN MICHAEL BENDIS COLLECTION, VOL. 1 TP
ISBN# 1-58240-583-2
$24.95

SIX GN
ISBN# 1-58240-398-8
$5.95

STUPID COMICS, VOL. 1 TP
ISBN# 1-58240-611-1
$12.99

ULTRA: SEVEN DAYS TP
ISBN# 1-58240-483-6
$17.95

WHISKEY DICKEL, INTERNATIONAL COWGIRL GN
ISBN# 1-58240-318-X
$12.95

For a comic shop near you carrying graphic novels from Image Comics, please call toll free: